The Tio Kingdom of the Middle Congo

VANSINA, Jan. The Tio kingdom of the Middle Congo, 1880–1892. Oxford, 1973. 585p il map tab (International African Institute). 32.00. ISBN 0-19-724189-1

Vansina makes another major contribution to the history of Central Africa. In spite of the importance of the Tio (Teke), who as middlemen in the Stanley Pool region were one of the main purveyors of the Angola and Congo coastal slave markets, almost nothing has been published on them. The only work in English of any consequence is the short section in Vansina's *Kingdoms of the Savanna* (CHOICE, Sept. 1966). This book is divided into three parts. The first contains a detailed ethnographic study of social structure, economic systems, and the Tio world view; the other two parts give some historical perspective on topics such as political evolution, Tio activities in the greater Congo trade network, interaction with French imperialists, and social change through the 19th century. Seldom has such a detailed work on a single African people been produced. This book, running to almost 600 pages, is packed with information on every line. It will remain the definitive work on the Tio for some time to come and should be acquired by libraries for graduate students.

THE TIO KINGDOM OF THE MIDDLE CONGO 1880–1892

JAN VANSINA

Published for the
INTERNATIONAL AFRICAN INSTITUTE
by
OXFORD UNIVERSITY PRESS
LONDON NEW YORK TORONTO
1973

Oxford University Press, Ely House, London W.1
GLASGOW NEW YORK TORONTO MELBOURNE WELLINGTON
CAPE TOWN IBADAN NAIROBI DAR ES SALAAM LUSAKA ADDIS ABABA
DELHI BOMBAY CALCUTTA MADRAS KARACHI LAHORE DACCA
KUALA LUMPUR SINGAPORE HONG KONG TOKYO

ISBN 0 19 724189 1

Printed in Great Britain
by Richard Clay (The Chaucer Press) Ltd.,
Bungay, Suffolk

Heureux qui comme Ulysse a fait un beau voyage . . .

En souvenir,

à Claudine.

Table of Contents

List of Maps

List of Charts

List of Plates and Figures

List of Diagrams

Preface

PEOPLES like individuals have their ups and downs. Now almost forgotten, the Eastern Batéké or Tio, as they call themselves, were known to many Europeans once. For travellers and geographers had heard about the mysterious kingdom of the great Makoko of Anziko since the sixteenth century and some of the Prester John stories even came to be attached to this realm. In time the Tio became one of the populations well known in the Americas, especially Brazil, as one of the main purveyors of slaves. They established themselves as middlemen at the Stanley Pool, at the hub of the great Congo commerce between the fleets from the upper Congo and the great caravans, ever since this trade began. By 1870 as much as one sixth of Africa's production of ivory may have passed through their markets. Then came the Scramble for Africa. In 1880 Count Savorgnan de Brazza signed a treaty with the Tio king Iloo, the French Parliament ratified it in 1882 and thereby initiated the Scramble in Equatorial Africa. From 1882 to 1885 the Tio kingdom became famous among the public for this Treaty while diplomatic circles scrutinized the extent of the realm and the validity of the Treaty.

After the Conference of Berlin concluded its deliberations, the Tio faded out of public view in Europe. Other events and developments in the Scramble were now more exciting. On the spot they were ousted from the banks of the Pool and the future capitals of Kinshasa and Brazzaville by new immigrants, they lost their lucrative trade and, even on the immensities of their plains, they were forgotten by the colonial administration itself.

Its past importance makes the study of the Tio kingdom and Tio society of great interest to the historian, and constitutes one reason for this monograph.

The anthropologist feels attracted to the study of a former state with an economy which in parts had gone far beyond mere subsistence, a system of descent, which combined bilateral and matrilineal descent in an unusual way, a political system which constituted the least centralized system of its kind in Africa, a religion which is still flourishing. Moreover the data available seem to allow for an analysis of this society at a given moment in the past, during the reign of king Iloo. Since some doubts have arisen with regard to the validity of studies based on observations made during the colonial period but which seemed to represent a pre-colonial situation, because abstraction was made of the colonial institutions and the ethnographic present was used, this could be a kind of test case. Was it really possible to gather data rich enough for a defined period in the past to allow for a satisfying description and analysis of a society?

Furthermore descriptive monographs are needed for as many of the world's societies as possible. The descriptive monograph has sometimes been maligned, perhaps because of the understandable preoccupation with the advancement of theory. Yet theory needs to be checked by data. Therefore monographs of a descriptive nature become as essential as bibliographies because they present the material to test theories with. Long, frustrating, and tedious as the work involved may seem at times, it must be done.

Descriptions record the state of a given society at a given time and become valuable documents themselves for the understanding of the social history of the area. There are no unimportant areas in the world. So every society should have its chronicler. For this reason, too, the book was written. It cannot but be incomplete, its interpretations may seem humdrum at times, it does not perhaps contribute in a major way to the development of theory, yet it had to be written.

NOTE: Congo Kinshasa is now Zaïre, since 1971, and the River Congo is called the River Zaïre.

Acknowledgements

THE Social Science Research Council (U.S.A.) awarded me the initial grant which made fieldwork possible and the Graduate School WARF Research Fund as well as the College of Letters and Science of the University of Wisconsin (Madison) supported much of the subsequent research and writing up.

Both I myself and the International African Institute are grateful to the Wenner-Gren Foundation for a generous grant towards the costs of publication which has also made it possible to include the considerable number of maps, charts, diagrams, and figures in this work.

In Brazzaville the Institut National de la Recherche Scientifique (ORSTOM) and its director Dr. Paulian helped me to get into the field with a minimum of delay. At this time M. Marcel Soret and M. J. Emphoux especially earned my indebtedness. Later Dr. J. Pauwels, Dr. O. Boone, Miss M. Karasch contributed some manuscript material, while M. Pierre Bonnafé not only made his field reports about the related Kukuya available, but read and commented on this manuscript.

Professor Daryll Forde, to whom I owe much of what I know about social anthropology, patiently annotated the draft of the text. His detailed and incisive criticism has been invaluable. I am also grateful to Miss Barbara Pym and Mrs. Hazel Holt of the International African Institute for the very considerable work involved in preparing the final revision of the text for the printer.

Then there are the Tio at Mbe, among them especially the late LIPIE who offered me friendship and shared his insights with me. I am grateful to all, old friends and new friends alike and hope only that I met some of their expectations.

The drawings in the field, the maps and the diagrams have been made by Claudine, who also contributed her own observations and insights about Tio life. I cannot acknowledge her share in this work because love cannot calculate. In any case it was a joint enterprise as our whole lives are.

Chapter I
Introduction

IN the 1880s the Tio on the plateau around the capital Mbe, as on the other Batéké plateaux, lived scattered in villages which were generally small in size ranging from less than ten inhabitants to perhaps forty. They practised agriculture, hunted, and gathered food and other commodities needed in daily life. Between the villages there were links of kinship and co-operation so that clusters of them formed what has been called the little society or the neighbourhood. In each cluster there was a centre constituted by the residence of a political chief which tended to be the biggest settlement in the area, although even the greatest chiefs seem not to have constituted settlements of more than one hundred to three hundred souls.

All the settlements were constituted essentially by the grouping of close bilateral kin around the leader or founder of the village. This was even true for the residences of the chiefs. The latter were bigger, mainly because chiefs had more wives, more slaves, and attracted more kinsmen. But when the leader was contested, or at his death, the village broke up and new leaders established new settlements. Even if the village survived, its social composition would change radically. In addition Tio men, even after marriage, did not stay for a whole life-time in a single village. They could found a new settlement of their own or often left one settlement for another where they hoped to gain more protection or enjoy more respect than in the village they had left. In this they were not bound to the neighbourhood, but, since most of their kinship links were ties with neighbouring settlements, that kept them in the area of one neighbourhood.

Such a little society occupied an area which might seem quite large since the distance between the most distant villages might be as much as forty miles or so. But the total numbers involved were still small, normally well under five hundred people. Its boundaries with other neighbourhoods were not formal so that in some cases villages at the edge might feel that they belonged to two communities of neighbourhood at once.

The little society was not self-sufficient, nor did it encompass all of the Tio institutions. There was the society writ large which politically included the whole realm of the kingdom, an area over two hundred miles from south to north and over one hundred and fifty miles from east to west. Economically the society was even larger since it

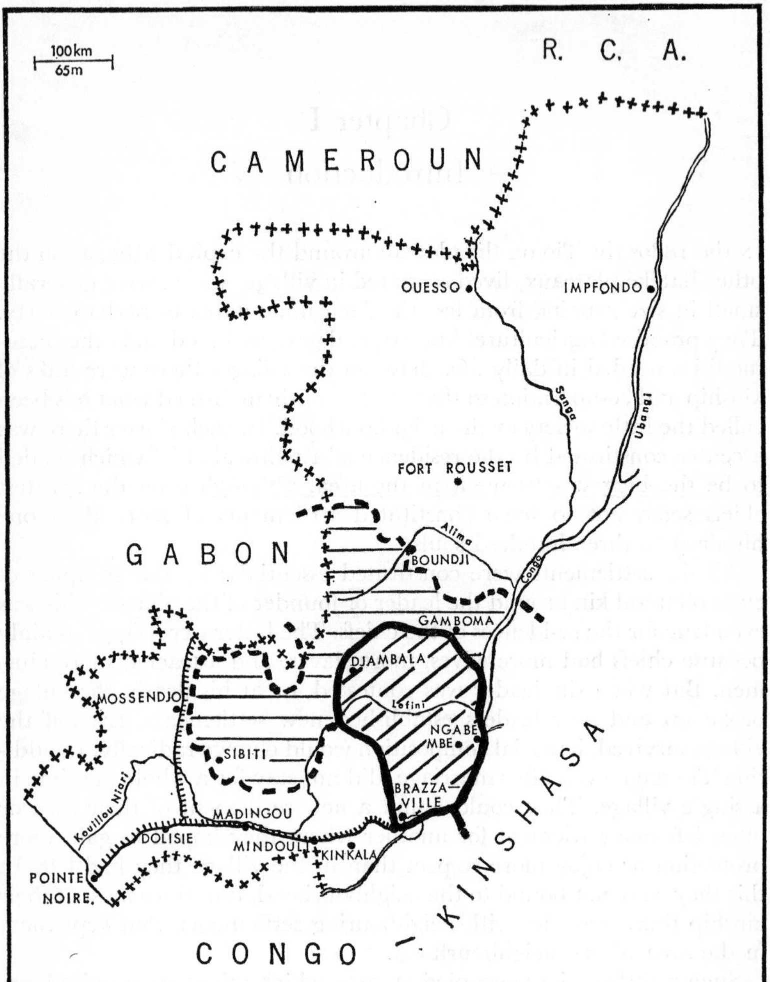

Map 1. *The Tio in the Congo Republic*

+++ : political boundaries ▨ : The Tio group (1963)

ııııı : railways ☰ : Other Teke

participated in a system of trade which reached from the coast to the upper reaches of the middle Congo. There existed, therefore, a large society of which the neighbourhoods were constituent parts.

In addition, the larger society included the riparian Tio as well as those who lived on the plains. Their mode of life was rather different.

The men were fishermen and traders, their neighbourhoods followed the course of the Congo river or the banks of the Stanley Pool. Their contacts with other neighbourhoods were much more intense, and so were the contacts with non-Tio peoples such as the Bobangi who had settled in villages in Tio neighbourhoods along the Congo, even sometimes in the same villages as Tio. Yet the social fabric within these settlements was essentially identical with the structure of the settlements on the plains.

This complex situation explains part of the babel of ethnic names available about the Tio. But the nomenclature is also linked intimately to the Tio conceptions about the geography of the environment in which they lived, and in turn this is linked to the question of density of population. So these three topics have to be considered in a section which must precede a discussion of the methodological procedures used for the reconstruction of the whole society as it existed in Iloo's times.

1. *The Tio and their country*

The Tio live in a very distinctive environment: flat elevated grasslands, dotted here and there with a few woods. In places one can walk a day 'crossing the unending plain where the eye only meets grass, grass, always grass. Not a tree, not a brook comes to break this monotonous crossing.'[1] The landscape leaves a profound impression. The uninterrupted horizons and the vast spaces without signs of human occupation convey an austere yet grandiose majesty. It is utterly different from the landscapes in the valleys or in the denser bush and forests. The expression 'Batéké deserts' used by more than one author, is opposed to the 'pleasant horizon' of Franceville.[2]

And the first impression of the landscape does not deceive. It is a very special environment. No one but Tio live on these grasslands and care for them. The Kongo and Nsundi, who since the 1890s have pushed the Tio away from the vicinity of Brazzaville, never climbed the escarpment to settle on the plateau. In the far south the Kongo neighbours of the Mfinu or the Yaka did not push into the great open plains. These are the home of the Tio and the lions. On the other hand, not all Batéké lived in such an environment. The Fumu and the Laadi lived in more broken country at lower altitude where there are more rivers and more trees. Neither did they climb the escarpment in the twentieth century when they were pushed out by the Kongo.[3] The Eastern Batéké or Tio proper lived on the plateaux and the Western Batéké dwelt in the lower country.

The geographer Sautter perceives the Batéké country as a unit with a regional character. He subdivided it in the plateaux of Mbe (his 7a),

[1] E. ZORZI, *Al Congo*, p. 385. [2] ibid., p. 480.
[3] G. SAUTTER, *Le plateau*, pp. 142–3.

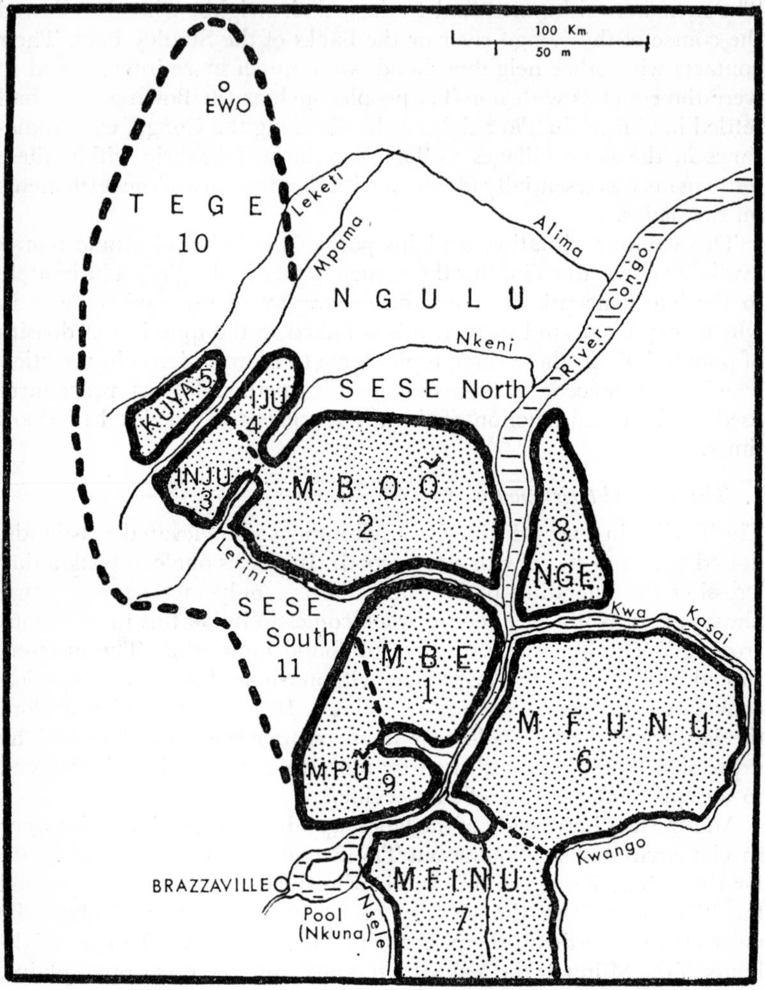

Map 2. *The Batéké plateaux*

Source: G. SAUTTER, *De l'Atlantique au fleuve Congo*, I, p. 144–149; own observations.

[dotted box] : typical Tio plateaux   [dashed line] : Idem after Sautter

MBE: name of plateau or region as seen by Tio

Notes:

2–5: Sautter's 7c
6–7: a single plateau
1+9: Sautter's 7a
10: Sautter's 7d
11: Sautter's 7b

of the Lefini (7b), of Nsah, Djambala, and Koukouya (7c), of the watershed Ogooué-Congo (7d), and included the narrow valley of the river Congo between the mouth of the Kasai and the Stanley Pool, a stretch called 'couloir' by the French and 'chenal' by the Belgians (7e).[4] He juxtaposed the Pool area to another great natural division, separating it entirely from the Batéké country. The Pool (6a) and the watershed of the upper Niari-Congo (basins of the Ndouo, Foulakary, and Djoué (6b)) formed the 'Transitional domain of the Lower Congo'.[5] But the Pool forms a strikingly original environment all by itself very different from the upper Niari-Kongo watershed. Like the plateaux it was inhabited by Eastern Batéké while the watershed was the home of the Western Batéké.

What makes the Tio grasslands so distinctive as an environment is not so much the general landscape as the fact that there are problems with regard to water. The plateaux are constituted by layers of a hundred feet or more of yellow or orange Kalahari sands on a granite base. The altitude varies from 800 metres for the Kukuya plateau to 600 on the Mbe plateau near the Congo river and even 500 to 400 metres towards the Nkéni river. There is then a slight tilt from the south-west to the central Congo basin. More striking is the lack of relief on the grasslands themselves. They seem to be absolutely level and there are very few rivers which cut them. Because of the porous nature of the subsoil and the lack of orographic relief, most of the rain that falls during a rainy season that stretches from September to May is lost in the sands which act as a huge sponge. The water either moves underground to one of the few existing rivers or stagnates sometimes in temporary shallows, if there is a layer of clay underneath as happens on the Wũ plateau.

The lack of water is not due to lack of rainfall. In fact the plateaux are better watered and receive rain for longer periods each year than the 'couloir' or the Pool area.[6] The problem is that no water remains on the surface. Brazza himself described a fight against thirst when going from the Lefini to the Congo[7] and after him many other observers also suffered from thirst. The Tio solved this problem in part by building eaves and utilizing huge waterpots to collect every inch of rainwater that fell on a roof.[8] They even invented a way of soaking cassava in a mere handful of water.[9] But their settlements were tied to the few rivers and streams that existed. For even though they cultivated the

[4] G. SAUTTER, *De l'Atlantique*, I, pp. 148–9.

[5] ibid., p. 146 and map p. 145.

[6] G. SAUTTER, *De l'Atlantique*, I map h.t. *Les pluies au Congo et au Gabon*; *idem*, *Le plateau*, pp. 134, 136–9; L. PAPY, *Les populations*, pp. 116–17.

[7] H. BRUNSCHWIG, *Les cahiers*, pp. 181–7.

[8] G. SAUTTER, *Le plateau*, p. 139. There were special huge pots for this purpose, the *otiele*.

[9] The so-called *idzia* technique. Cf. G. SAUTTER, *Le plateau*, p. 140.

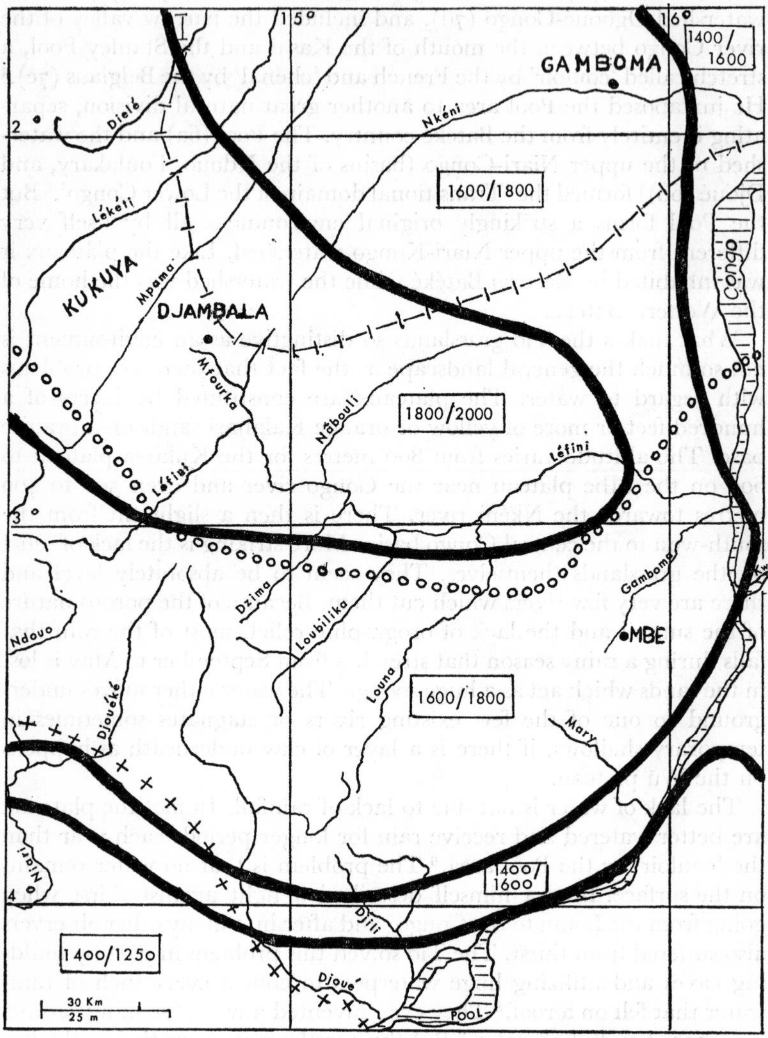

Map 3. *Rainfall on the Batéké plateaux*

Source: G. SAUTTER, *De l'Atlantique*, end map

1400/1600 : m/m per year between the boundaries

+ + + + + + : Four months of dry season South of the line

OOOOOO : Three months of dry season South of the line

—/—/—/— : Two months of dry season South of the line

plateaux, water for the households had to be carried from the rivers. The distribution of the population was severely conditioned by this factor. A Tio remembered how a village once tried to live so far from the river that the women needed a half day to get to the water. They would camp there and come back the next morning. But it did not last. After a year or so the site had to be abandoned.[10] It is understandable that the Kongo or other peoples who use water lavishly and as a matter of course would not stand the plateaux.

The flora consists of grassy steppes in which one recognizes *Hyparrhenia*, *Rhynchelytum*, some grass rubber (*Landolphia Thollonii*), and *Imperata* grasses. Tiny twisted trees dot the landscape such as *Hymenocardia acida* (like an oak) and *Annon arenaria* (like an apple tree).[11] From time to time one meets a copse of trees which are completely different. They are remnants of tropical forest. The huge forest trees arranged in two or three canopies are surrounded by smaller species which are especially fire resistant. This is the probable result of centuries of bushfires set by man. Some botanists feel that the species found in these copses are so varied and those of the savannah so few in number and of such common varieties, that the steppe must be fairly recent and the copses represent the remnants of the once ubiquitous equatorial forest. Others dispute this view and point out that in the steppe, too, relatively rare species can be found and can only be explained as remnants of old formations.[12] In any case, the landscape as it was in the 1880s, was substantially the same in the sixteenth century, since the open character of the landscape, the presence of lions, who live only in steppes, and the 'desert-like' character of the country, are all stressed in the early sources.[13]

The fauna is typical for open grasslands with forest animals living in the copses and along the rare river forest galleries. For the Tio the animal which predominates is the lion. Prides of lion were still numerous in 1963 and many travellers mention them.[14] Besides the king of beasts, great herds of buffalo were found in the nineteenth century on these plains. Countless numbers of elephants dwelled mostly near the rivers, such as the Lefini[15] but also on the plains and their ivory was eagerly sought. Among the smaller mammals a great variety of steppe antelopes must be mentioned such as the *nka* or the *ntsa*, and bush-rodents, described as rats, even though they are not. In the copses the Tio hunted the greyish *ntsee* antelope and other rodents, squirrels as

[10] Ookondzaadza. It happened on the northern part of the Mbe plateau.

[11] L. PAPY, *Les populations*, pp. 117–18.

[12] G. SAUTTER, *Le plateau*, pp. 126–7, holds the first view against L. PAPY, *Les populations*, p. 118.

[13] W. BAL, *Description*, pp. 55–8.

[14] N. NEY, *Trois explorations*, pp. 355, 364, as an instance.

[15] E. ZORZI, *Al Congo*, pp. 404–15. He counted forty-four elephants in a two-day trip down the Lefini. Coming up there had been fifty-seven of them.

well as more 'rat-like' animals. But wart hogs were also to be encountered.[16]

A major effect of the special nature of the environment was that on the plateaux themselves there were no mosquitoes and few flies. Sleeping sickness would develop only along the rivers, and people on the plateau were diseased only if they came too much in contact with the flies when fetching water. Malaria was also very rare, since the *anopheles*, too, was restricted to the valleys. On the other hand, diseases of the respiratory tracts, especially in the dry season, seem to have been much more common than in the lower lying and better watered areas.

The description just given does not apply to the environment of the riparian Tio. They lived along the water of the mile-wide sheet of the Congo river known as the 'chenal' or the 'couloir'—the channel, or near the shallow waters of the Pool. Their natural environment was forest on the banks and the water itself with the fish it contained. For them the seasons did not mean much in terms of availability of drinking water. But they remained important in terms of low and high waters because of the different fishing techniques used, and in terms of the prevailing winds, since in some seasons these often blew right against the current in the channel so that choppy waves made navigation dangerous or impossible for days.

On the Pool the seasons were significant in terms of trade. The numerous caravans which came to trade from the coast could mainly be assembled only during the dry season, when labour in the lower Congo was available for this. At the other end, the traders on the rivers were bound by seasonal factors of winds, high water, and cultivation cycles from where they came in the regions of the lower Alima river. Therefore the people in the trading towns at the Pool had to harmonize the lack of co-ordination in the ecological cycles of their partners in trade and sometimes buy ivory or other goods well ahead of the time they might expect to sell most of it. Compared with the channel area the environment at the Pool also offered more opportunities to hunt hippopotami and provided easier access to grasslands fauna because the forests surrounding the Pool were not as dense as they were along the channel and were absent along most of the south bank.[17]

The term Batéké is a Kikongo term referring to a group of populations which either belonged to a kingdom known as Makoko[18] or who appeared similar to populations which did. The term Teke is a deformation of Te(g)e, Tsio, Tio, Teo, by which most of these populations designated themselves and especially their language.

[16] G. SAUTTER, *Le plateau*, p. 144, notes that there are not herds of antelopes, only isolated animals. There were enough of them, though, to support the prides of lions.

[17] G. SAUTTER, *De l'Atlantique*, I, pp. 331–5, for a full description of the Pool area.

[18] Makoko and Mokoko are respectively Vili and Kongo forms of the Tio word *õkoo*: king. The 'kingdom of Makoko' has been known thus since the seventeenth century.

The core of the kingdom was located on the high plateaux north of the Pool. On the plateau just north the people were called Wũ[19] after the name of the plateau, which was named Mpũ. This area was bounded to the north by the dry valley of the Mary beyond which the plateau stretched to the Lefini river. That part of it was inhabited by the Mbembe, after the name for the area: Mbe itself derived from the term for capital, since the Tio capital was located here. The two ethnonyms referred to geographical areas and did not imply foremost a sense of identity which would oppose one population socially and culturally to the other. Both areas together form Sautter's plateau of Mbe (his 7a). Between Lefini and Nkéni the plateau was known as Mboõ and its inhabitants were the Aboõ. The plateau sloped towards the Nkéni and towards the upper Lefini and the people living on the slopes called themselves Sese, after *see*, meaning a slope on the side of a house-roof. The long narrow plateau bordered by the Mpama to the west, the Lefini and Nkéni to the east was known in its northern part as Iju, where the Jiju lived and in its southern part around Djambala as Inju with the Jinju people. Here the correlation between plateau and population was not perfect since some settlers to the west of the Nkéni near the land-bridge which joins the Boõ and Inju plateaux were also called Jinju even though they lived on the Boõ plateau. But the ethnic names indicated only geographical location and did not imply feelings of ethnic difference. To list these names as 'tribal names' and make different 'tribes' or 'peoples' out of each group as was done on the detailed ethnic maps of Equatorial Africa is entirely misleading. In fact all these people, with some variation for the Wũ and Jiju, were identical as far as society and culture are concerned and this study focuses mainly on them.

West of the Mpama the highest and most westerly plateau, Kuya, sheltered the Kukuya. North of the Nkéni a rolling grassland at much lower altitude called Ngulu, housed the Ngungulu, while east of the Congo but north of the Kasai the Nge plateau was the home of the Ngenge. South of the Kasai river but north of the Black river, the Mfunu plateau with the Mfunu, bordered on the Mfinu plateau which

[19] The spelling of Tio words does not indicate tone. Consonants are transcribed according to the International African Institute rules with the following exceptions. ŋ is transcribed *ng* and is always rendered as ŋ + g. Vowel length is indicated by doubling the vowel except for prefixes, nasalized vowels in last position, vowels before a nasal and consonant, which are always long. There are seven vowels, but since the dictionaries of the 1880s recognize only five there is often confusion between vowels of the second and third degrees. Occasionally we transcribe *ü* for what may be a combination *ui* but sounds like *u* in French *pur*, a centralized vowel of the first degree. Nasalization of vowels is indicated by ~. We regret having to reduce the vowel transcription to five vowels. Ethnic names are quoted without prefix. Geographic names follow the spelling adopted on the official maps of the Republic. Pitch is only rendered to distinguish between otherwise similar forms: e.g. *ngàà*: 'religious specialist', *ngáá*: 'master of'.

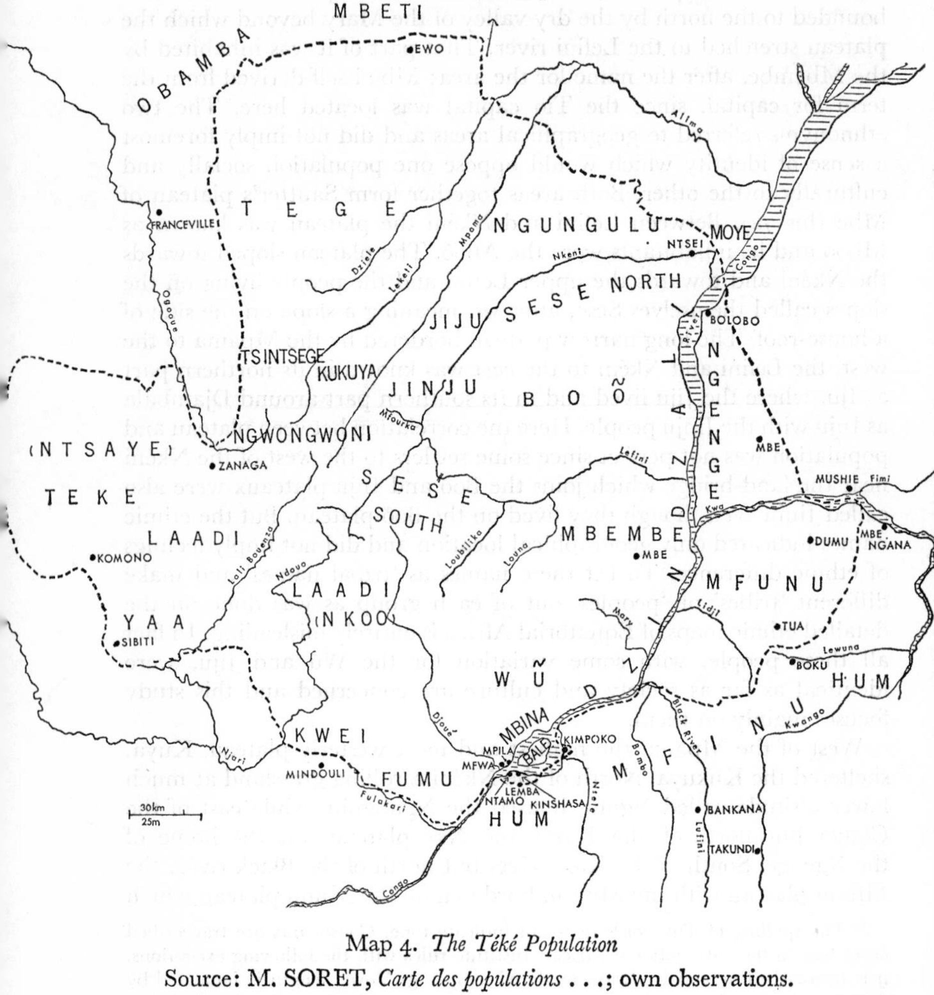

Map 4. *The Téké Population*

Source: M. SORET, *Carte des populations . . .*; own observations.

MFINU: Peoples

– – – – –: Limit of Téké groups excluding MOYE, MFINU and HUM

stretched away south of it to the watershed between the Kwango and Inkisi rivers in the far south. It was inhabited by the Mfinu. All these population names again express geographical residence. Among them, however, the Kukuya, Ngungulu, and Mfinu were socially and culturally distinct from the other populations whose way of life was identical to that of the people in the core of the kingdom.

People living in the Congo valley from the mouth of the Nkéni to the Pool were the Dzindzali, after *ndzali* the Tio name for the Congo river. Around the Pool itself the situation was quite complex. The settlement of Mpila on the north bank and those on the south bank with the exception of Kimpoko were inhabited by the Bale, a name derived from the Bobangi word Ebale, which designates the Congo river and the related *mubale*: 'fisherman'. They called themselves Nkoli.[20] The town of Mfwa and other settlements on the north bank of the Pool was inhabited by the Mbana or Mbina[21] and their western limit were the Djoué river. West of that river the people were called Lali by their eastern neighbours but called themselves Fumu. They stretched west to the Foulakary river beyond which lived various Kongo groups. To the north-west of the Fumu in the area of Mindouli was the area known as Kwei, whose inhabitants bore the same name. West of Mindouli towards Sibiti the Yaami (Yã) were found in an area of the same name. The region of Komono was the abode of the Tere often called Western Batéké proper in the literature. South-west of the Kukuya two open bush areas, between the forests of the Tere and the plateaux called Ngwoni and Tsege, housed the Ngwongwoni and Tsintsege, and the Laadi lived in the valley of the upper Laadi river. Finally, in the north on the plateaux west of the Alima lived the Tege or Tio Okali as far north as Eouo. All the populations mentioned in this paragraph were distinct from each other in their customs and way of life as well as in language, with the exception of the identical Bale, Mbana, and Mbina which form one population, and, perhaps, the Ngwongoni and Tsintsege who may form one ethnic population as well. As for the Dzindzali, their language and society was identical with that of the people on the high plateaux.

The peoples mentioned can be grouped by the anthropologist in the following basic groups: Western Teke including all groups west of the

[20] SIMS, *Mubale*: 'a fisherman'; *nkoli:* 'captive, prisoner' but *nkori:* 'paddler, . . . Mobali [*sic*]'. In quoting SIMS and CALLOC'H no page numbers are given beyond the entry in the vocabulary.

[21] G. SAUTTER, *De l'Atlantique*, I, pp. 364–5; M. IBALICO, *M'pouya kou M'Foumou*, p. 49. For the latter the Mbina lived in the area between the km 45 on the road to Mbe and the Djoué while the Mbana lived on the west side of the Djoué in several villages along that river. Beyond them lived the Fumu who also surrounded Brazzaville from the north side coming as far as Itatolo 15 km from the present town; TH. MENSE, *Anthropologie*, pp. 624–7, for the south bank and the Laadi; L. BITTREMIEUX, *Enkele*, pp. 666–7, for the most easterly group.

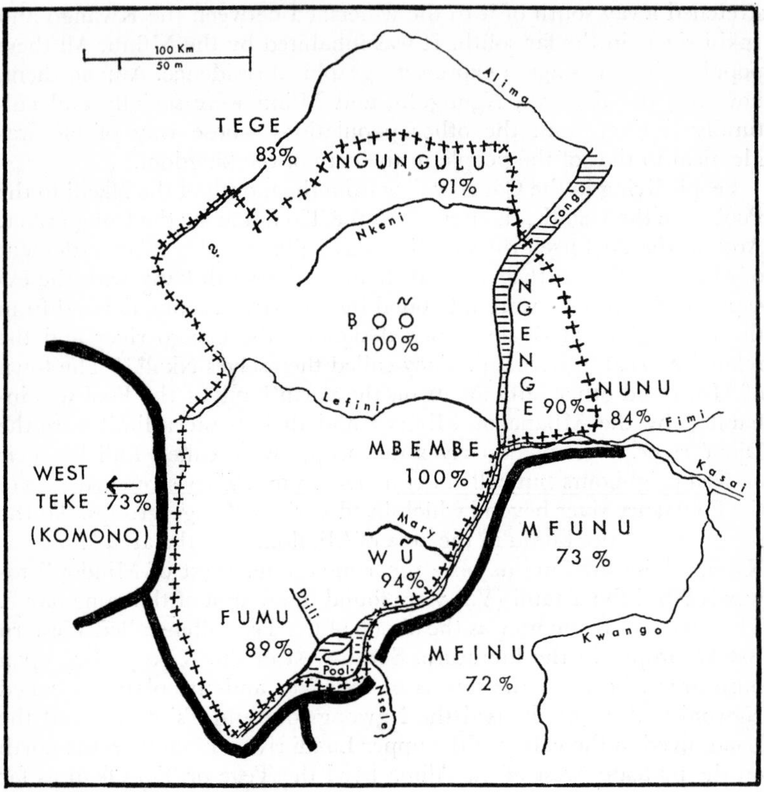

Map 5. *Lexicostatistics of the Tio*

NGUNGULU : Ethnic groups
% : Percentage of agreement with the speech at Mbe
+++ : Over 89% agreement
—— : Below the line less than 74% agreement

Djoué; Kukuya; Tege; Ngungulu; Eastern Teke including the populations of the Mbe, Nsah, Djambala, Nge, and Mfunu; Mfinu.

The peoples which surrounded this huge Teke cluster differed from them greatly in language and culture and are indicated on the map. Among them a group of peoples in the west (around Franceville) who spoke closely related languages and were organized in societies more similar to the Tio, is also known to Europeans as Batéké. Other peoples in the west and north-west, such as the Obamba, Mbeti, and Ngare, were close in language to the cluster. Nothing is known about their social institutions or their culture. Perhaps one or more of them should belong within the Teke cluster.

Besides the Tio there were also a few hundred Tswa who did not work the soil and were from the Tio point of view attached to different chiefs. They lived in the bush, were of smaller stature than the Tio and did not speak the Tio language but 'almost Tio'. They were to be found on the plateau of Djambala and near the limit between the Inju and Boõ grasslands. Like other such Central African groups they seem to have been pygmoids.

By cultural standards it becomes difficult to say where the Tio begin and end. If a political measure were taken to include all the people who lived in the Tio kingdom other difficulties would arise. Therefore it proved necessary to survey the literature about all the groups involved to see which groups shared social life and culture with those of Mbe, the capital. In 1880 these included all the Eastern Batéké. Culturally there were some differences between the dwellers along the Pool on the one hand and the plateau folk on the other but the Pool area was vital in the political and economic spheres, so that in these respects the area had to be included. As for the Wũ, the few existing slight differences have been taken into account. Thus there is good reason to include in this study specifically the Mbana, Bale, Wũ, Mbembe, Dzindzali, Boõ, Jinju, Sese North and Sese South, the Ngenge, and the Mfunu. Because, however, we are not quite certain that Ngenge society and culture as well as those of the Tege (Tio Okali) or the Mfunu are fully identical with practice on the core plateaux, references in the literature dealing with these groups have not been included and the reader should not assume that what is stated about the Tio is valid for these groups, even though most of it will be.

The Tio language enjoyed a considerable diffusion in the 1880s.[22] This explains why Sims started working on a vocabulary as soon as he arrived in 1883 for it was then the international language used on the Pool. Despite contrary assertions[23] the differences between the speech of the Boõ, Mbembe, and Jinju are very slight indeed. A standard lexicostatistic one hundred wordlist shows no differences. The differences with speech elsewhere are summarized in Chart 1 below.

CHART 1

Lexicostatistics of different speech communities among the Batéké

Mbembe/Wũ	94%	Mbembe/Nunu	84%
Ngungulu	91%	Tege	83%
Ngenge	90%	Mfunu	74%
Fumu[24]	89%	Mfinu	72%
Wũ /Fumu	91%	West Teke (Komono)	73%

Note: No data are available, unfortunately, for Kukuya. But Miss Paulian's work seems to indicate that it is surprisingly close, even in details, to Tsio, spoken at Kinshasa, and even more then to Mbembe.

[22] CH. DE CHAVANNES, *Avec Brazza*, p. 204, according to Sims and himself.
[23] A. JACQUOT, *Précisions*.
[24] Data taken from CALLOC'H, *Vocabulaire*, pp. 113–346.

The dialects mentioned in the first column with the addition of both Sese North and South can reasonably be labelled as the same language. In the second column the idioms compared belong to different languages. An indication of this is, for instance, that Mfinu scores just as high with Yans as it does with Tio. All of the languages discussed are included in Guthrie's zone B 70.[25]

The overall density of populations on the plateaux was very low. In 1948 Papy found 82,000 'Teke' in Congo Brazzaville for 80,000 km^2 of which 3,200 lived in Brazzaville. The small Koukouya plateau had 1,200 inhabitants at 30 per km^2. So large areas were empty and the density was well below one per km^2.[26] Later measurements were calculated by Gourou and Sautter. Gourou found for 0·3 to 1 person per km^2 for the plains in Congo Kinshasa north of the Black river, but including the people settled on the channel, and from 1 to 2 per km^2 south of that river and west of the Bombo, which includes settlements near Kinshasa and at Maluku of non-Tio. Between Bombo and the Kwango district the density was again 0·3 to 1 km^2.[27] Sautter calculated that the density of the plateaux including the channel, but excluding the densely populated Koukouya plateau, was 0·53 per km^2. Including the latter it rose to 0·75. On his detailed Table VIII, it appears that the northern half of the Mbe plateau and the whole Nsah plateau had around 0·5 persons per km^2.[28] Our own calculations based on the northern part of the Mbe plateau and excluding the population of Dzindzali and others on the Congo banks led to similar conclusions. Between the Lefini and the Mary river (including Imbãw) from Inoni (excluded) to the Congo valley (excluded), there were in November–December 1963, 563 people of which 328 lived in Mbe itself, for 1,343 sq M2 = 0·419 per sq M2 (3,425 km^2 or 0·16 per km^2) but it must be emphasised that we excluded people at the eastern edge of the plateau, as well as those living along the Congo. A population density then of one to one and a half per square mile (or, 0·5–0·75 per km^2) would hold true for the plateaux in the 1940s to 1960s. With a density as low as this, any shift of even a hundred persons in the area leads to differentials in the density.

The distribution of the population, then, has its importance. The

[25] M. GUTHRIE, *The Bantu Languages of Equatorial Africa*, pp. 77–80. For M. A. BRYAN, *The Bantu Languages of Africa*, pp. 29–32, Teke forms one single group with Yans thus adding Guthrie's B 70 and B 80. M. GUTHRIE, *The Classification of the Bantu Languages*, p. 33, had named the Teke group B 30 which is now superseded. Bryan's grouping together of Yans and Teke does not seem warranted to us according at least to lexicostatistical data. Cf. also J. ADAM, *Variations phonétiques*, and D. CASTEX, *Vocabulaire comparé*.

[26] L. PAPY, *Les populations*, p. 22.

[27] P. GOUROU, *Carté de la densité de la population*.

[28] G. SAUTTER, *De l'Atlantique*, I, Table VIII, p. 108 and Table VI, p. 107; end maps: *Densité par plages délimitées en fonctions des particularités locales du peuplement* and *Densité . . . par carrés pondérés*.

maps show that by 1960 all settlements lay near roads or near rivers and almost all near either a road or the Congo river. This was the result of French policies.

The population seems not to have been denser in the 1880s than it is now. The scarce data we have[29] show on the Mbe plateau an actual increase of population for 19 villages from 1935–8 of 2,304 inhabitants to 2,879 in 1949–52 and the demographic index calculated by Sautter gives 163·5 children per 100 adult women. The population was expanding. Its density therefore must have been lower before.

The situation is more complex however. Our own research has shown that there were important population movements between 1924 and 1934, during the period when the Congo-Océan railway was built. Almost the entire population which now lives on the plateau of Mbe immigrated at that time. We found only 7 men out of approximately 130 who were true Mbembe and not immigrants or descendants of the immigrants from that period.

Actually most of the population of the Mbe plateau went to live with its king Ngaayüo at Ngabe some time before 1918 and most people were killed by the epidemics of sleeping sickness[30] from which the channel suffered since 1887. To this was added the epidemic of Spanish influenza in 1918, cause of the death of the king among others, and several smallpox epidemics of lesser virulence.[31] People on the Nsah plateau and the Wũ were spared by sleeping sickness and the great distances hindered apparently the spread of smallpox and Spanish influenza.

It is therefore possible that the population in the 1880s was much higher than later on, and it is certain that this was true in the channel on the left bank. But there are also reasons to doubt this. In fact we believe that the density was below one person per square mile when the first Europeans arrived in 1880. The data are scattered but suggestive. Between the Pool and the Lefini in the channel there were only three Tio villages on the left bank of which one was of a fair size (say 40 inhabitants).[32] South of Mbe towards the Blue river there was only a

[29] G. SAUTTER, *Le plateau*, p. 150.

[30] L. MAILLOT, *Notice pour la carte chronologique*, pp. 45–54, noted that the epidemic in the 'couloir' stayed quite close to the river. Already in 1909 the relative immunity of the plateau dwellers was recognized even though the Nkéni valley had epidemics in 1908, 1947, 1950–51, but then the 'couloir' suffered these from 1887–1953 and again in 1954, 1955, 1958.

[31] H. BRUNSCHWIG, *Les cahiers*, p. 182, talks about an epidemic of smallpox.

[32] Cf. H. STANLEY, *The Congo*, I, p. 509; endmaps; H. H. JOHNSTON, *The Congo*, pp. 144, 151, 185. Cf. F. COQUILHAT, *Sur le Haut Congo*, p. 75; CH. DE MARTRIN DONOS, *Les Belges*, II, pp. 9, 126; HANSSENS, *Premières explorations*, pp. 13–14; *La tribu des Bateke*, p. 122; CH. LIEBRECHTS, *Léopoldville*, p. 526; H. BRUNSCHWIG, *Les cahiers de Brazza*, p. 191; CH. DE CHAVANNES, *Avec Brazza*, p. 148; endmaps—R. BUTTNER, *Reisen*.

settlement at Imbili (Atoro) near Imbã.[33] Along the Lefini there were four small settlements to Bouambé (Ngampo, Fafa, and two near Bouambé) and populations for three of them are given as 8, 30, and 12 people. The last one was also small.[34] From there to Mbe, then on the left bank of the Gamboma, there was but one village. Mbe itself was small and Ibali (royal graves) even smaller. On the other side the three villages of the three major chiefs Opontaba, Ngaliõ, and Ikukuri were bigger with a real concentration of population in Opontaba's settlement, which was joined with NgaAliõ's.[35] The number of villages and their size seems about equal to what was found in 1963. We have from the 1880s fourteen villages and in 1963, for the same area, fifteen. The size does not seem to have varied much from later practice, though the old Imbãw may have been bigger and the present concentration of population at Mbe should be compared with Opontaba's settlement. No wonder then that the travellers remarked regularly on the absence of population or about the 'deserts' of the plateau.

The point has been elaborated because population density is a major element of any social system, so that changes in density would almost certainly have implied major changes in the social system. Furthermore it is obvious that a kingdom with a density of one person per square mile constitutes an anomaly. But as will be seen, the whole of Tio social and political structure is predicated on such a low population density. For Sautter it was caused by the slave trade while only the spatial distribution of the people was affected by the availability of water.[36] Yet already in the 1580s the country was known to be a 'desert'[37] at a time when the impact of the slave trade could not have been pronounced. The low density must be considered as a stable factor caused by the total way of life of the Tio. The history of emigration from the plateaux since at least the sixteenth century seems to corroborate this. Even with the low density there was a feeling of 'over population' leading to emigration.

The situation on the plains by 1880 contrasts violently with the relatively important concentrations of populations around the Stanley Pool where the Tio numbered perhaps 10,000. Then, as now, the situation was better on the Nsah and Djambala plateaux, while the Kukuya plateau was already densely populated.

2. *Methodology*

To describe the way of life of an ethnic group during a particular period of time raises questions concerning the object of the analysis itself: what

[33] According to Mbalewa (NGAATAALI) who remembers the end of the period and became chief of the land.

[34] E. ZORZI, *Al Congo*, pp. 404–13.

[35] Attested by all travellers to Mbe from NgaNtsu, e.g. H. BRUNSCHWIG, *La Négociation*, pp. 22, 33; CH. DE CHAVANNES, *Avec Brazza*, pp. 156, 162–3.

[36] G. SAUTTER, *Le plateau, passim.*

[37] W. BAL, *Description*, p. 58.

and who is studied and questions dealing with the availability of data. The object is to describe Tio society. The full range of everything that can be said about Tio culture in the 1880s is not covered, and, since an analysis of the organization of society is the object, only those aspects of Tio culture which were closely related to this organization are included. Thus oral literature, for instance, is not studied, but the value-system is described. The latter is essential to our understanding of society, whereas the former is less closely linked to it.

The proper period of time for investigation would ideally be dependent on meaningful durations of time in relation to the institution involved. Thus the elementary family should be discussed over a period of 'one generation',[38] the state over a period such as a reign, agriculture by season and agricultural cycles, etc. These lengths of time vary from one type of institution to the next. The longest 'natural' periods involved are related to trade and politics. In practice it was necessary to find a common measure for all of these requirements. The unit of time to adopt had to be one of the longest 'natural' periods, and the political unit of the reign of Iloo seemed convenient. From the political point of view it represented a period over which the major lords of the realm as well as the king remained the same persons, at least from 1877 to 1892. The full impact of colonization was not yet felt, even though enough written sources are available about the major alignments in Tio politics. From the economic point of view, Iloo's reign coincided with the heyday of the ivory trade at the Stanley Pool from about 1870 to around 1898. Before 1870 the slave trade was paramount. After 1892 the Tio began to lose their monopoly as middlemen and this process was complete by 1899–1900. Thus the period chosen makes sense with regard to the economic and political data. It is long enough to include periods which are meaningful for other institutions. Yet at the same time this discussion shows the relative artificiality of the concept of 'integration' for institutions whose 'natural' durations in time differ so much.

The same is true when it comes to an examination of which unit of population must be the basis for research. When dealing with many institutions a small unit such as a village or several villages in a region, where customs seem to be homogeneous, would do. But in political matters the unit has to be the kingdom itself whether or not its citizens

[38] In fact we are not certain that a period of a 'biological generation', i.e. the time elapsed between the birth of a man and his oldest child is necessarily a good yardstick. Society is acted out by married adults who socialize the children. These may attempt to change the society later on but there is a distinct period in which men (the dominant element in Tio society) are the pace setters and that seems to lie between roughly ages thirty-five and fifty. Beyond the latter age they become 'sages' but no longer, in fact, carry the most active burden of making society work. If this holds true the timespan would be fifteen years and not thirty to thirty-five which would be closer to a true biological generation. But the transfer from one generation to another goes on constantly so that the evolution is continuous.

share the same social customs. As for the 'proper' unit for the analysis, as in the case of market-economy for instance, that could include a very wide territory beyond the Tio. The solution adopted here was to deal with the Tio of the capital and vicinity when dealing with kinship or small territorial structures, of the kingdom when examining politics, and of the whole geographic extent of the trade network when explaining features of the markets. The territories covered vary, therefore, according to the discussion but always include the core of the kingdom: the northern part of the plateau of Mbe. As it happens, all the Tio of the grasslands share the same social structures with regard to kinship and village. Yet this is not so by necessity and again the artificiality of the notion of 'integration' is brought out.

Still the concept of integration is valid, for on a given point at a given moment in time institutions have to coexist and often do mesh one with the other. The truth of this appeared when consideration was given to the plan to be followed for this description. It became quite clear for instance that most data dealing with ritual were best left in chapters dealing with the social context of the ritual, thus stressing how much religion interlocks with the other structures. Some institutions such as slavery impinge at once on social, political, and economic institutions. The dynamic links between the different institutions are best seen when one follows the careers of successful men.

The paradox of the situation is reflected in our sequence of chapters. The book deals first with the institutions which exist at a local level and for which natural time-lengths seem shorter. Social institutions, economic production and consumption, are followed by chapters dealing with the rituals of life, the role of the religious specialists and some considerations about the nature of religion. A second part is devoted to society writ large. In economic terms it is the market economy; in political terms it is the kingdom and its internal politics. A last part puts the whole analysis in an historical perspective.

A remark must be made about the ethnographic present. Anthropologists are now well aware of the dangers of this procedure.[39] Where-

[39] Cf., I. M. LEWIS, *History*, Introduction. A particularly clear statement was made by J. GOODY, *The Social Organization*, pp. iv–vii, where he concludes in the second edition that he is no longer satisfied that it is possible to analyse indigenous political systems relying solely upon the methods that anthropologists normally employ. To leave out a chronological record leads to '(i) insufficient emphasis on non-recurrent events; (ii) upon the institutions concerned with painful experience such as war and slavery (iii) and upon external relations (e.g. in communication with trade, the world religions, or in communications systems) in contrast to internal networks; combined with (iv) a tendency to over-emphasize the distinctiveness of groups and their social and cultural cohesion, for example in the interlocking of symbol, belief and social group' (p. vii). A synchronic analysis at one moment in time, even if it is dated to some past will not avoid these pitfalls. It is noteworthy that most anthropologists concerned with this problem have been preoccupied with problems of political anthropology. But the above makes it clear that the criticisms hold for all aspects of social and cultural study.

as, some years ago, we all believed it possible to use the ethnographic present without major distortion of the data and to give a view of a 'traditional' society by 'abstracting' the 'additions' or 'modifications' brought about by colonial rule, we now realize how unjustified this is. But is it possible to proceed otherwise? Goody has raised the question of whether it can be done at all. Can an anthropologist analyse a society for a period which falls outside his own fieldwork? It is obviously a matter of the sources available and the techniques to be used. The importance of this point explains why so much attention will be paid to a discussion of the sources.

This monograph attempts to break away from the ethnographic present both by examining a period through time and by defining this in terms of actual historical dates, 1877–92.[40] The reader will judge if this has been successful and if a better picture emerges from this approach than from the more traditional one.

The reconstruction is based upon written documents from the period, including some iconographic material, direct testimony from two informants going back to the period and oral tradition from other informants as well as from insights gained from fieldwork conducted in 1963–4. It was thus possible to understand the meaning of items mentioned by contemporary observers, but not understood by them. In addition direct oral testimony could be adduced for the decades following the period as well as some, but little, written material. Regrouping the data according to the rubrics, written data, fieldwork, oral sources, and others, the sources can now be examined more closely.

The Tio were the subject of much writing from 1880 to 1885 because of the power struggle between France and King Leopold over control of the Stanley Pool. Before 1880 direct evidence comes only from Stanley (1877). All the sources were compiled by outsiders but at least not all by outsiders of the same persuasion. First their nationalities were quite diverse and included Frenchmen, Italians, Belgians, Dutchmen, Swedes, and Germans. They included explorers, government personnel, missionaries, quasi tourists such as Sir H. H. Johnston, and traders. Among our witnesses were some who had had little formal training such as Pecile or Guiral whose observations are often of greater value than experienced people like Stanley. There are official acts of government, current archival sources such as letters and reminiscences.

But the material must mainly be evaluated according to two great categories. Those who wrote before the Act of Berlin came to be known at the Pool in April 1885 and those who wrote later.[41] Earlier writers of whatever nationality or profession tended to take sides with the

[40] Because of the nature of the data there is a clear bunching of information for the period 1880–5 (with a peak in 1884) and (from oral sources) 1890–92. Before 1880 little is available.

[41] CH. DE CHAVANNES, *Avec Brazza*, p. 276, for the date.

European government on whose territory they happened to be. Thus Johnston, for instance, derived his general information about the political situation in the kingdom from his host Janssen and represents the viewpoint of the International African Association. Pecile was wholeheartedly behind de Brazza's policies. The major point of dissension between the two sides was the extent and the nature of the political control exercised by the Tio king.

Documents dating from the years after 1885 tend to talk about the Tio in an incidental fashion and added little new except for data dealing with the economic evolution of the Stanley Pool area. The Tio were no longer of intrinsic interest to any European.[42]

Many of the government archival materials up to the beginning of 1886 have been published,[43] and there are almost no commercial or missionary archives. Most of the documentation since 1886 remains in the archives. Since, however, our aim is to analyse Tio society, rather than to give a blow by blow account of various incidents involving Europeans and, since the printed sources begin to show repetition after repetition in this period, it has not seemed profitable to try to cover these archives for the years 1887–92 even though, for instance, the government archives for Congo Brazzaville are now available after 1890.

In this it must be recognized that most of the reconstruction was arrived at from the inside, i.e. from oral traditions or verbal eyewitness testimony and that the written sources corroborated many of these data. The most valuable of the general European documentation was the description of the political power struggle around Mbe. This did not interest foreign observers after April 1885. Then there is the nature of commercial transactions for which printed data are available. For everything else the oral data were fuller.

One class of written documents proved particularly useful. This was the vocabularies collected by Dr. Aaron Sims, a physician and protestant missionary, before 1883 and by Calloc'h, a Catholic missionary, before 1911. Strictly speaking only Sims falls within the period. But given the nature of language it was possible to use Calloc'h as well. A third vocabulary, the one collected by Sir H. H. Johnston, was not much use since Sims[44] knew about it, undoubtedly checked upon it and declared that Johnston had included not a few Lingala words. The advantage of this sort of information will become clear further on as it is

[42] J. J. SURET CANALE, *Afrique Noire*, p. 97; C. COQUERY, *Brazza*, p. 129; P. AUGOUARD, *Trente-six années*, p. 16: 'The latter (Makoko) died in 1892 and the official Journal of the colony did not even shed a tear over this illustrious ally, who had been well and truly forgotten (*bien oublié*) since the partition operated at the Berlin Conference.'

[43] Cf. the publications of H. BRUNSCHWIG, C. COQUERY, M. LUWEL, CH. DE CHAVANNES.

[44] A. SIMS, *Vocabulary, English-Kiteke*, v. The words collected by Koelle were from west Teke according to Sims.

used. The basic concepts and the basic words used in connexion with social institutions appear in these vocabularies and confirm therefore their existence at that time. Even though they do not exceed 2,500 words or so and, given that the absence of a rubric is not surprising, it is remarkable that very few rubrics of importance escaped Sims and most of these did appear in Calloc'h. Hence these vocabularies are our best direct written data on kinship terminology, religious beliefs, and some points of the kinship structure.

Iconographic material and written sources are usually excellent when they deal with the material culture. The existence of a number of photographs, drawings, and etchings of the period by persons who had been there, especially those of Giacomo de Brazza, de Chavannes and H. H. Johnston, are clearly documents of the foremost importance in this respect. Also useful are catalogues of museums in which objects appear which were collected before 1892, especially those of the Royal Museum for Central Africa at Tervuren, and of course the objects themselves.

In other respects the written data deal mostly with easily observed superficial impressions or with trade and politics for which the Europeans showed a particular concern. Thus they testify clearly to economic production and exchange, to burials, to etiquette at the court of kings and major chiefs. Two descriptions of curing illnesses are available. But by and large the more intimate side of life remained unknown. There are good notations on the size of populations but almost none on the structure of villages and chiefdoms. Tio religion was not understood at all. Data about the operation of courts or the resolution of feuds are fragmentary. Even though collective action by a court was described when it involved Europeans, it was not realized what role it played in the operation of justice, nor was the procedure even understood. Data concerned with marriage and kinship are practically absent or untrustworthy. In general the value of written data will become obvious, when the reader sees what, in the reconstructions, is substantiated by these sources.

Ethnographic contributions appeared only after 1892 and the earliest took their substance from the written data discussed above. No anthropologist did fieldwork among the Tio even after Mme Annie Lebeuf Masson Detourbet wrote several articles about her visits to the area. Most of the numerous small contributions deal with material culture or art-objects. Later some were written by Tio from Brazzaville. The outstanding items of this bibliography are the publications of Professor G. Sautter and L. Papy. Without a period of fieldwork we could not have understood the general organization of Tio society on the grasslands of Mbe and Nsah.

Fieldwork was carried out from mid October 1963 to April 1964. Most of the time was spent in Mbe from whence visits were made to the near-by villages. But fortnights were spent in Ngabe and Imbãw.

Thanks to the kindness of Mr. Soret it was possible to pay a brief visit to Gamboma and the village of the NGIA. Despite the short duration of the field period and the fact that, even though I was learning Tio, I needed an interpreter all the time, a great amount of data were collected, perhaps because this was not the first time I had been in the field and perhaps because we remained in Mbe, a village of less than four hundred inhabitants during the entire period. All major events of the life-cycle, including the curing or treatment of illness were witnessed. We also arrived just in time for the planting season and left after the first harvest. We missed direct observation only of dry season activities such as hunting. Even so net hunting was observed during the small dry season. With the exception of the greatest political ritual—the seclusion of the newly chosen king and a royal funeral—we were fortunate enough to see examples of practically every social and political institution in operation, except of course for war and feuds which have been suppressed.

There is the question of how representative the results are since the study was concentrated in one place and checked only in two villages about 40 km (25 miles) distant: Ngabe and Imbãw. In the strictest sense the data are valid for the plateau of Mbe or its northernmost half. Yet the validity of the observations holds true for a much larger area. First, most of the inhabitants of Mbe were Boõ and Jinju, so that most of the Nsah grasslands were represented. Furthermore, visitors from distant villages were constantly found at Mbe, since it still functioned as the capital and, even more important, as a sort of centre away from town for the Tio living in Brazzaville. In addition one of the four wards of Mbe consisted of emigrants from the grasslands of Djambala and the Jiju group. There was even a resident Tege. Beyond that, systematic interviews were conducted with residents from all the Tio grasslands from Brazzaville to beyond Gamboma, including people from the grasslands on the left bank of the Congo river in Congo Kinshasa, south and north of the Kwa. Lastly it must be emphasized that we did not rely mainly on one informant or several, as often happens during fieldwork, nor only on direct observation, but that we did consciously spread out our interviews to all adult men of Mbe and some women and concentrated them later on in such a fashion that all interest groups, professions, and factions were represented. Among the main informants were Jinju, Jiju, Boõ, Sese (south), Mbembe, Wũ. Since these interviews with the same persons extended over months, we are fairly certain that almost all social and cultural differences between these populations came out, and there were very few.[45]

[45] Because the interviews were so informal and so frequent, they were taken down in longhand and not taped. Only one informant, Miandoo twice told us a long story in narrative form, for which taping would have been ideal. In all the other situations we felt better off without it.

We can therefore state with confidence that the fieldwork results are truly valid for the populations of the three grasslands: Djambala, Nsah, and Mbe, including the Wũ. They are not so for the Ngungulu of Gamboma, the Tege in the north-east (even though cultural differences are minor), the Kukuya, for which the first-class fieldwork of M. Bonnafé has given comparable data, or the western Teke. The Ngenge and Mfunu in Congo Kinshasa seem to be very close and the Mfinu less so, at least according to the reports we have about them. Uncertainty remains about the Teke Laadi also known as the Teke of Nkoo. Almost no data are available about them and the one informant we had about them did not originate from the area itself.[46]

The paramount value of fieldwork was first to give a picture of Tio society in action in 1963–4, only seventy years after the period we were studying, and secondly that it allowed us to discover informants for the oral history dealing with Iloo's reign. The informants were not chosen on a sample, nor by chance. From the genealogies and residential kinship structures plus career histories, it was possible to check carefully who could be an informant for the period, what he could contribute and what bias he might have, either because of his position now or because of the position of the eyewitness at the time. This could not have been done without fieldwork.

Without fieldwork it would have been equally impossible to understand Tio society since the other sources gave only scattered indications, but never a view on the whole. Still fieldwork was more of a necessary precondition than a direct source about the way of life seventy years before. We tried to avoid as painstakingly as possible just carrying anything back in time without proof. Of course the working hypothesis was that Tio society at that time resembled Tio society of the 1960s, especially in such sectors as religion[47] or economic production but this was never taken for granted. To use fieldwork data as a working hypothesis was found to be fruitful, both in case the hypothesis was confirmed or in the contrary case, when social change could be documented, or even when no data from the period could be found so that gaps in the reconstruction could be clearly seen.

Direct evidence for the reconstruction came mostly then from oral data. The direct testimony of the older informants was very valuable, but it had to be dated. From the career history of the informant it was gathered where he lived, when, and the when was established by reference to a set of events known to the Tio. These included not only the reigns of the kings in the colonial period but such items as the

[46] Data about Mbe in the appendices show the range of origins of the informants.

[47] On the northern Mbe plateau only one man was a Roman Catholic and one other (but he was a foreigner), Protestant. African Churches had made no inroads at all, in contrast to the villages on the *Couloir* where the creed of Dieudonné was flourishing. The Tio were proud of their own religion, quite open about it and not in the least afraid of being ridiculed. A rare situation for most of Central Africa.

passage of a comet and an eclipse of the sun, the accident by which a governor general lost his life in a plane crash, etc. The calendar and the list of all informants is given in Appendix I. Furthermore it was known that women married early, say when 15–17 and men very late, say when 30–5, so that when a woman informant stated that something had happened when she was still unmarried it could be dated between her age 10 and 17, whereas no such reasoning could apply when men were involved. Men, though, like girls usually married in order of seniority so that the ages of brothers or half-brothers could be roughly dated if it was known for instance that A had married and had a child when the eclipse of 1919 occurred, but that B was then still unmarried. In such a case it is safe to conclude that A must have been 30–5 and B 25–30.[48]

When people talk about their youth in general, 'when they were small boys or girls' it is necessary to establish an age range for the observation. From dated instances, but most of them are derived from non-Tio, we think that childhood memories can be dated between the tenth and fifteenth year of the individual, especially when fairly complex situations are involved. We did ask our informants not so much for general norms, which is the way they would invariably start, but for case studies with as many concrete details as possible. For instance: 'The village had two smiths.'—What was their name?—'X and Y' or 'I don't know'. The 'I don't know' statement did not mean necessarily that the testimony was suspect but indicated often that the childhood memory was of a simple and vague nature, maybe to be dated a bit earlier than other recollections. On the whole it was then decided that since ages could in fact be calculated within a 'window' of a quinquennium, the testimony was to be dated ten to fifteen years later, unless some element in it allowed one to be more precise.

By using this method the results of Chart 2 were obtained for eyewitness accounts to 1915.

From the chart it is clear that only one informant could really give an eyewitness account of the period of Iloo even though it is possible that NGAATALI as well may be counted in this group. The value of the other witnesses is that what they learned from their parents or elders belongs to this period as well: there is only one link in the chain of transmission for the oral traditions. For at the latest the younger informants of the chart were born around 1905 when their fathers were at least twenty-five. So the fathers were aged at least ten in 1890. Information from mothers also falls within the period for persons listed as 1906–10 since this implies that they were born 1895–1900. If the mothers were estimated at age fifteen or twenty when they married

[48] This calendar together with the full list of informants can be found in Appendix I. A second relative chronology involved the estimation of age by Tio over a man's or woman's lifetime. Most of this is given in the text.

Chart 2

Older informants: eyewitnesses 1885–1915

1885–1890: LIPIE:[a] Was adult, not married when king Iloo died in 1892. Believed by people to be the second or maybe the oldest living man on the grasslands.

1892–1897: NGAATALI: He was adult, not married, but no longer a child when king Mbandieele died in 1899. After LIPIE and a man from the village of Ibu near Ngo, he was thought of as the oldest man on the grasslands.

1900–1905: Ubwoono: Born under king Iloo but a baby when he died (1892). Remembers the comet of 18 May 1910. Believed to be the oldest living person in Mbe.

1900–1905: Abili Ndiõ: Maybe slightly younger than Ubwoono.

1905–1910: Ngateo: Saw the eclipse of 1919 when he was adult but unmarried. Ubwoono is his older half-brother. King Ngankia Mbandieele who started to rule in 1934 was his younger brother. Believed by the people of Mbe to be older than he is. This is due to his genealogical position. His descendants are very numerous and he leads the largest section of the town.

1905–1910: Mbali: Says that he does not remember the comet of 1910. But joined the army in 1914 or 1915. Born under king Iloo (before 1892). His genealogical position does give him a greater age than Ngateo, but genealogical age is notoriously difficult to go on.

1905–1910: Ngãkã: Leader of a village by 1933, which means he was born at the latest thirty-five years or so before. He had several wives then. A bit younger than Mbali. Believed to be older than Mbiinu Mbiinu and Okondzaadza.

1905–1910: Ngeikiere: Was married when Europeans arrived in Djambala in 1920.

1910–1913: Okondzaadza: Remembers events from before the foundation of Mpala, i.e. pre-1913.

1910–1915: Miandoo: Remembers king Ngaayüo who died in 1918. Was adult unmarried.

1910–1915: Alatsã: Married for some time at accession of Ngankia Mbandiele (in 1934).

Ba: Married and had two children before he stayed about four years at Bouambé. When he moved from there king Ngamvaala had died (1930).

Bilankwi: Was married and moved under king Andibi (1930–34).

[a] Small capitals are used to indicate titles as distinct from personal names.

their testimony reaches to the very end of Iloo's lifetime. Finally even testimony of these persons as eyewitnesses, especially the older ones brings us rather near the period chosen. When it deals with such slower changing items as bridewealth, for instance, testimony from Ubwoono or Abili Ndiõ can be accepted as valid at the end of the period studied. In most cases however reliance has been placed on what their fathers and mothers did, rather than what they remember from their childhood. An extreme case is evidence about a ritual, in which Ubwoono's mother was involved when she was pregnant with him. It belongs to king Iloo's period and allows no other interpretation.

For the period after 1915 many witnesses were available, but evaluation of what they said had to reckon with two factors. First it had to be established that the material went back to at least the level of the grandparents of the persons involved and, secondly, one had to be aware of the possibility that they had picked it up from the older persons of the village who were also interviewed. These have therefore been used mainly in a subsidiary fashion, with three exceptions, the informant Mbiinu Mbiinu, Ngambu alias NGANSHIBI, and Ngampiuo. The two latter are twins and according to a document of 1936 they were born between 1912 and 1917, probably nearer 1912. But they were educated by the famous queen Ngalifourou, who was an eyewitness for Iloo's time and Ngambu took over from Ngalifourou as NGANSHIBI. Mbiinu Mbiinu took over from the last NGEILIINO who was his uncle. He seems to have been born between 1907 and 1915–16. He turned out to be the most knowledgeable informant about the past of the Mbe area itself, because he had been taught by his uncle and the latter's predecessors.

The preceding explains why weight has also been given to titled office-holders when talking about their titles, for they learned their duties from their predecessors. Among them at least MOTIIRI and NGAMPO had derived information from persons who were coeval with king Iloo I.

Of the people mentioned on the chart only one was a woman. Of the thirteen persons there were two Mbembe, one southern Sese, one Jinju, one northern Sese, and eight Boõ. Places of origin, i.e. of birth, are spread all over the Djambala and Nsah grasslands as well as Mbe and Imbãw. The preponderance of Boõ in the number is not surprising since most people who lived in 1963–4 in the northern part of the Mbe plateau were Boõ by origin. Furthermore, already in Iloo's time and before, people moved from one plateau to the other. Thus Iloo's first wife was the daughter of a Jinju chief and he himself came from a Boõ family. Details about the life histories of all these informants were gathered, as for the others, but more intensively. These cannot be made public now. They did allow for the personal interests of the informant when assessing each piece of information. The insistence on concrete cases also diminished the dangers of biased information and many statements by one person could be checked by another one and, since sixty persons in all were interviewed, serious distortion of the reconstruction because of informant bias is not to be feared.

Part I
The Little Society

THE most elementary observation of Tio society in the 1880s obliges us to distinguish between a small-scale society and overarching structures which are political and economic. One would be tempted to distinguish with Tönnies between community (*Gemeinschaft*) and society (*Gesellschaft*), and at first the distinction seems to be admirably suited to the Tio data. Yet we have preferred to use the terms little society or neighbourhood and wider or large-scale society consisting of 'overarching structures' instead. For many of the characteristics attributed by Tönnies to both types of social groupings are not applicable to this situation without distortion. Face-to-face relationships remain important in the wider society, and kinship plays a paramount role in the operation of the political structures. The overarching structures moreover do not form one single 'Gesellschaft'.

With Redfield one might distinguish between a Great Tradition and a Little Tradition and indeed this is found in the Tio case. But Redfield's attention was turned more to cultural data, the transmission of ideas, emotions, values, and the like, which are not examined in depth in this work, because so many data about them are lacking for the 1880s. In addition there is more than one Great Tradition and the relations between Great and Little Tradition do not conform to Redfield's views. So we preferred to adopt a simple descriptive terminology which reflected the Tio situation better.

The available data about the little society force us to follow a description which deals first with kinship organization, then with settlements and marriage. After this sketch of the social organization, the economics of subsistence, which give its relatively closed character to the little society, are examined. After which the impact of beliefs, values, and cognition concludes this first part. This sequence is not intended to imply that it is our belief that available kinship groups moulded the economic organization or that either or both are the only true independent variables over time to which the 'superstructures' have to adapt themselves without ever taking any initiative. At this point the order followed merely seems the best suited for a clear statement, which focuses on the description of a society.

Chapter II
Kinship

SMALLER groups of Tio society were and are still organized around kinship relations. The principles underlying structures based on kinship can be best approached through an examination of the terminology of kinship. Indeed, a componential analysis of the Tio terms does show in what they differ from each other, which categories of meaning are combined to produce the whole set of terms covering the semantic field dealing with kinship. The Tio terms were clearly linked to status and roles, and from there one can move to a representation of the two major structures based on kinship, the *ndzo* or matrilineage and the *ibuuru* or bilateral group. An additional reason to start with the terminology is the fact that most of the terms are given by Sims and Calloc'h, whereas standard patterns of behaviour are not and the structures are not very well described.[1] Yet for purposes of presentation a description of the structures will be given first.

1. *The matrilineage and the kindred*

Three types of groupings based on kinship existed: the matrilineage *ndzo*, the bilateral kindred *ibuuru*, and the residential groups *ula*. The latter, being founded on residence as well, and more so than on kinship, will be left for the next chapter. For the former two groups, their structure, the institutions in which they played a major role,[2] and a sketch of the typical behaviour between members in basic relationships within the group are presented.

Ndzo, 'the house', was a corporate lineage group including all the living descendants in the matrilineal line of a common ancestor, usually not more than two generations away from the oldest members of the lineage. These ancestors were irrelevant for the group, except for one or more of the mother's brothers of the oldest living member of the

[1] It is conceivable that the semantic boundaries between the terms has varied since Iloo's time, without affecting the core-meaning of each term. This seems most unlikely however.

[2] The word function will be avoided as much as possible because of its ambiguity. In addition when it is used with the meaning: 'what a structure does' there is no control in reality over the number of different functions in society, where the boundaries between them lie, if they correspond to almost metaphysical 'needs', etc. We have tried to limit ourselves to an indication of participation by a social group in institutions (such as marriage, funeral, but *not* education . . .) which were clearly existing as separate entities. Purpose is not denied to social groups or institutions, but purpose cannot be demonstrated.

group. In fact, then, a matrilineage counted at most six generations in depth and four among the living, which was not rare because girls married early.[3]

There was nothing normative about the specific depth of a lineage, and sometimes *ndzo* would split up earlier, when the group had become too big, or harboured one ambitious man too many. In such a big group the struggle for leadership did produce tensions and splits, and when a death occurred it was attributed to the sorcery the would-be leaders used against each other. It was then time to split. But sometimes a group which was not very big would split, simply because there had been a violent quarrel. One case was remembered in 1963 when men quarrelled and split before they had grandchildren. The size of a *ndzo* was also variable. For a quarrel did not necessarily erupt when a *ndzo* grew large. Its leaders might get along well, or one of them might dominate the others so much that they did not want to break away.

The procedure for splitting off was to cut a banana tree *aaciir obiõ*, which also settled the quarrel which had led to the split. A banana leaf was given for both parties to hold. Then it was formally cut, usually by the chief of the land. Later the parties drank wine together to show they would not make each other fall ill. A split would be decided on only after the diviners had shown that one half of the *ndzo* was massively bewitching the other half, so that separation was the only solution. Lineages did not belong to clans. They were not identified by name, there was no praise name (*ãmbili*) attached to them, nor any food prohibition. Their identity was only marked by the fact that they had formal leaders: the 'chiefs of the house': *mpfõ andzo* or 'owners of the house': *ngandzo*. And when the *ndzo* had to be identified it would be named by the name of its head.

The *mpfõ andzo* was theoretically the oldest male of the lineage, an elder brother, mother's brother, or mother's mother's brother to the others. But, in practice, the son of such a man could be the head and such an arrangement was even preferred since he was then not part of the *ndzo* and therefore could not be a party to any disputes inside the group. Such a *mwaana be iboolo* 'child of a man' would also not be afraid of accusing members of the *ndzo* openly if they bewitched one another, which they did often. For the same reason one often appointed a slave of the *mpfõ andzo* to succeed after the death of his master. That the sons of the son of a *mpfõ andzo* or the son of a slave could ever succeed was in dispute in 1963. In fact houses such as Ubwoono's were known in which the succession since his birth around 1890 had been strictly

[3] Direct proof for both the matrilineage and its composition in Iloo's times was provided by both Ubwoono and LIPIE. Among the writers Calloc'h, 'neveu', p. 275, 'oncle', p. 279, 'chef de famille': *nganzo* is significant. The latter is a correct term for lineage head, still used in 1963.

matrilineal. It then became evident that cases where the succession was not fully matrilineal were hard to find. The ideal norm it seemed in 1963 was to appoint a son but in reality it was not done much.

Everyone dealt in fact with more than one *mpfõ andzo*. Besides the one in the matrilineage, there was the head of the house of one's father, where a person was *mwaana be iboolo*. This person was almost as important for an individual as the first one. Thus in the case of Marcel (1960s) his own *mpfõ andzo* Avila was much less relevant than Ngaayüo, the head of his father's *ndzo*. And there is no indication at all that this situation is of recent making.

Moreover, the term *mpfõ andzo* could be used by anyone to designate his own maternal uncle, or the eldest among them. By 1963 it was evident from an event that a mother's brother acknowledged some responsibility for his sister's son, but not for the sister's son of his sister's son.[4] The house must then be seen as a collection of small groups, comprising a set of brothers with the same mother and their sister's sons. Just as a person belongs both to a family of procreation and a family of orientation, he belonged to two such sets of mother's brother/sister's son. This vision would explain statements like Ngateo's: 'When the children are small, they replace the *mpfõ andzo* by those of their father and mother. Those can then make *okuu* (ritual).' The oldest brother would eventually become *mpfõ andzo* when the mother's brothers had all died.

The facts support the notion that the matrilineage operated essentially within two generations, mother's brothers and sister's sons, and in 1963 most of the *ndzo* of adults conformed to this pattern. The greater *ndzo* was an imbrication of the smaller ones, called *ipei indzo* 'pieces of the house'. The advantage of postulating such a structure is also that it explains why the specific role of the *mpfõ andzo* is so vague compared with the role of *nguboolo* 'mother's brother'. Furthermore the situation conforms very well with the strong insistence on alternating generations found both in the terminology and the general kin behaviour.

The *mpfõ andzo* and everyone's *nguboolo* fulfilled the same tasks. They represented the matrilineage at the inquest *okuu* which was held in case of severe illness of any of the members and where all the other members promised not to bewitch the patient or to desist from doing so, if they accepted responsibility for the illness. If one of the members was killed and a feud erupted both the *mpfõ andzo* and the *nguboolo* had to participate, even if they did not live in the settlement of the victim. Both also acted in matters of bridewealth, counter-bridewealth, and inheritance.

[4] In Appendix 10 the case concerning the quarter Uluuna shows a mother's brother being concerned about his nephew in court, but declining to take on any responsibility for the sister's son of his sister's son! The situation among the Kukuya is similar according to P. BONNAFÉ. The smaller parts of the *ndzo* are called *bataki*: 'those of one pair of buttocks'.

The inheritance of women and matters concerning bridewealth were in fact the only specific business related to the *ndzo* to the exclusion of the kindred. The *ndzo* were essentially a group of wife-takers and wife-givers. The inheritance of goods did not concern them. One other specific custom linked to the matrilineage was the habit of some to deposit goods and currency with their *nguboolo*. There was no compulsion. As long as the *mpfõ andzo* had them, he could use the funds for expenses he himself had incurred and even to defray costs incurred by another member of the lineage, but the latter practice required the explicit approval of the depositor. Further the *mpfõ andzo* seems to have collected tribute (*ingkura*) for the political chiefs and during the colonial period taxes were gathered this way, rather than on the basis of residence. In later years this was a prerogative of the *mpfõ andzo* not of all *nguboolo*, but it may not always have been so. For the *nguboolo* could sell his sister's son into slavery if he needed the funds and the child's father could not give them. He was, say the informants, supposed to get the agreement of the *mpfõ andzo*, but in the actual cases cited, no *mpfõ andzo* appeared beyond the maternal uncle himself. Lastly the succession to certain chiefdoms of the land, especially on the Wũ plateau, was strictly matrilineal. On the Mboõ plateau this was not a universal rule, since in some cases sons also succeeded.

Justice within the *ndzo* was administered by the *mpfõ andzo* or a *nguboolo*, if quarrels had erupted within the house, and according to the genealogical position of the quarrellers. A sign of the corporateness of the whole *ndzo* was also the fact that if anyone had been killed by another member of the *ndzo*, no feud could erupt and compensation was set by the *mpfõ andzo*. In addition most of the *mpfõ andzo* were 'big men' and heads of their own settlements. As such they often transmitted their leadership to one of their children as well as in other cases to one of their nephews. Whatever the case, they never clearly separated between the duties and privileges of being headman and those of *mpfõ andzo*.

Behaviour in this group was patterned on the roles of *nguboolo* (mother's brother)/*mwaan ankieli* (sister's son). The *mwaan ankieli* should like and greatly respect his maternal uncles who in turn should protect him, but could also order him around. Thus a mother's brother might pay the ritual fine for breach in etiquette to the father of a sister's son or might help with bridewealth if the boy or his father could not find the funds. But such ideal behaviour rarely obtained. People insist that in reality the *nguboolo* could lose their tempers, hit their nephews and abuse them. The *mwaan ankieli* tended to give his uncles a wide berth. A constant struggle was said to oppose them. The *mwaan ankieli* were believed to attempt to bewitch their *nguboolo* to kill them and take their place, whereas the older generation bewitched the younger one to enforce the recognized obligations on the younger members of the group and to maintain its position. It must be stressed though that the actual behaviour of uncles and nephews lay between the two extreme stereotypes given. Thus in 1883 Ngaliema, the leader of Ntamo went to Mpila to pay seven slaves and one tusk to free his nephew who had been accused of witchcraft there.[5] Had he not done this, the man might have been killed.

The stereotype reflects one important aspect about the *ndzo*. To a large extent fear of witchcraft was the sanction which kept it working. As long as both nephews and uncles behaved as they should, i.e. collaborated in the *ndzo* and had harmonious relations, they were not accused of bewitching each other. But if they neglected their obligations, accusations began to be whispered and public accusations might follow. So people tried to follow the prescribed norm. Moreover, every death rekindled the fear of actual witchcraft and revived the determination to fulfil one's obligations. As Ba had it:

'Formerly it was believed that when some one was ill, it was attributed to witchcraft. They said: he died because he was old too. But the close kinsfolk would never say that. They would start to think about who the witch could be, but they would not declare it openly. Sometimes they would not even go to the diviner, for instance if they believed an elder brother had done it.'

Of course they would go even less if it was a *nguboolo* or the *mpfõ andzo*, the arch-witches. These were followed closely by the mother's mothers who also killed people out of jealousy. It was said that when any single person in the *ndzo* was believed to have killed too many others in the *ndzo* he could be forced to commit suicide by hanging or the *ndzo* members would do away with him and fake it as a suicide. Cases dating up to the 1940s of the latter type were still known at Mbe. Once fear of witchcraft in the *ndzo* had reached this point it no longer provided a sort of negative solidarity within the group. It destroyed the group itself. For, after all, the effective *ndzo* probably numbered no more than five to ten male members.

Witchcraft also led the *ndzo* into feuds. Often, if a person in the kindred of one of the *ndzo* members was accused of having killed someone by witchcraft in the *ndzo*, the group refused to pay the counter-bridewealth for the mother of that member when it was requested. This inevitably led to a feud with the *ndzo* of the father of that member. To fight a common enemy united the *ndzo* but it also disrupted society in general.

When the poison ordeal was handed out by the political authority to test accusations of witchcraft, the *ndzo* had to put up three men as pawns to back their claim that their man was no witch and had killed no one outside the *ndzo*. If they won the ordeal, they returned the accusation against the accusers. If they lost they had to pay six men.

[5] C. COQUILHAT, *Sur le Haut Congo*, p. 361.

More positive forces for unification of the *ndzo* were the mechanisms of bridewealth, wife inheritance, and counter-bridewealth because they fostered common interests between its members. They made certain that every maternal uncle and every sister's son in the system had an advantage at times, in proclaiming the unity of the *ndzo*. However, the lack of identification marks, of *ndzo* ritual, of a corporation sole, all indicate that the *esprit de corps* did not go very far. This was a consequence of the internal make-up of the *ndzo* as sets of *nguboolo/mwaan ankieli*. But even more there was the fact that a person's whole *ndzo* was, for him, only part of a much wider group of kin—the bilateral kindred, the *ibuuru*. By 1963 almost all informants could be tricked into stating that their *ndzo* was their *ibuuru* and vice-versa. This genuine confusion resulted from the fact that for each man the *ndzo* only formed a part of his *ibuuru* in most actual situations. It may also have been a result of the weakening of the distinctive functions of both *ndzo* and *ibuuru* since the 1880s but we believe that the confusion already existed then.[6] *Ibuuru* was a kindred which included all relatives by blood of a given person. It was not corporate since it was different from person to person except for full siblings. The term differed from *baamukaana* or *baamuju* 'those of one species'[7] used for animal species and also to designate the social estates of aristocrats, commoners, and slaves. It included a kindred no more no less. It was not a patrilineage, nor a truncated patrilineage such as the *kitaata* of the Kongo, nor the matrilineage of one's father. It includes all half-brothers whether by the same mother or the same father, all cross cousins, cross cousins of the parents, in short, persons who would not belong to any form of unilineal descent groups. Furthermore, and quite normally, mixed descent lines were commonly cited when persons were asked to show how they belonged to the same *ibuuru*. It must be stressed because this combination of matrilineages of shallow depth with bilateral descent is not known anywhere else with the possible exception of the northern Lunda.

Two facts are unique here. First the *ibuuru* was recognized as a quasi-corporate group. It could not be truly a corporate group because its composition varied from person to person, except for siblings. But exactly as a family, which is also Ego-centred, still forms a well defined group during Ego's lifetime, so the categories of persons which made up the *ibuuru* were also well defined. Ego's *ibuuru* was not just the *ndzo* of his mother and his father or the *ndzo* of his four grandparents as the *ibuuru* is conceived among the Kukuya according to Bonnafé. If this

[6] A systematic inquiry was conducted among all informants old and young about this. The confusion was not greater among the young men than among the older people, as would be expected if there had been change. Judges and councillors were less confused than others.

[7] Sims, *kana* 'family, tribe, quarter in village, home'. Calloc'h: *kana:* 'famille' twa (*tcwa*): 'famille' p. 214. *Kaana* is certainly related to Kikongo *mukanda*, lineage. In Tio both words seem to mean 'species', 'tribe'.

were so, the structure could be reduced to the component *ndzo*. Here the *ibuuru* was thought of as the juxtaposition of extended families three or four generations deep, Ego's families of origin. Just as an elementary family is not the addition of part of one *ndzo* to part of another, this structure cannot be explained away in terms of its component *ndzo*. The other basic fact is simply that the *ibuuru* was involved in all social situations with the single exception of receiving bridewealth or counter-bridewealth. Thus the Tio *ibuuru* is not simply the equivalent of a collection of cognates of Ego, which may be assembled on occasional specific occasions as is the case in almost all human societies. To stress both the quasi-corporateness and the great functional load of the *ibuuru* we refer to kindreds as the kindred, in the same way the literature refers to families as the family even though it is an Ego-centred group.

Each person described his *ibuuru* by listing the forests (*idzwa*) of origin. These designated areas from whence his ancestors had come. In theory there should be a great number of these, but in practice people rarely went beyond a list of from two to four forests and divided their ancestry in 'quarters', not unlike the European nobility. In each generation a distinction 'on father's side' and 'on mother's side' was made and they rarely went beyond the four grandparents. In fact they listed six grandparents: father's father, father's mother, father's mother's brother, and mother's mother, mother's father, mother's mother's brother which is consistent given the existence of the matrilineages. Still most of these great-uncles had the same ancestry as the grandmothers and there were only four quarters of four forests of origin.

No one could establish the genealogy by which he descended from ancestors who had left those forests, so nobody knew who belonged to that group of descendants. So if people claimed to have ancestors which came from the same woods, they would recognize each other as kin. In practice however this recognition would remain meaningless and a rule of exogamy in this widest kindred, for instance, would not obtain.

For there existed a much better defined and smaller kindred. Just as the word 'family' in English can mean everything from a large kindred to an elementary family, so it was with the word *ibuuru*. It designated the widest kindred, the kindred on the father's side, the kindred on the mother's side, and finally 'the kindred in which one inherits' *ibuuru vyishiil iloo*. This encompassed all relatives by blood in the two ascending generations from Ego with all their descendants. Each person would view himself as belonging to two of these: one on his father's and one on his mother's side. Costermans[8] for the Tio of the Pool talked about a sort of familial grouping, the aim of which was the collective ownership and exploitation of goods. He noted in this context that a father had to buy off his son if he had been convicted as a thief and that married young men remained under the authority of the *paterfamilias*.

[8] B. HERMANT, *Les coutumes*, p. 297.

At this level the kindreds became more similar from person to person since half-brothers and parallel cousins shared one of the two 'kindreds in which one inherits'. Still there was no distinct name to designate these groups. Yet for a Tio they were easily recognized, for the personal name indicated one's ascendancy. In the mother's kindred, people would use a personal name which had belonged to a grandparent of the child in that kindred. In the father's kindred it would be designated with one of the names stemming from a grandparent on their side. Thus all Tio had two names. Ngaliema's other name was Itsi and the famous chief with the title NGOBILA was called both Ngantiene and Ngeimpãw.[9] This custom of naming can only be explained by reference to a kindred. Since names did belong to kindreds and since only one person was supposed to carry the name of that particular *nkaa*, homonyms had to be related, just as much as people who claimed to have come from the same forest of origin. In practice those who lived in the neighbourhood knew by the names of an individual exactly to what kindreds he belonged.

Beyond that, father's and mother's kindreds were indicated by the inheritance of food avoidances or *ngili* (*ngili*: 'forbidden thing', Sims). Each person kept three to five of these, so that some had to be eliminated at each generation, otherwise of course a person would have at least sixteen of these after a mere four generations. The limitations were due to the following practices. First all *ngili* fall in four sets and usually an individual kept no more than one of each set. The sets were:

1 white fowl or nightjar (*caprimulgidae*)
2 elephant or eel or hippopotamus or African oxpeckers (*buphaga africana*)
3 bushrats, eggs, wild cats, and eel or hippopotamus, whichever was not chosen in set two, *mbiene* rodent
4 rooster or water-turtle or bees (*sic*: honey may be meant) and weaverbirds (*philetaerus socius*). Very often an additional prohibition went with the weaverbird: not to walk in front of anyone during a thunderstorm[10]

[9] Other examples abound. Cf. H. STANLEY, *The Congo*, I, p. 304, Itsi/Ngaliema 349 Ngako/Nkow. The double names are the best indication of the existence of the kindred. Cf. also M. DELAFOSSE, POUTRIN, *Enquête*, p. 562, who believed one was a personal name and the other a clan name, and J. VANSINA, *Les noms*.

[10] The list is incomplete. In 1963 e.g., Avion had on the father's side: elephant, white fowl, Nile monitor, waterbuck (*mvuli*), and a rodent *mbiuu*; on the mother's side elephant and white fowl. The case shows that sets 3 and 4 are incomplete and that the mother's side had completely merged with the father's side. These avoidances were not 'totems' and R. HOTTOT, F. WILLETT, *Teke Fetishes*, use of *lisolo* as totem for this (instead of *ngili*) remains unexplained, p. 25. Calloc'h and Sims have both *ngili* as 'forbidden thing' and 'interdit', p. 244. But Calloc'h, p. 283, tantalizes with: '*li-solo:* pacte avec une bête' which could be much more than an avoidance!

Usually a person would drop the *ngili* on the mother's side which belonged to the same set as the one of the *ngili* on the father's side. If a man fell ill, the diviner would tell him to take it up again. Even if there was no overlap of category in the *ngili* inherited, a person could still try to drop one on his mother's side and wait for the results. It was believed that the punishment for non-observance would only be a form of mange, which was hardly a catastrophe. These were practices which obtained in the times of Iloo according to NGAATALI.

It is evident from the discussion that the food avoidances could not serve very well as identifiers of social groups since the list differed from person to person and also because their total number was much smaller than the numbers of food avoidances available in other, even neighbouring societies with unilineal descent. This reflects perfectly well the nature of bilateral structures where kindreds are not mutually exclusive, but overlap mutually to a fairly great extent.

Praise-names were also associated with kindreds. Since the latter were unnamed, they could not have praise-names. But the praise-singers would mention all the names of the ancestors in all lines of the person they wanted to glorify and the praises of the names of the forests concerned. Their songs consisted essentially in showing the connexion of persons with more or less illustrious forests. Nobility was defined by reference to a descent from one of four glorious forests and other places were famous because they had been the residence of mighty chiefs. The total effect of such a praise was comparable to the effect of a coat of arms, both with regard to its esoteric quality and its claim to belong.

Since the kindred was not a corporate group it had no head. But persons could be represented by the *mpfõ andzo* of their fathers and their mothers together and when needed all the members of one's 'kindred in which one inherits' could be assembled by Ego's father for his side and Ego's maternal uncle for his, such as for an *okuu* inquest.

The kindred in its widest sense provided a social status for its members to which personal names, praise-names, attribution of estate, and tribal identification were the components. This tribal identification meant that a person would describe himself as belonging to this or that plateau, as Mbembe, Boõ, Wũ, Jinju, etc. Usually one took the tribal name of one's father. But it did not matter much, said NGAATALI. If one did not know where one's father came from, one could simply take the name of the plateau on which one was living. Still a 1963 survey at Mbe showed that almost everyone listed his 'tribe' according to the origins of his father. It may have been true that formerly the identification followed that of the village in which one resided or in which one's father had resided.

The 'kindred in which one inherits' played a more important part in a person's life. Inheritance of goods, solidarity in feuds, in *okuu*, and the witchcraft ordeal were regulated by this group. But inheritance and sometimes political succession apart, all these institutions were shared with other social groups: the *ndzo* and the settlement groups *ula*.

The data on political succession from contemporary writers are rather mixed. Some like Brazza mention that 'brothers' succeeded.[11] Brazza also claims that 'sons' succeeded,[12] finally, most hold that 'sister son's succeed'.[13] In fact some chiefdoms had strict matrilineal and adelphic succession and in others the succession was bilateral since brothers including half-brothers with a common mother succeeded before sons. So the succession was not strictly patrilineal, but truly bilateral.

As for inheritance of goods, an almost contemporary source stated that at the Pool one half of the goods went to the sister's son, one half to the son, nothing for girls, and when the deceased was not a chief two thirds would go to the nephews and one third to the children. If the deceased were a woman half of her goods would go to her brothers or by default to her sisters and one half to her sons. If she had no children, everything went to her brothers and sisters and the converse was also true: if she had no siblings everything went to her children.[14] If a man had no heirs, a slave might inherit from him. The account is certainly not entirely correct. First a number of goods might be buried with the deceased, especially if he was a chief. Then brothers of men are not mentioned, yet there is very little doubt that they inherited; there is also no doubt that slaves were considered to be children when it came to inheritance and, finally, that men had very little to inherit, so that the provisions mentioned do not make much sense. The opinion of our informants that they left their valuable kitchen goods, such as metate stone for instance, to their daughters[15] and that the rest was abandoned seems much more likely.

In modern times the eldest surviving brother or half-brother of the deceased divided the inheritance. The brothers, the children and the nephews could all be among the heirs. In one case the eldest son took the gun and all the hidden money; the others had nothing; in another three brothers, all of one *ndzo*, divided the inheritance equally; in yet another case there was an explicit will: the child received a Petromax light and a phonograph, the younger brother a suitcase with pieces of cloth and the sister's son a sewing machine. In yet another case the gun was left to the son of a younger brother and the money divided among

[11] H. BRUNSCHWIG, *Les cahiers*, p. 182; P. AUGOUARD, *Trente-six années*, III, p. 19.

[12] H. BRUNSCHWIG, *Les cahiers*, p. 176; Sims, *kira uli tara*: 'succeed to father', p. 160.

[13] CALLOC'H, p. 275 'neveu'; M. DELAFOSSE POUTRIN, *Enquéte*, p. 562; P. AUGOUARD, *Trente-six années*, p. 19; C. COQUILHAT, *Sur le Haut Congo*, p. 61; H. STANLEY, *The Congo*, p. 375; W. H. BENTLEY, *Pioneering*, II, p. 19. It is possible that a preference for matrilineal succession did in fact exist around the Pool and one for succession from father to son among the Boō. But in all cases succession was adelphic.

[14] P. HERMANT, *Les coutumes*, p. 295 seq., according to Costermans.

[15] Iyene of Ampo thus saw a metate inherited from his mother by his sister. He thought that perhaps his mother had already inherited it.

the children of that younger brother, including an equal part for the man who had the gun.

The variation among the cases known in 1963 and the confusion of the reports of the time seem to indicate that there was also a great variation in inheritance. First the concept certainly existed since Sims has *mosolo*: 'inheritance' (to be used in the plural) and *yaa*: 'inherit'. Then Mbali summarized the principle he had learned when he became a councillor for the court. The guns of a *de cujus* were for his son; valuables in metal (*ngiele*) used as currency were divided between the brothers of the deceased and his children in the proportions of two thirds for the brothers, one third for the child and, within each category, half for the eldest and one half for all the juniors to be divided equally. Thus given thirty *ngiele*, the brothers took twenty, the children ten. The eldest brother took ten, the others divided the other ten. Among the children, too, the eldest took half, that is five *ngiele*, leaving five for the junior children. The eldest child received nothing however if he had inherited the gun. Goats and some of the household objects as well as part of the *ngiele* of the children could be given to sister's sons. Girls inherited as well as boys, but debts had to be settled before the estate could be broken up and, if they were not, the sister's son, but *not* the children or the brothers, was responsible to the debtors. The last point seems curious, but may be correct since the eldest brother who divided the estate was often a person from the same *ndzo* as the sister's sons.

Abili Ndiõ confirmed that women's objects went from mother to daughter. The household objects of a man went to his sons, which only half confirms Mbali. The house of the deceased was burned. If there were no sons, the household goods were left to the younger brother of the *de cujus*. In any case, some of these household goods were either buried with the man or broken and put on his tomb.

The Wũ were different, said Balewari. There the will of the deceased regulated the inheritance and involved sons, brothers, and sister's sons. Otherwise the younger brother, or, if none remained, the sister's son would take all, 'watch the children' and educate them. The *ndzo* there was more important than at Mbe where a brother would keep the whole estate only in trust and when there was a quarrel. Then the claims of all would be settled by the 'big men' of the kindred.

Solidarity within the kindred was fostered in part by the common inheritance, to the point that the Tio called this more narrow kindred *ibuuru vyishiil iloo*. The *esprit de corps* was also greatly strengthened by the respect the Tio had for their ancestors, the *ikwii*, that is for the shades of the deceased father, mother, and mother's brother of a given person. The cult of the ancestors however was in the hands of the head of the polygynous family, in which the father's shades were responsible for all members.

The kindred, even though it was not corporate, was an important social group. It played a part in the enacting of almost all major institutions. It included the *ndzo* and overlapped largely with the kin groups gathered together in a settlement, forming thus the core of cohesion within the *ula*.

2. *Rituals of kinship*

In the last resort people probably adhered to the kinship system because of an elementary need for security as well as a need for society. This element of security was represented by the shades of the dead, who warded off the calamities of life, that were believed to be the dark doings of witches. The cult of the shades and its requirements was therefore one of the strongest bonds especially welding the kindred together. The need for security itself was largely created by the belief in witchcraft which linked members of the *ndzo* together.

The *ikwii* (Sims: *Mukwi*: 'charm, ghost') were the shades of the dead and the word is derived from *kwa*: 'to die'. The shades of any person were his own father, mother, mother's brothers, or grandparents he had known when they were alive, and the grandparents were of minor importance. Thus most children had no *ikwii* since these relatives were still living. The cult for the *ikwii* was the privilege of married men or older bachelors whose older male relatives had all died and when married sons were living with their father he kept the altar and carried out the rituals for them. So the possession of a shrine (*kio*) was linked directly not only to the *ibuuru* and the *ndzo*, but also to the polygynous and even the extended family.

The shrine consisted of a table on which one would find statues (*itio*: Sims: *itio*, 'wooden figure used as a fetish') of the deceased relatives, together with the objects of the cult.[16] Besides the relatives mentioned one would find occasionally a statue for a deceased younger brother as at Mbali's or a grandfather, depending on the demographic situation and on the manifestations of the dead themselves. The only deceased who would never be honoured were persons who had died in war or as mad persons. For they became evil spirits *apfu*. Therefore the spirit of king Mbandieele who died in 1898, in what was considered to be a war against the French was never worshipped.

The statues themselves are well known from descriptions and collections. They showed sex, facial markings, a beard for men who had worn one, important men, and various headgear according to the fashion of the area and the favourite headgear of the deceased. Sculptors made them to order. The abdomen was hollowed out and filled with earth from the grave of the relative. Around it was wrapped a red cloth, that became even redder in time from all the kola that was spat on it.[17]

[16] Cf. drawing fig. 1.

[17] On the *itio* cf. Sims: 'wooden figure used as fetish'. TH. MENSE, *Anthropologie*, p. 625, claims they were used for curing on the Pool and made by the Hum for sale to

Besides the statues the shrine often contained one or more *otabi* (a kind of container), dedicated as *itiéé anciele* for a special category of children as well as *nkir'mbu* calabashes with a lid for living children in the household. A married woman's *nkir'mbu* would be at her father's shrine but her husband would pray for her. There could be a box in bark with medicine, the household *nkobi*,[18] and eventually one or more bundles of protective medicine *kaa* bound on a stick or a spear, although that could also be kept elsewhere in the house. On each altar there was certainly also a broom *onia*, a little long, cylindrical wooden rattle *õtsara*, and a rattle *libi* made out of a hardwood (borassus?) fruit and provided with little metal rings.[19] The two last objects were essential, since they served to call the *ikwii*, and different from the whistles with which medicine men could also summon *ikwii*.

There were variations to the shrine. In 1963 Okonzaadza kept an *itio* on the ground against the centrepost of his house and honoured it before an important act by blowing a *mvuli* horn and spitting kola on it. Some were too poor to afford an *itio*. The shades would not begrudge them this, but they still needed an altar. The statues were replaced by animal skins containing earth of the tomb wrapped in them. The proper skins were those of *mbala* (Sims: 'civet cat'?) and the rodents *ntsii* or *olongu*.[20]

Almost every day the master of the house would pray to his *ikwii*, usually during the evening. He rang the bell, shook the *õtsara* and began by calling them, whispering *shwii shwii* close to the statue or the skin. He could also use clicks the way women use them when they call the dogs. After a while he started to talk in conversation as if the relative was still alive. After he had spoken he chewed some kola and spat it on the statue or the skin for the *ikwii* to eat. Then he might pour some lustral water *ntsã* over the statue or the skin to clean it and pour wine afterwards for the *ikwii* to drink. When wine was poured, also on the

---

the Tio. This description is excellent. Cf. also J. DYBOWSKI, *La route*, p. 53, and for examples: E. COART, A. DE HAULLEVILLE, *La religion*, pp. 153, 260, fig. 466A; pl. XXXII, 466B, p. 261, figs. 468A and B; pl. XXXIII, p. 470; figs. 480, 481, 482, 483, 484, 485, 486, 487; H pl. XXXV, figs. 488, 489, 490, 491, 495, 496, p. 247; H. BRUNSCHWIG, *Les cahiers*, p. 215; H. BRUNSCHWIG, *La négociation*, p. 25; A. A. DE CHAVANNES, *Avec Brazza*, sketch opposite p. 161 which shows *itio, nkir'mbu,* and *nkobi*; R. HOTTOT, F. WILLETT, *Teke Fetishes*, p. 31 (some of his figures may not represent shades) and p. 27; L. GUIRAL, *Le Congo*, p. 290 (even king); J. MAES, *Fetischen*, pp. 48–50; H. MASUI, *L'état independant*, p. 82.

[18] Sims: *nkobe*: 'box stool'; Calloc'h, 'boite', p. 144; A box in bark sewn around a wooden bottom and top (for the lid). Contained kaolin and other ingredients. Besides the household box, there were powerful political charms with the same name.

[19] Sims: (*M*)*unyaa*: 'speaker's brush, stalk'; *liba*: 'rattle'; *mucaa*: 'medicine-man's rattle'; Calloc'h, p. 229: *mu-tsara*: 'gousse longue pour fétiche'.

[20] *Mbala* is a forest mammal, which lives in trees, with a brown skin and a black line on its back; *Ntsii* was a rodent from the forest with a black ringed tail, a pointed snout with whiskers, and a body with round spots. It was a fruit eater. They were not identified.

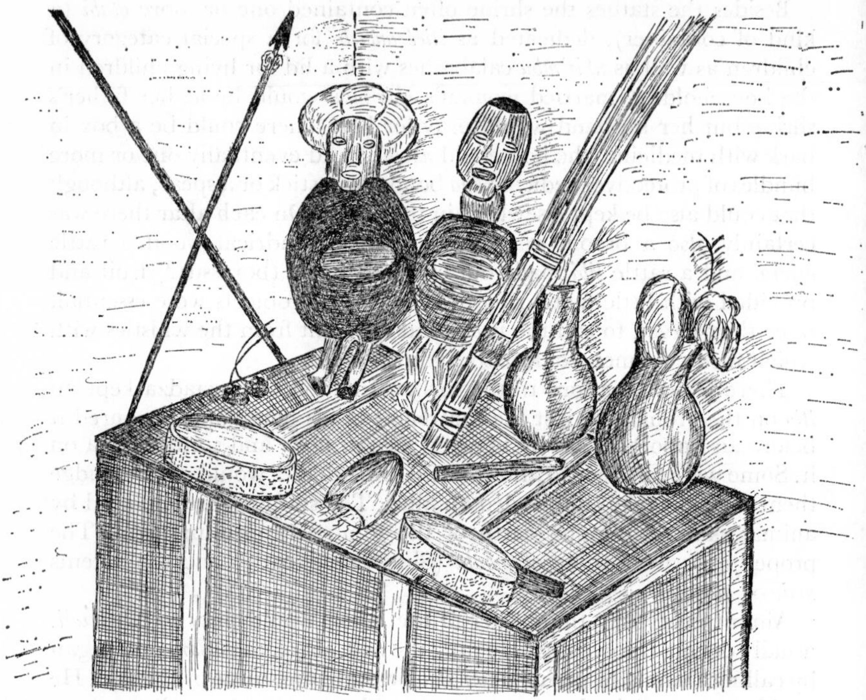

Fig. 1. Household Shrine for the Shades

NOTE: The two figures represent the father and the mother's brother of the deceased. Their bellies are hollow and filled with earth from the tombs. Each day kola is spat on them.

The pots are memorials for twins of the household owner who died. The feathers in one pot are for the eldest twin. They come from a rooster, probably sacrificed for the spirit.

The boxes are made out of bark and household *nkobi* containing white and red colours and medicine.

Between the boxes there is a wooden bell, *libi* and behind it a long rattle, *ôtsara*. Both are used to call the spirits of the shrine before praying.

On the wall the package near the head of the spear is a *kaa*, protective medicine.

cemetery, lustral water would be used first. It is worth noting that chiefs did not themselves perform the cult for their *ikwii* but appointed a special family to do it for them.

The *ikwii* were thought to be helpful. They would appear in dreams and advise. Thus, king Iloo consulted in a dream the grandfather of his grandfather about the treaty proposed by De Brazza.[21] They would come to help when people were ill and they were summoned, they

[21] N. NEY, *Conférences*, p. 159.

would certainly come when they heard their favourite songs played on the pluriarc or when the people sang at funerals or when the professional singers sang praises. They were guardians of the living yet sometimes they could become angry and would have to be propitiated. Usually they would not kill their descendants. For did they not belong to the same kindred? Even so, mother's brothers might send some severe illness and according to Mbali even kill someone of the household, whether it was a member of the same *ndzo* or not. The thing people feared more was the withdrawal of the *ikwii's* favours so that witches might get at them. Sometimes very old and forgotten *ikwii* would bring illness. One could only know if the diviner found out. But sometimes, when someone seemed sick without any reason, the head of the household might pray in the evening: 'Leave me alone, I cannot atone, I don't even know where your tomb is!' Atonement was certainly due when they dreamt of *ikwii* asking for food or drink[22] or when there was a bad omen, such as a nightjar crossing one's path, or meeting owls and chameleons. In short whenever something disturbing happened the *ikwii* might need propitiation. One could offer some copal (*oli*) to the shade and even deposit an *ona* or conus shell on the shrine. This was done when a person had died in anger and it was done only by the very great men for conus shells were rare.

More usually the *ikwii* felt neglected because their statue had worn out and been thrown on the rubbish heap and not replaced, or their plot in the cemetery had not been kept free of weeds, or they were just hungry for a sacrifice. Atonement then consisted in the sacrifice of a white fowl[23] or rooster or, if it was more serious, a goat, whichever was indicated in a dream by the deceased or by a diviner consulted about the illness in the family. Such an animal could be dedicated formally to the deceased and not killed on the spot. Some disreputable characters did sell dedicated animals to other persons afterwards and if they ate them and fell ill because of the anger of the offended *okwii*, that was their misfortune. Therefore white fowl for instance were not easily bought. Usually a dedication would do. And it would take the next misfortune or a persistence of ill luck to really sacrifice the animals.

The sacrifice had to be accepted first by the spirit. So one would hold the white fowl in front of the *kio* in a certain way by the neck and if the shades liked it, the fowl would strangle itself. Then the neck was cut and the blood gushed over the *kio* and the *itio*. After which it was plucked, cut up and left there during the night for the shades to eat with cassava and a little wine poured in libation. Sometimes the wings and legs of the dead fowl were broken and it was left there. Once we even saw a boy play with it just after the sacrifice. If the shade had eaten it, he would tell the master of the house in a dream. Then in the morning the

[22] CH. DE CHAVANNES, *Avec Brazza*, p. 166.

[23] White was a sacred colour in general. It was also associated with the dead.

family could eat the fowl. It should be prepared without spices and when the family ate it there should be no speech. For the *ikwii* would be there and partake with the living. This constituted a ritual of communion.

A goat would be brought near the tomb. It was accepted that the animal would fall on its knees in a certain fashion two or three times, if the *ikwii* agreed with the sacrifice. The throat was then cut and the blood flowed over the tomb. Some wine was also poured over and in the tomb by a tube connecting the surface with the interior. Then one half of all the internal organs of the animal was deposited in a hole near the tomb, in which one had first poured some of its blood. This was the portion of the shade. Then the officiant smoked a pipe in honour of the deceased. During the night the *okwii* ate and told the master of the house in a dream. Then the family would solemnly eat the meat of the animal in a communion ritual.[24]

If either for a fowl or a goat the shade did not send a dream the meat was left on the *kio* or on the tomb until such a dream happened. It was also possible for shades to refuse a sacrifice. They did so when they knew that the person who was ill and for whom the sacrifice was made could not recover, even though they might try to help. In such cases the wily would attempt to force the shade to co-operate by killing the animal despite the lack of acceptance.

The sacrifice thus comprised ritual steps of dedication, acceptance, the shedding of life, and communion. But the loss of life was not considered to be important. To give blood and meat was thought, at least in 1963 by medicine men such as Ikoli or Ngateo, similar to offerings of other foods like cassava or kola. The *ikwii* ate what was given to them. If they were never fed they would not die, but become mad and be capable of great harm, even death. They had to receive the blood first so they would see that the animal had really been killed for them and was not offered as an afterthought. In fact the sacrifice had some aspects of a contract since refusal of the animal meant inability or refusal to help the living.

Only goats, fowl and sometimes sheep (but they were rare) could be offered in sacrifice, so that goats and white fowl were looked upon as a link between the living and the dead. Other acceptable food was cassava maize, wine, and kola. Meat of pigs, ducks, and pigeons was not acceptable, but then in the 1880s those animals were only to be found at the Pool, and pigs like sheep also in small numbers among the Jinju. Poor people could give water instead of wine and fowl where others would give goats, for the deceased relatives realized very well what the living could and could not afford.

[24] A. MERLON, *Le Congo*, p. 99, for use of kola and pp. 114–15 for the smoking as an offering on graves. For kola cf., also Sims, *wana mûti*: 'spit upon kola-nut and talk to a fetish'.

Sometimes the shades wanted something else. They asked for a re-dedication of their altar or a general cleaning of the tomb or the building of a house, *ndzo ampiõ* on the tomb. Rather more frequently they asked for a little shrine *kio* to be built in the shape of a beehive, not at all like a house, in front of the home or on top of the roof. Such beehive huts were empty but served as memorials. If it was on top of the house on the ridge over the entrance (*kio ngaayuulu*) a little stick would pierce it on which an egg was affixed;[25] in front of the home the hut would be surmounted by a feather of a white fowl or of the prestigious *ndua* bird.

Thus we saw in 1964 a woman build such a hut. She made a tiny round floor in beaten earth, planted some twigs for a frame and covered them with grass which had to be of the *nshiel anciini* variety. She talked to her *ikwii*, sang and danced. When she tied the grasses together at the top of the hut with a ring of grass she counted three times nine. Then she put *tsuula* (red colour) on the ring, first prepared on a leaf with powder of camwood and water, purified with lustral water *ntsã* and offered maize beer. While she put the red colour on, her son called out *shwii shwii* for the shades to come. She then made fire by rubbing, but using a steel file. Then she planted some palm fronds near the *kio* and her son prayed and spat some kola near the altar. Normally she should not have built this shrine, because she was a woman. But she was a healer/diviner and she was acting only as a technician. Her son as the head of the household, prayed and sacrificed. He would now, after having built this altar, find many animals in his traps in the bush. For success at the hunt is a certain sign of the favour of the *ikwii*.

Women did not communicate directly with the shades, with one important exception. They could become *angkira*. A girl felt unwell. She would dream about her grandmother, less often a grandfather, never about any other shade. Always it was someone from the alternating generation. In the morning she announced the dream, dressed up carefully and added a touch reminding people of the deceased. Sometimes in the morning, but more often in the late afternoon they held a dance in which she would imitate to the music of the pluriarc the gestures of the deceased and sing a favourite song from the time the shade had lived. The performance would last nine days. Then the woman felt better and the spirit was propitiated. She might then build a little *kio* on the roof of the house or not according to the wishes of the *okwii*.[26] *Angkira* was felt by the men to be one of the typical female rituals in which men had almost no part. Why it was concerned only with *nkaa* is not clear. In contrast to the cult of the men, *angkira* benefited only the

[25] H. BRUNSCHWIG, *Les cahiers*, p. 171 mentioned a 'fétiche de poule'. E. COART, A. DE HAULLEVILLE, *La religion*, p. 216, mentions eggs on the roof but surmised it was a charm to help the laying of eggs. It is most likely a *kio ngaayuulu*. Calloc'h gives *ki-ba*, p. 153: 'case sur les cases'. This corresponds to Tio : *kio*.

[26] NGAATALI confirmed that this existed in Iloo's times. Such women might also be possessed by a *nkira* spirit.

person who danced it, not a group and it was a relation between a living person and a shade in which no antagonism was found. It was an individual personal relationship only. In this the worship at the *kio* by the head of the family and the *angkira* dance illustrate perfectly the differing worlds of men and women.

Besides the cult for the shades one other ritual was intimately tied to kinship structures, the *okuu*. It consisted essentially of an inquest about witchcraft. When somebody was gravely ill, the father would call upon all the kinsmen who could inherit, but especially the *ndzo*, for most bewitching was believed to be done within the matrilineage. The *mpfõ andzo* presided over the ritual. All members of the matrilineage had to be there, at least those of the sick man's generation, the generation below and the generation above. Otherwise they would be practically accused of witchcraft and suspected of not being willing to relinquish. The difference with the rest of the kindred is shown by the fact that not all kinsmen of the sick person had to be there. People who lived further out were excused. The reason for these rules of attendance was that kinsmen who were not members of the *ndzo* of the patient, nor close relatives, nor dwelling in the same village, were much less likely to have bewitched him.

When the *mpfõ andzo* arrived a special hunt was organized by the affines of the patient and the chest of all animals killed was given to the *mpfõ andzo*. Success in the hunt showed the disposition of the *ikwii* and the gift by the affines showed their goodwill to their in-laws. If there were new affines the *mpfõ andzo* had not yet seen, they came to him with a gift of wine and were presented. Then a meeting was held in front of the house of the sick person. The *mpfõ andzo* and the head of the house of the father of the patient began by making speeches to deny that they had bewitched the person, or to say they had, but they would now desist. Anyone else who felt like it, spoke afterwards to the same effect. Usually people, such as a *mwaana we iboolo* (patrilateral relative), would speak up because they were the prime suspects, considering their relationship to the patient. But a confession was not the truth. Some Tio in 1963 had it that when someone confessed he meant simply to let the true witch know that he knew who it was and would expose him if he did not desist! All dissensions, quarrels, and bad feelings were aired at the inquest and when it was over all witchcraft should have been taken from the patient. He should now recover, unless one of the witches present at *okuu* would not desist, or he had been bewitched by someone else. The main action in the *okuu* inquest was really a form of resolution of conflict. Here mention is merely made of its ties to both *ndzo* and *ibuuru*.

Taken together the rituals for *ikwii* and *okuu* formed a necessary underpinning in terms of beliefs and knowledge, values and emotion which gave meaning to the kinship categories and was perhaps the essence of the solidarity within them. And in so far as kinship was the unifying principle behind the formation of residential groups, these rituals also help to explain solidarity within the latter.

3. *Kinship terminology*

Consanguineal kin are *ibuur 'imo*, i.e. all people begotten (*buur*) by one common ancestor. *Iburu* for Sims is 'a relative'.[27] The term is clearly linked to Sims *liburu*: 'fruit' and Calloc'h, p. 230, 'graine, semence en général').[28] It contrasts with *abali*: 'in-laws'; a nominal derivation of the verb *bala* 'to marry' (Sims). People who were neither kin nor affines were 'foreigners' (M)*unzia* (Sims) (Calloc'h: p. 209) but the same term also meant 'guest' and 'foreigner' seems to be derived from 'guest'. They were referred to as *nduu* 'friends'. When de Brazza arrived at Mbe in 1880 the king addressed him: *Waanyi nduu* 'you came, friend/stranger'.[29] There is only one term of address or reference for the group of non-kin or strangers. Such was not the case for kin whether *ibuuru* or *abali*. Sets of terms for these categories comprised terms of reference and of address, but also often a teasing terminology (*itã*; *itaña*, 'play', Sims) of address. The other sets however were clearly based on the terminology of reference. The following list gives a definition for each of these terms, first for consanguineal kin, then for in-laws. Each definition should be an exact description of the semantic field covered by the term, using a set of underlying criteria which are shown by the whole collection of terms to be those by which terms are minimally distinguished one from the other.

A Set of consanguineal kin (*ibuuru*).[30]

nkaa/otioolu (*nkaa*/(*M*)*uteolo*: 'grandfather, rich chief/grandchild', Sims). A reciprocal pair of terms, the older person being referred to as *nkaa* when either both were two or an even number of generations apart including spouses of blood relatives, or by persons of the same generation if collaterals, i.e. if the common ancestor to both persons is in the third ascending generation. The descendant of the older branch is then *nkaa*. As a matter of prestige, co-wives can refer to each other by this pair of terms, the person first married being referred to as *nkaa*. The last case is only terminology of prestige since another special term of reference designates this situation.

[27] Terms noted in 1963 are given without reference. Terms taken from Sims or Calloc'h are indicated as such.

[28] A. SIMS, *A Vocabulary . . . Kiteke-English* is referred to only by the Tio word, which is the entry in the vocabulary. CALLOC'H, *Vocabulaire Français-Ifumu* is referred to by page. References to both authors are in the text.

[29] ONDONO, *Souvenirs*, pp. 14–15.

[30] Terms of reference are given. If the terms of address differ they are indicated in the text.

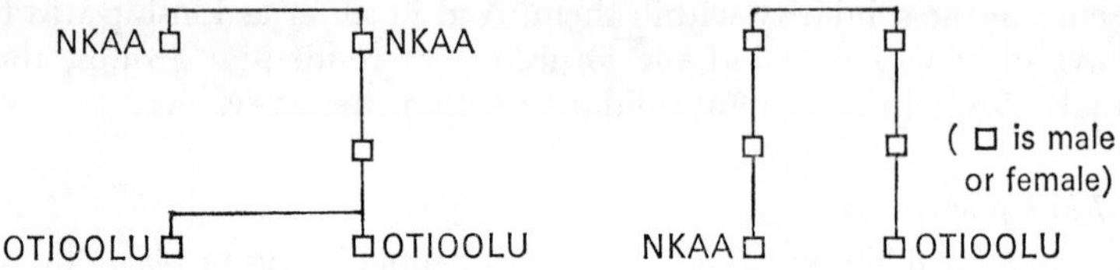

nnaana/mbwei (*yaa/mbwee*: 'elder brother, younger brother' Sims; note 'frère ainé, soeur ainée': *yaa, nana,* Calloc'h pp. 224, 325): reciprocal pair of terms, the younger person referring to the older as *nnaana*, between persons belonging to the same generation and of same sex, if they have a common ancestor in the first or second ascending generation.[31] A special term of address *ngaalu* (*ngalū* 'cadet', Calloc'h pp. 150, 257, a younger person whose name one does not want to divulge). *Ngaaluu* is an endearment used by the older to flatter the younger person. Thus: '*Ngaaluu*, give me five francs'. It means: owner of friendship and is related to the term friend, *nduu*.

nkieli/-(*nkele*: 'sister', Sims): 'soeur cadette': *nkele*, Calloc'h p. 325): self reciprocal between persons of the same generation and of opposite sex, if the common ancestor belonged to the first or second ascending generation.

mwaana (*mwana*: 'child, baby', Sims 'fils', 'fille', 'enfant': *mwana*, Calloc'h pp. 202, 218): any person in relation to any person one or an odd number of generations older, but also any child whether kin or not for any adult. This term shows that the terminology of kinship is not completely isolated from semantic sets outside it! In reference the composite *mwaan ankieli* is often heard. It refers to any child of a female called *nkieli* in relation to the male *nkieli*. Calloc'h p. 275, *mw-ana a nkele*: 'neveu', and he adds that the only 'nephew' known here, is the oldest son of the sister. He is usually the successor and the heir. In fact the usage is directly related to the existence of matrilineages where these persons are successors.

taara (*tara*: 'father', Sims): male in the first or any odd ascending generation from the other person if the chain which links the persons includes the progenitor of the latter. Often *taara* is the progenitor himself. Male spouses of blood relatives in this generation are included if the chain includes the woman who gave birth to the junior person in the relationship. Calloc'h p. 290, 'père': *tara*: remarks that the term is often used for reference or respect.

tooke: female occupying the position of *taara*. The term of address is

[31] In theory people in the same generation whose common ancestor belonged to the fourth generation backwards and further in time should be considered. This never occurred among the living in actual genealogies. Also the system is closed after two generations' difference.

taara. The term of reference means 'female *taara*'. Neither Sims nor Calloc'h mentions the term.

ngu (*nguu*: 'mother' Sims; 'mère': *ngu*, *mama* Calloc'h p. 265): female belonging to the first or any odd ascending generation from the other person. But the chain linking the two must include the woman who gave birth to the person of the descending generation and is often the woman who gave birth herself. The term of address is *mã* (*maa:* 'mother', Sims). Female spouses of blood relatives of the senior generation are included when the chain includes the male progenitor of the other person.

nguboolo (*ngubalu* 'uncle' Sims; 'oncle': *ngubalaga* Calloc'h, who adds: the only uncle they recognize is the maternal uncle p. 279): male person in the position of *ngu*. The term of reference means 'male *ngu*'. In address he should be called *mã* which in 1963 at least, and probably earlier, was much less common than the use of the term of reference, because the Tio are a male-dominated society and the use of a term associated primarily with females such as *mã* detracts from the respect due by the junior to the senior in the relationship, especially if both are male.

B Set of affines (*abali*)

ãkãw: betrothed. It is a term of reference designating females only. The name of the person is used in address. No such term designating males exists. Women are exchanged or obtained in Tio society, men not.

olõ/okali: (*mulume/mukali*: husband/wife Sims; 'époux/épouse': *mulumi/mukali*, Calloc'h p. 207): persons of opposite sex and same generation, one of which is an 'incomer' (i.e. the spouse of the other person or the spouse of a blood relative of the other person in the relationship). The terms are reciprocal *olõ* being used for the man *okali* for the woman.

In teasing, the terms are used between persons of the opposite sex, two generations apart whether they are blood relatives or not and if the younger person is a child in absolute age or also if the junior person is an 'incomer' (spouse of a blood relative) to the other person. The terms are also used in teasing persons of the same generation but opposite sex, who are linked by an affinal tie two generations below them:

OLÕ/OKALI

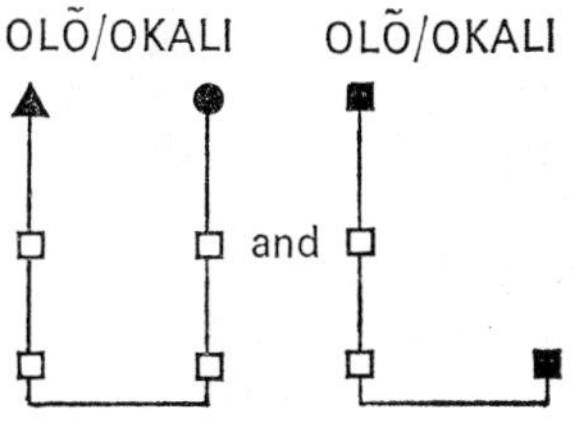

By 1963 *Okali* was also used as a term of non-reciprocal address to designate mother's brother's wife, at least by some. This usage, says Mbali, did not exist before and was introduced around 1920.

Sims has two other words for 'husband' namely *balo* and *ncwakiri*. The first one is a more correct form of *mulume*, the second however has not been found anywhere else.

mbàà/—: self reciprocal term used between females of the same generation coming in as spouses or blood relatives of the same generation, as spouses into a same *third* group of blood relatives. This therefore includes co-wives. The term is related to *ibàà*: jealousy. Neither Sims nor Calloc'h has the term, probably because there is no easy European correspondence as is also the case for the following one.

mbàlìkàlí/+—: self reciprocal term used between males of the same generation entering as spouses or blood relatives of the same generation as spouses into a same *third* group of blood relatives. The term is the male equivalent of *mbàà*. Note that there is no 'co-husbands' in Tio society though. Its etymology seems to be 'marriage/women' and it is not related to *mbàà*. In teasing the term is used between males of the same generation linked by an affinal tie one generation below them:

MBALIKALI

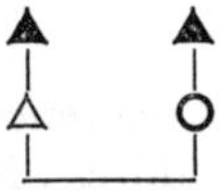

ondzali/—((*M*)*unzali*: 'brother or sister-in-law' Sims; 'beau-frère, belle-soeur'—*munzali*, Calloc'h p. 141): self reciprocal term used between persons of the same sex belonging to the same generation in which one is the spouse of the blood-relative in the same generation as the other person in the relationship. The term is complementary to *olõ*/*okali* since it is used between persons of the same sex and the other set is for persons of opposite sex.

In teasing the term is used between persons of the same sex two generations apart, *whether* they are blood relatives (but then the younger person must be a child in absolute age) or the junior person in the relationship is a blood relative of the spouse of a blood relative of the senior person. The affinal link must then be located two generations below the senior person at the same generational level as the junior person.

The term was also used in teasing between persons of the same sex and the same generation who are linked by an affinal tie two generations away from them, whether in descending or ascending order.

X + *okwo*/—(*uko*, *oko*, 'father or mother-in-law', Sims; 'beau-fils, belle-fille, belle-mère, beau-père': *bu-ko*, Calloc'h p. 141): reciprocal term added to any of the terms used between persons of adjacent generations who are blood relatives, especially *taara*, *ngu*, *mwaana*. The affinal link, however, must be in the junior generation. The junior person adds the consanguineal term to *okwo* which is the one used by the person in the chain who belongs to the same generation as he does, but to the consanguineal group of the senior person in the whole relationship. One can also state it as follows: the junior person identifies with the 'incomer' into his group *vis-à-vis* the blood relatives of that 'incomer'.

C. Remarks

In reference one can always be more precise by specifying seniority or juniority (*wookuru/wookiõ*) and sex (*waaboo lo/wuuké*: male/female). It was also possible to string sets of terms together to indicate precisely what the relationship was. Expressions current in the sixties were the *mwaan ankieli* mentioned and *mwaan ankaa* for collaterals one generation higher than the speaker, which avoided the use of the more honorific *taara*:

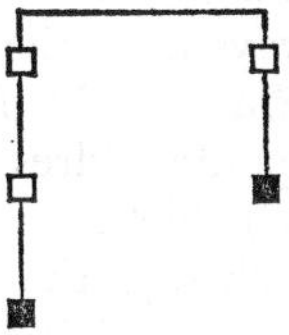

mwaan ankaa
speaker.

All kin, whatever their relationship, could be encompassed by the expression *mã* + possessive pronoun; e.g. *mã ame*, *mã andie*; my kin, his kin, etc.

From a change in the system, namely that *okali* is now used as a term of address for the mother's brother's wife when her husband is out of earshot with the intention, not of teasing her, but of claiming her as inheritance on the death of her husband, which was unheard of in the past, it could be deduced that kinship terminology was linked to status and rights. So it was, but other cases make it quite clear that the terminology reflects above all expected roles as patterns of behaviour and therefore relative superiority, prestige, inferiority, etc. This is evident in cases where choice of terminology remained possible. In 1963 for instance A could call a chief B by the term *nguboolo*. B was also related to A through A's mother and could call her *mwaana* so that A could call him also *nkaa*. He chose the latter since it implied a more comfortable and egalitarian relationship than would have prevailed if he had called him *nguboolo*. B reciprocated and called A *otioolu* because it suited him. He might have kept calling A *mwaan ankieli* and probably would have done so if A lived in his village or chiefdom.

This sort of conflict regularly occurred in a whole set of collateral

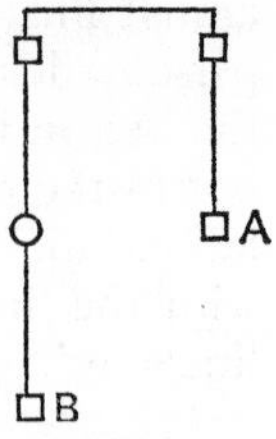

relationships summarized as follows: The senior person, usually a man, calls the junior *mwaan' ankieli* and hopes to be addressed as *nguboolo*. This implies that the junior should work for him and in all circumstances exhibit great respect for the senior. But the junior maintains that A is his *mwaana* and that he should be addressed as *taara* with all the respect that term implies. If she happens to be a woman her term of reference would be *tooke*. The junior person reasons that the senior one is *mwaan ankaa* of himself. *Otioolu* and *nkaa* are interchangeable because of the rule of alternation of generations which is very strong in Tio society. So a *mwaan ankaa* is a *mwaana*. The senior uses his terminology and the junior sticks to his own. In 1963 this was the case whenever this sort of relationship existed, at least if A was a man. When A and B were women that matter was almost irrelevant because among women relative prestige mattered very little. If A was a woman B did not object to see in her a *nguboolo's* wife, since a drive was on to make *mwaan' ankieli* heirs of these women. If all were men A called B *taara* and B called A *taara* nobody giving an inch. And this, it was said, had always been the situation. Indeed Calloc'h claims that consanguineal terms for the first and second ascending generation were often used as polite address.[32] Sims confirms this when he gives *nkaa*: 'grandfather, rich chief'.

Among his examples Calloc'h says that when called by the king, people answered politely '*taara* + king'. This was current and the chief NGOBILA in the 1880s was known to Europeans as *taara* NGOBILA to all. Obviously again the term chosen was one for which the expected behaviour coincided well with the role of chief. That this was the function of kinship terms also appears from the Tio custom of calling any stranger who lived in a village by an appropriate kinship term at least after a while. This again was a term from the first ascending or descending generation, depending on who was supposed to be senior or junior in the relation.

It is worth noting that the use of *taara* to designate chiefs or kings, was restricted to those who were not really fairly close kin to the chief. They used whatever term indicated the real blood relationship. Thus in 1963 an older brother of the king still addressed him as *ngaaluu* and referred to him as *mbwei*. The first function of the terminology was to indicate the relationship.

Pseudo kinship was also often established through affinal connexions. Thus in 1963 Marcel's mother married a second husband after the death of Marcel's father. This man had married Jean's mother, after the death however of Jean's father. Marcel and Jean were clearly not kin. Yet Marcel called Jean *mbwei* because of the connexion. This case

[32] CALLOC'H, *Vocabulaire*, pp. 60–1.

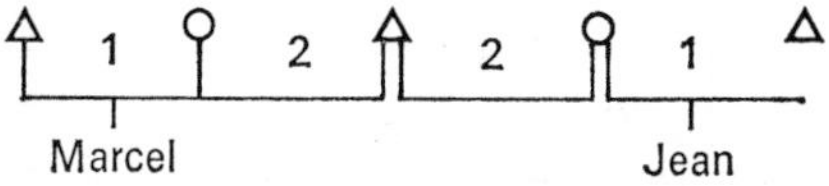

was again an example of something which occurred fairly often since most women were inherited and married more than once.

The following table shows the relation of the terms one to another in terms of meaning and establishes the principles which produce the minimal divisions within the semantic field of kinship terminology.

The principles underlying the terminology are evidently the difference between *affinity* and *consanguinity*, *generation* and *age*, *sex*, absolute and relative, *manner of procreation* (often called bifurcation) *collaterality*. They all seem biological but are of course all founded on socially recognized marital unions and socially attributed descent. Each of these is now discussed.

(i) Consanguineal and affinal kinship: This distinction is absolute and all-pervasive.

(ii) Generation: In the form of odd generations opposite to even or zero generations this principle too is all-pervasive. The actual difference of generation is only pervasive within consanguineal kin.

Age is only important within generation zero, thus carrying the idea of seniority to its logical conclusion. Since even twins are considered elder and younger, the pervasiveness of this principle is not surprising.

The manner in which the concept is applied clearly indicates the outer boundaries of the whole system. Among blood relatives it is only two generations deep (four if one reckons with an Ego and from his grandchildren to his grandparents), after which it becomes repetitive. This incidentally explains in part why Tio oral tradition lacks time depth. What happened in the life of a remote ancestor is reduced to two generations back from Ego in the life-time of his *nkaa*. The terminology thus puts a boundary to the felt depth of historical time.[33] Laterally the system is bounded

[33] N. NEY, *Conférences*, p. 159, claimed that Iloo had consulted the soul of his fourth ancestor, the grandfather of his grandfather. This certainly is a limit. In Tio traditions it is remarkable to note that IBALICO, *L'origine*, placed the story about the origin of the Tio of Mpila two generations back. Yet the same tradition had already been told by Luca da CALTANISETTA, *Relation*, p. 42, in 1698, as something which also had happened in a 'near' past. Another example was the moving of chief NGOBILA to the left bank of the Congo river, which was told to me as having happened at the time of the 'father' of the present chief and to Stanley as having happened at the time of the 'father' of the chief who ruled then and was a *nkaa* of the 1963 incumbent. Cf. H. STANLEY, *The Congo*, I, pp. 405, 510. The other factor explaining the lack of time depth is the importance of the *ibuuru*, which limited effective geneaologies to two generations as well.

CHART 3

Kinship terminology

	Blood relatives		Affines		
difference of even generations and zero generations for collaterals	*nkaa/otioolu*		*Sex: opposite*	*chain 1/2*	*similar*[a] *chain 1/3* *male* mbalikali/sr
difference of O generations	*Sex: similar* nnaana/mbwei	*opposite* nkieli/sr	olõ/okali in chain O one link	ondzali/sr	*female* mbaa/sr
difference of odd generations	*Sex: male* taara nguboolo	*female* tooke ngu *begetter/ bearer* mwaana	+okwo		

[a] Chain: The number of generations spanned by the chain linking the two persons is relevant here. If that number is zero or even, one set of terms obtains. Another when the number is odd. However the situation of odd generations is identical with the one created when there are two affinal links in a chain of zero generations. More than two such links are never recognized and two are only at the level of generation zero. Elsewhere only one is recognized. It is obvious that the affinal link must occur in the lowest generation of the chain. The situation reflects a polarity expressed in the alternation of generations and an equivalent alternation of affinal links.

first by the point where collaterals are handled in generation zero as if they were two generations away, when the common ancestor lived three generations ago. And for the affines the equation of two affinal links with odd generations indicates a counting of such links exactly as if they were generations. Kinship in a chain with three affinal links is not recognized. If it were the terminology should be equal to affines with only one link in the chain.

The alternation of generations which is so strong in the terminology was tied to several institutions of which inheritance of women was the most important. Adjacent generations inherited wealth, alternate generations inherited women. In terms of behaviour alternate generations stressed friendliness and adjacent generations stressed respect, prestige, and absolute seniority.

In the 1880s there was apparently no case where any one term was applied both to persons from odd and even generations. The distinction was then as rigid as the one between affines and blood relatives.

(iii) Sex: Sex is used in two different ways. The absolute sex of the persons (male/female) is used to distinguish persons in odd generations of blood relatives and for affines of the same sex self reciprocal when the chain linking them contains two affinal ties, or in the relation *olõ/okali*.

The similarity or opposition of the sexes of the persons in relation is also important and used in all affinal relations, where it is obvious but also for blood relatives in generation zero. One is tempted to attribute the spread of this principle to marriage and bridewealth practice. The behaviour associated with this type of relation is, however, much more important. In all these relations inequality is stressed again, with the men being by far superior to the women.

In fact the analysis shows that the similarity of sex is much more important than the 'absolute' sex of the partners in the relation. Thus in the odd generation the terms used in address did not make a distinction in absolute sex at all.

(iv) Manner of procreation: This involves actual procreation from a socially recognized man or woman. The principle, also called principle of bifurcation by many after Lowie, is used only at the level of the odd generation of blood relatives. Contrary to what many thought, manner of procreation does not *per se* establish the existence of unilineal descent groups, although this is most often the reason for its use. The following cases establish the point. The Tio expressed in 1963 (and it appears earlier too) this principle by their distinction *baana be iboolo* and *baana be ike*: ('children of maleness and children of female-ness'). They used these forms most to express the notions of patrilateral and matrilateral linkage. The

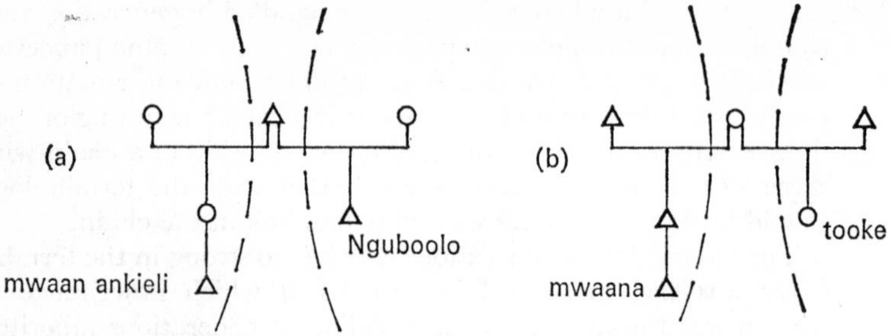

In case (a) *nguboolo* and *mwaan ankieli* do not belong to the same matrilineage; in case (b) *tooke* and *mwaan ankieli* do not belong to the same patrilineage.

Tio were matrilineal, yet the terminology cannot show by itself if they were matri- or patrilineal or even that they were unilineal. The usage of terms showed this as in Figure 1.

In fact the frequent use of the pair *nguboolo/mwaan ankieli* and not *tooke/mwaan ankieli* but *mwaana* was a reflexion of the matrilineal descent system which brought with it special behavioural roles for 'mother's brothers' and 'sister's sons'.

(v) Collaterality: the principle is implicit in the notion of numbers of generations over which a chain linking two persons can extend. The fact that the limit of collaterality is fairly narrow in the system indicates the possibility that bilateral kinship plays an important part in the system. And so it did. In fact the field covered by the terminology corresponds exactly, for the blood relatives, to the bilateral group in which one can inherit: *ibuuru vyishiil iloo*.

Kinship terminology does not form a completely closed semantic field. The terms of address involve the use or not of personal names and/or of political titles and personal names as well as titles from allied semantic fields. Terms of address refer to expected behaviour and the terms of reference with regard to a system of kinship. Titles refer to political structure and expected behaviour there, whereas personal names refer to the place of each individual in the total fabric of society since only one person at a time could bear a given name.[34] Their relation to kinship terminology can only be stated in general. Titles were used between non-kin and personal names were only used in address between kin when the partners belonged to the same generation or even generations and then only from seniors to juniors, not vice versa. Among affines of the same generation women could not use them towards men, not even their husbands, but other affines of the same generation could. The use of personal names in address was clearly linked with the idea

[34] A. ZORZI, *Al Congo*, p. 411.

of both equality and familiarity. The conspicuous absence of their use even as reference, as between a man and his mother-in-law, was a sign of respect. As for the relation between titles and kinship, terminology, the titles were always used in reference, but in address as has been seen, kinship terms denoting respect could be employed.

4. *Kinship behaviour*

There were three major patterns of behaviour: to behave with respect, to joke, or to behave neutrally. The first two roles were specifically recognized in that breach of respect led to the ceremony of atonement, *ipwooro*[35] and joking (or *itã itaña*: play, Sims) was a prescribed relation between other kin.

Ipwooro could be asked in principle by any senior kinsman from his junior if the latter had failed to observe the respect due to his elder. In effect, anyone, whether affine or consanguine who belonged to the generation just above that of the other person in the relation or to any odd generation above it, could require *ipwooro*. Within the same generation *nnaana* could require it from *mbwei* and even male *nkieli* from female *nkieli* although this was said to be very rare. Less rare was the requirement of *ipwooro* by husbands from their wives.[36]

The procedure consisted in bringing of wine and goods in the presence of witnesses by the guilty party. The aggrieved person accepted the gift and thus forgave the offence. A child who had aggrieved his father would bring his *mbwei* and *nnaana* as witnesses and his father would ask his wives and other children to be present. If a woman presented *ipwooro* to her husband she would bring her *nkaa*, or a *nkieli* or even a *nnaana* to 'speak for her'. For a woman could not 'speak for herself', in these circumstances. If *ipwooro* was not given, or the atonement was not accepted by the elder, then the spirits of the dead would be angry. In 1963 it was believed the deceased might strike with illness. But it was hard to know what the dead would do for no one had ever really refused to accept *ipwooro* or to proffer it.

If a child refused to pay *ipwooro* to his father, his mother's brother (the brother-in-law of the other man) could go instead and if the sister's son refused *ipwooro* to his mother's brother, the father could go. In the latter case the mother's brother could not refuse the atonement, for if he did so, the father could send his wife back to her brother and ask for a refund of the bridewealth. As for the wife, if she refused *ipwooro* to her husband, her father could pay for her.

What constituted an offence requiring *ipwooro* was not the same aggravation in different relationships. A wife using her husband's personal name would pay *ipwooro*, but not a *mbwei* using his *nnaana's*

[35] On behaviour the sources are indirect but the terms existed. Cf. Calloc'h, ***i-poro***: 'amende', p. 125.

[36] Also called (but in this case only) *ibwooni*. Cf. Ch. III.

name. Insults such as 'monkey', 'you have bad breath' addressed to a *nnaana* required reparation, but when addressed by a son to his mother they did not matter. The worst insult was to put oneself naked in front of a kinsman of the first ascending generation. This did happen, as in 1963 when a woman pulled off her wrapper in front of her mother's brother. She was said to be mad and the enormity of the act only reinforced the people's belief.

Just as the level of abuse changed according to the relationship, so did the amount of the payment itself. It varied from a bottle or calabash of wine to (in 1963) 200 or 300 Fr CFA, not a very sizeable sum. The exact amount was set by the aggrieved party. A *nnaana* could at worst only ask for a bottle of wine from his *mbwei*, whereas a father and certainly a mother's brother would require a much higher amount.

A joking relationship existed between blood relatives of alternate generations, among *ondzali* in a milder form and at its strongest, between *olõ* and *okali*, who were not man and wife. Horseplay would be allowed then. Typical banter with a brother's wife for instance would be: 'I want wine'—'I have none'—'You are poor'—'I don't like a poor husband'.

Between *nkaa* and *otioolu*, joking was strong if the *otioolu* were small children and of opposite sex to the *nkaa*. Grandmothers for instance loved to call their grandchildren little thieves and little husbands. When the *otioolu* had grown up, banter with sexual overtones was stronger with the *nkaa* of one's spouse, especially between the *nkaa* of a man's wife and himself.

A strong influence behind the joking was a pattern of esteemed[37] marriage, since one might marry siblings of one's spouse preferentially, especially after her death, and they could be inherited. A highly approved of marriage was a match between a person and the *otioolu* of his spouse, or between those *otioolu*. In former times no sexual banter was allowed in other circumstances. But by the 1920s banter also had begun to occur between men and their mother's brother's wives who claimed to inherit her. Joking relationships between partners of similar sex was milder. This type of behaviour united again blood relatives of alternate generations with in-laws of the same generation and only one affinal link.

The third major type of behaviour was a sort of neutral friendship. It implied about equal status, *ipwooro* could not be requested, teasing was not allowed. In this category fell the behaviour of only affines of the same generation, i.e. *mbalikali* and *mbaa*. The same sort of behaviour

[37] We are not using a terminology of prescribed and preferential marriage. Absolutely prescribed marriage did not exist. Preferential marriages were so in the ideal norm and we call them 'esteemed'. Whether this preference translated itself in a higher percentage of actual marriages is a moot point. In this regard preferential is too ambiguous.

could also be expected between elder and younger siblings of the same sex and between *nkaa/otioolu* but in both cases *ipwooro* could be requested and some mild joking was allowed, while this was not true for *mbalikali* and *mbaa*. This type of behaviour then clearly belonged to the fringes of the system.

A last type of behaviour was an extension of respect, namely avoidance. It obtained between a person and his in-laws of the first ascending generation, especially those of opposite sex. It was strongest between a man and his mother-in-law. The affinal link combined with the differences of one generation would explain great respect, but not such an avoidance because women are inferior to men and therefore avoidance between a man and his father-in-law should be higher. But the affinal nature of the link seems to be responsible.

The following table represents the four patterns of behaviour as a continuum with relations ranging from the most respectful to the most teasing.

CHART 4

The main patterns of kinship behaviour

	generation	*sex*	*senior partner*
avoidance	+1+affines	opposite	female
		similar	male
respect	+1 blood relatives	similar	male
		opposite	indifferent
	O+ 'incomers' (H/W)	opposite	male
	O+ blood relatives	opposite	male
		similar	male
Friendship	affines of affines	similar	none
banter	+2+blood relatives	similar	none
		opposite	indifferent
	O+ affines	similar	none
		opposite	male

Key: generation: indicates difference of generations between partners; affines or blood relatives

+1: one generation higher than Ego

+2: two generations higher than Ego

O: same generation as Ego

sex: indicates similar or opposite sex of partners

senior partner: indicates the sex of this partner, male, female, indifferent or no seniority should be shown

The structural criteria which play a part in establishing the type and intensity of the behaviour are consanguinity or not, generation, relative, and absolute sex. Of the others, manner of procreation plays only a small part (more respect is due to mother's brother than to father, but this was not really clear in 1963 at least) and the principle of collaterality simply implies that the more collateral people are, the less intense the relation will be, going towards the neutrality of 'friendship'.

The principle of alternation of generations is evident as is the analogy of the relation between blood relatives two generations apart and in-laws of the same generation. Since the most esteemed marriage was that between certain *nkaa* and *otioolu*, and since women were inherited by *otioolu*, the equivalence has meaning. On the other hand the counter-bridewealth *litsũ* circulated in adjacent generations, just as inheritance of material goods passed in adjacent generations.

When affines are involved all types of behaviour are more extreme and more formalized. The relation with the structural situations is obvious. The influence of the exchange of women is equally visible for alternating generations and in relation to similarity of sex. Here relations between opposite sexed partners accentuate the prevailing pattern of behaviour.

The table shows that males are dominant and indeed all authority used to be in the hands of males. The one exception where the female partner stresses its seniority confirms the rule. For this is usually a mother-in-law and her position is to be explained by the pattern of wife-exchange. If the senior partner is male the behaviour is more stressed, except in the case of affines of adjacent generations. This was obviously linked with the patterns of struggle for authority in the society.

The general roles discussed left much leeway for each individual to express himself. Everybody had his own ways of showing respect or friendship, to banter or avoid. Moreover there was a gap between the ideal and what was believed to be usual, what people believed they did. Co-wives should like one another, but it was believed that they were intensely jealous of one another. Then there was the real norm: the true average of actual behaviour. Were co-wives indeed on the average jealous one of another? This last norm can never be known for the nineteenth century whereas the two others can be transmitted by tradition and, in the case of co-wives, were.

It also must be underlined that imposed roles and the concomitant behaviour were no more of a strain, and maybe less, than imposed roles and behaviour are in our own societies. It should also not be believed that the terminology indicated precisely what behaviour was to be. It is not the whole truth in these matters. For instance many women might be called *mã*, but the intensity of the relation with the woman who had begotten a Tio changed the whole quality of that particular relation. This is exactly the point of the story about Ipubi, which certainly was told in the 1880s.[38]

[38] MIANDOO, had learned it from his grandfather.

Ipubi was a cruel chief. Once he went to a big village with many young children. He ordered to put all the mothers in a row and all the children in another line facing them. He then let the children run one by one to their mothers, to see how old they were. If a child ran to its true mother Ipubi declared: 'This one is old! They lie when they say that he is young' and he threw the child in the fire. If the child ran to another mother however, he was left alone, because he was too young.

The story shows that children learned gradually to discriminate between persons in one class. Despite the terminology and its classificatory character, the Tio individual looked at the world of his kinsmen from himself outwards. The importance of the *ibuuru* group which is defined outwards from an Ego plays a major role in this attitude.

Chapter III
Residential Groups

FROM the smallest to the biggest all residential groups were known as *ula*. Anthropologists distinguish between elementary family, polygynous family, extended family, and the village. But the Tio did not. When a particular family was to be designated, they said of a man and his wife: 'X and his wife' and of a man with a wife and children' X (the man) and his children' whether it was a polygynous household or not. In short, they all were called *ula* and *ula* designated a fraction of a kindred as much as a residential group. The non-corporate ill-defined kindred became corporate and well defined when it became in part residential. For the Tio saw people as living somewhere because they followed someone else. Most wives and children are there 'because' of their husband; the grandfather is the 'reason' for the settlement of his married sons; the mother's brother might have attracted some sister's sons besides his own children; the headman of the village had attracted everyone else in it. He was the leader, the man who had not followed anyone else because he had broken away from whoever he was living with. A special term *ikwei* has the meaning according to Ba of: 'It designates someone settled behind someone else, who has grown up, leaves and does no longer recognize the other man any more'.

The resulting groups are the polygynous family and the village inhabited by an extended family. These two basic groups are discussed in turn.

1. *The polygynous family*

The polygynous family was the rule among the Tio and it was small polygyny. Few had more than two wives except for the kings[1] and the major chiefs. This situation was possible because of the discrepancy in the age of marriage of girls and boys. Girls married early and boys very late. Because of the difference in age and taking a relatively high mortality into account there would then be far fewer men of thirty-five available than there were girls of fifteen. Inside the family there was a closer group comprising each mother and her children who lived in her house which also functioned as a kitchen. The husband lived alone in his larger house in front of the dwellings of his wives. The children were reared by their 'mothers', i.e. all the wives, not just the mothers

[1] L. GUIRAL, *Le Congo*, pp. 296–7; J. DE WITTE, *vie*, p. 32. Cf. chapter XII (*Lords*).

themselves, as well as by their grandmothers, aunts, and other female relatives. Pecile has a sketch of such a polygynous establishment and gives the following description of it. He mentions the collective education of the boys 'by all the women in the village', that chiefs have one house per wife, but maintains that commoners with one or two wives only kept a single house. Children were suckled until they were seven or eight years (?) old by all the women in the village who all have milk. Boys left the house at puberty to build their own. The women worked in the plantations, the men did 'nothing'.[2]

The most important function of the family was to beget and educate children. It functioned as well as a unit of domestic production and consumption. For this it was subdivided into groups of mothers and growing-up girls as opposed to the boys who worked together with or without their father.

The father was the only member common to the elementary families making up the polygynous family and he was the head. His leadership was seen not so much in his management, for economic decisions of planting and harvesting were very much left to the women involved. He did not show much leadership in the education of the children either. Only over boys did he have some influence and then not that much. His position of being head consisted essentially in being responsible in law for his children and wives, whenever damages had to be paid, and also to protect their health. He invoked the ancestors *ikwii*: the spirits of his father, his mother, and sometimes his mother's brother. He prayed not only for himself and his children but also for his wives. It was his job to see to it that an *okuu* inquest was held if someone in the family fell seriously ill and he would call on his brothers-in-law, the uncles of the children, and the brothers of his wife to get their *ndzo* at the inquest. It was in his house that the altar *kio* stood on a table with the statuettes *itio* for his ancestors. The statuettes were filled with earth taken from the tomb of the ancestor and then wrapped in a bit of cloth; with them were *nkobi* boxes with white earth and other paraphernalia relating to his ancestors. There he would also keep the family pharmacy with its medicines and charms. Women were not concerned at all with ancestors except for the *angkíra* ladies, who were possessed by the spirits of their *nkaa*, could sing and dance for them and act like them during a trance which recurred regularly. But that was supposed to help themselves only and not their families.

Within the family the main behaviour patterns were a reflexion of the structural relationships between its members. Wives and husbands should respect each other. The wife could never call her husband by name and he could impose *ipwooro* or *ibwooni* on her. On the other hand if he ill-treated her, her brother, father, or mother's brother could ask *ibwooni* to the amount of a fowl or two measures of wine (in 1963)

[2] E. ZORZI, *Al Congo*, p. 231.

from the husband. This was never called *ipwooro*, because a wife was inferior to a husband. *Ibwooni* as a technical term meant only payments between husband and wife to atone for errors made. This semantic difference makes it clear that women were inferior and in fact the roles of husband/wife epitomized the relative positions of men and women.

Men and women stood so far apart that there was almost a male and female subculture.[3] Men and women were rarely seen together. Only after dinner in the evening could they sit together around the fire. Women were supposed to be slow-witted, fickle, and unreliable. They could barely act on their own and had to follow men as dependants. They had little choice concerning their own marriages, were inherited as goods, and were held to be fit only for work in the fields and at home. Their heads were hard and so they were more able than men to carry things.[4]

But women had their own view of the world. They were often together since they farmed in groups, went to the spring together, collected firewood together, and spent their afternoons outside the village around their installations for soaking cassava (*idzia*). There they would gossip, affirm their values, feel themselves superior. They did not care much for men and believed that all young men were just dandies, good for nothing except for dressing up.[5] Often they were not much pleased with their husbands either and considered them a necessary evil. They cared for their brothers but not as much as for their sisters and mothers. There was a female solidarity in Tio life. They were not much interested in the world of men: the feuds and wars, the bridewealths, and counter-bridewealths, the court cases. They were affected by them, but could not help them much since they were frozen out of courts and councils, except when a divorce was discussed. So they talked mostly about the farm, the weather, babies and their mishaps, pregnancies, jealousies among co-wives, and very much about illnesses which beset them and for which they had their own collective rituals such as *itsuua*. The separation between men and women in fact benefited the women since it left them more freedom. Brazza remarked that they went around as they pleased among the Boõ in contrast to the Kukuya.[6] It is also not impossible that the fidelity of Tio women, which is reported later, has a connexion with this. Women were seldom together with men and very often in groups among themselves. To think however that there was less adultery because women as a group despised men as a

[3] The most detailed informant about this question was Abili Ndiõ. Her testimony dates to 1900.

[4] H. BRUNSCHWIG, *Les cahiers*, pp. 181–2. Women were used as carriers.

[5] ABILI NDIÕ and H. STANLEY, *The Congo*, IX, pp. 280, 375.

[6] H. BRUNSCHWIG, *Les cahiers*, p. 167. The case of the 'Queen' Ngalifourou also comes to mind. After the death of her husband, king Ngaayüo in 1918 she ruled alone for years and retained the title of *chef de canton*, until her death in 1956.

group would be wrong, but the general attitudes certainly had some influence.[7]

This whole attitude was obviously carried over into marriage. Wives and husbands were often antagonistic. They were allowed to hit each other, but a husband could not hit his wife before a third person or her brothers would ask for retribution. It was even worse, yet it happened, for a husband to tear his wife's wrapper off in public as a sign of supreme humiliation. Wives defended themselves well. In 1963 we saw one start an argument with her husband in the morning. She had to go to the fields, so she stopped, declaring she would continue it at night. When night fell, she suddenly began again with great fury and soon her neighbour, who happened to be her brother came over to side with her. Obviously this was a well controlled anger and she took advantage of the so-called irresponsibility of women.[8] On another occasion in 1964 a most important chief picked a quarrel with one of his wives. Soon a second wife came to the rescue of the first and then another and yet another one until all five wives were taking part in it. The chief was reinforced by his mother's brother and another relative, but the men were just outshouted and had to give in. The case shows how the solidarity of the sexes operated and how this quarrel became the occasion to express a mutual and deep-seated antagonism. It also illustrates that for women, men's hierarchies meant little, at least in domestic life.

But female solidarity did not always operate. There were cases where the wife would be helped by her brothers while her husband might be by her father, so that one found antagonists of both sexes on either side. The paramount exception to female solidarity was the relation between co-wives *mbaa*. They were often green with jealousy with regard to each other and the husband had to remain totally impartial if he wanted his household to function properly. Theoretically co-wives had to behave like *nkaa* and *otioolu* according to the date of marriage. It was believed to be an ideal second marriage to wed with the *otioolu* of one's first wife or, barring that, with her younger sister. It did occur that co-wives lived in harmony, especially if the difference of age was great. In any case the husband was supposed to ask the agreement of his first wife before marrying a second one and in principle many women liked the idea of a co-wife, because she could be a friend to do the work when the first wife fell ill. But often it did not work out and they quarrelled over the husband's favours.

[7] G. SAUTTER, *Le plateau*, p. 149. He mentions the very stiff sanctions for adultery as a reason. But these did not apply any more in the colonial period. Yet adultery even with relatively affluent outsiders remained rare.

[8] They argued about 100 Fr CFA she had borrowed to buy some facial cream during the absence of her husband. What enraged the lady was the charge that she once had spent 2,000 Fr CFA in this fashion. She claimed the charge was groundless and that furthermore her husband was much more of a spender than she was (which seemed to be the case!).

Among the wives of chiefs or headmen the first ordered the others around and eventually all the women in the village, according to the instructions of her husband. She would give him her private advice before any meeting of notables, and she would receive the best gifts offered to the chief's wives.[9] In such circumstances it becomes possible to see how someone like Ngalifourou, second wife of the king Ngaayüo could usurp his position after his death and with the help of the French play the role of king.

The brother/sister relationship (*nkieli/nkieli*) was complementary to the husband/wife relationship. A brother helped his sister under all circumstances, whatever the circumstances, even if for instance a divorce would result and the brother's kin might have to pay back twice the bridewealth. Since the brother never received any of his sister's bridewealth, this kind of action did not conflict with his material interests. Just as a brother always took his sister's side against her husband, he took her side in any quarrel between his wife and her. But here again in real life a sister might like one *nkieli* better than another one as in the case of Onini who had a very serious complaint to air. She did not tell her husband but left him to go to the village of her father's brother's sister, a *nkieli* and told him. She could have gone with less trouble to her full brother in Brazzaville, but she liked the other man better. He then took the necessary steps for her. A more complex situation was remembered by Miandoo, in which a man had carried on a feud because his sister's husband's sister had been killed.

Still the relation was not one between equals and a brother could exact *ipwooro* from his sister, but not the reverse. An element of distance between them was involved, since too great a familiarity would rate as incest and this was almost as bad as incest between parent and child. Still that did not prevent angry brothers or cousins from striking their sisters, but the contrary was forbidden.

The relationship between mother and daughter was usually much closer than that between mother and son. The mother would defend her girl by refusing to sanction a marriage planned for the daughter if the girl did not like it. She would have her daughter home for the birth of a second child since the first baby had to be born at the husband's place. If her daughter complained about her husband, the mother could make a love charm *ingali* for her (Calloc'h, p. 322: *i-ngali*, 'fetiche de séduction'). She was superior to her daughter all her life and could spank her even after the latter's marriage, whereas the girl could insult her mother but not hit her. This fairly free relationship meant in fact that most daughters and mothers understood each other well. After all, the little girl had been with her mother from babyhood and worked with her in the fields until her marriage and both confided much in one

[9] *Coutumes*, p. 43. This was the basis Ngalifourou started her career from, even though she was only the second wife of the king.

another. Yet, when the mother was old and widowed she would not go to live with her daughter, but rather with her sons, since her daughter was after all a dependant of her husband. Relations between all *ngu* and *mwaana wuuke* (girls) were patterned after those of mother and daughter in a less intense fashion.

Between mothers and sons the relationship was more strained. Sons did insult their mothers and, although they were not supposed to do so, they hit them on occasion too. In the latter case a mother could request *ipwooro*. But mother and son estranged rapidly, for at puberty he left his mother's house and built one for himself or roomed with a friend until marriage. A special feature of this relationship was that the worst insult men could hurl at each other was an allusion to the femininity of their mothers. This often resulted in violence and bloodshed. And such insults were by no means rare. It is true that mother/son incest was considered the worst situation in the world and insults of this sort were insinuations, but there may be more to it. The ambivalence of a world in which men thought themselves to be masters and where women were inferior beings was clearly tied up in this relationship. It was the only one where a man had to respect, to obey even, and sometimes to recognize publicly the superiority of a woman.

Sons and fathers were supposed to have a warm relationship, rather unlike the one the boy would have with his mother's brother. Once he was twelve or thirteen years old he had left the world of women and his father was supposed to teach him the lore of a man's world. So when the boy killed his first animal, a test of manhood, the leg or 'noble tribute' would go to his own father. If the father had a special training, as smith, diviner, healer, drummer, and the like, the sons could learn the trade if they wished to and many did. But in fact the boy lived more with his co-evals than with his father. His relationship with the latter would mellow with age and many sons came to be on comfortable terms with their fathers only after their own marriages, when they were in their thirties. Only then would they go with their fathers to the same fields and spend part of the day with them. Overall the relationship in practice seems not to have been as harmonious as the ideal required and few fathers felt the urge to utter efficient curses against their sons. That would result in a lack of success in hunting or when the son was falling ill. A diviner would make the diagnosis, *ipwooro* would be paid and the curse was then first acknowledged and then lifted in front of the boy's brothers. It was rare that a diviner would accuse a father of the death of his son and it was believed to be much less frequent than a bewitching by a mother's brother. Usually, not always, boys preferred their fathers to their mother's brothers and confided in them, although less so than mothers with daughters. They also felt that any slight done to their father was done to them. In 1963 an incident occurred in which an old man was sent on a useless errand by practical jokers. One comment was: 'Well the old man is only my father-in-law. If it had been my father, I might have fought over it.'

The relation was strongly influenced by prevalent patterns of authority. These were less rigorous than in the *ndzo*, but still as the head of the family the father exercised real authority, which his son might and sometimes did begrudge him. There were tensions over this and Mbali maintained that chiefs had sometimes scolded fathers when their sons had left the village: 'Why do the children go away? What did you do to them? Maybe you are bad (i.e. a witch).' So there was much less opposition between the relationships father/son and mother's brother/son than in strictly matrilineal societies. Much depended on the temperaments involved. A gentle uncle was 'better' than a stern father and so a son might even prefer to live with his mother's brother. In 1963, in fact, a third or so of the younger men lived with their mother's brothers and not with their fathers. But then again much depended on the status of the persons involved. Young men liked to live near chiefs or village leaders and would choose the parent who held the highest prestige.

Between fathers and daughters the relations were sporadic and neutral. This was not a copy of the mother/son relationship. First, father/daughter incest was considered much less evil than mother/son incest. Then fathers saw their daughters only sporadically and usually their most intimate contact occurred when the girl had to be married. After the nuptials the father always took the side of the husband because of the bridewealth and it happened that husbands would call on their fathers-in-law with a gift, to persuade them to talk their daughters into submission. The daughter did not get much out of the relationship since she could not express her opinions strongly at all. That was an insult and fathers tended to be quite authoritarian with their daughters, even more so than with their wives, who, after all, could talk back. On the other hand the element of striving for authority which obtained between fathers and sons was completely absent in this relationship.

Nnaana and *mbwei*, mostly elder and younger brothers, remained in a close relationship all their lives. There is a Tio name for a group of brothers, *isaani*, at least if they had a common father.[10] The boys could belong to the same *ndzo* or different *ndzo* but all belonged to the same polygynous family. The brothers, half-brothers, resident parallel or cross-cousins played together when they were young and formed a relatively tight group until their marriage. But after adulthood was reached, pressures for leadership became stronger. So it was thought that *mbwei* would not always meekly obey their *nnaana*, but often one

[10] *Isaani* designated a set of brothers or half brothers whose common father had died and who jointly directed the family in a single residence. Cf. Sims: *Isana*, 'foster child'; *maa isano*, 'stepmother'; *asaña*, 'half brother'. This contrasts with: *mutana*, 'stepfather'.

would try to bewitch the other and vice versa. This led to a kind of negative bond in the group whereby the limits of acceptable behaviour towards one another were carefully observed for fear of an accusation of witchcraft. Ambitious young men did quarrel with their brothers though, accusing them of witchcraft, thus often expelling their brothers or forcing them into submission. Many cases that occurred during the last thirty years were known in Mbe in 1963. It also happened that a man refused to pay *litsũ* for his mother on the grounds that his brother had been bewitching the other siblings. Stanley's account for the fight for supremacy between NTSUULU and his half-brother Ngako[11] is another instance. But it also happened that meeker brothers would rally behind their *nnaana* or that a weak *nnaana* would abandon the leadership to a *mbwei*. This however happened much more frequently if they belonged to the same *ndzo*, at least it appears so from the examples known in 1963–4, than if they belonged to different houses.

If *nnaana* and *mbwei* were girls the situation was radically different. They did not live together after their marriage and they married early, the oldest girl going first. In some cases two sisters would be co-wives of the same husband and stay together, but this was the exception. They had not to fight for common interests, so they got along much better than brothers. They would visit each other from time to time, lend each other food or foodstuffs if one was short and in general supported each other. A case was remembered among the Wũ where a man had killed his wife on the grounds that she had said that he was impotent. But her sister afterwards beat the culprit to a pulp, thus playing a role one would have believed fit for her brother. In general sisters helped each other most during these long visits which lasted for weeks, sometimes months. For then they could gossip during the farmwork, compare children, and jointly commiserate about the hard life their lords and masters made for them. Thus the groups of coeval women siblings were strengthened by the very separation between the spheres of women and men, the fact that it was a man's world, that there was no authority among women, and even the fact that normally women were separated and could not therefore daily get on each other's nerves, but would see one another on visits only.[12]

The enactment of the expected behaviour between members of the polygynous family, described in an impressionistic fashion here, sketches what sort of social group the family was. It stood at the core of the social system, not only because it educated the young, or procreated

[11] H. STANLEY, *The Congo*, I, pp. 348–50.

[12] Direct proof for these relationships during Iloo's reign is not available. Testimony from eyewitnesses or tradition is practically useless for this topic. A few cases remembered might be more exceptional and therefore of limited value only. Since behaviour is conditioned by the interests of the persons involved and ultimately by the structural features of the system which are known, the reconstruction seems justified and valid, even if it is derived from the later situation in 1963.

them or was at the heart of the kindred system. In economics it was the unit which produced and consumed most of the food and shelter needed for subsistence. For the individual it provided a home and constituted the fulfilment of the aspirations of most people. It set a model for all behaviour with people outside it, especially of course for collaterals in the same positions. And when the family became extended it also formed the basic unit of settlement.

2. *The extended family*

In time a polygynous family will grow into an extended family if the married children or some of them stay near the parental home. This was common practice among the Tio where, as they say, people live one 'behind another'. Most of the time the married sons stayed and the married girls left, but not always. There were some local endogamous marriages and in 1963 up to one third of the boys went to live with their mother's brothers. So the extended family has to be defined here by the following two characteristics: it encompassed three generations and it was a fairly stable residential group living in its own hamlet or quarter of a village. It rarely comprised all the married children and it often contained some of the married daughters as well as some married sons.

Such families existed in 1963 and one fairly often found them in isolated hamlets such as Isasiba. A similar settlement of a man with his two wives and children was known to Babet in 1933 and to all inhabitants of Mbe later on and in the 1880s Pecile noted that Ngampo's village counted eight persons including the head of the village, his brother, three women, wives of the two men, and three children. Not so long ago one wife and three babies had died.[13] Guiral found a hamlet with one old man, three younger men, two women, and one child and Stanley talks about the village of the 'fifer' of Ngaliema who lived in his own hamlet as a hermit halfway between Léopoldville and Kintamo.[14] It is clear that there were some hamlets, smaller even than an extended family. A polygynous family could live on its own. There were others where the third generation had died, but a set of brothers were still living together as in Ngampo's village. The latter was a normal situation for hamlets or quarters of villages.[15]

All these settlements were *ula* (Sims *ula*: 'village'). Bigger villages were divided into wards called *itwo* or *para* (Sims) and on the Pool (Sims) also *kana*, which meant at the same time, 'family, tribe, and

[13] E. ZORZI, *Al Congo*, pp. 408–9; V. BABET, *Exploration*, p. 38 note 1. He found two huts with one old man (NgeIbiõ) and his two wives. The fruit-trees of the Mbe abandoned in 1918 were still well in evidence by autumn 1933; L. GUIRAL, *Le Congo*, p. 301, mentions a hamlet with one old man, three men, two women, and one child.

[14] H. STANLEY, *The Congo*, I, p. 392.

[15] Cf. the terminology of Sims given in fn.10.

home!'[16] So the normal smallest but fully grown residential unit would be an extended family.

Both *nkaa* and *otioolu* were present in the extended family and their relationship was the element which distinguished this group from others. It was also a group which, unlike the polygynous family, had no head or representative *per se*. If only one *nkaa* remained he would act as head, because he was the head of his polygynous family, if several were present, there would be allegiance to the village headman and if the group lived in an isolated hamlet it would have its own headman, the person responsible for founding the hamlet. But he exercised authority, not because of his genealogical position, but because he was the leader of the settlement, and on more than one occasion he was not the eldest male person in the settlement. It is significant to emphasize this because the basic role of the extended family was one in which authority was played down.

In the polygynous family the respect associated with relationships between members of adjacent generations was prominent. The relaxation, the teasing associated with alternating generations was the keynote. Between *nkaa* and *otioolu* of opposite sex there was a joking relationship with faint sexual overtones which grew less as the *otioolu* became adult. The bond was stronger between grandmothers and smaller children than between them and their grandfathers, since most of the grandfathers were gone during the day and the grandmothers stayed in the village. When they grew older the relationships between *nkaa* and *otioolu* became more important. Sometimes a *nkaa* actually married an *otioolu*, considered as a smart marriage. Between partners of the same sex friendship was supposed to prevail. Grandmothers acted towards their granddaughters very much as *nnaana* to *mbwei*, but were more helpful. They would keep the babies, help with the tedious and long preparation of cassava flour and be ready with a helping hand without having to be asked. Between men there often grew a strong and genuine affection. The grandfather could impose *ipwooro* on his grandchild, but no one believed that a *nkaa* would ever bewitch an *otioolu* and that was remarkable. The old men needed the support of the young bloods in village or hamlet politics to keep their own sons in line and the grandsons needed the intercession of their grandfathers to adjust relations with their fathers if something went wrong and their help in matters of bridewealth or trade.

The quarter and the extended or polygynous family it contained was a social group of variable stability over time. In contrast to many villages, quarters were relatively stable. Thus the settlement of Nge-Ibiõ and his two wives lasted at least from 1918 to 1933 and the oldest

[16] Calloc'h, p. 303, 'quartier: village': *i-koro* and *nkolo*. Sims *ikoo*: 'enclosure, hedge, palisading' may relate to the Fumu word or not. Nevertheless, the Fumu too had wards within the village.

quarter of Mbe in 1963 was established there in 1934 and had already been a quarter in other places since, perhaps, 1925.[17] It had changed personnel but the group of brothers which had founded it after 1925 was still ruling it in 1964. By then it had grown into a much bigger settlement composed of other new quarters. Because of this stability the extended family represented perhaps the most significant social group based on kinship. It participated in all the major institutions, economic, social, and religious, of the society and, because it joined several polygynous groups, it could cope better than the latter group with the insecurity by the vagaries of social conflict and illness which endangered or incapacitated the whole group of some of its members. In feuds its size meant protection. In case of illness the presence of close kin meant that help would still be available to perform the essential tasks of house-building and agriculture. True, the polygynous family could often cope with these situations, but the extended family was better at it. On the other hand, the divisive influence of struggles for leadership of the group, which are typical of the village level were already perceptible at this level.

3. *The village*

Not far from the edge of a little wood, lost in a sea of high grass most of the year, a jumble of roofs announced the presence of a village. It might contain from ten to a hundred houses. The village was noticeable from far away, not by its buildings, but by the palm trees which often surrounded part or the whole of it. Its approaches were betrayed by the isolated banana trees sticking up above the grass near the *idzia* gardens. By the screen of palm trees one could guess the age of the settlement. If there was a whole orchard of them all around, it meant that the settlement was several generations old and it must have been the exception. However in 1963 Imbãw and Ãtoro were like that and it denoted a long occupation, dating from around 1900 according to NGAATALI. Then there were the villages where the trees were still young, but the banana groves were thick, and in the newest settlements even the banana trees were just planted, and the houses lay defenceless in an ocean of heat, light, and dust.

It was also possible to find villages completely hidden in the centre of the woods with small houses and no near-by plantations. This was a certain sign of troubled times. People had fled from the open savannah because of war or feuds. But they felt they could not stay for long in this situation. The fields and often the water supply were too far, there were too many elephants around, the forest was bad for the livestock. So

[17] This quarter Masala was founded by a group of brothers including king Ngankia Mbandieele, Ngateo and Ubwoono first as a hamlet near Inoni. In 1934 with the nomination of Ngankia it was moved to Mbe. Two of the other quarters of Mbe (which had four) were also first independent hamlets.

such settlements never seem to have been occupied for periods longer than a year, or, at the most, two.

A village should be relatively near the spring but on the plains, away from the mosquitoes. It should be near a wood because of the need for firewood, housebuilding, and tools and since the fields tended by the men were cleared in the woods. Also the cemetery was located at the edge of a wood, unmarked except for bits of crockery on low mounds, sometimes cleared of vegetation but often completely overgrown. Near the village there should be plenty of space for the different types of gardens and further away, but often only a few hundred yards, one had the main fields for the women. Most of the land was not of very good quality so that villages would be built, whenever possible, near patches where the presence of certain plants indicated a better soil.[18]

The village was arranged around a central courtyard in front of the house of the headman. But to the traveller this might often be lost in the scattered jumble of little groups of houses. Each ward built its quarter a little away from the next and if the settlement was fairly big, such as some Boõ, or Jinju villages, the total agglomeration could be considerable. At the Pool and among the Mfunu the normal pattern was to build fairly long, narrow houses around a circle with the shorter sides facing the interior of a circle. They looked then like the spokes of a wheel except that the disposition remained irregular and the whole circle might not be enclosed. Several photographs of the time show this disposition, which had completely vanished by 1963.[19] In other cases the centre could be more of a square, but never did one find one street with the houses of the men along it and those of their wives behind as is now the common plan. If the headman was a chief his settlement was recognized by a palisade built around his houses and forming a courtyard. In 1882 the household of NGOBILA, Lord of Mswata, occupied the centre with palisades and a courtyard around which the houses of his settlement were built. The other houses of the agglomeration were scattered without order or plan and seemed 'of revolting untidiness'.[20]

Even the capital was not very different. Brazza reports: '. . . The houses are enclosed in groups of straw palisades, which make easily defendable squares. Facing the entrance of the chief's (king) square, we stopped waiting for the chief to receive me. . . . The largest of the trees

[18] These data are still visible on the ground for villages from the period. In fact, features of the landscape can help determine the age of a site by such indications as how much of the orchard of palm-trees has remained, if the name of the village is still known or not and the condition of the palm-trees themselves.

[19] WHYMS, *Léopoldville*, p. 27, photograph of Kinshasa in 1881; E. HANSSENS, *Premières explorations*; A. CUREAU, *Les sociétés*, photograph XV, pp. 318–19. The photo may date from the 1890s. H. H. JOHNSTON, *Grenfell*, II, p. 732; 3. A. CHAPEAUX, *Le Congo*, photograph Ectors, pp. 536, 555–6; C. COQUILHAT, *Sur le Haut Congo*, p. 59; CH. DE MARTRIN DONOS, *Les Belges*, II, p. 113.

[20] E. HANSSENS, *Premières explorations*, p. 14.

stands in the chief's square.'[21] The only difference from an ordinary village was that all the hamlets were enclosed by palisades.

The size of villages varied very much. The smallest one mentioned contained eight persons and the largest were the great markets of (ki)Ntamo or Kinshasa[22] the population of which was loosely estimated to range from 2,500 to 5,000 inhabitants. In 1882 Mswata, one of the big settlements on the river, contained 290 souls and that included only 8 or 9 freemen, 85 wives of the great chief NGOBILA, and all the rest were slaves. It was big[23] then, but still essentially composed of probably no more than two or three extended families. The bigger settlements in the 1880s were Kinshasa, Kintamo, Mpila, Mswata, the residences of the chiefs OOPU, MUIDZU, NGE IMPÃW, the village of Ngampourou near the present Djambala and two or three other Jinju villages.[24] In such bigger agglomerations there were many headmen, considered the 'second headman of the village'.[25] And even these headmen ruled over several quarters. The situation was slightly more complicated in the residence of important trader chiefs because of the numbers of slaves they possessed. But elsewhere the basic quarter contained certainly less than fifty persons and one headman ruled over a few hundred at most. He was bound to take advice from the 'big men' of the quarters, if he did not want to lose people. At the level of the whole settlement the same principle remained true.[26]

The wards were then almost autonomous. They probably, in the 1880s as in the 1960s, cultivated land in separate places and were even built apart. But in some respects there was some integration, namely in the relatively high degree of village endogamy. In 1963 the origins of the partners in marriage was linked directly to distance. 46 per cent of the marriages then extant had been between people living within a radius of thirteen miles. Marriages were just as numerous between settlements as within settlements. There is no reason to believe this not

[21] H. BRUNSCHWIG, *La négociation*, p. 22; E. ZORZI, *Al Congo*, p. 386 confirms: 'un piccolo villaggio colle case cadenti e d'aspetto non molto prospero'. CH. DE CHAVANNES, *Avec Brazza*, opp. p. 161, shows a wall of the royal compound. The site of Itieele in 1963 confirmed that Mbe was small.

[22] Then named Ntamo or Ntãw and Nsaasa by their inhabitants. They are discussed in the section dealing with markets.

[23] TH. MASUI, *L'Etat Indépendant*, p. 81, following Hanssens (1882); E. HANSSENS, *Premières explorations*, p. 14.

[24] H. BRUNSCHWIG, *Les cahiers*, p. 168, for Ngampourou; L. GUIRAL, *Le Congo*, p. 305, on Jinju and mixed Jinju and Boõ villages.

[25] Calloc'h, p. 158; *mbyemo;* 'le second d'un village'. M. N. OBENGA, *Le royaume*, p. 35, may derive his information from Calloc'h.

[26] In Ntamo for instance there were nine chiefs for an estimated population of 5,000 of which many were slaves. That gave a population per chief of ±550–575. But these 'chiefs' again had to deal with the heads of extended families. When Ngaliema in 1881 wanted to accept Stanley he was compelled by the other chiefs, his 'followers', to abandon his plan. A. MAURICE, *Stanley*, p. 109, where these are described as 'the elders of Ngaliema and his chiefs'.

to be true in the 1880s. This implied that several women might be married into the same big village and choose to make their cassava soaking installations next to one another rather than each with the people of their husband's ward. Young men from different wards would band together for hunting (as they would from different villages if these were small and near enough) and friendships could flourish. So a large village remained very comparable to a collection of small villages a dozen miles or so apart from each other, but the processes of neighbourhood exchange were simply more intense.

Each village had a headman, *wookuru* 'the elder'. He was the leader of an extended family or wider group based on his kindred at the core of it. He often gave his name to the settlement he had founded or chose a name for it. Thus in 1963 the village of Okiene was named by its headman because he had ultimately been originally from a village north of the Lefini with the same name. Leaders were not chosen nor succeeded. They founded a village and those who wished went to live with them. At their death or before, the people might disperse again or someone of a younger generation might manage to keep part of the population in the village under his leadership. This was such a normal process that the term *ikwei* was given to a man who had split off from another village and founded his own. So the stability of a village was in reality not greater than that of a quarter. The psychology is neatly documented by Sims: *yalo*: 'cause to be revealed; cause to be found out'; *yalo ula*: 'emigrate'; *yalo mibi*: 'cause a thief to be known'. The witchcraft in the village was revealed and the victims left it.

A village headman was expected to protect the people who lived with him and to please them. He could settle mild quarrels between people belonging to his village. That meant that he would preside at an informal moot with the older relatives of the persons involved and voice the decision which in fact had been reached by arbitration. To the outside world he represented the village. He would lead it into a feud if a member had been killed and he would assist the political chief in reaching a settlement in which the aggravated party would receive a person as compensation, if someone had been killed within the village by another villager. He would also participate in the *okuu* inquest for anyone in his settlement, since he was related to everybody either by blood or as an affine.

Sometimes a *wookuru* would attempt to formalize his ascendancy through the acquisition of an *ibili* charm. These were charms made by the high priest in the kingdom, the LIPIE. He was in charge of the cult of the national spirit Nkwe Mbali at the Falls of the Lefini at Mbã. Anything that was washed ashore near the sacred falls would be picked up and he would make an *ibili* with it. That received a name and could later even be divided. Thus the *ibili* Ngamiõ acquired in the 1920s was divided after the death of the original keeper among two of his brothers.

One could go there and acquire an *ibili* against payment. It is not really clear if anybody could receive one, or if the applicant had to belong to the aristocracy (*baamukaana lilimpu*), and this confusion benefited the prestige of *ibili* holders. For they were easy to get, so easy that in spite of their claims, their possession did not mean much. Much more important as an indicator of leadership and authority was the ability of the *wookuru* to protect his people against illness and death. If people were healthy, stresses were low and the leader was judged able. Conversely, he was then respected because his spirit was supposed to help to keep the land quiet. But if there was much illness, he was judged to be failing in his duties as protector, his reputation declined and he might even be abandoned. On the whole, in normal times he had authority and was rather feared, for it was believed that if he was angry things might be lacking. He would not protect people efficiently any more and that could mean bad luck with harvests, the hunt, or illness.

Most *wookuru* had once been ambitious younger men striking out on their own, who succeeded in attracting thirty to forty persons around them. In chiefly villages relatives clustered around their kinsman who was a titled chief. But some *wookuru* managed to accumulate much more power. The most successful of all remains Ngaliema of Kintamo. Of slave extraction he succeeded in becoming *wookuru* and, without any other title or right, became the foremost trader in slaves and ivory around the Stanley Pool and one of the great powers among the Tio in the 1870–80s. In practice he had become indistinguishable from the great chiefs. It was not surprising considering that the trade created special opportunities for 'big men' but it must also be stressed that political techniques competitors used for leadership at the *wookuru* level were exactly the same as those used at all levels in the realm. Their discussion therefore is better left for a later chapter. Suffice it to say that there was intense competition within the bigger villages. For instance the history of Mbe from 1934 to 1963 was a succession of attempts to grab leadership or establish new leadership. Even the role of protector of the inhabitants of his village was not peculiar to the *wookuru*. It was even more apparent at the level of chiefs.

This need for protection was obvious in the village headman's ritual concerns. As soon as a spot for a new village had been found at the Pool the diviner was consulted. With the headman and the future inhabitants he went around and chased the evil spirits away with a great show of contortions. Then a strong stake was planted on the spot where the house of the headman would be built and on its top a ball of paste, made with several ingredients was deposited. In it the medicine-man attracted all the evil spirits which still remained in the area and imprisoned them by winding a piece of cloth around the stake. Then near the future centre of the village he planted some cassava, maize, and a hedge of *euphorbia*. The future prosperity of the village depended on the growth of these plants. This is why in the villages of the Pool there was always a stake topped by a flat stone and protected by an enclosure which 'kept the leopards and the jackals' away, clearly a protection against witches from the outside.[27] This is very much like the *nkiini* which was common in the twentieth century.

The *nkiini*[28] was installed on demand of the *wookuru* by a diviner healer. In larger villages there was more than one *nkiini*. Each ward might have one. In fact in 1963 even a section of the Masala ward in Mbe had a *nkiini*. Each settlement need not have its *nkiini* though, it all depended on the mood of the people and the *wookuru*. Where there was none, it often meant, however, not that the inhabitants were overconfident, but that they were poor and could not afford the price of a specialist. Where there was more than one in a ward or small village, it was obvious that that settlement was splitting.

The *nkiini* was a hole containing palm nuts and water and filled in, with a banana tree planted near by. Around this a circle was made and on the circumference black ant hills and trees were planted. Some specialists made an enclosure around it all and sometimes small gardens, especially of maize could be found within the precinct. The trees were all of species with which charms could be made for other purposes. They were the *obwooro* and *oto* trees, also planted on the tombs of chiefs in addition to *andooliõliõ* and/or *obolo*, *otsitsiõ,oiuneiuni* and others. The banana tree in the centre was called *õna* and the whole was the *nkiini*. The whole was a 'trap' for witches, a charm protecting the settlement against 'lightning, leopards, lions', and witches. The charm could only be effective if all the villagers had participated in its dedication and if all observed the avoidances connected with it. Usually these were the prohibitions against women bringing calabashes on to the village square if they did not carry them on top of a little *nkara* ring which is put on the head before putting any load on it. They could not also bring any firewood tied with a rope to the square. The prohibition in a particular case might be different, but it always involved the villagers and had to do with the square or *mbali* of the settlement.

To build the *nkiini*, the diviner/healer gathered all the inhabitants, dug the hole, chewed copal (*oli*), *liõ* grass (sanseviera?) and *lisisõ* grass, all sacred plants which give 'coolness' and are especially effective against lightning and witchcraft. He would then take a palm nut from every inhabitant, rub it against the person's forehead and throw it in the hole. The banana tree was planted, the hole closed and all the rest arranged. He then predicted the number of years during which no one

[27] E. COART, A. DE HAULLEVILLE, *La religion*, pp. 164–5.

[28] Calloc'h, p. 134; *nkina*: 'autel' may be this. The word and the shrine for villages are known from Mayombe to the Sakata and even further to the Kuba. It can be presumed to be old, especially since it is not remembered as a recent introduction anywhere.

would fall ill, e.g. three years. If his predictions came true, he would be called back the x years later to 'clean' up the *nkiini* and give some amulets (*kaa*) to the people then.

The banana tree of the *nkiini* grew and threw off shoots, after which its fruit could be eaten without any ceremony. The growth of the tree indicated simply that life in the village was healthy and normal.

The strength of the *nkiini* was attributed to an invisible animal like a lion, a leopard, or a snake left by the medicine man. When the *nkiini* was made, the medicine man did not pray to supernatural agencies but addressed himself only to the *wookuru* who had called him in. After the installation of the shrine, the *wookuru* occasionally sacrificed a fowl to his ancestors in particular and those of the villagers in general. On occasion, when they felt the need for it, villagers would offer a little kola to the *nkiini* to chase away the evil spirits (*apfu*). In this the ancestors of the *wookuru* acted as protective spirits for the whole settlement just as the *ikwii* of the father protected the whole household. It reminds one that the village was still built on kinship relations.

Protection by the headman was also visible and even dramatic for the villagers because he would dream about the dangers of his village. When this had happened he got up at sunrise and in the silence of the dawn proclaimed loudly what he had dreamt and what should be done, blaming those who quarrelled, exhorting all to remain peaceful, telling the witches in his village that they better remain quiescent if they did not want to be detected and punished. This technique of the talk to the villagers was impressive and effective, especially in times of stress, as could be witnessed when we were there.[29]

A last and indirect way to protect the village was to avert rain. Lightning was and is a major hazard during electrical storms on the plateau and it was lightning that was feared, for it killed people as an instrument, it was believed, of especially potent witches. Heavy rain and thunderstorms should be averted. Any man resident in a village could try it by blowing on a whistle, brandishing his magic horn, and telling the rain to go away.[30] The rain could be stopped in its tracks and sometimes the rainbow would show a certain sign that the medicine man had stopped it.

The mighty were supposed to be able to stop the rain. Thus king Iloo told Brazza that his NGEILIINO or first lord, Opontaba, had stopped the rain and the king himself had a small fetish dugout hanging over the door of his compound to stop lightning.[31] To charm away the rain

[29] This technique is widespread from the Kongo at least to the area of Lake Leopold II. It is not felt to be an innovation anywhere and may be taken as existing in the 1880s.

[30] E. ZORZI, *Al Congo*, p. 563.

[31] H. BRUNSCHWIG, *La négociation*, p. 24; E. ZORZI, *Al Congo*, p. 388 (the little dugout should stop lightning); E. COART, A. DE HAULLEVILLE, *La religion*, p. 216, where

(Sims: *yira ngawa*) most *wookuru* had a horn filled with magic. It would work only, like the *nkiini*, if one or more avoidances were observed by the whole village. Thus Ngateo remembered that no seeds of the trees *ĩkworambie ãsia* and *ntsuurnu* could enter the village. If anyone broke this collective taboo it might rain.

But unlike the *nkiini* any person in the village could have the equipment to avert rain. That was always put in a horn and prepared by a medicine man. There were also always avoidances with it and different medicine men would have different medicines and different avoidances, whereas one always imposed the same avoidance for a horn of similar importance. The owner of the horn went out, blew on his whistle to attract the attention of his ancestors' *ikwii*, brandished his horn and talked to his ancestors in his own words, not by any formula, conjuring them to keep the rain out. Then it would not rain. If it did rain after all, then either the charm was not strong enough because the owner had not paid enough to the medicine man, or perhaps the avoidance had not been observed. In a case like that, one would sacrifice a chicken and give some wine to the *ikwii*, pray to them and then the charm should work. For it was by the power of the ancestors, whether or not they use evil spirits (*apfu*) for the purpose, that the rain will be stopped. There were two types of charms, one with the horn of an antelope *ntsa*, to which kola was offered and one with the horn of the antelope *mvulimvuli*, to which no kola was given. Feathers were stuck in both.

Once again then the rituals for rain show the desire for protection and the fact that the *ikwii* of the *wookuru* should protect all. A new element in it is that competitors of the *wookuru* could also try to stop rain.

If the protection failed and lightning had struck, other magic was needed to put things straight. This ritual was not performed by the *wookuru* but could only be done by people in whose compound lightning had struck before. Three such people could be found in Mbe in November 1963 when lightning struck, showing how relatively often this event happened. There were two men and one woman in this case. They arrived on the scene chewing *lisisõ* (sanseviera?), just as a healer does when someone is ill, and spat it out on the spot where lightning had struck. They also hit the same spot with the central rib of a banana leaf to make the fire of lightning leave it. They also chewed copal (*oli*), considered an excrement of lightning, together with the *lisisõ* to make the 'animal' lightning come out. By this the effects of lightning were taken away and protection was ensured. If, however, it should have

the dugout is said to be a charm against drowning. Pecile is probably right. CH. DE CHAVANNES, *Avec Brazza*, p. 15, records the belief of NGANTSU that he had made it hail.

struck again and again, the community would then, through its headman, finally call in a medicine man from 'far away' who would find the cause and would point out who had been the witch/sorcerer[32] in the village. Precisely because he came from 'far away' he was not supposed to 'belong' or have local interests and could denounce a witch better than any local person. So once again, the headman ultimately had to protect his whole village by taking the necessary steps. As with the *nkiini* or when he told his dreams, the common enemy was always, beyond his changing shape, a witch from without the village or from within. All social and political tensions were thus projected as heroic fights of protectors against witches.

4. *Groups based on agreement and friendship*

Most of the social groups a person belonged to were given to him by birth. Ascriptive status played the first role, for any group founded on kinship was grounded on an ascriptive status. Yet individuals had some choice. For a bilateral kinship system left men much choice as to which side of their kindred they would choose to associate more with. The main choice to be made was the one of residence. Men could choose between different villages in which to live or they could strike out on their own. So, despite the fact that men's presence in a village could be explained by links of kinship, as having 'followed' so-and-so, except for the headman, it was equally true that there was a personal choice involved. Thus all residential groups could be looked on as built on achieved status as well. The mobility[33] of Tio men was one major way in which they expressed a great individualism. It may be, but cannot be proved, that the emphasis on bilateral descent had fostered unusual individualism. Be that as it may, common residence was also a major factor in the development of yet another set of social groups. For within one or neighbouring settlements there were groups based on common liking: on friendship. Here everything was due to achieved status. None of these was formally recognized by the Tio themselves, although friendship, the role which went with these, was. The tiny clusters based on friendship seemed to have little importance[34] for society at large. Yet it was essential for individuals, men and women, to have friends who did not have identical or opposed kinship interests. So whenever a settlement was large enough or near enough to another one, women would build their cassave soaking installations (*idzia*) in clusters so as to be able to be together and gossip part of the day. Yet, unlike the fields these clusters did not reflect kinship groups, or only imperfectly. Women

[32] The classical distinction between witch and sorcerer has no meaning among the Tio. So the terms are used interchangeably.

[33] R. HOTTOT, *Nomadism among the Bateke*, was apparently struck so much by this mobility that he talked of nomadism. His data go back to 1906.

[34] The only data on friends from the period are the word *nduu* itself, with the implicit testimony of LIPIE and NGAATALI that these patterns existed then.

built them near their friends. For those who had been married into the village, it had been possible to choose friends from among the other foreign women, married to villagers. This was a gradual process and one in which great freedom was left to the women, since they were not considered important enough to worry much about in this respect. The *idzia* were operated by each woman on her own and it was only the neighbourhood of the other *idzia* which was required to keep the friendship going. So no common interest was created and that seemed to benefit the stability over time of these little groups. Another stabilizing effect was the fact that such groups could include partners of differing ages.

For young men the situation was different. They came together for hunting. A drive with nets required hands and if, in bigger agglomerations, several groups of young men went out to hunt together, it was in the smallest settlements necessary to go and find some boys from other villages to team up for hunting. But the choice of mates for a hunting party was completely free and usually groups of friends developed out of these common ventures. But there were drawbacks. First with age, the common reason for the association would disappear and it would dissolve itself gradually. Also it differed fundamentally from the women's groups because the group had a common economic purpose: to hunt, and dissensions over the distribution of the spoils could and did easily arise. These groups were always much more contract associations. The young men would agree in advance of each hunt or series of hunts how the spoils would be divided and it is here that the technique of *itiõ* (*itimo*: revenge, Sims; *kitemo* in Kongo) later applied to a sharing of salaries in Brazzaville, had developed. Normally then men outgrew the hunting group and kept perhaps one or two friends they had met in the group and a young man changed groups fairly easily, because of a quarrel over the spoils.

Another form of friendship based on association for a common goal was the blood brotherhood which seems to have been prevalent mainly among chiefs and with the aim of trade. It was a partnership sanctioned by supernatural forces. Once one partner died, his fellow was believed to die soon after him. Since it is so closely connected with trade it will be further discussed there.

Beyond the above, friendship can be defined as a dyadic relationship. In this sense old and young among the Tio in 1963, and most likely in the 1880s, had friends. With age the relationship matured and deepened so that the role was most developed among mature and even older people. Friends were necessary and friends could not be close kin. *Nduu* or friendship meant to help the other person in adversity, to advise him, to tell what gossip had to say about him. One could count on a friend for help and one would help him without expecting strict reciprocity each time. *Nduu* could not bewitch each other, so one never had to fear them. Their advice had not to be taken with suspicion. For among Tio men suspicion was always rife. The most current saying in 1963 was '*attention, il faut se méfier*', invariably uttered in French by them. In Tio the expression was: 'not to have confidence'.[35] *Iminu* or confidence was a rare cardinal virtue. The French expression in 1963 reflected French attitudes towards the Tio, but it was a case of convergence since the constant struggle for better positions within the *ndzo*, the *ibuuru*, the *ula* by using witchcraft made suspicion a normal attitude.

Friends were especially important for the maintenance of prevailing norms of behaviour. They alone could advise and be critical. If one said: 'They say, you are going about with the wife of X and you should take care; there will be trouble', the other one might desist. Furthermore friends could mediate if two of their *nduu* quarrelled, they would give counsel with regard to marriage or bridewealth, etc. But their vital role was psychological: to provide some security, relaxation, and a confidant's ear.

Nduu were always of the same sex and usually, for men, of the same age. For women this was not quite true. The relation was also deeper between men, who needed it more than women. It was by its nature a relation between two persons, but it was not excluded that one of the two would entertain another friendship so that a chain of friendships could develop. This was more true, it seems, of women than of men who tended to be more exclusive. The social role was antithetical to behavioural roles tied in with kinship. It confirms the suspicions of tensions, ruthless competition, the fear of witchcraft as a negative solidarity which welded kinship groups together. Conversely it shows that no large groupings could be based on personal friendships alone and that kinship was essential for the formation of the necessary wider social groups.

5. *Conclusion*

The dynamics of the operation of the kinship system and the organization of the residential pattern were only possible because of the very low density of population. Land was without value and anyone could always leave and build his own home where it pleased him. The very vagueness of the kinship structure itself presupposed such a fluidity. Competition could rage unchecked because the losers could leave the game when they wanted to; in a dense area this struggle would have been a zero-sum game that might have been unbearable. In the smaller settlements, and they were the rule, people would split up long before they reached the level of actually fighting one another. In the larger settlements around the Pool the situation was different. There existed a limitation on favourable sites for creating markets and the struggle

[35] Calloc'h, p. 264: 'se méfier de' and p. 165: 'confiance': *i-minu*. Sims: *iminu*: 'belief, faith, confidence'.

may have been more intense, with actual strife and warfare occurring much more frequently.

Even within the *ndzo* the effects of the low density of population were evident. The tendency to consider one's matrilineage as consisting only of sets of mother's brothers and sister's sons could be attributed to the fact that other members of the *ndzo* would be spread over greater distances and that one did not see them often. This tendency gave a characteristic looseness to the *ndzo* which stands in sharp contrast for instance to those big and well segmented 'houses' of the Kongo.

The political organization impinged only slightly on the life of these social groups. Quarrels, feuds, conflicts of all sorts at the social level, were settled mostly without immediate recourse to the political administration. It is not surprising, given such a low density of population.

The striking individualism of the Tio, the importance of friendships are also part and parcel of what could be called a frontier situation, if it were not that the Tio had been living there for such a long time. The Tio adapted their society to the vastness of the land on which it thrived, so much so that Tio groups have emigrated for centuries from the plains, because they felt that there was famine and over-population.[36] As long as there were more wide-open plains to be colonized there was no reason to change the fabric of society. Moving was more traditional and easier. This, too, is a characteristic of a frontier society.

The other most striking point of this society was the wide gulf that separated women from men. Certainly a distance between men and women socially and culturally had been observed in other societies of Central Africa, but not such a devastating and aggressively negative view of each other. The reasons for this situation are not altogether clear. The exclusion of most women from the official management of social groups estranged them from many of the values and goals of men. Perhaps the very individualism of the Tio was involved. For pride (*orgeuil*) in men was called *ũpala*, derived from *õpala*: 'young man', and pride in women was *usiga* from *osiga* 'young girl'.[37] There was not even a common measure in haughtiness! But the major reasons may have been economic and the patterns of the division of labour.

[36] Which is at variance with the findings of G. SAUTTER, *Le plateau*, where the low density is explained as a consequence of slave raiding. There is no evidence for this in recent times. The profound adaptation of the social structure to a low density points to the existence of a low density for a long time. If the suggestions made are correct, there should be substantial differences between the Tio and the Kukuya who live on a plain with a high density of population.

[37] Calloc'h, pp. 247, 281.

Chapter IV
Marriage

TIO society knew two forms of transfer of persons from one kin group to another: marriage and slavery. The first was, in addition, the expression of alliances between kin groups and the occasion to forge new alliances, the shuttle which wove these discrete units into a common weave. The word marriage indicates both the making of a match and the union which results. Thus it is both a process or a sequence of events and a state or a union, which lies at the core of the family. These two aspects must be separated. So we deal first with the conclusion of marriage, then with marriage as an institution to end with the dissolution of the institution.

1. *Concluding a marriage*

The process by which a marriage is made involves a choice of partners, the exchange of a woman for compensation and ceremonies celebrating the match.

Marriage was forbidden between consanguines and for a second marriage with blood relatives of the first wife if they belonged to the generation of her father and mother, even if at the time divorce had been obtained from the first wife. This meant that the circle of alliances between lineages had to be widened at each marriage. It also meant that genealogies were not kept in great depth since marriage would otherwise become impossible. And they were not. The generation depth was only two or three generations deep from a marriageable person to the common ancestor. In fact it was agreed that people who were related because both of their *nkaa* were, could marry. Thus marriage within Ego's 'kindred in which one inherits' was excluded and so were sexual relations. Incest was worst with mother, then father, then full sibling. As a rule it was more serious the closer the blood relationship and worse if the senior partner was a woman than a man. Finally marriages may have been forbidden with Kukuya, Ngungulu, Tsintsege, Ngwongwooni, Fumu and Mboshi, Kongo, and all other non-Tio speakers establishing thus a measure of ethnic endogamy. They were certainly allowed among all the groups of the different plateaux and may have been with Tio Laadi, Ngenge, and Mfunu.[1]

[1] P. HERMANT, *Les coutumes*, p. 297, following Sims and Costermans on exogamy within kin-group. It is not strictly true that marriages were forbidden with the groups mentioned since some chiefs married, e.g. with Hum, and marriages to Bobangi seem also to have occurred. The information came from someone looking at the situation

At the limit of forbidden marriages lay the most desirable matches. For they renewed former alliances. Thus the Tio esteemed above all marriage between *otioolu*, i.e. persons related because both their *nkaa* were just beyond the limit of interdiction. What made it even more attractive was that in such a case no bridewealth had to be paid. The following situations were included in the term:

(i)

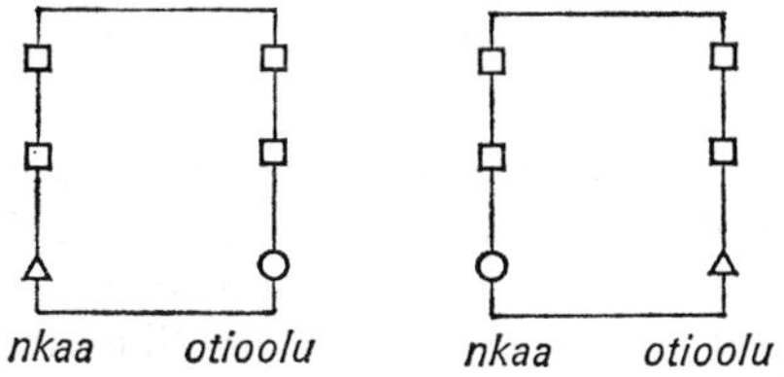

This marriage could be accepted or refused by the groups concerned. It came closest to incest. No bridewealth paid.

(ii)

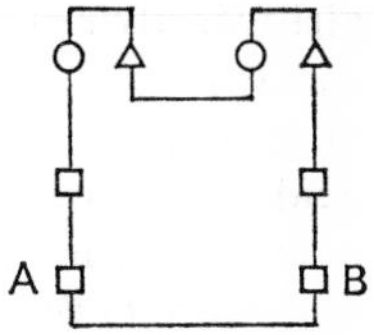

Marriage between persons whose own grandparents were siblings to persons who had been married. No blood relation existed between the candidates A and B. No bridewealth paid.

The rule seemed to be that whatever marriage reconfirmed a former alliance was desirable (if the former marriage had worked out) and bridewealth was not to be paid.

In the actual genealogies of persons such close but illicit marriages did occur, as is shown below:

(i)

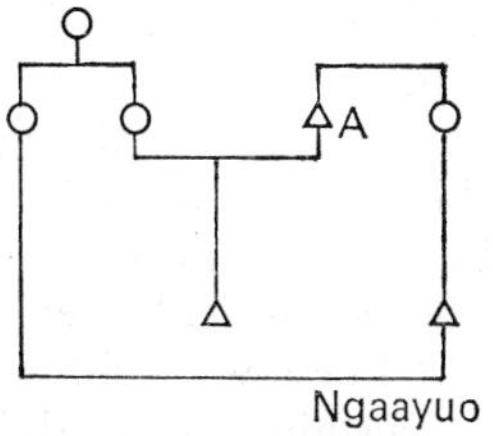

The marriage of Ngaayüo repeated the marriage of A. Bridewealth paid. (About 1925.)

(ii)

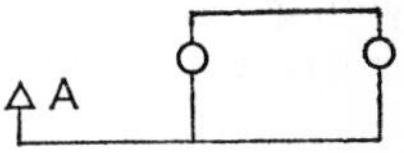

A married two sisters. He paid no bridewealth. (About 1880.)

(iii)

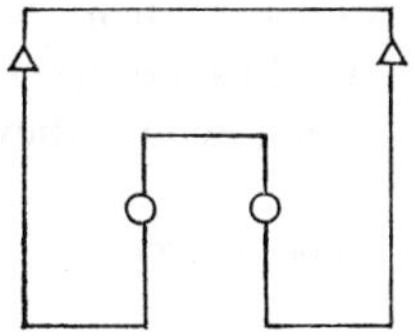

Both men married two sisters when they were full brothers. Two bridewealths paid. (About 1925.)

---

from the Mbe plateau. TH. MENSE, *Anthropologie*, p. 24, stresses the greater number of marriages between Tio and Hum and even Mfinu.

(iv)

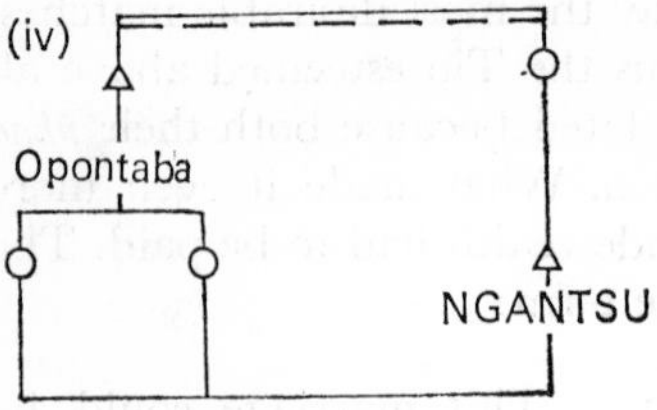

NGANTSU married before 1880 the two daughters of his mother's brother Opontaba (NGEILIINO). It is probable that the 'mother's brother' was collateral. If so it would be marriages between *otioolu* as in theory (i). In any case he married two sisters.[2]

The most liked form of remarriage or second marriage was with the wife's sister, as already noted, or other close affines of one's own generation. If a wife died childless her *otioolu* (obviously collateral) was given as a replacement without bridewealth or festivity. Since the older girl was always married before her younger sisters, a second marriage was with wife's younger sister or with brother's wife's younger sister or other sisters of incomers in one's 'kindred-in-which-one-inherits'. The evidence shows that marriages between close kin really occurred and marriages with the wife's younger sister or replacement of a deceased wife were current practice.

For chiefs desirable marriages should produce political alliances, so chiefs married one of their daughters to the neighbouring chiefs[3] and married daughters of chiefs themselves. Thus king Iloo's wife was the daughter of an important Jinju chief and Ngaliema of Ntamo married a bevy of Hum chief's daughters,[4] and of course NGANTSU had married the two daughters of the NGEILIINO, Opontaba. The results of such a policy were to keep the ruling group fairly inbred. They had the same effect as royal marriages in Europe.

Polygyny was normal and there was a great differential in the ages of bride and groom which made polygyny possible. Men, it was said, were thirty-five or older before they married and girls were not yet twenty. Adultery was rare, so there must have been another outlet for sex. Boys did have sweethearts *ãkãw* (Lingala *makangu*).[5] These were either very young unmarried girls or divorced women. Certain women did not marry very young and stayed single until after the birth of a child. After that their kin would insist on regularizing the situation and paying bridewealth. Divorced women or widows who managed to stay single would change lovers fairly often. They could have from four to six more or less all at the same time. The lovers would take them gifts. Some girls preferred to stay divorced and keep lovers, even if they had

[2] H. BRUNSCHWIG, *La négociation*, p. 51; L. GUIRAL, *Le Congo*, pp. 284, 293.

[3] CH. LIEBRECHTS, *Léopoldville*, p. 531.

[4] L. GUIRAL, *Le Congo*, p. 296; H. STANLEY, *The Congo*, I, p. 380.

[5] Sims: *musiu*: 'virgin, sweetheart' may have been the older term displaced by the Tio version of Lingala: *makangu*. CH. DE CHAVANNES, *Avec Brazza*, pp. 274–5 fn. 1; P. HERMANT, *Les coutumes*, pp. 294–5.

children.[6] Since divorces were fairly frequent *ãkãw* must not have been rare.

Sometimes girls were bespoken even before they were born. LIPIE told that when a woman was pregnant a man could go to her and give her a length of cloth with the words: 'If the baby will be a girl, she will be my wife; if it is a boy he will be my *nduu*.' Then nobody could marry the child unless he gave her up. Such a child was educated until puberty at her father's and then sent to her husband who proceeded to pay bridewealth. But this practice was mainly directed towards children in one's 'family', towards *otioolu*, and in that case there was, of course, no bridewealth to pay.[7]

In the preceding case it is clear that the girl could not give her agreement to the proposed union. In general the agreement of the partners to be married was not essential, but if one wanted to avoid a divorce, it was important to ascertain whether the girl liked the boy who came for her hand. The men chose girls, consulted at home and if their father's and mother's brothers agreed tried to get the consent of the girl's father. If there was disagreement between the girl's father and the girl's mother's brother the opinion of the former was decisive, despite the fact that so much of the responsibility about the bridewealth went to the mother's brother. In theory the agreement of the girl was required[8] but in practice Abili Ndiõ told us, many a girl was married by force. If her mother did not back her up in a refusal, she could be forced. Otherwise the mother would usually convince the father that the match was not good and the marriage was not concluded. If mothers did not like prospective candidates their only way to block them was to try and convince their daughters that the boy was no good. For formally they were never asked for advice.

Marriage partners were usually chosen from the same or among neighbouring settlements. If a suitor came from too far away the girl's father would refuse, claiming that they did not know the family. Indeed most older marriages recorded[9] conformed to the claimed pattern. Among the exceptions were political marriages and the one spectacular exception was a Tio girl, daughter of a wealthy trader, married to the head of a Bobangi village on the lower Ubangi river.[10]

Several types of marriages were known according to the type of exchange involved: direct exchange of girls, the giving of a girl in

[6] A situation similar to that of the village wife among the Lele. Cf. M. DOUGLAS, *The Lele of the Kasai*, London 1963.

[7] Confirmed by P. HERMANT, *Les coutumes*, pp. 294–5; CH. DE CHAVANNES, ibid.

[8] Abili Ndiõ denied this but P. HERMANT, *Les coutumes*, p. 294, confirms.

[9] Local endogamy at Mbe in 1963 for all marriages concluded was 76 per cent. For marriages concluded before 1920, i.e. by parents of older informants, the indication is that all of them were concluded between neighbouring settlements, or within the same larger settlement (e.g. Ntsaa).

[10] CH. DE MARTRIN DONOS, *Les Belges*, II, pp. 308–10.

return for bridewealth, which in turn would be used to acquire a replacement, which is indirect exchange, and the type known as *õke ampu*. Since the great majority of marriages involved bridewealth this may be described as the standard marriage.

The principle was simple. Two *ndzo* made an alliance in which one gave up a girl to the other and received goods in return. After the marriage was ended the bridewealth would be paid back. According to this view the goods given as bridewealth should be only obtainable by giving away other girls and they should go from one *ndzo* to the other. Here however goods used for bridewealth could be acquired in various ways and they were paid by the kindred of the man to the kindred of the girl. The implications of the situation will be examined.

The goods involved were 'currency' expressed after 1900 in terms of *ibuunu* or lengths of cloth,[11] even if other goods were actually given. Ubwoono remembered that first *mbula* shells[12] were given, then copper bars *ngiele* and finally *ibuunu*, whether Tio cloth such as the raphia wrappers *ndzu a tieeri* or the later fashion of *ndzu anna*. Among the imported cloth the most valuable were the red cloths known as *ãmbul atali*, now called *ãkã*.[13] Mahieu mentions bridewealth expressed in *ntaa* or raphia squares at the Pool.[14] In one precise case it was known that seventy pieces of cloth were paid around 1900. In another from the same date, the payment was in *ndzu anna*, and, still around the same time south of the Pool, payment was calculated in *mitako*, or brass rods as well as powder.[15] It is striking that the calculation was made in currencies. What was given were mostly also currencies, for Ngateo said that a hoe to the wife's mother, a gun to the wife's father could be given, and certainly wine had to be given as well. But no wonder that Guiral said that at the Pool they 'sold women'![16]

[11] Sims: *mubunu:* 'one thousand' and *ibuni*: 'account, sum, product'. Calloc'h, p. 292, 'pièce d'étoffe'; *i-mbuni*; 'cent mille': *mu-bunu*, p. 267. For him 'dot': *nzi*, p. 192, which was the basic currency. Sims labelled it 'money'. In the narrow meaning of the word, *nji* were shells of *olivancillaria nana.*

[12] *Mbula* were large *nji* shells.

[13] Calloc'h, p. 171, 'couverture': *mbullu.* Sims: *tala:* honour, thank. This *may be* the etymology. The term could also be connected with *Bulamatari*, nickname for Stanley and the agents of the Congo Independent State. Because of their red colour these blankets were better known as *nkã* (*nkami*) from the name given to the red ants *ãkã*. They were and still are very precious and were used and stocked by chiefs. Cf. G. SAUTTER, *Le plateau*, p. 155, and Sims: *nkama*: 'woollen cloth, blanketing'.

[14] A. MAHIEU, *La numismatique*, XXI, p. 15.

[15] YOULOU NKOUYA, *Une adoratrice*, p. 55. The king Ngaayüo paid this amount which had been the first bridewealth of Ngalifourou when she was married before. She had had four children before her marriage to Ngaayüo i.e., it seems before 1907. P. HERMANT, *La coutume*, p. 290, on powder and *mitako.*

[16] L. GUIRAL, *Le Congo*, p. 240; M. DELAFOSSE, CH. POUTRIN, *Enquête*, p. 568, say that guns, copper, powder, and cloth were given to the wife's father, a hoe, a goat, and dogs to the wife's mother. But formerly (i.e. in our period) the whole bridewealth was handled by the mother's brother only, which tends to confirm LIPIE.

The groom found his bridewealth among his relatives. His father was to pay for the first wife, his mother's brother for the second, and he himself for any subsequent wives. If the boy's father was too poor his mother's brother might contribute for the first spouse. It is possible that even in the 1880s some young traders managed to accumulate themselves the funds required. Even Jinju boys said Nge Ikiere would go all the way to Mpila to sell goats and raphia for currency. If so it was the exception. By 1920 it had become the rule. The amount required was high enough for the father to ask his relatives to participate in it. In fact it was necessary to do so, because the participation implied agreement with the marriage and expressed good harmony within the kindred, important facts to the kin of the bride to be. Then as now the amounts varied probably according to social status and fell in a range as the effect of bargaining was felt as well. The mechanisms by which the amounts were set and evolved in time were complex. Wives were not just commodities and people were at pains to avoid giving the impression that they 'bought' or 'sold' a girl. This seems to have depressed the price a little in relation to the general rise of prices. A few early indications have been given; a mean value of 100 *ntaa* (raphia), a case of 70 *ibuunu*, 3 to 4,000 *mitako* and 20 powder units or so[17] and 3 *ibuunu*. Other fragmentary data indicate in 1900 15 *ibuunu*, in the 1910s 9 *ibuunu*; a marriage around 1920: 20 *ibuunu*; about the same time 150 to 200 Fr CFA. By 1963 the sum involved was roughly 30,000 Fr CFA, a considerable amount.

The payments were always made in front of witnesses not related by blood to either party who kept a record of the transactions by keeping little sticks, each of which represented an *ibuunu* or a thousand *ngiele*. The bridewealth was received by the bride's father who kept about a third and handed two thirds over to the bride's mother's brother.[18] The simplest division was the case of Abili Ndiõ's first marriage. Three *ibuunu* were paid, one was kept by her father, one given to her mother's brother and one to her eldest full brother. Mbali claimed that 'formerly' the wife's father might receive 2,000 *ngiele* and the mother's brother 3,000, while her mother received a hoe and raphia square to the value of 5, 8, or 10 *ngiele*. The wife's father would give half of his share to his eldest brother, keep one fourth and divide the last fourth equally among his younger brothers. If he was the oldest, he kept half. The girl's mother's brother was the oldest of her mother's brothers. So he kept

[17] P. HERMANT, ibid. (according to Costermans); YOULOU KOUYA, ibid. The three *ibuunu* were what was paid for Abili Ndiõ. Elsewhere, though, she claims that this was a first instalment which was never followed up. Fifteen *ibuunu* around 1900 are for Nge Ikieere's mother and twenty *ibuunu* around 1920 were for his wife.

[18] LIPIE maintained that the wife's father received almost nothing; for Ubwoono he received much less than half. In fact one owed him only a costly wrapper *ndzu anna*, now replaced by a jacket and a lamp. NGAATALI thought he received perhaps up to half. All agree that the wife's father's share has been increasing.

half of the amount and divided the rest equally. If it was not the oldest among them who received the money he still had to give half to the oldest and divide the rest equally. The wife's father's mother should receive an *ibuunu* and two demi-johns (formerly jars of beer) to drink with her brothers, while the wife's mother's mother should receive a trifle as a gift from the groom for whom she was *okali*. If the oldest mother's brother had died, his share went to his sister's sons, that is to the girl's brother or maternal half-brother according to one version. The other less likely one had his share go to his children first and by default only to his sister's son, the brother of the girl.

For the marriage of Nge Ikiere's father, around 1895, five *ibuunu* went to the wife's father and ten to her mother's brother with three jars of beer to the mother's brother and seven jars plus the antelope *odzira* to her father, not counting the small gifts to her mother and to the *nkaa*. The division by the father and the uncle among their brothers was not remembered.

The groom's father paid for the first wife and he paid mainly to the *ndzo* of the girl. The bridewealth was divided among men of the first ascending generation, with only gifts for the others. In the period an evolution may already have existed by which the bride's father was receiving more than a token share and as much as half the bridewealth.

Marriages without payment of any bridewealth were possible as well. First the cases already mentioned of marriage with *otioolu*. Here however the position was simple: the second match was then merely the first marriage continued, just as if one was dealing with the wife's inheritance.

Informants claimed that it was also possible for two men to exchange their full sisters and be married by direct exchange without any bridewealth being paid. No case, ancient or modern, was remembered however. The statement is of interest mostly because it does confirm that the Tio consciously realize that marriage is an exchange of women.

A spectacular form of marriage where no bridewealth was paid is known as *õke ampu* or 'wife of authority'. A woman wanted to marry a man because he was 'handsome'. She 'touched' him and claimed to be his *õke ampu*. No bridewealth had to be paid. The name of the institution indicates that at one time this type of marriage could only occur when she chose a chief. Her case would then be similar to that of the man alone in the world who became a client (*isã*) of the chief. If the husband was a chief he would usually pay the bridewealth and the marriage was regularized. Its only anomaly was that it had been initiated by the girl. If he was not a chief and of modest means nothing happened. The enterprising girl's kin were unhappy about it, but there was little they could do. If she fell ill, her parents and mother's brother might refuse to come to the *okuu* inquest, although most of the time they were concerned and did come. If bridewealth had been paid they were obliged to come to *okuu*, however. The wife's family could not only refuse to come to *okuu* but accuse the husband of witchcraft and ask for an immediate return of the girl home. This was the best means of pressure they had. It is not quite certain if such a match was a true marriage, for if the terminology and behaviour between affines was observed, it was not clear whether adultery of the wife could be punished. Some claimed that the courts would award the normal stiff damages in such a case, the others thought not and thereby proclaimed this type of marriage to be a concubinage. Very few of these marriages did occur although there was a case in Mbe. Obviously it had to be a rare form of marriage or the whole principle of bridewealth would have come to nothing. Abili Ndiõ, who as a feminist rather approved of such procedures, maintained that such a marriage was valid and that adultery compensation would be paid. The children were recognized by all their kinsmen on the father's side and on the mother's side and in the case of *okuu* the mother's father could hold it at his place rather than at the husband's. She felt that many women had acted like this. If they were mistreated too much by their first husband, married with bridewealth, they would just leave him, go to a chief or another man and live with him. There would be no divorce. In effect then it was a form of concubinage used mostly by women who felt oppressed. Hence its exceptional character and also the acceptance by the women's kin.

Another form of concubinage also existed. In order to attract men to his settlement a chief (*mpfõ*) could give one of his sisters or one of his daughters or sister's daughters to unmarried men in his town so as to stabilize them. The man just made a payment of wine to celebrate the relationship but no bridewealth was paid. This was concubinage for there was no compensation for adultery and the chief could always take his relative back when he wanted to. The institution was known as *õke wuu yumpfõ*: 'woman from the chief'.[19]

The process of marrying was well regulated. The man first told his own father and the latter told his father, if he was still living, about the prospect. If the father agreed the boy then sent a *nduu* to the father of his girl with a small gift of tobacco and wine or beer. If this was accepted and the girl's father was friendly the next step could follow. Of course the whole community was agog and the matter was discussed among the different families. If no word reached the suitor that he would be rebuffed, he then went a second time with his elder brother or his *mbalikali*-to-be (the husband of the sister of the girl) and brought some tobacco, to a value in 1963 of 50 Fr CFA. The matter was

[19] H. H. JOHNSTON, *The River Congo*, p. 129, was offered the daughter of an old gentleman of Kinshasa for several lengths of cloth, which superficially looked like a genuine marriage with bridewealth. When he offered his wife after that for much less, it is plain that ordinary prostitution existed at Kinshasa in 1883.

discussed and the girl's father would indicate when the suitor could come back for the agreement of the girl.

Flanked by two witnesses the man returned on the appointed day with the *itieeri* or clothes for the girl. These consisted in 1963 of four *ibuunu* for the daughter of a commoner and six for an aristocrat. This was of course much more than what would have been proper in the 1880s. If the girl accepted the *itieeri* it meant that she agreed to marry the boy. If she refused, she turned him down. This actually happened in a case seen in 1964. The suitor had brought two *ibuunu* and gave them outside the house to the girl's father. He then remained outside the house near the open doorway. The girl was seated inside with a *nkaa* on her mother's side, a woman near her. In another corner the men were gathered. Almost every man of the hamlet was there, for they were all kin. She refused the cloth and a spirited discussion developed. The men pressed her but her companion stood firm. Finally the older woman rose with a *bw* of disdain and left with the girl in her wake. The men loitered a bit, agreed that they would try again and left. The two *ibuunu* apparently forgotten, stayed near the altar of the house. Later on, the two pieces of cloth were returned and the match was off. If the *nkaa* or the girl's mother had not supported her, she could probably not have withstood the pressure.

Once the *itieeri* had been accepted, the girl could go and sleep with the boy if he had a house in the village, but not yet openly live there. The next step was 'to sew the clothes' which consisted in 1963 in the bringing of another gift of palm-wine to the girl's father and up to six *ibuunu*. This was only a preliminary to the more formal gift of a *ntsa* antelope to the future father-in-law. This step was called *odzira*, 'the parcel, the bundle' (Sims: *muzira*, Calloc'h: *mu-dzira:* 'Cadeau de mariage'). It was a symbolic payment of meat to be repayed by the father-in-law at the wedding. At this meeting the date for the transfer of the girl to the groom was set.

At this point in the sequence of events, but according to the Tio without an intimate relation to *odzira*, usually came one or more general meetings of discussion about the bridewealth. The father of the boy and his brothers met the relatives of the father and of the mother's brother of the girl in front of the independent witnesses who acted as judges to debate the brideprice. The meeting was held according to the procedures usual at meetings where conflicts had to be resolved. They ended by settling the bridewealth price and the boy paid the girl's father in the presence of the company a token sum, 50 Fr CFA in 1963, earnest money or *uva* (Sims: *mfua*). The marriage was now established to the extent that it could not be stopped. The woman could only get her freedom back by a divorce and in all divorce actions the first gesture was to claim the *uva* money in return. At a meeting of this sort in Mbe we counted twelve men and the chief of the land was judge. From a demand of 30,000 Fr CFA they came down to 15,000 Fr CFA and one *ibuunu* and the husband paid 2,500 Fr CFA in addition to the *uva*.

A month later for a first marriage, or as little as a week later when it was a divorcée, the wedding could be celebrated. That day the wife's father sent a goat to the husband to raise kids. This was the return for the *ntsa* of the *odzira* and various symbolic interpretations can be attached to it: 'a wild goat' is given by the young man, 'a civilized goat' is sent back as a sign that he now fully belongs to adult society, or the young man sends sterile meat and the father sends his blessings for a fruitful marriage. The difficulty is that in 1963 nobody knew what the symbolism was actually supposed to be.

The women would come with her sister who came to 'sell' her and with her younger brother. If she had no younger siblings another relative might come. The groom invited his friends and relatives of the same generation. The girl arrived with parcels of food carried by people from her village or ward. Then in front of the witnesses the boy paid the largest single instalment of the bridewealth to the bride's sister and sent a *ntsa* antelope to his own parents. All the women of the village were there to greet the newcomer, to see if she was pretty, if she had a good temper, etc. The husband then gave a chicken to his wife who ate it with her companions and sent also some food or another antelope *ntsa* to the parents of the bride. There was no other celebration at Mbe in 1963. In the 1880s however there was a feast, at the Pool at least, with shooting and dances and singing. But it was not a big celebration, nothing comparable to a funeral say, and there was no ritual connected with it.[20] The bride afterwards lived in the house of the husband and cooked for him. The marriage was concluded.

2. *The marital union*

Most marriages developed into a family with children and even if they remained barren the couple formed a household which is best considered as a family. Matters pertaining especially to the marital union include residence at marriage, the expected behaviour patterns between affines, the rights over a woman as a wife and bearer of children and the rules with regard to adultery. To these we now turn.

After marriage the wife went to live in the village of her husband and his residence was often patrilocal. But he could also live with his mother's brother or another relative and this happened perhaps in one fourth of all cases. When the wife fell ill she often returned to her

[20] H. STANLEY, *The Congo*, I, p. 377; CH. DE MARTRIN DONOS, *Les Belges*, II, p. 115; CH. LIEBRECHTS, *Léopoldville*, p. 535. Beyond the shooting, said the latter, there was no ceremony. Sims: *swila bilamo*: 'give a marriage feast' and *bituoro*: 'marriage feast'. The process of marrying was not found in any of the written sources. NGAATALI confirms that it existed in the period.

mother for fear her husband be accused of witchcraft.[21] But the husband could also go and live in his wife's village, on a temporary or permanent basis and in 1963 such cases were found in all villages. Then people moved several times in their lives from one leader to another one. In the decision to move the husband's voice was dominant, even if the couple moved to the village of the brother's wife, father, or mother's brother. Residence after marriage then was flexible. Chiefs and leaders tried to exploit the situation to their advantage by keeping their married brothers and sons around them and trying to keep their married sisters and daughters as well. Their ability to do so was a direct measurement of the prestige of their leadership. This flexibility meant that relations between affines, certainly between the husband and his wife's kin had to be fairly smooth if the affines did not want to see the husband leave their settlement. This gave him a fair leverage, especially if his affines belonged to the core of the leading group in the village. As a consequence, cases were known where the affines dared not even insist much on a payment for the balance of the bridewealth if the husband lived 'behind them'. The advantages of having the family in the village outweighed the inconvenience of an unsettled bridewealth.

Perhaps the bridewealth was not intended to be settled rapidly, because the outstanding amount always reminded the husband and his group that they were wife-takers under obligation to the wife-givers. The behaviour between in-laws brought this out in a more subtle fashion.[22] The dominant relationship was between a husband and his female in-laws of the first ascending generation. The wife's own mother could not be seen by him and if he set eyes on her from afar he would run and hide. She transmitted her messages to the son-in-law through her daughter. He had to avoid her name. If he pronounced it when his wife could hear him or another daughter of that family they would consider it to be a grievous lack of respect. A quarrel would follow and she would tell her mother, who might claim damages. This was rather worse than if a man used the name of a chief rather than his title in addressing him. If there were homonyms of the mother-in-law, the son-in-law could pronounce the name but not if these women belonged to the village of the mother-in-law and might therefore be kin to her. This meant that uxorilocal residence in a village where the mother-in-law lived could be trying. Over time the relationship would mellow only a trifle, in contrast to relations between sons-in-law and fathers-in-law. There too a certain respect was due. In his presence the

[21] CH. LIEBRECHTS, *Léopoldville*, p. 531. Identical cases were found in Mbe in 1963.

[22] There are no direct written data about this. It is hard to see, however, how the situation described here could have been different and there is no feeling among the Tio that it was. The latter should not be stressed too much, for expected behaviour can change quite unconsciously. The main argument for reconstructing it this way is the connexion between this and everything else that is known about marriage and affines.

son-in-law could not pronounce his name and any off-colour jokes were better not told in front of him. But in time the relationship could evolve to become similar to that which existed between father and son. It did not quite become as close emotionally, though. Thus if a father-in-law was ridiculed his son-in-law was not necessarily bound to take up the cudgels for him. He might just stay outside the matter altogether.

Women did not avoid their in-laws and this reflects again that residence normally ought to be virilocal. They co-operated closely with their mothers-in-law, fetching water and hewing wood together, staying together when cooking the evening meal, but they rarely became true friends. The girl would for instance not have her *idzia* installation near that of her mother-in-law, and the relationship never became as close as that between mothers and daughters. Women did not avoid their fathers-in-law but did not pay special attention to them.

Between affines of the same generation joking relationships prevailed especially if they were of opposite sex. Horseplay and sexual contact was allowed. There might be an element of antagonism between wife-givers and wife-takers in it, but no typical banter which would bring this out was found. A special tie existed between a man and his wife's younger sister. They were *okali* and *olõ* by term of reference but addressed each other as *nduu*, friend, and she was of course a favoured second wife. Relations between men and the wives of their brothers were more teasing. The man would say for instance: 'I want wine.' She would reply: 'I have none.' He would snort: 'you *are* poor.' And she would conclude: 'I detest a poor husband.' This relationship shows that marriage was not an individual affair but that the brothers of the husband had a stake in his wife. The joking partners could never marry together, but behaved as if they were possible spouses.

Marriage gave an absolute right of paternity to the husband. All children born from his wife were his. But it did not give him exclusive rights over her sexual relations. If she had relations with one of his full brothers, a half-brother of the same mother, a sister's son, a mother's brother, or any male belonging to his matrilineage there could be no adultery and there was no punishment.[23] Still it was not considered proper if the relations were between mother's brother's wives and sister's sons. A fine of one goat and one *ibuunu* might be levied and the elder brother of the culprit as well as the offended mother's brother would help raise it. But it would be paid for the infringement of inheritance rights over that woman and would go to the heir. Sexual congress with the brothers of a husband, provided they belonged to the same *ndzo*, was allowed. This was consonant with cases where brothers swapped wives. In a recent case an elder brother had three wives and gave his favourite to his younger brother during the day, keeping her at night. But the younger brother wanted her at night

[23] According to NGAATALI, all this was practised during the period.

too and tried to kill his *nnaana*. In the court case which followed, only the fight mattered, for the girl was innocent of adultery since the boy was her second husband. In another recent case an elder brother gave up his wife to his *mbwei*, reasoning that if he did not, the boy would run around and he might have to pay heavy damages for adultery elsewhere! It is noteworthy that elder brothers were not allowed congress with the wives of their *mbwei*. At least that was said at Mbe in 1963. In recent times, it was added, such cases had happened and it had occurred that some angry younger brothers gave their wives completely up to their *nnaana*, out of spite. The rule may have been correct, for it fits with the general notions about seniority and the greater permissiveness towards unmarried boys. And in all specific cases mentioned the younger brothers were still bachelors. One recognizes in these rules the pressures of a polygynous society where men must marry late. But married men could also sleep with the unmarried sisters of their wife. Since girls were married off, if at all possible, by age, these were usually younger and the reasoning was that if the wife should die, the girl would replace her. In fact all these cases made it clear that marriage was not a union between one man and one wife, but a union between groups and that one group received a wife from the other. She was allotted to one man but his coevals had a share in her. This meant that the marital tie was not expected to be as intense or as intimate as it is supposed to be in Europe, for instance. And yet it could become so. For there are also cases known where an elder brother was so jealous of his *mbwei* because the latter went with his wife, that he killed the boy and passed it off as suicide. But those were the exceptions.

If a married man carried on with an unattached girl it was not adultery; if an unmarried man slept with a married woman, it was. Why the double standard? Because adultery dealt with the effects of congress: the woman might conceive and the man could not. What was important in the marital relationship was that it was an alliance from which children could be born, which would benefit both allied groups. Companionship was not the essence of that bond. Marriage was the transfer of a woman. Adultery was therefore the theft of a woman and the fine was to pay for stealing her.

The payment plainly shows this. The lover, if caught by the husband, could be sold as a slave or had to pay a fine equivalent to the bridewealth, if there was a witness, a lesser fine otherwise.[24] Common to both provisions was that the price to be paid was equal to the transfer of a

[24] M. DELAFOSSE, CH. POUTRIN, *Enquête*, p. 565; A. MAHIEU, *La numismatique*, XXI, p. 20. The lover became a slave of the husband or paid 100 *nta* (as much as the bridewealth) if there were witnesses. Otherwise he paid 40 *nta*. Confirmed by Ngateo and P. HERMANT, *Les coutumes*, p. 293. If the lover could pay the fine, he did not become the husband's slave. CH. DE CHAVANNES, *Avec Brazza*, pp. 274–5, says that the husband could keep the culprit as a slave.

person. The punishment was stiff but must be related to the late age of marriage for boys and therefore to their inclination to carry on affairs.

In one case a lighter fine was levied. If a woman had committed adultery with the half-brother of her husband from a different mother and a common father, the payment could be reduced to one goat and one *ibuunu*, if the father was still living. If he had died and the husband insisted on payment of the full fine, he would thereby cut the blood ties with his half-brother. This lighter fine testifies perhaps to the importance of the kindred, but mostly of one group within it: the *isaani* or brothers. For if a father had committed adultery with his son's wife he had to pay the full fine to his son.

3. *The dissolution of marriage*

For the Tio marriage ended with the reimbursement of the bridewealth in divorce or after the death of the woman. The death of the husband did not end the marriage since the widow was inherited and, even if the woman died, she could be replaced by her younger sister or *otioolu*. The three institutions are discussed in sequence: the inheritance of women, the reimbursement or *litsũ* and divorce.

Women were inherited by members of the *ndzo* of the husband and members of his own generation or the alternate generation of *otioolu*. Among the possible heirs the younger brother of the deceased was the first. Depending however on how many women there were to be inherited, the *mpfõ andzo*, if he belonged to the generation of the *nkaa* of the deceased or to the same generation, could claim some. If there were no younger brothers and the *mpfõ andzo* did not belong to the right generation (for instance if he was a mother's brother or a sister's son of the deceased) the women were claimed by the *otioolu* in the lineage; the sister's daughter's sons. Since their claim replaced that of absent brothers it had precedence over that of a *mpfõ andzo* and, if there was only one wife, the *otioolu* would receive her. However women could refuse to marry *otioolu*. If they were old, they could choose to remain alone uninherited.[25] In the first case the counter-bridewealth of the woman would be claimed almost immediately by the sister's son of the deceased. In the second the situation could remain unaltered until the woman had died. If a woman was to be inherited by an *otioolu* who wanted her but the sister's son of the deceased wanted to claim the counter-bridewealth, the right of inheritance took precedence and the marriage was not dissolved. Most known cases from the 1920s showed, indeed, an inheritance within the *ndzo* by a younger brother and in a case where several women were to be inherited, the *mpfõ andzo* took some. By this time some had begun to allot inherited wives to the sister's sons of the deceased.

[25] Abili Ndiõ claims that they could not refuse to marry a younger brother of the husband, however old they were.

Two informants pointed out that the inheritance was also conditioned by the origin of the bridewealth paid for the woman in the first place. Balewari, a Wũ, claimed that since the husband's father paid for the first wife, his sister's son could claim *litsũ* when she died, whereas the second wife, paid for by the mother's brother of the *de cujus* could be inherited by a brother of his *ndzo*, or his sister's son. If she refused, the bridewealth had to be refunded. In one case of unknown date two widows were to be inherited. One by the younger brother in the *ndzo* of the deceased, but the other by the sister's son of the father of the deceased. The latter refused her and asked for the bridewealth instead. Abili Ndiõ formulated the same general rule that the widow went to the group which had paid her bridewealth, whether it was the father or the mother's brother of the deceased. And the first wife would normally be paid by the father's side, the second one by the mother's brother. She added, however, that formally the mother's brother's side did furnish the bridewealth. According to her if the woman chose a half-brother in the *ndzo* of the *de cujus*, but the bridewealth had been paid by the father of the deceased, the inheritance would go through, but the second husband had to pay the bridewealth to a half-brother with the same father as the deceased. Otherwise that family would bewitch the woman; which means that the half-brother in the *ndzo* did in fact have a right to inherit.

Still it is evident from a few cases that when several women were to be inherited, and under unusual conditions, the half-brothers on the father's side did indeed participate. Around 1935, Ngateo inherited a woman from his paternal parallel cousin. The deceased had only left sisters and other girls in the *ndzo* behind him and the sister who inherited the girl gave her to Ngateo. When the counter-bridewealth is to be paid to the heirs of Ngateo they will pay one half to the heirs of the girl who gave the woman to Ngateo, so that in the long run their *ndzo* receives back one half of their rights. This was felt to be right since the woman had been *given* by the sister of the deceased who could have left her alone as a widow until an *otioolu* might marry her or a sister's son claim counter-bridewealth.

Another fairly recent case of this nature also shows the flexibility which existed. Ntsaalu was a paternal half-brother to the last two NGEILIINO's who were full brothers. When the first one of these died, his wife and children were inherited by the second one. When he died he left three wives. The one he had already inherited was old and left alone, one was inherited by an *otioolu*, Ngeingiere, and one went to Ntsaalu. He was king and his prestige may have helped, but it was also true that there were three women to divide. But after a short while the woman Ngankira inherited by Ngeingiere left him and took refuge with the *mpfõ andzo* of the house of the NGEILIINO's, Mbiinu Mbiinu, himself a sister's son (therefore not an heir) to the last

NGEILIINO. Whether there was or was not an intention by Mbiinu Mbiinu to keep the woman was vague. The *otioolu* considered the case a divorce and claimed bridewealth from Mbiinu Mbiinu. But then the king intervened, because all this happened at Mbe where he ruled. So he took the woman Ngankira to the remaining men in their *ndzo* who lived at Inoni. Mbiinu Mbiinu was doing that when the brother and the father of Ngankira arrived to see that any arrangement made was not going to hurt their relative too much.[26]

In all cases of wife inheritance the marriage persisted in that there was no reimbursement of the bridewealth. But the inheritance was a new marriage from the point of view of the children. Children begotten after the inheritance would have a different father from the children of the first marriage. There was inheritance of the alliance but not of the specific marriage.

The alliance could only be severed by a reimbursement of the bridewealth, the *litsũ*.[27] This would occur after the death of the woman unless she was replaced by a younger sister or an *otioolu*. The latter was common practice if the woman had died childless or if her children were young. The older the children the less the chance of replacement. *Litsũ* would also normally only be claimed if the husband had also died.

The amount of *litsũ* was the equivalent of the bridewealth paid, including the expenses the husband had had in providing clothing for his wife. It was gathered from all the relatives of the wife who had received a portion of the bridewealth or from their matrilineal heirs. It was claimed by the sister's son of the deceased husband or the heir within the *ndzo* of the husband.[28] The consideration was that the husband had paid a bridewealth which should return to him and his *ndzo*. Strictly speaking in most cases the father of the husband had paid the bridewealth and it should return to their *ndzo*, so the husband's father's sister's son claimed it. The wife's mother's brother, or if deceased, his matrilineal heir, and the wife's father or his matrilineal heir were responsible for gathering the amount and handing it over. Thus LIPIE received *litsũ* for his mother's brother, before Ngaayüo (1907) was king to the exact amount that had been paid for the wife of his mother's brother, and he later received again *litsũ* for his eldest brother. In the first case the amount was paid by the only survivor of

[26] No nineteenth century cases of woman inheritance were collected. They were probably similar to those cited with respect both to the complexity of situations and the flexibility of the rules used to solve them. Then as later the Tio individual tried naturally to bend or interpret the norms to his own advantage. Cf. M. DELAFOSSE, CH. POUTRIN, *Enquête*, pp. 564, 565.

[27] 'Dot après décès ou divorce' *li-tsumu* says Calloc'h, p. 192, and Sims: *Litumi:* 'wedding'. A. MAHIEU, *La numismatique*, XXI, p. 20, where it is maintained that *litsũ* was a little less than bridewealth (80 instead of 100 *nta*).

[28] *Litsũ* could be both asked and given by women in the absence of men.

the *ndzo* of his mother's brother's wife, her *otioolu* Ilaali. For his elder brother the payment was made by the mother's brother of the woman. Her father still lived but had not received the bridewealth so he was not accountable for *litsũ*.

The principle was simple but complications often arose, so that all cases were settled in an informal court by a chief of the land. To begin with much time had usually passed since the payment of bridewealth, there might be several claimants as heirs, and there were very often children of the marriage. If so, something should be given to them. If not they would consider all blood-ties to have been cut between them and their father's or grandfather's matrilineage and, for instance, could refuse to come to *okuu* called for members of that group. Finally matters of *litsũ* were dangerous occasions for quarrels. Non-payment of *litsũ*, whether the demand for it was refused or not, often led to armed feuds, which shows the importance attached to the matter.

The relation between the children of a deceased woman and the matrilineal heirs of her husband, their father, was often as follows: the woman's mother's brother had died so that his heir was her own child (A). The sister's son of the man (B) should claim *litsũ* from A. But, since they belonged to the same *ibuuru* and he did not want to cut blood-ties between them, it seems that he often did not ask at all for *litsũ* but waited until A and his siblings were dead to claim it from their matrilineal heirs C, *otioolu* of the deceased woman. Of course B could have died in the meantime and D would claim as his heir. If B asked *litsũ* of A, there was a strong chance that A would cut his ties and go to live with his mother's kin.

Since *litsũ* was to be paid immediately if a woman refused to be inherited, B had often to ask A for *litsũ* but then since A was a child of the couple, B would pay him half of the *litsũ* so the child would still recognize its paternal family.

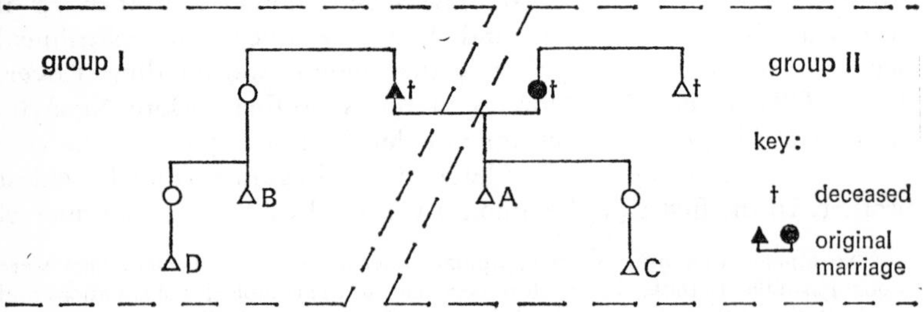

When *litsũ* cases finally led to feud and war, it was a situation in which the warring sides were very often the child (A) and his *ndzo* against (B) and his *ndzo*. Both A and B would receive help from their *isani* as well, i.e. their full brothers but also their paternal half-brothers and even parallel cousins.

The description of a few more or less modern cases shows the intricacies of the institution. Jean-Pierre was the child of Louis. But his mother divorced him and married Alphonse. Louis received *litsũ* from Alphonse for whom it was the payment of bridewealth. Since Louis had given nothing to Jean-Pierre the latter elected to stay with his mother and claimed Alphonse as his father. People admitted this, but still Jean-Pierre would never be allowed to marry in Louis' *ibuuru*. Louis remained his *pater* even if Jean-Pierre claimed that Alphonse was.

In 1960 François claimed in the name of his brother Ngangwo, who was in Brazzaville, *litsũ* for the wife Maabwoole of their mother's brother. He had died and she had refused to be inherited in that *ndzo*. He claimed the money from her half-brother with the same mother. A council was held and after negotiations which lasted nearly four years the half-brother of the woman paid 25,000 Fr CFA to François who gave 20,000 to his brother Ngangwo because he was the elder brother and 5,000 to the children of their mother's brother and the woman Maabwoole, so they would not cut the ties with their father's *ndzo*. In another similar case a mother's brother of a girl who refused to be inherited paid *litsũ* to the sister's son of the deceased husband.

Another fairly simple case shows the responsibilities of the wife givers in the reimbursement. The wife of Mpaani had died. He had paid 13,000 Fr CFA for her to the first husband of the woman and added another 3,900 Fr CFA as follows: 2 lengths of cloth to Itiere, 500 Fr CFA to Ngateo, 1,400 Fr CFA for Antswera. He also had paid three times one length of cloth to fasten onto the catafalques of three deceased persons among his wife's relatives. But he could not count those as part of the bridewealth. The sum of 16,900 Fr CFA was recognized as valid and was divided in two halves, one to be paid by Ndeela, one by Ngateo. Ngateo's half was divided into three equal parts for Ngateo, Angõ, and Ubwoono. This arrangement stemmed from the fact that the first husband had given one half to Ayu, the father of the girl whose *ndzo* was represented by Ngateo and one half to the mother's brother of Mangamvuba, for which Ndeela was responsible.

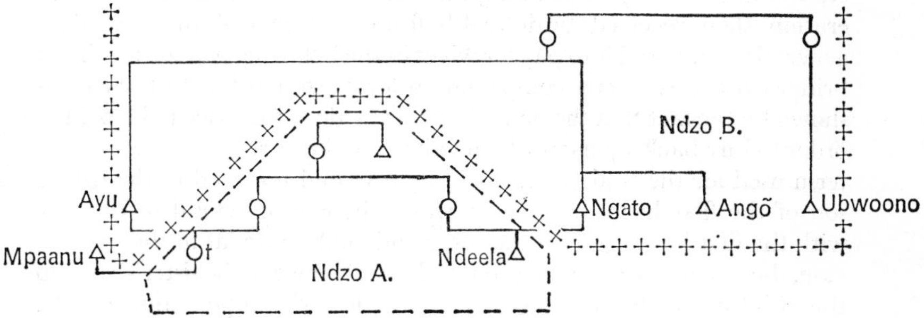

The story of Abili Ndiõ illustrates older cases and the confusion which could arise out of *litsũ* claims. When her first husband died, an *otioolu* of the husband inherited her. But it turned out that he did not belong to her husband's *ndzo* at all for he was in fact the son of the daughter of another wife of her husband. Abili Ndiõ did not mind but the people of her husband's *ndzo* did. The case went to court, a great chief decided. *Litsũ* was claimed but in fact her first husband had not paid bridewealth for Abili Ndiõ who was his second wife, beyond a first instalment. Her husband had no younger brother when he died, so she had to be inherited by an *otioolu* since both sister's sons and children could not inherit, and the only *otioolu* was Tutu, the one mentioned. Whether bridewealth had been paid for her husband's first wife, the grandmother of Tutu, she did not even know. Abili was inherited but divorced during the court case. Her bridewealth was calculated as the sum of the pieces of cloth or wrappers she had had from her husband and one cloth from the *otioolu*. That came to 10,000 Fr CFA. So on her side nobody but she herself had ever received anything (and obviously the value in Fr CFA had been quite inflated). Someone had to pay and it was the husband of the daughter of her daughter who did pay to Tutu and it was counted as *litsũ*. They could have asked *litsũ* of her but she would have refused to pay it with the dangerous consequences that might entail. All her other relatives in the *ndzo* had died. But it was not clear why the one who finally paid was under obligation to do so. For him it was a total loss. Abili's present husband did not pay bridewealth for her. And if he was going to, he would pay to the men on Abili's father's side but certainly not to the husband of her granddaughter, even though he had paid *litsũ*. For he did not belong to her blood relatives.

Litsũ was a formal breaking of the alliance and as such it was an act fraught with difficulties. The parties might quarrel, the children might leave, a feud might erupt. But it was a necessary evil since the recipients of *litsũ*, needed it most of the time to acquire a wife of their own. Normally there was an alternation of generations in this. The first descending generation could claim *litsũ* but the second descending generation had priority in claiming the inheritance of the girl. Each generation then received bridewealth from members of the preceding generation and used it to pay for wives in the following generation. That bridewealth was in fact compensation for a woman lost to her *ndzo* is shown by the fact that the name *litsũ* was used for the price to be paid in order to buy back a person who had been sold as a slave. It was also the term used for the bridewealth paid by a second husband to the sister's son of the first husband if there was a divorce or refusal to remarry with the first husband's brother or grandchild. Here, as in the original case, the amount of *litsũ* received was divided between the sister's son and the children of the first husband. The idea of compensation for the loss of a person is further reinforced by the fact that the amount of the fine for adultery was equal to a bridewealth payment, *or* that the culprit could be sold as a slave.

The rationale for using this system is clear. But it was cumbersome. It was not and could not be simplified since two *litsũ* could not cancel each other because the bridewealths paid had rarely been absolutely equal. In addition the system was dangerous since it easily led to conflict. On the other hand it is obvious that it allowed opportunities to men who could operate claims and by manipulating inheritances and *litsũ* hope to further their careers.

Divorce rates for the nineteenth century are unknown. In 1963 they were for the Mbe plateau: 52 per cent marriages ended in divorce per actual marriages, 59 per cent of divorce per all marriages ended (by divorce or death) and 38 per cent of all marriages actual and ended.[29] These rates seem high especially if one knows that bridewealth had to be paid back and that bridewealth was substantial. There were difficulties in paying it back and so the parents of the girl put pressure on her to stay with her husband. If the divorce did come the parents then wanted to escape the consequences and were very slow to reimburse, which often led to war between villages.[30]

A divorce was always pronounced in court which invariably tried to reconcile the parties first. If that was impossible the respective torts were assessed and the amount of the bridewealth to be refunded as *litsũ* was also fixed.[31] The principle was that if the woman left the man the amounts were doubled. The amounts included the value of clothing received during the marriage from the husband. The double amount was known in 1963 as *tike* from 'ticket'[32] but I was assured by NGAATALI that the practice was old. To wait for the bridewealth to be given by a second to a first husband, as happened in the case of Jean-Pierre, used not to be allowed, NgeIkiere said. The second husband remained unmarried with the girl. For if the first accepted the money, the children could, as Jean-Pierre did, refuse to recognize their erstwhile fathers any more and turn to the second husbands. So there had to be actual repayment and as long as there had not been a divorcée could not in fact really remarry. So that if the percentages given are close to the ones existing in the 1880s there must have been a sizeable number of divorcées who could be *ãkãw* to the sizeable number of adult but not yet married men.

[29] Cf. Appendix No. 6.

[30] P. HERMANT, *Les coutumes*, according to Costermans for the Mfunu, p. 290. This is very likely for the Tio as well and *litsũ* questions were remembered as the paramount causes of war by LIPIE.

[31] M. DELAFOSSE, CH. POUTRIN, *Enquête*, p. 564, speak of a council composed of both families. This was a court if a judge or arbitrator was present. The informants all insist they had to be and a chief would pronounce the divorce.

[32] From the expression: *elle lui a donné son ticket*; 'she bounced him'.

The bridewealth was paid back by those who had received it in the same proportion as they had received it and it was given to the husband, who kept it all without redistributing it to those who had given it to him. Supposedly he would use it again for remarrying. It was said that a wife's father would be prompt in reimbursing his part but that her mother's brothers would take much longer. They also had more to refund.

The causes for separation were in fact incompatibility for a wide variety of reasons. There might be sterility, theft, infidelity.[33] One of the favourite reasons, seldom stated in court, was the suspicion of witchcraft. Young Ngalifourou about 1900 divorced Mitsié because she felt four of her children had been bewitched by her husband's sister.[34] In reality no list of causes was important. The determination of either of the two spouses was paramount. If all conciliation failed they had to be divorced. There might be much misery as each of the spouses tried to make the other start the proceedings so as to make or lose on the bridewealth. The process was long drawn-out. The procedure was calculated to make certain that the determination was real, that the conflict could not be avoided. All sorts of mediations were tried first. The father of the girl or her mother's brother would try to coax her into resuming the marriage. The husband might propose to give her to a younger brother or they might suggest replacing her by an unmarried younger sister, if there was one available. It was only if all else failed that the divorce was granted.[35]

4. *Marriage as exchange*

Marriage was clearly an alliance between groups and these were the *ndzo*, not the *ibuuru*. But was marriage an exchange? Since a direct exchange of sisters was allowed it seemed so, yet it was the father (thus his *ndzo*) who paid the bridewealth for a son belonging to another *ndzo*. When that son died his heirs in the *ndzo* claimed *litsũ* from the wife-givers. It looked as if the father's *ndzo* was a complete loser in the operation. Other anomalies were that the father's kindred gave the bridewealth, not his *ndzo* and that the bridewealth was made up of items which were the currency of the day instead of being items with which one could only acquire wives as would have been expected. Furthermore one could ask why a counter-bridewealth, cumbersome and dangerous as it was? What did the pattern of alternating gener-

[33] P. HERMANT, *Les coutumes*, pp. 290–1.

[34] YOULOU KOUYA, *Une adoratrice*, p. 55.

[35] Cf. Appendix No. 10; for procedure, causes, and discussion. In a case of 1964 for 28,700 Fr CFA the bridewealth had been given to and was returned by: WF, WM, WMZS, W full B, WZ, WB, WMB, WMZS, WFBS, WFBS. Each had received amounts no less than 900 Fr CFA (except WMB who received only 500 Fr) and no more than 3,000 except for W full B 4,800 Fr and WF 4,100 and a *ndzu anna*, and seven *ibuunu*.

ations inheriting women and adjacent generations receiving or paying bridewealth mean? Why the exception with regard to the fines paid for adultery for certain members of the kindred? Why did a whole *ndzo* receive the bridewealth, but paid *litsũ* back to one man, the major matrilineal heir of the husband? The theory of bridewealth as a simple exchange for women seems to run into difficulties.

The chart shows the situation. In the operations marked (i) A, *ndzo* of the father of a member of B gave bridewealth in currency to C where it was divided between members of the *ndzo* and the girl's father. For a girl of the adjacent descending generation was given to B. Finally one generation later B in the shape of the sister's son of the husband claimed *litsũ* for the girl. The first fact to realize is that over two generations the operation amounted to the giving of a girl by C to B and of bridewealth from B to A. The *litsũ* B paid to A for a girl given in the previous generation (the mother of the boy who was husband in the operations (i)) was in reality the bridewealth for the girl received, for it compensated the A to C transfer of the previous generations. So far so good: bridewealth is paid and a woman received by B. But in the same two generations B itself lost a girl to A which is not compensated.

The real model implies a depth of four generations in which the two we discussed are numbers II and III. The case of *ndzo* C in the chart shows the full operation. In generation I bridewealth is received for a girl given in II. In III *litsũ* is given but a girl is received. Bridewealth is also paid here and in the next generation *litsũ* for that is received. The *litsũ* does not correspond to the bridewealth according to the Tio point of view but it must be taken for granted that bridewealths are of roughly the same amount. Since they were fixed by outsiders, this was roughly true.

If women were inherited it was by *otioolu* and the whole process was put back by two generations indicated in the chart by (III), (IV), etc. Sister's sons could not inherit women because then they could not claim *litsũ* but their sister's sons would, i.e. the *otioolu* of the married couple thus delaying reimbursement in the generation after the heaviest payment had been made (generation III of chart for *ndzo* C). One might also say that the exchange of women and of receiving bridewealth could not mix. Thus for *ndzo* C wealth was received in generations I and IV, women were given in II and received in III and all bridewealth was paid also in III. Since adjacent generations paid and received for women they are like affines and affines of these generations are twice so, as the terminology shows.[36]

From the point of view of a man's life, he could first receive a woman, then probably pay bridewealth for his son, marry his daughter and receive *litsũ* for his mother's brother, but pay it to his father's sister's son for his mother. He would end paying a bridewealth which

[36] Cf. Chart 3, Chapter II.

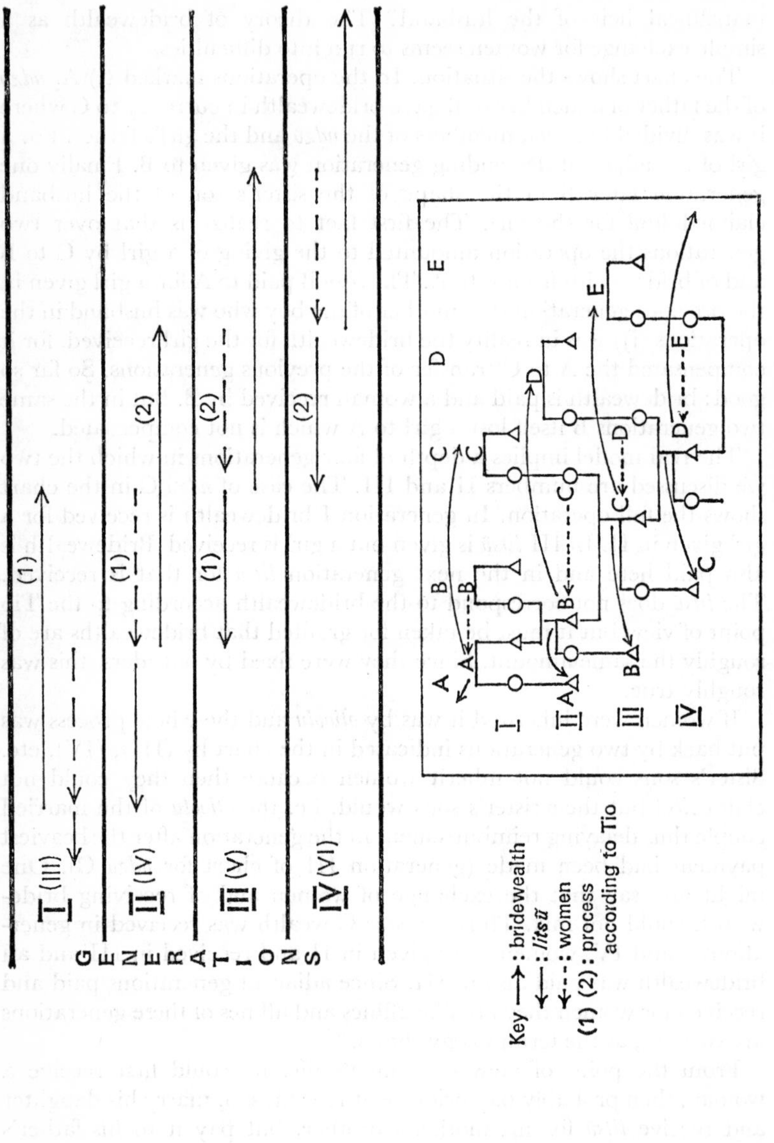

CHART 5 *The exchange of women*

was not reciprocated but had been when his father's *ndzo*, in fact his father, paid for him. Elders paid for younger men and enabled them to marry. This also gave them control over the actions of the younger people.

The alliance involved no less than five *ndzo* over a depth of four generations, i.e. the structural depth of the kinship system. The network was cast wide and included, in fact, for a person of the fourth generation in D three *ndzo*: A, B, C on his father's side, that is most of his father's kindred (not all because of the effects of polygynous marriages to begin with). This skewing of the relation is inevitable because the exchange of women as shown on the chart was flowing in one direction only from E to D to C to B to A instituting therefore a circular exchange system. But the circle was in fact often closed over fewer generations than it would take to go round all matrilineages in the country and this, despite the stringent exogamy requirements, because of the tendency to marry *otioolu* and to repeat marriages as with sisters.

The role of the kindred was recognized and is responsible, we think, for the complication of a system which needed four generations to even out. The man's father gathered the bridewealth either from his own resources or those of his brothers, *isaani*. These, given polygyny, did not belong to the same *ndzo*. But their compensation was almost immediate since the father would also contribute to his brother's sons' marriages. Cognates were also recognized in the payment made from bridewealth received by the girl's father, even if this was the smallest part in the 1880s. That was repaid when the *litsũ* for that bridewealth was required. The role of the kindred was further recognized by the lowering of fines, especially when they involved brothers whose father was living, i.e. members of the same extended family. The payment of part of *litsũ* to the children of the *de cujus* by their paternal cross-cousin was also a recognition of the extended family. Indeed in both cases if the full fine were asked or nothing given back on *litsũ*, it was felt that kinship had been cut.

The discussion of marriage showed that the *ndzo* played a more important part than had been surmised before. The kindred was recognized, but mostly in its territorial form: the extended family and, within the latter group, the key importance of a set of brothers, *isaani* was recognized. For indeed settlement was led by one who was either a grandfather at the head of his extended family or an elder brother in a group of *isaani* and their descendants.

Why was the bridewealth paid in currency? One could use it, not only to acquire another wife, but to buy a slave, to pay for adultery, or to break the sum up to trade with it at the markets of the Stanley Pool. This was possible because in fact women were replaced by women and bridewealth was only a temporary compensation. It was done because of the intense commercialization along the Stanley Pool. The Tio did not live by subsistence alone any more and this integration of the exchange of women into a commercial system allowed men to try to convert bridewealth into more wealth, so they finally had not only one woman in return, but perhaps an additional slave as well, or two women, if the trade had been favourable. The Tio exchange of women of the 1880s fitted only imperfectly in a closed subsistence economy. It is significant that of all the commercial 'signs' by which a woman could be acquired only one, raphia cloth, was produced in the communities of the plains.

Chapter V

The Economics of Subsistence: Production

TO find the food and the raw materials they needed to live, the Tio on the plains practised agriculture, raised small live stock and poultry, hunted and gathered wild produce. This was the job of a unit of production which consisted of the polygynous and extended families and the whole of these activities made up the production process of raw materials in the economics of subsistence, because they were the necessary basis of economic life, not because the unit of production was completely autarchic. The activities are examined in this order: agriculture, raising of animals, hunting, and gathering.

Fishing, the main activity of the riparian Tio is described at the end.

1. *Agriculture*

Agriculture was practised in three types of fields or gardens. There were the main fields in the savannah or *ncio*, where women cultivated the major crops: cassava, groundnuts, *voandzea*; the *ngwuunu* fields hacked out of the woods by men and planted by them with maize and tobacco; and the 'dawn-gardens', or *ibwõ* (Sims: bibuōmi, Calloc'h: 'petit jardin' i-bwomo(bi), p. 246), at the back of the houses which consisted of groves of plantains and bananas and of all sorts of plants in cleared spaces near by. A fourth, but minor type of garden was the *idzia* garden, a small clearing near the holes where cassava was soaked and where the plants of the *ncio* were grown on a very small scale, with some others, including an occasional banana. To complete the picture one must mention the shrubs and trees which dotted the village, the rows of stands of sugarcane like a hedge and the orchards of palm-trees behind the village or stands of them in the woods.

The basic equipment for tilling the fields included the axe, the hoe and the bush-knife. The axe was hafted to a piece of wood in which a hole had been made. The haft was then heated and the point of the axe knocked through it. Hafting a hoe was done in a similar way, the haft being quite short whereas the bush-knife was hafted very much like the present-day machete and like it had only one cutting edge. Produce was carried in baskets, the type of which was the women's *mutete*, a long fairly narrow object, built for porterage on the head (with a ring, *nkara*, of cloth under it on the top of the head). It was a long basket with a strong frame at the bottom and uprights. The sides were pleated almost like nets. Bamboo or whole vine was used for their

Chart 6

Crops and types of fields

Crops	*Type of field*
1 *Major crops*	
cassava: (Sims: *ncoo*)[d] (*lisoo*). Ubwoono claimed only 3 varieties were cultivated in Iloo's times	*nció* (savannah) mostly; *ngwuunu* (forest)
maize: (Sims: *masaa*) (*ãsaa likiini*). Much more planted in the 1880s than now	*ngwuunu*
groundnuts: (Sims: *nzu, liyu*). Three of the 4 major varieties at least existed. One (Sims: *wuwuo*; Ubwoono: *wowo*) was said to be introduced in 1880s but must have existed before	*nció; idzia* (clearing)
voandzea: (Sims: *pere*; 'large peanut') (*ãpiere*)[b]	*nció; idzia*
banana: (Sims: *kolitoro*) (*toro*: 'banana') 3 varieties existed	dawn-gardens, *idzia*
plantain: (Sims: *iculi*) (*nzal' aloo*)	dawn-gardens, *idzia*?
tobacco: (Sims: *kee, mfwaña*) (*ãke*)	*ngwuunu*
2 *Other crops*	
(a) *cereals*	
sorghum?: (Sims: *musabi*); millet or sorghum (*saalinsaa*) Miandoo at Imbãw. They still planted it a little	*ngwuunu*
(b) *root crops*	
yams: (Sims: *ikwa*: 'sweet potato, yam') (*ikwa*).[c] Sims saw two species of red yam and one other. In 1963 one species of red and one of white were recognized. Calloc'h; p. 638. 'igname' recognized seven species	*nció, ngwuunu*
sweet potato: (Sims: *ise, ngapiele*) (*ngaapiele wa mpiebi*). Plant abandoned since then[d]	*nció?*
(c) *gourds*	
calabash: (*osoo*) (Sims: *nganzoo*: 'vegetable marrow')	dawn-gardens, *idzia*
calabash var: (*lilabi*)	dawn-gardens, *idzia*
gourds: (Calloc'h: 'citrouille': *li-ta* (*n*), p. 161) small, green[e]	dawn-garden, *idzia, nció*

[a] One reference to sources is given, which is Sims whenever he mentions the plant. After his or Calloc'h's, in separate brackets, the term as noted in 1963–4.

[b] These were probably the 'pistache' Brazza mentions frequently. Cf., H. BRUNSCHWIG, *La négociation*, p. 33 where 'pistaches' are listed after *ngiu* (*ndzu*), quite separating them from groundnuts.

[c] H. BRUNSCHWIG, *La négociation*, p. 33 where Brazza has *Bicai*, following 'ignames'.

[d] H. H. JOHNSTON, *River Congo*, p. 295 lists them too. The Tio at Mbe in 1963 remembered the name but did not have the plant any more.

[e] Several varieties of gourds and calabashes were known. Since the dried fruit, the seeds and the plants all had different names, there is great confusion. Calloc'h, p. 161

CHART 6—*continued*

Crops	*Type of field*
(d) *vegetables*	
cabbage: (Sims: *ngwee*) (*ngwee*)[f]	dawn-garden
sorrel:[g] (*inkulu*)	dawn-garden
eggplant: (Sims: *incuma, mbono, yima*) (*liboono*)	dawn-garden
ãkieri: leaves were eaten	dawn-garden
ntiina: stem was eaten; like *broccoli*	dawn-garden
mbulidzu: leaves were eaten	dawn-garden
ãkio: fruit eaten of a planted vine	dawn-garden
ãntuo: fruit eaten of a planted vine	dawn-garden
okra:[h]	*nció*
onion: (Sims: *sabolo*; Calloc'h: *boli, maboli*, p. 279)[i]	*nció*
beans?: (Sims: *nkaa, nkasu*; Calloc'h: *kaya* (*ma*), p. 234)[j]	?
(e) *trees*	
safou: (Sims: *ncoo*) (*osoo*)[k]	woods
elaïs palm: (Sims: (*M*)*unkee*; 'palm-nut'; *nkene*: 'palm-nuts') (*iba inkéé*)	fringe village, woods
raphia palm: (Sims: *nkulu*: 'palm-nut' raphia) (*iba limpéi*)	fringe village, woods
Hyphoena palm[l]	near Congo River

('citrouille') gives six varieties, of which two only were known by name on our lists and under 'courge' another name is added. Sims adds three more unknown terms. We quoted only the varieties we saw and the Tio say these are old. Note the fruits are important in diet.

[f] H. BRUNSCHWIG, *Les Cahiers*, pp. 167, 172. Brazza surmised that they were a remnant of the influence of former missionaries; H. H. JOHNSTON, op. cit., p. 295 describes them as 'small and degenerate'. In 1963 they were all leaf and no heart.

[g] Calloc'h, p. 281: *i-nkulu*. Mentioned by L. GUIRAL, *Le Congo*, p. 297 as a favourite royal food.

[h] *Hibiscus esculentus*. We saw a few isolated specimens in 1963. They seem to be old, but direct proof was lacking.

[i] By 1963 small and rather sweet onions had become part of the diet and fairly large quantities were grown. Early travellers do not mention them. A. MERLON, *Le Congo*, p. 126 mentions onions downstream of the Pool. Perhaps they were grown on the plateaux as well. Unlike mango or tomato (Sims: *bono*, but Calloc'h, p. 334 *tomate* and 1963 *tumat*) or rice (Sims: *loso*) which were introduced in the early 1880s, onions like, e.g. pawpaws may have been older. Note that the fact that a name is given by Sims did not mean the plants were cultivated. For rice this is clear. It was the product shipped to the centres from abroad which was known.

[j] They may have existed around the Pool. Elsewhere they are totally unknown. Names seem Kongo. It is possible all vegetables are not listed here. Cf., A. DELCOMMUNE, *Vingt années*, I, p. 219 lists 'spinach' (a number of vegetables may be meant) and purslane; Cf., J. GHYS, *Etude agricole*, p. 127 where others are listed. All were cultivated in the dawn-gardens. The data of GHYS are from the Ngenge.

[k] Also mentioned by A. DELCOMMUNE, op. cit., I, p. 284.

[l] H. H. JOHNSTON, op. cit., p. 198. They made wine or '*malibu*' from it. A. MERLON, op. cit., p. 72 says the leaves were used like those of the raphia palm, upstream from the Pool.

CHART 6—*continued*

Crops	*Type of field*
borassus[m]	near Congo River
calamus palm: (Sims: *(M)ungele*)	near Congo River
bamboo: (Sims: *nkoki*) (Calloc'h: *li-tere*, p. 138) (*otieere*)	in, near village, near spring
Cajanus Indicus[n]	in the compounds, village
kola (*Cola Ballayi*): (Sims: *bilu*) (*ibilu*)[o]	in the compounds, village
(f) *shrub and small fruit trees*	
oranges: (Calloc'h: *samẽ* (*ma*), *sabole*, (*ma*), *limãgo* (*ma*), p. 280)	in the compounds, village
barbadine: (Calloc'h: *sia* (*ma*), p. 139) (maracuja)[p]	in the compounds, village
lemon: (Sims: *zamale*) (Calloc'h: *samẽ* (*ma*), *li-bãgo* (*ma*), p. 161)	in the compounds, village
guava: (Sims: *fufula*)	?
pawpaw: (Sims: *kapele*)[q] (Sims: *(M)umpuru*: pawpaw fruit, edible wood)	near Congo River
pepper tree: (Sims: *ntaba*; banduu 'pepper') (*ãdzuu*)	dawn-gardens
(g) *grasses*	
sugarcane: (Sims: *mufuee, munce, musuu*) (*ofwa*)[r]	*ngwuunu*, rows in bush near village; near *idzia*
pineapple: (Sims: *intu*) (*intu*)[s]	isolated in bush near paths
(h) *industrial plants*	
papyrus: (*ndzubi*): for weaving mats. Specialty of *Imbãw* area (Sims: *nzubi*)	marshy spots
cotton: (Sims: *(M)ufula nguo*: 'cotton cloth'; *fula*: 'fibre') (Calloc'h: *fula* (*ma*), p. 169). Miandoo claimed it was planted only to stuff cushions (*likuba*) with	isolated; on fringe woods

[m] H. BRUNSCHWIG, *La négociation*, p. 51. Brazza saw them on the right bank, on a former site of the village of NGOBILA. A. MERLON, op. cit., p. 71 notes their use from the Pool to NGOBILA's.

[n] H. H. JOHNSTON, op. cit., p. 295. The fruit is a sort of pea.

[o] In addition a number of trees were planted for fences such as euphorbia and a variety known in Mbe as *tulipier du Gabon*. Trees were also planted for shade and one type was left undisturbed, if found in villages, because it attracted edible caterpillars. In the woods, too, varieties of trees were favoured, by weeding around them.

[p] A. MERLON, op. cit., p. 107. Introduced by him in 1818 to Brazzaville.

[q] H. H. JOHNSTON, op. cit., p. 295. Lists pawpaw, not guava. Neither would grow on the plains. The first could not have been a European import at Mswata, because it was a tree and Europeans had barely arrived a year before Johnston visited. The same holds, *a fortiori* for oranges and lemons. For oranges see also Brazza in H. BRUNSCHWIG, op. cit., p. 33.

[r] A. MERLON, op. cit., pp. 108–9. True plantations were only found along the Kwa, elsewhere stands remained small.

[s] H. H. JOHNSTON, op. cit., pp. 196, 273, 295. The etymological theories do not convince.

CHART 6—*continued*

Crops	*Type of field*
Tephrosia Vogelii (*mboompo*) (Dupont: *Utanga*, p. 224).[t] Used to stupefy fish. (Sims: *mboo*)[u]	dawn-gardens
ntsana: plant used for washing	dawn-gardens
bwooli: shrub used for colouring cloth	dawn-gardens
ntsõ: plant used for colouring cloth	dawn-gardens
ngaaba: shrub for colouring cloth	dawn-gardens; in compounds, in village
oto: medicinal herb	dawn-gardens
mpiõ: medicinal herb, a shrub	dawn-gardens
bomba mpiõ: medicinal shrub	dawn-gardens
obwooro: leaves used to greet people on the holiday *Nkwe Mbali*	dawn-gardens

[t] E. DUPONT, *Lettres*, p. 224 saw this at Lishia. He describes the plant as papilionacaea with white flowers, which grew near the houses. The Latin name from J. GHYS, op. cit., p. 171 seems to apply.

[u] With the following the list is not exhausted, especially for the dawn-gardens, and with respect to medicinal herbs. These were also tended when wild, so that the limits between cultivating and not cultivating become vague. Note A. MERLON, op. cit., pp. 84–5 that the Laadi of the Pool made this soap from banana skins.

construction. As for storage either big pots (maize, groundnuts, sorrel, gourds) or big baskets (groundnuts) were used. The tools required for production were thus limited in number, simple, and rustic. Once given the metal parts any man or woman could make them.

A list of plants cultivated in each type of field is given in the following chart. Major crops yielded perhaps as much as 90 per cent of the total output of food. Yet the other plants were still cultivated, sometimes in one or two specimens per household, such as, e.g. okra. The vegetables were relatively important, since they formed part of the daily diet, but perhaps the most common vegetable was the young leaves of the cassava plant. The Tio were reluctant to abandon cultivation of any domesticated plant even if it had been superseded by another crop introduced later. So in any type of field one would find an odd plant here or there, so that some of the fancier plantations, especially in the dawn-gardens, looked like botanical gardens. Even when crops were replaced by others, the farmers did not abandon them altogether but restricted the cultivation of the ousted crops only gradually, so that their fields in 1963 were true museums of their own agricultural history. And this was done, very often, without any necessity. Thus the case of the people of Imbãw growing millet to offer to the local nature spirit, *nkira*, is an exception rather than the rule.

This cautious attitude did not mean that the Tio were unwilling to adopt new plants. There are the obvious examples of maize and cassava as well as groundnuts among the staples and the acceptance from the lower Congo of many fruit trees of European origin before 1880, but since then they have tried out a great number of new plants whether they were varieties of known crops such as cassava, tobacco or groundnuts, or new plants, mainly fruit trees and vegetables. The dynamism of this agriculture is shown also by the gradual disappearance of maize, which was a major crop in the 1880s[1] and had become a very minor one in 1963.

Despite all this the Tio on the plains were seriously undernourished. It was not only a matter of animal proteins but also a great imbalance in vegetable foods. Cassava had achieved such a preponderance in the production and the diet that undernourishment resulted. A certain sign of it was the cures for malnutrition, especially for women, known as *itsuua*, and the lack of muscular development.[2] There was thus a paradox between agricultural skills on the one hand and a clear lack of adaptation to the environment on the other.

The *ncio* were by far the major fields for food production. They were entirely cultivated by women alone. Spots would be chosen according to what the association of grasses revealed about the fertility of the soil. The grass was burned and the sod broken up by hoe in July and August before the first rains. By September, the women began to hoe small squares[3] an inch or two deep with the burned grass as fertilizer, stuck a few slips of cassava in the middle and surrounded the square with groundnuts of the *ndzu andzu* variety. A few of the squares might contain yams rather than cassava, an okra plant might be put where there was some more ash, some tobacco, some gourds *nta*, and some maize also could be found. All this planting was done in October. The women worked in groups[4] and hoed or planted their fields one after another, which they called *itiõ*. The fields were contiguous forming one huge rectangle or square for a whole ward so that the work, even if it was not collective, was done in close proximity to other women. After planting, weeding became important until the groundnuts were ripe late in December and in January with the advent of the small dry season. The nuts were harvested and their foliage was put on top of

[1] Cf. H. BRUNSCHWIG, *La négociation*, pp. 23, 33; H. BRUNSCHWIG, *Les cahiers*, pp. 167, 168; L. GUIRAL, *Le Congo*, p. 306; H. BENTLEY, *Pioneering*, I, p. 335. Maize was brewed into a light beer, of which great quantities were drunk as well as eaten in the form of a porridge (*oka*). It was not as prevalent as cassava since food given to travellers usually consisted of cassava and fowls. Since the 1880s the cultivation of maize declined sharply.

[2] This can be deduced from the fact that *wara* rings which are worn on the upper arm from the nineteenth century cannot be worn by men today. They are a direct reflexion of muscular development and an indicator of nutrition. *Wara*'s worn today by people on the plains cannot be used by the fishermen on the Congo nor by Europeans whose biceps are more developed.

[3] L. GUIRAL, *Le Congo*, p. 304, speaks of *plate-bandes*.

[4] N. BALLAY, *De L'Ogooué*, p. 263, saw women working in groups; *Les coutumes*, p. 23, calls this *kitémo* (*itiõ*).

each square. That was then hoed up into a round mound *õkala* (Sims: *mukala*, *ikala*) (Calloc'h: *mu-kalu*, 'butte', p. 149) sometimes waist-high. Thus they used buried green-tops as fertilizer but they did not employ the Kukuya's technique of burning these underground.[5] By the middle of February this work was finished and the main rains began. The cassava would mature and could be harvested as early as April, but since the roots remain good for two years after planting the provident householder picked up first supplies in the stands from the two previous years. After the last cassava was harvested, the *ncio* was abandoned having been in use for up to three growing seasons. There was land enough and no one bothered to come back to the exact spot of a former *ncio* field. There is thus no term for a fallow field in the savannah. Rights on fields were the rights over the planted produce and before that over the right to plant, once one had broken the sod. Rights over fields were derived from the general right over the product of one's labour.

January/February was also the time for the women to prepare new fields, called *ãtioo*, and to plant the variety of groundnuts with the same name. This was done on square, smaller mounds than for cassava or yams, called *ipa* (Sims: *ipa*: 'field, plantation, patch of ground'). This had to be finished a week or so before the end of February, in time for the major rains. The fields were smaller than those made in October. The crop was ready by the dry season in June.[6] A few groundnuts of the *ncio* reappeared a year after the January harvest and were harvested then. They were called *ibvuu* or *ibvuo*, like the fallow field in the forest. Similar second crops from the *ãtioo* field were ready by December, six months after the harvest of the main crop.

The *ngwuunu* (Sims: *ngunu*) were worked by married men with

[5] Size of the fields in the nineteenth century is known from A. MERLON, *Le Congo*, pp. 121–2, gives sizes of less than 10 ha of cassava and 30 ha of groundnuts for 100 hearths or 100 M2 and 300 M2 per 'hearth' which is comparable to the figures of 1963 but less. Since groundnuts were cultivated on cassava plots we can compare the 400 M2 to the 500 M2 of 1963. Perhaps maize made up for another 100 M2 or more in 1886 when the observation was made. In 1963 when the women had a tractor to break the soil for them, but had to pay for it, each woman's field was about 500 M2. The impressions of travellers would be notoriously incorrect about this because all the fields lay side by side; G. SAUTTER, *Le plateau*, p. 136, on fertilizer; N. BALLAY, *De L'Ogooué*, p. 263, mentions furrows but E. DUPONT, *Lettres*, p. 198, describes the planting of cassava best. On 27 September he noticed that they were making small mounds at a distance of one metre to one metre (about 3 feet). In each mound three slips of cassava were planted. After one to one and a half years there would be five to six roots of nine to eighteen inches, thick as a wrist. After two years in the ground they became three times as thick. In 1964 the mounds were waist-high and planted with three slips of cassava per mound. Hoed into the mounds are the ashes of the leaves of the previous crop of groundnuts.

[6] H. BRUNSCHWIG, *La négociation*, p. 23, in July; for he stated at the end of August: 'they have been harvested two or three weeks ago'. He could be wrong by a few weeks.

children.[7] They were cleared in the woods as early as July, each man working for himself. They were not neat like the *ncio* but had jagged edges and a rough oval shape. Stumps of great trees were still standing in the field, for those giants were burned down by forking fire in a hole made with the axe about four feet or so from the ground. Their area may not have been much smaller than a *ncio* field but each married man had only one *ngwuunu*.[8] The men would plant maize on mounds after clearing the bush in August/September in pockets here and there and harvest it in February. A few sugarcane and some cassava might be planted too. But the latter attracted the wart hogs too much. Tobacco had been prepared in nurseries on the fallow *ngwuunu*, called *ibvuu* or *ibvuwo* (Sims: *ibvuo*). It was replanted in the main field by December either on a *ngwuunu* which had not yet been used, or on spots where there was no maize. The tobacco plants had to have their leaves regularly pinched out until the crop came in by April and May. All the tobacco was dry and ready for use or sale in June. As for the maize, that was ready by February, and for a second crop by July,[9] which was planted by December/January and may have been the bigger one.

After the maize and tobacco had been harvested, the *ngwuunu* was planted with some cassava, despite the wart hogs, and reverted to fallow land. But unlike the fields in the savannah, ownership of the fallow land did not lapse. The man was expected to take it up again, when the trees reached the thickness of an arm, after roughly ten years. No one else could take the plot unless the previous owner had given permission. This reflects the relative scarcity of the forest as compared to the savannah and the greater amount of work needed for clearing. But, as for the savannah, a man could start a new plot on unused forest without asking the permission of anyone, even if it lay in the domain of a chief other than the one he resided in. This was a reflexion, not only of the relatively low density of population, but also of the relative lack of interest in agriculture as compared with hunting, since the domain was exclusive with regard to hunting.

The dawn-gardens were usually tended by women, although some men would plant a shrub and a few tobacco plants near at home and help with the planting of banana trees. The plants were generally put in at the beginning of the rainy season (October/November; February/March) and rotations were complex and left to the fancy of the owner. All the plants were useful and flowers were not grown at all. Most of the vegetables were not put in mounds, but an occasional mound, for instance for cabbage, was made. The garden was more or less fenced to keep the domestic animals out. It looked like a gigantic rubbish heap

[7] At Mbe in 1963 only eighteen men were working *ngwuunu* and among them only one bachelor.

[8] One measured in 1963 counted 600 M2 (611 M2 sq. approx.).

[9] H. BRUNSCHWIG, *La négociation*, p. 33.

with uncertain boundaries. Its fertility was derived from the night-soil and other refuse which was thrown there and the weeds often seemed to do better than the useful plants. Still, despite their unkempt aspect, the gardens produced well and were an essential part of the agricultural production.

Next to the garden was the banana grove. The plants were set in October and yielded fruit after six to eight months, continuing to do so during a year or more. New shoots were planted each autumn. The palm-trees next to the villages were planted occasionally and the nuts of the elaïs were cut when ripe. They were then crushed and the oil was collected. The rest including the palm kernel was thrown away. Raphia trees were much better tended than other palms. When the leaves were as long as the fore-arm, after four or five years of growth, they were used for weaving. When the tree was too old it would, like some other palm-trees, be destroyed. It was cut and the palm-wine was collected for about two or three weeks. Then it was cut to pieces to harvest the grubs *ãntswoolo*, which were considered to be a delicacy. Salt was sometimes made from the ashes of the inflorescence of the female fruit of palm-trees.

The kola tree was planted in prepared soil in the shade and constantly watched. It has a slow growth and produced fruit only after eight to ten years. It would produce thereafter for many years. The nuts played an important role in social life. They were given to the shades of the dead, eaten formally when friends met, and offered as tribute to chiefs. The safu tree on the other hand was not planted. When one was seen growing in the woods, it was merely protected by weeding around it.

Rights over trees were individual. The relatives of the person who had planted the tree could collect the fruit. Trees were divided individually at an inheritance. No one was allowed to plant any tree or shrub if he had not first received the permission of the owner of the land, i.e. the chief of the domain. This was in contrast to all other planting, which was totally free.

The last place where gardens were made was around the holes in which cassava was soaked: the *idzia*. Next to these women often planted one or two banana trees, as much for shade as for the fruit. There were calabashes and *nta* gourds as well as small cleared squares with groundnuts. Most of these gardens were tended by smaller girls under the watchful eye of their mothers. The *idzia* holes and the little gardens were strung out over the landscape like the beads of a rosary, connected by paths which went from one hole to the other. It gave some privacy to each of the women and allowed them to chat freely with others a few yards away.

The staples were produced to last from one harvest to the next and stored in jars for maize, groundnuts, and *voandzea*. Groundnuts were also stored in baskets (Sims: 'pea-nut basket'). These were left sealed in village trees if women could not keep them in their kitchen.[10] Their calculations were not always quite correct, but this was not really serious since cassava could always be harvested, but it was still a hardship. R. F. Kraft commented on the lack of foresight of the Tio by saying that each year they had only cassava in the ground left. They were short of maize, sweet potatoes, pea-nuts and bananas. Then they would buy from three to six bananas for one *mitako* (copper bar).[11] He probably exaggerated the lack of foresight but it shows the kind of hardship that was felt.

Work in the fields constituted much of the daily toil for women and older men. So much so that the same verb (Sims: *sala*) meant: 'work, labour, plant, clear away weeds'. Yet agricultural work was poorly considered and the contrast with hunting for instance is striking. The value system ignored how much life depended on agriculture, so the rituals for the fields were rather rudimentary. The ritual at the planting season for the *ncio* consisted of the giving of seeds of the groundnut to the chief of the land, the *mpfõ*, together with some kola. He put the seeds in the house of the shrine of the nature spirit for that domain and left them one night. The next day all the women came and he washed their hands and their hoes with lustral water. Then they could go and plant. Some chiefs went with the women and planted each third seed themselves for one field. Some avoidances (*ngili*) were joined to this. Thus on the plains of Nsah, the planting had to be done naked so that the elephants would not destroy the fields and one could not hail anyone in the fields.

The other ritual was individual. When a woman felt the need for it she could go to a *nciele* child or a twin, who were supposed to harbour fertility because of the manner of their birth and the close relation this meant to the *nkira*, spirit of the domain. The child would bless a pot of water and the woman could sprinkle it with a leafy branch all over her field. This she should do also before planting. It is worth noting that no charms existed at all to promote this fertility, in sharp contrast to hunting for which a great amount of amulets and charms were available.

If agricultural work was not valued very highly, the fields were still considered important and destruction of crops was a serious action. Thus when de Chavannes destroyed part of a cassava field by accident at Mfwa in 1885, the inhabitants fetched their guns and the damage had to be compensated.[12] For the Tio realized the economic importance of their fields for their subsistence, even if they did not value them highly.

[10] Cf. G. SAUTTER, *Le plateau*, p. 163; Brazza notes (H. BRUNSCHWIG, *La négociation*, p. 33) that huge baskets were used as granaries for cassava and sprouted maize; a month or so after the harvest there were still huge heaps of *voandzea* on the ground.

[11] E. DUPONT, *Lettres*, pp. 241–2.

[12] CH. DE CHAVANNES, *Avec Brazza*, p. 273.

2. *Domestic animals*

The only domestic animals (Sims: *mubuoli;* Calloc'h, p. 126: *i-bwoli*) raised on the Mbe plateau were chickens, goats, and dogs. At the Pool pigs, pigeons, and ducks were found as well. Sheep were rare everywhere.

Dogs were felt to be most important, mainly because of the hunt. They were fed on cassava and had personal names derived from proverbs or tales such as *nyi izur iwa*: 'wealth spells trouble' or other names such as *ãyele angambio*: 'the carrion eater', never personal names. No person would have more than four or five dogs and the women fed them and called them by clicks. They drank out of a little trough fashioned like a dugout. The men went hunting with them, but did not play with them or get very attached to any particular dog. Dogs were bought and sold. In 1963[13] an adult dog was worth 1,000 Fr CFA for a big one and a puppy was 300 Fr CFA. The prices varied by size but not by skill of the animal. An indifferent hunting dog was sold equally with a good pointer, for it was hoped he would follow the others to the hunt. It was known that dogs develop their skills with training but little or no training was given. No systematic breeding was attempted. Dogs slept in the house.

Whether cats existed in 1880 is doubtful. By 1883 there were some (Sims: *nganiauñ*) (*ngaaniõ*). They were still rare in 1963 but where they existed, they were fed cassava like the dogs.[14]

Goats did not have names and were not systematically bred. They could be sold like the dogs, but for breeding. Goats and kids were eaten. Most often they had been sacrificed first to the shades, for goats were sacrificial animals *par excellence*. Yet their position of 'mediator' between man and his ancestors did not give them any special consideration. Besides being sacrificial animals they were also one of the standard objects to be paid in fines. When sold, their value was geared to the value they represented in fines and in 1963 that was between 2,500 Fr CFA and 4,000 Fr CFA. Also every newly married boy was supposed to receive a goat from his father-in-law and start a herd with the kids. But large herds of goats were unknown and most households had just a goat or two and perhaps some kids. The whole herd was kept in a special solidly built house of logs during the night, to keep lions and leopards away.[15]

Chickens also were not kept in large numbers and eggs were rather rare. They too could be sold for breeding at about 200 to 500 Fr CFA

[13] Apart from its mention by most travellers only H. H. JOHNSTON, *The River Congo*, pp. 293–4 described it: 'a foxy head, prick ears, a smooth fawn-coloured coat, and a tail slightly inclined to be bushy'. They never barked and their masters were very attached to them.

[14] H. H. JOHNSTON, op. cit., p. 294.

[15] H. BRUNSCHWIG, *Les cahiers*, p. 191. For the pen see 3; L. GUIRAL, *Le Congo*, p. 201, where just such a structure is described as a pigsty in Jinju country.

in 1963. The eggs were mainly used by women and children and the meat was eaten when a chicken had been sacrificed to the ancestors. They had little coops, built about six foot above ground.[16]

Any or all of the above animals could be kept and cared for by others than their owners. No compensation was given to the keeper, except half of the litters born when he was in charge.

Pigs were known (Sims: *ngulu*) but not kept at Mbe although they were common both at the Pool[17] and among the Jinju.[18] Johnston describes them as 'black bristly, high-shouldered beasts, very like the Irish greyhound pig'.[17] They were kept for the meat and at the Pool freely slaughtered when needed. For the meat was not given to ancestors. Why the people on the Mbe plateau and many Boõ did not keep pigs is not clear.

'The sheep is rarely met with beyond the Stanley Pool; still it is known and named' said Johnston.[20] Sims called it *imeño*, Calloc'h had *i-mẽne*(bi), *i-ndomi*(bi), *indõnõ* which like its name in 1963, *imẽẽ*, are all onomatopoeic. For at the Pool they were rare, in fact almost absent. Guiral mentions only the animals belonging to Europeans and de Brazza claims they came there from the Ogowe; the ones Malamine possessed certainly came from there.[21] By 1963 they were not rare at the Pool and also found at Ngabe and Mpouya, but not on the Mbe plains. It seems that in the 1880s the west Tio, such as the Fumu, did have them but the people of the plateau kept none.

Ducks (Sims: *subi*) were found all around the river.[22] Later they were to be found everywhere, even on the waterless plains! They had probably already been spreading before the arrival of the Europeans at the Pool, but not for very long. Pigeons must have spread a little after the ducks. Even now they are not found in many places. Yet they were bred on the river in 1884 but not in many places since H. H. Johnston, who was a good naturalist, did not see them.[23]

[16] Chicken coops were called *mpo'ancwiu* by Sims. H. H. JOHNSTON, op. cit., p. 294, described fowl as small and mongrel-like. He noticed that the eggs were rarely eaten.

[17] H. BRUNSCHWIG, *La négociation*, p. 31, where the implication of the statement that there were pigs at Ncuna was that there were none at Mbe; A. MERLON, op. cit., p. 48, stated it explicitly in 1885–6; H. BENTLEY, *Pioneering*, I, p. 347; E. ZORZI, *Al Congo*, p. 433. Pigs were introduced at Mbe only after 1949 and left to forage where they wanted. They were half wild and to kill one when needed it was hunted and shot.

[18] H. BRUNSCHWIG, *Les cahiers*, p. 168; L. GUIRAL, *Le Congo*, p. 201.

[19] H. H. JOHNSTON, op. cit., p. 294.

[20] H. H. JOHNSTON, op. cit., p. 292.

[21] N. NEY, *Conférences*, p. 374; L. GUIRAL, pp. 232–3, 236. The five sheep of Malamine had been brought to the Pool by Brazza himself.

[22] H. H. JOHNSTON, op. cit., p. 294; E. ZORZI, op. cit., p. 433. Calloc'h, p. 151, calls them *shweshwe* and *vanaga*. A. BUTTNER, *Reisen*, p. 209, makes it clear that they were the fat mandarin duck still found now.

[23] E. ZORZI, op. cit., p. 433, and Sims: *tula*. Johnston did not notice any at Mswata or on the river. Sims is no proof they bred them for he also has *buru*: donkey; *ngomo*: cattle which the Tio never kept. But Pecile's testimony could not be explained away.

Domestic animals did not thus add much to the food supply of the Tio. The herds were too small for animals to be slaughtered regularly and so the necessary animal proteins had to be obtained elsewhere: from the noble chase and even more from the base collection of grubs.[24] As with agriculture, here again, an opportunity was missed to balance the diet and make food supplies more secure. For there does not seem any good reason why the herds of goats, sheep, or pigs should be limited on the plateau. The first two might feed on the admittedly poor mixture of shrub and grasses and the latter could have lived from the village refuse, and foraged around it as they now do.

3. *Hunting and trapping*

The Tio hunted in groups with nets and spears all the year round when the grasses were not too high, i.e. from July to January. A fire-drive hunt took place only during the dry season (May–September). Beside these enterprises individual hunting with a gun was practised as well, especially for tracking buffalo and elephant. Other individual hunts were directed towards monkeys and weaverbirds.

The communal hunt with nets was practised by the younger men with the aim of catching antelopes, especially the little *ntsee* (dwarf antelope) of the woods, the *ntsa* (*sylvicapra Grimmii*) or, more rarely, the larger ones such as *nka* (black antelope, the size of a small horse) and *mvuli* (waterbuck), the smaller black *ndzeio* antelope, and *mpfini* a smaller, reddish antelope. None of these ran in great herds, and two or three animals bagged was the expected result for every drive. The equipment consisted of spears (*yuo*), barbed spears (*yuo angana*) and the *likaana*, a forked stick in hard wood, used to kill the smaller antelopes, once they were entangled in the net. Knobkerries, just heavy sticks, almost unworked, were used to kill the animals as well as the big knife *onkù* with one cutting edge, whose handle was decorated and strengthened by round designs in ironwire. The nets were about 90 feet long and 16–20 inches high and obviously unsuited for catching big game. They were made by the men by cutting the wild plant which gave the thread. It was dried and peeled and the thread cut in lengths of about 20 inches, this they rolled on their thighs, knotted and meshed it. Sometimes nets were dyed. The nets were rolled around sticks so they could be staked quickly.[25]

A minimum of five or six young men were needed and an optimum seems to have been a band of about fifteen to twenty. So the younger men of smaller villages had to join forces with another village, sometimes even a village on another domain. The hunters left early in the morning and staked their nets end to end so as to cut off a corner of a wood, or right through it from one end to the other, or in a circle near a

[24] P. BASCOULERGUE, J. BERGOT, *L'alimentation.*
[25] H. BRUNSCHWIG, *Les cahiers*, p. 168.

curve of the wood, so savannah antelopes could be driven into the net or even into the impenetrable jungle at the edge of the woods.[26] The drivers kept contact by whistle and heard their dogs because they wore special bells. They went for several days at a time and camped at hunting camps (*õshie*) which were stations recognized by all. Thus in 1963 the domain of Mbe had five such stations of which Nganshiele near Ngantsu was the furthest while the others were located near the woods Imbali, Impei, Impo, and Isaala. These places were also the known fire-stations: the bush around them could only be burned with permission of the chief of the land and was reserved for the big fire-drives of the dry season.

The antelopes were divided according to rules agreed on before the hunt. When the drive was for *ntsee* a form of *itiõ* was often agreed on in advance. The first bag was for some named hunters, the second for others, etc. until all had had the proceeds of a bag. Otherwise and for bigger antelopes, the owner of the net in which it was caught received the back, the dog who had spotted the antelope received the neck and a bit of the chest, the one who killed it received the rest and divided with the others according to rules made in advance. The one who wounded a beast but did not kill it did not receive anything. A portion, usually a quarter of all the bigger antelopes or one of the *ntsee*, had to be set aside for the chief of the domain.

The fire-drive of the dry season mobilized all men, women, and children. They were set in prearranged lines through the savannah near one of the fire-stations. The chief of the land usually led the hunt himself. He gave a signal and a runner would light the fire in several places, opposite the line of people and their nets. All the animals fled and many were caught and killed. These were mostly antelopes, but rodents and rats, frogs, and other small animals were also killed by women and children. The bigger animals such as the occasional buffalo or elephants had to be killed by the guns before they reached the nets or escaped by breaking through the line.[27] The hunt was not often a great success. Thus Sautter went to eight fire-drives yielding only fourteen small antelopes on the Wũ plains. He calculated that this meant one antelope per 2 square km. Among the Wũ no one could cultivate in the areas set aside for this summer drive. This was not so among the Mbembe. There, as in the south, the chief of the land set aside some areas where the bush could not be burned during the whole year so that animals would take refuge there, which implied of course that people could not cultivate there. But these reserves might vary from year to year and were not, as apparently among the Wũ, according to Sautter, stretches of land which year after year were only used for

[26] G. SAUTTER, *Le plateau*, p. 145. Sims mentioned several whistles: *incinciño*, *ililiu*, and ferret bell: *limvuno*.

[27] H. BRUNSCHWIG, *Les cahiers*, p. 168.

this purpose. Still it is true that a great deal of the land was in fact only used for hunting. But these were the portions of the domains furthest away from the settlements and therefore not very practical for agriculture anyway.

Individual hunts or hunting with a few trackers for the same game or bigger game was essentially done with guns and the prime target were elephants for their valuable ivory as well as for their meat. Buffalo was a second good target, but at least as dangerous as elephants. The gun (*uta*) was a fire-weapon primed with flint like dane guns. For elephants the gun fired a spear *tswala* with a heavy head that could only be shot from very close quarters.[28] For other game the ammunition was slugs of ironslag *kiele* found at a few places where there must have been, long before, foundries, bits of lead imported from the Pool, copper and even little stones. Besides buffalo, all the bigger antelopes, especially *mvuli* and *nka* were favourite targets. Smaller animals and birds such as francolins or guinea fowl and their kin were not hunted, maybe because the use of power was deemed too expensive for such a small return. These hunts were usually made by specialist hunters rather than by young men and often hunting was done for the chiefs who provided part of the powder and hoped to sell the ivory.[29] The game was either tracked or the hunters lay in wait (Calloc'h, p. 121, *i-dzani:* 'affût (chasse)') along game-paths and near water holes. Other special hunts aimed at catching monkeys and some birds. Monkeys were shot with bamboo iron-tipped arrows (*liboi*). For this bows were used. These were small but Miandoo said they were bigger than the bows of children which are still found today and measure only 10–12 inches in length.[30] Children used these (*intampia*) and wooden arrows with blunt ends to shoot birds, especially the weaverbirds which lived in colonies in trees in or near the villages. Another children's tool was a bamboo, iron-tipped to hunt spotted rats in the bush and all the smaller rodents of bush and forest. These activities may scarcely be called hunting, but their yield in protein was steadier than the more spectacular chase, and should not be neglected.

Trapping lacked all the glamour of hunting. Yet it was widely practised. In part it was aimed at catching other animals than those which were hunted, such as the rodents, spotted rat, wart hog, Congo cranes, birds including guinea fowl, francolin, and similar birds. Others

[28] A very detailed terminology existed to designate guns and their parts as Calloc'h, pp. 225, 226 shows. The general term is *uta* (Sims: 'bow, gun'). It is clear that guns had been used for some time before the period we are concerned with.

[29] On hunting contemporary sources did not say much beyond mentioning the technology. Hunters for chiefs are mentioned by tradition (e.g. about Chief Nzãw Mbãw who lived before this period). A first general survey dates only from L. PAPY, *Les populations*, p. 125.

[30] L. GUIRAL, *Le Congo*, p. 211, mentions collective hunting of monkeys among the Jinju.

were intended to catch antelopes and other hunted game. Trapping achieved two things which hunting did not, in that it caught all sorts of animals which hunters did not get and it gave a much more regular supply with less expenditure of energy than hunting. Like agriculture it was not an esteemed occupation, but nevertheless a profitable one.

Five major types of traps were in use. The *iyila* or *ngira* was essentially a wooden frame set on one side and weighted with pieces of grey ant-hill and the like (in modern times also with bottles and trash). It could not fall flat because a stick kept the side up. But a trigger mechanism allowed the stake to be knocked out, with the result that this 'roof' would fall on anything that passed below it. There were different sorts of traps. The small and roughly worked models aimed at catching spotted rats and other small bush animals. Many were set up in the short dry season around February, when the bush was burned to clear it. Heavier traps loaded with logs were built near rivers or in the woods for wart hogs.[31] The most popular trap was probably the noose *omièrè* (Sims: *(M)umiero*). The bait in front of the noose was salt and urine for antelopes. The noose involved a trigger mechanism which when released pulled on the rope and tightened it. This simple trap could be adapted to catch all sorts of animals. It was very common for bushrats, but also for guinea fowls or francolins, or other birds (Sims: *swe*, *iswe*: 'a snare'; 'noose, knot, loop, bird-trap'); it was adapted for antelopes as well and even for catching large frugivorous bats.[32]

A bigger trap involving more labour was the *akiri* (Sims: *ukiri*: 'trap, pitfall, mine, hole, sand-pit'). It consisted of a passage way leading to a hidden pit in which spears or pointed sticks had been placed. It was especially used for wart hogs. Sautter calls these *kabri* and attributes them to Boõ and Jinju; one of my informants gave them a Ngungulu origin but in fact even the Tio near the Pool practised this technique, as seen by the references in Sims and Calloc'h.[33]

Even more collective labour was involved in the building of an elephant trap (Sims: *luo*, *ncuo*). A sturdy log in which a small but solid arrow-head had been planted, was hauled up between two trees along an elephant trail and held in place with vines. The ropes were released

[31] Sims: *lisua*: 'rat-trap'; *luba*: 'rat-trap'; Calloc'h, p. 292, has *lubi:* 'snake-trap'; G. SAUTTER, *Le plateau*, p. 163, mentions that the Kongo used this trap too. It seems similar to a Kongo-Laari trap described by R. JUNG, *Piège à porc-épic*.

[32] Cf. H. H. JOHNSTON, op. cit., p. 292 (for rats and birds); G. SAUTTER, *Le plateau*, p. 163, on bait; and G. SAUTTER, *De l'Atlantique*, I, p. 504, remarking that the technique was Kongo as well as Tio; G. LINDBLOM, *A noose trap*, about snares for bats which Calloc'h confirms, p. 292: *mu-ta* 'piège à chauves-souris'.

[33] Calloc'h, p. 221 *bu-kiru(ma)* 'fosse, piège'. Mbali and Ngaayüo at Mbe in 1963 thought the technique was *ngungulu* and had first been applied near Ngabe in recent times. It had been forbidden before 1963 because a number of accidents had happened with it. This story may show the affinities of the technique with northern practices; as a tradition it is either totally wrong or refers to a local usage established in Ngabe only.

if something stumbled over the stick which triggered it off. Along the Congo river a similar trap was used for hippopotami (Sims: *mpia*). In contrast to those described above, it is hard to believe that such a trap could be effective.

Certainly the bird-traps for which the Tio were and are famous were efficient. They burned the bush in the small dry season around February, laid the burned grasshoppers as bait for the birds and built many noose-traps to catch them.[34] The typical trap was a large bird-net put over the ashes and smeared with glue (Sims: *lima*: glue; *isuli*: 'trap; net of palm leaves'). In this season many Congo cranes were thus caught. They were not killed on the spot, but had their wings clipped and walked around the village like house storks until they were to be eaten. Other birds were also caught by this method but not in flocks.[35]

People put up traps where they liked. One did not have to ask anyone for permission to put a trap up nor did one need a blessing by the chief of the land. All animals trapped belonged to the builder of the contrivance. Practically no magic existed to help people catch more game. The only obligation of the trappers was to give a hind leg of some animals caught to the chief of the land exactly as for the hunt.

What a contrast with the hunt! First each hunter prayed to his *ikwii* before he left the house. Then he offered kola to the chief of the land, who gave it to his nature spirit (*nkira*) by chewing it and spitting it into the little charm house. The link between the shades and success in the hunt was close. Thus if people had renewed their shrines *kio* or had built a little house for the shades outside, they expected their luck in hunting to increase as a sign that their ancestors were happy with them. Good luck in hunting was a sign that all was well, that people were in harmony with the supernatural world. Consistent bad luck spelled impending doom. It had not to do with animals and their supposed relation to spirits of the other world, since success or ill luck in trapping the very same animals was of no account. It was hunting which counted.

Links between hunting and political structure were also close. Unlike trapping, hunting on domains belonging to a foreign chief of the land was forbidden and could become a *causus belli*. For both trapping and hunting public allegiance was shown to the chief by giving him the hind legs of hippo and all antelopes except *ntsee*, the tusk of the elephant which had struck the soil, when the animal fell, the hind leg and three ribs of the buffalo, the hind leg and the chest of the wart hog. The skins of civet cat, leopard, and lion also were noble tribute as well as the teeth of the lion. Among felines only the black genet did not have to be

[34] G. SAUTTER, *Le plateau*, p. 163.

[35] H. STANLEY, *Through the Dark Continent*, p. 544, on the western Teke (Fumu). The glue was made from the gum of 'sycamores'.

given up. To refuse this tribute on the hunt was tantamount to rebellion. Indeed it was the symbol of revolt.

Rules also existed for the pursuit of wounded animals. Any game wounded on one domain and killed on another one should be divided so that half a hind leg would go to one chief and half to the other. Quarrels often arose about this, but in 1963 no one could remember that such a case had led to war. And despite the fact that strangers should first ask permission from the chief, the hunting stations *õshie* were open to them. Presumably they first went to the chief's residence, asked his blessing and then took up their positions.

The relation between hunting and the political system was also shown in the ritual to deal with lions or leopards killed. As soon as the animal was dead something was tied over its muzzle, so the women would not see it. Otherwise their children might become carnivores (=witches?). The animal was brought whole to the village where a feast started with the performance of the *ngõ* dance in honour of the deceased chiefs of the land (*aakini maakuru*) and the appropriate songs, exactly as if a chief had died. The meat was not eaten because 'they were feared'. But the symbolic situation is clear enough. It must be added that the Tio feared the lion beyond all reason and thought that the king could send this animal in prides to attack anyone he disliked. To a lesser degree chiefs could call out the leopards against their enemies. The greatest of all nature spirits was called Nkwe Mbali: 'The Lion's Court'.[36]

To excel in hunting was apparently worth great expense and Sautter remarked that the most expensive charms were barely good enough to satisfy the craving of the hunters.[37] Such charms were of two general categories: those which protected the hunter from harm and those which assured him much game. Alatsã had learned his *ngaalimpfina* charm from his father. It was destined to attract game. The charm consisted not of a pill to be swallowed as some others are, but of a package worn at the belt or in later days in a pocket and it had to be wrapped in black cloth. Black stood for 'not being seen', i.e. being invisible. The charm (*ãti*) was made by taking special leaves and special earth and making a package (*oyuri*) for the client. The hunter put it in the fire, the first evening he camped out. Bending his face in the smoke he would say: 'I must kill x animals like the medicine man said' and he would begin to enumerate their names. The leaves were the ingredient which

[36] CH. DE MARTRIN DONOS, *Les Belges*, II, pp. 81–2, described the burial of a leopard after Janssen (1883). Normally the animal, draped in cloth, like a person, was buried with goats as food. On p. 112 Janssen told how he had missed a leopard with a trap and now had sores on his legs which the Tio attributed to the vengeance of the leopard. On tribute there are no direct data from the period in the written accounts beyond the mention that lion and leopard skins were emblems of kingship and chieftainship. But all informants stressed that the tribute was old indeed.

[37] G. SAUTTER, *Le plateau*, p. 147.

would attract the animals. And when the package was made, the medicine man would say: 'So-and-so has come to take the *oyuri*; he must kill many animals and he has wealth for me.' During the following night he dreamt how many animals would be killed and when the hunter came to fetch his package in the morning the medicine man told him. Sometimes he would not dream at all and warn the hunter that it might not work except perhaps by chance of God (Nzã). Food avoidances associated with this were that the hunter could not eat the heart, pancreas, or large intestine of the animals but should give them to the medicine man to eat. The latter should avoid putting the *ngaalimpfina* package on the ground. The herbs and earth put in the package were ordinary earth, ferns *oso*, seeds of the fruit *ntsunu*, the fruit *litari*, the leaf *ontsantsa*, the grass *ondonkula*, the grass *likoo*, and the leaves of *boompo* which was used to stupefy fish. Proportions did not matter. The seeds were grilled first and added to the package. Nothing at all from the hunter was required. It was not a personalized charm. In a more potent form of the same charm, the package was made and pills were made by grilling all the ingredients and pressing them together. The rest was put in a special magical package called *pfura*, and the hunter, before leaving, gave kola to his *pfura* and explained his needs. This *pfura* was usually given to persons who had had *oyuri* and done well. Payment for an *oyuri* was light, but for the *pfura* it was a lot.

As to the 'force' which activated both forms of *ngaalimpfina* it came not from the leaves or the formulae but from the *ikwii* of the medicine man and of the hunter. Yet the medicine man did not give anything from the spoils brought to him by the hunter to his *ikwii*. The hunter gave a chicken to be sacrificed for those.

Hunting involved risks and that was met by amulets or protective charms which enabled a person to fly away out of danger, or become invisible. *Akiro* was a charm to escape from lions. Hunters who carried it, put a patch of colour on their face when they went out. For another one, *inga*, four wild fruits: *ntsuunu*, *itiõ*, *intu iyuulu*, *sia* were forbidden. In yet another type the preparation and disposition of the charm was very similar to *ngaalimpfina* and the earth added was really *tsuula*, red camwood. It was left at the camp and the avoidance was that the hunter's wife could not eat the heart of the animal, otherwise she would not bear children. The hunter had an obligation to eat the heart. This gives one a glimpse of the symbolism involved, which is however also present in the other cases. There were many invulnerability charms since they were good not only for hunting but during war.[38]

[38] Again no direct data for the nineteenth century were available. Alatsã's father from whom he inherited *ngaalimpfina* may have inherited it himself in which case it was in use at the time of Iloo. We estimate the *floruit* of his father at 1900–20 however. Magic to protect oneself in hunting or in war was strictly forbidden by the colonial powers for obvious reasons. Still some has survived but is discussed with war since it formed part of the armament.

The value attached to hunting was obviously out of all proportion to its economic relevance. Sautter remarked how the men were waiting impatiently for the dry season to hold the communal drives, hoping to excel. For a man was judged by his behaviour during the hunt and true heroism was earned in the chase as much as in war.[39] The situation was not related to the value of meat *per se* since trapping did not have the same prestige. For the individual its attraction was not only the relief of daily boredom given by the unexpected situations and even the whiff of danger of a hunt, but it was also an occasion to display one's physical prowess and cunning. For men it was an ego-building process and this attitude fitted in very well with the very low density of population, the spirit of competition among these individualists and with their frontier mentality.[40] Yet there were serious disadvantages in this situation. The most obvious was that so much labour was lavished on such an unproductive pursuit and so little on other activities which could supply more food and more of the right kind of food. So that the love for hunting resulted ultimately in overwork and undernourishment for the women.

4. *Fishing on the plains*

The plains people fished in creeks, brooks, and rivers. They mostly fished for catfish buried under the roots of the trees near the edge of the water, putting up traps with a fish-hook baited on lines. This activity was mainly the concern of younger boys who always went hungry. Anything they caught was eaten fresh on the spot. There was no sharing as with all other food mentioned so far. Most of the fish was ferreted out with a stick rather than hooked on the line.[41]

In January or February a communal fishing party involving all the people of a village, or even of a whole chiefdom, would be organized.

[39] G. SAUTTER, *Le plateau*, p. 147, argued that perhaps this love for hunting would have helped to keep the population density low by giving a feeling of overpopulation as soon as hunting became less unrestricted. His argument to dismiss his own supposition is that such a situation would not resist a strong push from the outside or a vigorous internal demographic expansion. This is unconvincing, for other reasons (water, environment) did prevent a strong expansion to occupy the plains in the twentieth century. As for internal demographic expansion, as long as there were other plains one could migrate to, conflicts created by proximity would be avoided by migrating. This may have been exactly what happened. Love for hunting is not the whole explanation, but attachment to a way of life, requiring low density may have helped to maintain them.

[40] This situation is found in many societies in Central Africa. Historically it could be a reflexion of a value system obtaining before the introduction of agriculture, perhaps two millennia ago. But it would not have been retained if there were no continuing forces in these societies to make shifts undesirable. The division of labour between men and women with the acknowledged supremacy of men did, no doubt, contribute to this.

[41] G. SAUTTER, *Le plateau*, p. 163, reports that catfish was even brought from the Congo river to seed ponds.

The fish poison *mboompo* (Sims: *mboo*), cultivated in the village, was then used or a specialist climbed trees in the forest to gather the *nkunkwi* fruit. Each person received a part of the poison and cut the fruit up in pieces on the spot. The operation was not too dangerous for if some of the poison was swallowed the ill effects would be limited to severe diarrhoea. Everyone slept near the water and at dawn the poison, whether *mboompo* or *nkunkwi*, was thrown in the river. The water became dirty in colour and everyone ran downstream to his favourite spot with nets, scooping baskets, and items which looked like butterfly nets. Men, women, and children splashed about in the water trying to catch all the stupefied fish floating down on or near the surface of the water. Once the catch was finished the produce was divided in equal parts, with one quarter going to the maker of the poison, one to the chief of the land to which a person belonged and *not* to the one who owned the stretch of river or the pool, and one half was left to the person who had caught the fish. Fish was very much appreciated, so these parties often brought about quarrels or left bad feelings in their wake as people tried to steal fish.

This type of fishing with *nkunkwi* could only happen when the fruit was ripe during the short dry season of January. The fishing with *mboompo*, of which the crushed and pounded leaves furnished the poison, was used more in the great dry season, when the waters were shallow, the current weak and when there was not too much other work to do.[42] Unfortunately fish could not be caught thus all year round, for it was a major source of protein, which was one of the elements most lacking in their diet. The solution of carrying fresh or smoked fish inland from the Congo did not help much except quite near the river. For once twenty miles had to be walked the fresh fish was spoiled. Smoked fish was not sold to the people inland very much, for it was a popular item in the major trade at the Pool.

5. *Gathering*

Gathering was very important in the economics of subsistence, not only for such things as building materials, medicinal herbs, or firewood, which are quite common in Central Africa, but also for food. The distinction between hunting small animals and collecting grubs, for instance, becomes hair-fine and in practice the hunting or even raising of caterpillars by carefully up-ending the trees on whose bark they lived probably contributed more animal protein than hunting could. Like the Tio themselves most early observers did not comment much on this

[42] G. SAUTTER, ibid., said *nkunkusu* was used in dry season; L. PAPY, *Les populations*, p. 125, says fishing by women was practised in all seasons, by damming and then letting the river empty the area, by poisoning, in the dry season by putting baskets in the mud for catfish. Most of these applied to areas near the Congo river. Sautter is correct in his emphasis on the dry season but the stupefying agent then was *mboompo*, not *nkunkwi*.

with the exception of Ballay who noted the intensive hunt to collect rats, insects, grasshoppers, caterpillars, and winged termites.[43] The items were very diverse, so they are best set down in the form of a chart.

CHART 7

List of products gathered

A. *As food*

1 Animals

rats and mice: all mice and rats were caught except the house mouse (*ikaba*), and *mbiene* rats. The Jinju did eat the latter. Only children caught and ate the mice *mpimpuu*, *ancüwo*, *ofaana*. The animals were killed by clubbing them. During the dry season men caught *okwi* and *mpara* rodents.

otsiere: caterpillars. Hunted by children in October in the savannah. The first of the crop were given to the king. They were an object of trade.

ibii (Calloc'h, p. 159: *mu-biu*): caterpillars living on the bark of trees where they multiplied in wide colonies. The trees were protected and even planted in the villages for that purpose. Women collected them.

atoow (Calloc'h, p. 159: *too*): caterpillars of the forest, collected in February, by all.

inkiele (Calloc'h, p. 159: *i-nkele*): caterpillars collected beginning February in the forest and another variety collected in the savannah around the beginning of October, by all.

intswontswo: caterpillars collected in the forest beginning February, by all.

avura (Calloc'h, p. 159; *bvura*, 'generic name for caterpillars'): caterpillars collected in the forest beginning February, by all.[a]

termites: with the first rains in September the ant-hills were covered with a sort of roof and the creatures were caught when they flew out. To entice them drums were used to imitate the rain. Men collected them.[b]

anjié: grasshoppers eaten in the dry season when they are still young. Only one species was edible.

honey: collected even though bees were not kept and wax was not used. It could be gathered all the year round, but it was not collected extensively, and was little eaten or appreciated. When the moon was full it was forbidden to gather it.

[a] J. GHYS, *Etude agricole*, lists eight species of forest trees which harbour caterpillars. Calloc'h, p. 159 lists five species of caterpillars in the grasses and ten on trees. BONNAFÉ notes the great importance of their gathering among the Kukuya.

[b] G. BRUEL, *L'Afrique*, p. 142; G. SAUTTER, *De L'Atlantique*, I, p. 28.

[43] N. BALLAY, *De L'Ogooúe*, p. 263. Even if this observation obtained for the Tege rather than the Tio (it is not easy to distinguish here since Ballay was in both areas), it does not invalidate the point that gathering was very important. The situation of 1963 postulates it, even if perhaps colonial contact had led to the adding of one or another item to the list of products gathered. It is certain that after 1954 the water hyacinth was thus added. It spread on the Congo river after 1954 and by 1963 Tio women were already using it for packaging loaves of cassava. It was better, they said, for this purpose than any other leaf. Within nine years or less they had tried the newcomer, found it good, and harvested it. This certainly shows that there is dynamism in the gathering sector of the subsistence economy as much, perhaps more, than in the agricultural sector. For the related Ngenge, data published by GHYS, *Etude agricole*, in 1934 confirm that the attitude was not modern.

2 Plants

fruits: *inkworambie* (forest), *ayara* (savannah), *ãsia* (forest), *ikuli* (forest), *antsongu* (forest), *intu iyuulu* (forest), *ntsuunu* (forest), *itiõ* (forest). Most of these matured during one of the dry seasons and all collected them. Calloc'h, pp. 224–5 listed fifteen sorts of fruits, of which two were in village settlements. Two more are given on p. 261 as 'mangue sauvage'.

leaves: all were used as vegetables, except *soo ny' õnko*, and *ankooankoo* which were smoked as well as hemp. The leaves of *mpfõ* a plant found in the fallow lying fields in the forest was most appreciated and collected by the women. They also collected the following in the forest: *binu*, *nkaali*, *ntiina*, *ntsuankira*, *itswo*, *mpfũ*. In the savannah they found *ayara*, *angoono*, *balingei*, and *ãmbuwo*.

roots: several wild species of yams in the forest such as *nkieri* and *ikwembila*, a sort of wild potato, and roots of small shrubs used as spices.

mushrooms: (*buwo*) found both in the savannah and the forest. Harvested in the savannah in October and November and in March/April in the forest. Some were available all through the rainy season. Calloc'h lists thirty-three species, all of which would not be edible. Of eighteen species mentioned by Ghys only three were poisonous.[c]

3 Minerals

Earth from the houses and the yards was eaten by pregnant women and children, but when kaolin was available near by that was preferred.

B. *For other usages*

1 Minerals

Earth was used for daubing floors, clay for pottery and the iron slag of ancient workings for ammunition. Iron ore was not utilized in this period.

2 Plants

Medicinal herbs: a great many of these were collected and each medicine man would have his specialties. Some such as Sanseviera or the leaves of *ilibankie* were utilized on many occasions.[d]

vines: *libã*: in construction as rope, *likuya*: to make rope for hunting and fishing nets.

fruits: *nkunkwii* to make poison for fish. Cut by a specialist.

grasses: *ãshiele* from the savannah for patching walls; sword-grass (*imperata*) was used for thatching. Cf., Sims: *(M)ungili:* 'plant used in medicine and thatching'.

bark: of some trees from the savannah the bark was peeled to make boxes; the bark of the *nkei* shrub was used as a poison for the poison oracle.

marsh plants: *ũnkõ* and papyrus *ndzubi* were both collected to strip the stems and make mats.

wood: used for construction. Some, especially the long thin sticks needed, came from the forest, but much was cut in the savannah for shorter pieces. Furniture was made from savannah wood except for dugouts and wooden platters. Wood from both savannah and forest was used as well as firewood. This was gathered by women, whereas men would fetch wood needed for construction or carving. Men also brought back big logs of firewood when they had cut their *ngwuunu*.

[c] J. GHYS, op. cit., p. 122. Calloc'h, p. 156.

[d] J. GHYS, op. cit., pp. 122–3 gives examples of specific plants used to cure specific illnesses. For Tio drugs and ingredients used see Chapter IX.

Obviously gathering was still important to the subsistence economy and not only for purposes of healing or construction, for which it was to be expected, but also for food. The fact that all the food collected by women and men was used for the household, rather than eaten on the spot and that this applied for most of the food gathered even by the children, underlines the same point. The Tio knew their environment well and used both the products of the savannah and the forest which they found useful. The plants they used, even for medicinal purposes, however, were only a fraction of all plants known,[44] and the same was true of insects. There was nothing haphazard about the collecting. Finally, it is interesting that such a large place was given to greens which were already well represented in the dawn-garden. Some of the wild species such as *mpfõ* and *mpfũ* were helped to grow by weeding around them and for many of the greens especially the women practised what amounts to a form of vegeculture.

But the people did not realize how important the additional food received from gathering was to them in terms of proteins or fats or other elements. They underestimated the amount of time spent in collecting, because it was often done while people were going about for other purposes, such as fetching water or firewood or going to the hunt or the fields, etc. But in spite of the unawareness of the Tio, especially Tio men, the produce from this source remained quite important. It is hard to express in percentages how much food was gathered for how much was cultivated but one can surmise that most of the snacks (fruits), half of the greens, which were part of every meal, and most of the sauces came from wild produce.

Its relevance for purposes other than feeding was recognized and its position here was so dominant that it comes rather as a surprise to see that some industrial plants were cultivated or that bamboo for construction was planted.

6. *Fishing on the Congo*

The *adzindzali*, 'people of the river' all along the Congo river and the Stanley Pool had a different way of life. They were well aware of it and proud of being fishermen. One story about the origin of the Mbembe underlines it. It maintains that the Mbembe lived at Likulu, south of Ngabe together with the *Dzindzali*. However, they were afraid of the water and the dugouts and left hurriedly to push inland. Only chief NGOBILA and his water people stayed behind.

The environment of these people was the river and it affected not only their patterns of economic production but their whole life. Thus in the twentieth century, and doubtless earlier, people from the river

[44] The botanical knowledge of most Tio was much greater than mine and persons such as Okondzaadza or other older men were astonishing. They named every single plant and also used a whole terminology to designate associations of plants, indicating types of soil and types of vegetation.

would marry much further away than land-dwellers. They travelled regularly, and were living in villages next to Bobangi villages or were even mixed in the same village. Thus they had evolved a body of legal procedure to handle mixed cases involving both Bobangi fishermen and Tio. They were very much involved with trade while the fact that their major means of livelihood, fishing, required a sizeable capital, mainly in the form of dugouts, involved them even more in the economics of allocation, which was further away from autarchy than the way of life of the people on the plains. Here however the discussion must be restricted to fishing alone.

The major implements used were nets, paddles, dugouts, and traps. Nets were made by the men themselves who rolled first the fibres of the *likuya* plant and then knitted them into a net (Sims: *isia*, 'net, twine'), just as hunters did for their nets. These nets required constant repairing and the men made this their basic on-shore occupation. Paddles too could be made by the fishermen. They were made for paddling standing up, with the blade of the oar well over three feet long, while the handle measured a little less than three feet. The shape was pointed at the end, broadening out to reach the widest point about two thirds from the tip where the paddle had about fifteen inches in width to taper off towards the handle.[45] But many paddles were bought from the Bobangi. The dugouts were not made locally any more by the 1880s. They were bought from the Bobangi who brought them down from the Equatorial forest.[46] Thus one of the essential items for their occupation had to be acquired from the outside. The canoes used for fishing were smaller than the trading dugouts and were usually manned only by from one to three men. Weirs or traps were constructed in light wood or bamboo plaited with vines.

The techniques used were either spearing, using traps of various sorts and setting lines or nets.[47] One type of spearing aimed at catching

[45] *La tribu*, p. 122, and A. CHAPEAUX, *Le Congo*, p. 563, for photographs; C. COQUILHAT, *Sur le Haut-Congo*, p. 70, for method of paddling.

[46] Data on the price of dugouts and their trade in Chapter X. L. GUIRAL, *Le Congo*, described the boats as round-bottomed, long, unstable but fast. H. BENTLEY, *Pioneering*, I, p. 342, described a canoe carved with a wicker pattern with six paddlers and two steersmen. Boats of this size were used only for trade. The Tio did not have to buy dugouts for all along the river stands of trees were still plentiful at the time.

[47] Calloc'h, p. 288: 'pêcher': distinguishes 'aux herbes, aux arbustes, au filet': *baga*; 'à la ligne': '*lobo*'; 'à barrage' *yuba*; 'aux nasses': *dzuba*; 'au harpon', *tobo*; *mw-inu*, 'lance à poisson' (cf. Sims: *zuba:* 'catch fish by fence, trap or net'; *muzubi:* 'fisherman'; *loba*: 'fish with a hook'; *tobo*: 'impale, stab, transfix, tack, stitch'; *likala*: 'hedge made in the river for taking fish') for the Tio categories. We followed the organization of G. SAUTTER, *De l'Atlantique*, I, p. 426–41, which is a thorough study of fishing techniques on the Stanley Pool in the 1950s. He distinguished between spears, traps, dams and fences, lines and nets. This study has been used as background for this section. We have used Sims mostly to find out if the techniques attributed to the Tio existed in the 1880s. Since so many innovations were introduced later this is useful and necessary.

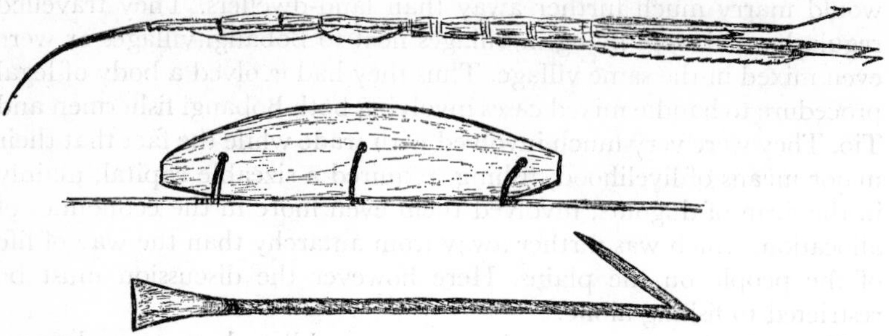

Fig. 2

Nine foot harpoon for hunting hippopotamus: details beneath it show the floats attached to a line leading to the iron hook, one of four which constitute the head of the harpoon. The hooks stick in the animal, the rope uncoils, the floats indicate the position of the animal and there is no line between the float and the canoe, which would capsize if pulled by the hippopotamus.

lungfish (*protopterus annectans*) and a few turtles, in isolated ponds or sheets of water during the dry season, in places where there was much vegetation, a thin layer of water and much mud. The grass was first burned and then a line of fishermen probed the mud back and forth[48] until they hit a fish. The art consisted in extricating the animal without getting bitten. Two types of spears seem to have been used (Sims: *muina, muswe*). At least one other type of spear with a multiple head was used (Sims: *isweo, nta mpi*) for spearing fish from a boat.[49] The most elaborate spear was a true harpoon (*inswei*) (Sims: *mpula*) used to hunt hippopotami with. When the animal was hit the head was detached from the handle, a rope unfolded between the two and the handle, on which a float was affixed beforehand, indicated the place where the animal had dived. Another rope connected the float with the boat.[50] Spearing fish was also done at night when some 'eels' and others were attracted by the light.[51] This was apparently a speciality of the channel and in vogue at low waterstands.[52]

[48] G. SAUTTER, op. cit., I, pp. 34–5 for a photograph.

[49] H. H. JOHNSTON, p. 292, mentions spearing, probably with a single spearhead. Since Sims speaks of a multiple fish-spear, G. SAUTTER, op. cit., I, p. 427, wrongly attributes this implement to a later date.

[50] See CH. SÖLNER, *Voyage*, p. 97, for a description. H. H. JOHNSTON, op. cit., p. 133, saw such a hunt being prepared only twenty yards away from the intended victim, ibid., p. 292.

[51] E. ZORZI, *Al Congo*, p. 428, maintains that when the fish put their heads out to see the light, they were chopped off. E. DUPONT, *Lettres*, p. 200. The observations were made at low-water season.

[52] Low-water season was from July to the beginning of September, with a second low water trough towards the end of March. Pecile's observation in Zorzi dated from the end of July. A. MERLON, op. cit., pp. 56–9, on spearing near Kwamouth. At the Pool he said small fish were also shot with bow and arrow.

The fish-weirs were remarkable constructions. They were used in high-water periods. The favourite were supple weirs in lattice-work of bamboo laths knotted with vines so that an inch or so remained between them. The two openings were folded inwards. In another model one wider net fitted over a narrower one which acted as a trap for fish that had swum through the first.[53] These weirs were set at high water in meadows of grass over submerged islands in the path of fish and attached to some grasses. Bigger models were anchored with stones and left for two or three days. The majority of fish was caught by these means.[54] They came in all shapes and sizes. The fish most caught were catfish (Sims: *ngolo*) and *distichodus*. More rigid frame weirs were probably also in use, especially a funnel type baited with a leaf which triggered a complete turn over of the trap. But how many of the fifteen types counted by Sautter existed in the 1880s is unclear. Sims names three: *mukweo*, *iloo*, *inta*.[55] Traps were often combined with fencing in corners or backwaters. This was done with a dam (Sims: *likala*, *mukamu*) or a fence, probably in bamboo (Sims: *Insuli*). The dykes were built in one day and were sometimes 30 inches high and 150 feet long. They were strengthened by sticks driven into the ground. The great weir, a funnel closed with a trellis of bamboo at the wide bottom *okwe* (Sims: *mukweo*), was used to block the passage of the fish and was put in place in the evening. During the night the fish was caught when it wanted to leave the backwater. This method was used at the Pool four times a year when the waters were rising or falling.[56] The work required about ten men to build and repair the dyke as well as to watch over the trap. The fence was put in place by one or two persons and the same traps were used in conjunction with it.

Fishing with a rod and a line was also practised but mostly by boys. (Sims: *loba*, 'fish with a hook') who used rods, lines, and floats.[57] This was, one fancies, more a game than an occupation.

The classic net was a seine (Sims: *infiere*: 'fishing net') (*imfiere*) built as a wall of netting with mesh two inches apart and weighted at the bottom with pottery weights or pebbles. The upper end was kept buoyant with floats (Sims: *mayuo*). The seine was dragged towards the shore by one or two canoes; it was also used to seal off the mouth of bays at low waters; or it could be fixed at one end and dragged by the

[53] G. SAUTTER, op. cit., I, p. 427, called these *nguino* for the Pool.

[54] A. MERLON, op. cit., pp. 58–9 says that some let the weirs float down the Pool instead of anchoring them.

[55] H. H. JOHNSTON, op. cit., p. 292, for traps, p. 148, he mentioned that some Zanzibari soldiers lifted traps and took fish. This almost certainly constituted a theft.

[56] Sims gives (*M*)*usano*: 'method of taking fish by closing a ditch at high water'. A. MERLON, op. cit., pp. 58–9, describes it.

[57] H. H. JOHNSTON, op. cit., p. 292, and he added boys used the equipment. A. MERLON, op. cit., p. 58.

other.[58] Another type of net was shaped like a huge butterfly net with a more oblong aperture and a very stout handle and was used for smaller fish.[59] Nets of all sorts would last a year, provided they were dried on poles and repaired diligently. Several nets could be strung together if need be; this was done when trawling. The boats went forward wide apart and against the current, slowly closing a circle. The net ballooned because it was dragged least in the middle and pushed back most by the current. When the circle was complete, the fish was trapped and could be caught by hand (not hauled up). There may have been a technique to catch deep swimming fish by hanging lines and hooks from a floating line. Yet that is called *ipanse* now at Ngabe, which is a Lingala name. Besides the *imfiere* and the butterfly net there were other types (such as Sims: *Likuoni*, *licele*, *ntinte*) but their characteristics are no longer known. For as Sautter has so vividly shown, techniques from all over the basin of the Congo river have come to the Pool and it is sometimes very hard to discern what was Tio and what was not. Thus a technique the fishermen of Ngabe described as *unteku* is what Sautter describes[60] as *moutekou*, which is said to have come from the Likouala. The round full bottomed net to be thrown, called *kasnet* was remembered in 1963 as being Kongo in origin but it may well be that it was introduced to the Pool from West Africa. This situation of borrowing between fishermen must have existed in the 1880s as well since Bobangi and Tio as well as Nunu fished in the same waters.

Most of the productive techniques mentioned and the usual techniques in working with nets required the co-operation of several people, up to six or seven in trawling. This number could still be recruited in any village among members of the same extended family and usually was, with the oldest acting as captain for the operations.

Fish was not all consumed fresh. Many were dried on sandbanks or on great frames and smoked with local salt.[61] The temporary settlements for this were called *õshie* like the hunting camps, another parallel, as with the spears and nets, between the technology of the fishermen with that of the hunter. The catch thus dried and smoked was then sold either for food along the banks of the river, if the fishermen were far from home, or at the greater markets, usually those of the Stanley

[58] H. BRUNSCHWIG, *Les cahiers*, p. 192; H. H. JOHNSTON, op. cit., p. 292; G. SAUTTER, op. cit., I, p. 434, makes it clear this must be *imfiere*. On the weights, pottery weights with holes were also used. This may have been the function of those little pottery bricks with holes found at Mafamba. Cf., J. EMPHOUX, *Mafamba*.

[59] H. H. JOHNSTON, op. cit., p. 292.

[60] G. SAUTER, op. cit., I, p. 435. Sails did not exist but were introduced by early Europeans. e.g. E. ZORZI, *Al Congo*, pp. 437–42, for such an early attempt. The technique *ikoso* another favourite at Ngabe in 1963 comes from the Ngungulu according to G. SAUTTER, op. cit., I, p. 438.

[61] H. BRUNSCHWIG, *Les cahiers*, p. 192 (smoked fish and salted with local salt); C. COQUILHAT, *Sur le Haut Congo*, p. 75 (smoked and dried on frames). (Sims: *itee:* frame for drying fish').

Pool. For at home the women of the fishermen cultivated, mainly cassava and the dawn-gardens, and some of the water people even made *ngwuunu* but on a small scale. Some of the women added pottery-making to their other tasks, since they were quite near the best clay to be found in the area. But the activities of growing food crops and fishing did not mix too well, since high-water seasons were the best for fishing but also for agriculture, with the exception of a few weeks in March where the secondary low-waters could overlap with the tail-end of the second planting season. So if the men cultivated they neglected their fishing.

Magic for fishing was practised as well. The charm *ipali* was also used to become wealthy. It is described later. The division of fish showed that the tending of nets was considered a special labour to be rewarded, but the ownership of a canoe, the major capital investment was not, nor was the task of directing the operations rewarded. For half of all the fish caught went to the owner of the net with captain and sailors dividing the other half and nothing going to the owner of the boat. In practice however the sailors were relatives and the boat belonged to one of their group. Still, in as much as the boat did belong to an individual and not to the group, but was used as property of the group, the division did not recognize capital invested. In this the Tio, at least the Tio of the fishing villages, were unlike the Bobangi or the Bangala where a plutocracy based on wealth had arisen. For in the bigger markets a plutocracy did exist, but it was oriented towards trade and trading canoes.

As for fishing with the construction of a dam or a fence, indeed any form of fishing where more than one man was involved, sharing was always by equal portions. Neither chiefs nor elders received any tithes in fish. The only spoils chiefs were entitled to were those of the hippopotamus hunt. One hind leg of the animal had to be given to them, as if it were a product of the hunt. Beyond that, any wreck or any other odd object found in the river along Tio territory down to the mouth of the channel in the Pool was to be brought to chief NGOBILA. Any complaints about lost property, fishing, or trading were to be lodged there as well. On the Pool itself a similar position befell, it seems, the chief NTSUULU of Kinshasa.

It should not be forgotten that the environment of these people which made them fishermen also made them traders and through this drew them strongly into the orbit of quite another type of economics. Moreover, sharing the waters with non-Tio made them more sophisticated and gave them a much broader outlook than that of most of the landlocked agriculturalists.

The production of raw materials by and for the households of the extended families at the village level on the plains met the basic needs of shelter and food. To complete the analysis of the economics of subsistence, the processing of these materials and their consumption by the same groups must now be set forth. Any analysis should also examine the economic factors of production. Since among these: capital, land, work, and skills, the first two have been shown to be negligible for the people on the plains, the last two only will be discussed in the next chapter.

Chapter VI
The Economics of Subsistence: Domestic Life

THE transformation of raw materials into finished goods still belongs to the production process. Finished goods were then consumed in the households to satisfy the culturally estimated needs for clothing and adornment, shelter, and food. With this domestic use of goods the description of the economics of subsistence is not yet complete. The uses of time, involving the production and consumption of intangibles remains to be examined. Any occupation can be seen as a productive activity from which goods or services flow. This would be true even of total inactivity since it produces relaxation or rest. Any action could be termed work. Work however is also the major factor of production in Tio society. It is interrelated with the other relevant factor, skills, in that the division of labour flows from the technical skills needed to produce certain goods or services. Work should be discussed as such, before turning to domestic consumption. Yet, from another angle any use of time is also a consumption for the person participating in the activity. Together with the uses of goods, the uses of time form the whole of domestic life in the Tio village. It was felt that a better understanding of domestic life would be served by discussing the topics in the following sequence: making finished goods, the domestic use of goods, and the domestic use of time.

1. *Making finished goods*

The processing of raw materials into finished goods sometimes required skills which were only held by specialists or semi-specialists, whereas in other situations the skills were available in every household. The artisans who produced the first category of goods were the smiths, potters, and weavers, while woodworking, basket-making, tattooing, were semi-specialties. As for the basic crafts of house building and cooking they were not specialized, nor was leather working. Strictly speaking the first category mentioned does not belong to subsistence economics since the producers were not the consumers. They involved allocation and exchange. Such specialists were not found in each extended or polygynous family, which were the producers/consumers concerned. There were however smiths and weavers in every neighbourhood, that is in every large village or cluster of settlements lying within a day's walking distance one from the other, and by the use of this group as a producer one could include these crafts in the discussion. The situation for potters was slightly different since they were found only in areas where clay was available. For most of the territory, then, the domestic units were not self-sufficient in ceramic products.

On the distribution of other specialists a few of the older citizens in Mbe testified about conditions when they were children. Okondzaadza lived in Aliõ (1910) where there were many people. The village contained no fewer than eight quarters. There was only one smith, but there were many weavers of raphia cloth. Woodworkers either made statuettes for the ancestors or wooden grinding boards. Wooden drums, however, were imported from the Kukuya and pottery came from the Kukuya or the market of Ntsei near the lower Nkéni. Abili Ndiõ remembered (1900) that the smaller settlement of Abili had one smith, one weaver, but no true woodworkers. Every man helped himself by making the basic tools in wood. At a later period Ba recorded a situation around 1920 or so when there was no smith at Nkwũ, his village, but there was one in the neighbouring village of Ngieluo. Several weavers lived in the village and in the neighbouring villages towards the Nkéni river, where there was more wood, there were specialists in carving drums, metate, and statuettes. Although all of these are later than the period under investigation there is every reason to think that a similar situation prevailed during the reign of Iloo.

These, then, were the specialists who produced goods. But other specialists provided services. Chiefs, medicine men, singers, snake-charmers, and certain musicians were also specialists. Since they did not provide goods but services, they are not considered here and only the crafts of smithing, pottery, weaving, wood-working, leather-working, basketry, tattooing, house building, and cooking are now outlined in turn.

The raw metal smiths used was not produced in Tio country. Abili Ndiõ remembered that the smith at Abili obtained it by buying lumps of metal from traders or by remelting old objects. By 1963 no one, including Bilankwi a smith of Mbe who had inherited the craft from his father, even knew what iron ore was and nowhere is there a mention of processing ore in Tio country during this period. The base metal was imported, iron as well as copper or lead which were all worked. The standard equipment included an anvil (*andzuunu*) (Sims: *nzunu*), two to four hammers of two different weights, both called *otiene* (Sims: *mutiene*), quadruple bellows or 'fly-whisks of the fire': *osèo ambaa* (Sims: *museo ambaa*) and a pottery nozzle in front of the bellows, appropriately called *ndzuu* or the kitchen pot. Split bamboo pincers or tongs (Sims: *mwinu*), and a file (Sims: *mukwaa*) were also used.[1] The tools were all made by the smith himself.

On the Mbe plateau raw iron was transformed into hoes, bracelets,

[1] E. ZORZI, *Al Congo*, p. 337, drew all of these except four nozzle bellows. He confirms, p. 391, that this was valid for the area of Mbe. Note especially the two types of hammers and file. Bilankwi inherited all his smithing tools from his father.

anklets, collars, adzes, axes, pipes, double bells *onku*, single bells *ba*, two types of throwing knives (which were no longer used for that purpose), hairpins, needles, several types of spears and spear-points, two types of daggers, different sorts of knives, including bush-knives with one edge, rather like a European kitchen knife,[2] a pocket knife with grooves in the metal, worn with a small scabbard, and a huge hunting-knife among others.[3]

The raw iron was melted over a fire of charcoal, made from the hardest wood available and constantly fanned by the bellows. The temperature was high enough to soften the metal completely but not sufficient to melt it outright. When the metal was soft the smith would first strike a dozen blows with his heavy hammer to get the shape. The metal might then be allowed to cool before it was heated again at a lesser temperature to be worked on with the lighter hammer, or this might be done immediately after the basic shaping. Final touches were added by filing when the object was cold. For working copper or brass the same technique was used. Often these metals also were only softened and then hammered into shape. Sometimes copper rods were melted down (Sims: *sua*: 'cast in a mould'). Objects in these metals were bracelets and collars for office-holders as well as other prestige items. They were worked carefully, chiselled with a white-hot engraving burin, which had been plunged into oil to heighten its resistance to heat.[4] Compared with peoples in the west and south the Tio were not particularly skilled as blacksmiths but their jewellery was as competent as the known products from Loango. Compared with the peoples upstream of the Congo river, the best blacksmiths of Central Africa, they were quite backward, and this was due in part to the fact that iron products were imported on a fairly large scale from there. A developing market economy had partly ruined the technological competence in this industry.

Smiths were paid for their work. Thus when de Brazza wanted a collar the royal smith asked for a dog and a goat as payment. Payment therefore may not have been made in the usual currencies.[5] For close kin, says Bilankwi, something like a hoe or a bush-knife would be given

[2] The form of the bushknife with one edge and handle parallel to the back and its method of hafting indicate old European influence. European knives were available at the court and at the Stanley Pool.

[3] H. BRUNSCHWIG, *La négociation*, p. 31, for trade. The 'Ancinciei', who lived upstream of the 'Ascimga' on the right bank of the Congo worked iron and made the big bells and the Tio 'sabers'.

[4] N. NEY, *Conférences*, pp. 351–2. Observations at the smithy of the royal blacksmith. Cf. hammers, bellows, and the melting of copper. See E. ZORZI, *Al Congo*, p. 391, for a drawing of copper work at the same smithy and the use of file and burin. Cf. also *Les colliers*, p. 63.

[5] N. NEY, *Conférences*, p. 351. Yet Bilankwi claims that payments were made in currencies: brass rods, *olivancillaria nana* shells (*mbula*), squares of raphia (*cul ikwo*) and rubber (for period 1899–1920).

free but for more products even kin had to pay. Smiths did not peddle their wares or sell them in markets. They made objects and stored them until someone came to buy at the shop. But their stock was never very great, so they mostly worked to order. It does not seem to have been a full-time occupation. In addition to metalwork the smiths were also often potters, making one product: the bowls of pipes.[6]

Smiths were still thought of in 1963 as *ngambaa imbatsa*: 'master of fire, maker of jewels' (Sims: *ca*: 'bangle, bracelet'). The craft was respected and it had connexions with royalty because of the king's eternal fire, the anvils in his kitchen, the anvils at the site of the national spirit Nkwe Mbali and the existence of a royal smith, who was one of the highest chiefs in the country. It was therefore a status as much as an occupation. People did not just become smiths. The craft was hereditary, often learned from one's father, and the tools were inherited from the father. People who practised the craft were sometimes called *bamukaana oculi*: 'those of the descent group of the smith' and this was a bilateral group. For daughters could inherit the tools as well, but not use them. Their sons might use them. If the trade was not learned while the old smith was alive, it was believed that the deceased *nkaa* who had practised it would teach the heir in dreams. When there was no direct heir, the tools could be inherited by someone in the same *ibuuru*, but then, says Abili Ndiõ, the heir had to pay others in the *ibuuru* for the tools.[7] The craft was thus limited to ascribed status groups, but smiths were not a caste, as in West Africa for instance, because they were free to marry whom they chose.

Pottery was practised by women only except for the fashioning of pipe bowls already mentioned. The raw material was the clay along rivers. A great variety of products was produced. The major categories were *ndzuu* (Sims: *nzuu*) cooking pots, water jars *mbio* (Sims: *mbio buu, ikaa, ikikaa, inkono*) ((*M*)*umuu*); trays and dishes *ikuõ* and *ãlõ* (Sims: *ikuono*); cups (Sims: *ikukuno, impimpini*); huge jars *otiele* (Sims: *mutiele*: 'Pot for cooking large puddings') used to collect rain and also to soak cassava in; fire-pots to be put in canoes (Sims: *nkie, ikuñu*); small vials (Sims: *ililii*); lids or saucers (Sims: *isa, isa nzaña*); and pottery sieves.[8]

[6] Data from Bilankwi.

[7] Data from Bilankwi.

[8] Added to this must be the pottery rings made to put the round-bottomed jars on and the pottery weights for fishermen's nets. Cf. H. BRUNSCHWIG, *La négociation*, pp. 33, 50 (*otiele*); In 1963 we saw some big *otiele* at Imbãw, which had been made by the Mfunu and imported in this period at the then existing village of Ibili, which confirms Brazza; H. H. JOHNSTON, *The River Congo*, p. 148; J. MAES, *Poterie*, pp. 23, 26, 42; H. H. JOHNSTON, *George Grenfell*, II, pp. 790–1, figs. 447, 448, 449, on exports of Tio pottery from the Pool; E. COART, A. DE HAULLEVILLE, *La céramique*, p. 18, No. 2 (pipe), p. 19 (weights), p. 25 (trade), p. 27 (form and decoration), p. 79 (decoration), pp. 95–6 (Mfunu water jar) (decoration made by turning the vessel on a wooden board when incising it), p. 105, II, pp. 143–5, figs. 150–72, pl. X–XI; pp. 143–4 (trade, p. 145). All specimens were collected before 1907. Most of the fine ware shown here disappeared completely. For sieves: *L'art congolais*, pp. 3–5.

For each type there were different wares according to their origins. For pottery was much traded on the Congo river and its affluents.[9] Thus pots with a rounded base came from the entrance of the Pool, pottery in kaolin with fine incisions around the neck was Mfunu, Moye pots had a typical decoration called *ngaluu*, etc.[10] The finer wares, especially the water jars, were works of art in shape and decoration and had all the variability of works of art. Yet the art had already lost ground at court for instance and around the Pool where imported European porcelain, glass, or crystal was deemed superior.[11]

The fabrication declined greatly in quality shortly after the end of the period. First the clay, sometimes pure kaolin for water pots from the lower Kasai, but more often other clays, was mixed with tiny grains of ground-up old pottery (*inkioonu*). Once the paste had dried, the bottom of the pot was modelled inside the bottom of an older pot or on the outside of an old bottom or even on a stone. Then the bottom was left to dry further in the shade so the process would not go too fast and produce cracks. Once the bottom was ready the walls, shoulder and neck were built up by the coiling method. After five to seven coils for a waterpot one came to the neck and mouth which were shaped by hand out of the last coil. The whole was then smoothed out with a palette (*ibeer indzuu*). Incisions could be scratched with the fingernail or a stiletto. Slips were also added to some pots. One form of painting consisted of drawing lines of a reddish mixture, probably with camwood (*baphia nitida*) as a base. Then the coloured place was rubbed with a pebble or a nut to impregnate the material with the colour. The pots were left for several days to dry again and then they were fired. Water jars at the Pool were plunged into hot palm-oil before baking.[12] A fire was started with very hard wood. The pots were put upside down on top of the fire. After about three hours, when the wood had been reduced to glowing charcoal, the fire was covered with straw. It all then smouldered for a whole night. The process was therefore always begun in the early afternoon. Pots were usually made in the drier

[9] And for a long time. Cf. J. EMPHOUX, *Mafamba*.

[10] Round-bottomed and small cooking pots came from the Pool and the Lari (i.e. formerly the Fumu). Kukuya and the markets of the lower Nkéni supplies all the Jinju and Kukuya pipes were famous everywhere. L. GUIRAL, *Le Congo*, pp. 242–8, on Bobangi pots.

[11] On the variability and the technique by which finer wares were made, cf. H. DEMETZ, *Les poteries*; J. MAES, *Poterie*, pp. 21–6; J. VANDEN BOSSCHE, *La poterie*; *L'art congolais*, pp. 306b, 307a, b. H. BRUNSCHWIG, *La négociation*, p. 29, for the crystal set of the king in 1880.

[12] J. MAES, op. cit., p. 26, claims to increase the impermeability of the jar; *L'art congolais* that their porousness was their great quality which kept the water cool. They were made more permeable. Cf. also H. DEMETZ, *Les poteries*, pp. 262–4, who gives no indication about the use of palm-oil.

season, not only because low water made access to the clay easier but also because of the strong regular winds which then prevailed in the channel and along the Pool.[13]

The wares were sold in the major markets and for currencies in general use. Trade was very brisk because there was specialization both because of the availability of raw materials and the differences in pattern and decoration.[14]

Tio men were weavers. They used a broad loom with oblique tension with which they wove only the simplest pattern of cloth, the *croisure toile*. The loom was not movable and the material used was raphia. Designs were obtained by using coloured threads and the Tio excelled in this technique. In addition their thread was well carded and woven very tightly so that the resulting cloth was supple and sturdy. But weaving itself was only the last step in a process that began with the preparation of the fibres. These were extracted from the leaves of the raphia. Fibres were tied in bunches and then carded. The resulting thinner fibres were then dried in the sun. After this the warp and woof were prepared on separate wooden rods and finally the loom was set up and the warp and woof rods were attached to the frame. The apparatus has been described by H. Loir in general and A. Masson Detourbet and J. Maes for the Tio.[15] Every time a new cloth was to be woven the loom had to be at least partly dismantled and set up again. Once a piece was woven it was smoothed out with a piece of wood in the form of a crescent, the *ikwoonu*. It was not beaten with pestles to make it more supple. The finished cloth measured about fifteen inches by fifteen.

Colours used for designs were red, natural white, yellow, and black. The thread was painted by pressing the juice from the leaves of the colours required over a bundle of thread or else by soaking the thread in the colour until it was dried out. *Bwooli* leaves were used for black colour, *ngaaba* leaves for the red, and *ntsõ* for the yellow.

Different types of cloth were the *cul ikwo*, which seems to have been a piece of four pieces of cloth by four, the *ndzu a tieeri* made up of three rows of ten, the *ndzu anna*, consisting of four rows of ten, the *vooro* or *liboo* which had twelve by ten pieces and the *ntaa*, the biggest of

[13] J. VANDEN BOSSCHE, op. cit., pottery was observed in Ngabe in 1963; E. COART, A. DE HAULLEVILLE, op. cit., pp. 95–6.

[14] They were more than probably paid for in currencies, even though no direct testimony is available, the size and volume of the market suggests it. Cf. Chap. X (markets).

[15] A. MASSON-DETOURBET, *Le tissage*; J. MAES, *Le tissage*. Two weavers, Iyene of Ampo, and the informant of Masson Detourbet at Etswali, Oshiakunu; N. NEY, op. cit., p. 150, on fine Boõ cloth; H. BRUNSCHWIG, *La négociation*, p. 34; H. LOIR, *Le tissage*, map IX, pp. 15, 57, 59–60, fig. 48. BONNAFÉ, notes that fibres were prepared among the Kukuya by the young people. It was possibly true for the Mbe and Nsah plains too.

all which was sixteen squares by ten.[16] The last two types were in use as forms of currency. Weavers were specialists and they sold cloth for other currencies, mainly copper or brass rods (*ngiele*).[17] Their cloth was much in demand in the Lower Congo and at the Pool so that in the 1880s many Sese and Jinju specialized in its fabrication to acquire currency. The product of this craft then was not merely destined for use in the circuit of subsistence, but primarily for use in the economics of exchange.[18]

The craft was less hereditary than smithing but it was so to some extent, because the skill was intricate and had to be learned and so usually younger brothers, sons, or nephews took over from their relative where they had first learned the job as an apprentice. They set themselves up when they knew the craft and, since there were no costly tools to be acquired as in smithing, this could happen whenever they were ready. Looms were the only machine the Tio knew and weavers were very proud of this. Even in 1963 one told me that his was a most difficult craft. For: 'if only one little part was missing in the whole, the loom could not work'. Which does show the appreciation that their instrument as a machine was different from any other the Tio knew. Being a weaver was an honoured occupation, less so perhaps than a smith but much more for instance than a potter or any other specialist.[19] It was also more of a part-time occupation than smithing. Cloth was thus stitched to other cloth and sewing was quite common. The men did this and sometimes used thorns but mostly well made needles with a flattened eye. The thread was often *kwoli*, a black thread growing in the crown of raphia trees or else raphia thread.[20]

Woodworkers all used the same tools: knives (*mbiele*), gouges (Sims: *musono*), chisels (*isoo*) (Sims: *isie*), and the adze (*nkiuere* or *ngwa*), which was their major tool. All men could carve a little and the fashioning of poles, beams, or the making of furniture with sticks and vines was done by all. Specialists were the makers of statuettes and others who made the wooden metate *ipo* to cut cassava. The latter also made grates, the little dugout troughs for dogs and a heavy smooth and

[16] Abili Ndiõ; H. LOIR, op. cit., p. 57, according to MAHIEU. In fact a *voro* amounted to four *ndzu a tieeri* or three *ndzu anna* was four times a *ndzu anna* and not only three times as Mahieu has it.

[17] Abili Ndiõ remembered only one in Abili. Earlier sources mention more.

[18] H. LOIR, op. cit., pp. 59, 60; H. BRUNSCHWIG, *Les cahiers*, p. 170: 'The people here (Sese) make much cloth of the country in which they trade. I saw bales packed in hide and prepared for porterage.'

[19] The cosmology attached to the loom and the weaver's craft which is told in A. MASSON DETOURBET, op. cit., could not be confirmed, and may well have been a construction made for her by the informant.

[20] L. GUIRAL, *Le Congo*, p. 265 fn., for needle and sewing. Sims: *ta* (throw) *iko*: 'to sew'. Later tailoring would be a craft of men who were weavers and sewers. Sims has also: *liwiu*: raphia thread (for sewing); *mukaru*: seam; *mbamo iko*: tailor; *bekero*; scissors. Those were certainly imported by Europeans after 1881.

round trough in which beer was brewed and which was also used as a cassava grinder. Boats were not made by the Tio but bought from outside. The other specialists carved only statuettes *itio* for the ancestors. In European eyes these were the only sculptors. For the Tio there was no difference, although they obviously appreciated and loved well-made statues.[21] But admiration did not carry over to the profession as a whole. Objects made by sculptors of both specializations were round or square stools for chiefs or the *mbara* backrest for chiefs or other people of prestige. Drums were made among the northern Sese, according to Ba. Elsewhere they were obtained by trade. As for mortars, it is not certain that any were used in the nineteenth century. Carving was not a prestigious occupation and in fact it constituted only a very temporary specialization. People learned it by trial and error and there was no apprenticeship or other formal training.

Every man could make simple mats by plaiting strand over strand with the fingers in sequences of 1/1, 3/1, 2/3; 3/2; 3/3 to the end where a hem was plaited. By using coloured strands designs could also be made ust as they could be made by jumping numbers of strand in the woof when passing the warp. The strands were made of marsh weeds and, for preference, out of papyrus *ndzubi*, of which the internal pale grey dermis was used. One obtained strands of an inch or more in width and seven to ten feet in length. Besides making mats such as the small *ikala* and the big *ngampa*, men also made the various traps and weirs. Still there were specialists in making mats. This time it was not because of the difficulty of the craft, as much as the fact that the marshes with papyrus were found near certain villages and not near others. In those settlements many men would take up plaiting as a spare time occupation.[22] Basket-making was much less tied to the presence of stands of papyrus, although some villages again seem to have produced more than others.[23] The most important products made were the carrying basket *mutete* (*otière*) with wide mesh, for carrying groundnuts on the head, later for tobacco and, with fine mesh, for all purposes; kitchen sieve (Sims: *musoo*), bag *mpari* (Sims: *mupaa*) for carrying, storage baskets *itunga* and the small *itutunga*, the big *imia* granaries for cassava, *olue* (Sims: *muluo*: fish-baskets) round working basket, its small

[21] R. HOTTOT, F. WILLETT, *Teke Fetishes*, discerned various styles in 1906 and the situation presupposed the existence of specialists everywhere. By 1963 only one sculptor was left at Poumako on the Mbe plateau and he worked for Europeans. The Tio made their *itio* themselves or bought them from Lari (Kongo). Still, they did appreciate art. e.g. One *itio* of exquisite quality could not be acquired in 1963 for any sum. Others were sold for low prices or, if old even given or thrown away.

[22] On mats cf. J. MAES, *La vannerie*. Among the Tio plaiting was done only by men (contrary to Maes) Calloc'h, p. 273 'natte' *i-kala*, generic term and a fine mat *li-bvu*, a small one *nkwali*(*ma*), or *ngampa*, a big one *i-mai*(*bi*). *Ikala* and *ngampa* are still used in 1963, the latter for better quality mats. Sims had only *tebe*; 'mat'.

[23] H. H. JOHNSTON, *The River Congo*, p. 148: 'basket work in all its stages is lying about' (at Mbila).

variants (Sims: *ililuo*), the true fishing baskets (Sims: *incano*) platters, *ituba* and general purpose baskets *itunga* and *itutunga* according to size.[24]

There were essentially two techniques in making baskets. The first was intertwining strands of bamboo as in plaiting mats and doing it over a frame of flexible twigs which was first built from the bottom up, variations in plaiting being used to produce decoration but also to help keep the shape of the basket at points of stress. The second basic technique consisted of making the bottom as before, but piling the bamboo strands one above the other, tying them together with raphia or other string often on a stiff frame.[25] In fact there were variations in the techniques according to the type of basket wanted. Stiffer wood for the frames, wider strands of bamboo or reeds, tighter or looser weaving, doubling, braiding were all used to best advantage. Decoration was common and executed either by variation in pattern or by weaving in coloured strands.[26] These were coloured like raphia thread. The Tio were exceptionally deft basket-makers and where other peoples would use objects in wood or leather, they made these in basketry whenever possible. Different types of baskets were often the speciality of particular men. It was, however, a specialization that seems to have been a minor occupation, to be done when there was time. In 1963 the specialists do not seem to have made more than about two specimens of baskets a month. This contrasted with the mat-making in which efforts were much more sustained. To acquire skill in basket-making was not so difficult and the craft was not hereditary but nevertheless, and unlike mat plaiting, it was definitely specialist's work.[27] Products were sold locally and information on media of exchange is lacking.

Practically no details about leather working are known. We do not even know if there was any specialization at all in the craft. Skins of wild animals and goats were cured (Sims: *yano*) by pegging them, stretched out in the sun, since that is the other meaning of *yano*. Skins were used for belts, as covers on wood sheaths of knives. Goat skins were used to sit on, iguana skins were wrapped around bows and whole—especially buffalo—skins also served for packaging raphia cloth.[28] Curing does not seem to have been very efficient and leather was not used extensively. It is probable that there were no specialists in this craft, but that all men cured a skin when they had hides. Products were probably not sold.

[24] J. MAES, *La vannerie*, Illustrations, pp. 13, 19, 25, including sieve. Sims has *munto* and *mbungi* as 'large baskets'. Note the two handled *ntsana* is post-1900 as are chairs.

[25] J. MAES, *La vannerie*, pp. 11–14, 20–2, on technique. The variety of techniques is not explained in detail anywhere.

[26] J. MAES, op. cit., p. 21, is very widespread.

[27] J. MAES, op. cit., p. 14, on decoration; TH. MASUI, *L'Etat Indépendant*, p. 81, says mats and baskets were much made at the Pool, but the frequency with which specialists worked or what their output was is unknown.

[28] H. BRUNSCHWIG, *Les cahiers*, p. 170.

In the nineteenth century the slavers knew the Tio as 'scratch faces' because of their beautiful facial scarification. These *ãncuo* (Sims: *anciu*) were cut by men on the face of all children of about two years old. This made them Tio and were thus a significant sign of personality as well as belonging to the group. Besides these there were other tattoos which were cut by women mostly on women at any time of life on the back or the chest. These were beauty marks. Called *njiele* (Sims: *anzele*), they took the forms of triangles with dots, lozenges, or exclamation marks. On the cheekbone one often carved a cross or a keloid in the form of a square dyed with the black colour *ndiõ*, which was known as *apopoo*. The keloid technique was to burn rubber, mix it with the ashes of the *owéia* plant, grind it, and put the mixture on the fresh cuts. The *ãncuo* and *apopoo* were free, but the *njiele* had to be paid for. What the women paid to the female specialist is unknown.[29]

Every man built his house, repaired it and built what was necessary for his wives. Most of the raw materials were carried to the spot by the man himself since perhaps only the ridge pole and the main uprights were too heavy to be carried alone. For these he had the help of his close relatives, fathers, brothers, or sons. The thatching grass (Sims: *ncelo*) was cut by the man or his wives and building itself could be done by one man. The sides were in fact basketry work in which the uprights were driven in the ground. Heavier poles were planted along the long sides. The semicircular roof was a frame covered with heavy layers of thatching grass. The only help needed was in planting the main posts. Still many men seem to have liked to work at their houses with someone else, to make the work go faster and have company. This work was strictly seasonal. For obvious reasons it could only be carried out during the dry seasons.[30]

Preparing and cooking food, like growing it, was women's work. This included the brewing of beer, but not the preparation of palm-wine *mali* (Sims: *malu*). Men climbed the tree (Sims: *ngoli*: 'fetters; tapster's rope'; *mpio* 'tapster's sling') to make the incision under the flower of the tree and hang the calabashes up. Or they collected the wine from felled trees. The wine was kept in calabashes and usually drunk the same day it was produced. But palm-trees were only well developed along the Congo river and the Pool. On the plains beer of maize, cassava and, it seems, sugar-cane wine replaced it. There was not much to the preparation of palm-wine, in sharp contrast to other food.

The major staple was cassava. The roots were brought to the soaking stations and in the *idzia* (Sims: *izia*). These were shallow pits, round

[29] One informant claimed that some had their *ãncuo* only cut after marriage, which seems scarcely believable, except possibly for girls. But it underlines the status value of the scarifications. On tattooing cf. TH. MENSE, *Anthropologie*, pp. 625–6 and fig. 1, p. 626; J. DYBOWSKI, *Le route*, fig. p. 53; D'UZES, *Le voyage*, p. 89.

[30] TH. MASUI, op. cit., p. 79, on houses.

and much narrower at the top than at the bottom. They were filled with a mixture of grass and mud made of sand to which some water was added. Once the cassava was put in them, the opening was closed with a stopper of grasses. A big *otiele* jar or a calabash could also be used for this purpose. The aim of this technique was to soak the cassava, using as little water as possible. It has been rightly cited as an outstanding example of the adaptation of the plains Tio to their environment.[31] After the soaking which lasted for a day or two, the roots were peeled, cut in big pieces and dried in the sun at the station. Then they were carried home where flour was made with them. First the pieces of cassava were cut in tiny pieces with a chopper, *ibieele*, a job which took a whole afternoon, and then it was ground into a fine white powder on the wooden metate *ipo* or on a stone metate *opioome* and *otaana*, which was a rare implement with a smooth uncut round pebble *obiooro* (Sims: *mucara*), or, lacking this, with a wooden cylinder *onkuli*. Occasionally the woman stopped grinding to chop recalcitrant pieces smaller until everything had become a fine flour (Sims: *ikele*). Often the flour was left for two days before it was ground again. Then it could be further prepared in two ways: in the form of porridge, by throwing flour into boiling water for two to three minutes, or by making cassava bread. For this it was kneaded with water into a loaf, wrapped in vine leaves and then cooked in a bain-marie, i.e. in the steam produced by a little water left at the bottom of the cooking pot. This produced the bread known on the river as *shikwange* (chicouangue) which could be kept three or four days and was therefore useful to fishermen and short distance traders. Other loaves were bigger, remained uncooked and could be kept for months, provided they were soaked regularly in water. These were only made at the Pool and on the upper Congo river. It was a Bobangi invention apparently and was the canned food of the long distance traders.[32] In fact Calloc'h pp. 160–1, recognized eight varieties of *shikwange*. Flour thrown for a few minutes into boiling water produced a sort of gruel (Sims: *itoo*; Abili ndiõ: *ito*) which was the standard dish.

This was sour and gluey and known as *bingolo*. A better preparation left air holes in it like Swiss cheese and that was *luku*. These could be consumed hot or cold. Other puddings and porridges, probably made

[31] G. SAUTTER, *Le plateau*, p. 110.

[32] E. DUPONT, *Lettres*, p. 199. Cf. G. SAUTTER in H. BRUNSCHWIG, *Brazza explorateur*, p. 138 fn. 2, and G. SAUTTER, *L'Atlantique*, I, pp. 272–3 for the 'canned food'; stone metate says Abili Ndiõ was *õpioonu* or *otaru*, the little stone *obioonu*. She contradicts Iyene who claimed these stones were still cut. For her only natural stones were used. Sims calls the small grinder *munsinsie*. Stone tools were important enough to be inherited; *on ipó* cf. H. BENTLEY, *Pioneering*, I, p. 334, who calls it a 'wooden trencher'. N. NEY, op. cit., gives clearly the three methods of preparation as listed by Jacques de Brazza: by *bainmarie*; like the Bobangi; as flour. Sims calls bread of cassava *intoo* (really a pudding) *lisoo* (really the root of the plant) and *ingwole*.

from cassava flour were listed by Sims as *kuli*, *mubala mpiño*, *mfuni*, and *tiere*.[33]

Maize was also ground to flour by the same method, but without chopping or soaking of course, and the resulting flour was called *mfumfu* (Sims). *Fufu* is the name now applied to cassava flour and the displacement of meaning confirms that the consumption of maize has indeed receded since the 1880s. The resulting gruel made with the flour was appreciated as a good food, fit for chiefs and kings and known as *oka* (Sims and Abili Ndiõ). But maize was also used to brew beer. It was poured into an *ipo* trough after the grains had sprouted and had been dried. After they had soaked in the *ipo* they were then crushed to flour or stamped in a big leather bag made from buffalo hide, sugar-cane was added for fermentation and the whole went back to the *ipo* or to great *otiele* jars which were then sealed as hermetically as possible so that the grain would ferment. After four to five days, the brew was filtered and ready for drinking.[34]

For each meal either maize or cassava was necessary. For at least one of the three meals[35] one added soup or vegetables. First palm-oil (Sims: *mali*), obtained by cooking and crushing the fruit, was added to the puddings or gruels. But there could be also fish or meat. There had to be vegetables in any case, possibly a stew of groundnuts, of which Sims lists two varieties *mokuru* and *imbwe*.[36] A broth made of palm-oil with doubtless some leaves added, perhaps calabash or gourdseeds, is also mentioned by Sims as *musoo*. The use of cassava tops as a vegetable with water or palm-oil, sorrel or other greens similarly prepared was a standard feature of the evening meal. All these plants were washed, sometimes plucked so the tenderest parts would be used. Then the leaves were chopped to pieces and grated before the tiny bits were cooked in water. The cooking pots, *ndzuu* had no lids. Two menus are reported from the 1880s. One consisted of cassava pudding in a ball, cassava leaves with water or palm-oil and sorrel, but that was said to be exceptional. The other describes a dish of smoked fish with cassava leaves, pimento, and cooked in palm-oil.[37] This was still a favourite recipe in 1963. Several ways to prepare groundnuts were used. They could be eaten raw, or they were sometimes roasted over the ashes of the fire in an old dish, with or without the shells. To cook them they

[33] H. H. JOHNSTON, *George Grenfell*, II, p. 149, on *luku*.

[34] H. BRUNSCHWIG, *La négociation*, p. 28, stresses the analogies with European beer; L. GUIRAL, *Le Congo*, pp. 242, 306; J. F. PAYEUR DIDELOT, *Trente mois*, p. 218. Sims: *ngingabu*, *ngangabu*: maize beer.

[35] Abili Ndiõ claimed that three meals (not two) were eaten at least since she was young and probably in this period.

[36] H. BRUNSCHWIG, *La négociation*, p. 28, on a snack of crushed *voandzea* or groundnuts, with chopped cassava toppings.

[37] Abili Ndiõ; CH. DE CHAVANNES, *Avec Brazza*, pp. 165–6; L. GUIRAL, *Le Congo*, p. 297.

were thrown, shell and all, into cold water and boiled. For another recipe the roasted and dried groundnuts were shelled and then ground to flour after which a little salt and cold water was added to obtain a sort of chocolate. All meat was prepared with oil first in a pot. When the oil had soaked the meat well, water was added and then the whole was boiled until the meat became tender. The water could be used as a broth. Meat was always dried before use and sometimes even smoked like fish. It was never roasted.

As well as maize beer and palm-wine, sugar-cane wine was also drunk and known as *ncuu*. It was extensively brewed on the left bank of the Congo river, especially north of the Kasai, but south of it as well. It remains unclear whether the Tio of the plains on the left bank produced it in appreciable quantities. A last drink is reported by Sims as 'malt': *nce*.[38]

Equipment for the kitchen comprised a variety of calabashes, baskets, and jars, as well as the grinding equipment in stone or wood. Grinding or crushing at the Pool was sometimes done with a pestle and mortar (Sims: *lipana*, *ilili*) but this was quite rare on the plains. Knives and bush-knives as well as wooden ladles or scoops (Sims: *liboo*, *ibiba*), pottery dishes, sieves of pottery or woven, and a winnowing comb (Sims: *sele*), used mainly for cassava and maize flour after it was ground and three ant-hills used as stones for the kitchen fire completed the equipment. Inland the pottery and the metal for all the iron tools had to be imported, while stone was very rare. No wonder then that in ordinary households metal, stone and pottery were replaced, whenever possible, by baskets and calabashes or wooden containers. The situation also shows that normal life was no longer possible in the autarchy of the household or even the village or neighbourhood. The domestic situation confirmed the situation in hunting and defence where the major weapon, the gun had also to be imported. But metal, pottery, and guns could last for a long time. This was not so with salt, which had to be imported from the coast or from the Kasai river since the Tio did not make it themselves any more. It was even more of a daily commodity than gunpowder, which was also consumed fairly quickly. Those products show that subsistence production was not a self sufficient system for all needs.

2. *The standard of living: basic consumption*

The basic needs of the Tio were dress, dwelling, and food. Their whole production was geared to satisfy these needs directly or indirectly. The concept of need is not used in an absolute or even in a biological sense but only implies that for the Tio these were necessities. Every person might expect to see these basic needs fulfilled. A decent living, a

[38] H. BRUNSCHWIG, *La négociation*, p. 38, for sugar-cane wine made by Mfunu. He mentions an item *ncheri*. Would it be 'malt': *nce* of Sims?

normal standard of living consisted of specified ways of dressing, living, and eating. Thus Tio needs were a direct expression of Tio values and needs dictated the chain of production and processing. So the whole economic system was geared to a value-system. That these needs were not biological necessities is obvious when dress is considered. For, most of the year, biology did not require any dress at all. Modesty required it and vanity added more. In addition there were cultural needs beyond the consumption of goods, such as the felt need for distractions in music, dancing, games-playing, which are discussed in the next section.

The essential dress for both sexes was a raphia wrapper knotted in front and held at the waist by a leather belt. Women brought their cloths up under their arms, covering the breasts and had no belts. Under the wrapper they wore a petticoat. In addition people sometimes wore lengths of cloth over their shoulders, especially in the colder dry season. Children were not clothed. The wrappers and other clothes varied according to occupation and wealth. Thus knee-long wrappers of raphia were used when going to the fields or hunting and women would either roll their long wrapper up around the middle or take off the kind of shawl they wore when it was colder. On holidays, men paraded with beautiful raphia wrappers with fringes at the edges of each row of pieces of cloth. These were soft as silk and square patterns of colours enlivened them. For chiefs, European blankets and yards of cotton cloth, linen, velvet, and even silk were already in use at the accession of Iloo. Thus when Brazza arrived on the Lefini he found that chief Ngampere wore a blue *molleton* cloth and had a red piece of serge as a shawl over his shoulders. By the later 1880s even the common people around the Pool wore mainly European cloth and had several pieces of it.[39] A large vocabulary designated the different types of imported cloth, the most prestigious of which was a red type of blanket called *ãkã* (Sims: woollen, blanketing). This was practically reserved for chiefs or wealthy men leading their own settlements. Even more prestigious were similar blankets with a design of a leopard, and better a lion, in a different colour. Most of those found their way to the king or at least to the five or six highest chiefs in the kingdom.

Social status in general was indicated by clothing. Maes reported in 1913 that the number of lengths of raphia cloth indicated the position. Slaves wore a small wrapper comprising two to three lengths, similar to the dress women wore when working on the fields. At home women wore a longer wrapper. For men dress was more ample and increased with their wealth or position so that a chief had a robe comprising

[39] H. BRUNSCHWIG, *Les cahiers*, p. 172. D'UZES, *Le Voyage*, p. 91 ill. 2, and p. 89 ill. Breasts are not covered and imported cloth is worn. P. AUGOUARD, *Voyage*, p. 140; *idem Le Congo*, p. 18, makes clear that the Tio did not usually wear European cloth, even in 1885.

forty-two pieces of cloth. And from the Kukuya it is known that their finest unrivalled raphia cloth was exported to the court of the king at Mbe.[40]

But the costume was only part of dressing. First the body was regularly anointed with camwood (*baphia nitida*) and palm-oil, the face was made beautiful by pulling out the hairs of eyebrows and even some of the eyelashes and by scarifications. The ethnic scarification was five or six shallow parallel lines drawn from the brows, down over the cheekbones to the chin; the other scarifications and keloids were only marks of beauty. The two upper front teeth were cut with a diagonal slant. The front and back of the female torso was also often decorated with scarifications.[41] White, yellow, red, brown, and black lines were drawn on faces and arms. The colours were obtained from camwood (red), lime, ochre, and charcoal. These were not idle coquetry but had a meaning. They were supposed to protect or heal people. Thus circles around the eyes were intended to help people see the invisible and were usually reserved for chiefs or *ngàà*. A striking example, probably an extravagant one of body-painting, was a woman wearing yellow on the right cheek, blue on the forehead, with one white eye, and the belly ornamented with many coloured circles.[42]

There were a variety of coiffures. For men it was regional. At the Pool the hair was tied into a bun (Calloc'h, p. 159, *i-mvu*). A wicker frame was hidden at the top of the head over which the bun was made. The hair was often pulled so strongly that a circular weal of flesh resulted. But near the temples the hair was left free and formed two points towards the eyes. One or two iron hairpins (Calloc'h, p. 206, *mu-ntuma*) could be worn. One variant, apparently for young, elegant men, was to divide the hair lengthwise in what Mgr. Augouard called slices of melon. The Boõ and Jinju men wore theirs like a rooster's crest (Calloc'h, p. 159, *mu-pani*), while at Mbe the fashion of the bun pre-

[40] On cloth: cf. CH. LIEBRECHTS, *Léopoldville*, p. 528; H. BRUNSCHWIG, *Les cahiers*, p. 169 and *idem*, *La négociation*, p. 46, where it is said women cover their breasts. In A. CHAPEAUX, *Le Congo*, p. 543 ill., has one woman covering her breasts and the other not; text p. 514, *La tribu Bateke*, ill. opp. p. 122 (man, woman, and baby), p. 122 gives size as about five feet by two; H. H. JOHNSTON, *River Congo*, pp. 136, 288 ill. of women. TH. MASUI, *L'état indepéndant*, p. 79; E. DUPONT, *Lettres*, p. 125; C. COQUILHAT, *Haut Congo*, p. 159; H. BENTLEY, *Pioneering*, I, p. 337; L. GUIRAL, *Le Congo*, p. 239; J. MAES, *Le tinage*, p. 104; P. BONNAFÉ; *Personal Communication*. For tattooing see p. 29 fn.

[41] On teeth: H. BRUNSCHWIG, *Les cahiers*, p. 167, with drawing; TH. MENSE, *Anthropologie*, p. 630. On anointing the body: L. GUIRAL, op. cit., p. 291, H. BENTLEY, op. cit., II, p. 18. On eyebrows: C. COQUILHAT, op. cit., p. 58; H. BENTLEY, *Pioneering*, II, p. 18; TH. MASUI, *L'ètat indepéndant*, p. 76.

[42] On colouring: TH. MASUI, *D'Anvers*, p. 172; H. H. JOHNSTON, *The River*, p. 128 (baby), pp. 152–4, 287; C. COQUILHAT, op. cit., p. 59; *La tribu*, p. 122; CH. DE MARTRIN DONOS, *Les Belges*, II, p. 18; H. BENTLEY, *Pioneering*, I, p. 342; H. BRUNSCHWIG, *Les cahiers*, p. 167; H. STANLEY, *The Congo*, I, p. 364; J. DYBOWSKY, *La route*, p. 62 (eyes of *ngàà*); R. BUETTNER, *Reisen*, p. 237 (*ngàà*).

vailed. Women had different and variable fashions. Hair frizzed and in 'rat's tails' is mentioned. Guiral says they made their hair white with ashes and made little pins with it and he saw a Jinju girl wearing a grass crown (Calloc'h, p. 171: *nkara*). With such hairstyles hats were never worn. In fact hats were insignia of authority and the term for political power in Tio as in Kongo is *mpu*, 'the hat'. They were skullcaps.[43] Ordinary people wore *ãkoo*, sombrero-like hats plaited in grasses.

Apart from political ornaments such as collars of office, jewellery usually consisted of arm-rings, ankle-rings, necklaces of beads in glass or not, and finger-rings. It was fashionable to let the little fingernail grow as long as possible. And men often wore a knife, axe, or a spear.[44] Men were most stylish at the Pool and Bentley remarked that dressing their hair, anointing their body with camwood and oil and completing their toilet, assisted by their wives, took a great deal of a man's working hours. Thus he rejoins Abili Ndiõ who remembered that in her youth 'all young men thought about was their toilet'.[45] It is also obvious from the descriptions that differences between wealthy and poor people showed up in clothing and jewellery. The latter was a certain sign of status, since it was included in the category of *unũ* or prestige items. Also remarkable is the fact that beads and pearls did not figure prominently in the costume, even at the Pool. Only the long hexagonal blue bead, *lie* (Sims: *lie*, long beads) which was worn under the chignon was prized. It was a mark of chieftainship until the market was flooded with cheap imitations in the 1880s.[46]

[43] CH. DE CHAVANNES, *Avec Brazza*, opp. p. 160, p. 161. TH. MASUI, *D'Anvers*, p. 61; C. COQUILHAT, op. cit., p. 59; H. H. JOHNSTON, op. cit., pp. 128, 152–4; H. H. JOHNSTON, *George Grenfell*, p. 585, No. 302, for a technical drawing of the bun. TH. MENSE, *Anthropologie*, pp. 625, 630, for the two men's styles at the Pool. H. STANLEY, op. cit., I, p. 364, mentions a crown worn on the head; cf. D'UZES, op. cit., pp. 89–90. A. MAURICE, *Stanley*, p. 94, for Augouard's description. Crest styles: R. HOTTOT, F. WILLETT, *Teke Fetishes*, p. 25, who mentions the two; H. BRUNSCHWIG, *Les cahiers*, p. 167 ('Le tortillon'). D'UZES, op. cit., p. 104. The only illustration in M. ALLAIN, *Encyclopédie*, II, p. 153, (Djambala) on female styles, cf. G. DYBOWSKY, op. cit., p. 53, fig. 19 with full description; L. GUIRAL, op. cit., pp. 240, 211; J. F. PAYEUR DIDELOT, op. cit., p. 217; H. H. JOHNSTON, *The River*, pp. 136, 288 ill. and text pp. 136, 152–4; *Tribu Bateke*, p. 42. Skullcaps are shown in DE CHAVANNES and another style is mentioned in H. STANLEY, *The Congo*, I, p. 297 'woollen' cap with decorative yellow, blue, and white woollen threads; This was also the style of NGOBILA at Mswata. Cf. CH. DE MARTRIN DONOS, *Les Belges*, II, p. 14 (ill.). N. NEY, op. cit., p. 358, ill. Calloc'h, pp. 159–60, did describe eight other styles, mostly for women.

[44] *Congo Illustré*, II, p. 285, II, 1893 opp. p. 110, for illustration of collar and finger ring; cf. H. STANLEY, *The Congo*, I, p. 364, for anklets and bracelets; H. BENTLEY, op. cit., I, p. 337, for anklets of iron and copper of Ngaliema; H. H. JOHNSTON, op. cit., pp. 152–4, for anklets and collars; C. COQUILHAT, op. cit., p. 59, for bracelets, beads, glass beads, and knives; A. CHAPEAUX, op. cit., p. 514, for all iron anklets.

[45] H. BENTLEY, op. cit., II, p. 18.

[46] ibid., II, pp. 20–1. Ngaliema even pawned his beautiful iron and copper anklets

Fig. 3
A Tio house of the 1880s

The houses were made of wood and grass and usually measured twenty feet in length by ten in width. They were built in a single dry season, but needed repairs every year. The door was on one of the short sides facing onto the courtyard. The roofs were ogival or semicircular. From a distance houses looked like covered wagons drawn up together around the courtyard like the spokes of a wheel. There were no compartments inside. Kitchens were separate, smaller houses, often part of the women's sleeping quarters, and boys had smaller sheds. Open sheds without walls were used for reception rooms by village leaders. All these constructions were simply frames of wood covered with thatching and walls woven like baskets over the frames with broader and longer types of grasses than those used for thatching the roofs. Occasionally a square house was mentioned.[47] Also on the Pool one

for these. Sims gives an extensive vocabulary about dress, jewellery, etc. The most interesting are: *saño saño*: 'loincloth with long fringe'; *iwini*: 'girdle, bracelet . . .'; *isisina*: 'purse'; *bibana*: 'sandals'; *(M)unkolo*: 'belt'; *za mulamo*: 'dress like Bobangi; tuck into girdle'. About jewellery: *wolo*: 'iron anklet'; *(M)unkara*: 'anklet'; and *nkanimali, iwoo*: 'bangle, heavy brass collar'; *ca*: 'bangle, bracelet'; *mulua*: 'bangle, bracelet'; *mulua akulu* or *mulua ikoro*: 'heavy brass collar'. This was the insignium of power. On care for the hair: *mukie*: 'hairdresser'; *isanu, iselo, nkala*: 'comb'; *ngouyili, ntuma*: 'hairpin' and *pfia*: 'hairpin, bone'; *ibara*: 'chignon' and *sura*: 'headdress'; '*bungaa*': 'headband' (Stanley's and Guiral's 'crowns'), *(M)uburu*: 'headdress, chaplet, waistband', obviously a band.

[47] H. H. JOHNSTON, *River Congo*, p. 151. NGANTSU'S village was built on piles; L. GUIRAL, op. cit., p. 294 drawing p. 228; E. ZORZI, op. cit., p. 387 with drawing; H. BRUNSCHWIG, *Les cahiers*, p. 172, for a square house; TH. MASUI, *L'Etat indepéndant*, p. 79. Note Sims *mvuno*: 'door', *inzinzo*: 'cupboard, hut, shelter'; *imia*: 'shed, boy's house, closet'; *(M)unkana*: 'shed, reception-room, kitchen, shelter, shed'; *ibvula* and *ifuri*: 'shed'; *isa nkana*: 'reception room or house'.

instance was reported where a house was screened off inside so that one third of it formed a separate room.[48] The furniture consisted of a bedstead with a wooden frame, with rope stretched across, anchored to the ground, on which matting and headrests were laid. People sat on mats or occasionally on the backrest and stool *mbara*. Cupboards did not exist but belongings were put on the ground or hung up from the walls in baskets or put on a shelf hung in the house above the hearth. A little table, like a raised bed was made for the altar of the shades and on or above it against the wall were found the charms of the house. A description of the king's own home according to Guiral gives a vivid picture of the inside of a home:

> Near the far end of the house and in a recess there stands a bed in front of which long European cloths hang, hiding it almost entirely. Near the bed, I noticed an oar decorated with copper; it was a trophy of the last war the Tio had fought against the Aban-Ho (Bobangi). The wealth of Mokoko is heaped in a corner of his house. There is a little of everything: cloth, European porcelain, collars made out of fifty or sixty little bells, several dane guns and the rifle which was presented the day before yesterday. The king keeps his precious objects (necklaces of beads, copper, etc.) in little wooden boxes decorated with cowries.[49]

Fires were made in the house, usually near the middle, but there was no chimney or any form of ventilation. This must have affected the eyes, especially when a company of people were gathered around the fire, smoking their pipes.[50] Women cleaned the hearth by removing the remaining charred bits of wood but left the ashes. Every day the house was swept clean with a broom by its owner and most dwellings were spotless except for the soot which deposited itself everywhere on the walls. This was not an unmitigated evil because it checked to some extent the multiplication of parasites and insects in the wall. From a functional point of view the houses were well adapted to the environment for they kept warm at night and were cool during the day-time. But they frequently needed repairs. Almost every year the thatching had to be redone and even the frame, attacked by termites and other pests lasted rarely for more than five to a maximum of ten years.

Sanitary installations are reported only by Brazza, who said that they consisted of a hole sunk in the houses. No one else reported it, neither

[48] H. BENTLEY, op. cit., I, p. 339.

[49] L. GUIRAL, *Le Congo*, pp. 294–5.

[50] Ill. of a bed N. NEY, op. cit., p. 372; ill of *mbara* backrest; H. H. JOHNSTON, op. cit., p. 295; H. BRUNSCHWIG, *La négociation*, p. 45; BENTLEY, op. cit., I, opp. p. 463, ill., II, p. 17 ill. On matting as furniture, H. BRUNSCHWIG, *Les cahiers*, p. 180; D. NEUVILLE, CH. BREARD, *Voyages*, pp. 265, 267; H. BENTLEY, op. cit., I, pp. 337, 339; Ngateo cited a sort of chair *ikola*, which may have been a round or square stool. Sims lists: *ntalu*: 'bedstead'; *mbara*: 'chair'; *likara* or *nkobi*: 'box'; *tebe*: 'mat'; *ikuoño*: 'brush, besom'.

foreigner nor Tio and it seems rather incredible. He also tells that there was a station for washing hands and face.[51] But this was probably located on one side of the threshold as it still was in 1963.

Around the house there were big jars for collecting the rain from the roofs. Eaves, held up by poles and made out of the inside of banana stems carried the water to these jars. Most houses had cleared courtyards at the front end and these too were kept clean. But at the sides and the back nothing was cleared or cleaned much. Dumping trash was usually not done there, but a little away in the vegetation beyond the back of the home. Hedges and fences were not used except around the compounds of the village leader, those of the chiefs and all the compounds at Mbe, the capital.[52] Fences were built like the walls of a house.

The possession of a compound was perhaps the only luxury powerful or wealthy men enjoyed over others. But one must remember that they had also one reception shed in addition to their dwelling and those of their women. Still differences in the standard of living between great men and small men were minimal. The Tio never developed a monumental architecture, not because they were not able to, but because they were not interested.

The major meal was eaten in the evening. In the morning and around noon people ate only what was left of the major meal, although most women would cook themselves a little snack around noon when they were in their fields. Beyond that at other times of the day snacks might be eaten.[53] Boys were trying to find fruits or edible things all day long. Men liked to drink palm-wine in the late morning and would ask for a snack at or after noon, if their wives were around. Men and women never ate together. In the evening when the food was ready everyone washed their hands and the wife would take the dinner out to her husband on pottery trays and little pots. They drank maize beer or wine with it according to season and supplies. As for the women they ate in their kitchen with their children. There were a variety of food preparations available, as is evident from the list of greens used as vegetables, but the basis of the meals varied rarely. On the plains it was not a usual occurrence to have smoked fish or meat. But something cooked in palm-oil went along with the main cassava or maize dish and greens had to be the third part of dinner. Food would vary by season according to the availability of maize and groundnuts versus cassava for the main dishes and also for the vegetables. Delicacies were prepared with groundnuts or *voandzea*, probably with the addition of

[51] H. BRUNSCHWIG, *Les cahiers*, p. 168; *idem*, *La négociation*, p. 50. The towel was made of banana fibre. The Tio say they also made it out of the *ntsana* plant. By 1960 no sanitary installations existed in any Tio dwelling.

[52] H. BRUNSCHWIG, *La négociation*, p. 22, for fences at Mbe.

[53] ibid., p. 50.

pimento, and bananas or plantains were in fact mostly consumed outside the evening meal. But the Tio cannot be said to have had a culinary culture.[54] They did not pay much attention to refinements as long as there was food and there was some variation.

Mighty men, especially chiefs dined together with their followers in their reception sheds or house and when they drank a complex ceremonial was observed. The latter was the major ordinary ceremony in which behaviour for chiefs differed from that of wealthy commoners. The latter had no drinking ceremonies, whereas the chief's etiquette was so organized that the exact status of each attendant to the ceremony was made clear.[55] Regarding food, however, the chief's table was not much better than that of one of his poor subjects, except perhaps that, because of the tribute on game, he enjoyed meat more often than others.

Food was then available in sufficient quantity. But, except for the riparian Tio, it was not balanced. Starchy foods formed the bulk of the diet and the preponderance of cassava was becoming disastrous. The men were slightly better off than women because they still had maize beer. Both enjoyed maize gruel from time to time but the cultivation of this crop was probably already diminishing, unbalancing nutrition even more. The greatest deficiency was of animal protein and, as has been said, no attempts were made to cope with it. Of course the Tio were ignorant of protein, but if they had been really interested in food, they would probably have translated their craving for meat or fish, which was genuine enough,[56] into a more balanced diet.

Men and women smoked or took tobacco as snuff. Commoners used short pipes either with pottery bowls and wooden stems or all in iron. Chiefs were proud of their five to six foot long pipes, sometimes with twin bowls and fashioned out of metal. Snuff was kept in little gourds or horns, hung from the belt. Tobacco was only cured by air and the leaves were then tied into ropes and left to dry out completely on the roofs of the houses. Hemp was smoked as well and the pipe often consisted of a gourd partially filled with water to cool and weaken the product.[57]

[54] There are no direct data available about recipes and culinary habits beyond the basics. But it is obvious that there was no true gastronomic attitude towards food. This did exist among certain peoples of Central Africa for instance among the Ntomba of Lake Leopold II.

[55] H. BRUNSCHWIG, *Les cahiers*, pp. 193–4, where the order of drinking and covering one's face or not is shown as very important.

[56] CH. DE CHAVANNES had been nicknamed *tara-niama* (father of meat) because he provided it and Malamine had ingratiated himself with the Tio chiefs mainly because he was an efficient hunter. All travellers reported the craving for meat of the Tio.

[57] Sims gives *kee* or *mfwaña* for 'tobacco to smoke' and *fuño* for 'snuff'. A snuffbox or horn was *ibibeo*; a pipe is called *mulii*, (now *key*) the bowl *mukoro* or (*M*)*unkoo*, also the name for a horn, its stem *muwubu* and the binding *ndaa*. On pipes and smoking: *Congo illustré*, 1893, opp. p. 110 ill. for a chief; A. CHAPEAUX, *Le Congo*, p. 543, for women smoking. On snuff H. STANLEY, *Dark Continent*, p. 536. Pipe bowls were found in

The greatest differences in the standard of living between people were seen in their personal appearance, in clothing and jewellery, thus the wealthy and the chiefs could show who they were. Beyond this, only the drinking ceremony and dining with followers were indications of status. The three situations stressed different aspects of social importance. The drinking ceremony rigidly indicated ascribed status, whereas appearance was a measure of achieved status. Since this stressed goods which were all foreign imports, wealth and wealth acquired in the market economy was thus stressed. As for the dinners, they indicated what the following of a person was and were a direct indication of power rather than wealth. The cultural choice of using only certain patterns of conspicuous consumption to stress status, implied that some things were important and others not, e.g. that the food one ate was unimportant but that it mattered who was there to eat it. In this way the social significance given to certain patterns of consumption intimately moulded the standard of living for the Tio.

3. *The uses of time: work*

Time is a commodity and its use is a consumption by itself. The various ways in which it is used are often classified as work or leisure. Although this distinction depends on the prevalent type of economy and one's theoretical stance, it is fruitful as long as the limitations are recognized and it has been adopted here.

Productive work is here defined as activity directed towards the production or processing of goods. It excludes services such as those rendered by religious or political specialists as well as by entertainers. It also excludes activities aimed in the first place at entertaining or relaxation. This view does not entirely agree with that of the Tio. For them *usala* (Sims: *sala*) meant according to Sims: 'work, labour, plant, clear away weeds' and *sala ifuna* was 'to clear a site'. Since then, the verb has been used for all activities which produce goods or payment if labour is hired, whereas it once meant 'to do agricultural work'.

The distribution of work entailed first a division within the household between boys, girls, men, and women. Women became responsible when they married, i.e. around twenty years of age and the same was true for men around thirty, maybe thirty-five years of age. Roughly, the division meant that women did the work on the *ncio* and the dawn-gardens, collected the vegetables, processed the food, cared for the babies, and cooked. Men made the *ngwuunu* fields, built and repaired

---

profusion on all recent or fairly recent sites of the Mbe plains. Cf. J. EMPHOUX, *Mafamba*. Hemp was smoked according to Sims: *zama* 'take hemp' (Calloc'h, p. 157: *dyamu*: 'chanvre') and the pipe for it *ntiba nzaña* or *ituri*. Valcke claimed it too. Cf. CH. DE MATRIN DONOS, *Les Belges*, II, pp. 73–4, calling it *iamba*, J. F. PAYEUR-DIDELOT, *Trent mois*, p. 222, denied this. Perhaps he was referring only to the western Teke or the Tege?

houses. Boys and young men were formerly warriors and hunters while unmarried girls helped their mothers by fetching firewood and water, tending younger children and working on the little gardens near the *idzia*. They also collected various insects. Men professed all specialties, with the exception of pottery. Finally older men and women who could no longer move so easily, stayed in the village. The older women did work around the kitchen and the dawn-gardens or looked after babies while the men kept an eye on the village and participated in village affairs. All men used much of their time to settle palavers of all sorts.

This distribution obviously shows an imbalance. Women were overworked from morning to nightfall and responsible for most of the production of food. They began early in life whereas men turned to agriculture only when past their youth. The result explains the bitterness of the women towards the men, especially the young men 'who cared only for their toilet', the frequent cases of exhaustion from overwork and undernourishment of the women, which were so well known that a special ritual or cure, *itsuua*, had been developed to cope with 'thin women', and partly the unsatisfactory nutritional situation. For maize was a product of the men's *ngwuunu*, whereas cassava came from the *ncio*.

Eleven months out of the year a woman's day began at around 7 a.m. with work in the fields until 12.30 p.m. They cooked and ate. After this there was work at the *idzia* or chopping cassava at home, getting water, and cooking the major evening meal, a job begun around 6 p.m., at dusk. Occasional afternoons had to be spent gathering wild greens and firewood. The major reserve of this was collected by them during the dry season. Men would bring some logs for their hearth, not for the kitchen. Married men with children left for the *ngwuunu* a little later than the women and came back only at 6 p.m., eating twice on the job. Then they did not do any more work at the village. But when it rained and on the official rest days (in some villages every other day), or in the dry season, they did not work on the fields. Women did not work in the fields every fourth day. The imbalance, as can be seen is not really so great between married men and women, when both went to the fields. It lies in the fact that the men went much less over the year and had less household chores.

Nor did men over the year and by taking specialties into account restore a balance with women. Most of the specialists had no *ngwuunu* or only small ones and, furthermore, there was no season in the year when men worked more than women. In August they were clearing the steppe for new fields and with the rains in September their agricultural year began in earnest. The last harvest of groundnuts and *voandzea* was only done by July. So they had about a month's respite from labour in the fields. But there was still cooking to be done and collecting as well as fishing took the place of agriculture. Men had no longer respite, for they began to cut the brush in July and clear their fields in September/October. They planted most of their crops (with the exception of tobacco) in November. Like the women they finished in July. But they had many more interruptions than women. The dry season saw them hunting, but this was mainly the communal hunt in which women participated too.

The flaw lay of course in the simple fact that men began to work the fields when they were almost middle aged, leaving the strongest part of the labour force, the young men, to be idle or to hunt, an occupation which did not give adequate returns for the investment of time it represented. Older men were not idle, because what time they did not use for agricultural labour they spent in activities necessary for the community or in work around the home that also had to be done.

The basic reason why young men were idle was that they were not held to be responsible persons until they married and they married late. This facilitated the practice of polygyny. Two major reasons can be given for the latter: the adequate spacing of births, of which the Tio apparently were aware and the economic usefulness of having wives, since they represented most of the economic output. A bachelor was miserable because he could not cook for himself and did not cultivate for himself. He had to scrounge where he could, with married friends or getting his pittance from a mother or sister. A man with one wife was always at the mercy of accidents, since she might fall ill, and often did. Who was then to continue with the fields, to provide food, etc? Or a woman might not have planted enough, or her harvest might have failed. Food could not be bought in the interior so a man had to receive it from friends in the same village or kin. For, as Abili Ndiõ said: 'One plants without calculating how much will be needed. Sometimes, there is too much, sometimes there is too little.' Having two wives equalized the production. It also made certain that when one wife was pregnant or had a small baby the work would still be done, because the other wife was bound not to be in the same condition, because of the spacing of births. Thus a sound economic case for polygyny can be made. Nevertheless, as a result, the whole food production process was left badly unadapted to the needs.

The rigidity of the sexual division of labour and the spatial separation involved also had effects on the household. There were in fact very few occupations both men and women could engage in. The rigidity of the separation helped to estrange husband and wife and this was emphasized by the fact that husbands and wives almost never saw each other. From early morning until dinner time they went their separate ways and did not eat together After dinner they might spend part of the evening talking if the man was monogamous. Otherwise custom dictated strictly which of his wives might spend the night with him.

Thus partly because of the division of labour the estrangement and even antagonism between spouses was increased.

Specialization of labour by craft because of skills was never total. A blacksmith never depended for his livelihood on selling his wares and buying his food. Food could not be bought and his smithing was marginal to the needs of his own household. The fields of his wives were more important and even his *ngwuunu*, if he had one, was more immediately relevant. No wonder then that no specialization, except that of chief, was a full-time occupation. They were all firmly embedded in the economics of subsistence. As for specialization due to the availability of raw materials in certain places only, the case of the mat-makers differs from that of the potters and fishermen. Plants for making mats were found in many more places and if they were not available second quality grasses could be used. In effect there was no great trade in these products beyond the neighbourhood, but there was in pottery and fish. Here specialization had clearly led to a strengthening of an economy of allocation involving marketing. With this exception however the organization of crafts confirms the analysis made of the economy as a closed system within households of polygynous or extended families and neighbourhoods.

As an occupation, rather than as a factor of production, work was one way of spending time, pleasant or not. For most women to go to the fields, hoeing, weeding, or harvesting was not much fun, but sitting near the *idzia* soaking cassava and peeling it, while gossiping with neighbours was much more pleasurable. Going to the river and bathing while fetching water and gossiping again in this little women's club was fun too. And similarly the work of men, girls, and older people had their satisfying moments as well as their hardships. As for young men, they were the only group to follow completely their inclinations with regard to their use of time. They only did what they liked and when they felt like it, whether it was work (hunting) or not, except in the emergency of war. For the others pleasure was only a very minor factor in their allocation of time to various activities. Nevertheless it remained a consumption of a commodity.

Beyond work, time had to be allotted for necessary social activities. Women raised babies, men sat in councils, in palavers, waged war, arranged marriages and funerals, and some administered their communities. Men cured some diseases and women others. Again, the amount of pleasure derived from these service activities was not very important in the decision as to how much time was to be allotted to them. They were a necessity and time had to be consumed for them. It is hard to assess the amount of time budgeted for this sort of activity. It was small for most women and highest for older people, women as well as men. This fitted in well with the fact that most of these activities involved little or no physical exertion. As for adult men, the proportion they devoted to this was, in 1963,[58] close to one fourth or one fifth of their time. Often they chose to carry out activities of this kind when it rained and they were confined to the village, or during the dry seasons when there seems to have been an increase in these activities.

4. *The uses of time: leisure*

After all the time for necessary activities had been deduced, there remained the portion that could be spent on leisure or physical relaxation. Some of this was not especially pleasant but again a necessity, such as sleeping. Leisure could be described as the activities whose main aim was not to produce goods, services, or physical relaxation, but to entertain. In daily life for adults the only time available for this purpose was in the evenings and it could be spent in games, dancing, singing, or simply watching the dancing and listening to the songs. For children there were games. Clowning was also done at dances or on special occasions.

A favourite game consisted in throwing four cowries three times in the air, playing heads or tails, while clicking the fingers when the cowries were in the air. If the slit side of the cowries showed in even numbers a point was made. It was a game of chance for adults, and was presumably played for small stakes, such as beads.[59] Another game, probably both for adults and children, consisted of making a hole in the ground with a little hole at the bottom of the first one, the threshold around the little hole being raised. The players threw two or three beads in the big hole as stakes. Then they rolled a big round bead. The aim was to let it roll round the threshold of the big hole, over the walls of the small hole and fall in. Players threw one after the other. It was not easy to aim, not only because of the threshold around the little hole, but also because the small beads often stopped the bigger one. Pecile termed it more a game of chance than of skill.[60] Then there was *inkeinke*, a game played on a board with twenty-four places, according to Sims. Known in 1963 as *isoli* the two players were seated across from each other and each commanded two rows of six holes. The aim was to capture the 'goats' of the opponent until he had lost all his tokens. It involved quick calculation and strategy.[61] Another game mentioned by Sims as *uculi* remains unknown. Yet another was a form of pitch and toss listed by Sims as *ta impene* or *zura impene*. For boys there was

[58] There were no direct data available from the period. It was perhaps greater then. The 1963 figure is also only an estimate.

[59] Miandoo and Sims confirms: *ta libee:* 'play pitch and toss' and the game of pitch and toss was called *libee*, which means 'cowry'! Calloc'h, p. 247: *li-bey*, *li-besi*.

[60] C. ZORZI, *Al Congo*, p. 427, Sims called it *ngaankee* or *ngaakula*, *kula*: 'to roll'. In 1963 the game was still played with a ball by children alone. Calloc'h, p. 247, *nganke*.

[61] A. CHAPEAUX, op. cit., p. 543, and calls it *isoro* (also illustration). *Inkeinke* probably has the same root as *ngaankee*; perhaps meaning 'token'.

wrestling (Sims: *ta intali*) and a kind of soccer game with a *kuli* ball (Sims: *ntila*) made out of the bark of a banana tree. It could be played with curved sticks and was thus more like hockey than soccer. Like wrestling it was mainly a game of physical strength.[62] There thus seem not to have been many games aimed especially at children, except perhaps a game with the hands while singing, Calloc'h p. 259, called *li-bwani*. Most of the time the young boys just ran around a lot, played at hunting or built small traps for bushrats or went fishing near the pond or river. Girls had not much time to play. They followed their mothers to the field and learned to farm very early. Young girls and boys did not play together.

Of the games which were remembered or mentioned in the literature most were games of chance. Skill was not very important and strategy appeared only in *isoli*. This predominance of games of chance, unusual for Central Africa, might be tied to the development of a market economy parallel to the subsistence economy.

The other regular distractions were the dances, organized in the evenings, when there was a relatively full moon. The young men came out, started beating the drums and began to sing, around a fire in a courtyard. The girls came, attracted as moths to a flame, and after the dancing was in full swing older adults would also come to watch more than to participate. Sims listed the dances: *(M)usii*, *ngasue*, *ngwane* (Calloc'h p. 247: *ngwani*: 'a game'), *impini*, *ikwene*, and *isiere*, which was a dance with knives, probably for men only. Calloc'h (p. 175) specified that *nkibi* was for men only, whereas *iya* involved both sexes. Most descriptions of dancing are of a general nature, one that is more elaborate is Pecile's:

> The only tamtam sounded and the dancers formed a circle. One of them left the circle and imitating a woman he began to turn around contortioning his body in the most provoking manner and doing as if he was lifting his skirt; he thus turned around the whole circle of dancers until he found one which pleased him, came near to him and they together did as if . . . Then the chosen person left the circle in his turn and played the same play. It seems that this figurative dance I saw done by men, is also done between men and women and that then happenings go beyond the limits of decency.[63]

Such clowning was indeed loved by the Tio, but was usually part of the dances performed during the day on festive occasions or at funerals.[64] Dancing was certainly accompanied by music and songs and it seems likely that steps, songs, and accompanying rhythms varied

[62] Miandoo said it was like soccer but Okondzaadza thought it was like hockey. Calloc'h, p. 247, mentions still other games *mpi*, and *ngaa*.

[63] E. ZORZI, op. cit., p. 392.

[64] *ta inkala:* 'to clown' according to Sims. Indeed this was still done in 1964 when at the funeral of a king's wife a few clowns performed contortions with great skill.

with fashion.[65] Steps for most dances at night were probably fairly simple with little aesthetic pretention.

The musical instruments for the orchestra included drums and trumpets made of the horns of *Tragelaphus gratus* and similar (*mvuli*) antelopes. Whistles, rattles, and iron clapperless bells, mostly single, but double bells when chiefs were present, were also used. Then there were hand-pianos (Calloc'h p. 272, *i-sanzi*; *ngere* was a bigger model) to be played alone with singing and no dancing, and what Sims calls 'concertina', *iyiño*, and which was probably *iõ* an orchestra of wind instruments, like those still found among the Kukuya. This was so closely related to singing that it has the same root as: 'to sing': *iõ* and singer or poet: *ndziõ*. The children moreover made trumpets from rolled up banana leaves.[66]

The instrument the ancestors were said to love most and certainly the one on which the melodies were best rendered was, however, never used in dances, but was confined to rituals. This was the *nguõ* (Sims: *nguomi*). It was always played alone to give according to one informant: 'slow and rather monotone melodies'[67] and according to Johnston 'melodies both quaint and touching'.[68] The instrument is a pluriarc with five strings attuned on what sounds to us like a pentatonic scale.

Most often the dancing was accompanied by drums and perhaps rattles alone. On one occasion, though, a whole orchestra was reported with drums, various sorts of trumpets and hand-pianos to accompany war dances where the warriors carried spears, shields, enormous knives, sabres, and quivers. The musicians wore feather hats and the chief was carried on the shoulders of a slave.[69] But such grand representations were not usual in every-day life.

[65] At Mbe in 1963 there were two 'societies'. The old men danced their dances and sang their songs: i.e. the ones their ancestors liked. CH. LIEBRECHTS, *Léopoldville*, p. 536. At every new moon and full moon people danced. All made wishes at the new moon not to be ill during the next month or not to be robbed when travelling, etc. The *nkibi* dance was imitated by certain statuettes. Cf. R. HOTTOT, F. WILLETT, op. cit., p. 28.

[66] H. H. JOHNSTON, op. cit., p. 297; CH. DE MARTRIN DONOS, op. cit., II, p. 290; TH. MASUI, *L'état indepéndant*, p. 82 (double bell). Sims notes *isanzi* '(hand piano) rattles': *ūciuciu, masamo, icaa*; 'trumpets in ivory' (*M*)*uñaa*, (*M*)*uñana*, 'traphelagus horn': *mvuli ambula* (not ivory as Sims claims) others *mubala, mfuño, mupari, iliri* and wooden trumpets *ipsara, nciño nganka* (*nciño*: whistle); drums *inzabaru, noma, nkunkuli, sima*, 'bell with clapper' *teño* (*tẽ*). One must add single bell *ba* and double bell *onku* to his list.

[67] *La musique*, p. 48, and also spoke of its 'often harmonious accents'.

[68] H. H. JOHNSTON, op. cit., p. 297 ill., and he speaks of 'real beauty of tone'. In 1963 Bilankwi among others was a virtuoso and the sound of the instrument was beautiful and haunting when played alone at night or during the curing of an illness. Cf. also J. MAES, *Les Lukombe*.

[69] CH. DE MARTRIN DONOS, op. cit., II, p. 290. The location was in Tio territory just north of the Lefini, but the description gives the impression of a Bobangi dance more than a Tio dance. These peoples borrowed a lot from each other.

When there was no dancing people stayed at home and told stories *nkõ* for children and grown-ups alike or people swapped proverbs. Some involved animals with the dwarf antelope *ntsee* playing the role of the trickster, some were hunting jokes. Some were believed to be true and were reminiscences about glorious and mighty chiefs, others were fictional and yet others were half true and half fictional. Very often a song, a saying, or a proverb formed the core of such stories.

Despite these distractions every-day life in the villages remained rather dull and people craved for something out of the ordinary. Spectacles of any sort were welcome. Thus a real element of entertainment was discernible (at least in 1963) at funerals, at marriage feasts and at more momentous occasions such as when medicine men drove the evil spirits out of the settlement in a grandiose and scaring hunt. The visit of a travelling troubadour or *ndziõ* (Sims: *nzima*, *nzini*) was common. These men[70] tried to find out where marriages or funerals were to be held, where palm-wine might be served on festive occasions, where their services would be in demand. Or a feast got under way simply because the troubadour was there![71] The drinking party of men (women discreetly invisible but within earshot) sat on mats, usually in the house and the troubadour would begin, encouraged by a small payment. He sang the praises of the chief, the head of the village, political titles if their owners were there, or about the men present. The greatest attraction was not the words but the song. Song is the highest art for the Tio and they sang well and often.[72] Troubadours used both head and chest voice and ornamented their melodies with intricate fioritura, thus allying complexity with beauty. They sang without any musical accompaniment. Still their texts were important to the persons who had invited them. For they were praise songs, listing their forefathers, the forests they came from, the titles associated with them and for each ascendant the exact relationship with the man honoured was quickly delivered *staccato* in between the melodies. Approval was greeted by clapping hands with extended fingers or by clicks. Disapproval took the form of grunts. The praises themselves (*ãmbili*, *ãntsili*) were very short, e.g. 'the breaker of skulls,

[70] Okondzaadza was a troubadour and son of a troubadour and the following is based on the description of his father's life. Confirmed by other informants too.

[71] Cf. for instance Sims: *lisoo*: 'marriage' and *za lisoo* 'have feasting and dancing together'. Since *za*: 'to eat', the connexion between marriage and feast is strong!

[72] Cf. Maalimwa who was our neighbour in 1963. She would sing by herself on all sorts of occasions and had a well trained voice. Yet she was not alone in Mbe. By 1963 the greatest pleasure of the Tio was to congregate around the radios when they were giving Tio troubadours' music. The singers, even from very far away were instantly recognized, criticized or extolled. Songs were very important to the Tio. To cure sick people, one had to sing because that would attract the ancestors and incite them to help. For special occasions there were special songs such as *kira*: a song of grief and *ikuña* for another type mentioned by Sims. Calloc'h, p. 157 has *bisima*: 'to sing for the wine'.

of the village of Ngwonkwaa's' referred to the great deeds of a warrior. It is clear that much of the enthusiasm for troubadours was directly linked with status and the competition between leaders, rather than to the purely aesthetic appeal of their singing. These men were specialists, who sold entertainment and glory to their consumers.[73]

Once in a while, in fact once a year at the capital and at irregular intervals at the residences of major chiefs, feasts were held during the day or several days. Drink and food were carefully prepared beforehand and everyone assembled on the village plaza to watch the dances, the clowning, the orchestra, and the singers. On these occasions people from villages all around the neighbourhood were gathered together and they spent much time gossiping, especially the women, and enjoying that just as much as the spectacle.

It is in the use of leisure time that the consumption aspect of the use of time is most apparent. As in feeding, housing, and clothing oneself, some uses were more approved of than others. For instance good singing by a troubadour was rated higher than any amount of dancing, and a rating by social significance tallies closely with the importance people attached to their entertainments. The biggest feasts were for kings, chiefs, or wealthy persons. *Nouveaux riches* such as Ngaliema in Kinshasa shot off pounds of precious gunpowder at the slightest occasion. The next class of entertainments were the praise singers who extolled status while performing stories. Clowning and dancing were more homely and more for adolescents and the young to whom routine was particularly dull.

But even in the choice of time for various occupations itself social significance dictated terms. Most of it went to work, answering the need for economic production. But not as much as economic policy would have liked. For of the four days in the week: *Odzuo*, *Okwe*, *Okila*, and Nkwé Mbali, the second and the last were days when agricultural work in the forest and the savannah was forbidden.[74] Nkwé Mbali was associated with the national spirit of the kingdom and the spirits of the dead. *Okwe* seems to have had a connexion with the leaders of the village.

[73] Not infrequently at courts and chief's villages or even at feasts there was competition between different troubadours. For an art which extolled competition this was only fair. Payment of the troubadour was given first in beer and then in 'gifts', not in currency. Those gifts were items such as raphia, bracelets, or pipes.

Another category of entertainers at great feast were the snake-charmers. All we know about them is they rubbed leaves in cuts of their hands as a serum against snake bites, that when they went to catch snakes they were never to shout and that when they had finished with a performing snake, it should be killed for fear it might bite people.

[74] CH. LIEBRECHTS, *Léopoldville*, p. 536, says that they had every fourth day off. Sims gives the days as *uzuo*, *ukweo*, *mukila* . . . but no fourth day. Calloc'h gives the Fumu days p. 262, under 'marché': *Mpika*, *Bu-dzuga*, *Bu-kweo*, *Mu-kila*. The Fumu had markets but the other Tio had none and the week was not tied to marketing institutions.

After the amount of time devoted to work most of the remainder was spent in activities of direct social importance and only the smallest share went to the most pleasurable occupation, entertainment. The uses of time thus confirm the pre-eminence of social needs and interests over economic or psychological necessities, which has been argued in the previous section. At the same time they show that time was an item of consumption.

5. *Conclusions*

The subsistence economics of the Tio contained several contradictions. On the one hand the Tio knew their environment admirably well. There was a remarkable ingenuity in adapting to it as is illustrated by the *idzia* to catch rain, the use of eaves and jars to collect rainwater and the ability to sink wells, or again by their uses of so many plants and animals and an agriculture that was loath to abandon any cultigen. Yet the Tio had not adapted fully to this environment. The most conspicuous failure was to obtain a balanced diet from it, which was due to the inequality of work-loads between men and women, young and old. In the most uneconomical way the heaviest burdens were laid on the physically weaker persons and on one sex rather than the other. Youth did not replace its lack of participation in production by other pursuits, even though most of the burden of carrying on vendettas and war fell on them.

The reasons for this situation were all social. It was the late age of marriage for men, in fact the desire to see the polygynous household as the basic residential grouping of producers and consumers that led to this situation. It may be added that technical activities did not create more than transient social groupings in themselves: the friends who went hunting together or the women who had their *idzia* near others were not groupings of significance. In addition the economics of the plains were basically subsistence economics. The producers consumed their produce yet were not self-sufficient. They depended on imports not only for trifles but important things like guns and gunpowder to hunt, salt to eat, boats to fish in, all their pottery, their raw iron, and many of their finished iron implements. This was the consequence of an historical evolution which had led to the development of a trading economy on the Pool, at the king's residence and those of the chiefs and all along the Congo river. The economics of subsistence on the plains were not the only economics. Indeed at the Pool where there was no cultivation at all, market economics were dominant. But nevertheless the small scale society on the plains stubbornly resisted converting to market economy in fundamental ways. It never allowed the sale of food for instance.

The relations between subsistence economics and social institutions were not all one way. Social values determined the consumption patterns and especially favoured those which allowed status to be expressed in its various forms. Cultural preferences, e.g. in fashions or art or etiquette also moulded demand. Production too was affected by non-economic considerations. Hunting thus played far too big a part in the system, perhaps because it too had been singled out to express status and political rights. But culture and society were affected by outside factors too. The low density of the country afforded precisely the opportunity for men to be in competition, for land was plentiful and free and losers could get out when they wanted to. The inequality of their burdens exacerbated the relations between the sexes which led almost to two sub-cultures: one for men and one for women. And finally the market economy had a profound impact on the political system and leadership patterns, that ultimately affected the small scale society as well.

Still at the level of the small scale society the corresponding economic organization was subsistence. The most remarkable fact here was the lack of close integration between social pursuits and economic necessity which produced some of the unpleasant stresses, such as malnutrition and quarrels between spouses, which plagued this way of life.

Chapter VII
Fortune and Misfortune

IN order to function, a society needs more than social groups with their norms and the economics of subsistence to support its members. For people fall ill and from the point of view of society must be cured to be useful once more. Since there is reason to believe that many Tio fell ill, the institutions which catered for the sick are significant. From the point of view of the individual they are even more so. The Tio did not resign themselves to accept illness, accidents, and death as a normal part of life. For them the ideal state of man was a blissful condition called *ngolo* (Sims: 'powerful, vigorous') in which good fortune favoured man and where calamities were unknown.[1] Happiness was striving for a better lot and such striving was grounded on belief in the efficiency of the religious specialists, called *ngàà,* the diviners and the healers (Sims: *ngaa*; 'medicine man, doctor').

Misfortune was due to ever-present evil and just as one had to cultivate constantly to obtain food, one had to fight evil to survive. Evil was always the work of witches and it was fought by the diviners who diagnosed, the cause of illness and death, and the healers, who could be the same persons, to cure diseases. Healers were also often medicine men who made charms to increase the good fortune of a person, in hunting, fishing, agriculture, love, the pursuit of wealth, etc. Diviners and healers were not the only religious specialists, however, since every chief of the land had his organization to care for the nature-spirit of his chiefdom. Since these occupations are tied up so much with political affairs their discussion must be left aside for now. Topics to be broached here are the causes of evil, divination, curing, and making charms, and finally the process by which people became *ngàà.*

1. *The causes of evil*

There were in the supernatural world, spirits similar to *ikwii,* called *apfu.* These were believed responsible for evil. Unlike nature spirits (*nkira*), which with few exceptions were restricted to a given area, they could roam everywhere. *Apfu* had a human-like temperament and a sex but unlike *ikwii* they were faceless: they had no name, they were no person anyone had ever known on earth. For Sims *mupfu* was a 'ghost,

[1] P. BONNAFÉ, *Un aspect,* p. 106, compares the related Kukuya concept *mpolo* to the Renaissance conception of Fortune. *Ngolo* and *mpolo* means 'health, good fortune, peace, strength'.

corpse', for Calloc'h (p. 186), who translated evil in Christian terms, they were 'devils'. The term has an identical root with *li-pfu* 'death' (Calloc'h, p. 176) and is the plural of 'corpse' (Calloc'h, pp. 179, 149; Sims) or 'ghost' (Calloc'h, p. 214). At one time no doubt it meant 'ancestor'. Interesting is its relation to *i-pfu* (Calloc'h, p. 241): 'inclination, disposition for goodness or badness', and 'temperament' (Calloc'h, p. 331). The Tio made a distinction in 1963 between the *apfu* which helped the diviners and healers which were 'good', as opposed to the *apfu* who helped witches and were 'bad', and the position was ambiguous. In fact the beliefs of practising *ngàà* about *apfu* varied from person to person beyond what has been stated.[2] In any given situation people knew what were *apfu* and what not. *Apfu* were to be detected during witch hunts and *ngàà* possessed them. The belief was clearly subordinated to the ritual in context.

Sorcerers or witches—no distinction was made—the *ngeiloolo* 'owners of witchcraft'[3] made people ill and finally killed them. The power of witchcraft required two elements: first the witch needed the *ifi* or *impfiri*, an organ by which he could operate. This was usually the stomach (Sims: *ifi*: 'paunch, gizzard'; Calloc'h, p. 208: *i-fi*: 'stomach')[4] or rather something in the stomach. But Bilankwi asserted that it could also be in the liver, the pancreas, or the thick of the calf. Without *ifi*, even though a person might be very jealous of someone else, he could not bewitch him. One was thus born a witch, for as well as other people, Nzã the creator, had made witches, mostly men but women also. Still there were people who had *ifi* and were not witches, perhaps because Nzã wished it. Those who were to be witches would start practising when young on animals, such as fowls, first; when they were grown up, they could attack people. The other necessary thing was to have *apfu*. A child witch could not really operate because it had not yet acquired *apfu*. How witches acquired *apfu* was said to be unknown.

All serious illness and all deaths were in practice attributed to witchcraft.[5] Witchcraft was the ultimate cause. Thus in 1963 Likubi explained that even accidents were due to witches: 'Even if one rode a bicycle for the first time and one fell and killed oneself it was the work of witches; white people also must have witches, whatever they say. For

[2] Cf. Chapter IX for details.

[3] *Iloolo* reduplicated stem iloo from *loo*: 'to bewitch'. Cf. Sims: *ngailoolo*: 'possessed by evil spirit'; *muloo*: 'wizard, devil, cannibal' (cannibal because witches 'eat', i.e. destroy people); *loo*: 'bewitch'; Calloc'h, p. 260: *ilo*: 'maléfice', 'donner maléfice': *loo ilo*; also p. 326, 'sorcier': *mu-logi, ngaa bi-toli*; 'sort': *i-lô̧go, i-toli*; 'jeter un sort': *logo ilõgo, loo iloo*. The variant of Sims (*M*)*unkebe*: 'witchcraft' may be Bobangi.

[4] Sims who was a physician has *mupaa*: 'stomach' but note Calloc'h, p. 326: 'sorcellerie'; *imfiri*; Sims: *imfiri*: 'covetousness, avarice, a pinch' may be the same word. Cf. E. COART, A. DE HAULLEVILLE, *La religion*, p. 165, says that the Tio call *likundu* (witchcraft substance in Lingala) *olaghi*. It is located under the heart where it produces a fleshy protuberance.

[5] TH. MASUI, *L'état indepéndant*, p. 82.

else, why would they die?' Ba, who was older, stated that in former days too death was attributed to witchcraft. They said sometimes: 'He died because he was old. But the kinsmen would not say that. They would look for the witch. They would have an idea as to whom it was, but would not state their suspicion. They might even not go to the diviner to find out for certain, when it was feared to be a close member, such as a *nnaana* perhaps.'

Ba certainly put his finger on the important phenomenon. Deaths were felt to be attacks on the kin and residential groups to which the deceased belonged and concerned only them. Others might poohpooh the affair but they had to defend themselves against the witches of their enemies or disappear one after the other. And since witches were evil in the sense that they killed people who had never harmed them in any way, blameless innocent persons, no responsibility could fall on the survivors. At the same time the absolute nature of evil and misfortune was established.

That absolute evil was shown in the fact that one of the favourite gambits of witches was to profit from the slightest dissension between members of a social group to attack a person involved so that the responsibility would fall on the other party. This ploy meant that people should do all they could to live harmoniously in their social groups and often deterred them from dissent. The evil of witchcraft was also shown however by the fact that witches attacked above all people in their own *ibuuru* and especially their own matrilineage. In fact all witches, said Ngateo, began within their own extended families, but if the men in the kinship groups proved to be too well armed against witchcraft they would turn elsewhere. Favourite victims were the small children of one's own sister, which obviously translates the tensions within the *ndzo*.

Accusations of witchcraft themselves whether founded or not, were a most potent weapon to destroy enemies. Since all leaders and chiefs as well as all *ngàà* had mysterious powers to stop witches, some believed that they had to be witches themselves. For the *ngàà*, Mbiinu mbiinu, a *ngàà* himself, thought that *ngàà* probably held their power from the *ikwii* of the persons they had first killed as witches and turned these *ikwii* into his *apfu*. As for chiefs, all Tio believed that when the king was introduced he had to kill twelve people by witchcraft to find the strength to rule. And how much more was this suspected of successful leaders? The latter even claimed to be witches in an indirect sort of way as Ngaliema did when he retorted: 'If I have a knowledge of witchcraft in my heart, who can take it out?'[6] No wonder then that such accusations against political enemies were always believable. They could only be efficiently answered by drinking the poison ordeal *nkei*, but that implied an even risk of death. A leader could also flee and thus hand his group over to his rival, and competition for leadership being as fierce

[6] H. BENTLEY, *Pioneering*, I, p. 346.

as it was, these accusations became a major weapon. On the other hand, even if the situation was calm, every death would arouse suspicion and thus create tensions in the social or political groups concerned. The beliefs made practically certain therefore that there were always tensions.

In practice, whenever a person fell ill, his kin were summoned on both sides to a ritual meeting or conjuration called *okuu* to solemnly disclaim responsibility or to swear that they would desist. If that did not help, or even before, a *ngàà* was sent for to detect the witch and attack him with his own *apfu* or make a bargain with the *apfu* of the witch so that they would desist.

When a witch was detected and killed by the poison ordeal he was thrown into the bush or the river but his *ifi* was cut out and hung in a tree for all to see. It was so evil that flies would not touch it. The poison ordeal succeeded every time in killing a witch, except when the *impfiri* was located in the calf of the leg. One could thus accuse anyone who had survived the test again and then the poison would be put on the person's calf. If he was guilty he would die. In practice it meant that persons who had survived the test were given a clean bill of health and probably for a long time.

In this whole context the role of *ngàà* was awesome.[7] For not only was their responsibility to heal, but they first had to divine and in case of death to accuse. Their power nevertheless remained limited because their own position was ambiguous because of the presence of social leaders and political authorities, but perhaps most because of their own numbers. No settlement was left without at least a minor *ngàà* and in Mbe in 1963 every leader was a *ngàà* in addition to several other men and women. For, there were many gradations in the craft, and many tried their hand at a bit of curing and perhaps divining.

2. *Diviners*

The Tio opposed diviners *ngàà vaa*, *ngàà bwaa*, or *ngàà waa ngoonani* (Sims: *ngààbwaa*: doctor) to healers: *ngàà waa libuu* (Sims: *buo*: 'to doctor'). According to the technique they used several sorts of diviners were recognized. There were those who (i) looked into water or into a mirror and saw the face of the person responsible for the misfortune; there were (ii) the *ngàà mpiaari*, (iii) the *ngàà mbulu*, owners of the *mbulu* or jackal skin who used trance, the diviners who used (iv) dreams, and those who operated with (v) a charm *kaa*. Among them were the most powerful personalities as Dupont noted: 'They designate the culprits and exercise an influence over internal affairs.'[8]

[7] E. ZORZI, *Al Congo*, p. 230 'The medicine man can by means of rituals based on deviousness and charms kill a man, find a thief, find a supposed poisoner. They are believed (the *ngàà*) and much feared, for they know poison well.'

[8] E. DUPONT, *Lettres du Congo*, p. 212.

1. *Divining by looking into water or into a mirror.* These specialists used the reflexion (Sims: *izilazili*: 'shining, reflexion' or shadow *ijilajili*; Calloc'h: *i-dzil'adzili*, p. 279: *ombre d'un corps*) a person left invisibly on the surface of the water in a pot, or on a mirror (Sims: *izili*: 'mirror'). By 1880 there were certainly not many mirrors in the country and since this was the technique *par excellence* of the *vàà*, troughs filled with water were used most frequently. As mirrors arrived in sufficient quantity they were used instead and the name of the mirror clearly shows its relation with the word for shadow. The pot or mirror was seen as a huge charm of the *kaa* variety. The client told his case, the diviner looked into the mirror or into the water and in the latter case he threw either *imbul'ngwo*, small seeds like a coffee bean, or old palm kernels in the fluid to watch their movement in the trough. From these he saw what the cause of an illness was and told the client.

With a mirror the *ngàà* often began by putting white and red stripes of earth on each side of his eyes and a large spot on his forehead. He took the mirror and put it on to his magical bag *pfuura*; he then shook his *õtsara* rattle, looked, and told the client what happened. The colours were to enable him to see into the unknown and with the rattle he called the *ikwii* or *apfu* to assist him.

Once the client had been told, both he and the diviner snapped their fingers and the *ngàà* gave his prescription. If it seemed a serious, almost desperate case he would advise that an inquest *okuu* be held; if not, the *ngàà* would indicate a healer and if it was a case for the ritual *itsuua*, he would say so. Sometimes he prescribed himself to drink this or that drug *imiõ*, especially an infusion *itiéé*. But he could not give him proof of divination or *ampia*.

2. The *ngàmpiaari* (Sims: *ngaampiaru*: 'witch, doctor, diviner'). The diviner received the necessary information from the client, then rubbed some of the drug *mpiaari* into his hands and spat some chewed pimento and peanuts on to it, after which he started reciting a list of suspects while rubbing his hands. When he arrived at the name of the party responsible for the illness his hands would cross, but before he came to it he would question the oracle of his own hands about particulars which narrowed down the field of suspects. Then each time his hands crossed the answer was positive. If the *ngàà* then named the culprit, which was rare, he gave the client no proof or *ampià*. If not, he would give *ampià*.

The technique was based on the *mpiaari* drug. When the diviner swallowed it, he had to be nude and alone. The charm would work only if it was addressed before each operation by such words as: 'Here is the wealth (money), here is the case' (then follows the exposition of the case). A good diviner asked his questions several times over to be certain.

Even though he might refrain from naming him, the *ngàmpiaari* described him in such a fashion as to leave the client in little doubt. Once the latter knew the identity of the supposed culprit he went to find a hunter with the information. The hunter then told his gun: 'If X is guilty, the animal at which I shall aim, will be hit; if not, it will escape unhurt.' Were the animal to be killed he would give the hoof or *ĩkwa* as proof or *ampia* the client could exhibit when he lodged a formal complaint. When there were four or five *ĩkwa*, they went to the suspect and gave the *ampià*. The suspect went to the chief who sent suspect, accuser, and witness to a great *ngambulu* who would divine and reveal the name in public saying: 'X, you are a witch.' As soon as the *ngambulu* named another person than the suspect, the latter was acquitted forthwith and the accused had to pay a fine. If not the accused could request the poison ordeal. The whole procedure apparently existed in the 1880s since Sims gives also *ngaambiu*: 'hunter, one who foretells matters of sport'. Rather than a tipster, it is probably the hunter described by the Mbe informants in this procedure. The word certainly means hunter (Sims: *mbiu*, 'hunt, stalk') and someone tried to tell Sims how hunters collected *ĩkwa*.

3. *ngambulu* (Calloc'h, p. 190, *mpolo*: 'divination'). A *vàà* who owned a jackal (*mbulu*) skin could use the mirror technique, but often preferred the trance. He talked and sang to his bag of jackal skin and sometimes he danced. Singing, he might break into a recitative and suddenly mention names. He then opened his bag, sniffed his *õtsara* rattle to call the *apfu*, sang, and spoke again. When he had finished singing, he no longer recalled what he had said, so it was up to the client to catch the name or the names when they were uttered. The *vàà* had been a medium for a message from the *apfu*. Some *vàà* could remain conscious nevertheless and were able to explain after the consultation what had happened and who the witch was. This form of divination could only be done with a *mbulu* (jackal) or *ndzùbì* (mongoose) bag and was the most important of all divinations since courts used it as a check. The payment for the operation was designated by the special name *õsul avàà*.

4. *Dreaming*, *ulwooro* (Sims: *Luoro nzoli*: 'dream'). The diviner simply placed his charm *kaa*, his medicine bag *pfura* or the charms called *ãti* near his bed and dreamt during the night. It is this technique which De Chavannes mentioned as a usual one and he added that the suspect was then killed without further ado.[9] The *vàà mbulu* never used this technique and the *ngàà* who did could not give proof. The technique worked, it was believed, because of the efficacy of the charms used. Many Tio did dream about such situations anyway, especially in connexion with their own departed, their *ikwii*, so it may have been a widespread home remedy. The consensus in 1963 seemed to be though that such an accusation could not entail the immediate killing of the accused, and De Chavannes who heard about such cases after long delays may have been mistaken

[9] CH. DE CHAVANNES, *Avec Brazza*, pp. 235–6.

in the procedure. An advantage of the *ngàà* over other people was that he could cure at the same time. His dream would tell him what drugs to use or he could send his *apfu* to the *apfu* of the witch to argue the case and, adds Ngateo, also a former *ngàà*, 'if Nzâ allows it, you will heal'.

A variant of this would make use of a statuette *itio*, like an ancestor statue but filled with earth from the grave of the *ikwii* of the *ngàà* from whom it was bought. The client told his case, paid, and *ngàà* dreamt with the statuette next to his bed. He would then know if the patient would recover or not, but he could not indicate the witch. To confirm the diagnosis the client then went to a hunter and if the patient was to recover, the hunter would miss his prey and give *ĩkwa* as proof. Ubwoono who practised this art in the past added that the *ngàà* sang, clicked his tongue to call the *ikwii* and invoked the *nkira* or nature-spirits (of the domain presumably) before he went to sleep. Mbali added that a *ngàà* held the statue, put ashes around the eyes (to see the unseen) held the *õtsara* rattle to call the *ikwii*, held also a leaf *andzo ankwei*, a sort of fern, and looked at the statuette. This would gain power of encouragement from the rattle. Sometimes the statuette trembled, the *ngàà* also. These statuettes were very small and called therefore *ititĩõ*. The *ngàà* would then not sleep but speak with a high-pitched voice according to his statuette. Some of these did not speak at all, and divination went by dreams. Both techniques, the trance and the dream, said Mbali, existed 'since he was born'.

5. With *kaa*. The charm *kaa* was put on the ground facing two objects. The diviner heard the case, addressed his *kaa*, told him that he had been paid and added: 'If X is a witch go to object one, if not, go to object two.' He shook his *õtsara* and held the *kaa* in the hand. It would drag him to one of the two objects. A set of questions and answers revealed the complete explanation. Okondzaadza who explained this technique in 1964 used *kaa*. He claimed that certain days it might not work because the *apfu* of the *kaa* were too tired. If it worked the *kaa* moved in his hand. He would first find out if the patient was to recover or not before trying to establish guilt. Once he found that party he described it in general. His diagnosis also remained general: it was an illness or a case for *itsuua* treatment. One of Okondzaadza's patrons told us that he began by going to the patient's hut and coughing very loudly. He then set his *kaa* to work. The result of the consultation was that the patient would not really recover, but would not die. Two *apfu*, i.e. *ikwii*, that of the father's father and the one of the mother's mother of the patient, had 'attached him' for reasons unknown. Since the diviner did not discover what the negligence of the patient towards these shades had been, nor how to atone for it, the consultation remained incomplete. Although the case dated from 1964 it is clear that divining in the 1880s must have proceeded in such a general fashion, although the

method of the *kaa* itself is not reported for that period, Sims has *ta bwaa*: 'use charms to discover a witch'.

The *kaa*'s avoidances had to be honoured if it were to work. They were to avoid taking a stick from the fire as a torch for lighting or to keep water in the house all night. Anyone could become a *ngàà* by buying the charm. The instructor would tell the buyer if they had to paint their faces or not and in what colours. The *kaa* could not be operated at night. It had to be offered something, usually kola, and it operated with a simple formula such as: 'Here is the money (wealth) and the case is . . .' The *kaa* could be used for dream divination like the statuette in the previous technique.

Sometimes the *kaa* did not function properly. In which case it had to be returned to the instructor who would settle the matter. One would also always send it back when, as sometimes happened, it made an error. For the *kaa* one did not give proof *ampia*. After it the proof by hunting *ĩkwa* was usual. With this technique the name of the witch could not be revealed to the patient either. The technique was used in cases of witchcraft or for theft but not, for instance, for adultery which was so serious a matter and potentially so full of trouble that only a poison oracle or the so-called *lindaa* oracle could settle it.

For some occasions, such as theft, other ways of divining still existed. For instance, to discover a thief divination by rain could be practised. Anyone having a rain charm could say of an approaching rainstorm: 'If X stole the goods it will rain, if not the rain will go away.' Perhaps the friction board oracle may have been in use too in the 1880s but the Tio did not claim to have seen it in 1963 although they had heard of it, perhaps in the city.

In fact divination seems to have concentrated only on finding out witches by the techniques mentioned, adulterers, and on occasion thieves. Theft at the commercial centre of the Pool must have been considerable since Sims has an unusual number of expressions dealing with it. It was of course a sign of the commercial economy and it is not surprising that in addition to general divining, special milder and quicker forms of divination existed to deal with the problem.[10]

It is obvious that the techniques described corresponded to several levels of divination. In general all diviners attempted to diagnose an illness and to tell a patron what to do. In addition most would add something about the cause of the illness which was attributed either to

[10] *yalo mibi*: 'cause a thief to be known'; *bwaa uta*: 'to find out a thief'; *ta mukwiu*: 'divine, find out a person who stole or who made another one sick'; and *mukiu*: 'oath' and 'to swear an oath', *loo mukiu* which seems to indicate that oaths were also used to designate thieves. The verbs *ta* and *loo* are 'to throw' and 'to bewitch'. Cf. also *loo kwani*: 'revenge, work a charm (*kwani?*) for detection of a thief, etc.'; perhaps using a technique with a *kaa* charm called *kwani*? Also *kene mibi*: 'to find out a thief'. The long enumeration reflects the problem of thefts on the great markets, a concomitant of a developing market economy.

witchcraft or to neglect of the *ikwii*. In the latter case atonement could be made by building a little shrine, *ngayulu*, on top of the house, or a shrine in front of the house or by cleaning the tombs, making offerings or sacrifice at the altar in the house or at the tomb.

The epitome of the diviner, the true *vàà*, was the *vàà mbulu*. The most impressive of his divinations was known as *ta vàà*: 'to throw divination'. He put the *mbulu* next to himself and, with the spirit of the *mbulu* in him, he would simply tell the client. A hair of the jackal skin attached to a leaf was proof. This prestige was due to the close link between the diviner and his spirit Obuu waalua, a sort of nature spirit which lived underground everywhere under the earth and who was superior to any other spirit except the national spirit of the kingdom Nkwe Mbali. To become a *vàà mbulu* the diviner had to spend some time underground in the realm of Obuu waalua a spectacular and fearful performance.

By 1963 there were still some diviners of this class in the area and most were women, which contrasts sharply with the generally subservient status of women. In former times though, it was said that there were as many men as women. Thus Ubwoono claimed that his mother went to Obuu waalua when she was pregnant with him, i.e. around 1890.

Vàà mbulu had other powers as well. They could foretell the future, to forecast, for instance, if a chief was about to die or not. Information of this nature came to him in dreams and he always announced such information unasked—another sign of his awesome knowledge. Only one person could do this sort of thing with even greater prestige and that was the chief LIPIE who served Nkwe Mbali himself. In a minor way illness could be predicted as well. When rain was threatening the diviner would state: 'If X is going to be ill, it will rain, if not it won't.'

It is therefore of interest to see that even if a *vàà mbulu* had ventured his prestige and had designated a person as a witch, in front of a witness of the chief, the suspect was not executed forthwith. Instead the procedure foresaw next the application of ordeals, especially the poison ordeal. Since ordeals were administered by courts they are better left for discussion when all the procedures for solving conflict are handled. For in contrast to divination also they did not merely indicate a culprit, they punished him and thus solved the conflict created by his deed and the desire for revenge of the wronged groups.

Some *ngàà* diviners were even more powerful and prestigious than the *vàà mbulu*. These were always men and never locals. They were summoned by political authorities to chase the *apfu* away and kill them during a grandiose and spectacular fight at which all the residents of the village were present. They claimed to find out all the witches in the settlement at once and to destroy their *apfu*. In fact this procedure and the circumstances surrounding it was a political act and a direct intervention in the conflicts within the chiefdom. It was both a dramatic struggle and a spectacular way to attempt to solve all internal conflict. Again, therefore the discussion of this must be left for the general discussion of conflict resolution.

3. *Healers*

Most diviners were also healers and the term *ngàà* referred to both. But there were many more healers than diviners, from modest persons who happened to have a single remedy and were known only in their settlement to specialists for individual illnesses and more professionals still who held medicine-bundles wrapped in a *pfura* (Sims: *pfuro*: 'a fetish') package of ordinary cloth, a *nkobi* box of bark or in the jackal skin.

They had much to do, for illness was frequent. Sims, a doctor, noted the terms for smallpox (*icwele*: 'fresh smallpox'; *bakuri*: 'smallpox marks'—*akuri*: Calloc'h, p. 341 'variole'; and *izimi*: 'smallpox marks'). In addition he mentioned sleeping sickness (*luo tolo*) which began probably after 1884, yaws (*bilu angara, bikilu angara*) jiggers (*mupfiu*) also a recent introduction (1882–3), scarlet fever (?: *imina karu*) and ague (*libvu*), probably malaria. These can be taken to have been the main diseases on the Stanley Pool with helminthiases and dysentery. (Calloc'h: *mu-co*: 'ver du corps', p. 342) (Sims: *mpula*, 'diarrhoea', Sims: *musere*: 'hernia, tumour, rupture, ganglion, hyrocele, diarrhoea, loins' and *musere mu ila* (litt. in the intestines): 'spasms, wind aching in the stomach'; Calloc'h *mu-sere*: 'dyssenterie'). On the plains one must add to these malnutrition and some pulmonary diseases. It is not known whether the severe forms of tuberculosis which are encountered there today were prevalent or not. On the other hand both sleeping sickness and malaria were practically absent during Iloo's reign, because of the particular nature of the environment. If chief NGAATALI of Imbâw is to be believed, leprosy was known (Calloc'h, p. 253, *kyaga*: 'Lèpre du pays'?) but rare and both tuberculosis and cancer were not unknown. Smaller discomforts such as lice, accidents or symptoms of the major illnesses such as headaches as well as the ubiquitous sores (Calloc'h: p. 113, 'abcès': *i-bimuga*; 'à la tête': *bu*, 'au pied': *i-nso*; 'à la cuisse': *i-cŵe, i-bana bana*; 'à l'aisselle': *mu-tere*) (Sims: *ibana bana*: 'abscess, swelling') also had to be cured.[11] The health situation seems not to have been very good and, as in 1963, it may be surmised that the working capacity of many persons was hampered by one or another illness. No wonder then that there was a real need for healers and consequently diviners.

The Tio had a general knowledge of anatomy, derived from observation and the cutting up of mammals, but their empirical knowledge of disease may not have been very extended. The theory seems to have been that good health (Sims: *kilikili, uwama*, Calloc'h: *psala*, p. 233,

[11] H. H. JOHNSTON, *The River*, p. 173, mentions jiggers, also pp. 237, 182 whooping cough.

'guérison, santé) was deranged by fever (Sims: *mukana*). A passing fever was called *mbaa* like the fire (Calloc'h: 'fièvre passagère', *ba*, p. 218 and the same word meant also 'unmerciful, cruel' (Sims: *mbaa*). Fever was heat and conflict and it could be cured only by peace and coolness. As heat and fire are chased away by water, fever could only be eliminated by induced diarrhoea.[12] The theory fitted very well with the notion that illness was due to witchcraft, itself the sign of tension. That was the ultimate cause to be corrected first, by bringing back peace before any cure would work.

The case of accident or flowing blood excepted, it seems that the recognition that a person was ill came when there was fever and the notation of Calloc'h seems to indicate that it had to be persistent fever. That was the sign for a person to take over the role of being ill (Sims: *(m)uluu*: 'sick person'; *lua*: 'be sick'). A healer (*ngàà waa libuu*; Sims: *imbu*; 'to heal': *buo*) then had to intervene.

But healing was not restricted to illness. Rain-makers or people who stopped rain were designated by the same term. Healing may have been thought of as a technical process which aimed to replace misfortune by fortune. To achieve this there were rituals, charms, and drugs for the major illnesses as well as for the minor ailments. Any charm was known as *ãti* (Sims: *uti*)[13] and there were three kinds: *imiõ* (Sims: *(M)umiño*) which were drugs to cure, *kaa*, protective charms (Sims: *inkiele*: 'protective charm'?) which could also be used for divining, and *osel'beene* or charms for good fortune. The classification corresponds well with the notion of good fortune: the first class of charms brought fortune back, the second class maintained it and the third improved upon it.

The rituals for curing are best approached through a series of examples. De Chavannes reported on a cure he saw at Mfwa.[14] Three sick women were being treated by a healer, Ngantsibu, and two helpers. The accessories were a fetish box (*nkobi*) with all sorts of odds and ends such as bits of bone, shells, ashes, earth, seeds of fruits, bits of different metals, a medicine bag (which is a skin with contents similar to the box) and a little trough containing water, two fruits, a bored stone, and a shell. The meaning of all these paraphernalia remained hidden to the observer. The *ngàà* ran his fingers over all these objects and then laid hands on the heads, the arms and the chest of his two assistants, before repeating this on the three patients. The officiating

[12] Mbali. The preparation *itiéé* was used. There may be a link between Calloc'h, p. 260: *bu-byelo:* 'maladie' and Sims' *Ubele*: 'hatred' in that the Tio word *may be* identical. Confirmation is lacking from elsewhere.

[13] *ã-ti* has a prefix class six for fluids or bulks and the stem *-tí*: 'tree, vegetation'. Medicine-bundle is therefore a good translation. Sims also gives *isuno* and *mumiño*. The former word may refer to a particular cure.

[14] CH. DE CHAVANNES, op. cit., p. 226. His supposition that there was Catholic influence because of the imposition of hands and because all concerned dipped their hand in the water of the trough is not warranted.

persons then bent one towards another, took each other by the hands for a few seconds, then separated suddenly, shaking their hands and declaring: '*kilikili*', thus rendering a verdict that the patients would be restored to good health. Then Ngantsibu took a seed from his box and ate it while the two assistants put the four elements which had been in the trough into their mouths, passing them on one to another. A few words of exorcism followed and the ceremony was over.

The operation seems fairly straightforward. The healer ran his hands over the magical objects and laid them on the patients. He did some divination with his helpers, perhaps studying the behaviour of the two fruits in the trough, and declared that the patients would be cured. But only an explanation of each of the objects in symbolic terms would yield a more complete explanation.

The second case was described graphically by H. H. Johnston.[15]

Approaching his residence (of Makôlé who was ill), we see that something very special is taking place. The palisaded compound round Makôlé's huts is festooned with great palm branches, interlaced at times so as to form arches of greenery across the pathway. The entrance to the principal house, where the ceremony we have been invited to see, is going on, is a veritable bower, so thickly do the upright palm fronds cluster about it. Thirty-nine people, all crammed into the interior, which is about twenty feet by ten. They are all playing on drums, 'marimbas' (hand piano) and a rude sort of lyre (pluriarc), and singing at the top of their voices, their nearly naked bodies streaming with sweat, for in addition to the exhausting nature of their occupation, there is a roasting fire burning in the centre of the hut, and its smoke mixes with the steam from the human bodies and produces a thick mist through which various details of the interior can but dimly be discerned. At one end of the hut however, we can see Makôlé, who is sick, seated under an overarching canopy of palm branches, with the soles of his feet turned towards the blaze. On one side of him, a wife crouches over a dish of food that she is preparing. All this time, her husband, a stout, well-made man in the prime of life remains perfectly motionless and silent, the perspiration streaming down his body, and we are informed that it is an important condition of the cure that he should not give utterance to a sound while the charm is working.

At length there is pause for refreshments, and all the occupiers of the hut musicians, wives, and patient, turn out into the open, panting, laughing, and wiping the sweat from their glistening bodies. Jars of sweet and pleasant tasting palmwine from the Malebu or Hyphoene palms is brought in by slaves, and all present, including ourselves, take a drink, Makôlé participating freely. Although he is bound to keep silent, he makes up for want of verbal welcome by the most effusive grins: in fact his face is wreathed in fatuous smiles, for he is evidently highly selfconscious, and imagines himself to be an interesting figure to the white men who have come to witness his 'cure'. His friends tell us he is suffering from headache and to corroborate this, he himself points to his temples and forehead which are painted with white pigment. But probably

[15] H. H. JOHNSTON, op. cit., pp. 197–8.

the whole affair is got up to serve as an excuse for a bout of malafu drinking and a grand function.

The scene in the house was exactly such as the one I witnessed eighty years later at an *itsuua* ritual. The only difference: the patient was a woman and not a man. This allows us to give some explanations not supplied by Johnston. The palm fronds indicated that the patient was a man, otherwise it would have been wild calabash vine that would have decorated the house. The people were there as well-wishers who actively helped to cure the patient and Johnston's presence was interpreted in that light. The songs sung were probably most ordinary, but it was the singing which was important and the use of the pluriarc *nguõ*. It was played only on ritual occasions.[16] It was believed that the shades *ikwii* loved its sound and were irresistibly attracted by it. The songs too were for the *ikwii*. That is why they were the ordinary dancing songs, with only a few specials thrown in by the first singer, who was a medicine man. Johnston was right. It was an occasion to break the monotony of humdrum life, but even more so for the dead than for the living. The presence of the *ikwii* would make certain that they would help the *ngàà* to fight the *apfu* of the witch. Obviously the illness was not simply a minor headache. Headache was a part of it and the kaolin lines, kaolin being the colour of ritual, indicated this. It must have been a severe illness to justify this kind of gathering. The man was motionless and perspiring. He was perhaps, as was the case in 1964, waiting for a trance which did not come. And then everyone went out into the courtyard. Now the *ngàà* explained to me that this was done so that his *apfu* could really get through. For the crowd in the house could be such that they could not get to the sick person. In 1964 people went back into the house and finally the trance came. In 1863 Johnston did not stay, so we do not know.

The third example dates from 1964 and illustrates a smaller private ritual, almost a doctor's visit. The day before there had been an *okuu* inquest to deal with the stubborn illness of an old woman. It was evening and the *ngàà* came in, leaving the door open, so that one could see in the glow of the fire which had been kept burning brightly by the son of the house. One *itio* had been set carefully against the centrepost of the house and the patient was in bed. The *ngàà* talked a while to her first and then the other man began to play the pluriarc and to sing. The *ngàà* meanwhile chewed *ãmpõ* herbs, including copal, *lisisõ* grass, and the *niõ* fruit, all cooling elements, and spat these on the patient, on the floor and near the door to cure her. He also shook his *õtsara* rattle to call his *apfu* and came from time to time to the door to spit and so encourage them to come, for the *ampõ* are like kola, an offering. They went on like this for some time and then the player of the pluriarc

[16] J. MAES, *Les Lukombe*, pp. 241–2 states that it was the instrument of 'intimate life' (1913).

stopped and the *ngàà* began to sing. He explained afterwards that this first song comes from the *apfu*, who will cure the patient. A clever person can understand what it says, for it is an ordinary song used as an omen. The song indicates the state of the illness. If it is 'good' there will be recovery, otherwise not. After a while the *ngàà* neared the fire and threw some Bengal powder on it, transforming the orange glow into the most fantastic colours. The effect was a notable success. Asked the reason for this innovation he merely said that it gave power to his *ãti*. He bought it at Brazzaville and used it to cure. The spectacular effect was made not so much to impress the patient, which it certainly did, as to impress the *apfu* and make them stay. This is why the Bengal fireworks were repeated more than once. After four hours of playing, singing, spitting, and making fireworks the *ngàà* left. Early next morning he returned and was given a white fowl. Sitting on the bed of the patient he suffocated it in the proper fashion as if it were a sacrifice to the *ikwii*, then he dropped a little of the blood on the woman, the *okwii* and the threshold (Sims: *Bula cwa ñakila*: 'sprinkle blood on a drawn figure'). He did this because the *apfu* of the witch were there and they had agreed, he told me, to take the life of the fowl instead of that of the woman. This was the result of the bargaining that had been going on between his own *apfu* and those of the witch. In addition to these visits the healer also gave the woman on each occasion some *imiõ* to take. And in his mind there were other good *apfu* behind each of the leaves which had been ground into the drug to make the woman well.

A curing ritual then always began with the calling of the *apfu* by making music and singing, by the spitting of *ampõ* and occasionally by being called. *Ngàà* used a special whistle *ikiri mbulu* or the horn of a *ntsa* antelope for this. The *ikwii* of the patient were also supposed to come to help the good *apfu*. They could not be called by name as during an *ikwii* ritual for the shades. Once all were there, including the bad *apfu* who caused the illness and were always near the patient, bargaining could begin. The family would now put *ibuunu* (and more recently money) near the head of the bed as a fee: *iluuõ* (Sims: *iluoño*: 'doctor's fee'). The money was supposed to be an offering or a bribe for the bad *apfu*. Good and bad *apfu* now bargained about the price and the *ngàà* would ask the family sometimes to make it higher. More often the family began by claiming that the initial price asked was too high and the *apfu* bargained with the *ngàà* announcing the results of their palaver to the people. The *ngàà* did not take the goods which were left near the head of the bed until the patient was cured. Then only could he take them as his payment. These payments were high. In 1963 the minimum was 2,000 Fr CFA and one *ibuunu*, but they might reach as high as 15,000 to 20,000 Fr CFA, *i.e.* a price as high as bridewealth or the payment for a slave, a ransom of life in the most literal terms. The *apfu* took the invisible substance of the funds and very often a fowl had to be sacrificed to them too, so that they would have to 'eat' and desist from 'eating' the patient (Sims: *museme*: 'sacrificer, one who offers animals in fetish rites').

After the bargaining there remained only the giving of the medication. There might be a resumption of singing with more forecasts about the evolution of the illness. Thus if a song went: 'it rains, oo, it rains, oo, with great drops, with great drops' (*mvul ano, oo* (*bis*) *tswolé, tswolé*) the patient would die. Another dancing song such as: '*ke* fish, oarsman on the river, bring me over, bring me over' (*ke obala ndzali, dzu me, dzu me*) might be a good sign.

In serious cases one would always begin with an *okuu* and then only would the *ngàà* come. He might decide to tackle the question in a different fashion, especially if the person was already in agony. Then he called his *apfu*, took his *õtsara* and ran out of the house singing: 'if you are a *ngàà*, heal!' (*okali, ngàà, buwo*). He then ran to the corner of the village, a favourite spot for bad *apfu*, or even to the cemetery as in despair, pursuing the evil *apfu*. Then he came back to ask for a goat to be put near the head of the patient and sent his *apfu* to tell the others: 'leave him alone; they give a goat as well as the money'. If the others agreed the goat would be sacrificed. If they refused, it remained there and there followed an invisible fight of the *ngàà*'s *apfu* with those of the witch. This was highly dangerous and made a hero out of the *ngàà*, for his own *apfu* might be killed in the fight, he would remain unprotected and he too could die. In the visible world all this was translated by the wild running around of the *ngàà*, who often took his gun and could start shooting at the bad *apfu* where he 'saw' them sitting. Thus curing illness became an exciting drama whose climax was either death or recovery.

It seems that formerly no payment, except a sacrificial fowl for his *apfu*, went to the *ngàà* in case the patient died. By 1963 several *ngàà* had different opinions, some claiming that the fee for the *apfu* was theirs whatever the issue.[17]

Besides the general rituals described above some others were used only for illnesses which resulted in the patient becoming a *ngàà* himself if he recovered. In the Mbe area two such rituals were known, *olũ* for future *mbulu* diviners, and *itsuua*,[18] called *nkira* by the Wũ women

[17] No written testimony about this is available for Iloo's times. On the whole procedure and its meaning Ikoli, Ngateo, Ubwoono, and Mbali (all *ngàà*) agreed that this was in use at the time. They also agreed that in the case of death no fee could be claimed at that time.

[18] Calloc'h: 'esprit'; p. 208, has *i-cuwa* among them. Calloc'h is the earliest written reference to it but Ngalifourou underwent the ritual after an illness when she was already married to king Ngaayüo in the first or second decade of the century. Cf. YOULOU KOUYA, *Une adoratrice*, p. 55. Ubwoono's mother went to *itsuua* and that was likely to be in the 1880s or 1890s. Sims: *cuu:* 'exhausted, tired' has the same stem, if its tones were identical.

whether they suffered from malnutrition, as was most often the case, or from illnesses varying from angina to tuberculosis. The diagnostic was that they had to feel exhausted and they had to become emaciated and to cough. Conventional medicine was tried first and did not help. Once there were several such women and a *ngááyuulu* or mistress of the ritual was available, *itsuua* could be held. The *ngááyuulu* had to be a woman who had been through the ritual herself and as a result of it had 'taken' the medicine basket *nkobi* which went with it. It was entirely a woman's affair even if on occasion an immature boy was also taken in if he showed the proper symptoms. He could in any case, never become a *ngááyuulu*.

In the case observed in 1963 the instruction was given by a woman from the Wũ, Ngontsuo, and the ritual was aimed at one patient in particular who had become very thin and was to die shortly. The beginning of the ritual was absolutely identical with the description given earlier of Johnston's observation. The aim was to get the patient to enter into a trance. Every ten minutes or so the music would stop and Okondzaadza a male *ngàà* or Ngontsuo would advise: 'Do *itsuua*, the witch must step aside, the illness will go away, she will take the *nkobi*, she will heal.' Ngontsuo had her trappings, a bundle of inedible *osõ* leaves, which the *ngàà* holds in her hand or puts on his head, a stick *okaana*, which is the lower part of the *okõ* vine, the upper part having been eaten (Sims: *mukana*: 'staff') and a whistle made out of the horn of the *ntsa* antelope with which to call her *apfu*. Indeed she left the house regularly, turned around in front of it—the moon was full—whistling. Then she came back and told the assistants what to sing. It was hot in the room so she asked that *ntsã* or lustral water be given to the *apfu*.

After an hour or so the organizer of the *itsuua* for the family of the sick girl came in with the greeting: *nkira va iniinie*: '*nkira* spirit sit down and rule' and all answered *nie*, *nie*: 'rule, rule' as was customary. He repeated this twice and the third time he asked 'what for?' and then the assistants began to play and sing really well. But the girl was not seized by the spirit of *itsuua*. Towards ten o'clock the music-making was so vigorous that they broke a drum, but even that did not stop them. Just as someone was leaving to fetch another one, the patient rose slowly out of her sweating total immobility, stretched her arms, turned around, picked up the first medicine basket *nkobi*, and went out. All shouted encouragement, *wooloo*. She went out with Ngontsuo. She caught hold of the wife of the organizer of her kin group and a co-wife of her husband and brought them back into the *itsuua* with her. Then she started to dance at the sound of the new drum. She took the second *nkobi*, went out and took two other women, a co-wife again and her mother-in-law, to sit with her in *itsuua*. But she did not enter. She put the *nkobi* on her head, turned around the house and all of a sudden climbed on to the roof, the *nkobi* still on her head. Her brother was behind her to catch her if she fell and all encouraged her, *wooloo*. Now she had been seized by the spirit. She had been 'upstairs' and was truly *ngáàyulu*. If she recovered she was a *ngàà* for *itsuua*.

The women all came back inside. She sang by herself while all the women took cold white ash from the hearth and daubed their faces with it, justifying another name, *ngáàlifura*, which was the *itsuua* name taken by the queen of the 1920s, Ngalifourou. The ashes were symbols of the *ikwii* and the gesture was to thank them and the spirit of *itsuua*. Then the patient gave names to the women she had caught, calling them 'mother of healing': *ngu abuo*, 'weeper': *ngeilili*, 'smiler': *ngeisã* and *adzondzali*. The women were to keep these names for nine days only, the time *itsuua* normally lasts at Mbe, in contrast to the Wũ country where it goes on for two or three months. The names were supposed to show the alteration in personality brought about by the *itsuua*. Only the *ngáàyuulu* name was permanent because only that woman had been seized by the spirit and thus really been 'altered'. Even if she had not taken the basket she would have changed names for *ngeikara*: 'the idle one' or 'the cripple' a scathing comment on her failure. Now she had succeeded and could cure by imposition of hands and use of ashes. The *ngáàyuulu* Ngontsuo was to make a *nkobi* box for her and of course she would heal.

It is not surprising that her kin brought much to drink and that the continuation of the singing took on a holiday air. And yet on occasion, Okondzaadza had to push people away from the door so that the *apfu* of Ngontsuo could get in to help the cure. The celebration lasted until past midnight. The next day one woman left, but the others who had been caught decided to remain for the remainder of the nine days and the new *ngáàyuulu* who came from the Wũ was to stay much longer. As for the woman who had left, she came back after her work in the fields every evening for nine days, which was not very logical since one of the features of being in *itsuua* was the absolute ban on working in the fields. The difference between theory and practice became even clearer the next day when two other of the women in *itsuua* followed this example. As for the first patient, she stayed. Every morning and every night there was a dance. Soon these became small affairs, attended mostly by conscientious elders, while the frivolous youth had been enthralled by something else. The patient stayed a month, but did not gain weight. Then they gave up and she died shortly afterwards. So even though she had been *ngáàyuulu*, the witches had been too powerful after all.

The women in *itsuua* were considered to be of chiefly status. They wore the royal red and drank behind a blanket like chiefs or kings. The spirit of *itsuua* was believed at least among the Wũ to be a powerful nature spirit such as great chiefs and kings control. The house was framed with the wild calabash vine, symbolizing femininity, and two palm fronds. The women in seclusion had nothing to do but rest, relax, and talk and Abili Ndiõ claimed that formerly they all liked to go to *itsuua* for a rest from the back-breaking toil in the fields. There was little discomfort, the only avoidance being that they should not eat cassava on the days of Nkwe Mbali and *okwe* which were sacred. As for the *itsuua* illness itself, that was supposed to manifest itself only by a fever just before dawn, but no drugs must be taken and the fever died down of its own accord. Many women liked to go, and formerly the chief patient would catch her friends to sit through it with her, whether they were emaciated or not. When women were barren they could enter with the others even if they were not called. Perhaps the most unpleasant feature for the companions of the sick woman was that after the nine days were over, the ceremonial ended with the formal handing-over by the *ngàà* of their hoes, so that they could go back to work.

Since the ritual was aimed mainly at exhaustion and malnutrition, resting made sense and the long period of rest enforced in the Wũ area much more so than the short ritual nine days at Mbe. Since the major aim was to cure, this is an important point. But for the women this ritual provided a focus. It was their ritual, one way for them to become *ngàà* and the only time when women were treated like chiefs.

The ritual by which one became *mbulu* was similar in that it began with illness and ended in death or the acquisition of a new status. It was open to women, but it was not closed to men. Compared to *itsuua* by men in Mbe, it was felt to be much more important and indeed so was the resultant status. But compared by women, it was considered barely equivalent and not half as much liked.

In the nineteenth century some other similar rituals existed near the Pool. The most important one was *ndembo* only in use at Kinshasa, Ntamo, and Kimpoko, the three settlements south of the Pool. It was probably a ritual taken over from the Hum or the Kongo, similar to the *nkita* of the latter. It was a form of initiation for adolescent boys and girls or perhaps even young married people and the ritual was resorted to when general misfortune had struck. The twenty or fifty people who joined in an initiation were kept in the bush from three months to three years. Again *nkira* spirits were responsible for the transformation of the participants who emerged, as in *itsuua*, with new personalities.[19]

North of the Pool the river people knew a cure for women called after nature spirits named Uma or Nzuma, if they were suspected of having been impregnated by these spirits. The cure consisted of food avoidances and the drinking of drugs prepared by a medicine woman. After birth the baby was also treated and eventually the mother did not take any more drugs but still had to observe the avoidances until the

[19] C. COQUILHAT, *Sur le Haut-Congo*, p. 59; E. COART, A. DE HAULLEVILLE, op. cit., p. 199, says specifically it is teke, but adds p. 204, that it was identical with the *nkita* cult in the Kongo hinterland. The vocabulary seems Kongo; Calloc'h, p. 153, *nzo ankira, nzo a mbaa:* 'case de circoncis', along with a name: 'house of men'. This could be *Ndembo*, were it not for the circumcision. By the 1960s (and perhaps long before?) the cult was no longer in use.

baby was grown up.[20] If the spirit was Uma, the expectant mother had to drink a solution made from leaves gathered at the bottom of a brook and four other sorts of plants: the roots of a sort of grass, two types of leaves, and spines. The drink was mixed with palm-wine and taken, three times every morning except on unlucky days, *okila* and *odzuo*. For Nzuma the drink was made with bark of three trees, one of which grew only in the plains, mixed with kaolin and palm-wine and drunk as in the other case. Uma, the male spirit, was thus associated more with water and forest and Nzuma, a female spirit, with the savannah. When the baby was born it took the same drink once a day. The avoidances of the mother fell into five groups: pork was forbidden for both Uma and Nzuma. For Uma the others were: porcupine; *ntsili* fish; hot cassava to be eaten with anyone else but her husband. For Nzuma they were birds; any fish that had prickles; palm-oil and goats. To that corresponded any game caught during a hunt with a dog wearing a bell for Uma. Details regarding the behaviour these women and their babies were to observe if they did not want to fall ill, seem to be explained by the supposed temperament of the spirits.

The drugs *imiõ* were prepared in the form of infusions, pills, inhalation, and paste for local external application or in raw form for passing over the body. Food avoidances and sometimes other avoidances as well were always part of the treatment. The major preparation against fever was called *itiee*, after a piece of calabash in which they were presented. The *ngàà* collected leaves from the plants *ikuru*, *oshioonu*, *itweeni*, *ankooankoo* and cut these up while 'talking to them', asking them to cure the patient. Once cut he put them in a sherd of calabash with water, and added colours, kaolin and a type of red, and allowed the mixture to settle. When he made the *itiee* he could not have intercourse with his wife the night before, presumably because intercourse was fire and conflict, which the *itiee* was supposed to remove. Other avoidances or *ngili* (Sims: *ngili*) were that the *ngàà* alone could touch them and that the leaves could not fall on the ground. The mixture was prepared a day ahead, for the *ngàà* left them next to his *ikwii* to ask for their inspiration in dream. The *ikwii* would tell him to proceed or to leave the patient alone. The infusion was to be drunk four or five times a day. When the leaves were rotten, they were thrown out. The first time *itiee* was drunk the *ngàà* was present, made an invocation and sang with the pluriarc. After the person had drunk he would forecast if the patient would live or not.

For specific illnesses, specific preparations were made according to

[20] M. IBALICO, *La thérapeutique*, pp. 17–18, is the only one to mention all of this. But among the Fumu *nkira* were held responsible for certain illnesses as is evident from R. HOTTOT, F. WILLETT, *Teke Fetishes* and Calloc'h: 'esprit'; p. 208 (*ma-kani;* cf. note 10 *kwani*; and *kaba*); cf. Calloc'h, p. 260, 'maladie' where *nkira* are specified as spirits of illness.

the diagnosis. Leaves or pieces of bark could be cooked in a pot decorated with colours and then infused. The patient drank often three similar preparations in succession. The *odzuuru* technique, which is the one presumably used in the description of De Chavannes, consisted of putting the leaves in tepid water and 'drawing' them (Sims: *kila*: 'put on medicine') over the body of the sick person with invocations and singing. Pills *ãtiõ* were obtained by mixing scrapings of bark grilled over the fire and then stamped into powder, mixed with palm-oil and pressed by hand. For pills there had to be admixture of some other element, usually animal, which would come out of the medicine bag, *pfura* or *mbulu*. Finally inhalation *idzubi* consisted of having the patient inhale the vapour of water heated in a pot which contained a mixture of vegetal elements.

A list of common materia medica of Mbe in 1963 contained fifteen sorts of bark, of which three only came from the savannah and one from a tree which grows in both environments, savannah and forest. There was one sort of seed, roots of banana and four fruits as well as six common types of leaves all from savannah environment. Some of the latter were cultivated in the dawn-gardens. Items such as palm-nuts, palm-oil, toppings of cassava and the vegetable *mpfũ* or pimentoes which are common foods, were also used in medicine.

The principle on which a remedy was prepared was to look at the symptoms and for each of these, e.g. headache, fever, rash, belly ache, a specific ingredient was mixed in. Illness was thus not conceived at this level as a specific whole but as a combination of ailments and it follows that most treatments must have been evolved very much by the trial and error method. For some symptoms nothing was given, but a *ngili* imposed for an avoidance was just as much treatment as a positive ingredient. Thus for coughing, one avoided palm oil. Some symptoms warranted blood-letting (Sims: *ncwa*: 'cupping calabash'), especially headaches.[21]

Specific examples of treatments are, e.g. a medicine to kill lice (Sims: (*m*)*umweño*); the avoidance of cassava toppings for pains in the kidneys; blood-letting plus the avoidance of *mpfũ* leaves and cassava toppings plus sometimes painting a band of colour (usually the sacred kaolin) around the head for headaches.[22] For mumps there was inhalation with leaves of the mango tree[23] and *ompirimpiri* leaves. For vomiting,

[21] Bloodletting could be something which diffused to the Tio from seventeenth-century European medicine, but local origins are also possible. An item not mentioned are enema's. Given Tio theories of fever, they would be expected.

[22] J. GHYS, *Etude agricole*, p. 122, gives a partial list of plants and their medicinal uses among the Ngenge; three out of seven were used to make dressings for wounds, two (the first mentioned) to fight constipation, one against sore throats, and one to cure elephantiasis.

[23] This is definitely recent, since mangoes were planted after 1880. Mumps are recent too. The *materia medica* remains dynamic.

ngwantsoo, buds of banana trees were cut, the pieces packaged in two or three ordinary leaves and infused for a day, a treatment called *véé*.

The above examples show some good sense at first sight. For cassava toppings or *mpfũ* leaves which are too old provoke pain in the kidneys of healthy people. They also contain obvious symbolic elements such as the painting around the head. Most items could be one or the other. Banana buds, fit in very well with the symbolic role of the banana in almost all rituals, but perhaps the treatment also had some effect. Only pharmacological studies could determine this for most of the *materia medica* in use. Yet one can state already that this pharmacopaea was inspired at one and the same time by experience in curing and by symbolism, the hypothesis being that the Tio classified plants in a few general categories such as forest and savannah and also had symptoms classified so that experiment took place only with a portion of the available vegetation: that portion which corresponded to the category of symptoms. Thus often the plant chosen might be effective and symbolically correct. For example we suspect in the case of mumps that mango leaves were used because mumps was introduced by the Europeans as was the mango tree, along with some others. The eruption of mumps was then handled with an old known treatment for a rash *ompirimpiri*, but mango leaves were used.

If this is correct it follows that the Tio may have been much better adapted to cope with some of their ailments than an analysis of symbolism alone would suggest. But the general symbolism and the ritual was necessary both because of their world view and to act as a *placebo*, an important part of every medicine.

Most *ngàà* had stocks of leaves, seeds, roots, animal bones, shells, and the like in their *nkobi* or medicine bags and treated all sort of illness. But there was some specialization. Thus by 1963 there was one specialist on the plains of Mbe for mental disease and at least one other who set bones. And then there were the simple home remedies inherited in every family where one or the other acted as *ngàà* for things like healing sores or binding small wounds. Even so the number of *ngàà* who practised in a wider circle was relatively great in Mbe by 1963 and probably even greater in the 1880s. This situation also means that experimentation with *materia medica* was brisk.[24]

Authors of the early period do mention 'fetishes' or 'idols' and these were not in use at Mbe by 1963. The suspicion is that these statues were either used for divining or simply represented the *ikwii* of the *ngàà* or the patient. Yet Hottot mentioned in 1906 a specific type of statuette made to cure disease brought about by the *nkira* spirit Makani. This was con-

[24] E. ZORZI, *Al Congo*, p. 426 and p. 230 on the stocking of medicines in a *nkobi*. The situation in the 1960s was probably similar to that in the 1880s since we found no indication or reason to believe that the number of *ngàà* had increased during the colonial period.

nected with cults such as Uma or Nzuma, which are not in existence on the plateau. This was also the case for statuettes connected with Kiba or Mbuma other *nkira* spirits, responsible for specific diseases.[25]

Kaa were charms used after recovery from illness or by anyone who felt threatened and needed protection. Unlike *imiõ* which were specific for each symptom, *kaa* were identical for all illnesses, although they changed from one *ngàà* to another. In the 1880s almost all men seem to have worn some of them. Liebrechts claims that amulets were made daily and that certain houses of chiefs along the Pool were filled with them. They were made by the *ngàà* and wrapped in a bit of cloth or an animal skin, often with the feather of a rooster sticking out. They were thus rather like a medicine bag. Each charm had its own aim and a fresh preparation was poured over it when needed. For chiefs the *kaa* were kept in pots or animal shells.[26] The different aims were not different illnesses but to ward off different enemies. A simple *kaa* in 1963 for example was the wearing of a lion's tooth as an amulet by a child. It protected the child if the *apfu* responsible for his disease was someone to whom the necklace from which the tooth was taken had belonged. But if this was a direct ancestor of the child, it would not work, for *kaa* were directed against *apfu*, not against *ikwii*.

Kaa always contained *lisisõ* grass against lightning and snakes, bark of the *ilibankie* tree, leaves of the same tree, and some earth taken at its foot. When gathering this central element the *ngàà* told the tree: 'let us go to the village, to heal people, to settle the land'. That earth was taken, which was never done with the plants used in *imiõ* showed that the *ilibankie* was a tree of the nature spirits *nkira*. The spirit of the domain in which the patient lived was thus asked to help him. Hence the expression 'settling the land'. Then he added *akoo* grass tied in a knot to tie up the activity of witches. This grass was then cut into pieces and acquired the name *ampirimpiri*. In addition each *kaa* could include some other parts of trees or other grasses, according to the *ngàà*. But in

[25] E. ZORZI, op. cit., p. 230, 'idols in wood' which probably refer to ancestor statuettes. But not so among the Fumu and perhaps the Sese or a part of them. R. HOTTOT, F. WILLETT, op. cit., p. 31, say that all *nkiba* statuettes lacked the typical abdominal cavity of the sculpture for ancestors and claim the *kiba* to be an inferior *bongàà* spirit. (Calloc'h, p. 216, has *bõgaa*: 'fétiche'.) For Sims *inkiiba* was a bee-hived fetish in front of the house. Calloc'h, p. 260, mentions *kiba* as a *nkira* spirit responsible for illness V° 'maladie'. Calloc'h, p. 208, has *ki-ba* as 'esprit'. R. HOTTOT, F. WILLETT's makani statuette (pp. 26–7) corresponds to Calloc'h's p. 208, *ma-kani* 'esprit' and perhaps Sims' *kwani* in *loo kwani* (fn. 10). R. HOTTOT, F. WILLETT's secret society *bumu* is very likely Calloc'h's *mbuma*, p. 260, V° 'maladie'. The conceptions of *nkira* in the whole area varied considerably. The Fumu usage seems to be what Tio call *kaa*. Fumu data stem from 1906–10.

[26] CH. LIEBRECHTS, *Léopoldville*, p. 533. For *kaa* objects cf. E. COART, A. DE HAULLEVILLE, op. cit., p. 233, pl. XXV, figs. 403–4, 406, p. 233 figs. 410–11, 413, and note also the borassus bells from Kimpoko pl. XII, fig. 699, which are *libi* and used mostly for the *ikwii* cult.

all preparations there had to be one *nji* or *olivancillaria nana* or a cowry for 'strength' or rather good fortune, since *nji* was a symbol of commercial wealth while the cowry may have been a symbol of fertility.

After the ingredients had been gathered, they were kneaded with a portion of an animal which had to be added and then the *kaa* was tied in a piece of raphia or cloth that should be red or black, or in a skin. Finally earth, water, and the feather of a rooster or of a *ndua* bird, a symbol of authority, had to be added as it was also on all shrines.

One particular *kaa* in 1963 contained kola, pieces of banana tree bark of the variety *atoro* which would close the way to the witch, since it had been cut into three pieces, a *nzi*, a piece of elephant's skin with the hair of its tail, both to strengthen the *kaa*. The ingredients of *ilibankie* were there with *obwooro*, *owõ* and *oshuu*, and preparations of trees connected with *nkira*, *obwooro* even with the *national* spirit Nkwe Mbali. Earth from the crossroads was put in to throw the witch off the track and a feather added. Another preparation of 1963 contained *ilibankie*, *lisisõ*, *iloolo*, a grass named after witchcraft and *iuwere* leaves, also from a *nkira* tree. In yet another the feathers were of the *inkuo* bird (plantain-eater), also a symbol of authority and the *kaa* was put into two horns each of which had been affixed to a stick. This was in fact common and *kaa* were thus kept attached to the shafts of spears or knobkerries, placed on or near the altars in the houses.[27]

The ritual by which a *kaa* was made included first the invocation at the foot of the *ilibankie* tree. During the kneading the *ngàà* addressed the *kaa*, singing:

> *Inciele*, bug of the underground, *inciele* of the *nkira*

or:

> dung beetle, the one who whispers, his neck will break.

The first song calls on the *nkira* and a bug which was linked to it, while the dung beetle was linked with a witch since witches can use them or flies to bewitch for them.[28] The song was a threat to the witch. The *ngàà* always added: 'you threaten to destroy (eat) me; if you do, there will be trouble'.

After soaking, the animal skin was added and it was always the skin of a feline, the animals of *nkira*, but apparently not of either the leopard of chiefs or the lion of kings. The skin and hair of the tail of the elephant could be substituted. Then the *kaa* was given a name, different from that of the *nkira* of the area, and a rooster was sacrificed to it, the tail-

[27] The ritual for making *kaa* is described after several informants including Ngaatali and because of the latter's testimony may be taken to represent practices at the end of Iloo's reign without major changes.

[28] In fact flies and mosquitoes brought both malaria and sleeping sickness and the dung beetle was conceivably a factor in the spread of helminthiasis and dysenteries. Thus the symbols of witchcraft were rather representative.

feather of which crowned the whole, if not feathers of *nduo* or the plantain-eater.

During the preparation the *ngàà* had observed certain avoidances. He had not slept with his wife the night before, he had also not eaten recently of a wild fruit such as *ibu isià, ingè, ntsùunu, ncwii*. They were all blood red and each *ngàà* only avoided one of those species.

Now the client could come. First the *kaa* was paid for and the *ngàà*, received a fowl to replace the one which had been sacrificed.

The payment was a minimum of half a length of cloth by 1963 and thus much less than the payment for treatment of illness. The client was to observe some avoidances. Usually he could not light a torch at night from the fire in his hearth, which was a hot element and an element of conflict. Or he could not light a torch of grasses because the fire was bright. He could not stand up naked in his hut, since witches roam about naked at night. He could not put the *kaa* on the ground or use for fuel any wood or grass which had gone into its composition, since that was a lack of respect. He should take the *kaa* with him on trips since he would not be protected otherwise. He could not rub blood of a fowl on it, but could otherwise give it kola as if it were an *ikwii*. Finally if a dung beetle dropped on one's head when travelling, a very unlikely situation, that was an omen and the client should return home at once. Moreover the *kaa* would make him dream from time to time and thus give him instructions. For instance if one dreamt at Mbe that the king gave either a hoe (woman) or a matchet (boy) to you, your wife was pregnant and the child would be of the sex announced by the object; if one dreamed of a military parade, the client should not go to the forest or near the village, according to what he had planned; if one dreamt of a crowd on a path, one could go to the village if one had wanted to.

What the spirit in the *kaa* was, remained a little unclear. It was connected with the *nkira* and for NGAATALI, a chief of the land himself, it was the *nkira*. For others such as Mbiinu mbiinu, also a chief of the land, the power came first from the *nkira*, but actually the spirit of each *kaa* was an *apfu*. Such dissensions of opinion about religious belief were quite common. They contrasted with the unanimity about the rituals to be observed.

Kaa and *imiõ* were thus very different. And yet one case was noted in 1963 where an *imiõ* was made with ingredients which usually go into a *kaa*, excluding however the *ilibankie*, and including the dung beetle! Obviously the ingredients had been chosen for their symbolic value and the fact that they appear in *kaa* was not an obstacle for making a pill with them.

There seems to have been another type of *kaa*, *ikõ* (Sims: *ikuñu* 'magic') used exclusively for women. So far little is known about them except that at Mbe they were rare in 1963. One woman possessed one because she was a *nciele* child, having been born in a special way and supposed to possess more than usual powers of fertility; on the other hand she might have acquired it to avoid having to confess her lovers before childbirth. It may have been a female counterpart of *kaa* since women do not seem to have possessed *kaa* and that *ikõ* was made specifically to protect them.

If *imiõ* cured and *kaa* protected against illness, *osel'beene* furthered good fortune in hunting, in fighting, in war, in trade, in love affairs, in fishing, and in obtaining rain. This was what Sims indicates as: *impa* 'magic, deceit' because it often meant furthering one's own good fortune to the detriment of someone else. Yet, despite some of its obvious anti-social effects, the Tio declared in 1963 that *osel'beene* was 'good' in essence, thus translating no doubt their own individual points of view.

The main categories were *ipali* for gaining in love, wealth, or success in fishing, *ntsankã* for rain, and *ĩkwi* for war and hunting. There were other charms too, less widespread, such as *ocwe*: 'the head' for winning in fighting or wrestling and so named because the owner had to avoid eating heads of animals, and *imbuuni* in war.

Most of these have been discussed in the situations for which they are used, so that only one example of *ipali* is necessary here. On the day before one would like to go fishing one took *liko* grass and *ontsantsaa* grasses and salt. A package was made and in the evening one burned this and inhaled the smoke. In the morning fishing should go without a hitch. The only avoidance was that one should not let the ingredients fall on the ground, for part of the mixture was not burned but kept in *apfura*. Kola was given to the package (Sims: *wana m̃uti*: 'spit upon kola-nut, and talk to a fetish') and an object called *linkani*, consisting of vine plaited in such a way as to make the tiniest dish in the form of a tri-lobed flat knot. This was used to offer kola to the *pfura*. One had to be a *ngàà* to make this or conversely if one could make it, one was *ngàà*.

Osel'beene as a category of charms designating bottles with medicine and grilled leaves, that were prayed to when one bought the preparation from the *ngàà* and the avoidance of which was that no woman loved by the owner could touch it, are modern. They are made for love, to acquire wealth, or to make a friend give money. However the only new thing about it seems to be the glass or plastic bottle. Formerly exactly the same items were sold by the *ngàà* in *pfura* packages or tiny gourds.

The type of charm was very similar to *kaa* but it involved no *nkira*, only *apfu*. By 1963 some were made to bewitch one's enemies and it was virtuously claimed that this was never done before. This may be true in that, if it were an old practice, a distinction between witch and sorcerer with magic would have arisen. It did not. The matter must remain uncertain, however, since chiefs or wealthy traders might very well have used such means against their adversaries.

4. *Becoming a ngàà*

The craft of healing was very often learned from father or mother along with the secrets of the *imiõ* used in that family. Fathers could train promising sons and associate them with him in his practice, as happened for instance with Ikoli who began his career in this way as an apprentice in 1948. His father knew many *imiõ* which he inherited and perhaps he added some new ones to them.[29] One advantage of this procedure was the belief that when *ngàà* grew old and weak, their *imiõ* also became less effective, thus pointing to a tie between the efficacy of the charm and its maker. The young apprentice reinvigorated the old recipes. In this way especially families who specialized in such things as mental illness, the handling of fractures, snake-bites, and other sorts of accidents maintained the skill. They usually passed it on from father to son, because sons lived with their fathers and nephews did not live with their uncles. When the old man died his ingredients were passed on. If there was no heir, they would be deposited in or upon the grave.

Sometimes a child had not learned the craft but inherited the equipment. Just as in other specializations, it could then happen that the *ikwii* of the *ngàà* would visit him in dreams and urge him to take up the craft. In such a case the living man was usually requested to apprentice himself to another *ngàà*. It was claimed that only the knowledge was transmitted directly by dream. But such an apprenticeship did not last long. The apprentice paid a fee, stayed one or two weeks with the teacher, learned the rudiments of the art and went back home. If his *ãti* were still weak, or becoming weak in the course of time, he could return for a refresher course, which undoubtedly must have happened to those who wanted to take up the craft seriously.

There was a whole scale of *ngàà* from the owner of one *ãti* to the accomplished healer and diviner. But to become a great *ngàà* more formal calling was needed. Most often it began when a boy or a girl fell ill and almost died. He recovered, but began to act in a strange fashion, straying here and there and finally disappearing into the forest (not in the savannah) where he might stay for weeks or even months. When he returned, he had recovered his balance and declared himself *ngàà*. He then became an apprentice and stayed with his teacher until he knew everything the other person knew, unlike the previous type of *ngàà*. It also happened that they did not apprentice themselves, but started practice right away and it was then supposed that the *ikwii* of their deceased father had taught them. This whole procedure applied usually to men. Women *ngàà* acquired the craft after having entered *itsuua*, emerged *ngáàyuulu* and stayed with the woman who had directed

[29] No written data from the nineteenth century are available on these first ways in which the craft was inherited. The oral data do not go back to the period. Yet it makes common sense succession and is so similar to succession in crafts such as smithing that it can be accepted for the 1880s.

the *itsuua*. But, like men, they could also become *ngàà* by going to *olũ*.

The *ngàà mbulu* were the most revered among the *ngàà*. They could only achieve this status by a prestigious and spectacular ritual in which they searched for their *mbulu* in a ritual called *olũ*. This began not unlike *itsuua*. A person fell ill and while they were singing and playing the pluriarc in the house he suddenly began to dig with his hands in a corner of the house. The hole became deeper and deeper and finally the person disappeared entirely into it. A mat or some cover was put over the hole, once he was in it. The people waited for nine days for his return drumming and singing all the time, if the kin group of the candidate *ngàà* was big enough. Meanwhile he was underground and moved under the earth to the spirit Obuu waalua who would give him the *mbulu* skin and the *iliri* whistle with which he could detect who was ill and attacked by witches when he whistled. If he blew on it later, Obuu and all his ancestors would come to help him.

Obuu was a great *nkira* and he gave *nkobi* or boxes with drugs along with the *mbulu* skin. Some, near the Congo river, believed that he lived under the whirlpools created by the current and the sand of sandbanks was his sign. People collected it and put it in little bark boxes, *nkobi* as being from him. Inland, some people believed simply that he lived underground in an unknown place, or everywhere underground, or that he came from a place *alua*. In the nineteenth century Obuu meant either the Congo river itself (Sims: Mubu: 'The river Congo') or the ocean;[30] *Obuu waalua* meant Obuu the healer.

After nine days the *ngàà* emerged from a hole some distance away from the house and carried the objects with him with perhaps also a *nkobi*, the objects *oshwi* and *olũ*, after which the ritual was named, wealth in the form of squares of raphia and a stick *okaana*, like the one used in *itsuua* rituals. This variety of *ngàà* was called *ngàà mbiere* and was superior to the *ngàà olũ* proper who had not dug but stayed in the house, rather as for *itsuua*. Only the first one was a genuine *ngàà mbulu*. He emerged a *ngàà*: before he could not cure people, now he was a master at it. The *ngàà* who had first treated him when he began to dig and who had actually helped to make the hole and cover it with cloth now became his *taara*. He would now avoid eating cassava in its *ito* form, eating only chikuange. If it did not work out and the candidate did not start a hole or stopped digging, he would stay in the house nine days, dancing much of the time, and would receive the skin, the *iliri* and the *nkobi*,

[30] H. BRUNSCHWIG, *Les cahiers*, p. 166 and *idem*, *La négociation*, p. 43. Brazza first identified Obo as the ocean among the Kukuya, but stuck to this at Mbe. For him the Congo was Olumo. Calloc'h, p. 278, gives *nzali mõgwa*: 'the salt river' for 'océan' and that is the usual term. Yet all peoples of the Lower Kasai, east of the Tio as far away as the Kuba identify *mbuu* as the ocean.

As for *waalua* it is obviously derived from Sims: *lua*: 'to be sick', so the name is 'Obuu, the healer'. The belief has similarities with the beliefs about Kalunga to the south.

when he came out. But he had not made the dangerous journey underground, where *apfu* were lurking to kill, and his prestige was therefore limited.

All informants in 1963 agreed on this account and some said they had assisted in their youths at such rituals where the man came out away from the house. Ubwoono's mother did this and disappeared when she was pregnant with him, i.e. during Iloo's reign. So obviously, and for the first time in this account, some conniving must have taken place among the *ngàà* at least. A tunnel had to be built and a person be hidden for nine days.

The one *ngàà mbulu* at Mbe was a woman who had been in the house but did not dig a hole. She had learned her trade from the *ngàà mbulu* who put her in the house. And from her account it was clear that the ritual was planned in advance but that it was unknown to the assistants whether or not the candidate would dig the hole. Most *ngàà mbulu* certainly belonged to the second variety, whose prestige was still greater than that of any other *ngàà*.

The status of *ngàà* was largely achieved. True, in the case of curers, though not of diviners whose power lay in their *kaa* or the help from their *ikwii*, one needed to have had a *ngàà* among one's forebears. This very often happened, given the bilateral system of descent and the great number of modest practitioners. But this was only a prerequisite at best. Great *ngàà* became famous by achieving the *olũ* ritual and showing success in curing and in divining. The latter was more prestigious than the former but both went together in the persons of famous *ngàà*.

That status was also based on a public image fostered in part by the *ngili* avoidances the *ngàà* upheld and by the degree of spectacular behaviour he put on when officiating. Most *ngàà* had to be a little ascetic. They could not eat more than three kola nuts or bananas in a row while another delicacy, sugar-cane, was forbidden altogether to them. Often they could not sleep with their wives, and sometimes they should sleep next to them but not have intercourse. The latter also reflected on the sacredness in which they often found themselves when officiating. The sacred was cool and aloof. It feared defilement. Thus *ngàà* could not enter the house of a woman who had given birth, because an opposite form of fertility was too strong there. He should also behave with a maximum of decorum when not officiating. He should avoid anything that witches do, like going about naked. And this was even more important in that many people believed *ngàà* to be witches themselves and thought they had acquired their powers by killing people whose *ikwii* they used as *apfu*. In all of this the image of the *ngàà* was like that of a chief or a king and the attitude of people towards him was reminiscent of their behaviour towards great chiefs, a mixture of respect and fear. A final touch to the *ngàà*'s image was a certain mystery. He was said to be able to see the unseen, so that if he stared into the void, people were intrigued. Some *ngàà* talked to others by means of grunts and clicks like those with which *ikwii* or *apfu* are called, which was received with awe. Certainly the best local *ngàà* were leaders in their community as much as the chief was.

Some rose to higher eminence. If among most of the *ngàà* actual mystification did not exist, the thirst for more prestige brought it about by some. It is typical that mystification must have been part of the ritual to become the highest ranking class of *ngàà*. For such ambitious men tried and often succeeded in being called in to cases far away, where some politically tense situation had created a difficult case for divining. Such a man began on arrival by astonishing the local people by reciting all the knowledge he had gathered about them, before launching himself into some unorthodox but always highly spectacular witch-hunting. This type of man was of the same stamp as the great traders or the greatest chiefs and the positions he tried to gain or the conflicts in which he competed go beyond the terms of reference of this part of the book.

Most *ngàà* stayed in their community, belonged there, divined and attempted to cure the misfortunes of their neighbours. Their status was higher than anyone else, excepting only the local chief of the land or the most energetic leaders of bigger settlements, but that was because they fought witches. This is also the reason why their status was so much higher than that of any artisan. Even in economic terms it was understandable that it should be so, for many were ill and had to be helped along to remain productive. In social terms they were essential as the leaders, because of their role in playing down conflicts or at least arbitrating in them through divination, thus being in fact a counterweight to political leadership.

Before the ideologies on which local Tio society was built can be described, there still remains another class of rituals to be dealt with: those which concerned life itself, rather than the restoration or the improvement of a good life which has been discussed here.

Chapter VIII

The Flow of Life: Birth and Death

THE events of birth and death are life itself. They created a person's existence or transformed it from that of a living thing to a shade. Ascribed status flowed from birth and all status was destroyed at death. Nothing was more important for people. These events were important to social groups also. True, groups arose in other ways, such as through marriage or following scissions in lineages or in villages, and membership of groups could be altered by admitting slaves or selling members, but basically birth and death determined the evolution of the kin group membership. Thus the rituals surrounding these events were not merely an enactment of the passage from one status to another for the individual but also conveyed the meaning of these happenings for society. Nowhere else can the relation between individual and society be better grasped than on these occasions. Before birth and death can be described however we must first turn to the notion of life or the cause of life *mpiini* as the Tio call it.

1. *Mpiini*

Everyone lives because of or perhaps with two *mpiini*, a word that means both life-container and that which makes someone live. Besides this force and a body there was also a shadow *ijilajili* (Calloc'h: *i-dzil'a dzili*, p. 279; Sims: *izilazili*: 'reflection'). The theft or destruction of the latter could be imagined but had no great import, whereas the capture of both *mpiini* and their destruction was death.

One *mpiini*, the dominant one, was received from the father and the other from the mother. The father's *mpiini* consisted of an arm-ring or other object which the father put in a box or a calabash with a lid *nkir'mbu*.[1] This ring *ilua* (Sims: *mulua*), usually made out of copper, had a mysterious link with one specific but unknown animal in the bush. People only knew who their animal double was when they were about to die. If the animal was killed, the person would die. But the correspondence remained imperfect, for if the person died, the animal survived. It would begin to behave in an eccentric fashion. If it had been an elephant it would go off alone as bull elephants used to do and it

[1] Sims: *nkira mbu:* 'a calabash with lid to store cloth in'. It was a small round calabash cut in half. The lid part fitted on the bottom part by indentations at the edges. It was closed by a cord round the top of the lid. *Nkira mbu* were used, not only for *mpiini* but also for keeping women's jewellery. Any container of *mpiini*, on the other hand, could be called *lipfuo*.

became very easy for men to kill them during a hunt. If it had been a wart hog it would go off and start eating cassava, etc. And in the reverse case only some people believed that a person would show the same symptoms as the animal which had been killed or died, e.g. would complain of pains at the spot where the animal had been wounded. Most Tio seem to have believed that when the animal had died a person felt ill and died too. In practice this situation never arose since persons were always thought to have been killed by witchcraft and their *mpiini* animals always came to mourn them by coming quite near to the village. If they were lions or leopards they would roar out at the moment of the death of their human double.

Mpiini animals were hippopotamus or crocodile, and they could be any feline, elephant, buffalo, wart hog, jackal, hyena, *nka* antelope, python, or a black forest snake. They were thus the biggest and most dangerous game. The double animal had the sex and the idiosyncracies of the person. If the person was a glutton, so was the animal; if he judged well, so did the animal, etc. Wherever the person went the animal went with him but at a distance which made it invisible. For that matter a person could never kill his *mpiini* by accident at the hunt for it would stay out of the way. And he did not have any avoidance to observe because the person would not know what even the species of his animal was.

It was not clear in 1963 whether the *mpiini* was in the animal or in the bracelet the father designated for it and it obviously did not matter. For the object: *mpiini* too had effects on the human it belonged to. If it came to be lost a person would be very ill and might even die, were it not for the *mpiini* inherited from the mother, and in such case a medicine man could make a new *mpiini* by making a brew and having one person drink it. That which he drank was now his *mpiini*; in fact it is clear that the bracelet was merely the container of the *mpiini*, for if it fell, or if the person fell, the *mpiini* could be caught on the ground by a medicine man. In other circumstances too such a man might steal a person's *mpiini* and blackmail him or let him die. For medicine men were the only ones who could see the *mpiini* and the *mpiini* animals.

Still the father designated a ring and kept it for his children until he died, after which each child took his own ring and kept it.

At Mbe the *mpiini* on the mother's side was the umbilical cord or a ring in a *nkir' mbu* of her own. Usually it was the cord. This was buried near or under a banana tree planted at birth and if the tree flourished, so would the child who could never eat its fruit. The whole spot was called *nkira* like the spirits of nature. All *mpiini* could be called *nkira*, but only as a metaphor for glorification and because to mention the word *mpiini* in public could be dangerous.

Some healing drugs *imiõ*, which became the *mpiini* and were somehow also connected with the animal in the forest, could be made. The aim of such a preparation, which was dangerous, since it could be stolen, was to keep people always in good health.[2]

Despite the divergences in the accounts, the Tio notion of life, for that is what *mpiini* amounts to, was something individual a person received more from his father than from his mother and which could be strengthened or weakened during his life-time. Thus it reflected the bilaterality of the social structure. It also stressed the uniqueness of each individual.

2. *Birth*

The Tio held that a person existed before birth, some indeterminate time after conception. Thus Ubwoono told us that he was with his mother at an *itsuua* ritual, meaning that she was pregnant with him. As soon as the pregnancy was ascertained the mother had to stop all relations with any lovers she might have had, on pain of seeing the child die. Later sexual relations with the husband were also forbidden and she began to observe avoidances which seem to have varied from one woman to another.[3] For instance in 1963 expectant mothers were not supposed to drink water standing up.

When a first baby was about to be born the mother had to be in the village of her husband. For later children she had the choice between her husband's home and that of her mother. As soon as the pains began the women neighbours came to help. A huge fire was built up and the husband was called home. He could no longer leave the village and was restricted to his house for nine days after the birth, just as his wife was: a mild form of couvade. Before the birth actually began, the woman had to confess if she had had any lovers, a ceremony called *ikia*. Then the midwives hung (Calloc'h, p. 177, *yiliga li-nsangi*; 'décorer une case de femme en couches') a yellow wild calabash vine (*iwambe mbãw*) around the door a sign that a female ritual was in progress. The birth itself took place in a squatting position in front of the fire. The midwives intervened only to support the mother and if necessary to push on the belly to accelerate the birth.[4] The child was collected on a banana leaf, the symbol of the individual in Tio rituals. The afterbirth and the ashes of the fire were collected together on a woven plate *ituba*. Immediately after the birth the child was washed and the umbilical cord cut with a little knife *biina* in spatula form, also used for the circumcision a few

[2] The Ngungulu called the umbilical cord *nkira* and that was the mother's *mpiini*. The father's *mpiini* was a package which the child deposited with his mother's brother. The father's *mpiini* is very similar to the package of *imiõ* at Mbe which could be the *mpiini*. Perhaps Calloc'h, p. 238, *li-solo*: 'pacte avec une bête' concerns the *mpiini*. If so it is the first notation about it.

[3] No direct data were available on this except observation in 1963–4. The avoidances usually aimed at preventing the child from looking like someone or to facilitate parturition.

[4] CH. DE CHAVANNES, *Avec Brazza*, pp. 274–5 fn. on birth.

days later. Immediately after birth the umbilical cord, the afterbirth and some of the ashes were buried outside and on that spot a banana tree was planted whose fruit could not be eaten later. The place was called *nkina*. The growth of the tree in the first year prefigured that of the child. As for the umbilical cord it was called *nkwũ* (Calloc'h, p. 276, *nkumi*: and also *nkira*) just like the word for personal name *nkwũ*, (Sims: *nkuño*: 'name') thus symbolizing personality. In fact the Tio held in 1963 that the banana tree was part of the personality complex of the child, his *mpiini*. After the event mother and child stayed for nine days, a ritual number, in the house and the fire was kept burning fiercely.

De Chavannes claimed that there was no ceremony at birth, not realizing perhaps that the birth itself was a ritual. He meant only that there were no festivities and such was also the case in 1963. Liebrechts said that the birth was followed by a salvo of muskets. In Kinshasa a medicine man or diviner examined the baby to see if it would bring evil to society or not. If it did, it was killed on the spot. He foretold also what the baby's lot would be. There the same author also reported that the baby would sometimes be killed so that the woman could resume sexual relations with her husband, which are forbidden during the suckling period which lasted for years. De Chavannes said only that all sexual relations were forbidden to the mother until the child was strong enough to go by itself to the spring to fetch water, which the mother then drank ceremonially. Then the child was weaned. The murder of babies to avoid this long period of abstinence must have been exceptional indeed.[5]

The first days of his life the baby remained unnamed until someone in the family of the husband and someone in the family of the wife would 'dream' a name. This was the name of a deceased person in the alternating generation of the child, i.e. in the generation of its grandparents. Because the name had remained taboo ever since the person died, the child was thus assigned a vacant position in the total system of names.[6] The name indicated the precise status of the child with regard to all other people on his father's side for one name, on his mother's side for the other. And everyone in the village recognized immediately to what groups he belonged by the mere mention of the name. Hence the Tio designation: *nkwũ ula*: 'name of the village'.[7]

[5] CH. DE CHAVANNES, op. cit.; CH. LIEBRECHTS, *Léopoldville*, p. 535.

[6] CH. DE CHAVANNES, op. cit., p. 241, had from the wife of chief Nghia the story that the great chief Opontaba believed de Brazza to be a reincarnation of the father of the king. But reincarnation cannot be deduced simply from the fact that an ancestor tells someone in dream to give his name to a child. And in 1963 no person stated even the principle of metempsychosis. De Chavannes' testimony is rather indirect, as well as exceptional.

[7] CH. DE CHAVANNES, op. cit., pp. 274–5 fn. says that the boy was given the father's father's name and the girl received the father's mother's. He adds however that 'both' names were sometimes joined. This is obviously misunderstood. Cf. J. VANSINA, *Les noms*. Chavannes adds that often the name of a chief was given to the child of a friend of the chief.

Hence also homonyms had to be related and acted as if they were, despite the fact that names could be acquired in other ways, at least at the Pool where De Chavannes claimed that the child of a friend of a chief could be given the latter's name.

North of the Pool among the Bale two other ways of naming children were current in the 1880s[8] and no doubt long before. A baby born under exceptional circumstances might be given a new name alluding to the events. Beyond these symbolic names others were given when it was suspected that the woman had been impregnated by one of two nature spirits, Uma or Nzuma, rather than by her husband. This was recognized, says Ibalico, by the behaviour of the baby in the first months after his birth. Six moons after the event he was named by a female medicine man. On an auspicious day, six months after birth, the day of *Okwe*, the name was given with the following ritual.

After a feast that lasted the whole night in front of a fire fuelled by nine bundles of wood the medicine woman wished the child well in a song and asked for her fee. Then a hole was made in the wall of the house and the child was brought out through it for the first time. If it was a boy, he was put straight on the butt of a gun. Outside, the woman proposed Uma names until the family agreed to one. A meal was eaten made up of food kept during the six months since the birth of the baby, including nine baskets of food and nine fowls (four chickens and five roosters, one of which was to be burned until it was totally consumed by the fire). This was in honour of the shades of the dead. Once the ritual meal was finished people went on dancing for the whole day. For the Nzuma names the ritual was similar except that once the child was outside the woman diviner carried it on her back three times around the house. The mother followed with one or two burning sticks in a basket and a branch of the *nsanda* tree. Then the naked child was put in the middle of the village, the father and the mother knelt down, one in the direction in which the sun rises, the other in the direction where it sets. They then started running on their knees towards the child. The first to arrive there received a white fowl paid by the other party. A claw of the fowl was cut and with the blood the child was anointed on the forehead and chest. The name was given and the fowl was eaten by the kin of the mother or the father, whoever had won the race.

Of these rituals, reported by Ibalico, no trace was found elsewhere and it is more than likely that they were confined to the Bale only. Another naming ritual reported from the Kinshasa area had a villager called *lema* for the occasion to impose a name, after which there was drinking and a fowl was eaten.[9]

[8] M. IBALICO, *Origine et sens*, p. 44, for the following. He collected information in the 1950s but claimed that it described the situation sixty years earlier.

[9] E. COART, A. DE HAULLEVILLE, *La religion*, p. 163. This was reported as a Tio custom but it seems more Hum. The *lema* would have been the mother's brother.

Small children did not yet have a full personality and were not addressed by their names even if these had been given. They were called *ngaaliboo*: 'baby boy' (Sims: *ngaliboo*) or *ntsoono* 'baby girl' (Calloc'h, p. 202: *nsono*). Boys were circumcised a few weeks after birth without any ritual (Sims: *cira mpulu*: 'circumcise'); the coming of the first teeth was awaited with some trepidation, since a child whose upper incisors appeared first showed that either his father or his mother was a witch. In time the babies learned to walk and talk. Yet none of these occasions was used to stress the growth of their personality. Indeed there were still taboos which set them apart from other people. Thus their mother could not take them to a funeral wake, for birth and death had to be kept separate; also no one who had eaten cassava leaves, a very common dish, could touch a baby. The situation came to an end when the child was weaned, after it had brought water to its mother who drank it. This happened roughly two years and six months after birth. The mother could now resume relations with her husband which was called 'to lift up the child': *sene mwana*, following Sims. Now the child could be addressed by its name and had become a full person.

Another effect of these rules was that in this way births were spaced rather more than three years apart which was wise, given the difficulties of nutrition on the plateau. The first months after weaning were nevertheless dangerous for the child because the cassava offered as a substitute weakened it.

If children were now full fledged persons their socialization had, however, barely begun. The girls would begin to follow and later work with their mothers while the boys spent more and more time with their fathers and later with their cohorts. Teaching by example, by use of reward and very little by punishment (Tio children seem to have been spoiled) was very gradual. And it is remarkable that no ritual at all marked the full socialization of the boys and that the marriage ceremony which gave the status of adult was so simple.[10] Perhaps the absence of ceremonies was related to the fact that babies, children, and adolescents were like all the other boys and girls. There were no status differences among them. Since achieved status loomed so large in Tio society it was the differences between status of persons in the same categories of ascribed status which seem to have mattered most. Even at birth achieved status began to differentiate people. Thus twins and the abnormally born occupied a special place in society.

A baby born in an unusual position, such as right foot first or a breech-birth, was called *nganciele* and had a special relationship with *nkira* or nature spirits which gave him a special status. The baby was supposed to influence directly the fertility of the fields and to be a *nkira* in his own right. When such a child was born the father took an *otabi* jar and placed it on the altar of the ancestors. If the child died,

[10] CH. DE CHAVANNES, op. cit., on sexual education.

unlike the case of other children which were not mourned, the father anointed himself every Nkwe Mbali day with *oshüene* (red line on the face).[11]

Nciele individuals held rituals of fertility. One modern variety consisted in the washing of a spendthrift individual with lustral water, so that 'the 5 Fr which entered into the house by one door would not leave by the other'. He could also bless the hunt by washing the gun or the net. But most often his powers were connected with the fields. If a field was not doing well the diviner could discover that it was due to a *nciele's* opposition. The woman who owned it would then pay the *nciele* who would wash her hands and her hoes exactly as the chief of the land did after having prayed to his pot *otabi* or *anshiele*.

If *nciele* were asked to promote fertility beforehand, they either gave the woman palm leaves and the vines of the wild calabash, i.e. the symbols of male and female, to be put on the fields or made a special preparation of plants. Both were known as *nkira* and the woman who had applied them to her field said: 'I have put *nkira* on it.' The special preparation involved the roots of the banana tree *ãtoro* and the *izooli* plant, crushed, pounded, and mixed with water brought by the *nciele* as well as by the client. The mixture was put in a pot and the faces of the clients were decorated with red and white, the basic colours of the Tio. The client used it when she wanted to without observing an avoidance but praying to the *nciele* and offering her charm water or kola. Thus *nciele* were in effect a variety of medicine men or women for increasing fertility.

Twins also enjoyed a special status, and were called *nkira* because of a connexion with fertility similar to that of the *nciele* but weaker. In the unequal Tio society they were moreover an almost perfect expression of equality. The *ambu* (Sims: *bambu*) or twins had special personal names. The older was *ngambu* (Sims: *ngambu*) or 'the owner of gemelleity', the younger *ngampiuo* (Sims: *ngampiu*). So even for twins, seniority was maintained. Triplets were also called *ambu* and the elder children bore the names of twins whereas the third was called *maatieere*: 'the third one'. Despite the stress on seniority, twins were a pair and their parents were now named *maabwoole* and *taarabwoole*: 'mother and father of two'. The child that had preceded the twins was also renamed *waabiir ituba*: 'you carry the platter with ashes', since this child carried the ashes of the fire of the birth of the twins to their ritual place. At the end of the nine days of lying in, a place was prepared at the edge of the settlement where banana trees were planted in two parallel rows and there the ashes and the umbilical cords were buried. There were two banana trees per child and one plate of *ituba* per twin,

[11] According to Mbali, the father of a *nciele* child. But he wore the markings on *odzuo* day when he told this. The pots on the house altar for these children are also called *iti anciele*.

a simple adaptation of the ritual for single children.[12] Children born after twins were still influenced by the special status accorded to twins. They received the following names by order of birth: *Ngampfira* or *Mpfira* for a boy, *Ngeiloolo* for a girl, *Njiila* for the next child, then *Ngeikuu* and *Ntsaalisie*. All these names were known as *nkira* names. They indicated a relation with the *nkira*, just as a woman who had been possessed and healed in the *itsuua* ritual took the *nkira* name *ngáâyulu* among the Mbembe. The allusions contained in the names are only partly clear. The child after the twins is called a witch or a deceiver and the last two of the set have names alluding to a sort of ant-hill (*ikuu*), a symbol of fertility and to lustral water.

For each of the twins the father, as for a *nciele* child, made a *nkir' mbu* filling them with *nkira* things, such as white kaolin and large *olivancillaria nana*, and *mbula* which were used as currency. A special ritual took place at their birth and that of all subsequent children until Ntsaalisie. It consisted in a dance led by the father of the twins in which the songs were the current songs with the exception of a few more salacious ones, but the dances were obscene and symbolized the fertility which had come upon the village. It was believed that if these dances were not held, the mother of twins would not be able to succeed in her plantations. Once again *nkira* is thus specifically linked to plantations and much more so than to success in hunting or the accumulation of commercial wealth.

The gemelleity of the twins was expressed in the teknonyms of the parents, their banana trees and pots, their own names and their whole daily life. One twin was supposed to do as the other did. Their clothes, pots, dishes, food, utensils were all as equal and identical as possible. This equality ran contrary to the basic tenet of Tio society and it is certainly for this reason that it was stressed so much with twins even though at the same time seniority did apply: the oldest twin married first and inherited as much as the other twin and younger children together. But he was still a twin and as such a symbol of equality, perhaps of the negation of authority based on age, perhaps simply of the negation of the relevance of ascribed status.

Thus the case of twins was similar to that of the *nciele* child in their exemplification of fertility, and both were extremes of what normal birth also meant. But the case of twins went beyond this in its implication of an equality which threatened seniority, hence the additional complications in the ritual. All the rituals of birth implied that life and personality were not believed to be identical, for people acquired their individuality gradually. The process began before birth and naming was the obvious attribution of personality. Even after the name was

[12] Burial sites for the placenta of twins are different from others. Two parallel lines of trees are planted next to the banana trees for each placenta which face each other.

given, a long time elapsed before the name could be used and the child was recognized as an individual. Furthermore the lack of differentiation in the ritual showed that it was not an occasion where social variables such as status or wealth were emphasized. The child of a king was not handled differently from that of a pauper which shows the limited role of the Tio attributed to ascriptive status. Indeed, the only differences in the rituals of birth were related to the manner of birth and could be said to reflect already achieved status, were it not that they so clearly reflect first the quality of fecundity, that quality society needed for its very survival.

3. *Death*

Death meant passing away from the living to the status of *ikwii*. It was the only occasion in a man's life where the whole sum of his life's achievement was shown to all. So no two funerals were exactly the same and ambitious Tio men were very concerned about their obsequies. This explains Ngaliema's insistence that Stanley furnish him a costly and as yet unseen sort of coffin.[13]

After death there had to be mourning to acknowledge the gap left by the departed and the deceased had to be integrated with the *ikwii* while the mourners had to be reintegrated into society. Death was not overcome however until the widower or widow had remarried, the inheritance been distributed, and the name of the deceased been dreamed of and given to a new child. Then only was the death wiped out.[14]

Death also represented a crisis for the social groups to which the departed belonged. For its cause was always witchcraft and it represented temporary defeat in the ceaseless struggle of these groups against all others. Hence the dramatic atmosphere. For every death was followed by an inquiry into its cause, accusations of witchcraft developed and tensions were thus increased in the community.[15] The analysis of this conception about the causes of death must however be left for another section.

The rituals of death include the dying, the preparation of the corpse, the wake and mourning, the burial, and the end of the mourning period, a sequence which could take up to a year for a king.

As soon as the palaver of *okuu* had failed to improve the condition of a patient, as soon as the diviner-healer abandoned medication, everyone expected the patient to die. If the illness became too long it was

[13] A. MAURICE, *Stanley*, photo. opp. p. 121, p. 125. It was to be forty-two inches in diameter and twenty-one inches deep, black sheet-iron imitation of a Tio coffin.

[14] M. IBALICO, *Origine et sens*, pp. 30–1; J. VANSINA, op. cit., E. ZORZI, *Al Congo*, p. 409, for a mention of the taboo on the name of the dead.

[15] TH. MASUI, *L'état indépendant*, p. 82, stated that death always resulted from crime or witchcraft and was followed by poison ordeal for the accused. This is probably an over-generalization.

necessary to make the patient die. For this a rope was attached to the arm of the patient and the other end was brought outside the house. The whole family would pull on it. Then the eldest *nkieli* or child cut the rope and the person died. The husband or wife of the deceased, indeed any of his affines could not be present. The rope was held by the children, brother and sisters (all *nkieli*, *nnaana*, and *mbwei* present), and his sister's sons, his parents eventually, but never his mother's brother. If there were no *nkieli* or children, the sister's son cut the rope. According to other indications in 1963 this rite was performed for anyone who was about to die.[16] In this way a biological event was willed and a new role set for the patient. Actual death was proclaimed some time after when respiration had stopped and no heartbeat could be felt. It is significant that the affines were not allowed to 'kill' a person, nor a mother's brother, nor any grandparents. It was primarily the duty of the members of the nuclear family, which might normally be expected to be free of any guilt in bewitching the patient. The one who cut the rope was a sibling of the opposite sex and the reason for it being one of the opposite sex is not quite clear. One is tempted to link this to marriage; one cannot marry one's sibling of the opposite sex and therefore an alliance with an outside group must be entered into. Now the alliance is finished for the deceased and his sibling can replace the spouse. The cutting of the rope by a child or a sister's son by default of a sibling is logical since they were the major heirs.

As soon as the death had been proclaimed, all left the house, again with the exception of one or two women whose duty it was to wash the corpse with the juice of mashed banana trunks and to clothe it. The banana represented a person and the juice stood for blood. The others outside immediately started to wail and howl and weep against the walls of the house with the arms crossed behind the head. The women shouted *taaro, maamaame*: 'my father, my mother'. On hearing the noise the villagers rushed to the scene and immediately joined the mourners, weeping, wailing, and beating their breast. The less close kin they were the shorter time they stayed. After a decent interval they left and as soon as they had turned the corner, the tears ceased running, clothing was straightened out and they went about their work in the village adding perhaps a banana frond to their clothing as a sign of mourning. If the deceased was a man, no one was allowed to go to the fields on the first days after death. There could be some delay between the actual moment of death with the first wailing and the arrival of the first outside mourners. In a case when a child died in Mbe in 1963 the mother started weeping four and a half hours before death occurred and the mourners arrived more than two hours later when the men were already making the catafalque.

To make the catafalque the corpse was first put in an 'N' shape with

[16] This ceremony was not observed directly in the 1880s.

flexed arms and legs and tied tightly in this shape before *rigor mortis* could set in. The corpse was clothed before this. Then lengths of cloth were tied around it as tightly as possible to prevent it from swelling or breaking the bonds. It was then put on a round support in wood or wickerwork and another support was prepared to be put over its head. On the head a copper dish was put for a cap. Dried banana leaves were put all around the corpse between it and the wall of the catafalque which was made out of more cloth. The wall was stitched then to the bottom and top parts and this structure was the coffin. The first pieces of cloth used had been those which belonged to the deceased. The others were attached by close kin and the usual sign of condolences was the giving and accepting of cloth to be sewn on the catafalque. By 1880 these were already mostly imported cloth at least at the Stanley Pool even though *ndzu atieeri* or *ndzu anna*, the *ntaa* were still in use.[17] The brothers of the deceased man set the numbers to be given by the in-laws. If they set two, said Mbali, the child would give five, even ten, each according to his possibilities, but more than two. The brothers-in-law gave the number set by the brothers of the deceased. Others might then give from one to three pieces of cloth. (Calloc'h, p. 150, *kura*, 'cadeau de mort'.) The catafalque was made by the children, the brothers-in-law, and the fathers-in-law of the deceased.

In a case at Mbe in 1963 the father of the deceased child gave two lengths, his brother and half-brother each one-half of a length and the mother's brother of the mother of the child two. Since it was a child no others were added. The three wives of the father of the deceased wept all day along with the wives of the mother's brother of the father and the father himself. The others left after one hour and a half. The makers of the catafalque were the father's brother's daughter's husband and two husbands of two daughters of two of the father's half-brothers and one mother's mother's brother's daughter's husband, i.e. all belonging to the theoretical generation of the child on the father's side and one generation higher on the mother's side. The main point is that all were affines; in fact they were the closest affines of the deceased child and in his generation. It is worth noting that one of these men was in this position by a putative relation only which allowed him to claim residence at Mbe. In this case where the death had occurred in the early morning, the mother stopped weeping at twelve and began again at two in the afternoon but was left almost alone until the formal mourning began with a funeral dance in the evening. And all during

[17] A. MAHIEU, *Numismatique*, 1928, XXI, II, p. 120; E. ZORZI, op. cit., p. 393, CHEF DISTRICT BRAZZAVILLE, *Décès*, p. 3. The corpse was not embalmed and smoke was produced to keep the flies away only near the corpse. Medicinal herbs *tsantsako* were burned, to protect the living against evil and the death in general (17 sq.). To refuse a length of cloth (as happened at Ngalifourou's funeral) was a great insult, tantamount in fact to an accusation of witchcraft.

the day, even when they were working at the coffin the men discussed the possibility of witchcraft.

Other funerals were similar and data from the period confirm the general pattern. The catafalque was prepared in the same fashion. For men 'warpaint' was first added on their faces.[18] The catafalque was probably prepared by the in-laws, the brothers-in-law being most indicated.

For certain categories of persons the funeral rituals were different. When a child was very small, practically no ceremonies were held. Ibalico attributed the absence of ritual for firstborn children among the riparian Tio of the Pool to the belief that if a child were buried with pomp and much cloth, it would not be reborn again if it happened to be a *nkira* spirit. Some of the nature spirits incarnated themselves in children in the hope of being buried in great state, after which they would refuse for ever to be reborn. The belief certainly exemplified the great prestige funerals held for the Tio.[19] No reason for simplifying funerals, burial, and mourning for children was given in Mbe, the obvious one being that these persons had not yet acquired much individuality and much status. For once children were two years old or more and weaned, a regular procedure was probably followed.

When a woman died in childbirth or during pregnancy an autopsy was performed. The child was buried separately. But if the mother showed a suspicious swelling, i.e. a sign of being a witch, the corpse was beaten by the people present and it was thrown in the bush, wrapped in one piece of cloth that also surrounded the child and the ends of which were tucked in round the mother's body. Similarly when someone died without apparent reason an autopsy was made to reveal if there was a suspicious tumour or not. If there was, the corpse was handled as has been mentioned. Witches could also be weighted with a stone and simply thrown into the Stanley Pool according to Chavannes. Johnston reported that somehow their skulls were retrieved and set on poles in the village to remind malefactors of their ultimate punishment. As late as 1964 a death with suspicious swelling afterwards was handled swiftly. A person passing through Mbe died there under these conditions and even though he had seven close kinsmen at Mbe was immediately buried. He died late in the evening and by sunrise he was gone. Murderers were also thrown into the bush, Johnston affirmed. Slaves and paupers were thrown in the bush or the river.[20]

Women and children were usually buried with the minimum of pomp

[18] CH. DE CHAVANNES, *Voyage*, pp. 83–4; *Idem*, *Avec Brazza*, pp. 163–6; *Les tissus*, p. 211; E. ZORZI, op. cit., p. 393; CH. LIEBRECHTS, op. cit., pp. 535–6.

[19] M. IBALICO, op. cit., p. 31.

[20] A. MAHIEU, ibid., p. 120, for pregnant women and cysts; CH. DE CHAVANNES, *Avec Brazza*, I, p. 164, for paupers and slaves, and p. 536, for drowning a woman witch in the Pool; H. H. JOHNSTON, *The River Congo*, pp. 179–80, on witches. Also H. H. JOHNSTON, *Grenfell*, p. 658, for murderers.

for the funeral, the mourning period, and the burial. For chiefs and kings or even aristocrats it was different. First the catafalque was built differently: instead of banana leaves a special bearded grass, *iyaala*, was used, while the vine to pack the bier was of the *iwa* plant. On the coffin a *ndzo ancweli*, a construction of no direct use, more or less like a cone set on top of the coffin, was added and also placed at the bottom of such a catafalque. It is what De Chavannes called a large 'pompon de fibres' on top of the coffin.[21] On this wickerwork frame skins of smaller felines were fastened, especially those of *mbala* and *ntsii* which were also used in the cult of the *ikwii*. When a king or great chief had died *iyaala* and *ndzo ancweli* were used and in addition the head was cut out of all the banana trees of his residence, an obvious symbolic gesture. For other aristocrats, including queens, only the *ndzo ancweli* was built. Beyond this though, the major differences between one funeral and another lay in the size and make-up of the catafalque itself. The more important the deceased the more people came to attach cloth to his catafalque. Mahieu claimed that in this way in the area of Kinshasa some accumulated up to 9,000 pieces of raphia cloth. He saw a catafalque which was so big and high that the front of the house had to be taken out to get it out. The bier was six feet high. For a woman he noted, there were never more than twenty *ntaa* or sixty pieces of raphia cloth. A catafalque for a wife of the king we saw in 1963 measured six feet by three and represented less than sixty lengths of cloth, but included some of the coveted red cloth. In 1913–14 a bier was measured at Ndolo, near Kinshasa which measured eight feet ten inches across and nine feet seven inches high.[22] Such large biers existed also in the 1880s or early nineties since one is recorded measuring seven feet across by eight feet one inch in height.[23] Sixty-five men were needed to drag this catafalque and the author estimated that two-thirds of all imported cloth in the lower Congo and in the region of the Cataracts was used for burials. For the Tio of Kinshasa it would not have been less.

Variations in the size of the catafalque were also shown by the estimate of the numbers of carriers required to move them. Pecile in 1884 says four were enough for an ordinary burial, De Deken in 1897 estimated thirty to forty carriers, and elsewhere (1892) twenty to thirty carriers were deemed sufficient. But Chavannes mentioned only six carriers for a relatively important man in 1884. These were relayed by other teams of six.[24] Other authors also commented on the enormous amounts of cloth used. Coquilhat met a huge boat on the river with the catafalque of a chief, on which they had tied *all his cloth* and they would

[21] A. MAHIEU, op. cit., p. 120. [22] J. MAES, *Tissage*, p. 403.

[23] *Les Tissus*, p. 211; CH. DE CHAVANNES, op. cit., pp. 163–6, gives three feet in diameter for one foot four inch to five feet in height.

[24] E. ZORZI, op. cit., p. 394; C. DE DEKEN, *Lettre-Missions de Chine et du Congo*, 1897, p. 440a; A. DE CHAVANNES, op. cit., p. 164; *idem, Voyage*, pp. 83–4; *La tribu Bateke*, p. 123.

bury with him all his guns, his wealth in trading goods, and his copper rods.[25] Liebrechts says that a great deal of a chief's wealth was buried with him. They tied an enormous quantity of cloth around the bier and attached plates, guns, and all sorts of European items to it in 1887 at Kinshasa.[26]

There was also competition around the Pool for the best funeral. Ngaliema had begged Stanley, whatever the cost, to get him a metal cylindrical coffin from Europe and a few years later the chief of Mfwa, on the other bank, wanted De Chavannes to make a sort of wooden tub for him and one for his wife.[27] This was certainly to emulate Ngaliema.

Such attitudes towards funerals resulted in great expenditures, as the evidence indicates. Yet the data should be viewed critically. Earlier observations tended to give the lesser sizes of biers and numbers of carriers required and observations made on the plateaux show that the catafalques were far less lavish than on the Pool. It could have been expected, since cloth was commercial wealth and was obviously in greater supply at the Pool and there supplies increased greatly after 1882, if only because the Association Internationale Africaine and the Mission pour l'Ouest Africain vied with each other to buy the allegiance of chiefs with substantial gifts.

Yet there remain the assertions that much of the wealth of chiefs was buried with them and here the statements of Coquilhat, Liebrechts, and *La tribu des Bateke*, that the stock of cloth in 1892 was used above all for the burial of its owner, are explicit. It is on statements such as these that Sautter based his contention that the chiefs of Mbe had depopulated their core area to pay for the cloth that was later destroyed when they were buried.[28] Yet it is clear that on the plains there were very few expensive burials of this type before 1885 and that authors on the Pool tended to exaggerate or at least to mention only the largest burial they had witnessed. Most of these were observed after 1884 as well. When a great chief Bwabwa Njali was buried in September 1884 Giacomo de Brazza was not struck by the great size of the bier.[29] Yet this chief had received gifts from every traveller since 1881, not counting the income he derived from his ferry on the Djoué. There had been two nights of shooting, rather than only one or a few hours, which was reported by Brazza from north of the Lefini, but the chief was buried rapidly which was not the usage later when the corpse of a chief remained on view for as long as a year to allow his subjects to pay their obligatory contribution in cloth.[30]

[25] C. COQUILHAT, *Le Haut Congo*, p. 64.
[26] CH. LIEBRECHTS, op. cit., p. 534.
[27] Cf. fn. 12; CH. DE CHAVANNES, *Avec Brazza*, p. 252.
[28] G. SAUTTER, *Le plateau*, pp. 154–9 and especially p. 155.
[29] E. ZORZI, op. cit., p. 426. [30] *Les tissus*, p. 211.

Still there is little doubt that there was a complex of conspicuous consumption even before the arrival of the Europeans and that the death of the greatest chiefs, kings, or wealthiest merchants did destroy a sizeable amount of goods. The effects of this practice on trade, inheritance of wealth and power must await the discussion of Tio society at large. Suffice it to say here that the practice showed the intimate links which existed between trade, prestige, and power, whether legitimate or not.

The event of death itself was a crisis and in the first hours after it happened, people might be afraid of developments. Grief-stricken kin could become convinced that so and so had committed witchcraft and avenge themselves instantly. Thus de Brazza was believed to be responsible for the death of the eighteen-month-old son of NGAANTSU. The visiting Bobangi at the village were 'not at ease and generally distant'.[31] In another case Amelot was believed by Ngambiele, head of Kimpoko, to have bewitched and killed one of his wives. The situation deteriorated rapidly in an attack on the post of Amelot and it had to be evacuated.[32] Perhaps the atmosphere is best rendered by the following passage from de Brazza:

> Great weeping comes from the village, when I return. Every one shouts and weeps. The brother of the chief, who was ill, has just died, which explains the preoccupation of the chief which had given some weight to the false alarm of the Bobangi. The women take their wrappers off and wear instead banana leaves the rib of which forms a belt. They are painted white. But new miseries are awaiting me while they carry baskets of palmtree moss (the thing that one uses for the lighter) to surround the corpse with. My guide comes to me mysteriously saying that the men who came from the other bank are no good. They have caused the brother of the chief to die. We talked among ourselves about that, he said and some said the white man had done it but Ngampe (headman) had said no, that the white man had brought here only words of peace and that he had given many trade goods. Certainly, it was not him who had made the fetish which had killed his younger brother. He ended saying not to eat what the people from the other bank had brought with them. The corpse, once it had been folded in four, wrapped in cloth and mats and well packed up, was carried to an empty space between the huts and there, placed on a mat, kept sitting by the close kin, while everybody wept around it and told [glorified] what he had done in his lifetime. [and] After having wept and made tam-tam all night, they simulated a fight with oars [they were *Dzindzali*]. Then when day came they buried him near the village.[33]

Once the funeral bier had been made, at least for the ordinary citizen, mourning in a more formal manner began. The wives, the sisters, and the mother of the deceased sat around the catafalque with

[31] H. BRUNSCHWIG, *La négociation*, p. 52.

[32] CH. DE MARTRIN DONOS, *Les Belges*, II, pp. 181–4.

[33] H. BRUNSCHWIG, *Les cahiers*, pp. 195–6. They also fired salvoes of muskets. Note that burial on the day of death was extremely fast. Compare the ceremony with CH. DE CHAVANNES, *Voyage*, pp. 83–4.

their backs to it, silent or smoking a pipe.[34] They put on banana or other leaves (Calloc'h, p. 154, *i-pula* and leaves *mu-fuli*, *i-sili*) and painted themselves. From time to time they got up and circled the house, wailing and lamenting. If a chief had died they painted their faces with ashes, wore a black wrapper and twisted their hair up into little balls consisting of blackened grease and clay (Calloc'h, p. 163, *mfuluga*; 'coiffe de deuil'). In the evening there was a wake, unless of course the person had already been buried as in the case cited by de Brazza.

The women, hair shaven, advanced shuffling with their feet, half dancing, half walking, in front of the gap in the wall of the house in which the catafalque had been set up. The mother of the wives still walked all round the village in a dazed condition, white ashes on the face and bare-breasted, lamenting the deceased. Their appearance told of the drama, for ashes and shaven hair were the symbols of death, the extinguishing of the fire of life, the bareness expressing grief and the banana leaf showing that a person was involved. They carried leaves and vines of the wild calabash *iwambe mbãw* as baldrics. This was the plant of femininity, but also the plant that was hung around the door when a child was born. It showed that the ritual concerned life itself. Furthermore the main women mourners carried *õtsara* in their hands as if they were invoking the *ikwii*.

Then the men came with a garland of palm fronds, the symbol of men, but this may perhaps have only been worn if the deceased was a a man. They had drums and horns, but no pluriarcs and started to dance and sing all night long. The older men merely sat there and visited. Before the dancing got under way a speech was made, by the father of the deceased, or a father's brother or by his eldest sibling, acting as *mpfõ andzo*. The speech would conjure people not to quarrel, not to fight; it urged the men to dance all night; it forbade them to bewitch one another and cautioned them at the same time to be on their guard, saying for instance that he who has a cup should not share it (for fear of poisoning people). In essence the conjuration delineated the crisis and gave direction as well as some reassurance to the mourners, for it was understood that if witches roamed about or fights broke out the *ndzo* would react corporately.[35]

The dances were those people liked, although a funeral dance or a war dance may have been included. Most of the songs were ordinary ones which were also sung for instance during healing and were intended for the living as much as for the dead. A few lamentations were sung by the women such as '*mama, pi enzo*': 'mother, be quiet in the

[34] Cf. photograph in H. LOIR, *Le tissage*, p. 57, dating from 1913. The attitude of the mourners was still the same in 1963. Note that no banana leaves were worn any more but a wrapper. On dress for mourning a chief, cf. J. DYBOWSKY, *La route*, p. 54.

[35] The written sources gave no data on conjurations.

house'.[36] Guns were also fired from time to time and the men drank beer or wine. There may have been associations of men dancers in the larger communities; in Mbe by 1963 there were two—one of the older men who sang the songs and danced the steps the deceased of their age would have liked, and one of the younger men. This may be a modern phenomenon since the reason for the two 'societies' was said to be that they could not agree on the music to be played.[37]

These dances and songs were repeated in the following afternoons and evenings until the burial. The participants had to be fed and given drink as on the first night by the close kin and thus a long burial period could consume most of the fortune which was not lavished on the bier itself. Visitors from other villages came to dance too. This the deceased had expected and the length of the festivities, the numbers and quality of visitors who had to be entertained and who added cloth to the bier, were all signs of the status the dead person had enjoyed in life. Thus Stanley describes the enthusiasm of Ngaliema, the ex-slave, when describing how guns would be fired for several days and there would be a big catafalque of cotton cloth, woollens, silks and satins, including no doubt the famous red blankets. His funeral would truly be worthy of a king with singing warriors, wailing women, and young men from villages all around to shoot off their muskets and dance. In this way the length of time the body was exposed was directly related to the wealth of the deceased.[38]

This period varied from one day, but more commonly nine days, to three weeks or a month or two. For a king it had to be a year or close on it and then the date of burial was set so there would be many people and much to eat. For instance Ngalifourou died on 8 June and the burial was planned for the following February because there would be less rain then and the harvest of maize (and groundnuts) would be in.[39] Periods longer than nine days were almost certainly exclusively customary for wealthy chiefs of settlements or great political chiefs only.

It is not known whether mourning at a distance was usual in the 1880s. By 1963 it was. For instance when the death at Brazzaville of a kinswoman was learned in a compound at Mbe there was mourning by the grandfather collateral to the deceased and his wives, who kept

[36] H. H. JOHNSTON, *Grenfell*, p. 724. The observation dated from 1907.

[37] CH. LIEBRECHTS, op. cit., p. 135. In 1963 at one funeral the women danced a Ngungulu dance, for Ngalifourou's funeral Mboshi dances were in use. Fashion seems to have determined what was danced.

[38] CH. DE CHAVANNES, *Avec Brazza*, pp. 164–5, where it was two months; H. STANLEY, *The Congo*, I, pp. 392–3, on Ngaliema; CH. LIEBRECHTS, op. cit., p. 536, who stresses that visitors had to be given food and drink.

[39] CHEF DISTRICT DE BRAZZAVILLE, *Le décès*, pp. 2, 4; E. ZORZI, op. cit., p. 393 (three weeks; immediate for a child); CH. DE CHAVANNES, *Avec Brazza*, p. 263 (two months); *idem*, *Voyage*, p. 83 (eight days to three weeks: he means nine days); *Les tissus:* one year for chiefs. In 1963 the normal length was nine days (a ritual number par excellence) for adults. For queens, chiefs, and kings, it was much longer.

weeping and mentioning the taboo names of all the deceased people they had known to help them weep even more. This lasted but one evening. The practice of mentioning taboo names did exist in Iloo's time since Sims has *zula*: 'to mention the name of a deceased person; to dig a grave, to writhe'.

The burial itself, if not on the ninth day after death, was fixed on one of the two favourable days: *nkwe Mbali* or *okwei*. The bier was put on a stretcher and the bearers took it to the cemetery followed by the whole village and kin from elsewhere. During the procession, drums played and all danced and sang including the bearers who made the catafalque dance with them. The women brought food with them. If the person was important, there had been an all-night dance with various festive dances and perhaps clowning preceding the burial which was then held shortly after sunrise. The burial ground was a cemetery in the woods. As soon as they came near the place the bearers dropped the catafalque and all fled. Coming back later one of the bearers struck the bier, waited and shouted that the dead person was now truly dead, whereupon the food was brought into the cemetery to the head of the *ndzo* officiating, who distributed some to all participants. This funeral meal consisted of, in the case reported by Chavannes, fish with pimento and cassava leaves with palm-oil. It is probable that cassava and perhaps also groundnuts were forbidden to the mourners. The head of the procession did not eat in this instance and perhaps not in others.

Then the tomb was dug by the women who made it a round shaft of seven feet or so in depth. The bier was lowered into it, a stick put from in front of the mouth of the deceased through the top of the bier to above ground level and then the women threw their belts into the grave. This was then immediately filled and the earth stamped down. A small tumulus of earth and ashes marked the emplacement. Then the stick was taken out so that there was now a hole from the mound to the mouth of the deceased through which libations could be offered.[40]

Writers report that for chiefs human sacrifices took place at the tomb. Pecile specifies one boy and one girl killed for even ordinary men;[41] this may have referred to the Tege. But the description of the burial of a leopard after the fashion of a chief lends credence to the reports, for when the leopard in his coffin, was lowered into the grave, some goats and he-goats were slaughtered to accompany it and be food

[40] E. ZORZI, op. cit., p. 394; CH. DE CHAVANNES, *Voyage*, pp. 83–4; *idem*, *Avec Brazza*, pp. 165–6; *Les tissus*, p. 211, and observations in 1964, filmed by ORTF. On an auspicious day cf. YOULOU KOUYA, *adoratrice*, p. 54. The dances for her were *kimbalambala* and *njobé* which are Mboshi and perhaps even Kouyou in origin.

[41] CH. LIEBRECHTS, op. cit., pp. 527, 530, 535–6; *La tribu bateke*, p. 123; E. ZORZI, op. cit., pp. 230–1; *Les tissus*, p. 211, where he claims that the victims were now replaced by figurines [now was 1892]. Already Liebrechts claimed that near Kinshasa and the Europeans the custom had been abandoned, but then as administrative head of Leopoldville in 1887 he could hardly claim otherwise.

for it.[42] At Mbe no sacrifices of this kind were mentioned either by authors or informants.

Burial was in a vertical hole and in the cemetery. One later writer claimed that unlike free persons who were buried in foetal position slaves were buried upright.[43] Bentley differed from others in claiming that a man was buried in the floor of his own house, among the Tio north of the Pool.[44] All others mentioned cemeteries except for the kings.[45] On the graves a little house was often built to protect crockery or jugs left on the mound with ashes that formed the tumulus. The fetishes of the owner were either buried with him or left on his tomb, at least some of them.[46] Burial of a child may have taken place near the house as in 1963.[47]

Around the tombs one planted *oto*, *bwooro*, or *oliõliõ* trees as a sign of recognition for the cemetery rather as for a *nkiini*.[48] For kings regular houses were built over the carefully fashioned high mounds and many of their objects of pride (*unũ*) were displayed on the tombs. Guiral thus saw two tombs in one house. The tumulus in the form of a dome was 'hard as cement'. Remnants of painting on these remained and a Toby statuette was set on top of one. In front of each tomb there stood a *mvuba*, or iron sign of authority, and along the walls hung used cloth. In other houses nearby there were smaller tombs, and the keeper of this royal cemetery explained that the size of the tomb and the composition of the tumulus varied with the rank of the deceased. Ordinary men had only earthen tumuli. On the tombs of the kings deceased since

[42] CH. DE MARTRIN DONOS, *Les Belges*, II, pp. 81–2. Of course one could claim that the animals were the equivalent of food offered to an *ikwii* but food was *not* offered at the burial elsewhere.

[43] E. COART, A. DE HAULLEVILLE, op. cit., p. 180, among the Tio of Kwamouth; H. H. JOHNSTON, *Grenfell*, II, p. 653; A. MAHIEU, op. cit., p. 120.

[44] H. BENTLEY, *Pioneering*, I, p. 253. Cemetery was in 1963 *ampiõ* (Sims: *ampino*) the plural for a grave; CH. DE CHAVANNES, *Avec Brazza*, pp. 165–6, described a cemetery as did E. ZORZI, op. cit., p. 426.

[45] L. GUIRAL, *Le Congo*, pp. 302–3, for royal tombs at the time. Since 1918 at least, kings' tombs all were isolated and near the village where they ruled last.

[46] On *tumuli* and grave furniture. Cf. CH. DE CHAVANNES, op. cit., pp. 105–6; E. ZORZI, op. cit., p. 426 (fetishes left on tomb); R. HOTTOT, F. WILLETT, *Teke Fetishes*, p. 35 (buried with owner); CH. LIEBRECHTS, op. cit., pp. 535–6 (wealth of deceased buried with him); E. COART, A. DE HAULLEVILLE, op. cit., p. 182; TH. MASUI, *D'Anvers*, p. 61; E. ZORZI, op. cit., pp. 411, 430, for *tumuli*. The grave of Opontaba (who died 1893/6) in Mbe had only a small earthen tumulus in the cemetery, but a Toby statuette was still on it. Other tombs showed dishes and jugs from this period. According to Mbali all prestige and costly objects (*unũ*) were buried with their owners. This is not true since we saw a ring *unũ* that had been inherited from the grandfather (a chief) of the owner in 1963.

[47] E. ZORZI, op. cit., p. 411, where one woman and three children had been buried in the village. But this was almost a cemetery by itself.

[48] No *õna*, a sort of cactus, could be planted however. This made the essential difference with the plantation of the *nkiini*.

1918 one finds similar items such as, e.g. a very long single iron clapperless bell, and cloth with the coveted drawings of lions and leopards on a red background against the walls.[49]

In the period following burial, the dead became *ikwii*, when was not known exactly, but it was certainly after burial. They could come to the living in dreams to tell them their needs as they would later, but also to accuse the person who had bewitched them. They could send misfortunes just after their death. Thus Ngalifourou did not like the day of her burial, because the crowd was too small, and sent a great downpour which did not stop the funeral. This happened frequently, since many dead made it rain on the day of their burial. Tornadoes ravaging the plantations and an epidemic among the goats at Mswata were attributed by the chief to the angry spirit of Janssen who had drowned in the river. He had, it was believed, rejoined Europe downstream but he was angry that no monument had been built for him at Mswata.[50] After burial, however, this manifestation of the dead person's behaviour ceased, to be replaced by the usual characteristics of *ikwii*.

The rituals of death were not over with the burial. Mourning (Sims *upfile*; Calloc'h, p. 185, *mu-pfili*) continued and it was only when this was formally abolished that the obligations had been fulfilled. It has been seen that during the first days special dress was required and that no one in the village was allowed to leave it to work in the fields. As long as the coffin stood above ground this was enforced for all close relatives, even though other villagers seem to have been able to go back to their occupations and resume normal dress quite quickly, perhaps as soon as the day after the coffin had been built, or the second day after death. The chief mourners were father, mother and/or spouse of the deceased, as well as the children: in short, the members of the elementary family. They could not eat cassava, or any vegetables, but only bananas.[51] The first days the mourners should also go hungry to show their grief. Then special food avoidances began to appear. For instance if the husband was a hunter, the widow would avoid meat and if he was a fisherman she would not eat fish. The husband would not eat grasshoppers, caterpillars, or the *mpaari* rats, which were mostly collected by married women. Clothes after the first days became a red *vooro*, stained with palm-oil or a black cloth. By 1964 this had become black

[49] L. GUIRAL, op. cit., pp. 202–3. The tomb of Ngankia Mbandieele (died around 1938/9) in Mbe was very similar, to the tombs described by Guiral. The house however was no longer closed, but a shed.

[50] CH. DE CHAVANNES, *Avec Brazza*, p. 535; YOULOU KOUYA, op. cit., p. 54; Likubi believed in 1963 that all deceased people sent rain on the day of their burial. On Mswata, CH. DE MARTRIN DONOS, *Les Belges*, II, p. 279.

[51] E. COART, A. DE HAULLEVILLE, op. cit., p. 184, claimed at the Pool no vegetables, no chikouangue could be eaten but raw cassava could. This seems unlikely because of the nature of even so-called sweet (unpoisonous) cassava. The uncooked leaf of cassava bread might be meant.

clothes or a white sheet. The hair was shaven, the nails were left growing and bathing was forbidden in the river. All of these symbols are obvious. The rags express grief as does the general neglect, this particular shade of the colour red denotes misery (and not power), the nails symbolize continuing life.

The first ceremony to remove mourning[52] consisted in the washing of the chief mourners in front of the houses, in the presence of members of the extended family of the mourner and of the deceased as well as the in-laws of the same generation who had helped to build the coffin. The mourner was washed, his nails were pared and he resumed ordinary clothing. The date at which this took place varied again according to the rank of the deceased, usually from three to five months after death.

The washing was undergone by the husband or wife for a spouse, the parents for an unmarried child. As soon as it was finished and the person clothed, drink was brought for the guests and a meal served. But the chief mourners, just washed, could not yet eat cassava or meat. At night there were dances with the special dance *otiere aakwó*: 'the head-basket of bananas'. This may have been an allusion to the continuing food avoidance or to the coming back of bananas, i.e. the replacement of the deceased by a new child shortly; we do not know.

The second and final end of mourning (Sims: *lisoo*, p. 160, funeral feast, but p. 68, marriage) took place never less than six to ten months after the death and often as much as two to three years later. A man invited all his kin and all the relatives of his deceased wife. A woman invited only her kin, not that of the deceased husband. The guests arrived with contributions, in 1963 ranging from 100 Fr CFA to 500 Fr CFA, which were called *ãloo*. All the big men of the settlement were there too. There was a great dance in the evening after food and drink had been served to the guests. The dances were of the ordinary kind but *otiere aakwó* was also danced. If the deceased had been a chief all the men of the settlements on his lands were invited too and came with their drums. The next day all were fed again and the principal mourners ate cassava and meat. The women donned new clothes. Once this feast was held the widow married the heir. A queen NGAASAA at this time underwent ritual bathing which took the queenship away from her. The widower too could remarry.[53]

The funerary rituals clearly showed the importance of rank, status, and competition in Tio society. In sharp contrast to the ritual for birth there were infinite grades by which again and again wealth, power, status were displayed by the number and quality of people mobilized,

[52] Travellers did not report on these celebrations to end mourning.

[53] Calloc'h, p. 343, *mu-pfili, mfi*: 'veuf, veuve'; Sims: *mfi*: 'unmarried' (and *isani*: 'widow'). The confrontation of both rather makes the state of widowers and widows clear. All sexual relations were forbidden before this last ceremony. Cf. Calloc'h, p. 343: *x. ku mfili apali lobu*: 'X left widowhood today'. The term is identical with mourning (Sims *upfili*, Calloc'h, p. 185, *mu-pfili*).

the length of the proceedings, and the objects used. In a less obvious way they also illustrated the passage of a person from life to the state of *ikwii*, having his close kin accept death, then imagining the possible anger of the deceased and his desire for revenge as well as the fear of the people in the face of death itself at the burial. Gradually he then becomes a 'normal', i.e. mostly benevolent, *ikwii*. And finally the theme of crisis, of loss to a group and the desire to counter-attack is also enacted just after death has occurred.

Birth and death are biological facts with a social significance. The groups concerned are the same in both cases and the elementary family plays a prominent role in the events. Other groups seem not to have participated in the ceremonies at birth at all and played only a minor role in the funerary ritual except just after death and when the *mpfõ andzo* led the burial. Their participation indicated not merely the concern over a loss of a member but the promise of protecting the others. This attitude was also the one these groups took when illness first struck. The role of the family was much more intimate both in birth and death. They lived with the person and formed his most immediate and intimate social surroundings. This tends to underline again the genuine individualism of the Tio and their feeling that they were connected to larger groups only for protection and the fulfilment of needs an individual was hard put to fulfil alone.

But the great differences in the treatment of birth and death did not flow only from the difference between the events. The equality in birth and the inequality in death were stressed. Death for the Tio was indeed the 'final reckoning' and ambitious Tio men hoped to show a dazzling account. The overwhelming importance of achieved status associated with the values of competition and ambition are thus expressed, while prescribed status was almost absent. It showed only at death in the right of aristocrats to have *ndzo ancweli* and was conspicuously absent in birth rituals. Much more visible at funerals were the signs of wealth, the number of retainers which flowed from real power and real wealth. It comes as no surprise that a discussion of death had to take into account the patterns of consumption of trade goods, for it was through trade that the big men in this period had established their power.

These rituals involved no religious specialists at all. This provides a marked contrast to the detection of evil and the prevention of its consequences, barrenness, illness, and death. Then specialists could fight, but once people were born or had died, evil had been averted or had succeeded and the technician of the fight against evil had no further role to play.

To round off the description of the small-scale society, a sketch of the major premises by which the Tio regulated their behaviour and thus made social life possible is needed. This involves a discussion of Tio ideas and values, to which we now turn.

Chapter IX
The Inner World

THIS study must include at least a sketch of some cultural features such as religion, world-view, aspirations, and ethics of the Tio. For if institutions are recurrent behaviour and if society can only exist when the behaviour of its members can be predicted, something must be said about the *primum mobile* of this common and recurring behaviour. Tio religion could not have been omitted and has in fact already loomed large in previous chapters. For religion is a pervasive phenomenon and it has therefore been necessary to describe many rituals and beliefs when the situations were discussed in which they figure. The task here is to pull these descriptions together into a more formal discussion of religious belief, ritual and symbol which will lead on to world-view and ethics. Few direct data, beyond those already used, exist to document these topics at the end of the nineteenth century, but it seems reasonable to attempt at least to sketch the general outlines of religion, both from rituals described and terms known from the period.

Religion concerns all beliefs, rituals, and symbols, which imply a relation between man and supposed supernatural beings or forces. No distinction at all is made between magic and religion and within the complex of beliefs, symbols, and ritual, it is claimed that ritual is the essential element. Furthermore there is a 'constellation' involving religion and latent symbolic categories which form a world-view. Out of religion also flows the general principle of ethics or normative behaviour in relation to what is considered good or bad. The whole constellation forms the 'ideological superstructure' of society: in plain language: a constellation of knowledge, belief, and emotion, common to all Tio, which exercises a deep influence on their social life.

1. *Beliefs*

Tio beliefs in *ikwii*, *apfu*, witches and *mpiini* have already been touched upon. References to *nkira* have been made but the notion must be discussed further. Nzã, the Creator, has not been mentioned so far. For Sims *Nzaña mpuu* was 'God', while Calloc'h translated 'Dieu' (p. 187) by *Nzami* or *nkira*. In connexion with the translation of Sims, Coquilhat reports that the Baptists held that the Tio believed in God but that he was indifferent to man. The Tio were more occupied with their fetishes and charms, rather. The statuettes they had they did not adore and they had only a vague belief in an after life.[1] This thumbnail

[1] C. COQUILHAT, *Sur le Haut Congo*, p. 60.

sketch speaks for itself: it is no more trustworthy than the one Johnston gave, according to which there was no ordeal, no witchcraft, no religious specialist, though when one was needed for legal questions or for a few obligatory ceremonies he could be borrowed from another ethnic group. They had almost no religion although there was a mild form of ancestor worship; they had a shadowy idea of God, but the term given was the sky.[2] Such statements reflected the ignorance and prejudices of outsiders more than any reality. All it means was that the Nzã of the Tio was not readily recognizable as the God of the Christians.

Nzã could be described as the First Cause of all created things or as a Creator of everything that is 'normal'. But he could equally be considered to be the first of the nature-spirits *nkira*, as Calloc'h apparently did. Bilankwi held that Nzã was a *nkira* and had created all the *nkira*, and Ngateo declared that 'the ancestors' thought that Nzã was the sun and the first of the *nkira*. In 1963, as in Johnston's time, he was still connected with the heavens, although this expression may very well have derived from missionaries and Europeans, including Johnston!

There was certainly very little ritual for Nzã. Bilankwi recalled only one prayer: 'God, look at the things, *bu, bu*': *A, Nzã, tal iloo*; *bu, bu*. There was no ritual for him, no sacrifice, only this and perhaps other short prayers which might or might not be answered.

Beyond this there were variants in beliefs by 1963, and no doubt earlier. Bilankwi still believed that Nzã was not endowed with all knowledge: 'There are things he does not know about; if he did, we would know them too.' God created everything, including evil. So the witches are his messengers, for Nzã decides when one will die and the messengers carry out his will. But they also take more people than they are allowed to; then, afterwards, 'Nzã may be angry'. And the same man also declared: 'God created all the names of the twins and that is it.' Those names are all related to an identical *nkira*, so he visualized Nzã as a *nkira* of First Causes. Ngateo held that Nzã was concerned with man and did intervene. He could for instance refuse an *apfu* to a *ngàà*. He could not however send misfortune. Without him 'we would all be in the earth'. He made the things and persons which are considered normal and that excludes witches and misfortune, though if there were to be an accident one would say: 'Nzã is bad, for he opened the road to the witch.' Nzã, thinks Ngateo, was omniscient.

Another typical statement came from the singer Okondzaadza when he said that the praise poems (*ambili*) are first learned from Nzã and that others can learn the poem from the first to whom it was revealed. It shows once again the tendency to use Nzã as a First Cause.

In short the notion had to do with a purely cognitive structure of a world-view. It was the answer to all 'why's'. It is not known whether

[2] J. JOHNSTON, *The River Congo*, pp. 289–90.

this notion was influenced by Christianity,[3] and if so when. The Tio even in 1963 had a name for the Capuchins of the seventeenth century. They were, said Bilankwi, the '*ĩdieele Antoni*'!

There was more to Nzã. Seen as the first of all *nkira* with his residence in the sun, he was identified with this symbol of life-giving force. On the other hand he was not regarded in an anthropomorphic way, as all other *nkira* were. Everyone in 1964, except Bilankwi, agreed that Nzã was never angry or in a good temper: he had no temper. He stayed the same and he did not send illness, although he 'opened up the road' so that witches could harm man. And Ngateo was emphatic to attribute this all to what the 'ancestors' thought about it, i.e. what he learned probably as a child.

It would be tempting to go beyond the sketchy data and to affirm for instance that Nzã was the spirit everyone invoked when he was in 'individual' need. After all, it was true that everyone *could* pray to Nzã without any intermediary, but few prayers are known and it seems that Nzã's name was only one among many used in oaths. Calloc'h, p. 61, mentions '*apfu*', 'my mother', 'your wrapper', 'my hair', 'the ashes of the dead', and 'listen you', all as equivalent exclamations or oaths, so the prominence given to *Nzã* in recent discussions should be attributed to the interest of Christians in this name and it can be surmised that he was considered in the 1880s to be a First Cause and nothing more. He was like the *nkira* and dwelt in the sun. Moreover, and it is important that no ritual at all was associated with this belief, no symbols were connected with it and it was thus different from all the other beliefs in non-human entities.

It might in fact be compared to the vague beliefs the Tio held about the moon. Oddly enough the moon was *not* the seat of a spirit, but there was ritual associated with it. The first night of every full and every new moon there were dances, and at the new moon all made wishes for a prosperous month such as not to fall ill, not to be attacked when travelling, etc.[4] The moon was apparently a symbol of fortune, but no one knew why. As a paradox with Nzã, which is only a belief, here is a symbol with some ritual (the dancing) but without real belief. How all this came about is an historical question to which we may never know the answer. The situation certainly did not interfere with other beliefs or organized rituals, which explains why it *could* develop. But like folklore, both the belief in Nzã and the dances and wishes at the new moon, are a case of raw materials for religion which the society did not exploit.

[3] There has certainly been some diffusion because the juxtaposition of two words as, e.g. *Nzambi mpungu* in Kongo, *Nzã mpwuu* in Tio and *Ncyeem pwoong* among the Kuba with similar terms for the whole area west of the Kuba to the Kongo is too much to explain by coincidence. To say the content of these terms is common and derived from missionary teaching is however quite a different proposition.

[4] CH. LIEBRECHTS, *Léopoldville*, p. 536.

Nature holds the most powerful, the most beneficial spirits, *nkira*, who lived in the shadow of the cool woods, hidden near the murmur of a brook or rarely on the open dusty, hot, glare of the savannah. These spirits had names and were considered to be persons with a ghostly sort of white body, mostly invisible and with no real personalities: *nkira* spirits were not easily swayed by passions such as love and anger. The Tio plains are divided into chiefdoms and in each of these a *nkira* had taken up its abode and exercised his power over the same domain over which the chief of the land ruled. It was the privilege and the duty of the chief to be the master of the *nkira*, i.e., to ask of it blessings and fertility on behalf of the community. The cult was complicated by the fact that the chief himself did not pray or sacrifice to his spirits but had a 'prayer' in one family and a 'sacrificer' in another to carry out ritual for him. The latter lived near the spot where the *nkira* dwelt, while the former lived in the chief's village and tended the shrine, also called *nkira*, which stood in front of the chief's house. This shrine was a model of a house, big enough to enter, but still only on a scale of one to four or thereabouts compared with a real dwelling.

At the level of the kingdom there was the national *nkira* at the Falls of the Lefini, associated with the king and holding sway over the whole realm. To him each fourth day was consecrated and the day like the spirit was named with awe: Nkwe Mbali: 'The Court of the Lion'.[5] So *nkira* meant, it seemed, a spirit connected with ritual, a shrine, symbols, and a certain level of social organization. The situation is perhaps comparable to *ikwii* who had their shrine, ruled in the household and were prayed to by the heads of the families.

Yet it was not that simple. Sims translates *nkira* as 'whirlwind, charm, box of charms, twin', *nkira mbu* as 'sack, package, calabash fitted with a lid to store cloth in' and *nkira adza* as 'spring of water', while Calloc'h (p. 260) had *nkira* also listed as 'spirits of illness' and linked to a ritual of circumcision (p. 153, *nzo a nkira*: 'case des circoncis'). True, some of the meanings given by Sims are manifestly only places where *nkira* are, such as whirlwinds and springs. The other meanings accord with some already mentioned in previous chapters. These included the umbilical cord, the banana tree planted on the place where the placenta had been buried, the navel (Calloc'h, p. 276) the maternal *mpiini*, objects associated with twins or *nganciele*, and also the power of these children to increase fecundity. The same stem with another prefix, *ãngkira*, designated women who danced, when in trance, in honour of some of their *ikwii*. *Nkira* also designated Obuu waalua and Nzã. Finally the *kaa* charms were obviously activated by the *nkira* spirits of the forest.

[5] ibid. Each fourth day was a holiday. This was known on the Pool as *mpiu* (Sims), *mpiha* (M. IBALICO, *thérapeutique*, p. 19), and *mpika* (Calloc'h: 'marché', p. 262), all regular derivations of the same word, but none related to Nkwe Mbali. It shows that a part of the ideology of kingship was not accepted in these areas.

What then did the notion *nkira* really mean? Not 'sacred' for there were sacred items or beings who were not *nkira*, e.g. *ikwii* or *ãti*. The word referred on the one hand to spirits and was linked with fertility on the other. The dance of women is explained by Ngaatali who claims that formerly, in Iloo's time, this dance was also performed if the women were seized by *nkira* spirits. This leaves the following:

CHART 8

Spirits, persons, and objects called nkira

spirit or person	*objects*
twins or *nganciele*	their pots (*nkir'mbu*)
mother's *mpiini*	umbilical cord or navel
	banana tree
nature spirits	shrines in chiefdoms
special spirits:	
Nkwe Mbali	shrine at court
Obuu waalua	
Nzã	
(spirits of illness)	

It has already been stated before that the belief in *nkira* spirits as the carriers of illness was restricted to the Fumu and perhaps some of the Sese.[6] The ritual, *itsuua*, on the plains was not believed to be connected with the *nkira*, while it was around the Pool. Moreover it is worth pointing out that it was a ritual for barren women and women who had grown 'thin'. For it is clear from the chart that the concept had two facets: land and its fertility connected with spirits was one, the fecundity of women the other.[7] Among the Tio of the Mbe plains healing was only connected indirectly with the complex with the one *nkira*: *Obuu waalua*. The Fumu, Sese, and perhaps others had directly incorporated healing as the work of *nkira* too, since this also was restoring or augmenting fortune. The Mbembe simple acknowledged the *nkira*'s role, not so much in curing as in preserving from illness by the link with the *kaa*. For them *nkira* meant a supernatural entity that brought, preserved or increased fecundity; for the Fumu it also restored fecundity.

Guiral describes some of the Boõ and Jinju reactions to *nkira*. He himself was believed to be supernatural and villagers brought their children to be touched and so strengthened by him. In another village a man started by excusing his father, the leader, because he was old and could not come, for his legs were not strong enough any more. But the leader had heard that 'Le bon Dieu' (the translation was from Malamine who knew Tio quite well by this time) was passing by and he wanted to offer fowls, maize, and cassava. Since Guiral was in a hurry

[6] Cf. Chapter VII fns. 20, 25.

[7] Also P. BONNAFÉ, *Un aspect religieux, passim.* But in its manifestations the *nkira* was very different among the Kukuya.

and had not accepted any gifts, the young man concluded that Guiral did not want to eat what the land produced, that all the men of the village and the crops would perish, for Guiral was angry.[8] There is little doubt that Guiral was taken to be a *nkira*. The connexion with fertility of the children, the fields, and the people was clear.

The various facets of the concept *nkira* were linked by the Tio notion of the good life: fecundity of the land, be it agriculture, fishing, or hunting, a life in steady good health and the birth of children, in short fortune or the good life: *ngolo*.[9] NGAATALI put it in a nutshell: 'They said formerly [in the 1890s] that the *nkira* gave children, the animals and the plants; also that they all grew and that the animals were killed.'

Of the other spirits the Tio recognize the *ikwii* and *apfu*. The *apfu* were attached to both the notion of the occurrence of misfortune and the restoration of fortune. They were the spirits of the abnormal events, while the *nkira* dealt with normal fruitfulness. The role of the *apfu* among the Fumu and their neighbours was slightly different, since the concept of *nkira* there had usurped part of the responsibility for abnormal events.

Yet despite what has been said before, one should not consider that the Tio had a system of beliefs in the supernatural. There was no system. Beliefs were linked to ritual and symbols and ritual was tied to specific situations. This is why it has been necessary to describe some of them in almost every chapter concerning their work. That there was no system of beliefs is evident from the variability in the beliefs between one person and another. Because of lack of data from the 1880s, data from *ngàà*, practising in 1963, must be used. And once one went beyond the notions of *ikwii*, *apfu*, *ngeiloolo* to ask, for instance, who was responsible for the efficacy of the charms, the answers differed widely. For Okondzaadza *apfu* could move and lived everywhere as a separate but invisible human race with men, women, and children, begetting for themselves and living all over the forests and the savannahs. The Teke Laadi believed that they had villages but the Boõ and Okondzaadza with them did not believe this. The *apfu*, he said, were not *ikwii*, but yet they were, for they were *ikwii* of the *ngàà*, and that is what gave force to all charms made by the *ngàà*.

Ngateo disagreed: *ikwii* and *apfu* were quite different. The *ngàà* inherited his *apfu* from previous *ngàà* and Nzã had created *apfu* along with people. Moreover he thought the *ngàà* only had the good *apfu*, the bad ones being those of the witches with their *impfiri* which *ngàà* never had. It is this sort of good-angel *apfu* which made charms work. Mbiinu-Mbiinu disagreed. *Ngàà* were often sorcerers with *impfiri* and *apfu* could be good or bad, depending on who used them, for they were

[8] L. GUIRAL, *Le Congo*, pp. 305–6.

[9] *Mpolo* for the Kukuya (Sims: *(M)umpolo:* 'reward') where it also meant good luck, a combination very different from that among the Tio as will be seen.

not linked to specific persons. They were in the things. Every leaf in the forest, every grass on the plains had its *apfu*: there were myriads of them. The combination of those whose objects were mixed in charms or even *kaa* cured. Others were caught by witches and worked for them. The *ikwii* were a sort among the *apfu*. The *ngàà*, often a witch, used his victims to be *apfu* for him, and the witch found his in a similar way. *Apfu* were mainly in vegetal matter and there were none in stones, sand or kaolin, except the earth of the cemetery. Perhaps, he did not know, some could be in animals too. He gave the example of how a child could be protected by a lion's tooth from a necklace of one of the very ancestors of the child. In other words the *apfu* in the tooth was in fact an *ikwii*. Ngateo said this could not be for *apfu* really were not, and this is a second opinion, really the *ikwii* of witches. If anyone died and talked like an *apfu*, he should be burned so as not to become one.

Alaatsã knew only that witches have *apfu*, that they were bad in principle and that they were not at all *ikwii*, except for the *apfu* of the *ngàà* and this opinion was roughly also that of Bilankwi, while Ikoli held a version similar to Mbiinu Mbiinu: the *apfu* were in the things, in every little thing the *ngàà* uses.

And an equal variability existed with regard to other points. One remembers how some informants believed Obuu waalua lived in the whirlpools of the Congo river and others, of the same household as a matter of fact, thought he was under sandbanks; for another one he dwelled only under one particular sandbank, for others he was everywhere underground, and still others did not know.

An equal kaleidoscopic and imaginative number of beliefs, or should they perhaps be called suggestions, would spring up when one inquired as to the relations between supernatural beings, rather than what they all were for, or all did to man. Here it was obvious that informants had never thought of this and began exercising their imaginations. What then had informants in common? Basic notions as to who the sorts of spirits were and what they were responsible for in terms of situations and rituals. For the rituals were held in common, ritual action presupposed some common acceptance of the presence of other worldly spirits and they were named in it. Therefore all held this too in common. But once one went beyond this, everyone was free to believe what he wanted to. The Tio had no sacred books, no dogma, no catechism, no compulsion to believe the same things as long as they participated fully in the same rituals. And the very variability of beliefs, even among specialists, is proof of this attitude.

There is no reason to hold that this situation was new in 1963 and untrue for the 1880s, since if there had been change it would have been in the direction of becoming more dogmatic as the religion was attacked by foreign missionaries. But then missions had no success on the plains and even in 1963 there were only two converts to Christianity on the Mbe plain: the gardener of the former missionary and the Protestant catechist. Nor was this attitude due to the mixed origins of people living in Mbe. After all they were mostly western Boõ or Mbembe and the differences did not follow areas of origin. The variability can only be explained by the fact that details of beliefs were not drawn into the social religion. Everyone was free, because it did not matter.

In addition there were no theologians. The beliefs came to life in everyone's mind when rituals were held or misfortunes discussed, in concrete given situations of planting and harvesting, giving birth, hunting, falling ill, in accidents, and death. In fact this characteristic explains why it would be completely misleading to build up a complete Tio system of belief from Nzã to the *ikwii* and with full details about the ghoulishness of witches and the finer distinctions between good and bad *apfu*. Such a construction would completely vitiate any understanding of Tio mentality. The simple but powerful facts that situations called for common action, which had to be common ritual, which entailed a basic common belief would be lost. Why and how Tio religion was an affair of the community would be lost. This surely is the most important point for both analysis of what religion was to society as well as what the nature of this religion was.[10]

2. *Ritual*

Why did the Tio have recourse to rituals in certain situations and not in others? First it would seem that they only had recourse to them when danger threatened or when misfortune had actually struck, whether they also took practical steps or not. In addition there were rituals to handle passage from one status to another. One group among these dealt with situations involving passage from one specific status to another, e.g. to become *ngàà mbulu*, or king, while when such passages involved general status, other types of rituals or rather ceremonies took place, for in these cases no immediate reference to a given supernatural entity was involved. Lastly there were some rituals which were meant to increase already existing good fortune, or to bless a practical enterprise which was about to be undertaken, e.g. blessing with lustral water before starting cultivation.

In all these the importance accorded by social consensus to different activities was the major key and this is especially true for rituals of passage dealing with specific status and rituals of fortune. For instance

[10] There were also no complex religious myths contrary to A. MASSON DETOURBET, *Le tissage*, A. LEBEUF, *Le role de la femme*, *idem*, *Aspects de la royauté*; at least none were told to us despite our insistence on this point. In our opinion Tio religion is similar in this to others. Cf. J. VANSINA, *Religion et sociétés*. Cf. what Bilankwi and Ngateo said about the relations between Nzã and witches. Neither had really thought about it beforehand it seems, so problems, such as the relation between Creation and Evil, were never raised because religion is encapsulated in the social situation.

ngàà mbulu underwent a ritual but smiths or ordinary *ngàà* did not and blessings were given before the start of cultivation but not before pottery was being made or cloths woven, for instance. Thus rituals were closely linked to both Tio perception of the world and the commonly held social goals.

An internal study of ritual could start from a morphology of the various rituals existing. This attempt leads to both recognition of the great variation between them and to acknowledging that rituals formed a 'system' in the sense that there were recurrent actions from one ritual to another. Thus the ritual for coping with lightning involved calling persons whose houses had been struck previously by lightning. These arrived, chewed *lisisõ*, a grass that *ngàà* also often chew and spit out as an offering in the treatment of illness. They also chewed copal, *oli*, which is 'cold fire' to 'cool' the spot where lightning had struck. Again this is found in other rituals. But then they also struck the ground with the rib of a banana leaf as a rod to drive out the fire of lightning. This action is unique, even though the general symbolism of the banana tree was found in many other rituals. To summarize: as in other rituals the area was 'cooled' off to drive out misfortune and specifically the lightning was driven out. Finally, the fact that only people who had had experience with the same misfortune before could perform the ritual, recalls the initiation of *ngááyuulu* through *itsuua* or to a lesser degree that of a *ngàà mbulu*. For the example it is clear that each ritual should have besides its recurrent features a unique action to cope with the unique specific situation in which it was used.

In practice it turned out that the best approach to discover basic patterns was to arrange rituals in classes, according to who performed them, as in the chart on p. 230:

Four groups of rituals exist: a great variety handled by *ngàà* which should include women dancing *ãnkira* and *liséé*; the *okuu* inquest by itself; rituals of passage dealing with general status, such as rituals for birth and death; a last group consists of either praying, dedicating, or sacrificing for a spirit or blessing with lustral water, in the name of *nkira* power, since the water comes from the Falls of Nkwe Mbali (for the king) or derives its power from the *nkira* of the domain (chiefs), twins or *nganciele*.

The variety of rituals performed by *ngàà* is not surprising, since he was the specialist called in the greatest variety of situations. Many rituals of the *ngàà* had to be spectacular and unexpected which explains the embroideries on basic patterns, as for instance in healing ritual. But the basic commonest element in all *ngàà* ritual was prayer, dedication, and sacrifice, as in the last group. This group includes *liséé* because that ritual is very much more complex than but similar to both initiation into specific status, as for the *ngàà mbulu*, and the giving of *ãti* by a *ngàà*.

CHART 9

Classification of rituals by performers

performers	*rituals*
Ngàà: without change of status:	making *nkiini*
	making all *ãti*
	divining
	healing
	handling ordeals
	chasing witches out of the settlement
with change of status:	*itsuua* (women)
	lightning (women, men)
	mbulu (women, men)
	becoming parents of twins and dance for twins
other specialists:	
political for chiefs:	praying or sacrificing for the *nkira* of the domain (similar to ritual for *ikwii*)
political for kings:	installing a king in ritual of *lisee* (also for Lords of the Crown)
	praying or sacrificing for Nkwe Mbali (similar to ritual for *nkira*)
heads of kin-groups:	offering, dedicating and sacrificing to *ikwii*
chiefs or *nciele*:	blessing with lustral water of women in connexion with fields
chief LIPIE:	blessing the king with lustral water (similar to previous)
by heads of *ndzo*:	*okuu* inquest
by individuals:	praying, offering, sacrificing to *ãti* or *kaa* (similar to ritual for *ikwii*)
	rituals for passage for general status
	praying to Nzã
by women only in trance:	dancing *ãnkira* for *ikwii* or *nkira* (similar to dancing in trance in *itsuua*)

Okuu was held by the head of the *ndzo* and consisted in talking. In form this incantation was similar to both a court palaver and a ritual, because conjuration of witches was involved.[11]

Rituals of passage concerning the life cycle have already been described. Again they can often hardly be called rituals, because the reference to other-worldly beings is so slight. This is most noteworthy in death, burial, and mourning rituals.

In the last group, the giving of lustral water was a simple ritual to preserve fortune. But the rituals of misfortune, from praying to saci-

[11] To be described in the chapter on conflict.

ficing, are obviously the most central in Tio religion, either to cope with misfortune or to avert it, whether the performer be the representative of a social group or a religious specialist like a *ngàà*. It consisted of four stages which could be performed separately if needed. These were praying, offering, dedicating, sacrifice, and communion.

Prayer was a straightforward address to the spirit or *ãti* involved. Its attention had been called by whistling, or using the rattles *õtsara* and/or *libi* while saying *shwiii*! Then the applicant chewed some kola, perhaps some *lisisõ*, and spat it out as an offering on the appropriate tomb, altar, figure, or charm; for *ikwii* wine was also poured, but not for other spirits. Meanwhile the man would simply say: 'Here, spirit, here is the case . . .' or if it was a *ngàà*: 'Here is the money, here is the case . . .' There was no appeal, no impassioned invocation, just a statement of the case and a straightforward request for help.

If it was necessary the suppliant would bring a white fowl, in more serious cases a goat, and dedicate it saying: 'This is your fowl (goat)', and the animal could never be killed except as a sacrifice to the spirit it was dedicated to. Usually however this was done only for *ikwii*, since they alone would accept this compromise of a delayed sacrifice.

The sacrifice itself began with an act showing that the spirit had accepted the gift. The neck of a fowl was squeezed by the officiant and if the bird choked, the spirits accepted. A goat had to fall three times on its knees in front of the altar, tomb, or place where there was an *apfu* or *nkira* house, as a sign that it was accepted. The throat of the animal was slit and the blood poured over the sacred place, since spirits drink blood. The meat was prepared with cassava and left overnight as an offering to eat. Why the blood should flow first was not clear. Ngateo held that thus the spirit could see that the animal had not already been killed for some other purpose, but it seems a poor rationalization.

Some sacrifices were mere offerings of blood and meat, just as one offered cassava or palm-wine. These were for the *ikwii* who wanted to eat, and who had usually indicated this in a dream. But even so there might be communion. The next day the members of the household would eat the remaining meat without salt or pimento, because the *ikwii* were eating with them and afterwards they would be benevolent.

In sacrifices to *apfu*, however, it was not a matter of food but of exchanging the life of the goat or the fowl for the life of the sick person. For *apfu* must eat to exist and they eat people, but can be satisfied with goats and even sometimes fowls. They too could come to a communion with members of the stricken family and then let the sick person heal—if they were paid off.

In all these actions the amount of deeply symbolic actions and words was small. It was believed that spirits heard when they were called and really came, that they really killed animals and really ate the blood and the meat. Only the white colour of the animal and the day chosen for sacrifice (*Nkwe Mbali* or *Okwe*) had symbolic significance at all. The rest was a straightforward action in reality. There was nothing symbolic about it in the sense of doing things 'by analogy'. For them sacrifice was real in the sense that transubstantiation is not a metaphor, but a reality for Catholics.

This realism, or rather an imaginary representation in realistic terms, is also strong in other rituals such as those already described for healing. People must be cured by drugs and *apfu* bargain with *apfu*, fight with them or cajole them into accepting—it all really happens and if the bystanders stand too closely packed they leave no way for the *apfu* to come. In these rituals charms, drugs, ornaments, music, all had some symbolic value, but at the same time they were supposed to have real 'true' effects. The music might be an omen, for instance, but *ikwii* liked music and would come to listen to it. *Apfu* could not resist the graceful melodies of the *nguõ* and when the instrument is sounded they throng to the spot and become really enthralled; the dance of the *ãngkira* woman, in which she imitates her deceased grand-parent, is watched fondly by him and the dancer imitates the little mannerisms of the deceased to make people remember. It is the kind of realism which also puts the little signs on *itio* to make them, though conventionally carved, the image of a particular person. At a time when research on symbolism is making such strides, this basic fact of the realism of ritual and sacrifice must be stressed. It is the first and most important feature of all Tio ritual, even to the beating out of the animal lightning out of the ground!

Realism explains another feature: familiarity. *Ikwii*, *apfu*, *nkira* are actually there, eat and drink, listen to conversation, and talk in dreams. The long bargaining matches between good and bad *apfu* might seem to lack reverence in the eyes of Europeans but there was no question of reverence among the Tio. There was participation, the participation which may strike fear, as when *apfu* are fighting, but no awe or piety. Respect was shown to *ikwii* or *nkira* but it was the kind of respect accorded to older persons or to chiefs. Thus public rituals were also feasts and distractions and people assumed the attitudes one has on a holiday. Johnston for instance was struck by this fact[12] and what he took to be the curing of a minor ailment may well have been a major cure, despite the 'laughing and joking and panting' of the assistants.

Rituals never failed because of a lack of piety. They failed because there was no acceptance of a proposed sacrifice, no agreement to be reached between bargaining *apfu*, because of breach of contract, as when a food avoidance was not observed, or by the interference of another ritual. Thus rain charms might not work if someone else was using rain at the same time as a method to divine if X would fall ill or not. The rain would respond to divination first and the charm would

[12] H. H. JOHNSTON, op. cit., pp. 197–8.

not work. Finally charms might not work if the person who made the charm was too old or if it had already been used often. There would be a quality of attrition about it which meant that the *apfu* were no longer happy with it.

The connexion of ritual with social groupings was close, not only because most ritual was performed by a group, or at least concerned in it, nor only because occasions for ritual were occasions deemed to be important by social consensus, nor even only because rituals protected members within a group and were an expression of solidarity by the group, but also because of the essential imaginary realism of the act. The following chart illustrates how close the connexion was.

CHART 10

Ritual and social groups

social level	*sacred place*	*typical ritual*	*typical belief*
individual	banana tree	charms	*mpiini*
family	*kio*, tombs	praying-sacrifice	*ikwii*
ndzo	none	*okuu*	witches[a]
village	*nkiini*	installing *nkiini* holding rain[b]	*apfu*
chiefdom	*nkira* house *nkobi*	praying-sacrifice lustral blessing	*nkira*
kingdom	*Nkwe Mbali* package	*liséé* lustral blessing praying-sacrifice	Nkwe Mbali

[a] Witches were linked with *apfu* and meant divining rituals and often curing to follow. They are only typical of *okuu* in that no other spirits were involved.

[b] Most often charms to avert rain belonged to and were worked by the village leader. The avoidances were collective to the settlement.

It is clear from the chart that *okuu* was a ritual to a lesser degree than the others. The *ndzo* was not really associated with either a sacred place or a typical spirit. As for family and village, often the village leader was also the head of the one or two families in his settlement. Furthermore it must be noted that at each level of increasing social complexity typical beliefs of previous levels were involved with their rituals. Thus kingship involved protection against witches and *apfu*, calling on the *ikwii* of the king, using charms, and Nkwe Mbali was a *nkira*. Finally it was not so much the ritual alone which differentiated between social levels as the sacred places and, to a lesser degree, spirits. Typical of rituals was that charms especially for furthering fortune were found at the individual level and used only by men, whereas praying-sacrifice was associated with social groups, and with rituals to correct misfortune. Group ritual for furthering fortune did not exist at the kinship or village levels. Lustral blessing was a prerogative of the political level and its *nkira*, even though *nkira*-endowed people such as twins and *nganciele* could dispense blessings to women at the individual level. The following chart illustrates this:

CHART 11

Rituals of fortune or misfortune and society

fortune	*misfortune*
men: Charms (individual)	prayer/sacrifice + curing (collective)
women: *nkira* (individual/collective)	prayer/sacrifice + curing (collective)

It follows that the collectivity alone could correct misfortune or avert it when it threatened, whereas fortune could be sought individually. Women did so rarely and it is still in question whether individual appeals to twins or *nganciele* were ever made or if the women of a settlement all came together, since they all made their fields next to each other. In any case the spirit *nkira* was closely associated with the collectivity. In general women were more inclined to collective action than men. Men did seek fortune individually and one recognizes here a reflexion of male ambition which also led to conflict and was in a sense anti-social. But male aspirations were checked once misfortune had occurred, since they then had to rely on social groups to help them.

Ambition in its worst form was of course the activity of a witch. On the other hand, belief in witchcraft was a powerful negative force for the definition and promotion of social groups, since all tensions within the group and even more supposed dangers from outside the group could be projected upon witches. The rituals to protect against witches at each social level enacted social solidarity in a dramatic form. Necessarily at the same time social solidarity was re-established within the group after strife by casting out the losing contender and his followers and branding them as witches.

3. *Symbols*

The realism of ritual action seems to exclude metaphorical symbolic action. Yet at the same time latent symbols were present in almost all ritual as in other ceremonies. Whenever rituals have been mentioned some common symbols have nearly always been noticed. Thus a banana tree represents the life in a person. If the tree dies, the child will die, its withered leaves are used for packing corpses in their catafalque, when lineages split a banana stem is cut, banana ribs drive out lightning, etc.

Other latent symbols are the *ngili* or avoidances, some of which are directly connected with ritual such as the avoidance of bringing firewood into the village square if rain and lightning charms are to work since firewood belongs to fire and the charm tries to avert it. Some form a set related to social groups and these are the food avoidances people inherit from their parents.[13] Symbols were both an integral part of ritual and outside of ritual and religion. They operated on another, deeper level where they expressed the meaning of the situations, statuses, or actions with which they were connected. They were thus the expression of values and feelings about society, life, and the individual.

The essential features of latent symbols should be examined briefly. The most obvious one is that the degree of pervasiveness varies incredibly. Thus banana symbols were found in most rituals and it seems to be perhaps the most pervasive symbol in Tio culture. On the other hand a symbol such as the dragon-fly occurs only once. In recent times it was the avoidance one had to observe if one wanted to be a sucessful goalkeeper in the soccer game! This plasticity is readily explained by the other features of Tio symbols.

Symbols could come alone or in sets, and sets could be dual or complex. There were obligatory sets and free sets. Thus the hoe representing a female always came with the cutlass which represented a male, whereas in the set, palm frond = man, wild calabash creeper = woman, each element could appear independently. When it did, it changed meaning: the creeper alone was a symbol for life itself, as at birth; the palm frond alone seems to have been only a sign of sacredness such as kaolin is. When the two occurred together, e.g. at a healing ritual, they might then carry a double meaning. Complex sets were for instance the colours: white, red, black, or the *ngili* avoidances of kinship groups which fell into four categories with several variants in each category. As for colours, a rash statement would be that white represented sacredness and peace, and *ikwii* red—life, blood, power, fire, and conflict—with black being in recent times the colour of death, which it already partly was (with red) in the 1880s. The statement would be rash because (i) symbols are latent and one could 'guess' at their meaning only if all circumstances in which they appear are catalogued, and (ii) because each colour or colour combination could mean different things in different situations, because the set, like all complex sets was 'free'.

This leads us to a third and perhaps the most important feature of symbols. Since they were latent they were only held partly in common. As long as they figured in ritual or ceremony their presence was common, but not the meaning. One person might see one meaning in them which another would dispute, whereas yet another accorded them no importance whatsoever. In fact the effect of most symbols seems to have been different for everyone according to the degree of transparency it had, the previous occasions on which a person had seen it used and the emotions recalled by those previous occasions, and perhaps the amount of thought he had given to it. In this symbols may

[13] Cf. Chapter II, section *ibuuru*.

be compared to poetry. The social effect of this was of great importance and explains why rituals entailed symbols. For the interpretation of a symbol was personal and it was a function of feeling as well as of reasoning. It involved a person and thereby made a ceremony or ritual meaningful to him as an individual in a most intimate way.

The ambiguity of the meaning of symbols is a feature linked to the previous one. This level varied. Sometimes the link between sign and meaning was stable and practically overt: dung beetles were a sign of witchcraft, nine, the perfect number. But these were often the least important symbols. The more powerful ones were ambiguous and there were many meanings for a given sign at different occasions or even at one and the same time. Thus songs at a healing ritual were omens but first they might mean different things to different people. 'The smith forges, *we, we*' might mean that the person would heal just as the smith makes a new hoe out of old iron or that the person would die, for the smith is the master of the fire and fire kills. One could look at it on this one level only or one could discover yet other meanings in it. The smith represented the *ngàà* since he controls fire; the ringing noise of the hammer is similar to that of the bells used in war, etc. The ambiguity was of course even more pronounced when symbols were part of free sets, since meanings could then be heaped one upon the other. If an *itsuua* woman put white ash on her head, that reminded them of death (ash + white), of *nkira* (white) and of fecundity, of fire (ash) of coolness and peace (kaolin), etc.

A last feature of symbols was that they did not really form a system. Like words in the language they formed only an open-ended series. New symbols could be invented, old ones dropped and it would be impossible ever to draw up a complete list of symbols for a Tio community, since symbols were only partly held in common. It would be impossible even for an individual, since everything could have a symbolic meaning, and if the person were required to make his latent symbols conscious he could add infinitely to it. In a latent way new symbols did arise essentially by analogy or association. The first process is well exemplified by copal. Copal came from under the water and was cool. But it was almost transparent and looked like frozen fire. Therefore it was fire and yet the opposite. No wonder that it was used to 'cool' a person or a place struck by fire. Association was based on correlation. Since certain illnesses always strike when flies or mosquitoes are present the mosquitoes become a sign for the cause of the illness, witchcraft.

Symbols were then metaphors used in a latent fashion by individuals in their own ways. Some occurred consistently in rituals and ceremonies and thus linked society and the individuals since they had acquired a collective meaning. Some were so pervasive that they were almost transparent in meaning, even though there was no sharply defined common meaning held by social consensus about them. How could such a consensus arise? Why would it? The answer is obviously that like language and the basic categories of observation, symbols were taught unconsciously to every child, for these symbols were as much a part of a world-view as the basic categories themselves.[14]

4. *The world-view*

Some Tio symbols belonging to dual sets are so widely held and so invariable that their meaning is obvious to the observer. In addition links between these sets are also to be found. Objective evidence, either, e.g. particularities of the language such as right = 'male side', or concurring statements by several informants make it possible to draw up a table of these, to which have been added some correspondences felt strongly to exist by the observer, but not truly authenticated.

The first observation about the table is that when direction and space, time and seasons, meteorology and heat and sex are involved the evidence was clear. These groups, except for the two last, are clearly basic categories of observation, similar to those called categories by Kant and Durkheim. There is no doubt that they are taught in an unconscious fashion to babies and children. The inference is that the remaining groups were also taught and form a real category. This can only be claimed by inference for group III, inference meaning probably extension or consequence. Still the whole table clearly shows a dual constellation, one desirable, the *ngolo* constellation, one undesirable but occurring, the conflict situation.

The very fact that such a set of basic categories remained latent, although held by all, reinforced the acceptance of these categories of perception as well as those dealing with moral values. Thus the basic categories become perhaps the strongest normative power in society. The aspirations of all were to have *ngolo* and it should then follow that all would avoid conflict and competition and concentrate on the opposite values to achieve the good life. Yet this did not happen, mostly when men were involved. Therefore there must have been equally strong forces to allow them to evolve different aspirations.

The basic dualism should however not lead one to imagine that one half should prevail without any of the other. In fact the table shows that the relation is something like *yin* and *yang*: both halves exist, both complement each other, both are unavoidable. In fact one could state that fertility and fecundity belonged to the women's half, yet the *nkira* are in the men's half; or that *ngàà* were the witches they had to combat, and so on. How deeply the realization of this essential complementarity

[14] Tio culture was not studied in depth. For the 1880s this is practically impossible for lack of data (cultural materials are among the most altered data in transmission or even the memory of the eye-witness). The intrinsic difficulties are great. Most of the symbolic culture being latent, techniques are required to bring them out in as 'objective' a way as possible. This research requires a considerable amount of time and an excellent knowledge of the language.

CHART 12

Dualism

direction:	left: East	right: West (by sun)
and space	left half of	right half of
	sky at night	sky by day
	downstream	upstream
	'tail' of village	'head' of village[a]
	down	up?
	behind	in front
	savannah	forest and village[b]
time and season:	wet season (hot) (*mvula*)	dry season (cool) (*otsaa*)[c]
	wetter dry season	high dry season
	(dry season of women)	(dry season of men)[c]
	(*otsaa wuuke*)	(*otsaa waa boolo*)
	days *odzuo, okila*?	days *Nkwe Mbali, okwe*?[d]
group II		
heat and sex:	female	male
	heat	cold
	fever	good health
	fire	water
	moon	sun
	sex	abstention
meteorology:	lightning	no lightning[b]
	rain	dryness
group III		
values:	conflict	peace
	anger (*mpuuru*)?	harmony and 'good life' *ngolo*?[e]
	Misfortune?	Fortune?
spirits:	*apfu?*	*nkira + ikwi?*
religion:	witchcraft?	*ngàà?*
ethics:	evil, broken?	good, whole?
colours:	red?	white?
	ndzo?	*ibuuru?*
kinship groups:	adjacent generation?	alternate generation?
	affines?	affines of affines?

[a] Villages were built in circles. The orientation was taken from the leader's dwelling.

[b] Some triads do occur but are reduced to dual oppositions. Perhaps this should be applied to rain + lightning versus dryness which takes a zero term out of the table.

[c] Seasons are in fact counted as four: *mvul ãtsõ* 'first rain', then *mwaa otsaa* 'small dry season', *ndwoolo* 'great rains', and *otsaa* 'great dry season'. But the dualism is explicit in *mvula* rain vs. *otsaa* dry season. The fourfold division could of course be reduced to two pairs and one would expect *mvul ãtsõ* = male, *ndwoolo* = female; *mwaa* = female, *otsaa* = male. Note that Sims *mukali* and *mulumi* has this pair reversed!

[d] Again a fourfold but alternating division with two 'lucky' and two 'unlucky' days.

[e] The following are all speculation although for red and white the evidence seems especially convincing.

was rooted in the conscience of the Tio we were unable to discover. That the complementarity led to ambiguity is obvious and this was present, e.g. in the rituals dealing with twins, where suspicion of fecundity due to witchcraft and fecundity as an expression of *nkira* were mixed.

Dual opposition means that there must be marginal elements. One may also wonder why there was only dual opposition. In fact triads existed, such as the division of space in village, forest, and bush where villages and forests had names and bush had not. This indicates an underlying dichotomy. Some classification, such as that of the seasons, was by four, but that could be and was reduced to two pairs. Then there were the taxonomies of cognition: the classifications of animals and plants, for instance. Here as many classes were recognized as were necessary.[15] Thus Ngateo's fundamental grouping of animals comprised ten groups. Binomialism had no place here, and essentially empirical categories were recognized.

In this way dualism was restricted to a view about the world and basic categories, which acted rather like the unconsciously applied grammar acts on language. It helped to classify not empirical experience but symbols and values. Its social significance is evident since this shaped the expression of ethics, values, and aspirations. Its relation to social stability as a goal is moreover striking.

5. *Ethics and values*

Evil for the Tio was, in the absolute, witchcraft and the notion implied a link with religion. No wonder that Sims has translated *ilolo* as 'devilry, evilspirit, gizzard (because of *impfiri*), evil, mania, sin' when it means 'witchcraft'.

But other expressions denoted wrong-doing. Thus *nkini*, which is derived from *nkina* (Sims) 'tabooed thing', and *kina* 'be stopped', and thus means (Calloc'h, p. 337) 'transgression' is defined by Sims as *nkini* 'evil, sin, mischief, desire, insubordination, valour, oppression', and the abstract *ukini* 'courage, bravery, boldness, brave, fearless'. Calloc'h (p. 288), calls *nkini* 'péché' (sin), and *bu-kini* (p. 341) 'vaillance'. In a catalogue of undesirable behaviour the inclusion of 'desire' and 'valour' are rather surprising. *Lineño* for Sims is 'wickedness' and for Calloc'h (p. 341), 'vantardise' (boasting) something which was linked to valour among the Tio. Then there was *mpuru*, which for Calloc'h (p. 263), was 'méchanceté' (wickedness) but also 'force, fort' (p. 221), and we know that it means angry as well. Sims has it as

[15] These were: birds, fish, 'animals', caterpillars, snakes, rodents, turtles, lizards, spiders, flies and mosquitoes, grasshoppers. 'Animal' included domestic and wild mammals. Further subdivisions of that class were made according to where the animal slept. The Tio have a vast taxonomy for animals and plants which requires considerable knowledge of these fields to investigate.

I

'angry, severe, fierce, enraged, painful, passionate', thus expatiating on the word desire.

No other terms describing wrongful behaviour in general occur[16] in the dictionaries. So it seems that behaviour linked with ambition and forceful aspirations was considered evil. And no wonder, since it was certain to lead to accusations of witchcraft or to suspicion of witchcraft in the one endowed with valour and ambition. Clearly linked with this was the mention of dissatisfaction and insubordination. Further it must be stressed that lack of mercy was also thought to be evil. Sims also gives: *ncoo* 'pitiless, mischievous, mania mischief, sin (?)'. Mercy was to be shown especially to kin and neighbours and blended with gentleness and peaceful behaviour. Mercy was the opposite of ambition.

All of this confirms what has been adumbrated about *ngolo* 'the good life', 'fortune'. The aspirations of people should be to live in peace and harmony, being co-operative, doing things collectively, being partly passive, meek, in need of protection, and unambitious. To be all this was to be 'good'.

Women often lived up to all this, but men did not. In fact their aspirations were often completely 'wrong'. They wanted competition, bargaining, insecurity as long as it meant opportunity to advance in status. This clashed as much with the ethics as it did with the basic categories of the world-view.

Signs that this 'wrong' tendency was deeply engrained abound, however. To take one: the conception of evil as witchcraft did away with the notion of responsibility by oneself and of chance, since a rigid causality was always involved. Yet the Tio loved games of chance and were anxious to have the future foretold, as if they could alter something in it. These traits were signs of status mobility. Chance itself was a notion that could be tinged with unhappiness as in Sims: *suro* 'slip down, fall, get untied, do anything by change' and the derived *isurisuri* 'accident, chance', or it could mean luck as in Calloc'h (pp. 156, 221, 236), where *bweo* was 'chance', 'fortune', 'heureux' (happy). The notion written down by Sims squared with the world-view and the ethics that ambition and anything out of custom could only be an accident while the notion Calloc'h recorded was in fact very close to happiness itself, even if it was morally all wrong.

What happiness should be is indicated by Sims: *Ise* 'joy, happiness, gentleness, gentle, kindness, politeness, correctness, happy, pleasant, good, right, kind, salty, whole, not cracked', and the reduplication *isise* 'happiness' and *isisie* 'joy, happy', all confirmed by Calloc'h

[16] Calloc'h, pp. 288, 259, 215, has *i-pfuma* as moral wrong or error Sims gives *asuma*, *asumu*, and *sumu*: 'sin, guilt' and *uyuu*: 'sin, misfortune' [*sic*]. Calloc'h, p. 260, also has *fina*: 'malfaisance, malice' and Sims *mfina*: 'waste, murder'. Note that all these are distinct from terms meaning shame of which there are two: *nconi* and *upfuru*.

(p. 145): *i-se* 'bonheur'. This ideal refers again to what should be and is quite opposed to the *bweo* just mentioned.

The two aspirations were obviously both deeply rooted in the make-up of the society in the 1880s, and yet they clashed completely. One ideal was to parade oneself dressed up with followers, to have one's praises sung, to be laden with 'objects of honour', to be respected and treated with a sort of awe. The other was to be lost in the crowd.

The clash can only be explained by reference to the environment which allowed great mobility, to the dominating place of achieved status, to an economic and political situation which encouraged ambition and allowed status to be achieved. But these things have not been prominent so far. For they were not prominent in the small-scale society as much as in the greater tradition: the whole Tio world. This whole 'outer' world was so strongly linked with the small-scale society that despite the basic world-view, the metaphysics of evil, religion, and ethics, the ideal of ambition and opportunity had been accepted.

Part I
Conclusion

THE Tio neighbourhood was a tightly integrated whole based on kinship groupings whose dominant mode of economic production was the economics of subsistence, even though certain essential items such as salt, iron, guns, powder, and pottery were unobtainable locally and had to be exchanged for other goods produced in the neighbourhood. Religion and rituals dovetailed neatly with the social and economic structures of the small society. The picture of the neighbourhood is not yet complete. The chief of the land or squire should have been discussed and so should the different forms that conflict took, whether it was feuds, *okuu*, ordeals, or the local court. These topics were left aside because they are common to both the local society and the larger world. It could be argued that they formed in fact part of this level of society and that their presence at a higher level was merely an extension of their role for the neighbourhood. This position is plausible, with the proviso that the ideology of chieftainship contained certain elements derived from the larger society.

And yet it is not possible to view the small-scale society as a world closed unto itself. There are for instance incidents such as the *apfu* bargaining for wealth to rescue a sick person. Such behaviour was wholly alien to a closed society living in a subsistence economy. It is an indication of the deep impact of the wider world on the neighbourhoods. In fact the analysis of Tio religion brought out that a set of values clashed head on with the ideals of modesty, submissiveness, meekness, and gentleness which belong so obviously to this little society. The central values of the wider world had pervaded the neighbourhood, to its most intimate core. The conclusion must be that the little society represented merely a sub-system in the wider society, albeit not only a distinguishable but also a fairly autonomous sub-system.

At one level the little society was an integrated whole. Its institutions were intertwined and fitted together like gears in a machine. The major kinship groups were the major producers and consumers, the values related to the perpetuation and the smooth function of the social groups and institutions. Very few internal discrepancies existed, even though changes in economic production distorted the distribution of labour and relations between men and women. The passage of time affected this integrated whole and produced expectable discrepancies.

At another level the little society was not a whole at all. For the political structure was the outgrowth of the social organization, the economics could not be understood without taking the commercial economy into account and to every Tio religion and ideologies represented both the smaller sub-system and the whole. The larger society was not just an extension of a conglomeration of neighbourhoods. It was as integral a part of every segment of society as the neighbourhood itself was.

Part II

The Wider Society

THE wider society consisted of two major overarching structures: the Great Congo Trade system and the Kingdom. The economic structure is presented first since it is not really possible to understand the Tio political structure completely without reference to it, while the operation of the commercial economy may be sketched with only marginal reference to the political structure. This represents an interesting paradox since not only does the commercial system encompass a much larger area, but it involves non-Tio intimately in the picture. The problem of description thus points out already that in the operation of the Tio political system some non-Tio elements must be considered to be of great relevance. What exactly is involved, to what extent the paradox is true, and what it implies will become clear from the presentation of the data.

Chapter X
The Great Congo Trade

COMMERCE was most important to the Tio in the 1880s, since it was the source of wealth and one of the sources of power. But the trade of the Tio represented only a segment in a widely flung network involving many peoples, a network linked itself at the coast of the Atlantic ocean with the world markets. A presentation of the operation of this trade among the Tio opens with a general sketch of allocation as a system of distribution to be followed by descriptions of the great Congo commerce, the organization of the markets, and the commodities.

1. *Allocation and exchange*

Allocation of goods and exchange of goods are quite different operations. Allocation is a transfer of goods without direct reciprocity in goods or services; exchange is a transfer of goods for a direct return of goods or services. Gifts, and transfer of inheritance are allocations; a sale, the payment of tribute, or of fines are exchange. Payments made for the acquisition of titles are also exchange and so is the transfer of persons whether as slaves or in marriage among the Tio.

Allocation occurred simply when gifts were presented. The action was called *kaba* (Sims: *kaba*: 'to allot, divide, present') and a gift was *kabo* or *kabu* also *kingolo* (Sims) or *ngolo* (Calloc'h, p. 231).[1] This makes the nature of the operation evident enough. Gifts were usually divided, i.e. allotted to people who had some right to them by their quality of being a kinsman, a friend or a neighbour. Only certain goods were given in this way, usually food or food products. When there was no famine, food could not be 'paid' for nor was it 'sold' in the countryside, although it was on the markets. In the early years of this century food was given to a woman whose plantations had failed either because of miscalculation or as the result of illness. Her kinsmen or co-villagers, her 'friends' gave it without any idea of a specific return. According to Abili Ndiõ no reciprocity at all was expected and even less of a check was kept about them than is the case for 'social obligations' or even the exchange of Christmas cards in Europe or the

[1] Calloc'h gives the meaning of the word also as 'gratis, for nothing' the partial equivalent of the Lingala word *mpamba*: 'nothing'. This *ngolo* is *not* the same word, as the one Sims translated as 'powerful; vigorous' and we called Fortune or 'The Good Life'.

In this chapter data from Calloc'h will be used sparingly since in commercial matters the situation changed greatly between 1880 and 1910 when that dictionary was completed.

United States. This type of gift and the fact that it dealt mainly with food is characteristic of the dominant rural mode of production: subsistence. This was no longer true on the market places. Those did not have a subsistence economy, in itself an index of the intensity of the market economy of which these places were the focus.

Travellers mentioned gifts in valued goods, probably what Sims called *kiibuni*: 'gift, present' related to *ibuni*: 'account, sum, product'. They were paid in trading goods and reciprocity was expected in goods and almost immediately. These were not gifts at all but the introductory exchange of marketing.[2]

Inheritance was not considered by the Tio as simply allocation, for the same verb (Sims: *kira*) was used to describe this (*kira uli taara*, p. 160) and trading, probably because trading goods were involved in many instances. Tribute, taxes, and bridewealth were all 'paid' (Sims: *fura*) and thus also fell outside simple allocation.

Exchange in the local communities involved inheritance, bridewealth, fines, tribute, and also payments for goods made by professional artisans in local trade, as has been shown.[3] It is typical for the importance of the subsistence economy here that sometimes payment was still made in goods other than currencies or that close kin received some goods without any payment at all. In all these transactions however the rural small scale society was 'invaded' by the operation of a market economy. Only the production of food and housing remained free of this.

2. *The Great Congo Commerce*

The expression 'Great Congo Commerce' has been used by Sautter to designate the flow of trade between the coast and the Stanley Pool and from there up the Congo river and its tributaries. The designation is apt because it translates both the extraordinary geographical extension of the network as well as the great intensity and astonishing scale of the trade.[4] By 1880 it was fundamentally a trade in which ivory was exchanged for goods imported from Europe. The Tio were middlemen between the suppliers of ivory and the suppliers of coastal goods. On each segment of the network however a host of local products were traded as well, giving a great flexibility, complexity, and density to the whole system.

Earlier in the nineteenth century trade had been based on the export of slaves but the transition to the export of ivory had been

[2] *Ki-ibuni* 'pledge?' is identical with the other two words given by Sims and renders its meaning better. For instances: cf. A. MAURICE, *Stanley*, p. 110, where the return of the original 'gift' of Stanley by Ngaliema meant a breaking of the agreement made; cf. also H. BRUNSCHWIG, *Les cahiers*, pp. 165, 168, for the sending of 'gifts' ahead of time and the refusal to accept because Brazza feared he could not reciprocate.

[3] Cf. Chapter VI: para. 1, *Making finished goods*.

[4] G. SAUTTER, *De l'Atlantique*, I, pp. 265–78.

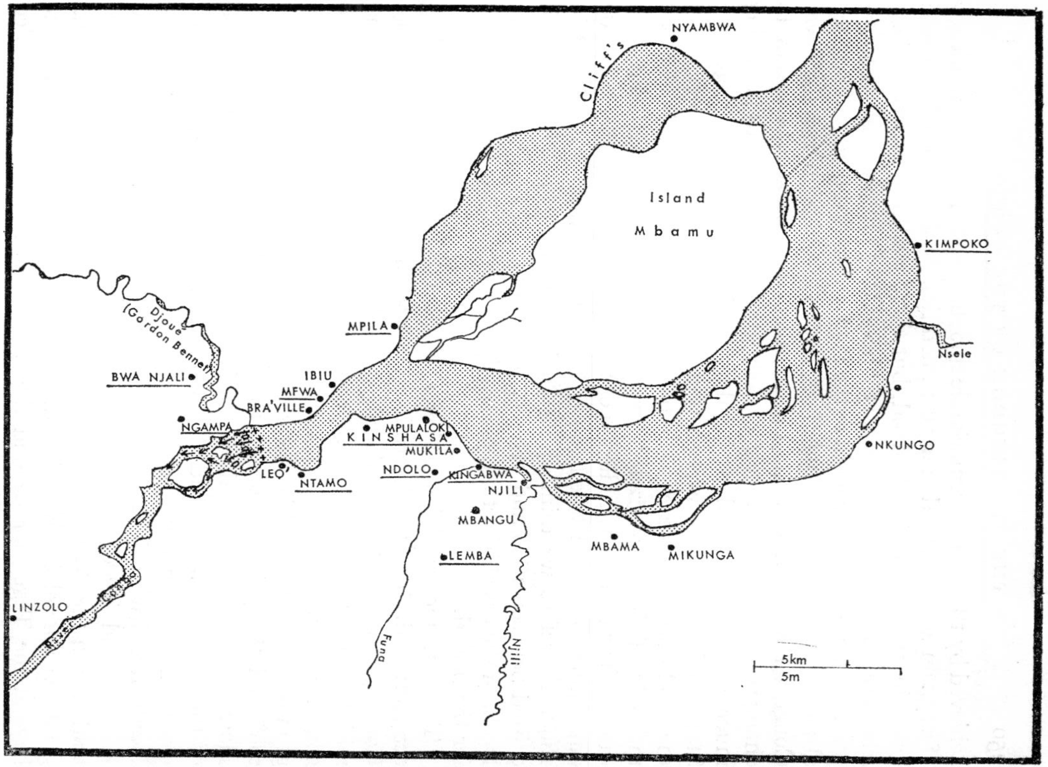

Map 6. *The Stanley Pool in the 1880s*

Ntamo: residence of chief and market

Notes: Kinshasa was the residence of the overlord NTSUULU, Ntamo of Ngaliema, Mfwa of NGIA, Mpila of Ngaamakono. These were the four major markets.

Kimpoko housed Ngambiele while Ngampa and Bwa Njali gave their names to their settlements. Ndolo belonged to Bankwa and Kingabwa to Lekibu.

The Hum paramount lived at Lemba.

achieved by 1870 with a remarkable smoothness, owing to the resiliency of a system which carried many commodities. At the coast palm-oil and groundnuts were also in demand, but there was little export of these from areas far in the interior partly because of the problems of transport.[5] Slaves were still brought to the Pool and traded there but became absorbed in the African populations, both Tio and peoples of the lower Congo on both sides of the Congo river. The situation was not to change essentially until well after 1885, from imported goods becoming much cheaper with the dumping done by the agents of the Congo Free State as of 1882 and the French as of 1884 to win both the allegiance of the Tio lords and a share in the trade at the Stanley Pool. But in 1888 the bulk of the ivory trade there was still in Tio hands[6] and even though their portion dwindled over the years, the basic pattern of trade only came to an end when the railway from Matadi was finished in 1898. Therefore we think it justified to describe the situation as it existed between 1880 and 1885–7, but also to assume much less than has been the case hitherto in this study, that later indications are valid for the period.

The first and crucial question arising in discussion of the trading economy of the Tio is to determine which segments of the Great Congo Commerce should be considered. It has been said that the Tio were middlemen between the coast and the interior. This does allow us to consider them as a natural segment in the system. But which Tio groups were involved? The sketch map indicating the routes commerce took and the points at which there was a break in carriers clearly shows that the coastal goods reached the Tio via the Soso, or the chiefs of the Manianga area and Mindouli, or the Teke Laadi. The first two groups traded with the Pool where there were market-places, the Laadi traded with the Pool but also directly with the Sese, Jinju and Kukuya and Tege by caravans and by peddling. The Kukuya traded with the Pool as well via Sese country. The flow of the coastal goods over the plains from the lower Congo does not seem to have gone beyond the Tege, nor beyond the Boõ; these areas could be called

[5] J. JEANNEST, *Quatre années*, pp. 55–63, 121–2; map opp. p. 274, about the ivory trade; and p. 267, on palm products and groundnuts. The importance of the ivory trade can be assessed by his estimate of 100 'tonneaux' of ivory a year being exported between the River and Ambriz, with most coming from the Pool. In 1885 a calculation allows for eight tons of exports a month from the Pool or ninety-six a year, going to the harbours both north and south of the Congo estuary. This makes the Pool, certainly as of 1870, by far the biggest marketing area in Central Africa.

[6] A. THYS, *Au Congo*, pp. 44–5, and map. Thys had just been to the Pool to examine economic conditions for the *Cie du Congo pour le commerce et l'industrie*, a branch of the *Société générale*. He assessed the competition and stated that the trade in ivory at the Pool could not be lured away from the Africans. After 1887 the commercial steamers, he hoped, would be able to buy ivory at the sources and bypass the carriers on the rivers. They still had to cope with the transportation problem to the coast, which the African 'chiefs' had solved by their existing organizations.

minor termini of the trade. But on the Pool the goods were carried by river to a breaking point at Bolobo and the lower Nkéni on the Congo river, to Mushie on the lower Kasai. The settlement of Mswata was no breaking point for carriers but a political centre and a centre for the exportation of foodstuffs affecting the Pool area.

Bolobo was a great market-place and from there or directly coastal goods came to Ntsei, along with goods from the upper Congo. There they were sold to Boõ who came to that market. But some Bobangi canoe-men went up the river Nkéni beyond Ntsei, peddling their wares to other villages on the Nsah plateau. Beyond Bolobo and Ntsei a major nucleation of the trade on the Congo river was the Likuba area from where trade flowed up the Alima and to the Tege who derived both coastal goods and products from upper Congo by this route. It remains to mention that the area of Mbe traded overland with the Pool and also by water over Mpio a Bwaani (Ganchu) and Mswata, and that products from the upper Congo arrived at the plateau of Mbe either directly from canoe-men stopping at Mpio a Bwaani and Mswata or from the Pool. The Sese, Jinju, and Kukuya also received most of the upper Congo products from the Pool although a few filtered through from the market at Ntsei. Perhaps a few Tege passed some upper Congo goods on to the Kukuya, although there many of the commodities (iron, e.g.) from the upper Congo regions competed with similar produce the Kukuya derived from their western neighbours in Gabon.

Thus the trading economy can be studied by reference to three centres: the Laadi trade in the west, the Ntsei with its market in the north, and the great market of the Pool in the south.

3. *Organization of the markets*

The dry season, especially the month of August, was the period of the great Tege caravans, numbering hundreds of people, who left well armed and with full protection of charms for the south, to Laadi country, which took about twenty to thirty days. Once arrived there each trader went to a Laadi man with whom he was a business relation to sell the slaves he had brought with him for salt. During the wet season the Laadi came up to the Tege. Trade with the Sese and Jinju may have gone on all the time. Groups of fifteen to twenty Laadi came in search of slaves. Guiral even saw two Laadi merchants in Sese country doing their business. Most goods were carried on the head, but salt, which was the main trade item beside cloth, was slung in bags over the shoulders.

Whenever a group of traders entered a new territory they sent a man ahead with a gift of a piece of cloth to the important political chief of the area.[7] The Tio remember that all trade had to begin at the residence

[7] H. BRUNSCHWIG, *Les cahiers*, p. 165.

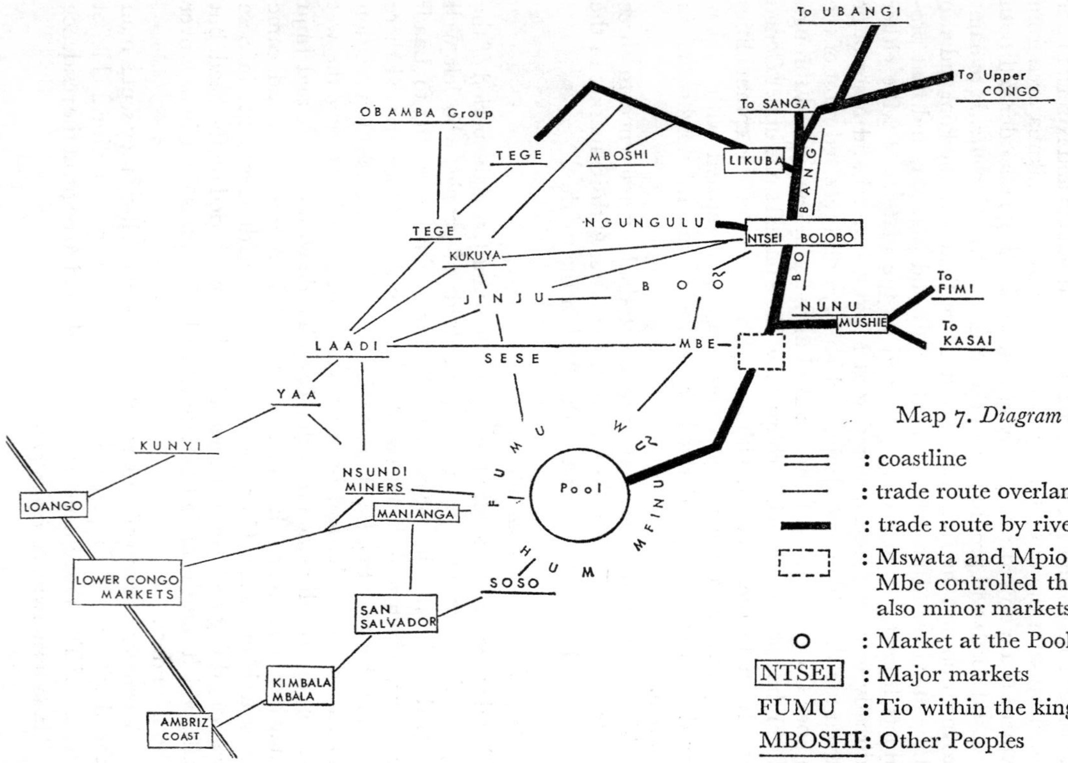

Map 7. *Diagram of Trading Network*

: coastline
: trade route overland
: trade route by river
: Mswata and Mpio a Bwaani, where the Lords of Mbe controlled the traffic on the Congo River; also minor markets there
O : Market at the Pool
NTSEI : Major markets
FUMU : Tio within the kingdom
MBOSHI: Other Peoples

of the political chief. From there the visiting traders swarmed out.[8] Unlike the Tege, the Jinju and Sese did not conduct caravans to Laadi country although small parties were sent. Whenever a village, says Ngelkiere for the Jinju, had collected two tusks it went to the chief who sent two to three men to sell them. The profits would be divided into three parts: one for the chief of the land, one for the political chief who sent the men out, and one for the finder of the 'dead' ivory, for the Jinju did not hunt these beasts. Professional hunters went only after buffaloes for meat. Before the benefits were divided the chief had already given a part to the men he sent for selling the tusks. They went to Nsundi and bought cloth for it. Besides ivory, the Sese apparently carried their raphia to the Pool,[9] also perhaps in small parties.

The Laadi visitors and others for Miandoo, Abili Ndiõ, and Ngelkiere all remember some Vili (*aloã*) and Kongo stayed mostly with the chiefs who acted as their brokers with the right of first buying and selling. Some seem also to have made business friends in other settlements and those then acted as landlords and brokers for them. Men in this relationship were usually blood brothers. Traders bought their food on the spot, another source of income for their landlord, and therefore they tried to stay as short a time as possible. Unless they were a bigger caravan they did not stay for more than a few days at any given settlement. They came all the year round, but the slack season must have been in the dry season from May to October, perhaps, for that was the time when the Laadi formed their caravans in the direction of the coast. The Vili however may have come only during this season.

Protection for the travellers as well as decisions in commercial quarrels were given by the political chiefs, even though it could and did happen that the chiefs themselves would rob a bigger caravan.[10] Feuds and wars also hampered progress sometimes, but this was only a minor problem since most 'wars' were intermittent feuds only.[11]

The pedlar trade of the Bobangi on the Nsah plateau was organized in a similar way. Each Bobangi trading 'chief' was a blood brother of the Tio chief he visited regularly. In this fashion Bobangi frequented

[8] L. GUIRAL, *Le Congo*, pp. 169–70, 220, for trade with the Tege; H. BRUNSCHWIG, op. cit., pp. 166, 168, 172, for evidence of Laadi trade to the valley of the Lefini as far east as the river Lubilika.

[9] H. BRUNSCHWIG, op. cit., p. 170.

[10] The Tio at Mbe remembered an attack by a chief of Djambala against a group of Kukuya which led to war. The vulnerability of the traders was recognized and charms were made to cope with it.

[11] H. BRUNSCHWIG, op. cit., p. 165, for a short delay due to a feud or a minor war. L. GUIRAL, op. cit., p. 193, was not allowed to proceed to chief 'Nhempourou' of the Jinju because of a war over a woman between his host and the Jinju. This was, however, exceptional in that African traders did not need to recruit porters as Guiral did. For it was fear that the porters would be attacked by the enemy that made his host decide to send him along another route.

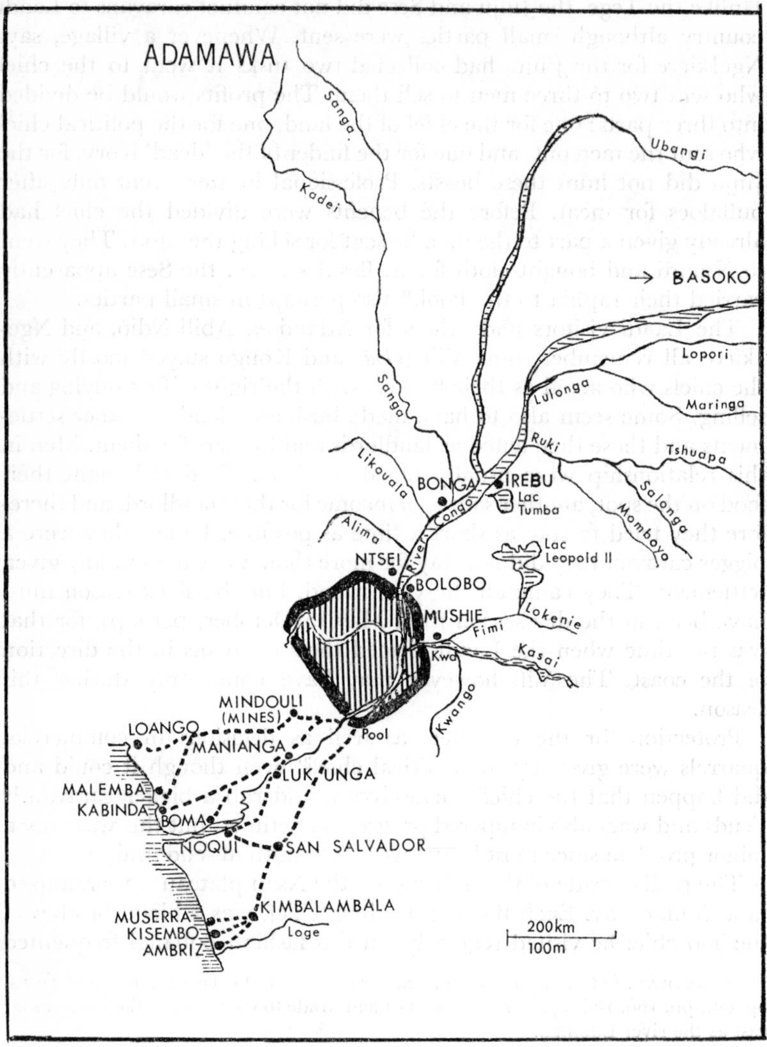

Map 8. *The Great Congo Trade*

: Area controlled by the Tio Kingdom

: Atlantic Coast

ADAMAWA : geographical region

----- : route to the coast

the residences of all Boõ and Jinju chiefs on the Nsah plateau, north of the Lefini. Froment noted among the Bobangi that their chiefs entered into blood brotherhood to create an alliance or a reconciliation and that commoners did so to create secure trading relationships.[12] A crucial difference between the Laadi and the Bobangi trade was that the Bobangi all came from the markets of Bolobo and Ntsei.[13]

Jinju and Boõ in return visited the Ntsei market. Little is known about its organization, however. Tio tradition regards it as the biggest single market after those of the Pool. It can probably be identified as the market of the Nkéni river, described by Ponel, since Tio and Ngungulu put it near the mouth of that river. Ponel mentions only that there were two markets held side by side. In one the women dealt in foodstuffs, while the men sold all other commodities on the other. These included, as the Ngungulu of Mbeya remembered, products from Europe such as the prestigious Toby jugs, and ironware from the upper Congo. Ponel added that Bobangi brokers, under the leadership of a 'friendly chief', traded overland in the countryside.[14] The market was obviously under the control of the chief NGÃBÕ, or of the ritual head NGIA.

The markets at the Pool were the hub of the whole system; on the north bank Mfwa with the hamlet of Ibiu and Mpila and on the south bank Ntamo and Ntsaasa (Kinshasa). The Tio controlled all these markets and were the middlemen through whose hands all the goods exchanged had to pass. The ferries over the Djoué were under the control of NGAMPA and BWABWA NJALI, probably Fumu chiefs, who also traded but on a much smaller scale. The bulk of their revenue came from operating the ferries.

The relative importance of Ntamo, Kinshasa, Mpila, and Mfwa in terms of population varied continuously as people moved from one to the other. Any estimates must therefore be relative. Perhaps Stanley's estimate of 5,000 for Ntamo alone is exaggerated and Dupont's figure in 1887 of 2,500 might be more correct although by then the Tio were beginning to leave a town that was too close to the Europeans. Kinshasa was often estimated at about 5,000 persons. De Chavannes estimated Mpila at about 3,000 persons and perhaps 1,200 houses while for Mfwa

[12] E. FROMENT, *Un voyage*, p. 190, described a situation at Liranga, near the mouth of the Ubangi river, among Bobangi. Tio tradition remembers ties of blood brotherhood between Bobangi chiefs and Nzã Mbã a famous chief, earlier in the century who lived on the Nsah plateau. ONDONO, *Souvenirs*, p. 15, claimed that king Iloo had wanted to become a blood brother of De Brazza when the latter arrived first at Mbe, but the explorer refused.

[13] C. COQUILHAT, *Sur le Haut Congo*, p. 84. In November 1882, Ibaka, chief of Bolobo was on the river Nkéni buying ivory. H. BRUNSCHWIG, op. cit., pp. 165–6, for trade between the great chief NGEIMPÃW at Abili and the Bobangi and also for general relations between Bõo and Bobangi.

[14] C. COQUERY, *Brazza*, pp. 340–1. Ponel specified that they bought iron from the Kukuya and brought it from there to Ntsei.

Stanley gave the estimate of 150 men which could not mean much more than 600 inhabitants. Perhaps Ibiu had not been estimated with it.[15] Yet Guiral held that the market at Mfwa was in 1882 by far the most important one on the Pool and Tio informants of the plateau talk more about Mfwa than about Mpila. Yet by 1885 Mpila had become the major market, probably in part to stay away from the new French settlement.[16]

All in all, then, there were probably no more than about 10,000 Tio around the Pool[17] and a variable number of Bobangi which one can perhaps estimate in the rainy seasons at about 4,000 to 5,000 with less than half living there permanently. For a country with a low density of population this was, comparatively speaking, a metropolis!

Most of this population no longer lived in a subsistence economy since they did not cultivate but bought foodstuffs from the area of Mswata upstream and from their hinterlands. In Kinshasa, and probably elsewhere, some men were still fishing but most men lived from market activities alone. For women the change was greatest and they seem to have had a great deal more leisure time than their sisters in the villages, even though here they made pottery and prepared heaps of *chicouangue* for the traders. They also attended food markets, where women of the villages in the hinterland came to sell their produce.[18]

The most remarkable difference between the organization of these market towns and the villages was that so few free men controlled so

[15] G. SAUTTER, op. cit., pp. 367–8.

[16] A. MAURICE, op. cit., p. 135, for Stanley's claim that Mpila was also a market. Kinshasa was not and the much smaller Kimbangou was. Clearly Stanley's informants belonged to Ngaliema's entourage. It is clear from L. GUIRAL, op. cit., p. 242, that there was a market at Kinshasa in 1882 and all evidence from French authors goes against the notion that there was a big market at Mpila until 1886. Cf. A. MERLON, *Le Congo*, p. 30. By 1891 J. DYBOWSKI, *La route*, p. 52, makes clear Mpila had become the preferred market. A. BUETTNER, *Reisen*, p. 222 (end 1885), held that Mfwa and Ntamo were still the major markets.

[17] CH. LIEBRECHTS, *Léopoldville*, p. 526, for estimation (1887) of only five thousand Tio south of the River. There may have been more in 1881 but not a great many more.

[18] L. GUIRAL, op. cit., pp. 239–72, describes trade at the markets and travelling by boat with a trader. All authors stressed the lack of cultivation as he does, p. 240. W. BENTLEY, *Pioneering*, I, p. 19, states: 'They kept their women in laziness.' All this is still exaggerated except for Ntamo. There was some cultivation and women attended food markets. Cf. CH. DE CHAVANNES, *Avec Brazza*, p. 273, for fields at Mfwa. On fishing, e.g. H. STANLEY, *Through the Dark Continent*, p. 535, and H. H. JOHNSTON, *River Congo*, p. 128, at Mpila and Kinshasa; the strongest proof that this was not a subsistence economy comes when L. GUIRAL, op. cit., p. 242, says that food, alone of all commodities, could not be exchanged for merchandise, but only for currency, whereas in the villages food alone could never be exchanged, except for sale to strangers. W. BENTLEY, op. cit., ill. opp. p. 396 for chicouangue; A. BUETTNER, op. cit., p. 223 (not even cassava fields at Ntamo; import by women from inland to food market).

many slaves.[19] The great leaders owned hundreds of slaves and perhaps as many as twenty women. The slaves were trusted retainers and manned the caravans to the coast. As for the women, some wives were the visible signs of alliances between the leader and other leaders in the area, such as Ngaliema's marriages to the daughters of the Hum paramount at Lemba and the leader of Kimbangu.[20] All these settlements were composite. Mfwa consisted of several separate villages, Kinshasa consisted of seven settlements fairly spread out from Kalina to Ndolo and Ntamo also had seven, eight, or nine chiefs.[21] In each of these clusters there was a principal leader and Stanley lists Ngaliema at Ntamo, NTSUULU in Kinshasa, NGIA at Mfwa and Ngaamakono at Mpila. The other chiefs 'followed' the leader just as was the practice in smaller settlements. But in fact they seem to have functioned as a council and if the great leader displeased them too much, they could move away to another market. This was apparently what one of them, João Makabi, did when he crossed from Mfwa (Ibiu) to Ntamo.[22] Each of the second-level leaders had probably also his own establishment of slaves and wives with very few free men, mostly relatives as in the villages. The effects of trade then were to make these secondary units much more cohesive, to accentuate division by social status between slaves and free men in them and to intensify rivalry between leaders. As an economic concern each town could and did act as a corporate group on important trade decisions such as preserving the monopoly of the Tio as middlemen or the admittance or rejection of European establishments.[23]

Seasons did affect the markets even though they were open every day of the year. In December and from March to May, i.e. during the rains, the boatmen came to bring the ivory and slaves to the Pool in

[19] Cf. Chapter III, fns. 20, 21, 24; H. STANLEY, *The Congo*, II, p. 372, states that the nine chiefs of Ntamo had eight hundred slaves. TH. MENSE, *Anthropologie*, p. 625, Ntamo grew by buying slaves.

[20] H. STANLEY, op. cit., I, p. 350, for the political marriages of Ngaliema; A. THYS, *Au Congo*, pp. 44–5, for carriers being 'les propres sujets' of the leaders; P. AUGOUARD, *A la suite*, p. 41. In 1882 he bought carriers at the coast from caravan leaders.

[21] L. GUIRAL, op. cit., p. 228 (Mfwa); W. BENTLEY, op. cit., pp. 350–6 (Kinshasa), p. 346 (Ntamo). A MAURICE, op. cit., p. 113 and H. STANLEY, op. cit., I, pp. 306, 350 (Ntamo) and pp. 295–6, 299–300, for Mpila which was said to have five chiefs.

[22] A. MAURICE, op. cit., p. 134, for enumeration of leaders; For Makabi, W. BENTLEY, op. cit., I, pp. 341–2; H. STANLEY, op. cit., I, pp. 295, 306, 392, 490, II, p. 191. He apparently moved in 1881 from Ibiu to Ntamo and quickly became the foremost leader there after Ngaliema. Also A. HANSSENS, op. cit., p. 66 (1882).

[23] A. MAURICE, op. cit., pp. 109–10, shows common action against Stanley by the chiefs of Ntamo who brought back their part of the presents the latter had given to Ngaliema. They forced Ngaliema's will in this matter but acted in unison. For enforcement of monopoly on ivory at Ntamo, p. 135, where a Nunu convoy of twenty-five boats was prohibited from selling to Stanley. In fact the chiefs of Ntamo took the ivory into custody.

much larger numbers than at other seasons. But most of the coastal caravans travelled during the dry season, leaving the Pool at the earliest towards the end of April and at the latest by the end of September. There was thus little overlap between the two streams of trade and it explains the absolute necessity for middlemen who could stock and hold the merchandise. This explains why leaders needed to have stores of coastal goods on hand to pay for the ivory. It is improbable, but not impossible, that they held these on credit. Another mechanism was one remembered at Brazzaville. The ivory was handed over to the Tio leaders who sent the young men of their settlement to sell it in Kongo country probably at Manianga. Only when the sellers returned was the ivory paid for. Goods and ivory or slaves then moved from the orbit of one regional market into another one still maintaining ultimately a link between the coast and the Pool. But all goods brought to the Pool from up-river by March would be destined to go with the great caravans of the dry season.[24] And at all seasons there was a light canoe traffic on the river as well, if only to bring food to Mfwa and Mpila from Mswata.

The trade on the river was carried by Bobangi, whether called Apfuru, Yanzi, Bobangi, or Likuba, terms all designating the same people and also by the Tio riparians all along their stretch of the Congo river. Canoes came down either singly or in groups as large as twenty-five and perhaps more on a trip.[25] Delcommune described the standard trading boat as 15 m long (16 yd) by 80 to 90 cm (3 ft) wide, deep in the water with trading goods packed one metre higher than the sides and extending over the whole length of the boat. The captain stood on a small platform at the back with a rooster, a part of every Bobangi naval outfit, and in the shade of a multicoloured umbrella while others

[24] CH. JEANNEST, op. cit., p. 95 (coast); G. SAUTTER, op. cit., p. 377 (Pool). On fashion of selling Sautter is confirmed by TH. MENSE, op. cit., p. 627 and A. MERLON, op. cit., p. 28. Some traders evidently came at other times from the Lower Congo. e.g. A. MAURICE, op. cit., pp. 109–10. By November, Zombo and Kongo traders from Ambrizette were still at Ntamo. W. Bentley arrived late in February but was anxious to get back before the rains made rivers impossible to cross. E. TRIVIER, *Mon voyage*, p. 53, states that October and November when the main winds came from the south-west made the Pool unusable for dugouts and that during those months there was no carrying of goods to the Pool. R. BUETTNER, op. cit., p. 234, who travelled late in October and early November saw no traffic at all in the channel until he neared Mswata when only six boats were seen, all Bobangi. On stores of Kongo trades in Tio villages cf. A. VEISTROFFER, *Vingt ans*, p. 100, for two open sheds with powder kegs and cloth, being stores of Kongo caravans 'which come each year to trade at this time' (August 1885) (CH. DE CHAVANNES, *Avec Brazza*, pp. 322–33).

[25] L. GUIRAL, op. cit., p. 256, started out with a lone Bobangi trader, but soon joined (pp. 261–2) a group of other Bobangi boats, cf. fn. 22 for the Nunu convoy of twenty-five boats. R. BUETTNER, op. cit., saw a typical group of six, with white roosters on their prow, a sign that they were Bobangi and not Nunu. All other travellers who mention them counted from two to ten boats in a typical convoy. The biggest convoys were rare and may have been Nunu rather than Bobangi.

protected the other members of the crew. Before the umbrella came into fashion mats protected the crew from the cruel glare. The range capacity of a canoe can be set at 2–3 tons and 1½ to 2 tons useful load. Every afternoon or evening the crew landed on a sandbank or on the bank and organized camp; they put the long oars in the ground and draped the mats which covered the trading goods during the day, over them. These mats were relatively watertight.[26] Along the water route the greatest danger for the navigators came from piracy. The Bobangi complained that the Tio of Mswata and NGANTSU's frequently engaged in this and that they had to send retaliatory expeditions until the outbreak quieted down.[27] The trip down the river took three to five or six days from NGANTSU's to the Pool depending on the wind and in reverse direction five or six days must be allowed.[28] In a matter of two to three weeks, then, the Bobangi could travel all the way to the mouth of the Ubangi river and their settlements furthest upstream. Control over the river trade in Tio territory belonged to chief NGOBILA at Mswata for the up-river and to chief NTSUULU of Kinshasa for the Pool. Complaints about robberies and losses as well as stray finds and of abandoned boats or other goods were to be reported and deposited with them. But since NGOBILA's people were also inclined occasionally to piracy everyone trusted to his charms for his personal safety. Thus the boatman of Guiral had an object in dried clay like a cylinder which he rubbed with palm-oil when danger threatened. The rooster of the Bobangi boats was also supposed to be a protective charm. But beyond this the navigators relied on travelling silently at night to get by dangerous places and also on their guns.[29]

The range of the whole trading system up-river was great. Via several intermediaries goods went up as far as the Aruwimi near Basoko, to the middle Ubangi river and up the Sangha and Alima rivers. The extent of penetration on the Ruki and its affluents is unknown. Trade also went up the Lulonga and affluents, the Kasai,

[26] A. DELCOMMUNE, *Vingt années*, I, p. 217; A. THYS, op. cit., p. 44, on careful stowing; L. GUIRAL, op. cit., p. 260; CH. LIEBRECHTS, op. cit., p. 508, estimated two to three tons for the load of a boat with 200 kg (400 lb), food and a crew of twenty to forty. E. ZORZI, *Al Congo*, p. 376 and E. FROMENT, *Trois affluents*, p. 461, compared would give a tonnage of two tons eight per load per boat, but if compared with, G. SAUTTER, op. cit., p. 270 (Chavannes), the average load is only half: one ton four per boat, which seems more likely. Pecile considered one ton and a half not to be excessive. P. AUGOUARD, *Le Congo*, p. 18, gives a smaller size as usual: 6 to 8 metres by 0·50 to 0·60 but this was a fishing boat.

[27] L. GUIRAL, op. cit., pp. 245, 270. He mentions all the riparian villages, but it is clear that only the two mentioned in the text had the power to carry out such raids.

[28] H. BRUNSCHWIG, *La négociation*, p. 34. He took coming down three days, of which one was spent entirely in the Pool. L. GUIRAL, op. cit., pp. 256–75, took seven days going up, of which two were spent in the Pool but he travelled rather leisurely. He stopped at Mswata. The same amounts of time were still estimated in 1963.

[29] L. GUIRAL, op. cit., pp. 274, 270.

Mfimi, Lake Leopold II, Lukenie, and perhaps the lower Kwango and Kwilu rivers also. But the Tio did not go further than Irebu and the mouth of the river Ubangi. They did not go up any of the affluents as the Bobangi did. And a third people, the Nunu from Mushie, also traded all the way from the Pool up the Kasai to the Kwango and the exit of Lake Leopold II.[30]

The Bobangi were the main traders. They came to the Pool in large numbers in the rainy seasons, except for October–November, and in the dry season they navigated up the Alima and the Lulonga, bringing down some 20 to 40 tons a day of cassava for their settlements from the Alima alone where there was little or no agriculture. They were always fishing or trading, mostly both at the same time. They were the only people to do this and they were also the only ones who had villages on the banks in Tio territory beginning with Mpila. More than one village was in fact mixed Bobangi and Tio.[31]

Data on the caravans are much less clear. A caravan for the Tio was a herd (Sims: *mu-kya*). The main traders south of the Pool were the Zombo (Zomo, Soso) and people from Manianga (Kwõ, Nsundi, Manianga). In 1870 caravans arriving on the coast south of the Congo could count from 100 to 500 souls and carry 200 to 300 tusks. 500 men was also the largest number seen in 1887 by Dupont.[32] North of the river the Laadi caravans were certainly much smaller. The only caravans which could probably approach those of the Zombo in size were the dry season ventures of the Loango. In this direction, both north and just south of the river, were the intermediary trading centres of Manianga, the mining area of Mindouli and even the Yaa villages who acted as brokers between the Laadi and the Kunyi. Many more small groups or even individuals travelled to the Pool from the Laadi, Kukuya, Sese, and Jinju areas than south of the river.[33]

Carrying was done on the head, except for salt and for ivory, which was carried over the shoulders wrapped in rags for small pieces, or

[30] TH. MASUI, *L'état indépendant*, p. 80, for Aruwimi; C. COQUERY, op. cit., pp. 463–4 (Pradier, 1886) for Likouala and Sangha, pp. 107–10, for the overall trade; G. SAUTTER, op. cit., I, pp. 265–71 (the overall trade and especially the Alima portion); M. STORME, *Ngankabe, passim*, for the Nunu.

[31] L. GUIRAL, op. cit., pp. 282–3, for an example of a mixed village. H. JOHNSTON, op. cit., p. 151, felt that the Bobangi were not yet settled downstream from the Kwa (with the obvious exception of Mpila) and that upstream of that river the settlements of Tio and Bobangi alternated, thus forming a cosmopolitan river culture. Cf. also E. ZORZI, op. cit., p. 404, on their internal organization for trade. Cf. J. DYBOWSKI, *La route*, pp. 95–6.

[32] CH. JEANNEST, op. cit., pp. 55–63; E. DUPONT, *Lettres*, p. 149. These carriers were all slaves. Cf. G. SAUTTER, op. cit., I, p. 371; A. MERLON, op. cit., gave two hundred men as a high figure (1885–7).

[33] L. GUIRAL, op. cit., pp. 196, 212, 216, 202. The only major caravans of several hundred he mentioned were Tege going to the Laadi, pp. 169–70. Cf. C. COQUERY, op. cit., p. 406 n. 1 on Yaa (Jacob, 1894).

slung under a pole carried by two men for big tusks and which was not always trusted to slaves taken along for sale.[34]

Head porterage was not very efficient and loads seem to have been rather less than 60 lb which became the standard load with the European caravans. At night the caravan camped in shelters made on the spot. Since the bigger ones travelled during the dry season rain was rarely a problem either on the march or at night. Food was bought as far as possible along the road, often for relatively stiff prices, and the great southern caravans paid tolls to the chief of every territory they crossed. In the north ferries over the Djoué were paid for, but that seems to have been all until the staples were reached. The Loango caravans paid tolls all the way from the coast to the valley of the Djoué. Once the toll had been paid the chief had a man escort the traders with his bell through his dominion.[35] The caravan leader was obviously given great responsibility since he did all the negotiating and decided all matters about the route, as well as making charms for the caravan and maintaining internal discipline. Unfortunately no data are available on the relations he had with subgroups within the caravan, or even about the existence or the makeup of these subgroups or on the police he may have had to enforce the regulations he imposed. These problems of organization did not exist for the small groups who went out on their own. On the other hand a really large caravan did not often have to fear much for its security.

The Tio themselves did not participate in this caravan trade except for short stretches and in small numbers. It is true that by 1885 we learn about caravans sent out by Ngaliema, but this development may well have occurred after the opening of the trails by the International African Association. It is unlikely that larger Tio caravans went out long before this.[36]

The differences between the trade to the coast and the carriers upstream consisted then essentially in the much slower pace of trade over

[34] A. ROBERTS, *Nyamwezi Trade*, p. 61, points out that this was a skilled task best performed by young men. The generalization that slaves were bought to carry the ivory and then sold along with the tusks on the coast is perhaps untenable. For the Tio, cf. G. SAUTTER, op. cit., I, p. 377, where tradition claims that young men from the entourage of the leaders carried the ivory for sale. These did include mostly slaves, but slaves who were part of the domestic life of the leader, not slaves for sale. Yet P. AUGOUARD, *A la Suite*, p. 4, bought slaves used for carriers and claimed this was common; A. MERLON, op. cit., for mode of carrying ivory. H. BRUNSCHWIG, *Les cahiers*, p. 170 (salt carried on stick over shoulder by Boõ).

[35] C. COQUERY, op. cit., pp. 401–2, for a trip starting in Loango. Other and earlier authors such as Augouard or Bentley confirm. Cf. PH. MARTIN, *The Trade of Loango*, pp. 153–4 after Pechuel—Loesche. For an idea of the amount of toll. D. NEUVILLE, CH. BREARD, op. cit., p. 213; P. AUGOUARD paid forty fathoms of cloth. J. JEANNEST, op. cit., pp. 121–2. The trip from Ambrizette took from three to four months.

[36] Cf. G. SAUTTER, op. cit., I, p. 373. For 1887 and A. THYS, *Au Congo*, pp. 44–5. R. BUETTNER, op. cit., p. 227 (1885 guide of Ngaliema to go to San Salvador); A. MERLON (1885–7), op. cit., p. 31

land, the greater expense from tolls, the much greater amount of manpower needed, and the exclusion of the Tio from the trade towards the coast. The latter may well be linked with the manpower problem. Even with their slaves, the population around the Pool would be hard put to organize caravans of hundreds towards the coast, to keep control of the markets at the Pool and still to participate in small group trade to the plains and on the river. Before the arrival of the Europeans it was clearly not a profitable enough use of their manpower to enter into competition for the carrying business to the coast.

Once the foreign traders arrived, they camped. The fishermen settled on beaches set aside especially for them at Ntamo, and perhaps Kinshasa, or at Mpila.[37] The coastal caravans settled inland behind Tio towns. Trade was conducted almost daily. The market lasted more or less half a day. The wares were displayed on the ground in the open air except for ivory and slaves. Once the market was finished the seller took his remaining merchandise and left for a neighbouring market. As Guiral describes it:

> the goods were displayed in the open as in the fairs of Europe and all around circulated buyers and sellers. From time to time a group detached itself from the crowd and disappeared into a house; these were interested parties who went to settle the details of a deal started at the fair. But it was impossible for me to be present at these talks. One heard continually shouting from merchants who announced their arrival or called others in this fashion. On the river the boats were going along: some landed near Mfwa, others disappeared in the direction of the villages on the left bank.[38]

Before the Bobangi landed his wares he agreed with a Tio to sell and received earnest valuables from the Tio. Once then landed he could not sell to anyone else. The bargaining might take days or weeks however during which the Bobangi was fed and housed by his Tio host.

Bargaining took hours and had become formalized to a point.

[37] CH. DE CHAVANNES, op. cit., pp. 229, 243. There were five Bobangi chiefs there; W. BENTLEY, op. cit., I, p. 350, saw the beach of Ntamo empty but he arrived in the dead season; otherwise *idem*, p. 461, mentions the beaches for Bobangi and for Nunu; cf. A. HANSSENS, op. cit., p. 7, mentioned that chief Mangui was camping (in 1882) on Ngaliema's territory with his Bobangi and sold ivory to the latter.

[38] L. GUIRAL, op. cit., p. 229, and for other details p. 242. Ivory was not traded in the open, cf. p. 243. Later reports from Kinshasa to this effect are thus confirmed, and this was not a reaction to the presence of Europeans. In fact most of the deals done in the privacy of the houses were probably concerned with ivory. Since those were important transactions the settlement of the amount, sort and quality of goods to be given in return needed a long debate. It is likely that slaves were also sold in this fashion, which would help to account for the fact that the trade is mentioned by so few Europeans. Cf. also CH. LIEBRECHTS, op. cit., p. 523. On ivory cf. A. MERLON, op. cit., p. 32. The tusks were kept buried in the ground, where they were supposed to 'grow'. Merlon claims that in one day at Mpila four hundred tusks could appear from nowhere if a buyer was found.

The buyer decried the merchandise, the seller stressed his loss in the transaction and the efforts he had deployed to get the merchandise. During the process the goods were carefully checked, prices were compared, means of payment discussed, eventually credit was arranged and when it was all over buyer and seller snapped their fingers together in unison, which formalized the contract. No further changes were allowed after such a formal agreement.[39] If disputes arose they were referred to the chief of the town.

Regular clients and chiefs were welcomed differently. They were put up in the house of their Tio 'friend' and very often became blood brothers (Sims: *za makwani*). The ceremony itself consisted in crossing the hands of the brothers in front of witnesses, making an incision in their crossed arms, putting salt on it and mixing the blood of both by rubbing arms. Stanley and Ngaliema did not drink the mixture but this was the next step. Then the medicine men of both parties arose to detail all the horrors that would befall a faithless blood brother. The essential nature of the pact is well brought out by the fact that the term for it derived from *kwani* (Sims: 'revenge') and meant 'to eat feuds to avenge'. Blood brothers did not only have to help each other, they were also expected to stand actively by in each other's feuds.

A ceremony of alliance, amounting to near blood brotherhood was the exchange of charms, *kaa*, such as Stanley and Ngaliema concluded in 1877 and which was considered by 1881 to be tantamount to blood brotherhood. The blood pact also had close ties with trade and the compact between Stanley and Ngaliema in 1882 was the conclusion of an agreement over ivory sales, which mattered much to both of them. The bond thus formed was not truly unbreakable, since if one partner felt that his charms were stronger he might try to defy the sanctions for breaking the pact. The community around the Pool disapproved though. Thus, even though the compact had been founded only on an exchange of charms both a Hum chief and his own son reproached Ngaliema in 1881 for wanting to attack Stanley. In fact the pact was the strongest means available to protect a foreign trader and it usually seems to have been honoured.

Blood brotherhood was believed to be a pact that lasted till death. If one partner died, the other was supposed to follow him soon to the grave. Thus a Tio leader who wanted blood brotherhood with Dolisie declared: 'You are young, I am old; soon I will die; make the blood compact with my son and successor.' This aspect of a pact unto death and beyond is also well known from the Kwango.

[39] The business acumen of the Tio was well known and feared by most Europeans. One of the standard clichés about them was: 'They are very able commercial brokers'; TH. MASUI, *L'état indépendant*, p. 76; W. BENTLEY, op. cit., II, p. 15, linked Tio bluff and their despising attitudes to the bargaining process. Calloc'h, p. 165: 'conclure; faire claquer les doigts pour conclure un marché'; A. MERLON, op. cit., pp. 28–30.

Lasting partnerships between chiefs did not always imply blood brotherhood. Brazza was told by a Bobangi chief at NGANTSU's that the fathers of chief NGANTSU had given the right of way to them. He was a friend of NGANTSU's father and when NGANTSU was young he had urinated on his foot. Then when the boy's father died he recommended his son to him and now they consider NGANTSU as a father. And another chief Okeme came to NGANTSU to show him his son and tell him: 'If tomorrow I die, he will replace me.'[40]

The Tio landlord benefited as well since he acted as middleman between the traders from the coast and those from the upper River. The caravans from the coast sold their wares to the leaders of the settlements, rather like Bentley in 1881. Guiral states that the Tio either received goods to sell from the Bobangi or bought them and then entered into business relations, with the Kongo (*Bakouyas*) or Zombo (*Poutou*), sold the goods and kept a commission on the price. This corresponds well with what Tio told Sautter about selling the ivory in Kongo country and then returning to pay the Bobangi.[41] The situation seems to have been that when the great caravans from the coast came, the Tio leaders had a stock of ivory sufficient to buy all the incoming goods. In the off-season they then traded in local markets west of Ntamo and Mfwa. Indeed the great coastal caravans would have lost too much time and expense for buying food, if they had had to wait to sell their goods and buy their ivory piecemeal. Their needs give a special economic role to the really wealthy town leaders, who alone could accumulate the necessary amount of ivory and slaves required.

The role of the local markets (Sims: *nkana*, Calloc'h; p. 262: 'marché' *yu*) to the west remains obscure. West of the Djoué Calloc'h indicated that by 1910 the major markets alternated on different days of the four-day week, forming a cycle. In 1916 the system had spread under the influence of the immigration of Kongo speakers in the upper Djoué and also because of the rubber trade. It is not even certain that market organizations based on cycles even existed among the Fumu before 1892. The only minor markets mentioned then were the ferries of Bwabwa Njali and Ngampa, just as Mswata and NGANTSU's and Lishia's were up river.[42] One more market was mentioned, that of

[40] D'UZES, *Le voyage*, p. 133 (pact unto death); L. DE SOUSBERGHE, *Pactes*; H. STANLEY, *Through the Dark Continent*, pp. 536, 538 (1877); H. STANLEY, *The Congo*, I, p. 385; and A. MAURICE, op. cit., pp. 112, 122, 150–2 (1881–2). H. BRUNSCHWIG, op. cit., pp. 46, 51.

[41] L. GUIRAL, op. cit., p. 244; G. SAUTTER, op. cit., I, p. 377; TH. MENSE, op. cit., p. 627.

[42] *Les marchés indigènes, passim.* He remarks pp. 95–6, about the total lack of such markets on the Tio plains. The Teke names for the days of the week given by him correspond to those of Calloc'h but the latter's *Bu-dzuga* lost the *g* which makes it closer to Tio. Even if they did not have the markets and the cycle, the Tio on the plains

'Mokoko, the little one', who lived near the Falls well downstream from Ntamo. In fact it is possible that the big markets listed by Guiral, Mfwa, Kinshasa, Ntamo, and the small Mokoko, were rotating by day of the week. He states only that 'markets were held practically every day on one of the points of the Pool' and remarks that after a market the sellers try the next one. He mentioned *four* markets; so does Stanley who gave Ntamo, Mfwa, Mpila, Kimbangu.[43] Such a market organization would help to explain price-setting. It also gave a reflexion of power relations on the Pool since the dominant leader would hold his market on 'the fourth day of rest'.[44]

Details about the financial nature of the transactions, such as partnership in buying, brokerage, conversion of currencies, benefit margins, must wait for a sketch of both currencies in use and commodities traded, to which we now turn.

4. *Commodities*

The variety of commodities circulating along these trading networks can first be classified in groups according to points of production, then the exchanges typical for the different areas of trade will be sketched before a discussion by commodity concludes the section.

Goods coming from the coast included European cloths, guns, gunpowder, crockery, mirrors, beads and shells, candles, brass goods,

---

had the week. The days are given according to the *marchés indigènes*, p. 99 (both Kongo and Tio), Calloc'h, Sims, and our notation in 1963.

Sims:	1916	Calloc'h, p. 262	1963		Kongo (1916)
Mukila	*Moukila*	*Mu-kila*	*okila*	(3)	*Nkila*
Mpiu	*Mpiga*	*Mpika*	*Nkwe Mbali*	(4)	*Mpika*
Uzuo	*Boudzoua*	*Bu-dzuga*	*odzuo*	(1)	*Nkoi*
Ukweo (*Mukwéo*)	*Boukwéo*	*Bu-kweo*	*okwe*	(2)	*Boukondzo*

The numbers indicate the sequence from (1) to (4) as it existed in Mbe. Days two and four were propitious and more or less sacred. The name for day (1) however is derived clearly from *dzuo*: 'to close'. The over-all correlation with Kongo names is close. In fact there is total correspondence with the names used by the Ngungulu and in the Kwilu by the Yans. The same set of names with only one change from the Tio/Yans model is then found all the way to Kasai. This would be proof for trade in this area, were it not that the week is unconnected with trade (because no markets) on the plains, but has a slight religious meaning. The obvious indication seems to be that the plains Tio accepted from an area where markets existed, probably around the Pool, a week (Sims: *muluña;* Calloc'h, p. 322, *mu-luna*) to be used mainly as a way of organizing time. M. N. OBENGA, *Le royaume*, p. 43, follows Calloc'h, but adds that the market Tsaba was held only every eighth day.

[43] A. MAURICE, op. cit., p. 135; L. GUIRAL, op. cit., p. 242. Note that the order of Mfwa and Ntamo differs in both sets, otherwise one might well hold that the market at Kinshasa coincided with Mpila and the small market at Kimbangu with that of the little Mokoko.

[44] CH. LIEBRECHTS, op. cit., p. 536.

whether in the form of raw material (rods, bangles, wire) or finished objects, and iron wares, such as knives, but no raw iron. Goods manufactured along the coast were salt and objects of pride (*unũ*): luxury objects in engraved brass made in the Loango region. Slaves came from the lower Congo area, but were bought there as well.

Goods from the mining districts of Mindouli and Boko Songho included lead for bullets, perhaps still in bars, as well as red copper in raw form.

The plains produced some ivory, groundnuts, slaves, raphia, goats, fowls, game meat (especially buffalo), tobacco, rubber, foodstuffs, such as cassava, maize, maize beer, bananas, and basketry work. Among these raphia came especially from the Kukuya and the Sese.

The peoples west of the Kukuya produced raw iron, iron goods, wooden drums, pottery, and leopard skins, which formed a distinct flow of commodities.

Goods produced by the Bobangi or acquired by them further upstream in the Sangha, Ubangi and Congo rivers were smoked fish, a variety of pottery, canoes, fishing gear, iron implements and iron objects of *unũ*, mats, a special variety of palm-oil, slaves, camwood, and copal. To these may be added products from the Kasai river and upstream, whence especially salt from Sakata country and fine pottery from the Mfunu, as well as harpoons for hippopotami, smoked hippo meat, sugarcane wine, fine pottery and smoked fish from the Nunu joined the other commodities. Hippo meat was also traded by the riverfolk.

The Pool itself produced fine pottery and pottery pipes, finely engraved copper or brass objects and perhaps metal pipes. Pigs were also raised there, and some fish was caught.

The immediate hinterland of the Pool, i.e. the Hum to the south, the Fumu and Wũ to the north as well as the Mfinu and Mfunu as far away as Mswata, produced food for the great markets and the travellers: maize, banana, fowls, groundnuts as well as white and red kaolin, a little tobacco, some slaves, and some local ivory.

The south-west with its Laadi, Loango and Kongo traders brought goods from the coast and the mines of Nsundi in return for slaves, rubber, groundnuts, raphia cloth, goats, fowls and game, perhaps also tobacco and ivory. Groundnuts and rubber were not sold to coastal caravans anywhere else. No doubt because their bulk and low price made it prohibitive, not to speak of the fact that both products could be gathered much nearer to the coast. Tobacco was carried because it was a high priced crop, even then. From the area covered by the Laadi pedlars small quantities of groundnuts and rubber could however be carried over a short distance to be sold in the Yaa markets.

The north-west and especially the market of Ntsei brought quantities of coastal goods, special palm-oil, a great variety of pottery and ironware from the Ubangi and the Congo upstream, as well as products west from the Kukuya to the Tio in return for slaves, ivory, and tobacco. The local food market at Ntsei had fowls, grasshoppers, and larvae of white ants on sale along with salt and fish. This trade in contrast to the market in other commodities was kept by women and it is unclear who furnished which foodstuffs.[45]

All along the river to the Pool there were exchanges, between river-folk and land-lubbers, of foodstuffs for smoked fish, on occasion salt, coastal goods, fishing gear, or wine, in short any of the river products, were also exchanged for ivory, slaves, or tobacco. Also the Tio fishermen and traders acquired all their canoes and paddles from the Bobangi or Nunu.

At the Pool itself all the products from the coast and the lower Congo were exchanged for all the products of up river. In addition commodities made at the towns themselves, food brought down from the hinterland and products from the plains of Mbe and Mpũ, mainly ivory and slaves, reached this market zone. But slaves also came from the west and raphia from the Sese. The only products of the whole system not traded here were: groundnuts, rubber, Bobangi mats, special Bobangi palm-oil, as well as salt from the Kasai or from the upper Congo river. The better coastal salt, as well as local salt, was available and the Bobangi products mentioned fetched lower prices than all other products that these traders could carry.

The first feature to note about commodities imported from Europe is that the coastal areas themselves competed with products made locally. The imported cloth vied with raphia, the metals with local iron, steel or copper products, the crockery with fine pottery, the guns with spears, the coastal salt with the potassium salt made along the Congo, the objects of pride for chiefs (*unũ*) with similar items imported from the upper Congo. Of major imports, the beads were, perhaps with the cowrie and *olivancillaria nana* shells, the only products which were not directly competing with indigenous products. Imports were clearly getting the upper hand, for cloth, salt, and certain items of crockery, and spears and bows had been almost completely replaced by guns. Local iron and copper were still competing, but losing ground. The basic reason was not the market price, for the African product was still usually cheaper than the European one. It was the quality which had made these goods accepted first as luxury items and then in the towns of the Pool only as items for daily use. The result was a growing dependence on imports, the gradual loss of certain technical skills and an overall reduction in the degree of self-sufficiency in Tio communities.

[45] C. COQUERY, op. cit., p. 341 (Ponel, 1886), pp. 459–60, details the trade further up near the Alima and to Bolobo. This included the other goods produced by the Bobangi.

The second feature of the coastal imports, and this is an index of their value as luxury items, was their extraordinary variety. The Table below lists only those which Sims included in his word list.

CHART 13

Coastal goods for sale at the markets of the Pool by major categories

1 *Metals*

metal basin, pail, tin teapot (the latter two only for use by Europeans): *tele*
brass wire, iron wire, ring, thimble: *lindaa*
brass nail: *linconso*
brass rod: *litoo*
brass rod: *lingele* (*ngiele*: used as currency. *mitako* in Lingala)
brass nail; chair nail: *inkwambani*
rod; iron, or metal: (*M*)*ungiri*
knife: *mbiele*

2 *Cloth*

handkerchief: *leso*
shawl: *mfumfula*
calico: *mbinsa*
covering, sheet, robe, mosquito curtain: *ntaa* (cf., also used for a large piece of fine raphia cloth)
linen: *mese*
fine cloth, silk, banner: *likee* (Calloc'h, p. 219 'flanelle')
cloth, border of cloth: *limbala*
blue cloth: *ngapi* (Calloc'h 244: blue with dots: *niã̄ka*)
woollen cloth, blanketing: *nkama* (always red; name from *nkã̄*: red ants) the most prestigious cloth all chiefs and leaders wanted to have. (Calloc'h: 317: *nkami*)
napkin: *ikini*
white cloth: *Ikali ibubi* (Calloc'h, p. 292: *mu-bubu*: piece of cloth of eight fathoms)
calico, white cloth: *furo* (Calloc'h: 'calicot', *fuma*, p. 150 same cloth?)
whole piece of cloth: *cina*
shawl: *ncaro*
shawl, thin cloth, heap (sic!): *muzu*[a]

3 *Beads and shells*

beads: *misaa*
string of beads: (*M*)*unkali* or in general *loo misaa*
string of beads, necklace: *mulele*
girdle of beads: *mucara* (only for women)
string of beads, tattoo marks, tribal marks: *nzele* (underlines role as jewellery)
string of beads, hoop iron, lamp wick: *muzi* (all three imports!)
white beads: *bincaa biicicilo*
blue beads: *lisisaa*
red beads: *lincononcono*

[a] Calloc'h, p. 209: 'étoffe' listed twelve varieties in 1910 and G. SAUTTER, *De l'Atlantique*, I, p. 377 tells that Tio in the 1950s still remembered five basic varieties.

long beads: *lie*. These were imitations of ancient long hexagonal beads, which were very rare. At first exaggerated prices were paid for them. Cf., W. Bentley, op. cit., II, pp. 20–1
large, button: *sio*
small button: *isisio*
cowry: *inkolo*
large cowry: *liji* (in fact *lizi*: *olivancillaria nana* and *nji* the plural or any currency)
cowry: *limbuli*[b]

4 *Crockery*
bottle: *mulii* (also copal!)
drinking glass: *ifila*
drinking glass: *itenõ*, *ititeno* (probably crystal, because the diminutive also means little bell)
saucer, cup: *isisa*
plate, lid, saucer, dish, pan: *isa*
spoon: *foo*
teaspoon: *ififoo* (this and the preceding may have been only for Europeans)
glass: *mubweo*[c]

5 *Fire arms*
powder barrel: *inzeze*
powder horn: *tue limbaa* (ladle of fire)
gun: *uta* (Calloc'h, pp. 225–6 lists Tio names for forty-four parts and items connected with the gun. It confirms how fully integrated the weapon was in 1910, and no doubt already in 1880)[d]

6 *Others*
salt from the sea: (*M*)*ungwa* and *musio*; it came in blocks *bula* (Calloc'h, p. 144) and *Mungwa* was coarser than the fine salt *musio* (Calloc'h, p. 122)
candle: *mukaño*
mirror: *izili*, *itali*

[b] Calloc'h, p. 290 gives eight varieties of beads, but one is the *olivancillaria nana*. In fact the Tio were not as interested in beads as many other peoples further inland. 'Beads have no value': Pradier in C. COQUERY, *Brazza*, p. 462.

[c] Calloc'h twenty years later added: 'carafe', 'cuillère', 'faïence', 'flaçon', 'verre'. Glasses were more important than dishes, mainly because transparent objects could not be made locally but also because drinking was more important than eating. The Toby jugs were in great demand as *unũ* objects. One still adorns Opontaba's tomb at Mbe.

[d] PH. MARTIN, *The Trade of Loango*, p. 153 estimated the import of guns along the Loango Coast reached 50,000 firearms a year for the second half of the eighteenth century. Even though it may seem an inflated figure, even half that number brings home the truth that guns were a standard weapon by 1880.

This list does not exhaust all goods that were imported but includes all the more usual items. One category which is obviously missing is alcoholic beverages, such as gin and rum, which seem to have filled some of the bottles mentioned.[46] The surprising omission among goods carried to the Pool are the big brass bowls or pails called *neptunes*.

The units of measurement for these commodities were the unit except for the following: for cloth there were standard lengths the fathom and the *cortade* of 3 fathoms and thickness was taken into account. Width was calculated as standard or double; metal wire or rods were evaluated by length and thickness, gunpowder by barrel and perhaps by the ladleful as oil was, and for salt by standard block, which looked like a little bag 20 cm long and 'as thick as a little finger'. Slabs were used by the Laadi, some being of a weight of 6 lb and others of 40 lb.[47] The attention paid to measurement in general (measure; *imiu*: Sims) is another indication of a market economy, for the more precise the measurement, the more exact the price will be.

Nearly every sort of goods that reached the Pool from the coast could go further. But each population up river might like different styles in cloth, beads, and shells, while glasswork and porcelain moved upstream only in small quantities. Pradier reported that at Brazzaville the red or blue flannels sold best, then handkerchiefs, then blue or red prints with large colourful patterns. At Bonga, near the mouth of the Alima, which is probably a good indication for conditions at Ntsei, cloth, which was worth double the price at the Pool, had to be cheap, so that light cloth even of bad quality was sold best, although cotton stuffs of a better grade were marketable. He then mentioned two definite types of prints and two types of handkerchief which sold well, and went on to mention the same two flannels also sold at the Pool, mentioned yet another type and concluded by stating that white calico (which was in demand at Bolobo) fetched no price at all. Empty bottles were highly priced, white beads twice as valuable as blue beads. Bells, knives, salt, mirrors, copper chains (an article for wear by leaders), guns, powder, and springs were apparently fairly cheap.[48] Tio traders at Irebu sold beads, white *americani*, prints, blankets (flannels), and such items as a brown porcelain jug and a buffalo leather belt adorned with ten little bells, which belonged to the *nkumu* leader of the Mpama, downstream from Irebu. Cowries and the special blue bead *lie* (called *nkange* here) also came from the Tio.[49]

Just as Pradier and other Europeans wrote up reports about local conditions, calculated the demand, and were quick to transmit

[46] CH. JEANNEST, op. cit., pp. 58–83, gave a detailed account of goods landed and sold on the coast. In addition to articles mentioned, such items as swords and old clothing and *curiosa* were also sold. One third of a payment was always calculated in guns, one in cloth, and one in powder kegs. Cf. also A. MAURICE, op. cit., p. 102.

[47] Calloc'h, pp. 252, 206: 'mesure étoffe' and 'épaisseur de tissus' for cloth; L. GUIRAL, op. cit., pp. 243, 170 fn. 1; C. COQUERY, op. cit., p. 97, after Pradier; P. AUGOUARD, *Voyage*, p. 113 (the Cortade measure as used west of the Pool).

[48] Report of 1886. Cf. C. COQUERY, op. cit., p. 462 (Pool), p. 471 (Bonga).

[49] A. SCOHY, *Notes*, p. 4.

information about changes in consumer demand, so the African traders transmitted information and calculated prices and profit margins. This applied especially to the beads and trinkets, followed by cloth, because they were dependant on fashion and a luxury. The very success of the Tio middlemen at the Pool shows that they had fully mastered the vagaries of supply and demand in this tricky market. The fickleness of the market associated with the variety of goods offered, thus constituted the third major feature of the commodities imported from Europe, with the exception of guns.[50]

The trade in guns and powder needs no further comment beyond a mention that it was perhaps the best indicator of the general flow of trade since the demand was great anywhere and the product uniform. For instance the Kukuya received their guns from the Pool but also from the Yombe area, showing that the connexions with the Pool were more frequented than would be supposed at first sight. Also it must be remembered that like salt, gunpowder was a commodity that was incessantly consumed, not only in hunting and war but perhaps even more at funerals. Even in Bobangi villages below Bolobo it had become *de rigueur* to fire at least one salute at a funeral.[51]

Coastal salt did not oust local salt because of its higher price, which made it, for instance, less economical to use in the preparation of smoked fish, but also because salt made from marsh plants or the male flower of the palm-tree was a different product in which potassium rather than natron predominated. The major centres of production of local salt were first the Sakata along the Mfimi where, during the dry season, men and women only prepared salt for export by the Nunu and the Bobangi. The latter used a good deal of it themselves to smoke fish. The Moye of the marshes of the Nkéni and Alima were also great producers and the Bobangi of Likuba also made this product. It was traded to the plains and it is possible that the packages of 40 lb of salt, mentioned for the Tege, were river salt. It was also brought to the Pool itself and sold there, partly in competition to coastal salt. The very fact that it was considered worthwhile to bring it to the markets there indicates that it still held a place next to the import. Unfortunately no data are available to indicate if it was a lower price or a different usage which was responsible for this.[52]

[50] TH. MASUI, *L'état indépendant*, pp. 496–7, lists the demands for 1897. It is obvious that major changes had occurred, especially in the taste for beads.

[51] L. GUIRAL, op. cit., p. 202, for the Kukuya, H. H. JOHNSTON, op. cit., p. 178, on gunpowder. At the Pool kegs were used for musketry salutes on every occasion. Cf. e.g. A. MAURICE, op. cit., p. 123, when 150 lb were shot by the chiefs to celebrate an arrangement reached with Stanley.

[52] *Le Sel*, p. 135 (sample), pp. 154–5, 163; C. COQUERY, op. cit., p. 97; W. BENTLEY, op. cit., I, p. 460, European salt was sold everywhere along the rivers Congo and Alima, at Ntsei as well as by traders below the Pool. Cf. E. FROMENT, *Trois affluents*, p. 463; H. BRUNSCHWIG, *Les cahiers*, pp. 180, 191 (along the Congo); C. COQUERY, op. cit., p. 460; G. SAUTTER, op. cit., I, pp. 276–7.

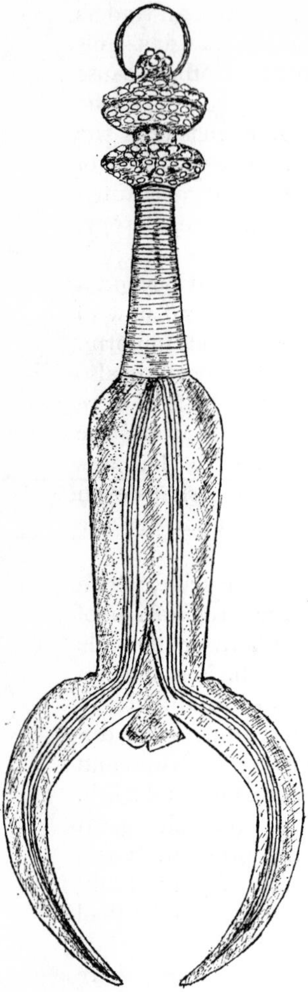

Copper and lead were only found and smelted in the mining district of Mindouli and west of there. Ingots of both were made (Sims: copper ingots: *bikulu*; lead: *boli*) but copper was fashioned in rods or bangles called *ngiele* and used as currency. Some of it was transformed into jewellery. The major use of lead was to make bullets, but since it was expensive, apparently because of its rarity, little of it found its way up river; some of the mines had even been abandoned by 1880. Copper which by 1870 may have been finding its way to areas as far away as Uele, suffered from the competition with imported brass and by 1880 brass wire had already become the major currency. Copper declined because the customers seemed to prefer the shinier brass and in addition copper could apparently no longer match the price of brass.[53]

The Tio had to import all their iron. Three major sources for this product are mentioned in the literature, although there were perhaps others. First there was the land west of the Kukuya near the upper Ogooué. From there ingots (Sims: rod iron or metal: (*M*)*ungiri*) were carried to the Kukuya, whereas similar rods from Nsundi arrived at the Pool and were sold to the plains south of the Lefini. The iron from

Fig. 4 Knife of Honour: *Unũ*

These were imported from the Ubangi River where the Ngbaka make them. They symbolize female genitalia among the Ngbaka, but this meaning is not apparent to the Tio. For them they are 'objects from afar', endowed with prestige, and owned by wealthy men or lords and so an indication of high status.

the Kukuya was then bought by Bobangi who carried it to the market at Ntsei. But this market was probably also furnished with iron from Bolobo. In the hinterland of Bolobo it was smelted and then fashioned into weapons and tools—knives, axes, and spear heads—and sold to

[53] On lead W. BENTLEY, op. cit., I, p. 401; H. BRUNSCHWIG, op. cit., pp. 222, 223, On copper G. SAUTTER, op. cit., I, pp. 374–5. H. BRUNSCHWIG, *La négociation*, p. 48. where de Brazza remarked at Mpio a Bwaani that the copper and lead bullets there were far bigger than those used on the Alima against him. This is a direct consequence of supply and transportation costs.

the Tio. Some of the iron imported from the upper Ogooué was also similarly sold as finished products rather than in raw ingots. More was transformed by Kukuya smiths into luxury products such as double and single bells with or without clappers, pipes, and knives. Some metal objects came from a distance. Thus a bell in European style at Imbãw seems to have come from the Boko Songho area.

This trade faced the competition of finished iron goods imported from Europe, mainly bush-knives which Kongo traders sold on the southern plains, but in the early 1880s the imports had made only small inroads, especially because the iron smelted in the region of Bolobo was of an exceptionally good quality because of the high temperatures reached with the use of 'hard' charcoal there. Beyond this, luxury objects in iron, objects of prestige such as chiefs' throwing knives, came from the lower Ubanghi and similar state knives from the upper Ogooué, but not from Nsundi or from Europe. European swords which were also prized seem to have been imported in very small numbers and none are attested on the plains or beyond the Pool.[54] The raw iron seems to have been used most to make hoes and axes. Worn-out tools were also melted down for re-use.

Just as important but for different reasons was the trade in pottery, which flourished despite the limited competition of imported crockery. The great centres for fabrication were among the Moye and beyond the Bobangi near the Alima, in the towns of the Pool itself, among the Mfunu and Nunu along the Kwa. The products were sold at the Pool, at Ntsei and all along the Alima and Congo rivers. Pottery was exported from the Pool to the Bobangi area but also from the Bobangi to the Pool. The explanation for this is cultural preference. People wanted to have certain products such as fine jugs from the Pool, others from the Mfunu, small pots from the Pool, big jars for catching rain from the Mfunu and others from the Moye. Braseros and cooking pots of other types came from the Bobangi, as well as some types of dishes and yet different sorts of jugs. Even pipe bowls were traded over great distances. Thus all the river people both made and bought pottery and the Tio on the plains imported them from all the centres.[55]

[54] L. GUIRAL, op. cit., pp. 161–8 fn. 1 for the Ogooué and drawings facing p. 160, for spearheads, axes, and state knives from there. C. COQUERY, op. cit., p. 341, where Ponel specifies it was smelted by the Mbete and Ndumbo; Tio informants had a clear recollection of this trade as well as of the flow from the Pool and from Nsundi. For Bolobo cf. H. H. JOHNSTON, op. cit., p. 175. For prestige objects cf. TH. MASUI, op. cit., p. 81. The many types of Tio knives were mostly imported. For bells and the like Tio informants were specific. It is of course possible that the Kukuya bought them ready made from their neighbours.

[55] C. COQUERY, op. cit., p. 460; L. GUIRAL, op. cit., pp. 241–2, 260, 264; TH. MASUI, op. cit., p. 72; W. BENTLEY, op. cit., p. 460; H. BRUNSCHWIG, *La négociation*, p. 50; G. SAUTTER, op. cit., I, pp. 277–8; H. H. JOHNSTON, *George Grenfell*, II, pp. 790, 791; E. COART, A. DE HAULLEVILLE, *La céramique*, p. 25; TH. MENSE, op. cit., p. 628. Tio informants were specific and many old specimens of pottery survive in

The river people in turn bought raphia cloth from the plains people. The standard lengths of cloth were even used as a currency on the Pool, in the area downstream to Manianga and on the plains. Cloth was produced everywhere on the plains, but in small quantities except among the Sese, which exported it in specially prepared bags, and among the Kukuya. The latter were the only people to have created orchards of raphia palms and thus to have organized a special production process with it. Their cloth was also the finest and according to the Kukuya the best of their cloth went to the court at Mbe. During the reign of Iloo and probably before, competition with foreign cloth began to give the latter a decisive advantage, even though among the Sese and Kukuya the production was maintained. Perhaps the quality was improved to meet the competition for by 1913 the raphia cloth had become an item of luxury and survived.[56]

The main commodities for sale against the coastal imports were ivory and slaves. The first of these seems to have been the mainstay of the whole trading system during the period studied. Whenever trade is mentioned by contemporary authors, or the value of it assessed, they speak of ivory. Perhaps they neglected slaves to some extent but it is evident that by 1880 ivory was paramount. Tio country and especially the lower valley of the Lefini still housed considerable numbers of elephants, even if they roamed in small herds. Thus in two weeks de Brazza saw about one hundred elephants on the lower Lefini.[57] The Tio of the Pool or the Mbe area did not hunt them systematically, but the Boõ and Jinju chiefs did and had professional pygmy hunters as well as Tio to track both buffaloes and elephants. The existence of special traps and of a gun that shot a special spear to kill elephants also indicate that the technique of production had reacted to demand.

The Tio chiefs controlled all ivory sales. The ground-tusk, i.e. the tusk which touched the ground when the elephant fell, was theirs in any

cemeteries and elsewhere. The decoration and execution of each type of vessel allows identification of the area of origin.

[56] A. MAHIEU, op. cit., XI, p. 20, for use as currency; H. LOIR, *Le tissage*, p. 59. Her fig. 49 shows a 'book' of pieces of cloth called by the Tio: *muti iko* (Sims) and used as currency. C. COQUERY, op. cit., p. 111; N. NEY, *Trois explorations*, p. 150 (*Boõ*); P. BONNAFÉ, personal information; H. BRUNSCHWIG, *Les cahiers*, p. 170 (Sese), p. 191 (sold on Congo river to Bobangi); J. MAES, *Le tissage*, p. 393 (in decline by 1913 at Pool and Mfunu, but they bought from Congo Brazzaville, p. 394); luxury item, p. 403.

[57] N. NEY, op. cit., p. 239; E. ZORZI, op. cit., pp. 405–15. Brazza, claims Ney, saw 101 elephants and Pecile mentions 57 going up the river and 44 coming down. Even near the Pool elephants were still living in sizeable numbers. The low density of the population was favourable to the presence of the pachyderms. H. H. JOHNSTON, op. cit., pp. 262, 263, noticed that there were many elephants on the 'Upper River'. One was killed at Mswata more or less by chance since they were not hunted by the Mfunu.

case. In addition all tusks were brought to the political chiefs among the Jinju, says NgeIkiere who sent two or three men to sell each pair of tusks to the Nsundi (Laadi?). He paid the messengers and then the proceeds were divided in three parts: one for the hunter, one for the chief of the land, one for the political chief. Tusks were also sent to the Pool and to Ntsei or bought by itinerant Bobangi.[58]

The great majority of tusks for the Pool did not come from Tio country. Tusks were said to be rare even at Ntsei. The major sources of the Bobangi lay up the Sangha and Congo rivers. European travellers comment on the abundance of ivory on the Bonga market or believed it to come from 'Bangala' or 'Upoto'. In fact it is likely that there was no intensive hunting in any region but that collection of the ivory over the very extensive area spanned by these trade routes assured a steady supply.[59]

The value of a tusk depended on its weight, its absolute size, its condition, whether cracked or not, its curvature, and its diameter. Since these characteristics counted in Europe, they obviously influenced the market in Africa. The Tio distinguished between *ncĩmo* (Sims: 'tusk, ivory') and *isoo* (Calloc'h, p. 246, 'escravelle') which was a substandard size. They weighed the pieces with a *iyele* (Sims: 'balance, olive beads') perhaps a system in which the weights corresponded to the multiple of the weight of a seed. In any case, because of the high value per unit the bargaining was especially stiff and could be stretched over more than a day for exceptional tusks.[60] Once again, the Tio mastered the intricacies inherent in the trading of this article, and made handsome profits with this commerce.

[58] The Tio were quite clear about the collection and sale of tusks. LIPIE and Nge Ikieere mentioned that the hunters of the chief did not go after elephants especially, but more after buffalo. NgeIkiere volunteered the information about the sending of young men to sell at Mpila. This agrees with G. SAUTTER, op. cit., I, p. 377, who comments on the practice of sale there. But Ngateo when commenting about the great chief Nzã Mbã, who lived earlier in the century, stated that he sent his hunters after elephants. Those who did not come back with tusks were themselves sold as slaves. True or not, the story shows an awareness by the Boõ of the possibilities for additional revenue open to chiefs. In the same tradition one also talks about young men and slaves being entrusted with ivory and other goods for the market at Ntsei. Note C. COQUERY, op. cit., p. 340, for the statement that ivory was rather rare though at Ntsei.

[59] H. H. JOHNSTON, op. cit., p. 263, E. DUPONT, op. cit., p. 669. L. GUIRAL, op. cit., pp. 242, 260, 264, 271; W. BENTLEY, op. cit., I, p. 460, disagreed with all other authors when he stated that the Bobangi brought little ivory to the Pool. A. MAURICE, op. cit., p. 135, has Stanley reporting that he would wish to establish his central factory for ivory among the 'Wyyanzi' (Bobangi) and he was very interested in this trade, so much so that he (p. 158) kept a trading journal of ivory.

[60] C. COQUERY, op. cit., p. 470, on the importance of the Sanga. TH. MASUI, op. cit., pp. 328–31, about the European market in ivory (1897). There are no olives in or near Tio country. The seeds mentioned by Sims could be from *arbus precatorius* and in West Africa as in India there existed a system based on its weight. The carrying of tusks overland was a delicate operation.

In the 1880s slaves had just been ousted by ivory as the main commodity traded at the Pool, and Pecile, Guiral, Brazza, Mense, and Trivier still found the slave trade important.[61] The flow of trade presented some peculiarities. Thus Guiral claimed that slaves came from both the lower Alima and the Kukuya or Laadi area to the Pool to be sold to Kongo. Yet Storme cited one case of a Tio from Mfwa who was sold *upstream* to a person in Mushie, and Reynaert says that the Ngenge sold locals into slavery to the Bobangi or at the Pool but bought from the Tio as well as from the Mbelo, Bolia and Boma. The Tio remembered sales at Mpila and towards Ntsei. Hanssens stated for 1882 that Ngaliema sold ivory for gunpowder, guns, *and slaves*, brought by the Kongo from the San Salvador area.

Mense confirmed Hanssens and claimed that the Ntamo settlement had grown after the end of the slave trade and its replacement by ivory through the buying of Kongo and Hum slaves by the Tio. He added also that there was a great exchange of slaves among the settlements at the Pool between the Hum, the Tio of Ntamo, and the Bale. Trivier described the sale. The person to be sold was brought into the house: the buyer looked at his teeth, examined the eyes, made him walk, run, lift weights, and prices were discussed. This procedure is identical with the one described by Miandoo. Trivier added that if the price was too low locally the slave would be sold to the Bobangi for resale in Ubangi where they were eaten. The procedures surrounding the sale show coastal influence and are identical with the examinations in the eighteenth century by the ship's physicians. In the 1880s much of this examination was probably superfluous because most slaves were required to perform only domestic chores. It was much more relevant then, at least at the Pool, where the slave hailed from and what sort of special skills he might possess.

The demand for slaves was not surprising, since retainers were needed to man the caravans and to be a successful leader a person had to invest in slaves for his own town—to defend it, to man his canoes, to do household chores, sometimes to cultivate, and often to trade. There was no labour for hire and thus labour could only be provided by slaves. On the coast and on the road to the coast demands for manpower

[61] E. ZORZI, p. 231: Pecile ranked slaves as more important than all other items of trade, including ivory; L. GUIRAL, op. cit., pp. 169–70, 220, also ranked them first for the Tege, p. 241, at the Pool, and p. 271, at the mouth of the Alima where they were bought by Bobangi who sold most of them at the Pool and kept the others; p. 242, at the Pool he mentioned slaves coming from the Tio of Mbe and from the Bobangi, but speaks of troops of slaves coming from the Kukuya (Bakouyas); N. NEY, op. cit., p. 150 (after Brazza), said they and raphia cloth were very important for the Boõ; H. BRUNSCHWIG, *Les cahiers*, p. 170, a slave with yoke and p. 172 for kidnapping. Cf. G. SAUTTER, op. cit., I, pp. 313–14, 370–1. E. TRIVIER, *Mon voyage*, p. 43, described the actual sales; TH. MENSE, op. cit., pp. 624–5, commented on its volume.

were similar. So a trade to the Pool and beyond would be understandable, just as one sees why the Bobangi kept some of the slaves they captured for themselves.[62]

Another major current of slave traffic towards the lower Ubangi river is to be explained, partly in terms of a need for manpower and partly because these populations were cannibals.[63] But it was practically necessary to sell the person 'far away' so that he would not be able to run home to his former kin. This is why every group exported slaves, even if they also imported them. Tio slaves would be bought by the Zombo and Zombo by the Tio. Slave exports were mostly men but women also were enslaved and their fate would be different in that they became concubines of the buyer. Great chiefs acquired many women this way. A curious case is a Zanzibari girl whom Opontaba probably bought at Mpila and kept among his women.[64] Obviously the buyer and seller had not looked upon her as another standard slave. In fact there was no 'standard slave' and the negotiations for sale were as complex as they had been on the coast earlier in the century, since every slave represented a different value.

Thus the slave trade was still flourishing in this period, basically because of the need for manpower and followers. And it was, among the Tio, a trade wholly controlled by the chiefs. For no one could be sold as a slave unless he was first brought to the chief of the land who ascertained first that there was a right to sell the person and he had, as when European commodities were offered, a first option to buy. This means that with regard to the three pillars of the long distance trade—coastal imports, ivory, and slaves—the Tio chief of the land, and how much more the political chief, held a semi-monopoly.

The major trade in ivory, slaves, and coastal goods would not have been able to spread over such great distances if there had not been a subsidiary trade in foodstuffs to accompany it. Most important were cassava and fish. Sautter has described the great cassava production of the Bobangi on the Alima river and makes the telling point that the product was comparable to canned food. The package of prepared cassava, dozens of pounds in weight, could be kept edible for up to three months by mere immersion in the water of the river from time to time.

The Bobangi thus carried their staple with them and cut down

[62] C. COQUERY, op. cit., pp. 460, 470, confirms Guiral; M. STORME, op. cit., p. 74, fn. 5; REYNAERT, *Asservissement*, p. 9. Tio information about chief Linganu of Mbe Nkulu (around 1850) and Nzã Mbã (1800?). J. HANSSENS, op. cit., p. 7; E. TRIVIER, op. cit., pp. 43–4; TH. MENSE, op. cit., pp. 624–5. P. AUGOUARD, *A la suite*, p. 41 (bought a person of Mfwa in 1882 near Loango).

[63] Cf. G. SAUTTER, op. cit., I, p. 314, and this is confirmed by A. DELCOMMUNE, *Vingt ans*, I, p. 326, on the Lulonga. In any case a fair number of slaves went up the Ubangi river.

[64] CH. DE MARTRIN DONOS, *Les Belges*, II, pp. 76–7.

sharply on the need to stop for food *en route* or even more on the cost involved in buying fresh food from day to day.[65] But since there was little cultivation on the Pool itself, there was need and call for the hinterland to provide the extra food. Thus Mswata supplied Mpila and Mfwa while the Mfunu villages downstream, especially Lishia, seem to have functioned as food-markets for the canoes on the river. Whereas Mswata sold canoefuls of cassava loaves to Mfwa, the other sites did not sell cassava but greens, eggs, bananas, and local fruit. These articles in the towns and at Lishia could only be paid for with currency, while higher on the river the Tio villages from NGANTSU's and upstream usually sold these goods and some fresh cassava for fish. Fish was not in demand near the Pool because every one fished and did not need to buy it from the passing navigators. In the hinterland of Kinshasa the Hum villages and the Kongo beyond grew all the food that was necessary for Ntamo and Kinshasa. They also provided all the domestic animals needed as food there.[66]

The role of the Tio on the plains was not only to sell at the riverside, for the Mbembe, Wũ, Jinju, and Sese did send cured meat, especially buffalo meat, to the Pool. This came from individual hunting but mostly from the hunters of the chief. At the Pool it competed with the hippo meat the Nunu and some courageous fishermen from the Pool itself brought to the market.[67] In addition goats were sold at Ntsei to travelling Bobangi on the river and to Kongo traders or Laadi among the Sese and Jinju. The pedlars from the south-west also bought the buffalo meat. The sale of buffalo, which was still a Tio speciality in the 1950s, is not surprising, but the sale of goats is. For the ratio of goats per person was in the 1960s very low and there is evidence that even in the

[65] G. SAUTTER, op. cit., pp. 272–4. At the Pool the Bobangi seller was fed by his Tio host.

[66] CH. LIEBRECHTS, op. cit., pp. 521, 527; H. STANLEY, op. cit., I, pp. 295, 319–20, 393; R. BUETTNER, op. cit., pp. 223, 232, for towns south of the Pool; L. GUIRAL, op. cit., p. 241, for towns north; for the evolution at Ntamo, where Ngaliema finally managed a monopoly of food supplies; W. BENTLEY, op. cit., II, pp. 19, 143; and CH. LIEBRECHTS, *Souvenirs*, pp. 189, 191; C. DE DEKEN, *Lettre*, p. 60. Bentley said that in Kinshasa the local population sold fish for the food (cassava) of the Hum; H. STANLEY, op. cit., I, p. 510; R. BUETTNER, op. cit., p. 236, for Mswata. Even in 1892 that town was a major supplier of foodstuffs. Cf. e.g. CH. LEMAIRE, *Voyage*, p. 48. On Lishia and other riparians, H. H. JOHNSTON, op. cit., pp. 145–6; 149, 183, 185; L. GUIRAL, op. cit., p. 266; J. DYBOWSKI, *La route*, p. 89; NGAMPO described trade at NGANTSU's as selling bananas, greens, and cassava. H. BRUNSCHWIG, *La négociation*, p. 35, where Brazza comments on the price of cassava at the riparian villages and linked it with the growing of cassava in the Alima, as well as to the founding of Bobangi villages on the road to the Pool; CH. DE MARTRIN DONOS, II, 9, p. 11, on Pool; also the curious statement of Brazza in H. BRUNSCHWIG, op. cit., p. 54.

[67] L. GUIRAL's statement on buffalo game, p. 241, was corroborated by Ngateo, LIPIE, Ngelkiere, Miandoo. On market hippo meat in slabs of 6 to 9 lb cf. A. MERLON, op. cit., p. 43.

1880s goats were considered, as they are now, to be sacrificial animals.[68]

A special branch of the food trade went in the other direction. The Bobangi always fished on their trips and whenever possible, smoked fish for sale. The fish dried on frames, salted with river salt and smoked remained in good condition for a long time and was used not only as another preserved food but as the major means of payment for small purchases all the way down to Mswata and then again on the market at Ntamo and Kinshasa as well as Mfwa and Mpila for sale to the people inland. This trade Johnston described as 'immense' and mention of smoked fish occurs in most descriptions of markets. It must have used up quite a quantity of river salt from the Kwa and from the Moye.[69]

A last speciality was the sale of beer. The Tio on the plains sold maize beer and a little sugarcane wine both at Ntsei and at the Pool, whereas great quantities of sugarcane wine from the Mfunu, Ngenge, and especially the Nunu, were sent both upstream and to the Pool. The standard unit of trade in sugarcane wine seems to have been a six or ten-gallon pot and many were brought down. Merlon claims that the Nunu kept regular sugarcane plantations for this purpose and sent canoes out twice a month to sell the product upstream at Bolobo, downstream to the Pool. It is only a suspicion that the disappearance of the maize beer trade was a sizeable factor in the subsequent decline of maize cultivation on the plateau. This trade, even more than trade in meat, foodstuffs and tobacco, may have been of real significance in bringing currency and thereby the ability to purchase in the wider commercial network to every household. We know that ordinary foodstuffs were sold by women, meat and tobacco probably by men. We do not know who sold beer, but suspect that the women did. This product would, especially on the plains, have given them a source of steady income. Since maize was however cultivated by men, the proceeds may have been shared.[70]

[68] H. BRUNSCHWIG, *Les cahiers*, p. 191; Ngateo (to Ntsei) NgeIkiere (in the southwest). Brazza even declared that there were many goats at Ngampei. On low number of goats among Kukuya, personal communication of P. BONNAFÉ after L. BASTIANI and B. GUILLOT.

[69] G. SAUTTER, op. cit., I, pp. 274–6, for fishing itself; C. COQUILHAT, op. cit., p. 75, for smoking; H. H. JOHNSTON, op. cit., pp. 128, 132, 142–3, 171; W. BENTLEY, op. cit., I, p. 460, II, p. 19; L. GUIRAL, op. cit., pp. 141, 267–8; C. COQUERY, op. cit., p. 341; TH. MASUI, op. cit., p. 72; H. BRUNSCHWIG, op. cit., pp. 192–3. Because of the salt the Nunu were even better placed in this trade. Cf. TH. MENSE, op. cit., p. 628.

[70] L. GUIRAL, op. cit., pp. 241, 242, 260, 264 (a whole load from NGANTSU'S only with beer) (Pots of 25 litres = 6 gallons); H. STANLEY, op. cit., I, II, pp. 407–8, 512 (ten-gallon pots). W. BENTLEY, op. cit., I, p. 460. G. SAUTTER, op. cit., I, p. 370, suggested the production was a speciality of the Congo 'channel'. But it is clear from Abili Ndiõ and Guiral that beer as well as a little wine was brewed on the plains. The Kwa and the area north, all the way to Mbandaka, are still renowned for their sugar cane wine. The product was therefore more widely made. Cf. also N. NEY, op. cit., p. 327; H. BRUNSCHWIG, *La négociation*, p. 51 (40 litres = 10-gallon pot). But data on wine in A. MERLON, op. cit., pp. 108–11.

Groundnuts were also sold, but probably not more than other foodstuffs, except perhaps to the Laadi. Palm-oil was brought to the Pool, probably from the west and another centre of distribution was the Bobangi oil which was marketed at Ntsei and on the Alima.[71] More important was tobacco, which was grown everywhere on the plains and sold to the traders of the south-west, the pedlars of the Nkéni, at the markets of Ntsei and the Pool. Even the women at the Pool grew it. The most renowned tobacco was that of the Tege which went down the Alima and from there even to Lukolela, itself a tobacco-producing area. The product came in spiralled rolls of standard lengths. The Tio tobacco itself was of medium quality and packaged as bundles of leaves or braids. It was exported along with ivory to the coast and with beer was a product that men could produce in small quantities in every village. And like the maize for the beer, the production presupposed the cultivation of *ngwuunu*. Given what has been said about agriculture, it would seem as if the older men produced these commodities and the younger men brought them to the market, or traders came to fetch them in the village.[72]

One other product of daily use was brought down from the north, especially from the Sangha and the Kwa. This was the red camwood *ngula* (Sims) which came in slabs (Calloc'h, p. 144, *mu-bununa* 'bloc de Tacoul'). It was sold at the Pool and used there. Small quantities may have gone south to Ambrizette but not west, since the tree also grew in Mayombe. The Tio on the plateau used it only as a colour to rub on the body and not to make a general ointment. For them this trade was of less importance and so probably was the trade in kaolin.[73] The same is true for the limited trade in copal,[74] rubber, and kola. It is certain that

[71] G. SAUTTER, op. cit., I, p. 277. There were few palm-trees on the plains and some of the oil was imported, although there is no evidence for it now. At the Pool oil was probably traded since Sims gives *tue*, *ititu*, and *ibubaa* all as oil measures. They seem to have been ladles with varying contents. The exploitation of the oil-palm at Mbe in 1963 was so little known that only one man out of seventy could even climb a tree. True this represents a deterioration compared to the 1880s, but the situation was probably never brilliant.

[72] E. FROMENT, *Un voyage*, p. 213; C. COQUERY, op. cit., p. 341; CH. LEMAIRE op. cit., pp. 49–50; H. BRUNSCHWIG, *Les cahiers*, pp. 191, 180; Abili Ndiõ, Ngateo, Ngelkiere, Miandoo; L. GUIRAL, op. cit., p. 241. There is evidence for the Boõ, Jinju, Mbembe, and Wũ. The Kukuya who now produce along with the Boõ an excellent tobacco, worked less at this crop in pre-colonial days according to P. BONNAFÉ. Cf. also TH. MASUI, op. cit., pp. 466–7; G. SAUTTER, op. cit., I, p. 278. *La tribu batéké*, p. 123. Clearly to grow tobacco was better business than to plant food crops at the Pool; A. MERLON, op. cit., pp. 113–14.

[73] C. COQUERY, op. cit., p. 470, where the importance of this trade comes out. W. BENTLEY, op. cit., I, p. 460 and *Panorama du Congo* fasc. 2, last page left, middle row photograph for Kinshasa. Kaolin, both white and red [*sic*] was found at Pic Mense, south of the Pool and sold there: A. MERLON, op. cit., p. 142.

[74] L. GUIRAL, op. cit., pp. 241, 242; H. H. JOHNSTON, op. cit., p. 175: his *onkoli* that came from the hinterland of Bolobo may well have been copal which was found

some rubber was produced in the south-west and sold to the Laadi or Loango, but little trade was transacted at the Pool, at least by 1882. There is only one mention of kola on the markets of the Pool, yet this was a prized product. Probably the available production on the plains was barely sufficient to cover needs and this may be true for the upper river and for the lower Congo. Further research might well attest a limited flow of kola from Gabon and Mayombe to the plains.[75] Local trade in other products such as copper and brass ornaments or statuettes for *itio* is not well documented.[76]

Evidence for the volume of trade in different segments of the network and for the different commodities is fragmentary. Some of it, dealing with the size of transportation units, has already been indicated. More precise data concern mainly ivory. Since they are often expressed in terms of value, the evidence will be left for the next chapter.

At this point the general description of this commerce has been sketched. It remains now to analyse the commercial economy itself.

---

in the rivers near Lake Leopold II, Lake Tumba, and in the hinterland of Mbandaka. Cf. TH. MASUI, op. cit., pp. 415–19, for its use as a gum and varieties.

[75] H. BRUNSCHWIG, *La négociation*, p. 43 and L. GUIRAL, op. cit., p. 241, were explicit that no rubber was traded on the river. Yet rubber and kola were presented to Stanley when he opened his shop in 1882. Cf. H. STANLEY, op. cit., I, p. 384. Stanley was probably tested with new products by sellers who hoped a market might develop. A. MERLON, op. cit., pp. 98–9, mentioned both white and red kola but was emphatic that it was not a product for sale in 1885–7. Its social role was immense since kola was exchanged at each important social or political gathering and used to sacrifice to shades and for charms as well.

[76] It was probably of small importance. On sale of metal collars, rings: D'UZES, *Le voyage*, p. 90, and such sales are implied in L. GUIRAL, op. cit., p. 241. Over the years fabrication of these objects for European tourists may have begun to become significant. For the fabrication and sale of statuettes to represent shades by the Hum to the Tio of the south bank, cf. TH. MENSE, op. cit., p. 625. Other products such as leather items, mats, baskets, etc., may all have been present on these markets.

Chapter XI
The Commercial Economy

TO examine the sort of commercial economy that existed among the Tio at this time, it is essential to discuss successively the currencies used, the prices, the volume of the trade, and the role of Tio traders in it before its major features can be perceived. The chapter will conclude with a brief sketch of the impact of this commercial system on Tio society.

1. *Currencies*

The market at the Pool dictated which currencies were acceptable to the Tio over their whole territory. By 1880 these included a copper unit, the brass rod: *mi-tako*, (Sims: *litoo*) a cloth unit, the *ibuunu* for imported cloth and the *ntaa* for raphia cloth, the *nji* which was the *olivancillaria nana* shell and perhaps still a lead ingot. The situation was dynamic however and within a few years after 1881 the *mitako* had supplanted all other currencies as a standard of value. Payments could be made with these currencies or objects might be bartered directly once their value had been assessed in terms of currency. This implied that there were ratios of value between one currency and another. Only foodstuffs could not be acquired, at least in 1882, by barter but had to be paid for in currency. There were often relative shortages of these, and they were essential for survival which may explain their special status. To account for this by arguing that their low value per unit made them difficult to exchange, seems less convincing.[1]

Lead ingots, stated Bentley, who arrived early in 1881, were at one time indispensable for the purchase of ivory at the Pool. Ingots of lead and copper ingots arrived there from the Nsama mines which he situated sixty miles north-west of the Manianga market.[2] They had lost out completely to other currencies well before 1881. Copper rods from the same area came to the Tio probably directly via the Laadi. From the mines they also came to the Pool where they were resold to the Bobangi. They are described by Mahieu as being cylindrical, thick as the little finger, and one inch or so long. The Bobangi and the Tio also used another copper rod, half an inch in diameter and three inches long and bent at the ends, which was molten in Manianga. These were and are

[1] L. GUIRAL, *Le Congo*, p. 241; N. NEY, *Trois explorations*, p. 327, for J. de Brazza stating that foodstuffs were never bought for cloth at NGANTSU's because the loss on conversion would be too excessive.

[2] W. BENTLEY, *Pioneering*, I, p. 401.

called *ngiele* by the Tio and were used as currency before the brass rod (*mitako*) replaced them. De Chavannes made it three and a half inches long at Mfwa with a circular section of one square centimetre, (little less than half an inch). By 1880 the first type of one inch was still in use among the 'Bangala', but they were replaced by *mitako* as soon as the Europeans arrived. At the Pool itself they were ousted before 1881.[3]

Nji means now 'money' or any currency in Tio, but it specifically referred to *olivancillaria nana*, often called *nzi mbuli* at the Pool,[4] which the Tio on the plains called *mbula* for the larger shell and *nji* for the abstract notion of money, as well as for the smaller among the *olivancillaria* shells. There is no doubt that they were in use on the plains and among the Mfunu, the Ngenge and perhaps the Bobangi, if this is what Guiral labelled 'cauris' and which he said was a currency.[5] It was in use at the Pool whence the Tio received most of their *mbula* and *nji* and it seems to have been reserved mainly for paying or calculating small amounts in terms of value. It corresponded to a unit of currency in Manyanga, the Cataracts region, which was a short blue hexagonal bead, a quarter of an inch in length and also called *nzimbu*.[6] In March 1884 De Brazza was buying cassava at NGANTSU's with these beads.[7]

Raphia cloth was a standard of value on the Pool in the form of *ntaa*, which were thirty squares sewn together in a wrapper. Each square was standard because of the standard measurement of the loom: sixteen inches by sixteen inches. They were sewn together in three rows of ten, of ordinary quality. Twenty *ntaa* made a *luni* (*ibuunu*?) which was a multiple of the standard. Cloth of much better quality and finer texture, which, it is said, took seven times as long to weave had five times the

[3] G. SAUTTER, *De l'Atlantique*, I, pp. 374–5. Citing L. GUIRAL, op. cit., p. 242, he argued that the copper rod was still a currency by 1882. It is more likely that Guiral wrote 'copper' for 'brass' in view of all other sources. Cf. A. MAHIEU, *La numismatique*, No. 12, p. 13 and XXII, No. 1, p. 11. The first copper currency was *muzanga* and the longer one *ngétélé* for the Bobangi. Mahieu arrived only in 1894, but made a hobby of this. He mentions brass only for the Pool, specifying the copper currency had been ousted. Chavannes (Sautter) in 1884 already labelled it as the 'old rod' and Bentley (fn. 2) in 1881 also seems to discard it.

[4] *Lizi*, the singular was: 'large cowry' for Sims. The Kongo term was *nzimbu mbudi* and both *mbudi* and *mbuli* derive from *bugio* (Portuguese) called *boesje* by the Dutch. The Kongo expression meant *olivancillaria* being large and resembling cowries. The use of *olivancillaria* antedated the arrival of the Portuguese on the coast and it was probably the first currency for the Tio since *nji* came to stand for all currency and money.

[5] E. D'ARTEVELLE, *Les N'zimbu*, pp. 157, 158; AUGUSTEYNS, *Notes*, p. 1; A. MAHIEU, op. cit., XXI, No. 11, pp. 16–24; XXII, No. 1, p. 11; L. GUIRAL, op. cit., p. 243.

[6] W. BENTLEY, op. cit., II, p. 20; A. MAHIEU, ibid. CH. JEANNEST, *Quatre anneés*, p. 25, mentioned them as currency in Ambrizette around 1870.

[7] N. NEY, op. cit., p. 341. It is evident that at NGANTSU's food was being traded for commodities unlike what happened at the Pool. The beads were described as 'best liked' but not as currency. Two of them paid for a loaf of cassava. However, on p. 327, there too, he says, food was bought with currency, e.g. brass rods.

value of the standard. Other sources claimed that the standard at the Pool was either the raphia square or ten of them. They also stressed that it differed from the huge wrappers, fine as silk, decorated with fringes and dyed in stripes. Raphia squares were also used as currency in the area of the Cataracts and west into Mayombe, where they were known as *mbadi* and *bongo*. On the markets of the Cataracts, mainly those of Manianga, they had been abandoned, but elsewhere in that area they were retained, primarily for standardized social payments. The Tio of the plains and the Mfunu also continued to use them, but among the former the *ibuunu* of European cloth was replacing raphia. This meant a setback for the producers, mainly the Kukuya and the Sese.[8] As in the case of the *nzimbu* it is known that the raphia square had served as a currency north of the river Congo for centuries.

The unit for imported cloth was a cotton print of standard size, called *ibuni* or *ibuunu*. It was the only currency used by Loango, Laadi, and Nsundi traders in the south-west of the country, and Mgr. Augouard remarked in 1881 that cloth was plentiful north of the Pool, but was used not for wearing but for currency. This was certainly an effect of the coastal trade from Loango where the *cortade*, a piece of four yards of cotton print, folded into three, was the standard unit. In Nsundi the *cortade* was three fathoms. Unfortunately the standard size of the *ibuunu* is not known for certain, but may have been only two yards, half a *cortade*.[9]

Ibuunu were not used directly to pay for many goods since their value per unit was high. They were primarily a standard of value for accounting as Bilankwi and Abili Ndiõ pointed out. Like the raphia cloth they replaced, they were used for social payments, mainly bridewealth, fines such as for adultery, and sometimes tribute. In all of these the calculation was made in *ibuunu* and at least part of the payment also included them. And it should not be forgotten that many *ibuunu* were lost when used to drape around a catafalque and to be buried with it.[10] Because

[8] *Le tissage*, p. 329a; A. MAHIEU, op. cit., XXI, No. 11, pp. 16, 20; H. LOIR, *Le tissage*, pp. 59–60. The relation between labour and value given by Mahieu is obviously too vague for any deduction, beyond the fact that labour was taken into account.

[9] Miandoo, Ngelkiere, LIPIE all held that only *ibuunu* was used as currency in the west. Mbali mentioned *ngiele* brought by Laadi. These were the old bent copper *ngiele*. Some *ibuunu* along with *nji mbula, ngiele* came from the Pool; For Cataracts see A. MAHIEU, op. cit., XXII, No. 1, p. 11; NEUVILLE, CH. BREART, *Voyages*, p. 216 (Augouard); C. COQUERY, op. cit., p. 402 (*cortade*): Dolisie in 1884 was advised to use 'short yards' and cheat like everyone else. The plains Tio called the standard piece of cloth *ibuun' anji*, which stresses its role as currency. Cf. CH. JEANNEST, op. cit., p. 33, for *cortade* at Kinsembo but not at Ambrizette. P. AUGOUARD, *Voyage*, p. 113 (*Cortade* in Nsundi).

[10] Sims: *ibuni:* 'account, sum product' thus says it is a standard of value; Calloc'h, p. 292: *i-mbuni:* 'pièce d'étoffe'. Its use for social payments was still important in 1963 as, by all Tio accounts, in the 1880s. Its limited role as currency because of its high unitary value is clear from *Les marchés indigènes* (1916: cloth sold only in first-class markets) and J. de Brazza, this chapter fn. 1.

they were currency the Tio did not mind receiving low quality stuffs.

But the most important currency and even, according to Guiral, 'the only money' was the brass rod called *mitako* in the literature, *ngiele* by the Tio. Earlier *ngiele* had designated the copper ingots from Manianga but now the name designated the *mitako*. The latter were imported brass wire, known on the coast in Ambrizette by 1869 as *ntakou*.[11]

The *mitako* was always of about the same diameter variously reported as $\frac{1}{7}$ inch (Bentley) = 3 mm, 50, 3–4 mm (Mahieu), 2 mm, 50 (*la monnaie*), 2 mm and 5 mm (both J. De Brazza) 2 mm (*les marchés*: 1916), but its length was variable from place to place and by year. In 1882 and even until 1884 it was reported to be 65 cm or 26 inches long (Stanley) 60 or 65 cm (J. De Brazza), 60 cm (De Chavannes). It was 30 inches in early 1881 (Bentley). Then it became 52–5 cm (*la monnaie*) after having been 50–60 cm (Mahieu), 50 cm (Mahieu) which was the official size of the Independent Congo State for a while, probably in 1886. In late 1887 it was 40 cm (Dupont) but in January 1889 it was quoted at 52 cm (Trivier). By the end of the period in July 1891 it had fallen from 0·33 to 0·28 cm (Dybowski), always at the Stanley Pool. By April 1893 d'Uzes gave it at 0·15 cm. By 1916 it was only 10 cm long on the markets of the upper Djoué,[12]

Successive owners did cut down their *mitako* and this obviously contributed to the deterioration, especially the further one went upstream. Still Jacques de Brazza in 1884 at NGANTSU's had them at 65 or 60 cm in length. The practice moreover shows a keen commercial sense, but this does not explain the rate of deterioration. It is obvious that the movement was worse than the mean from 1881–4, close to the mean from 1884–9 and less thereafter. An increasing influx of coastal goods culminated in 1885 because of the rivalry between France and King Leopold. The progressive competition between Tio and European traders after 1885, the food shortages at the Pool, the manipulation by both the French Congo and Independent Congo authorities of large quantities of *mitako* and their use by 1886 at the latest to pay labour may all have exercised some effect on the *mitako* unit, through the

[11] CH. JEANNEST, op. cit., p. 320 (vocabulary: *ntakou*): L. GUIRAL, op. cit., p. 242: 'la barrette de cuivre, *seule* monnaie du Stanleypool'. For the Tio designations: A. MAHIEU, op. cit., XXI, No. 12, p. 13 (*longele* sing. of *ngele* = *ngiele*).

[12] E. ZORZI, *Al Congo*, pp. 231, 384; L. REYNAERT, *Asservissement*, pp. 9–10; W. BENTLEY, op. cit., I, p. 461; H. STANLEY, *The Congo*, I, p. 374 (also 65 cm) and stating that they are being cut short; A. MAHIEU, XXII, No. 1, pp. 13–14, XXI, No. 12, p. 13; *La monnaie*, pp. 34–5 with a picture of a *mitako*. N. NEY, op. cit., pp. 327, 341; *Les marchés indigènes*, 109 n; G. SAUTTER, op. cit., I, pp. 374–5. De Chavannes and Dybowski cited in Sautter. L. GUIRAL, op. cit., p. 263, talks about 'fil de cuivre' rather than 'laiton' and because it is wire, it could not be the old copper currency. So he mixes the two terms. In the Independent Congo State payments were still made in *mitako* by the Government in 1901, and in Brazzaville Klobb reported in 1896 (Sautter) that only cloth and *mitako* were acceptable. The Bentley figure is probably more the statement of a norm than of practice. Cf. also graph.

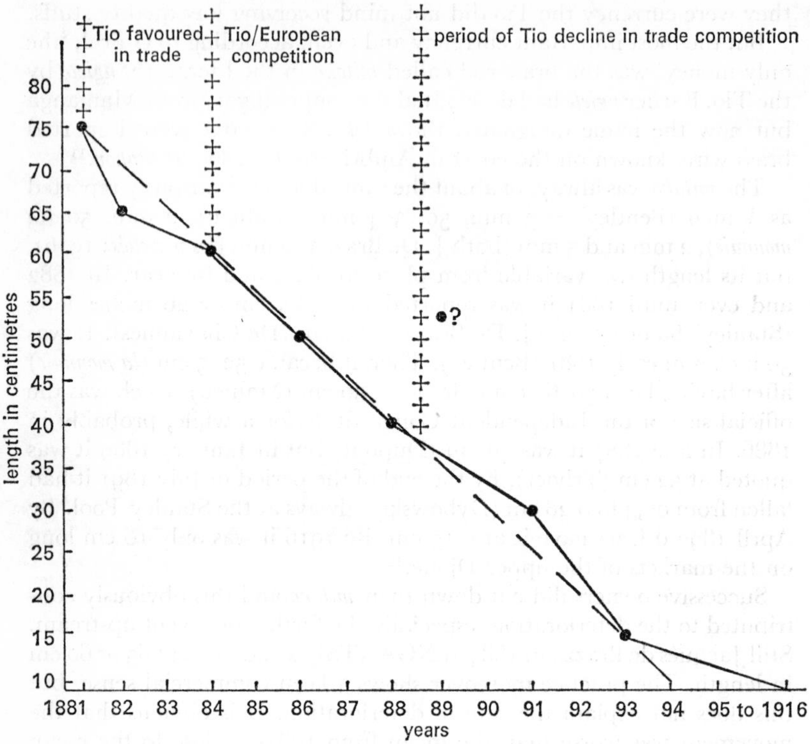

Note: Only the quotation by E. Trivier does not fit in well with the graph

++++ : boundaries between periods of time

— — — : average decline 1881–94

CHART 14

Decline of the mitako in length: 1881–93

inflation of prices and by multiplying the amount of rods in circulation manifold. The *mitako* had become an official currency of the Independent Congo State as of 30 July 1886 for the whole area upstream of Kinshasa on the Congo and the Kwa, and even if things were less formal at Brazzaville it became an official currency there, perhaps even earlier. After 1888 the Tio of the south bank were eliminated and the curve may reflect the steady decline of Tio competition.

Why were there multiple currencies in the early 1880s? One can first point out that cloth was the biggest unit, rather similar to the raphia *ntaa*, and that both were used more as a standard of value than as a means of payment. For caravans from Loango it was the best currency since it was the one they used at home and all the way to the Pool, including even the raphia variants. The brass rod and the shells were light and had small unit values. The rods were the principal means of payment. Their nominal value was much higher than the *nji* which had devalued over centuries of use, whereas the brass rod was relatively new having replaced the older copper and lead currencies. They had become the one item that served currently for both calculating value and making payment, just because the value per unit was neither too low nor too high. As for *nji* they held their ground because they were in use in Bobangi country among the Yaka and equivalent to the blue beads of Manianga.

The data indicate clearly that both cloth and *mitako* remained 'money' throughout and long beyond this period. The other items are accounted for at once by the particular historical evolution and, like the rods and cloth, by the fact that they were used as currency elsewhere and therefore were needed at the market on the Pool. Conversion clearly was made in the markets between cloth and *mitako*. Why then did not one of these take over completely? Essentially because the spheres of exchange for both commodities were slightly different. Cloth was used for social payments and *ngiele* bangles were considerably less prestigious.

Reported rates of exchange between currencies were 100 *ngiele* for 1 *ibuunu* and 100 *nji* equal to 1 *ngiele*, said Abili Ndiõ. This is almost certainly only a rough indication. One *mbula* for her was equivalent to one square of raphia. Data about *nji* gave 10 to 1 *mitako* at Tshumbiri (Bellington) and 25 to 1 at a later date among the Sengele in the hinterland of Bolobo, 150 *nji* for a fathom of indigo drill among the Mfunu behind Lishia, and only 300 for 3 fathoms of cloth. The data are too fragmentary for any analysis but do establish that the value of a brass rod stood about midway between a fathom of cloth (1 *ibuunu*) and the *olivancillaria nana*. This allows one to postulate a single system in which different currencies were all pegged one to another in different orders of magnitude, as Abili Ndiõ does.[13] Yet this is not the whole explanation.

Thus Guiral noted in 1882 that slaves were bought for cloth, guns, and powder. Ivory was sold for hundreds of yards of cloth. A tusk of 60 lb was worth 200 fathoms of light Congo cloth, 10 guns, 20 powder kegs, 60 *mitako*, and some pottery. At about the same time Stanley paid for ivory in cloth and *mitako*, and regretted that he could not sell guns.[14] From these data it appears that the main commodities expected as payment for ivory and slaves, the mainstays of commerce, were a part in cloth, a part in powder and a part in guns, which was also the mode of

[13] E. D'ARTEVELLE, op. cit., pp. 157–8.

[14] L. GUIRAL, op. cit., pp. 243–4. A. MAURICE, *Stanley*, pp. 102, 116–18, 135–6, where he based plans for buying on the import of *mitako* only, p. 151 (sale of two tusks after five and a half hours of bargaining for silk and *mitako*); p. 175 (complaint that he could not compete with coastal traders in guns).

payment at Ambrizette in 1870.[15] Thus the different currencies were not just multiples one of the other and equally exchangeable without gain or loss. This is confirmed by the information that on all the markets of the Cataracts area and the Pool there were people (Sims: *musobe*, 'money changer') whose living consisted in exchanging other 'values' into *mitako*, beads, or cowries to make smaller purchases possible.[16] If it was a source of livelihood, there were obviously gains to be made. This could only be because the different currencies did not buy the same goods. They were perhaps theoretically universal standards of value but restricted means of payment. An examination of prices and trading practice in general will show what their limits were.

2. *Price*

Quoting prices as given by travellers for the different markets yield the kind of data which by itself has relatively little value. These data must be supplemented by information with regard to profits themselves reinforced by an assessment of the volume of trade involved. Further evidence will then follow about both the traders and their financial practices.

Known prices, fragmentary as they are, follow:

CHART 15

Price by market on Congo Upper River: 1880–92

date	*market*	*goods*	*price*	*source*
1880	Pool	1 keg with copper	5 pieces cloth (5 fathoms?)	Brazza (Brunschwig, 53)[a]
1882	Pool	2,500 lb ivory from Ngaliema	12·500 *mitako*	Brazza (Maurice, 134)
		(or 1 lb ivory)	5 *mitako*	
1882	Pool	2 loaf cassava of 5 lb (one feeds 1 man, 48 hr)	3 *mitako*	Brazza (Maurice, 1, 374)
1882	Pool	2 tusks, together 140 lb	353 yd silk 970 *mitako*	Brazza (Maurice, 151)
1882	Pool	per lb: tusks over 30 lb	23–30 *mitako*	Brazza (Maurice, 158)
		per lb: tusks under 30 lb	8–12 *mitako*	
1882	Pool	1 haunch hippo whole	80 *mitako*	Guiral, 233, fn. 1
1882	Pool	1 haunch hippo cut	160 *mitako*	Guiral, 233

[a] First the name of the observer, then, if different, in brackets editor or writer and page. References to Stanley are all to *The Congo* and for Liebrechts to *Léopoldville*.

[15] CH. JEANNEST, op. cit., pp. 58–83 (G. SAUTTER, op. cit., I, p. 372). Before ivory it had been standard payment for slaves.

[16] A. MAHIEU, op. cit., 1929, No. 1, p. 16 fn. 5.

CHART 15—*continued*

date	*market*	*goods*	*price*	*source*
1882	Pool	1 whole buffalo	400 *mitako*	Guiral, 233
1881/2	Pool	1 house	300 *mitako*	Guiral, 232
1882	Pool	1 boat, seven paddlers	150 *mitako*	Guiral, 233
1882	Pool	cassava loaf: 1 man, 24 hr	1 *mitako*	Guiral, 243
1882	Pool	near 1 litre palmwine	1 *mitako*	Guiral, 243
1882	Pool	1 bag salt 20 cm long	1 *mitako*	Guiral, 243
1882	Pool	1 big fish	4 *mitako*	Guiral, 243
1882	Pool	60 lb ivory	200 fathoms cloth 10 guns 20 powder kegs 60 *mitako* pottery	Guiral, 243
1881/2	Pool	1 slave woman	460 *mitako*	Guiral, 244
1882	Pool	1 slave	guns powder cloth	Guiral, 243
1883	Pool	1 lb ivory from Bobangi to local:	11 *mitako* (80 cents)[b]	Stanley, 1, 384
1883	Pool	1 lb ivory from Bobangi to Stanley:	27 *mitako* 5 (2 Fr)	Stanley, 1, 384
1884	Pool	1 sow and 1 pig: a piece	130 *mitako*	Pecile (Zorzi, 439)
1885	Pool	1 slab of redwood	1 *mitako*	Froment, 468
1887	Pool	12 kerchiefs (4 fathoms)	30 *mitako*	Dupont, 182
1887	Pool	fowl	6 *mitako*	Dupont, 182
1887	Pool	goat	60 *mitako*	Dupont, 182
1887	Pool	cassava loaf for caravans	8 *mitako*	Dupont, 213
1887	Pool	cassava loaf for Leopoldville station	2 *mitako*	Dupont, 213
1887	Pool	cassava loaf for locals	1 *mitako*	Dupont, 213
1887	Pool (Mfwa)	fine to Bobangi for bloodshed	500–600 *mitako*	Dupont, 257

[b] In Belgian currency.

CHART 15—*continued*

date	*market*	*goods*	*price*	*source*
1889	Pool	bottle rum	4 *mitako* (2·0, 80 cts)	Liebrechts, 524
1889	Pool	1 lb ivory	35 *mitako* (=T Fr 20 cts) per *mitako*[c]	Liebrechts, 524
1891	Pool	slave male child	600 *mitako*	d'Uzes, 90
1891	Pool	slave female child	1200 *mitako*	d'Uzes, 90
n.d.	Pool	slave	40–80 *mitako*	Sautter, I, 377
n.d.	Pool	murder	200 *ntaa* gun 1–2 goats some fowls	Mahieu, XXI, 20
n.d.	Pool	bridewealth	100 *ntaa*	Mahieu, XXI, 20
n.d.	Pool	adultery + witness	100 *ntaa* slave	Mahieu, XXI, 20
n.d.	Pool	adultery-witness	40 *ntaa*	Mahieu, XXI, 20
1887	Lishia	one small goat	12 yd cloth	Dupont, 225
1880	NGANTSU's	1 ten gallon jar wine	one gun 4 wrappers (fathoms?)	Brazza (Brunschwig, 51)
1880	Mswata	1 metre long fish	80 *mitako*	Buettner, 268
1880	Mswata	1 piece local salt + pinch imported salt	20 *nji*	Buettner, 50
1884	NGANTSU's	12 kerchiefs (4 fathoms)	25 *mitako*	Brazza (Ney, 347)
1884	NGANTSU's	1 cassava bread	2 Congo beads	Brazza (Ney, 341)
1884	NGANTSU's	1 fathom best cloth	6 *mitako*	Pecile (Zorzi, 396)
1884	NGANTSU's	1 fathom 2nd best	4 *mitako*	Pecile (Zorzi, 396)
1884	NGANTSU's	1 fathom 3rd best	3 *mitako*	Pecile (Zorzi, 396)
1884	NGANTSU's	1 fathom least best	2 *mitako*	Pecile (Zorzi, 396)
1884	NGANTSU's	1 gun	40 *mitako*	Pecile (Zorzi, 396)
1884	NGANTSU's	1 boat (*una bella piroga*)	250 *mitako*	Pecile (Zorzi, 396)
1884	NGANTSU's	1 pot (30–40 l) wine	25–30 *mitako*	Pecile (Zorzi, 429)
1885	NGANTSU's	2 slabs of camwood	1 *mitako*	Froment, 468

[c] In 1886 the *mitako* was at 15 cts officially, but in 1889 Cambier like Liebrechts had it at 20 cts (128).

CHART 15—*continued*

date	*market*	*goods*	*price*	*source*
1886	Kwamouth	30 lb ivory	2 *pieces* of kerchiefs (2F. 50)[d]	Merlon, 36–7
1886	Kwamouth	1 pot (50 l) wine	30–35 *mitako*	Merlon, 111
1889	Kwamouth	1 boat, 14 metres	1000 *mitako*	Cambier, 128
1885	Bonga	3 block camwood	1 *mitako*	Froment, 468 Pradier (Coquery, 470)[e]
1886	Bonga	5 fathoms light colour cloth	10 *mitako*	Pradier (Coquery, 471) (not by Froment)
1885	Bonga	1 fowl	2 *mitako*	Froment, 469
1885	Bonga	1 mat Likuba	2 *mitako*	Froment, 469
1885	Bonga	1 cassava loaf (Alima)	2 *mitako*	Froment, 469
1885	Bonga	50 bananas	3 *mitako*	Froment, 469
1886	Bonga	medium size bunch bananas	2 *mitako*	Pradier (Coquery, 47)
1886	Bonga	1 litre palmoil	1 *mitako*	Pradier (Coquery, 47) (not by Froment)
1885	Bonga	male slave	400–500 *mitako*	Froment, 469
1885	Bonga	female slave	300–400 *mitako*	Froment, 469
1886	Bonga	female slave	200–400 *mitako*	Pradier (Coquery, 47)
1885	Bonga	red or blue flannel one fathom	25 *mitako*	Froment, 469
1886	Bonga	red and black flannel one fathom	25 *mitako*	Pradier (Coquery, 471)
1886	Bonga	red or blue flannel one fathom	20 *mitako*	Pradier (Coquery, 471)
1886	Bonga	print 'dog'; 1 fathom	8 *mitako*	Pradier (Coquery, 471)
		print 'black woman' 1 fathom	12 *mitako*	Pradier (Coquery, 471)
1886	Bonga	kerchief (unit?)	12–15 *mitako*	Pradier (Coquery, 471)
1885	Bonga	empty bottles	6 *mitako*	Froment, 469

[d] Merlon, 113 had the *mitako* at 12 cts 20–30 lb of ivory came to ±21 *mitako* only; less than Stanley paid per lb at the Pool in 1883 (!). This does not seem in line with the other available data.

[e] Pradier copied Froment, but gives different figures for some articles at Bonga.

CHART 15—*continued*

date	*market*	*goods*	*price*	*source*
1886	Bonga	5 Gras cartridge case	1 *mitako*	Froment, 469
		2 glass coloured beads	1 *mitako*	Pradier (Coquery, 471)
1886	Bonga	1 white glass bead	1 *mitako*	Pradier (Coquery, 471)
1886	Bonga	10 cowries	1 *mitako*	Pradier (Coquery, 471)
1884	Mokémo	1 boat, very big	1450 *mitako*	Pradier (Coquery, 471)
	(1½ days South of Bonga)	1 boat	1000 *mitako*	Chavannes, 1935, 210–11

It is not possible to compare prices for one article in the same market at a given time, so fluctuations of this type remain undetected: the data are too scanty. But they can be examined (i) in relation to different commodities at the same time, (ii) to one commodity on different markets, and (iii) to the same article through time. With Pradier three clusters of markets are recognized: the Pool, NGANTSU's-Mswata-Kwa-Bolobo, and Bonga[17] and because the data are scarce it will be necessary sometimes to combine time place and commodity.

The most obvious feature about commodities is that they fall into three sharply distinct classes of value. The first and cheapest class at the Pool was never more than 8 *mitako* at any moment of time. It included foodstuffs, camwood, fowls, rum, salt, and interestingly enough, cloth, by the fathom, although not the set of twelve handkerchiefs. Payment was or could be made in *mitako* and in shells. Only one example of payment in shells is known as there is one only of payment in beads, both from NGANTSU's. By 1884 the value of the best cloth was per fathom no more than 6 *mitako* at NGANTSU's and probably less at the Pool. This was not likely to have been the standard print used for currency, which may be set at about 4 *mitako* per fathom. As a currency then cloth did not, after all, have a much higher value per unit than *mitako*, although for most small purchases it would either be awkward, as when a fowl had to be paid in 6 *mitako* or one fathom and one yard, or too high.

In the middle range of goods between 40 and 130 *mitako* one had guns (40), 10 gallon pots of wine, goats, whole hippos and pigs, in short, guns, wine and meat, although cut up meat, such as the haunch of hippo given cut up at double the value of the whole haunch, was, *per unit of sale*, probably cheap enough to fall into the lower range of prices. The case of the haunch taken in conjunction with other indications, such as the sale of a pinch of salt at Mswata, makes it clear that one characteristic of the trade at that time already was to subdivide the

[17] C. COQUERY, op. cit., p. 470.

units for sale into minute portions for commodities everybody needed on which a very high profit was taken. This is still typical for retail markets in the area today. We surmise that it was typical for the women's food market in the 1880s.

The expensive commodities listed at the Pool were a house, a buffalo whole, a slave, boats, and ivory. Houses however were rarely sold except to Europeans. The buffalo is obviously the top price for meat. Ivory and boats varied enormously in price according to the size of the unit presented. One 1884 boat already cost 1,450 *mitako* at Mokémo upstream! Similar prices or values were possible for tusks over 30 lb. On the other hand some small size units could be cheap, such as a boat for two or three paddlers would be, or a tusk under 30 lb at 8 *mitako* a pound. Prices for slaves were much more standardized and seem to have been tied to the payment for blood-money.[18] The high price asked for boats was not only due to a cost of production compared to other items. Cambier noted: 'After ivory what the black man values most is his boat.'[19] For the people on the river it was their capital investment; they could not be without a boat. So the high range of prices included both the major exports—ivory, then slaves and the necessary capital good to export them, then the dugout. Moreover slaves furnished the best part of the labour force as well.

On the market of Bonga the division between lower priced and high priced goods was even more extreme since there is no middle range at all indicated. Slaves, boats and probably ivory were almost a different market. This ties in again with the practice at the Nkéni to hold the markets for foodstuffs and other wares separately. Still prices for many products remain unknown and some were sold on the market for commodities. Cloth is obvious, but pottery or mats are also good examples: there might be two financial spheres and two spheres in the market place but they did not overlap completely.

A last range of prices at the Pool was not quoted in *mitako* at all but in *ntaa*. It dealt with bridewealth, fines for adultery and murder: all social payments. Obviously *ntaa* and raphia squares had become a restricted currency to be used only for these occasions and those on which, for instance, inflation because of over production would have little effect because of the symbolic nature of the payment. But it was not a sphere hermetically sealed off from the other. For in any murder or adultery case the culprit had to pay fowls and goats as well and there is one example on record of a blood debt by a Bobangi that was assessed and perhaps paid in *mitako*, as ordered by the chief of Mfwa. This shows that the market currencies began to pervade spheres other

[18] Cf. section on slaves, Chapter XII. Bridewealth also had a similar value. Note that the indication given by Sautter's informants seems either worthless or else to apply to an early period when *mitako* were rare.

[19] E. CAMBIER, op. cit., p. 128.

than exchange of goods on the market and that one force in this was the presence of non-Tio who were there only as traders. As will be seen later, imported cloth and *ngiele* or *mitako* as well as *nji* figured in court fines and in tribute but only sporadically, on the fringes, so to speak.

Comparing the fluctuations of prices over time can be done only if one remembers the constant devaluation of the *mitako*. The *mitako* of 1890 was only half the rod of 1884! Despite that the *mitako* made better rates of exchange with the Belgian franc. In 1883 Stanley rated one rod at 13.75 cts, in 1886 it was put at 15 cts and by 1889 Cambier reckoned one at 20 cts. True, the calculation must not be taken too seriously, since it is not clear for 1883 or 1889 whether it was calculated according to cost price of the rod or official selling price as the 1886 quotation is. Still, we think they all refer to selling price and indicate an increase in value of almost 100 per cent between 1886 and 1889, bearing in mind the shortening of the rod. Another way of stating this is that rods became more expensive to buy in terms of francs. But such an increase in production costs in Europe or of transportation costs would be unimaginable, so the importers, whether official or private, must have gradually increased their prices to make profit on the exchange of francs to *mitako*.

All this makes the fluctuation of prices in time and expressed in *mitako* rather difficult to assess. Then there are questions with regard to the commodities. Few are listed for the same or even different markets at different times and some vary so much in size (e.g. boats) that one does not know what one compares. But even the cassava loaf at the Pool could not be compared because the 1887 data do not give any indication of quantity and in 1882 Guiral listed a loaf for one and one day at 1 *mitako* while Stanley had double the size of loaf for 1.5 *mitako*! So nothing can be said except the obvious, that caravans paid many times more than did residents and Europeans or their dependants twice what locals paid, at a time when there was actual food shortage. The one obvious comparison is between wine at Kwamouth and NGANTSU's 1884–6. Considering the quantity to be identical one finds an increase in price of 17 per cent (35 as a base) which is exactly equal to the depreciation of the *mitako* (60 as a base)! The price had remained stable.

Data can be discussed for cloth and ivory. One notes first that prices were very low in 1884–5 when the International African Association and the French were engaged in a dumping struggle. Guns, for example, were then being sold for less than their cost price.[20] Cloth in-

[20] E. ZORZI, op. cit., pp. 395–6, for calculations of cost by Pecile who was then selling at the government shop in NGANTSU's village. They operated at a loss. Cf. also N. NEY, op. cit., p. 347. Stanley had started by trying to buy ivory as cheaply as possible but clearly was forced by Ngaliema to overpay. Cf. A. MAURICE, op. cit., pp. 134–5 (Stanley's reasoning at 5 *mitako* per lb), pp. 151–2, for the first actual transaction, which still left a benefit of £ 28–0–2 on a sale worth in England £ 65–14–0.

creased in price between 1884 and 1887 as would be expected. Twelve handkerchiefs at NGANTSU's for 25 *mitako* in 1884 may have been only 20 rods at the Pool. In 1887 they were at 30 rods at the Pool. With 30 as a base the increase was over 33 per cent while the depreciation of the *mitako* had been of 9 per cent in length. A composite increase of 22 per cent results.

Ivory prices for Europeans rose dramatically from 2 fr in 1883 to 7 fr in 1889 but in *mitako* at a 20 cts value for 1889 the rise was 21·5 per cent roughly the same as for cloth! However if the *mitako* had been at 15 cts in the 1889 price the rise would be 41·50 per cent, well over that for cloth. It is clear that the data are unreliable. But perhaps one may say that to the Tio the rise in the prices of ivory and cloth was similar and that they had probably maintained the number of yards of cloth and guns per lb of ivory, paralleling the situation for wine at Kwamouth. To Europeans the increase in the price of ivory seemed immensely more than the increase in the price of cloth, but playing on the rate of exchange for *mitako* turned this into a gain for them. The real cost in francs per *mitako* lay much lower than the conventional value.

Roughly then the market at the Pool did not substantially worsen for the Tio, but by playing on the exchange rate *mitako*/franc the Europeans nevertheless managed to make substantial gains on ivory.

All of this is borne out directly by Dybowski and d'Uzes. The latter complained that Dolisie had been obliged to pay the *mitako* up to 30 centimes (French) when the value was no more than 10 centimes (French) in April 1893. The traders then explained that *mitako* sold might mean that it would not be possible for them to buy ivory. Dybowski was quite explicit. The Tio sold ivory and rubber (1891) to the European shops and maintained the prices by the possibility of having to sell to Kinshasa rather than to Brazzaville or even to the Kongo. Ivory was then priced at 16 to 18 fr (French) to the kilogram but payment was made in goods (we think mainly cloth, by then) the cost price of which was raised substantially. So the benefits did not flow from the buying of ivory but from the mark up in the selling of European commodities. Obviously the artificially high rate of exchange of the *mitako* for European currencies played a part here. Dybowski notes that the value *attributed* by the traders to the *mitako* was 0·15 cts (French), that they counted in *mitako*, but paid in goods: cloth, knives, and different utensils.[21]

But he gave a rather rosy picture of costs, not counting, for instance, wages for Europeans engaged in this. It still seemed to him good business even though, p. 158, he had to list the price per lb between 8–12 and 25–30. Later the need to counter French dumping raised the prices beyond cost-price for cloth and guns, but there may still have been a profit-margin on ivory.

[21] J. DYBOWSKI, *La route*, pp. 51–2; D'UZES, *Le voyage*, p. 251.

The shortening of the *mitako* worked to the advantage of the European traders since the cost price per unit went down. But the Tio caught up with this and in fact maintained prices. In 1889, if the data are to be trusted, the same quantity of cloth still bought the same amount of ivory. In addition the graph shows that they too benefited by the shortening of the currency and more than the traders. This was because of its use in the other spheres of trade. For the traders it seems that the gains made on the *mitako* came mainly from a lowering cost for hiring labour (Kongo) and higher benefits from selling *mitako* to other Europeans. But the gains made by the commercial houses after 1886 were much more the result of their buying ivory upstream than of a dramatic change at the Pool. The most dynamic trader, Mr. Gresshoff of NAHV, had sensed this from the beginning and spent more and more time up river, first at the Falls and later in Ubangi.

The mechanisms of prices will undoubtedly be much better known once more archival material becomes available. The data given however indicate clearly that the system operated as a port of trade in which a European economy based on money enmeshed with a Tio economy based on *mitako*.

Comparing prices for one commodity at the same time in different markets shows consistent rises in price between the market nearest the input of the good and the market furthest away from it. The 1885 data on a block of camwood are typical. Paid five or four to one *mitako* in Ubangi, the rate became three to one at Bonga, two to one at the mouth of the Alima, Bolobo, and NGANTSU's and one to one at the Pool. The value of cloth in the Sangha beyond Bonga was almost double its price at the Pool. Ivory paid 7 fr at the Pool in 1889, was paid 4 fr in the Lulonga. This ratio of prices characterises a similar number of markets in relation to the Pool.[22] These data do not indicate direct gains because of the costs of transportation and food and also because the persons who sold upstream products also bought and resold products from downstream. Still it is obvious that the profit margins between one market and another were an economic force which kept the trade moving.

3. *Volume of the trade*

The profit margins also explain the volume of the traffic. This volume can be roughly assessed by the numbers and tonnage of canoes involved as well as by the flow of ivory available for sale at the Pool. Indications of its variation over time are unfortunately not available.

The dry season trade on the Alima for cassava was astonishing. Pecile compared it with the 'civilized trade' and he came from the hinterland of Trieste. In one week he saw one hundred boats loaded

[22] C. COQUERY, op. cit., pp. 470, 471; E. FROMENT, *Trois affluents*, pp. 468–9; CH. LIEBRECHTS, *Léopoldville*, p. 525; R. BUETTNER, *Reisen*, p. 222, is clearly incorrect.

with cassava and evaluated each load at $1\frac{1}{2}$ tons, each package being 25 kg, that is, 150 tons or 21·4 tons a day. Froment spoke of 40 tons a day being ferried from April to September in convoys of 10, 15, 20 boats, each manned perhaps by a boy and a man, going down the current. Coquery thus assesses it at between 20 and 40 tons.[23]

Since the trade down to the Pool was at its height during the wet season one may infer that many, if not most of the Bobangi who cultivated in the Alima then came down to the Pool. There was also another centre for plantations in the Lulonga as well, but one cannot simply transpose indications of volume on the Alima to the Congo river.

The indications are scattered. First none of the authors who commented on the traffic in the Alima seems to think that it was equally great per day on the Congo river, because they did not comment on it. But then they saw the Alima before they saw the trade on the Congo. Stanley noted in 1882 the arrival of a convoy of 25 boats in March with 25 great tusks; Liebrechts claims that the average boat had 20 to 40 paddlers, 200 kg of ivory and food for 8 days, the total bulk being 2 to 3 tons loaded, a higher average than Pecile's. De Brazza probably saw all the traffic up and down assembled during 3 days together at NGANTSU's and counted 16 boats in September 1880, manned by about 200 people, men and women. In the two weeks before, convoys had varied from 1 to 6 boats at a time. Guiral counted on one night in May 1882 about 10 boats going down. From the different authors it is clear that every day one or more boats went to the Pool and came up from it with complete families aboard. Liebrechts may exaggerate the size of the boats slightly since 30 paddlers was deemed by De Brazza to be a big vessel. De Brazza also stated that each boat going down carried about 10 to 20 big tusks which is at sharp variance with Stanley. All in all though, it is clear that at all seasons some boats, at least one a day, went down and one went upstream and that in the wet season the traffic was heavier. Day in day out one ton of goods perhaps went to the Pool and in the wet season convoys with over 35 tons (25 boats) came down, so that the maximum flow may not have been much less than on the Alima.[24] Merlon claimed 300 tons of ivory passed by Kwamouth per year (1886) and calculated the tusk at 40 lb, which makes it 50 tusks per ton in a year! At 30 lb this gives 225 tons a year or 19 tons a month

[23] E. ZORZI, op. cit., pp. 371, 376; E. FROMENT, op. cit., p. 461; C. COQUERY, op. cit., p. 97; G. SAUTTER, op. cit., I, pp. 267–8.

[24] A. MAURICE, op. cit., p. 135; CH. LIEBRECHTS, op. cit., p. 508; P. BRUNSCHWIG, *La négociation*, pp. 43–6; L. GUIRAL, op. cit., p. 268; many other scattered indications can be found since almost every traveller mentioned something about boats. But they are often very hard to interpret. A. MERLON, op. cit., pp. 36–7; the same author, p. 11, claimed that fourteen jars of wine made 1,800 litres, when at 50 litres a jar they give only 700 litres, and loaded a boat. So his calculation on ivory may be inaccurate as well.

of ivory alone. Since each boat was more heavily manned than on the Alima one may estimate that the biggest convoys carried as many as 300 adults at once. No wonder that the Bobangi at Mpila alone were estimated to be 3,000 to 5,000 persons, all of them there on trading trips.

Such indications as there are on the outflow of ivory confirm the magnitude of the trade. Two general indications first. Jeannest claimed that ivory caravans in the dry season carried from 50 to 200 to 300 tusks each. The total export amounted around 1870 to 5,000 to 6,000 tusks from Ambriz to the mouth of the Congo river, most of which came from the Pool. To compensate roughly for those which came from elsewhere one should take the sales of ivory from the Pool on the Loango coast from Banana to Loango into account. In weight this amounted to about 100 tons, about one-sixth of the world production then. In 1889 Liebrěchts evaluated monthly traffic at about 8 tons to which must be added what was handled at Brazzaville which Froment gave as 3 tons a month for 1888 or 1889.[25] That gave 132 tons of ivory a year for the traffic over the Pool, half of the claim by Merlon. The production was climbing because of the despatch of commercial steamers since 1886–7, yet the total is not out of line with the estimate derived from Jeannest. One hundred tons at 200 kg a boat represented 500 vessels a year or 41 per month, which again does not seem too much, compared with what was said about traffic, especially since some ivory came over land.

With this background the estimates about ivory and the value of ivory at the Pool become more credible. Stanley thought in March 1882 that there might be 200 tusks on the markets. They were sold rapidly because the Kongo and the Zombo went back and forth between the markets. Ngaliema had a store of about 50 tusks. Elsewhere he claims he could buy 50 tusks a day, if he had the men to carry them out and the merchandise to pay for them.[26] Indeed in 1884 he told the Berlin Conference that there was a stock of 3,000 tusks at the Pool. If the Pool produced 100 tons a year or 6,000 tusks, 500 should flow through the market each month and probably a higher number in March when the Bobangi arrived in numbers. The 50 a day may be exaggerated, but it is not impossible at the height of the season, for it represented only 3 to 4 boatloads. And Stanley was not alone. The penny-pinching Mgr. Augouard waxed eloquent in August 1881 when he claimed that at Mfwa 80 to 100 tusks a day were sold and that the

[25] CH. JEANNEST, op. cit., p. 55. Maximum size of caravans was 500 porters; CH. LIEBRECHTS, op. cit., p. 525. E. FROMENT, *Un voyage*, p. 215 fn. I. A. WAUTERS, *Le Congo*, pp. 58–9, for imports to London 1856–63. Tonnage was between 500–600 tons a year, without rising. Atlantic Africa yielded 1,140 tons.

[26] A. MAURICE, op. cit., p. 117 (November 1881: 50 tusks a day, but the contexts allowed for rhetoric; pp. 134–5 (200 on the markets) is a careful calculation from the context. A. WAUTERS, op. cit., p. 60.

Pool was, without any doubt, the foremost market for ivory in the whole of West Africa.[27]

A few estimates in currency exist as well. In June 1884 Pecile sold the equivalent of almost 1,000 *mitako* of goods within a few days at NGANTSU's. And Stanley's shop sold for Ł500 the first day of operations and for Ł300 the next.[28] No wonder that Stanley and Leopold II evolved the fantastic idea to pay for the 'Founding of the Congo State' by capturing the ivory trade at the Pool. It did not work out, since the Tio and Bobangi could not be dislodged and the merchandise to buy it and the porters to carry it to the Pool were lacking.[29]

The volume of operations in the south-western quarter of Tio country is much less well known. The biggest caravans were those of the Tege to the Laadi and vice versa, numbering several hundred, to sell slaves during the dry season, but they did not come near the plains. The number of pedlars is impossible to assess; in small numbers they criss-crossed the country constantly during the dry season. How much they brought in or carried away cannot be calculated.[30]

4. *The Tio traders*

The very size of the great Congo Trade involving thousands of persons is testimony to the gains to be made. These were of three sorts. First in the retail trade, handled probably by women at the Pool and connected with the bigger trade in foodstuffs which yielded good profits all along the river and at the Pool, where by 1887, cassava was increased in price eight times when sold to members of a caravan, though both of these types were ancillary to the movement. It was clearly the gains to be made by moving merchandise from one market to another which yielded handsome returns. But only if the organization was right. True, cloth almost doubled in value on the Sangha or the Lulonga and ivory doubled at the Pool while smaller items such as camwood allowed a mark up of 400 per cent even, but there were costs. The operating costs on the river were boats, paddlers, and food. This market system had not developed any form of wage labour, so manpower had to come from one's kinsmen as happened much among the Bobangi, who lived

[27] G. SAUTTER, op. cit., I, p. 369; NEUVILLE, CH. BREARD, *Voyage*, p. 213, where the ferry costed forty yards of cloth at the Djoué; p. 215; he sat on a stock of twenty-five tusks in the house of the chief of Mfwa. P. AUGOUARD, *Voyage*, p. 141. By coincidence C. COQUILHAT, *Haut Congo*, p. 73, also saw twenty-five tusks at the home of that chief, in December 1882. A. MERLON, op. cit.: Mpila could produce four hundred tusks any day (p. 32).

[28] Z. ZORZI, op. cit., p. 403; H. STANLEY, *The Congo*, I, p. 380.

[29] A. MAURICE, op. cit., p. 119, fn. 3, where king Leopold II asked for the organization of the ivory caravans to cover the expenses of the expedition. p. 117, Stanley proposed chasing Brazza out of the country by taking over the trade, p. 118 he clamours for men and merchandise to do it. Also pp. 135, 148 (one must bypass Tio and Bobangi), p. 166.

[30] C. COQUERY, op. cit., p. 97; L. GUIRAL, op. cit., pp. 169–70.

in whole families off the trade, or from slaves. Caravans were even worse off since the manpower problem was so much greater. In order to reap the benefits an initial outlay was necessary. But, if the kinsmen were not banded together in the venture, the acquisition of slaves required amounts of capital.

Thus there were only two ways to be launched on a trading career. Either one began over short stretches with a fishing boat, selling local goods, such as pottery and wine, and fishing as one went along in the hope of reaping enough benefit from this operation to acquire first a few men and then a big boat. The other way was to have the ability to commandeer men. This political chiefs had and they were thus already favoured in this respect, even besides their semi-monopoly on the sale of slaves or ivory. A variant of this latter way to become a big trader was to grow up in a trading establishment and take it over, as Ngaliema did.

For there were trading establishments. NGANTSU's, Mswata, Mfwa, Ntamo, and most of the settlements of Kinshasa were all characterized by a structure in which a few free men ordered a few kinsmen and a great number of slaves about. When on their way for their masters, the slaves did a little business for themselves. Certainly the women did at the Pool where they cultivated tobacco, sold in the retail market and produced pottery. Elsewhere along the river at Lishia, Mswata, NGANTSU's, and other villages they sold food.[31]

The Tio who did not live along the river or the Pool traded in a different fashion. The kings and chiefs did send down men with ivory, as NgeIkiere remembers.[32] The establishment at Mbe also sent major lords to the Pool in order to collect tribute and when they were there they did a brisk trade themselves.[33] There was even a new road over the plains from Mbe to the Pool, built after the cessation of the slave trade, inhabited by former slaves of the king, who welcomed official

[31] This has been shown for all except NGANTSU's. Cf. there H. BRUNSCHWIG, op. cit., p. 51: 'all the men of the village are the slaves of NGANTSU' and he had even married his sister to a slave. Those slaves manned the boat, laden with beer, that L. GUIRAL, op. cit., pp. 263–4 met. Perhaps their women had brewed the beer, perhaps they had bought it themselves in the Kwa.

Data on food markets have been presented. For Lishia L. GUIRAL, op. cit., p. 266. The market was held at fixed dates. Later during the period all these places grew wealthier by selling food to the steamers as well. The expensiveness of food explains why the Bobangi had organized the food production of the Alima. Even when they arrived at Kinshasa, says CH. LIEBRECHTS, op. cit., p. 508, they still had food for sixteen days. Slaves could earn on their own but paid a tithe on the benefits to their owner according to the same author, p. 530.

[32] E. ZORZI, op. cit., p. 435. The king had sent down three men to sell ivory.

[33] H. BRUNSCHWIG, op. cit., p. 53. In 1880 NGAALIÕ had been at Kinshasa for a year 'to do his business and represent the authority of the king'. After he left and until 1885 his brother the great chief Opontaba replaced him at Mfwa.

travellers and if they were great chiefs would pay slaves and goats as tribute.[34] The wealthiest man of the whole area, outside of the Pool probably, was believed to be a kinsman of Opontaba who must have travelled himself, since he married his daughter to a Bobangi chief on the Ubangi river.[35] But this was the exception. The sources and the oral data all agree that chiefs sent their men to the Pool to trade or to Ntsei, but did not go themselves. Yet the kinsmen of the king at Mbe traded and even claimed to receive their food free when travelling.[36]

Then there were the young men. Ubwoono remembered that when he was young the unmarried men traded. His own father also did this. They wanted to acquire *ngiele*. Mbali and Sautter's informants in Brazzaville confirmed this. But these young men were probably the ones sent by chiefs and have already been mentioned. It does not seem that they often traded on their own, and if they did it could not have been in slaves or ivory.

Lastly, on the plains there were also the sales of food to passing pedlars, and tobacco or beer were prepared for them. In sharp contrast then to the river people all these forms of trade were occasional; they were neither a major occupation, nor were they carried out on a regular basis. The contrast is even more marked when one knows that from the Pool to the Kwa only one small village, Nyari, was reputed to consist of fishermen who did not trade much. In all the others all the activities, whether fishing, brewing beer, making pottery or cultivating, were intimately intertwined with trading and at the Pool as on the River one can no longer speak of a subsistence economy. After all: 'The Bateke do not cultivate much; their harvests would not suffice for their keep. They have to buy part of the cassava they consume: they only reap tobacco . . . and make objects for sale.'[37] A sharp contrast with the plains people, where what was not really much cultivated was tobacco.

The difference between the two—inland Tio and water people—is perhaps best shown by their handling of gains. The Pool people sold ivory which did not belong to them to the Kongo or Zombo and then retained one quarter of the sale as commission; the inland people paid the costs of those who went to sell ivory and then divided the return between a political chief, chief of the land, and the killer of the elephant or the finder of the ivory; or the inland chiefs took tribute. The first were in a market economy, the others in a subsistence economy where distribution channels followed clear social and political norms. Of

[34] ibid., p. 55. This text clearly contradicts the same author, p. 37, where it is claimed by Bobangi that the trade formerly went overland to Mbe and from there to them, unless a much earlier period was meant. Cf. also G. SAUTTER, op. cit., I, p. 378.

[35] CH. DE MARTRIN DONOS, *Les Belges*, II, pp. 308–16.

[36] L. GUIRAL, op. cit., p. 297.

[37] L. GUIRAL, op. cit., p. 240.

course, it helped that the river people dealt mostly with 'foreigners', but then their whole organization had been adapted to trade,[38]

The Tio attitude to trade at the Pool is best preserved in the commercial vocabulary. The word for price (*ntalu*) was derived from the verb *tala* to 'calculate'.[39] A price was first bid ('spoken': *liele ntalu*). Then 'thrown around' (*ta ntalu*) sometimes lowered ('smooth out, excuse': *kwee ntalu*) because the merchandise had been 'discredited' (Calloc'h: p. 177), or raised *luia ntalu* to be finally set, i.e. 'cut' *tsira ntalu* rather like judges set the price of a fine after arguments have been heard (*cira ndoo*). Once agreement was reached, there was a contract, given by Calloc'h as *mu-kele* (p. 336), and concluding a contract was *bere mukele* 'to hit a contract' (Calloc'h, p. 287). This was also done when people entered into partnership (*ubvuo*, *ibvuu*) for instance when Tio took over the ivory of a Bobangi to sell it upstream. To dissolve the partnership again was *kaba unkira* to divide the trading. Sometimes the price was right but the buyer had to borrow *õsuomo* and was given credit (*zima*) after he left a pledge *isuò* (1963 = Sims: *isuo*). This was supposed to be always of lesser value than the 'debt' that remained to be paid and this was always paid in slaves when ivory was concerned. When the time came to 'return a loan' (*loo*) the pledge was redeemed (*nyano neno*). Thus Ngaliema once pawned his beautiful anklets to Bentley and redeemed them in time.[40]

Trust (*mukalu*) was not prevalent. Cheating was very common. *Mitako* were pared down, the *cortade* or the fathom of cloth was shortened and sometimes there were attempts at outright stealing. At Mswata Janssen saw some ivory dealers arrive from NGANTSU's, who left the ivory, crossed the river, then later came back to take the ivory away and return the cloth, because the price was not right. But they had cut away part of the cloth and when this was discovered, they were pursued and caught. Finally they had to settle for the terms of the first sale and 50 *mitako*.[41] And there was cheating with ivory, with measures of all sorts. The net effect, though neither Europeans nor Africans realized it, was to push prices up and devalue both merchandise and currencies. *Koro* means 'chief, proprietor, trader' and 'to snatch, to steal, to hide!'

Once a deal was closed a statement of accounts (*swiba*) was made and the gains (*nkali*, *ndanu*) could be assessed. People traded for profits

[38] Ngelkiere for the distribution inland; G. SAUTTER, op. cit I, p. 377, for the Pool. The mentality is better rendered by tradition than by the many statements that the Tio were the brokers of the Pool.

[39] All the terms are from Sims unless Calloc'h is mentioned. The latter was rather avoided since his information dates from 1910. Compare with M. N. OBENGA, *Le royaume*, p. 43.

[40] H. BENTLEY, op. cit., II, p. 21. The pair was mortgaged at two hundred rods. A. MERLON, op. cit., p. 28, about slaves as pawns.

[41] CH. DE MARTRIN DONOS, op. cit., II, pp. 62–71.

and a trader was either *ngankali* 'the man of profits' or *ngankira* 'the man with trade'. The latter word came from *kira* 'to inherit' and also 'to trade'. The implication is obvious: 'to receive wealth' and a business or a shop was *nkali* or *i-nsuma* (Calloc'h p. 274). The first means profit and the second is more obvious; it derives from *suma*: 'to buy'.

On occasion people ran into debt *ibumũ*. If the debtor could not pay the creditor tried to pass the debt on to another person: *ta ibila*, 'throw a debt' rather in the fashion in which feuds were passed on. When the debt had become a 'back debt', *ibimũ iyili*, the parties might end by settling on a composition fee: *mfuo* from *fura*, 'to pay'. One might pay in instalments: *mpebele* (Calloc'h, p. 185). Often when the creditor claimed his debt: *tamua* (Calloc'h, p. 308) the debtor complained that it was too high, which action was *yamo* (Calloc'h, p. 308). The opposite of gains was: 'to wipe off currency', *yala nzi*.

The terminology reflected the psychology of buying and selling and its importance. The great number of entries concerned with it in both Sims and Calloc'h is a reflexion of the importance of the market-place. And if one is struck by the variety of terms, and the existence of some to signify rather precise operations such as 'to render accounts', one must also be struck by the absence of any terminology related to 'interest on capital loaned' and on sales or loans of labour and land. In fact all the terms meaning to pay wages for labour are derived from such words as 'to pay a fee to a *ngàà*' or 'to make a gift for services rendered'. So the terminology also reflects the limits of this economic system.

5. *Major features of Tio commercial economy*

Buying and selling operated much as in European markets and gains were also the *primum mobile* of Tio traders. But there was no true money-market. Interests were not charged, loans being given only against pawns. And currency could not buy either land or hire labour. Labour could be bought permanently, of course, by buying a slave. Thus both Malamine and De Chavannes bought houses, but not land. The latter specifies that he paid 900 *mitako* for fields and houses on the spot where he proposed to build. Nor did Stanley buy land. As for labour it became a cliché in the literature that the Tio at the Pool, wealthy because of the ivory trade, did not deign to work, i.e. to hire their labour out. The reason is not the low prices paid. Labour was cheap since Pradier paid only 1 *mitako* a day to his Kongo Lari workers, which was just enough to buy food. But the Tio also regarded wage labour as equivalent to slavery, since slave labour had been the only labour that could be bought or sold. By 1889 at Kwamouth there is even a case on record where Cambier hired the slaves of a chief for 1,500 *mitako* a week to work for the mission. Perhaps this had been going on before 1880, though it is unlikely. At any event this was the Tio answer to the demand for hired labour.[42]

Thus the economy was unlike a market economy in that although the trading sector was fully developed, there was no money market. Currencies were not money. Although they allowed trade and the making of profits, they were not an instrument of exchange for *all* goods and services. Even the *mitako*, which the Europeans turned into a universal currency, was not. The limitation of the currencies to particular spheres of circulation, even though conversion was possible, was the crucial feature which prevented the development of a money market.

The following chart summarizes the different spheres of circulation.

CHART 16

Spheres of circulation of currencies

spheres of circulation			*goods*	*subsistence economy sector 'currency'*	*market economy sector 'currency'*
I			food — meat retail	gift	*nji* (beads, *mitako*)[a]
II			social services (bridewealth, fines, etc.)	*ntaa* (raphia, cloth)	—
III			death gifts	cloth (raphia)	—
IV			fine, bridewealth, smiths,[b] ritual, and social service	fine, bridewealth, smiths?[b] goats, fowls	
V	a)	(i)	manufactured goods, e.g. beer per pot, pottery, redwood, meat, etc. crockery, mirrors; (tobacco?)	—	*mitako* (cloth)
	b)	(ii)	guns, goats, fowls prestige objects *unũ* (usually metal) (*lie* beads)	—	*mitako* (cloth)
VI			ivory, slaves (boats?)	—	gunpowder guns, cloth (*mitako*)[c]

[a] The articles in ( ) are secondary currencies making inroads by 1880: The sign — indicates penetration by the other sector, whether market or subsistence; The sign ═══ shows blocks of spheres according to unification in both sectors.

[b] In one case, the royal smith asked a goat from Brazza for a *unũ* collar.

[c] Note that ivory and cloth were particularly closely linked.

[42] CH. DE CHAVANNES, *Avec Brazza*, p. 169; Pradier in C. COQUERY, op. cit., p. 462; E. CAMBIER, op. cit., p. 157; CH. LIEBRECHTS, op. cit., p. 527. Because the Tio at the Pool did not hire their labour, they were ultimately crowded out of the cities, especially Brazzaville. By 1886 already, if not before, Kongo Lari were at work there.

In terms of commodities, the spheres are self-explanatory, once it is known that goats were always used in major sacrifices, for bridewealth, and in fines. They were almost a ritual animal such as cattle for the Nuer. In Sphere I retail trade occurs of course only in the market economy sector. The typical means of payment were *nji* but *mitako* and beads were infiltrating. This was the range with articles of small value.

The social services sphere and the death gift sphere show the subsistence economy sector dominating the market economy sector completely, although cloth began to make inroads against *ntaa* for social services and had supplanted the latter in burials on the Pool and for the wealthy. But no currency was yet established. A clear link existed with sphere VI when persons were concerned, since payments for bridewealth, fines for adultery, bloodmoney, and the price for a slave were all harmonized. This 'people sphere', where persons were exchanged, cut across II and VI, because in the latter sphere the sale of slaves had been completely absorbed by the market economy.

The sector of goats and fowls was special in that they changed hands usually because of social or ritual action in the subsistence sector, but were a source of meat for the market economy and fell in the middle range of value goods there which includes the whole of sphere V. The subspheres were real in that *unũ* objects became associated with titles and prestige, moving in a subsphere of politics and power. Guns circulated like other goods but since they were singled out as means of payment for ivory and slaves they were part-currency. In sphere V the market economy sector dominated completely. *Mitako* were especially associated with this. The last sphere requires little explanation. It represented the high range of goods with the *possible* inclusion of boats. If not, boats were part of sphere V, (i) and really usually paid for in *mitako*, whereas in this sphere cloth and guns were indispensable, with *mitako* making only inroads.

From the point of view of the relation between currencies the situation is clear. *Nji* to be used in sphere I, *mitako* in spheres IV and V, cloth in III and VI, while raphia held out in sphere II. Overall *mitako* and cloth had about an equally wide distribution, but since cloth was much more used as a commodity or destroyed (burial) than *mitako* (only jewellery and not destroyed) and *mitako* occupied the crucial sphere of goods with a middle range value, it gained the upper hand as a universal currency. Its small bulk may have helped, especially when the Europeans arrived on the scene.

Conversion between currencies was possible but because of the unequal role of currencies losses and gains were entailed. Thus to convert *nji* or *mitako* into cloth was a gain because cloth allowed the acquisition of people, could be used for burials and increasingly for bridewealth and adultery fines, or as bloodmoney. *Mitako* were not quite as good. But it depended not only on the general and abstract picture but on the particular situation. Somebody who, like J. De Brazza and Pecile, had to buy food was penalized if he bought with cloth. He had to convert down which would be one step to *mitako*. The person who made the conversion gained on it, provided he did not need food, for he had made cloth out of *mitako*. The same was true in all other spheres. One rather suspects that the smith at Mbe who asked for a goat rather than for *mitako* or cloth, may have needed a goat badly for a sacrifice. For obviously for an *unũ* object, such as the collar was, he could have obtained either. Guns, goats, and fowls were obvious intermediaries in converting 'up' from *mitako* to ivory and slaves or 'down' from *mitako* to ritual or social services.

It is interesting to see that at the Pool people produced goods with middle range value (pottery, tobacco, metal *unũ* objects) and bought part of their food. This is a clear case where a calculation of different returns for equal labour comes in. Because vegetable food was in the small value range of goods, and required as much work as planting tobacco and perhaps more than the other activities, the time budgets were accordingly allotting as little time as possible to agriculture. In the subsistence economy on the plains it was the reverse. There agriculture paid off because there was a demand for the extra food and at home one strove for autarchy.

Converting 'up' is related to the notion of capital and capital investment, but also to general social values. The accumulation of wealth presupposed capital investment in boats and men and an increase in the rate of investment would result in a corresponding increase in returns. So from the economic point of view, what was needed was bought labour—slaves. This was true wealth. Women married into the household of the trader and children born in it were all equal to slaves in so far as they increased the labour force by an equal amount. Because they could work more, male slaves cost more than females at Bonga, despite the fact that females could reproduce, while at the Pool, especially later, females were twice the price of males. In addition an accumulation of people also meant political power, especially if they had guns.

The aim of trade, indeed its very nature, as may be seen from the terminology, was to make gains. And the aim of gains was to become wealthy. Ambition for wealth and power were the psychological movers of the whole system.

Poverty was not having many kinsmen, being alone and powerless, as genealogies of poor people in 1963 attested. The latter's genealogies were invariably a small fraction of those of important or wealthy people. So, even in 1963, the number of followers still counted. Sims has the following terms for poor persons:

muwene: 'one who has nothing'
-unya, -unyaa: 'poor, uncivilized'

-umboni: 'poor, uncivilized'
-uwelo: 'poor, destitute, barren'
(*myuwelo:* 'servant, one with no property')
-ncana: 'unmarried, wretchedly poor' (it meant: 'commoner!')
nko uwelo: 'servant, poor person' and *nko* alone: 'aversion'

Contrast with wealthy people:
mupfuli: wealthy one. Calloc'h, p. 60, also polite interjection to answer first wife and thus honour her
mvwama: rich, affluent person
akuru: rich, wealthy (it meant: 'senior, older, more respected')
munaa: 'rich man, king'

To become wealthy was a compelling dream, for wealth and power were one. Calloc'h, p. 302, has *manama*: 'power stemming from the men one has bought or acquired'! So conscious were the Tio of the links between wealth and power. Charms to become wealthy were made and bought by political chiefs but also by people who had begun to accumulate wealth. One of these, according to Angõ *yil nkwi*, was a *pfura* and a fowl (*yil nkwi*) given by the *ngàà* after the client had already had an *oyuru*, some herbs received and put on the evening fire of which the smoke was then inhaled. The *pfura* received kola and the client would become wealthy and gain wives and inherit and succeed to political offices. To achieve this aim some people did not hesitate. Payeur Didelot may have exaggerated when he claimed that some on the Pool were so greedy that they would sell their wives if they had no goods and poison their neighbours to inherit from them[43] but that poisoning may have been purely sorcery. And there was so much distrust about people who were becoming rapidly wealthy that Calloc'h reports: *lyeme*: 'ordeal to be undergone because one becomes too wealthy'. This desire for wealth produced greed which has often been commented on. Even the king could not refrain at one point from telling Guiral: 'that the Commandant (Brazza) should come quickly with his gifts'.[44] Besides this wealth also produced inordinate competition among men for the desired power which was the aim of it.

It is thus important to know if wealth could be inherited and if in this way at least a class of powerful people had come into being. The composite noun *ngáá* + *noun* meant: 'master of', 'the one who is in control of', 'owner of'. Wealth was amassed in raphia squares and in the bigger *olivancillaria nana* which were kept by whole big rain jars (*otiele*), claimed Bilankwi. That however was typical for the plains people, who still lived mostly in a subsistence economy.

[43] J. F. PAYEUR DIDELOT, *Trente mois*, p. 217.

[44] L. GUIRAL, op. cit., pp. 300–1, and for example also chief NTSUULU, pp. 254–5, Opontaba competing for gifts with the king, pp. 288, 292. All other travellers commented in the same sense. Thus Pecile in E. ZORZI, op. cit., p. 220. 'The local people here (NGANTSU's) are haughty and presumptuous, because they are too rich . . .'.

For the squares were of greatest use in the sphere of social payments and acquisition of wives. Okondzaadza commented that wealthy people paid their fines quickly, acquired wives, and dressed well, but otherwise hid their wealth. This again is typical for the plains economics. At the Pool or on the river really wealthy people could hide neither their slaves, nor their stocks of ivory or merchandise.

In the plains stores of cloth and other wealth were inherited since little of it went on the catafalque of the deceased with the exception of a relatively small number of raphia cloths. Only chiefs were really given big burials. But on the Pool when a truly rich person died a great deal of his movable goods, as has been seen,[45] were put on the catafalque and destroyed by burial. Another part was lavished to pay for the singing and dancing by mourners but that may have been compensated by gifts brought by the mourners. Still, most of the stocks in cloth went with the deceased. The slaves seem to have become free and were thus lost as property. If not, they as other goods, mainly *mitako*, guns, and ivory, were divided according to the inheritance rules and at best the next heir had only half of the estate, minus the cloth, of the deceased. Thus no hereditary aristocracy of wealth could arise there. And with the major chiefs inland, the same situation prevailed. Here the loss to the heirs was even greater, since most of their fortune, as that of king Iloo himself for instance, seems to have been converted into cloth.

Sautter has argued that the whole Tio economy aimed at converting into cloth and that the essential movement was an export of slaves, caught by the crudest means, and an import of cloth for lavish burials. The depopulation of the plateau resulted.[46] One cannot agree with this. First, slaves were not caught wholesale and even when one chief, Linganu at Mbe Nkulu, tried it, people left the town but did not flee the plains. The Mbe profited more from the trade at the Pool and at NGANTSU's and Mswata—the 'famous pirates' of Guiral—than was realized. Finally big funerals on the plains were given only to major chiefs and between 1880 and 1892 none of those seems to have died. The rate of destruction of capital in cloth on the plains was thus limited. At the Pool it was much higher, but the opportunities of the Tio middlemen in the trade constantly made up for this. Even there many goods were redistributed after death and served as new seed money to begin another accumulation of fortune. In addition people were added as wealth increased so that in the ivory era at least wealth repopulated. The slaves sold at the Pool were by and large probably not sold to the caravans, but mostly to the local wealthy men such as Ngaliema.[47]

[45] Cf. Chapter VIII, section on funerals.

[46] G. SAUTTER, *Le plateau*, pp. 154–9.

[47] TH. MENSE, *Anthropologie*, pp. 624–5, is specific about the increase of population by buying slaves after the end of the slave trade.

The relation between both sectors, commercial and subsistence, is now clear. The subsistence sector derived some currency from the external sale of products like raphia, tobacco, a few slaves, food, and ivory, with their chiefs reaping the main profits which they converted into wives, slaves, and guns. The distributive nature of disposing of returns must actually have discouraged people from trading, for at best they received only a third of the proceeds or a carrier's tip. But enough small currency, mainly *nji* and *mbula* and some cloth, flowed into each household so that some imported goods were becoming standard. Cloth was on its way to becoming a standard item in each house, and items such as coastal salt while still a luxury were becoming more and more part of the standard of living. Necessities were gunpowder, guns, knives and ironware, and pottery, all traded inland or bought at the markets by the plains people. The latter were not unaware of the commercial economy and had taken over some of its values, but the mechanisms of social and political control still discouraged more active participation. The major chiefs were happy with this since they benefited.

The commercial sector was wholly integrated in the great Congo Trade and economic ties with the plains Tio were weak. But in the social sphere most of the patterns of the inland Tio had been kept and persisted, which reflects the basic fact that the ties between the two communities were not economic, but social. They married one with another, they belonged to the same political system, they subscribed to the same kinship system, similar or the same rituals and almost identical values, except on economics! Another difference was that some of the European trade goods which were still luxuries inland, were daily necessities at the Pool. The situation had not progressed to the point where all, or on the north bank even most, people dressed in cloth, or that everyone needed European crockery, but there was more of this than on the plains. For instance more European knives were in daily use, yet the bulk of the European imports, for which all the ivory was sold, were semi-luxury goods ultimately destined for some chief or leader somewhere in the vast Congo system. Because the system was so extensive no particular local economy felt a great drain of its productive resources, Tio economy least of all, since the Tio lived well off the vast volume of traffic generated outside their territory.

6. *The impact of the Congo trade on Tio society*

The major economic effects of the commercial economy have been described. Two major consequences resulted from it. First Tio economy became much more dynamic as a whole and liable to serious changes over shorter time periods. The shift from slave trade to ivory trade in the 1850s or 1860s had been an example and the various changes from 1880 to 1898 were other signs. Currencies fluctuated, supplies and demands for different goods varied and there is therefore a history to the commercial economy under king Iloo's reign.[48] The changes in the subsistence sector were much slower and scarcely visible over this period. The more obvious change in the latter sector had been its loss of autarchy, which was the other major consequence of the commercial economy. The loss of autarchy led to a loss of technological know-how. It was a slow movement, started long before this period. But by king Iloo's reign the Tio did or could no longer smelt iron, build canoes, hunt with bows and arrows. In a certain way the plains Tio were thus becoming a poorer rural countryside.

The social effects of the trade system were spectacular. Although the ideology and the language of social structure were still the same, the structure itself was not. River settlements were towns, peopled with large numbers of slaves and women depending from few masters. Almost every adult free man represented the apex of a trading house. A town like Ntamo may have had only eight of these. Further study, if still possible, of these places may yet help to reconstruct internal relations in these 'trading houses'.

The major effect was the development of social classes or social estates. Distinctions in style of living and in wealth between the very wealthy and the political chiefs had vanished: witness chief NTSUULU and Ngaliema, but the difference in mode of living, values and occupation between these men and the great number of slaves were bigger than ever before. A slave might disobey king Iloo, as happened,[49] but not Ngaliema. Between the two classes the small number of free men and the large number of free women were different from slaves only in that they could not be sold. So the rift between the rich and the poor grew wider and a growing dichotomy between women and men evolved. Most women were herded in large polygynous households. As free as on the plains, they pursued their own trade though probably bitter about a lowered social status.

The trade obviously had a deep impact on politics. Wealthy men had guns and power and retainers. They were 'big men' who could compete with the chiefs for control. In fact by 1880 it seems that the foremost lords of the kingdom had less power than Ngaliema. So the chiefs and the kings tried to participate in the trade or mulct traders of tribute to acquire guns. They could use free men for retainers and needed less wealth than the traders who had to acquire slaves. Chiefs along the river all participated fully in the trade and, with the single exception of Ngaliema, dominated it. As for the establishment at the capital, in theory, according to ideology, it was supreme. Some of this still lingered and the chiefs of Mbe were received with some consideration at the Pool. They even collected tribute, but that was because they had set up close kin as chiefs in at least Mfwa and Mpio aBwaani. At Mbe the First Lord Opontaba acquired a power so much greater than that of

[48] Cf. Chapter XV. [49] L. GUIRAL, op. cit., p. 294.

the king that the Europeans could fear for a time in 1884–5 that he would oust Iloo.

But perhaps the biggest impact of trade on politics was in the field of values. Ambition had always been a cardinal virtue of politicians, it would seem, from village leaders to kings. Competition had always existed. But now the flame of envy was fanned by the nature of economic competition and the power which flowed from it. Competition and striving for power were exacerbated from 1881 to at least 1885.

In spite of this, however, the commercial economy did not at these times subordinate politics or the politicial structure completely to its patterns, for the nucleation of political power remained different from the nucleations of the trade network and did not even shift.

Culturally the trade brought many changes. Some, like the development of greed and cupidity, were visible in the value system, but there was also a sense of adventure and a will to take changes. A major change had been the rise of a great and a little cultural tradition. The Pool was the hub of the former, which could be found all along the river. Tio and Bobangi had borrowed so much from each other's culture that Sir Harry Johnston in 1883 had difficulty keeping them apart up river. Their clothing and housing were similar, they spoke Bobangi up river and Tio at the Pool, they lived in mixed villages. Lingala had already evolved as the language of acculturation and one sees the traces in Johnston's vocabulary.[50] Unique institutions had arisen to cope with the situation of mixed living. Thus the Tio in any mixed village always sent an observer to the Bobangi court when there was a case among the Bobangi to learn their customary law. The latter did the same with regard to the Tio. When a mixed case involving Bobangi and Tio occurred, it was tried by the observers of both communities acting as judges, since they knew the customs of both parties.[51] At the Pool Tio, Hum, and Bobangi had so mingled on the south bank, that it became difficult for outsiders to distinguish between them. There were also on the south bank overlaps with Kongo culture such as the taking over of the *nkita* rituals. The settlement of Europeans at Léopoldville and Brazzaville during the period, unconsciously accelerated the movement. Much of the common culture of Kinshasa City, now the pace-setter for a nation, grew out of this mixed culture.

During Iloo's reign this cultural elaboration had already produced

[50] A. COURBOIN, *Bangala*, p. III, VII, is conclusive about this, at least for the Alima river. Lingala did exist there. At the Pool both Tio and Lingala seem to have been spoken. Tio was important which explains why Sims devoted his first linguistic work to this language. Cf. also CH. DE CHAVANNES, *Avec Brazza*, p. 204.

[51] Information obtained at Ngabe in 1963. Both the local Bobangi and Tio claimed that it went back to remote times (although not at Ngabe which was founded around 1918). Acculturation in such matters as fishing, the use of certain common types of pottery, etc., was even then evident from the descriptions, especially H. JOHNSTON, *The River Congo*, pp. 124–210; 281–end, incl. vocabulary.

a great enrichment of the texture of life. Instead of a few fishing techniques, many were now available.[52] People had a wide choice of pottery from different areas and the buying of foreign pottery at the Pool was becoming a cultural necessity. Nunu or Bobangi beer flowed freely and camwood from the far off Sangha was in great demand. Life became thus much denser, not only because the agglomerations were large, but because the objects and the behaviour associated with them diversified so much. In short, the towns at the Pool were becoming the most sophisticated settlements perhaps in the whole of Equatorial Africa. And correspondingly the cultural appeal of the political *élite* at Mbe must have declined.

[52] G. SAUTTER, *De l'Atlantique*, pp. 424–46, for a description of the wealth of techniques brought from everywhere to the Pool by the 1950s. Many existed in the 1880s or were brought then.

Chapter XII
The Protectors: Lords and Squires

THE widest reference in space of the Tio political structure was the kingdom as a whole. Below this, only one clear territorial subdivision was recognized: the domain of the chief-of-the-land whom we call the squire. Proceeding from the smaller units to the bigger one must necessarily follow up the earlier discussion of the settlement and the neighbourhood with that of the domain, the political expression of the neighbourhood. Next another authority must be introduced: the chief-of-the-crown, or the lord. Lords held no sway over territory but ruled varying numbers of squires. Besides this, both types of chiefs were distinguished one from another most clearly by the ideologies on which their claims to authority were based as well as by their style of living. Both acted almost in an identical way in their essential role of chieftainship: to provide protection, as well as in matters of administration and justice. From this angle lords were overblown squires. Because of the identity in essential roles as well as the contrasting parallelism of the ideologies both sorts of authority are better discussed within the framework of a single chapter.

1. *The squires*

Tio geography was seen by its inhabitants as consisting of a series of plateaux. These in turn were conceived of as sets of woods (*idzwa*) as islands in a sea of grassland. The woods were named and between them there was emptiness. In the political realm a portion of a plain was set aside as a *ntsii* (Sims: *ncie*: 'country, earth'; *nsi* (*nci*): 'soil, earth') ruled by a squire (Sims: *ngancie*: 'ruler' litt. 'in control of land'), the *ngántsii* or *mpfõ antsii* (Sims: *ngancie*: 'ruler'; *mfumu*: 'chief, king'). That such a domain was really a set of forests is clear from the enumeration of forests made when a squire is asked to indicate the extent of his domains. Thus in 1963 chief NGAMPO reeled off a list of thirty such woods, adding some places which were now deserted (Map No. 9).

Boundaries were roughly recognized. Another squire described the boundaries (*ondil antsii*) as bounded by the spring of A, towards the woods B and C, towards the wood D, including the former settlement of E but not of F. Boundaries were only fluid lines between woods as Sims indicates (*mubilu*: 'boundary mark, tribal mark, drawn line, space of time'). With such a low density of population this is not surprising.

It was also not very useful to define the domain by the settlements it contained since village structure was fluid and consequently settlements

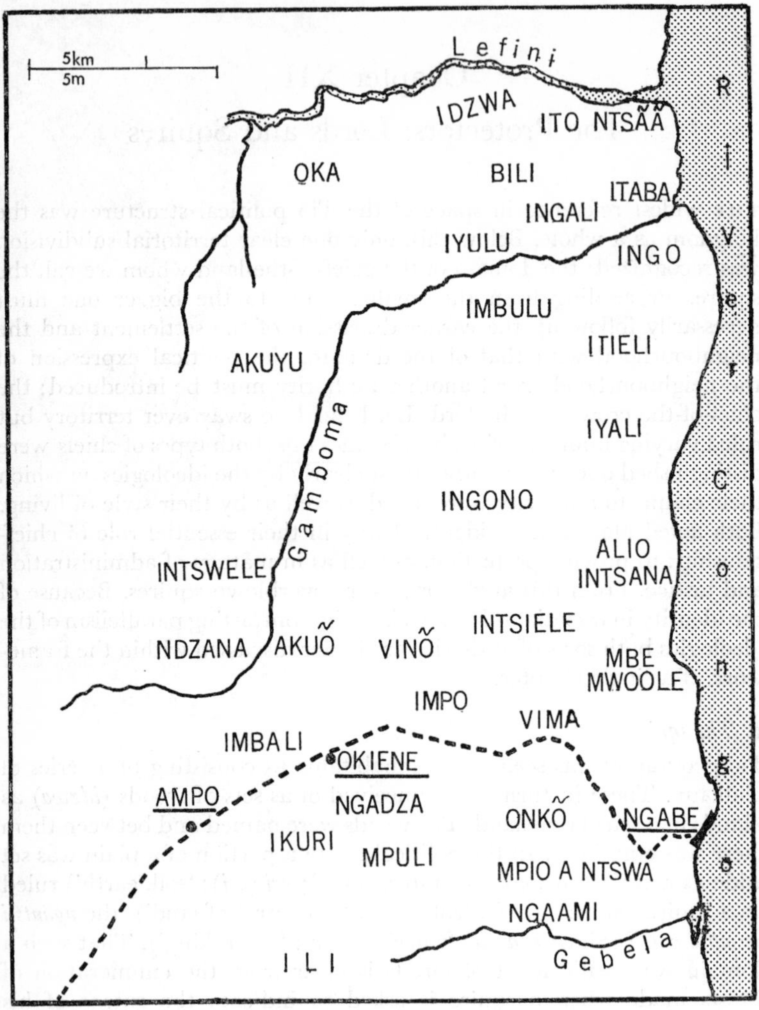

Map 9. *Domain of Ampo*

- - - - - : Motor road Mbe-Ngabe

ILI : Woods

● OKIENE: Villages (1963–1964)

Notes: Beyond the named woods to the West, the next patches of forest belong to the domain NDUA; to the South the first woods of the domain MBE appear below Ampo. But both on the South and to the West the border remains uncertain within a limit of several kilometres in the savanna.

were unstable and shifted. Moreover usually the squire's village was the only one located in the open land, while others were built in the woods and stockaded against surprise attacks. The insecurity of which this was a consequence stemmed from the numerous feuds. The situation meant that a list of settlements coincided with part of the list of forests.

There were about sixty domains between the Pool to the south and the Nkéni to the north. Map 10 gives a sketch of the ten chiefdoms occupying the plateau of Mbe proper as distinct from both the plains of Mpũ and Mboõ. The territories of the domains here and on the other plains were much larger than among the Fumu and near the Pool proper where seventeen are listed in the immediate vicinity of what is now Brazzaville.[1] This is explained by the much denser human occupation. On the south bank the situation was more confused, but there seem to have been four Tio squires, and perhaps four or so Hum squires as well, so that the territory of present-day Kinshasa consisted of no less than eight domains, and perhaps more.

The legitimate basis for the authority of a squire was his mastership over the *nkira* spirit of the domain. Usually his abode was in a wood, although one case of a *nkira* dwelling in a depression near Imbãw was known. *Nkira* were anthropomorphic and carried names. Their name preceded by the compound substantive *ngàà* 'owner of' often formed the title of the squire, such as NGAATALI at Imbãw. Different *nkira* might have the same name so there could be squires with the same title. There were also squires with titles which were not clearly derived from the *nkira*'s name. But there were no squires without title.

The *nkira* helped to ward off catastrophes and to protect the inhabitants of the domain, and provided sanctions for the squire, whom the spirit helped to rule with success. Worship for the *nkira* was institutionalized. Each squire had a kindred in charge of the upkeep of the little house, also called *nkira*, in front of his yard. The house contained a package or a box with the objects of the *nkira*. Hence Sims: *nkira*: 'charm, box of charms'.[2] The head of this group could enter the shrine, open the package or box and sacrifice kola or wine there while praying on behalf of the squire and on his orders. Another kindred was in charge of worship at the *nkira*'s own abode in the forest. In serious cases they went there to pray on behalf of the squire and

[1] Calloc'h, pp. 323–33: 'terre': *nsye* listed as the most important 'quarters' of the vicinity of Brazzaville in 1910: Bikyo, Ibwa, Ingolo, Malima (Mpila), Mukaru, Inkyeno, Impaga, Itaatolo, Nga ibina, Nduo, Bambu Nčwele, Nsa Manzo, Ingwali, Ime, Ibiligi, Mbuambuli. He added Nkwe, Mpumu, Mbulankyo, and Mbe which is probably not correct. This dates from 1910 and several names of portions of the town may have been added such as Ibiligi: 'place of the Belgians'. The territory described seems to have extended around the town for about ten to twelve miles only.

[2] Also 'twin'. Cf. Chapter IX.

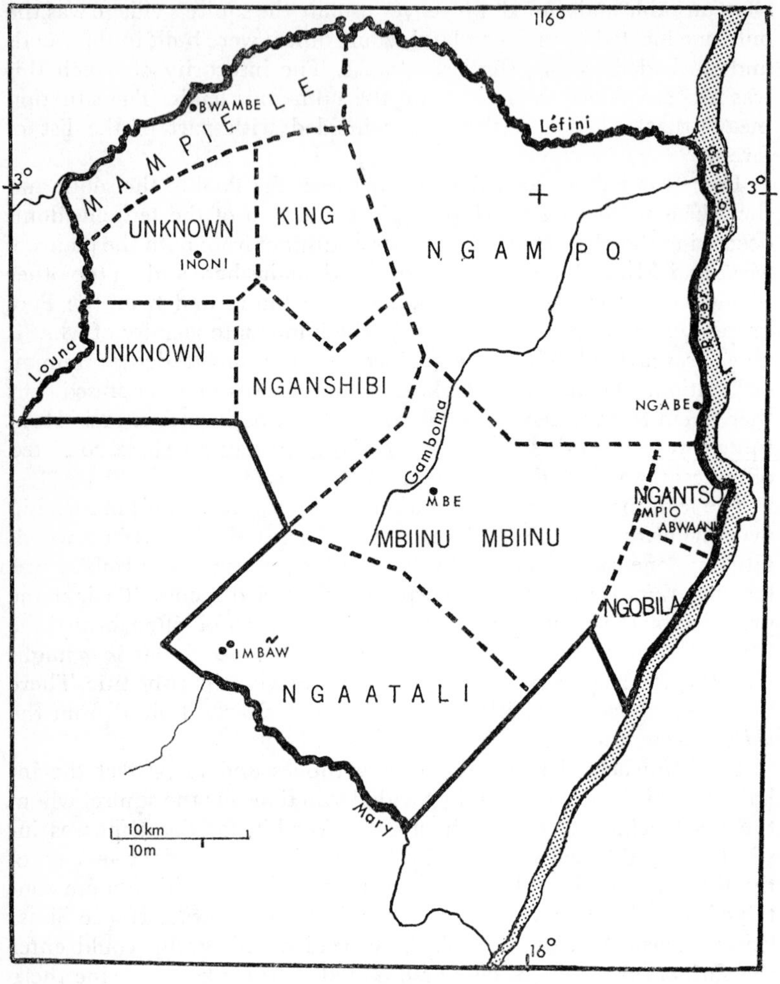

Map 10. *The Ten Domains of the Mbe Plateau*

——— : Boundary of the plateau

- - - - : Boundaries of the domains

sometimes to sacrifice a goat offered by the latter. No one except the family who opened the *nkira* package or box knew what was inside, but besides white earth and perhaps some *olivancillaria*, these were objects found at the site where the *nkira* dwelled.

Anyone disobeying a squire's orders or disregarding his rights might be taken ill without other cause than the *nkira*'s anger. In addition the squire could curse: 'I curse X on the earth' and the guilty party or the whole domain would be stricken by misfortune. The culprit had to apologize and bring a gift, whereupon the squire removed the curse by having his *nkira* prayed to and a sacrifice of a fowl was made near the *nkira* house. Then the squire chewed the bitter *oshioonlu* plant and spat it out over the hands of the suppliant and also over the *nkira* objects to cool the anger of the spirit.

Because of the connexion with the *nkira*, the squire was entitled to a tithe of the hunt: (Sims: *(M)ulani*; 'chief's share of anything'). All animals had a general connexion with the spirit. So a haunch of all trapped or hunted animals, except for the *ntsee* caught during the drive with nets, had to be given. If the animal was wounded on one domain and killed in another one, one half of the haunch should go to each squire, said Ngateo. Often there were quarrels about this, because the boundaries were so vague. Refusal to give a haunch resulted, it was believed, in lack of success for any further hunt. Generally it was said that it would also lead to war, for the offended squire would attack the culprit. If the chiefdom lay along a river one fourth of any catch of fish was for the squire also, if it had been caught near the bank. In the middle of the rivers Lefini and Congo there was no domain. The connexion between earth and hunt was also shown by the obligation to hand over to the squire the tusk that first struck the ground when an elephant was killed.

Consistent with the value system, is a contrast between the rights of the squire over the hunt and the relative lack of rights or interference with agriculture. Thus no one could hunt on his domain without having permission and the squire, especially in Mpũ, reserved the right to give the signal for the annual bushfire drives. But to cultivate no permission was necessary. Indeed even to settle on the domain did not require authorization. True, the squire could ask an objectionable group to leave his lands but the group might refuse, stay, and fight. Just such a war was remembered by Ngateo. It had occurred on the domain of the squire of Ntsaa. The immigrants won and they stayed. Such an occurrence however was rare, for most squires knew well that people brought power, not empty land, and did their best to attract immigrants just as any headman at the settlement level tried to attract settlers. Yet if people left, the squire was powerless. They did not fight to compel even settlements who migrated to come back. This is due to the extraordinary low density of population and the structure of Tio settlements where internal strife led men to wander off and start their own village.[3] On the other hand migrants feared to disregard the owner of the land. They would 'find' a goat or a fowl and wine to give him, so that things would go well with their installation. They also liked to hunt and for

[3] R. HOTTOT, *Nomadism*, went so far as to claim that the Tio were virtually nomads. It shows that by 1906 the mobility was still very great.

that the squire was needed. In addition trees could only be planted with his approval and fruit, especially kola, was expected to be given to him.[4]

Ritually the squire could help with the hunt by blessing the hunters beforehand with kola. As for the fields the women would come with kola and seeds. He put the latter in the house of the *nkira*. The next morning he washed the hands and the hoes of the women to drive out the fire of misfortune and then gave them the seed. In some domains he would plant the third seed on each field himself.

Squires had to behave so as not to endanger their domain. For instance they could never run, even during a rainstorm. It was undignified and harm might come of it. They often had some *unũ* prestige objects and imitated the lords as best they could. Thus squire Ngampei in 1880 was announced by a drum, sat on two leopard skins as the lords do and had his elbow resting on a cushion, rather reminiscent of the *likuba* cushion of the king, upon which sat a child. His wife sat at his right side and his daughter at his left, again in imitation of the king whose two major ritual wives sat next to him.[5]

The insignia were not standardized. Bracelets or anklets of copper and beads, necklaces with leopard's teeth or made of beads, fly whisks made from the tail of a buffalo, a very long iron pipe, sometimes with a double bowl, and above all a red blanket were prestigious items and any squire who had those would show them. They were also allowed, like the lords, to have their arrival announced by a costly iron bell (NGAMPEI had it done with the drum). In addition squires sought wealth at least to the extent of being polygynous. The number of wives indicated wealth and their *ndzo* and kindreds would sustain the squire in case of war. But polygyny beyond two or perhaps three wives was beyond most squires and NGAMPEI even had to be content with one.[6]

One ceremony indicated precisely who was legally master on the domain: the formal drink. Brazza witnessed NGAMPEI drinking his cassava wine from a large jar. An assistant sang first and the population kept time by knocking pebbles one against the other. NGAMPEI covered himself with a cloth (it should have been red, but he had none). Meanwhile his wife sang his praises. After that, his guest, a *wookuru*, also drank with his knife of *unũ* on his shoulder but not covered. Only the highest authority at any gathering could cover himself thus.[7] The whole was a modest imitation of the ceremonies performed by lords and kings.

[4] *Coutumes* mentioned, p. 18, that only Tio strangers could settle. If the land was received from a simple kin-group leader, they gave him a fowl. He would then go with them to the 'chef politique'. If it was the latter who authorized installation, he was given a goat or a calabash of wine.

[5] H. BRUNSCHWIG, *Les cahiers*, p. 189.

[6] *Coutumes*, p. 42.

[7] H. BRUNSCHWIG, op. cit., p. 193.

The role of a squire was essentially to keep the peace and prosperity politically. He acted exactly like a *wookuru* at a higher level. Thus he settled disputes between members of different villages on the domain or different kinship groups. He might call for an ordeal to be given and supervise its operation. He admonished people when he felt they were straying into behaviour that could provoke quarrels; he was present at the settlement of most cases of *litsũ*, which were notorious for their potentiality to lead to feuds. He assisted also at most *okuu* inquests. He approved of the placing of hunting camps and set aside parts of the bush for this purpose and in the dry season he took the initiative to open the hunt there. His rule was informal however and shared by the inhabitants of his own village often the largest on his domain. Despite the limited etiquette he felt obliged to observe, he worked like any villager. In fact he behaved entirely like a village leader. He was judged by his constituents above all else by his speeches. *Wookuru* in their settlements and squires were wont to appear at the crack of dawn on the plaza of their village and announce in a voice, rendered more ringing by the stillness of the night, that the village was menaced, because of disunity, that such and such had been announced by dream and that people should behave. If the situation was really tense, such speeches and orders (Sims: *musiu*: 'law') could also be given before nightfall at dusk. Since this was the essence of rule and no entire data exist some examples of 1963 are given.

'Witchcraft now surpasses all. The witch must stop. Never was this seen under the old kings. First lightning fell on the school, last Monday, and now someone became mad at Osabi. I have dreamt badly. The *ikwii* of the Earth (*nkira*) has said: "There must be no quarrel neither among the men, neither among the women, otherwise someone will die. Lightning had been sent by foreign chiefs." '

Current gossip about this said that the day before the squire had been to Osabi with two *wookuru* for *okuu* and that there must have been witchcraft there, in the kindred of the sick person. As for the lightning the blame was laid at the door of a coalition of lords and others who were the enemies of the king and happened to be very active at the time.

A day later in the evening the squire announced that no one would go to the fields the next day. Next morning he sacrificed a white fowl and kola to the *nkira*.[8] He asked for the people to be preserved. There was no attendance, but everyone knew he was doing it. He also promised then that the graves of the former squires would be cleaned by the women of his village.

A month or two later the same *ngántsii* declared when a number of disputes had broken out:

[8] Because of altered conditions the squire was in 1963 the head of the kindred which prayed and sacrificed to the *nkira*.

There is an epidemic among the small children, so they have to stay at home. It is not due to the witches, but just an illness. However I am *ngantsii*, I must protect the village against the witch from outside the domain, who could well come to gain from this situation (he meant the quarrels as well as the epidemic). So there should be no more quarrelling, for that opens the road for witchcraft.

And a pathetic appeal to save a baby who was desperately ill:

Listen then: The one in the child, that he keep quiet. Since I have come to live here there always have been epidemics. But now, now because there is fever (quarrels) in the village, you want to eat the children. The village is now in danger. Everyone must lock his children in at dusk (when the witches go around). I do not want any more wailing in the settlement. The village must now rest peacefully. The witch who is throwing discord in the village, must step back. He must let this epidemic alone. Don't mix in this, leave the children alone. I want this village to be quiet. How can one have peace and good life among many, if one eats (bewitches) the other!

The implication of such a warning was that the squire would take whatever steps were necessary to flush out the witches, either by calling a *ngàà* in to rout them or by appealing to his *nkira*.

These speeches were recorded in 1963 but there can be little doubt, as NGAATALI confirmed, that they were also, perhaps more, used in the reign of Iloo. They give the quasi-heroic dimension to the role of protector and stress both his affinities with *ngàà* and his major concern about the welfare of all in his domain. No wonder that people evaluated their *ngántsii* by their speeches . . . and by the relative number of deaths striking his domain.

A last duty of the squire was to collect tribute *ingkura* (Sims: *inkura*: 'King's share of meat'; Calloc'h, p. 168: *i-nkura*). The term meant really 'that which is tied' and referred to all types of goods given to the king via the lords as tribute of the people. He taxed the heads of *ndzo* who lived on his domain and they in turn collected it from their members, whether or not they lived on the domain. The amount was not fixed. If the *mpfõ andzo* for instance came back with only three eggs the squire cursed him until more came along. If there was much, he might leave something for the head of the *ndzo* to keep. Thus it was as representative of the higher authority that he collected tribute and passed it on but he might himself retain some of it. It was a source of income, but not as much as the fines, *iã*, he collected in cases judged in his court. The sources of income from both were rather low. Real wealth came to some squires mainly through trading, because they had first choice in the sales of foreign goods, controlled the sale of slaves and ivory and also could sell some of the haunches given as tribute. But such squires were a minority for they themselves were usually controlled by the lords, who took most of the trade and its profits, who judged cases in appeal and through whose hands the tribute went up towards the capital.

The net result was that in appearance squires seem to have been almost as poor as their subjects. They were respected and any insult to them was felt to be an insult to the domain if it came from an outsider. But they only differed in style of life from their charges by the few trappings they wore and the ceremony for drinking.

Squires did not rule alone. They worked with a council, which acted also as court. There were two, perhaps three council members besides the squire and he chose them. They were the *amieene*, known for their wisdom and moderation; a reputation acquired by the very fact that they headed the largest residential kin-groups of the squire's village. He chose them, but they chose him. Any defection of such an important *wookuru*, with all his folk could be a very serious blow and it was rumoured that some squires were not above handing out *mbula* and even *ibuunu* to attract or to keep such leaders. This entailed that the council discussed matters on a footing of real equality, even though the squire was given such marks of respect as hearing his remarks being greeted by a respectful clapping of hands, before the debates began. In fact even the highest and mightiest lords or the kings had to live somewhere. And in their settlements their *amieene* were crucial. Thus Guiral saw the king consult his councillors and the powerful NGOBILA took advice from his men when a difficult palaver had arisen.[9]

Squires could come from only certain kinship groups which were collectively known as *baamukaana lilimpu*: 'those of the kindred of authority'. These were the kindreds to which the lords and the king also belonged. They constituted a political aristocracy, opposed to the *antsaana* or *ankieri*: 'the commoners' (Sims: (*M*)*unkere*: slave). In this, the Tio were similar to the populations east of them who divided society into an aristocracy, commoners called *antsana*, and slaves. Commoners could be *wookuru*, councillors, they could trade and grow wealthy, but they could not rule, at least not with authority. In Tio society, where so many statuses were achieved, this was still the prerogative of ascribed status. But then there was a spreading of the quality of aristocracy among all in a kindred and since marriages between aristocrats and commoners were frequent, the successful commoner could always hope to marry an aristocrat and beget potential rulers by her, or to have his female kinsfolk marry into the nobility.

[9] CH. DE MARTRIN DONOS, *Les Belges*, II, pp. 62–8 (the quarrel between Janssen and the ivory traders already alluded to). L. GUIRAL, *Le Congo*, p. 295. Guiral says they were former slaves. Since the word *nsuo* also meant 'councillor' as well as 'person given as pawn' (slave) according to Calloc'h, pp. 166, 266, this might explain it. But if the term is really identical, one would not expect the great power of councillors, which was stressed by Tio, laymen, councillors, and chiefs alike. There is something not right and Sims compounded it by giving (*M*)*unduo*: 'adviser' and *nduo* 'orders, learning'. Neither Sims nor Calloc'h reported *amieene*.

There is even a question as to whether squires really had to belong to the aristocracy. Speaking of the Boõ, two older informants, the MOTIIRI, a high official, and Bilankwi maintained that squires were not necessarily aristocrats, even if they were usually. This only emphasizes that the political régime was open for participation to commoners and thus strengthened their support for it.

The rules for succession were however not hard and fast. Succession to the office of squire went usually from father to son only after all male siblings in a generation had succeeded. An older sibling might be passed over if he was not mentally fit or if a younger sibling had become much wealthier. For it was felt that wealth was needed, if possible, to pay for the acquisition of more wives. Most of the squires appointed their heir before they died. The ideal was to pick the successor when he was still a boy and had shown himself to be a smart child. He was then trained, assisted at meetings and court cases and learned the secrets of the *nkira*. If a man died without successor, one was appointed and expected to learn about the *nkira* by dreams.[10]

But NGAATALI inherited from his own sister's son, who held the office from his mother's side. So the succession had not only been matrilineal but it descended a full generation. And his case was not unusual. Mbiinu Mbiinu stressed that between a younger brother, a sister's son and a child one often preferred the one who was more intelligent, but weighted this preference by considerations of age. A lord from the area of the Pool held that sisters' sons never succeeded but that one could have an *otioolu*, son of a daughter, for successor. Another one confirmed and stressed that women could never become squire, but there are cases on record of women squires. One ruled at Mpu aNdzã. Concrete data show cases of succession by anyone in the kindred except for the father's sister's children of which no examples were found. Sons and *otioolu* enjoyed a certain preference and there may even have been preferences on different parts of the plains. Thus in Mpũ *otioolu* seem to have had the advantage, at Mbe strict patrilineal succession was observed in some cases, and near the Pool a case or two where sister's sons did succeed are known.

In fact the data indicate only that the one in the kindred to succeed should have achieved the most impressive status in terms of reported ability, following (for the Tio a measure of ability) wealth and perhaps preference by the office-holder. The rules differed slightly from region to region, without being hard and fast anywhere. The part of achievement, competition and power politics in all of this is evident.

Once the successor was chosen and the predecessor buried, there was

[10] This mode of operation is not directly attested in any way, but was reconstructed as the most logical one. Somebody had to 'choose' and neither the other squires nor the lords did it. It is striking to see from the written sources how little was reported about squires compared to lords!

a feast to which all surrounding squires and the lords of the region came. They received wine and goats from the new office-holder who told them: 'See, today I am *ngántsii*.' Whoever came to the installation thus recognized the new squire. No formalities were observed. Once chosen by the main settlement of the domain, the man was squire. The choice had certainly involved discussion among the *amieene* and eventually other leaders of settlements. It was announced informally by them as soon as they reached agreement.

The data on succession show that despite the mystical link between *nkira* and squire, this was a political office. The office did carry authority and power, albeit on a modest scale. Politics overruled ideology sometimes, as becomes clear in a few cases known where new domains were created altogether, *nkira* and all. A former king, Ngateo told us, had thus given the forest *nciel a mfini*, which was 'empty' to Ondzaala and made him squire of Ontsuo. He even managed to convince an older man and his kin to settle there 'to give haunches' to the new squire. Ondzaala found a *nkira* in the forest and organized its cult. Obviously the 'empty' land had been taken from someone, a chief at Nkõ near Olwoono who had granted permission to the king for the amputation of part of his domain. Given the known military weakness of kings, it may have happened in this fashion. In this case anyway the new squire kept one haunch for himself and gave every second one to Kurukuru a political lord at Impe! This happened before Ngateo had grown up, at the latest then around 1910. Ngateo suspected that it happened before. There is no reason to doubt this story, because of its precise nature and the fact that the informant was not grinding any axe. Such stories are very rare because events of this nature gave the lie to the belief of a special innate link between squire and *nkira*. Therefore no one cared to remember such events.

Even in 1963 people believed and wanted to believe that the authority of the squire derived from the 'unbreakable mystical bond' which had always existed between the squire and the *nkira* of a domain. The role of power politics was pushed aside in order to preserve intact a faith that gave such backing to an authority that had little physical power behind it, a faith moreover which gave comfort and security to the inhabitants of every domain. They were protected.

2. *The lords*

Lords ruled over squires and over other lords. Their authority was recognized in all the domains which brought them *ingkura* and the number could vary with a switch from one lord to another by one or more squires. There were two levels of lords. Lords of the first rank received tribute from other lords as well as from squires. But even these high lords, as most of the others if not all, were squire somewhere in their own right. Squires or lords who paid tribute to other lords were his *nkani*. To be *nkani* further entailed that half of the tribute collected by the lower echelon be brought to the *nkani*'s lord, that the *nkani* went to the residence of his lord whenever called and conversely that the lord 'attach' a piece of cloth to the catafalque of his deceased *nkani*. For the whole kingdom there were no more than eight lords of the first rank and perhaps no more than twenty of the second level, although some at this level, notably Jinju chiefs such as NGWAMPOLO, were just as powerful as lords of the first rank.

Lords were ranked by the status of their *nkobi* in the hierarchy of *nkobi*. For their authority was grounded on the possession of a sacred object, the *nkobi*, kept always in a box, similar to the possession of a *nkira* by the squire and of the spirit Nkwe Mbali by the king.

The *nkobi* was an oval box made out of the middle part of the base by which palm leaves are attached to the tree. Lid and bottom were made separately. The top and bottom proper were made out of wood and the sides of palm-leaf were stitched to it. Any such box was a *nkobi* and anything could be kept in it, but usually it was a receptacle for charms or other sacralia, hence Sims: *inkunkobi*: 'box'. The *nkobi* of the lords were very much bigger than others and about as high as a pail since the wall was built up by stitching several overlapping lengths of palm leaf on top of one another. Along the Congo river at Mswata and perhaps among several Tio settlements on the right bank some *nkobi* had developed into regular box-stools, i.e. items shaped like a bobbin for yarn. One could be seated on the large wooden top of the box and the equally large wood bottom stood on the ground. This is what Sims called *nkobe*. These items were used by chiefs who concealed protective charms and other objects in their stoolbox. It fulfilled the role of the *likuba* cushion among the Tio of the plains. It is therefore not yet the *nkobi* of authority, the *nkobi* of the lords.

The *nkobi* was kept in a separate shrine house and covered with red cloth.[11] The contents were an absolute secret, even to the master of the *nkobi*. Only the kindred of those who opened the *nkobi*, an hereditary position in that kin group, could know. They alone could also transfer the contents to a new box, once the old bark box had become decrepit. No one could take anything from the contents and no one could add anything. At least that was what most informants contended in 1963. One, NgeImpio, held that one could add from time to time, but not take anything away. All were adamant about the fact that really no one but the opener of the *nkobi* knew its contents. According to LIPIE, these actually consisted usually of kaolin, camwood, three other sorts of red obtained from different type stones, *olivancillaria* both small and big ones, conus shells (*ona*), *Egeria Congica* shells, (*itibi*) originating in the lower Congo. Another lord, who had actually seen the contents of a

[11] Cf. figure no. 5 of *nkobi* in a house, with tiny ex voto's for it; also sketch of such a box next to a familial *nkobi*.

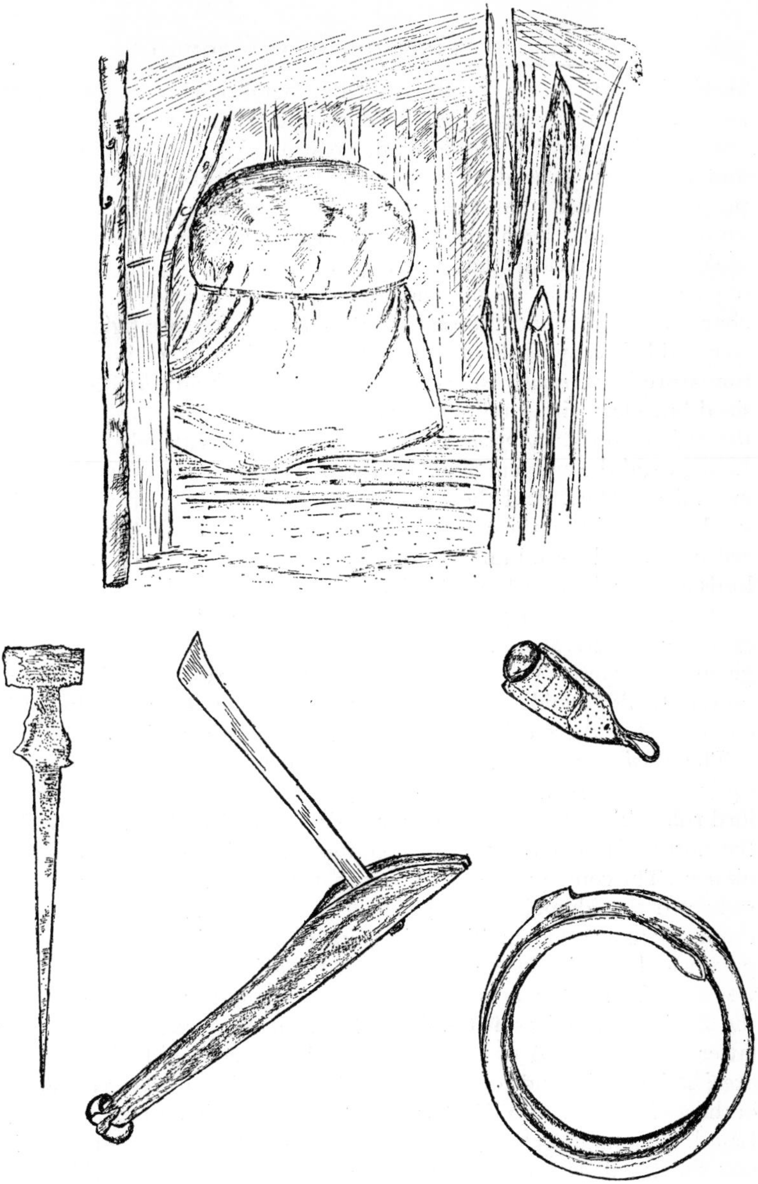

Fig. 5 *Nkobi Mbamwe* of NGAMPO in its shrine at Ngabe (1964)

(i) The *nkobi* is covered with red cloth. It is a lidded box with top and bottom of wood and sides of sewn bark. (ii) Other depicted objects, kept with the *nkobi* to honour it. They are: a model anvil (*ndzuunu*) sign of the greatest lords; a miniature bell with a clapper, also a sign of a lord; an adze, the insignium of office of lords and squires east of the River Congo, also in miniature; a brass wrist-ring of Vili manufacture representing a snake coiled upon itself, which is an object of *unũ* because it comes from the far-away coast.

nkobi, claimed there were also *viele*, i.e. metal objects, in these boxes, such as hammers, anvils, imported manillas called *ntsaa* (Sims: *ncaa*: 'authority'), *wara* bracelets and anklets worked in Nsundi and Loango, and necklaces of beads and cowries. It is important to realize that people contended that these objects had never been put there by humans but had been given in an original box by the spirit of the *nkobi*. Yet it is clear that the objects were *unũ* objects and sacred objects, such as the colours and shells which were also found in other charm boxes. Around the *nkobi* in its shrine, a few prestigious objects were added as symbols of its importance. These were items such as miniature bells, *mvuba* (signs of authority, lords held), anvils and full-sized bracelets, either red copper *ngiele* of a type known as 'the ring of the *ntsii*' or ordinary *ngiele* as well as brass rings with relief worked at Loango and the emblem of justice the *onia* broom. One of each was put around the *nkobi*. And these are no doubt objects which were added gradually as *viele* to the contents of the box itself. The fact that so many reflect *unũ* and were imports suggests a link between the power of the lords and the long distance trade.

It was crucial for the *nkobi* system that ordinary people, and perhaps even the masters, should not really know what the actual contents of a given *nkobi* were. The mystery enhanced its prestige and supposed power. It also avoided embarrassing questions as to the origins of its contents! For there existed official myths as to their origins.

The *nkobi* were linked with a *nkira* spirit, but unlike the case of the squires, this spirit did not necessarily live in the area over which the lord ruled. The spirits of the major *nkobi* south of the Lefini all lived to the north of that river and were connected with places on the Ntsaa plateau. The consequence of this was that the power of the *nkobi* was not restricted to a domain as was that of the squire's *nkira*. The political implications are evident. The *nkira* spirit of the *nkobi* was propitiated by prayer and sacrifice in the same way as the *nkira* of a squire was. There was a kindred of 'openers' at the shrine and another which lived near the abode of the *nkira* spirit and could be ordered to sacrifice there. The latter were supposed to know exactly where the *nkobi* had been. For *nkobi* had histories and could travel.[12] Thus the *mbuuru waashiõ* ('prayer') of the *nkobi* Livi of NGE ILIINO at Mbe lived at Etswali, north of the Lefini. The man in charge in 1963 was Inõ and the abode of the *nkira* was the wood *Mvula*, located just outside the domain in which Inõ lived. At Mbe the *mbuuru waadzulu*: 'opener' was the kindred of

[12] The 'prayer', i.e. the man near the abode of the *nkira* would recite the places where the *nkobi* had been when addressing the *nkira*, at least according to Ngateo. Mbiinu Mbiinu claimed the 'prayer' recited the name of all the previous masters of the *nkobi* he could remember and it was not necessary, nor in fact the case, that all the successive masters were remembered. Note also that when the *nkira* was not prayed to for a long time it became ineffective. 'It was said that it was dead' claimed Mbiinu Mbiinu.

Mbiinu Mbiinu and the latter was in charge. Since the last NGE ILIINO had never been replaced, Mbiinu Mbiinu had taken over the charge of squire for the domain Mbe and was thus both master and 'opener'.

The prestige of the *nkobi* was further enhanced by its titles. Names are very important to the Tio. The *nkobi* had its own name, e.g. Impãw, and its master also had a title, e.g. NGEIMPÃW. The latter did not necessarily have to correspond with the name of the *nkobi* although it often did: for example, the *nkobi* Ondzaala was kept by OPUU. In addition the *nkira* of the *nkobi* had its own name as well, and its abode was named too. To the *nkobi* Impãw corresponded the *nkira* Ngaalitõ which lived in the forest Kõnõ. Around each *nkobi* there was a basic lore. When, like Impãw, the *nkobi* was famous, stories both about its *nkira* and about its past had arisen. Ngaalitõ was supposed to live in a house with 'nine or twelve walls' (rooms) in the depths of the Kõnõ forest. What happened there according to Ngaayüo is typical of the mystery surrounding those mighty *nkira*:

I have heard about the house of Ngaalitõ with its nine rooms. The one who saw it, was Ngwamba, who cooked and had his house nearby. There were also other cooks (but no one else dared go there). When time for meals had come, Ngwamba went to the first room and rang the iron bell *mpã*. He entered and when he arrived in the next to last room, he left the food and went away. When he came back all was eaten. That is: they put the food in a huge bowl called *angambe*. The *nkira* ate and divided the food in two parts, placing the feather of the *inkuo* bird (a royal emblem) on one. This he then ate. The other part was for Ngwamba. When the *nkira* had finished, he too rang the *mpã* bell and the food was taken out.

Other things might belong to the body of folklore. Thus both for Ondzaala and Mbamwe thefts of the *nkobi* itself and miraculous happenings associated with that were remembered vividly. Whatever people said about *nkobi* was intended to show how important they were, how powerful and how interesting. In a sense these stories were foundation charters for the *nkobi*. To stress the power and the mystery there was also the fact that each new master had to go into isolation with the opener of the *nkobi*, usually for a ritual nine days. During that time he was initiated into the secrets of the *nkira*. It was a dangerous proceeding for the master, who might be killed by the very power of the *nkobi*, and for the people because he might kill people by witchcraft to offer them to his *nkira*. The ritual was called *lisee* exactly like the installation rituals for a king.

These awesome *nkobi* were graded according to their importance and a lord's rank followed accordingly. This was done not only with regard to lords who were *nkani* one to the other, but also for major lords who were not directly related in the hierarchy. It expressed thus the competition between the major lords. By 1963 the classifications were not uniform but expressed a person's political allegiances or beliefs rather than reflecting any concrete reality of hierarchy. The great *nkobi* were twelve in number and any list ideally gave twelve even if it turned out in counting that more were included. Two such lists are given below.

Clearly the rank of the *nkobi* derived to a large extent from the prestige of the lord who kept it. There were exceptions. The most famous *nkobi* kept the glamour associated with their history and thus helped to increase the rank of the lord who owned them. Then there were 'mother' and 'children' *nkobi*. The ingredients of the latter had come from the former. Evidently strong lords had created *nkobi* to reward followers and cement a *nkani* relationship or, more simply, to receive great gifts in return.

To mention, even in 1963, the creation of *nkobi* was as formidable a heresy as to admit that one knew the contents of a *nkobi*, and no doubt it was so during Iloo's reign. Yet NGAALIÕ himself told that one of his predecessors had taken the ash of the holy fire which the NGAALIÕ's have, put it in a *nkobi* and given it names, *nkira* and all, for a small NGAALIÕ, a minor lord in Mpũ. One of the major reasons kings 'invented' small *nkobi*, and the most powerful lords as well, was to increase the tribute system. A lord with a *nkobi* could request the *ingkura* from the squires. If too many squires depended from too few lords for an effective collection it was simple to create more lords by making more *nkobi*. And the very mystery of the *nkobi's* contents helped to disguise its origin. Also any talk in the open about its derivation was very quickly suppressed to preserve the political credo.

The *nkobi* ideology in its very complexity facilitated political instability. For myths were adaptable. Lords who rose in power struggles simply saw their *nkobi* rise on the political stock market, and conversely the *nkobi* of one who was on the wane came in for severe depreciation. The *nkobi* acted in Tio ideology very much as *baraka* did in northern Africa. The ideology was always adapted to the political reality and the myths, even about individual *nkobi*, were adapted as the need arose, not by any fiat but by the rumours among the people who saw that it did not work as expected.

A last and psychologically crucial point about the *nkobi* was that the one who held it bore the title, enjoyed the privileges, and received the power of its *nkira* as if it were a charm, provided only that he was an aristocrat. A celebrated case in Iloo's reign was the stealing by the great chief Ikukuri of the *nkobi* Mbamwe and the title NGAMPO, one of the highest in the land.[13] NGAMPO, the heir of the *nkobi*, said in 1963

[13] Brazza knew him as Ekukuri. Cf. H. BRUNSCHWIG, *La négociation*, p. 14. The story must have happened before 1880 when he had become one of the major lords near Mbe. The tradition is evidence for the role of the *nkobi* at this time, a role no writer heard about then. The quarrel between NGEILIINO and Ikukuri which some traditions link to this episode is of course directly reported as of 1884.

CHART 17 *Ranking of* nkobi

1° Mbiinu-Mbiinu

name of nkobi	*Lord and place kept*	*comments*
1 Nkwe Mbali	King	not a *nkobi*
2 Livi	NGEILIINO at Mbe	Mbiinu Mbiinu's own
3 Muyu	MUIDZU at Ntsaa/Abili	
4 Impãw	NGEIMPÃW at Abili	*nkani* of MUIDZU
5 Andziõ	NGANDZIÕ at Imbãw	not a *nkobi*
6 Ampo	NGAMPO at Ampo	the *nkobi* was Mbamwe
7 Liõ	NGAALIÕ at Opontaba's	not a *nkobi*
8 Ngampei	NGOBILA at Mswata	
9 Ondzaala	OPUU at Nkwũ	*nkani* of MUIDZU
10 Ngie	— at Mbe andzieli	minor *nkobi*
11 Oka	NGANTSU at Mpio a Bwaani	minor *nkobi*
12 Mvula	King of Ngenge at his Mbe	

No 1–3 reflect general hierarchy; 4 comes in as a *nkani* of 3; 5–7 gives further hierarchy of the major Lords on the Mbe plains; 8 and 9 are sudden remembrance of two major chiefs; 10 is a purely local *nkobi* of a now (1963) abandoned capital; 11 is an association with 8, and 12 is a great *nkobi* because the king of the Ngenge was practically independent. This is also the reason why it comes last. Note the emphasis on sites and titles associated with the Mbe plains. Mbiinu Mbiinu is Mbembe. His long stay on the Congo left some influence also, but he hid his political affiliations well.

2° Ngateo (second version)

name of nkobi	*Lord and place kept*	*comments*
1 Nkwe Mbali	king	not a *nkobi*
2 Liõ	NGAALIÕ at Opontaba's	
3 Muyu	MUIDZU at Ntsaa/Abili	
4 Ondzaala	OPUU at Nkwũ	*nkani* of MUIDZU
5 Impãw	NGEIMPÃW at Abili	*nkani* of MUIDZU
6 Mwangãw	MAYALA at Okuu	minor *nkobi*
7 —	IKAYULU at Ãkã	minor *nkobi*
8 Andzobo	NGANDZOBO at Impo	minor *nkobi*[a]
9 Likuba	NGAALIKUBA at Ibu	minor *nkobi*
10 Sinõ	MAMPIELE at Buambe	

[a] He reassessed Andzobo as the smallest one.

1 and 2 deal with major Lords at Mbe; 3–6; 8–9 are major and minor *nkobi* of the Ntsaa plains from where Ngateo came; 10 on the passage of the Lefini also can be seen as a chief of that plateau. Only 7 belonged to the south, in fact to Mpũ.

In his first version Ngateo with the five major *nkobi* of Ntsaa, followed it up by a set of three *nkobi* whose lords were linked in *1963* as one faction in a major political struggle, followed with four minor *nkobi* of Ntsaa and then six from Mpũ, to end with a major title around Mbe. After saying he was naming the twelve great *nkobi* he thus ended with nineteen names. Both the influence of his environment and past as well as political preference were clear.

that a diviner Nto put everyone at the residence of the NGAMPO to sleep with a spell and robbed the *nkobi*. He claimed it was stolen from a child of Ikukuri and the king ordered it to be returned after all the lords had met. The NGANDZIÕ in 1963, heir of the enemies of NGEILIINO Opontaba the great political opponent of Ikukuri had it that Nto stole it from Ikukuri and gave it to Opontaba. The leader of their faction NGANDZIÕ, who was allied with Ikukuri, had all the chiefs join and the *nkobi* returned. The NGAALIÕ of 1963, a descendant of the faction of Opontaba, had it that Ikukuri stole it and kept it. The truth seems to be something like the version of an old woman, Ngobabi, at Ngabe where the *nkobi* is kept. She said that the village Intali paid tribute to one of Ikukuri's children. At the death of the lord there, whose career had been in constant decline, Nto brought his *nkobi* to Ikukuri, after having put the mourners of the late *mpfõ* to sleep. All the lords met, but accepted the *fait accompli*. All the narrators agreed that whoever had the *nkobi*, held its power.

This was not an isolated case. Another major *nkobi*, Ondzaala, was stolen also after the death of the owner. The point in citing the different versions was to indicate again how myths about *nkobi* could be twisted. Even after eighty years, the original power struggles were still voiced by it. And in turn the story was one of the elements which kept the cleavages alive over all this time since 1881 when they started.[14]

Thus the detailed ideology of the *nkobi* was a glorification of power politics. Yet at the same time the *nkobi* provided a mystical basis for the authority of the lords, in a fashion similar but superior to the relation between *nkira* and squire.

The foundation myth for all *nkobi* develops another aspect of the ideology, while reinforcing the supernatural and mysterious attributes it had.

A first set of versions held essentially that one day a huge *nkobi* appeared at the king's capital after people from all over the area had been waiting for a very long time for it to appear. So many people had gathered that a famine ensued so that the Jinju left before the distribution by the king of the twelve *nkobi* inside the big one began. That is why they have none. The *nkira* who had 'given' all these *nkobi* was Nzã, the Creator himself or the *nkira* Obuu.[15] In this set of versions the

[14] By 1963–4 the NGAMPO was no longer a major factor in the opposition to the NGEILIINO, nor was the latter title even in use.

By then NGANDZIÕ, the weaker ally of Ikukuri, had become the focus of opposition to the king who had rallied the supporters of the NGEILIINO's. The beginning of the enmity dated back to 1881–2. For in 1880 both Ikukuri and Opontaba sided together to advise the king not to sign the treaty with Brazza (Ngateo). Two years later the power of Ikukuri was challenged by Opontaba. Cf. L. GUIRAL, op. cit., pp. 297–8.

[15] A set of versions, for in details and arrangement all sorts of variants were found. The myth was still living. Erudite Tio also combined it with other sets of versions.

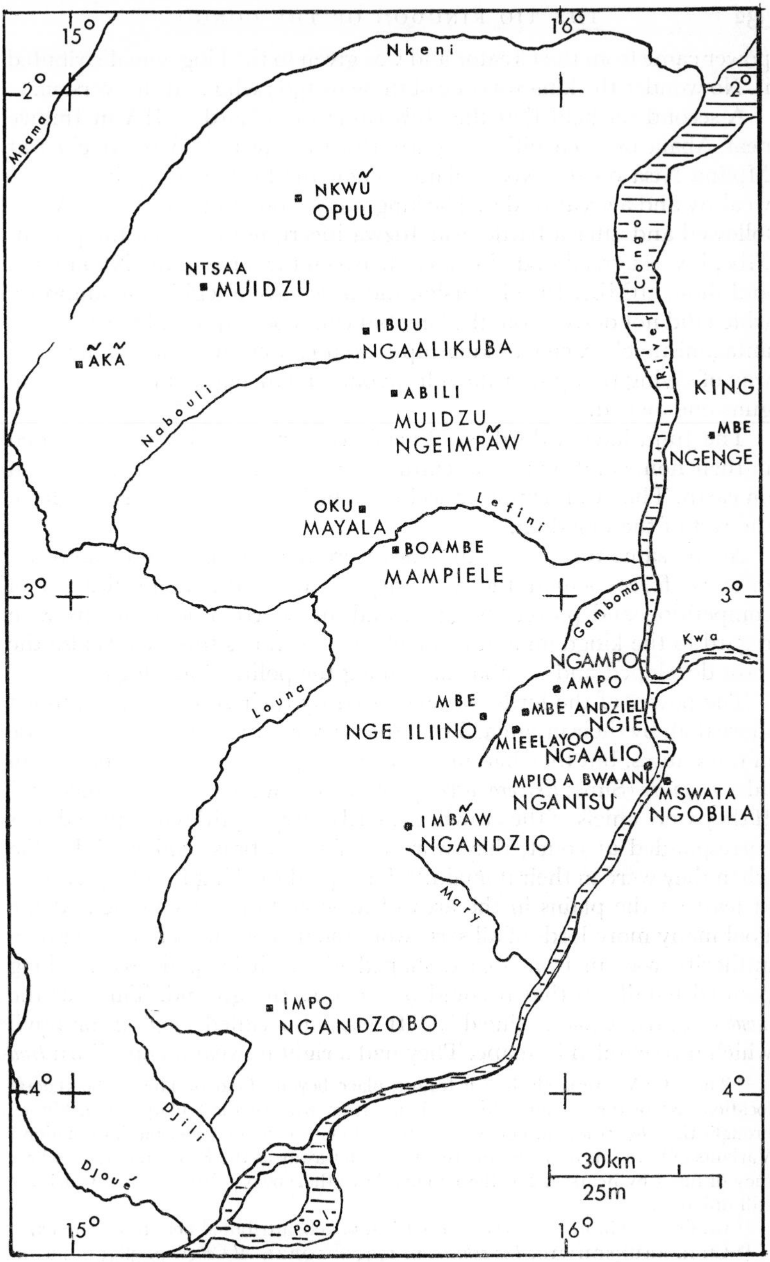

Map 11. *Spatial distribution of the nkobi ranked in Chart 17*

■ Ntsaa : Place names

MUIDZU: Titles of the major *nkobi* holders

power came from the Creator and was given to the king who distributed it. No wonder the king was one of those in 1963 who told this version.

A second set held that the *nkobi* came from Lord NGIA in Imbwe near Abala or even ultimately from further away.[16] A great chief at Mpiina Ntsa on the Ntsaa plain bought the twelve *nkobi*, for he was wealthy and a great trader. The king was jealous and stole them. A war followed and after a battle near Idzwa itieeri, not far from the present Mbe, it was agreed to divide them between the lords of the Ntsaa plain and those of Mbe. In this version the *nkobi* gave a legitimate authority which did not derive from the king but could be acquired by wealth. Its antagonistic character to kingship is well expressed. It was a mythical way of saying that power flows from one's following and the number of guns one owned.

The Jinju have a third set of versions. For them they were divided in their homeland by a local culture hero the NGANSHIBI, first man on earth. They thus express a feeling of being different politically from the rest of the kingdom.

At the same time, then, the *nkobi* were the legitimation of power, a mystical force behind the authority of the lords, a glorification of competition and power struggles, and an assertion of autonomy with regard to the kingdom and its ideologies. In Iloo's time it was also the most developed and flamboyant among the political ideologies.

The power of the lords was expressed by their style of living, much more than by their insignia. The latter were essentially the same as those of the squires, but they had more objects of prestige. Most lords had an adze *nkwuere* (Sims: *likwero* 'adze'); which was worn over the shoulder.[17] If they were chiefs of the crown, i.e. lords carrying titles to which duties corresponded at court, they wore the famous brass collar of the Tio when they were in their domain.[18] They paid the king for this privilege, at least on the plains in the area of Mbe and on the channel. At the Pool many more lords of all sorts wore them. The emblem of their own authority was an iron object, shaped like a little spade with a long pointed handle so that it could be stuck in the ground. This was the *mvuba* (Sims: *mvuba*: 'shield').[19] It was also called *ndzuunu* or anvil which it resembled in shape. They had a right to wear a cap (Sims: *lipu*

[16] The NGIA ultimately had it from a place beyond Okoyo. This is the general location also of the mythical Me Lo Kima from whence the Kukuya hero, Mubie, brought the *mpu* (titles, authority), according to P. BONNAFÉ (personal information). Variants of both sets of the myth are found as far away as the Kukuya plateau where they diffused by hearsay. For the Kukuya have their own political myths which are still different.

[17] Cf. drawing in H. JOHNSTON, *The River*, p. 298, attributed here to Opontaba.

[18] Cf. H. BRUNSCHWIG, *Les cahiers*, p. 173; E. ZORZI, *Al Congo*, p. 385; H. BRUNSCHWIG, *La négociation*, p. 30, where Brazea claimed that NGANTSU had paid a slave to obtain one. Cf. figure no. 6 of collar.

[19] H. BRUNSCHWIG, *La négociation*, p. 45, for a drawing (a double *mvuba* above a palm-tree).

s.*mpu* pl.), 'cap, hat, power'), a circular affair embroidered with threads of imported cloth, which is seen on the portraits of all major lords such as NGOBILA, NGEILIINO Opontaba, NGAALIÕ. Then there were the necklaces formed of brass or copper chains with long links, *mpaa*, the *wara* bracelets, the small necklace (Sims: *mukolo*) the staff (Sims: *mukana*), the fly whisk (Sims: *museo*, 'sceptre', the beautiful anklets of brass inlaid with lead or with iron, the long ornate pipes, the bracelets made with hair of the elephant's tail, and the red blankets which were very expensive. Then there was the exceptional object, such

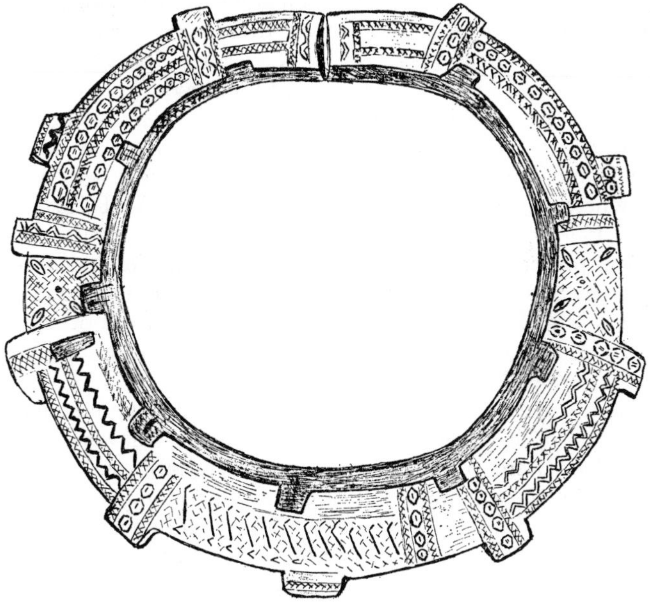

Fig. 6 The collar of the king's office: *õlua*

as NGANDZIÕ's bell made after the fashion of a European church bell, probably somewhere in the mining district. It had been cast in an alloy that looked silvery and was decorated with geometric lower Congo type motives. Toby jugs also belonged to these wonderful objects. The fact that they, rather than regular emblems, translated the lord's office fitted perfectly with the basic fact that the real foundation of any lord was the power he himself had been able to muster, just like his collection of curiosities. Similarly the state knives of Ubangi origin were *unũ* objects for many lords.[20]

[20] Cf. J. DYBOWSKI, *La route*, p. 55, ill; and figure no. 3 1963. These objects are said to be Ngbaka in origin.

Around the Pool other *insignia* were customary and most if not all lords wore them. There was the bun of hair with a long blue *liee* bead in it and ivory needles stuck into it. And then there was the cap with feathers (Sims: *sala*; 'state head dress'—really 'feathers'). These included the feather of *ndua*, blood red and of the highest rank, that of the bird *mbie*, an eloquent bird, the *nkenkene*, a bird that sees the future, the parrot which symbolized obstinacy and work, the *lindiandié* (swallow) which could help its master flee instantly from danger by soaring high in the sky together with some of his followers, symbolized by the *Bintsui-na-ntsui*, and the *libankoli*, or water eagle, an emblem of high authority just as the rooster's tail feather was the emblem of lower authority. All these feathers of the state dress were worn because these qualities were conferred magically on the wearer. For the same reason all Tio lords wore painted circles around their eyes. This allowed them to see in the other world. These chiefs of the Pool wore the brass collar, the fly whisk in the left hand and the adze or an axe of state in the other.[21] There the wearing of the shell *Egeria Congica* was also mentioned, whereas in the channel area, notably by NGANTSU, box-stools were in use.[22]

Magical protection was needed to ward off enemies and to increase one's power. Some lords were so loaded that they reminded de Brazza of 'Aeneas with his father and the palladium and the other gods of Troy'! In addition great lords always had a *ngàà* at hand, when they undertook serious business.[23]

The status of the lords was also shown in their ceremonials. The important lords had speakers and a throng of followers went with them.[24] They were preceded by music, if possible an orchestra of horns, metal bells, whether single or double and trumpets, an ensemble called *iõ* (Sims: *iyiño*, 'concertina'). What really mattered was the ceremony of the great salute (Sims: *buono mfumu*: 'prostrate to a king') whereby men and women and lesser squires or lords all came to kneel and bow to the ground, giving one hand into the hands of the lord, thus recognizing his superiority. This was known as the salute of the

[21] For the Pool area M. MAPULA, *Les chefs*, pp. 17–18; see an axe in A. MAHIEU, *La numismatique*, XXI, No. II, p. 21 photo. He mentions *mop̃a* (Sims: *mupaa*) p. 20, a shoulder-bag, the symbol of the power to collect tribute. This was a copy of the kongo *lukhoto*. J. DYBOWSKI, op. cit., pp. 62, 53 fig. 18, for head dress and clothing of Lord NTSUULU.

[22] E. D'ARTEVELLE, *Le N'zimbu*, p. 30; CH. DE CHAVANNES, *Avec Brazza*, p. 153. Drawing in P. AUGOUARD, *Le Congo*, p. 82 ill. (no origin given; it could be Bobangi too).

[23] H. BRUNSCHWIG, op. cit., p. 51 (citation in Italian); C. COQUERY, op. cit., p. 349.

[24] C. COQUERY, op. cit., p. 348 (speaker); H. BRUNSCHWIG, op. cit., p. 25. King Iloo told Brazza not to stay where he was because Opontaba was arriving and should see him only surrounded by his men.

mpfõ or of the *ntsii*.[25] Then there was the wine-drinking ceremonial in front of a numerous attendance with praise singers and assistants, described by De Brazza at lord Ngamfourou's (NGWAMPOLO?):

Then a major operation begins. The chief is about to drink. The beer is passed in a cup made of a calabash. A man sets himself back to back with the chief leaning his back against a third person [*sic*!]. A high official once again filters the beer and drinks a few mouthfuls, not from the cup, but from his hands. A fourth sticks a long needle [the *mvuba*?] in the ground next to the chief, on top of which a leaf rolled up as a funnel is put. A fifth takes two iron bars in his hand, which sound out. The person who supports the chief's back takes a leaf in his mouth and the operation begins. A praise singer sings. All the company sits down. The chief takes the cup, covers his head and his torso with a cloth, which he holds high with a knife. The one who holds the rods beats them one against the other and marks time. All the people present beat time. After having poured a few drops of beer next to the leaf, the chief drinks. The whole ceremony reminds one somewhat of the horses . . . to make them drink. Finally, only the chief has drunk; he spits three times the last draught next to the leaf. I forgot that before the ceremonial begins the chief has knotted a rope on his left hand, which is held respectfully by a man at the other end to prevent the chief from becoming drunk or rather, so that if he becomes drunk his head will not leave the body [*sic*].[26]

The great lords surrounded their houses with a palissade and a labyrinth. An iron bell hung from the door. Inside there was their courtyard, the *mbali* (Sims: *mbali*, 'yard, enclosure', 'place for sitting and assembly'). There they listened to court cases and palavers. When they were about to eat a little boy would ring the bell and anyone who wanted to could come and sit with the chief. If the lord was wealthy he would thus give food every day in porcelain dishes. The lord sat on his leopard skins, the others on mats. Music was made, everyone but the lord drank together and praises were sung.

Lords had many retainers. Their messengers would go when ordered bearing the lord's adze, his *mvuba* or any other personal object such as a comb[27] to bring his orders to squires and village leaders. These were not always slaves, for NGAALIÕ and the major lords on the Ntsaa and Djambala plains had groups of Atswa (Sims: *mucwa*: 'pygmy, bushmen') or pygmies as hunters and messengers. His *angabira*

[25] Calloc'h, p. 320: *li-bya:* 'grand salut pour le chef'. The great lords performed it for the king. Cf. H. BRUNSCHWIG, op. cit., p. 34, where NGOBILA refused to salute NGANTSU whereupon the latter decided he would not leave his house. Yet in theory he was *nkani* of NGOBILA. Cf. also pp. 46–47, when Bobangi came to greet Brazza. This text is the clearest in showing that the act consisted of kneeling and stretching one's hands to the lord who put his hands over those of the person paying homage. Many other references deal with the ceremonial (called N'ché by De Chavannes) at the court of the king. Lords had no right to the 'abject' homage the king was entitled to.

[26] H. BRUNSCHWIG, *Les cahiers*, p. 168. Many other descriptions exist. The next best with a drawing of the cup is E. ZORZI, pp. 389–90.

[27] CH. DE CHAVANNES, *Avec Brazza*, p. 235 (comb of NGANTSU's).

(Sims: *pira*, 'chief, captain, steward') as those helpers were called, were also sent on business to the markets.

Lords also kept a dozen wives or so. At the Pool only their daughters and wives could have their backs tattooed.[28] This grand style of living could not come simply from the tribute collected. It came not only from court fines but from the trade and the control the chiefs had over the exports of slaves and ivory and the imports of cloth. One story about the hero lord Nzã Mbã, who lived long before Iloo's reign, underlines not the splendour of his court but his ruthlessness. He ordered men to go hunting elephants and come back with tusks for the market. Anyone who did not come back with the tusks of an animal he had shot himself was taken away and sold as a slave. Whatever happened, the lord had an income. The same lord was known for making charges of adultery with one of his numerous wives against men, only to be able to sell them. The splendour and lavishness in food and drink had to be paid for by trade and the labour of the lords women and slaves. It was they who had grown the ten tons of groundnuts that Brazza saw lying more than a month after the harvest in the *mbali* of NGOBILA.[29] And then there was the labour he could require from any group of men in the area where he lived to repair his fences or build houses, clear paths, and carry goods.

Essentially then the style of life of a lord was linked to his revenue and revenue was a direct consequence of his power in men and guns, both to control trade and command people to work for him. As for the people they accepted this régime. To live without chiefs was to live like a flock of sheep[30] and to live near a great lord, was not only to bask in his glory but to be better protected against the vagaries of feuds and wars, even if the lord imposed his exactions. For after all, even lords needed people and could not overdo it, if they did not want to see the population of their villages melt away and the squires go to other lords to ask for protection.

The style of life was almost as important a foundation for a lord's authority as his *nkobi*. For success remained unchallenged. So the same term may mean: 'to rule a country' and 'to emit sparks' (Sims: *nie*). At any event people believed that when a lord was about to die a comet would fall at Mbã, at the Falls of the Lefini. For their style of rule was spectacular.

The rights and duties of lords were much vaguer than those of the

[28] D'UZES, *Le voyage*, p. 90: A Lord on the Pool had seventeen wives of which only one was free, the others being slaves. The first wife was a slave-woman; J. DYBOWSKI, op. cit., p. 54: Lord NTSUULU had ten wives installed in a closed palissade at Mpila by 1889; P. AUGOUARD, *Le Congo*, p. 19: NGOBILA had thirty wives, living in several enclosed compounds; TH. MENSE, *Anthropologie*, p. 626: Lord's daughters and wives only wear scarifications on their backs.

[29] H. BRUNSCHWIG, *La négociation*, p. 50.

[30] CH. DE CHAVANNES, op. cit., p. 161.

squires. They seem to have emphasized the protection they afforded in the same way as squires, by going out at dawn and dusk to address their village. They had councillors called *nkula mbali*: 'on the way to the court' and these had influence for the same reasons they had it with the squires, if less so. They received messengers from higher lords or from the king and transmitted the tribute, keeping half for them as the squires had done below them. They judged, often in appeal from the courts of the squires. Unless they were squires as well as lords no haunches were due to them but they received perhaps one hundred kola when the harvest was in and they could decree a tribute on meat. Thus Ngaliema wanted a pig that had been given to Bentley to be killed on the spot so that he could claim a shoulder.[31] What distinguished them from most of the squires in their rule was the frequency of the struggles with other lords in which they were involved. War as much as trade was their way to become more important. But otherwise essentially their rule was much like that of the village leader in his settlement.

The succession of lords was as indeterminate as that of squires though two predictable differences existed. Competition tended to be more frequent and more brutal. Thus when Opontaba died around 1895, NGANDZIÕ tried to take the title and the *nkobi* and give it to one of his children, according to Miandoo, a NGANDZIÕ supporter. NGANDZIÕ was matrilineally related to Opontaba and thus held a claim. But Opontaba's children prevented this: there was war and a fight at Ingiõ. The successors were Opontaba's children and NGANDZIÕ was thwarted.

The new lord had to be confirmed in his title, but not in his *nkobi*, by the king, if he held a royal title and would normally be entitled to wear a brass collar. Thus Opontaba's successor had to be confirmed, but not Ngaliema's, who was not a royal, but a slave grown wealthy. Most, in fact all, known lords except Ngaliema were also chiefs of the crown. And the succession gave some power to the king. The king had to send the collar, a *ndzu anna*, sign of the investiture and two bracelets, and his representative then gave these insignia to the successor in the presence of all the lords and squires of the area. All present then kneeled in front of the envoy, usually a lord of the capital Mbe and performed homage, the new lord included, after which they executed a special dance in front of the envoy, declaring that they were the 'wives', i.e. the *nkani* of the king.[32] In the case of Isu, king Ngaayüo went north of the Lefini and bargained there with the lords, taking gifts from two candidates

[31] H. BENTLEY, *Pioneering*, I, p. 351; *Coutumes*, p. 21.

[32] A. DOLISIE, *Notice*, pp. 44–5; E. ZORZI, op. cit., p. 385; H. BRUNSCHWIG, *Les cahiers*, pp. 173, 191; CH. DE CHAVANNES, op. cit., p. 368. The ceremony Dolisie describes probably took place in 1884 and is the one De Chavannes refers to in connexion with NGIA. Only members of the French establishment stressed the importance of collars. Congo Free State officials believed the king had no authority.

to the post and promoting the one lord to the post, then filling the now vacant post of that lord with another claimant. But he had to go with an armed retinue.

One effect of the system of succession was to allow very powerful lords or kings to collect titles of chiefs of the crown with the *nkobi* attached and to form a closely knit aristocracy which for one generation or two dominated the whole or the larger part of the kingdom. This is what Iloo's father seems to have succeeded in doing. He captured all the four major titles on the Mbe plains, and apparently those north as well, while the Jinju chiefs were drawn into the orbit by marrying the son to the daughter of the strongest lord (NGWAMPOLO?).

The squire was a village-leader writ large and the lord was like the squire in this. Both had the benefit of an ideology linking mystical forces to their rule, which the village leader had not. But in many other ways they were ruling in a very similar way. Their role was to protect, to make the good life possible. They should ward off witches, they should shield their people. The meaning of the feathers worn as emblems at the Pool shows what a good chief should be: to be a good orator and a good judge, to foresee the future, to be a persevering worker, to have the magic to flee danger with the people around him, all in addition to fighting witches and human enemies. At each level the role of being a protector is only made bigger.

Despite the mystical basis for authority, the politics of power were the same from the settlement to the level of the lords. It was always the same problem: to keep rival leaders from coming up in the settlement. Perhaps the best example is the case of 'Parrey' who went with Stanley to the Kwa, returned to Kinshasa and came home to Mswata in 1882 loaded with presents and basking in prestige. He was now a 'big man'. Rivalry between him and NGOBILA had to follow. After all, there were only eight free men in Mswata. Parrey's wife died. The diviner ruled that Parrey had done away with her. Parrey did not undergo an ordeal, but grew thinner and thinner. He fled to Opontaba finally and dying urged the latter to avenge him. Meanwhile the field was left to NGOBILA.[33] And only a few years earlier, NGOBILA had succeeded in ousting his brother who was the lord. Whether mad or not, the latter had killed too many people and everyone had taken refuge with the younger brother who finally took over the settlement, title of the crown, and *nkobi*.[34] Numerous other cases are reported.

So the situations, the reasons for conflict, the splits, and their outcomes, were much the same at all levels, because the aim was the same: to acquire power by taking the residence of the current leader. There were differences. In fact the lords had much greater power because of their slaves and their guns and this gave them a firmer nucleus than

[33] CH. DE MARTRIN DONOS, op. cit., II, pp. 122–5.
[34] H. JOHNSTON, *The River Congo*, p. 197.

either squires or village leaders could count on. The squire still had some authority from his *nkira*, but the village leader always had to work with an unsteady coalition of kinsmen that could fall apart at any time. So there were more splits, fusions, and scissions at the village level than in the domain or at the lord's residence.

But the greater power of the lord worked in other ways too. At this level, more than at others, external conflict threatened and attacks by other lords were potentially worse than those by squires or feuding villages. So the lords were more protectors than the squires and much more than the village leaders.

Beyond that lords had a unique role again because of their nucleus of force. They alone had the power to stop feuds and small wars, because their force was a deterrent, and because of their alliances with other lords to make the deterrent effective. In this fashion they represented law and order.

Chapter XIII
The Resolution of Conflict

STRIFE in Tio society was resolved through arbitration by assemblies, functioning now as court now as council, all using a similar procedure, the palaver. The inquest, *okuu*, was called to quieten conflict. Ordeals were a final peaceful but dramatic way to settle conflict. Force occurred in two major forms: feuds and wars. The major consequence of these techniques to resolve conflict, especially if force had been used, was to alter social status. For if a few people gained by it, many more drifted down into slavery. Slavery is so closely linked with the settlement of strife that it is added to a discussion of the palaver, the inquest *okuu*, the ordeals, feud and war.

1. *The palaver*

What political scientists call the decision-making process was for the Tio *ndoo*: 'words', the palaver. Matters were discussed in a group according to a set procedure whether the group was a set of kinsmen discussing bridewealth or *litsũ*, a court or a council. The description which follows discusses in particular the squire's or the lord's *mbali*. The procedure however is identical at the other meetings.

Pronouncing justice and being a chief of whatever order were closely related. The most unambiguous emblem of chieftainship, the broom *onyia* (Sims: *(M)unyaa*: 'speaker's brush')[1] was the emblem of the judge, who led court trials. Many cases never came to court. A quarrel within a single *ndzo* could be arbitrated by the *mpfõ andzo*, even in the case of manslaughter. The *mpfõ andzo* proposed a solution and the other members agreed to it, rather than break the solidarity of the group, bringing the case into court and having to pay court fines *iã* (Sims: *fura yaña*: 'pay for a crime'; *wolo yaña*: 'accept a fine'). In cases where two *ndzo* were involved in the same or near-by communities an informal moot involving *mpfõ andzo*, the village leaders and often the squire, would attempt to settle the matter before bringing it into court. The distinction between informal and court settlement is most difficult to make here however, because the procedure and the people participating were identical. The only difference was that the meeting was not held at the *mbali* but at another place. *Mpfõ andzo* also settled inheritance cases and presided over discussions about bridewealth and, more important, the counter-bridewealth *litsũ*. Cases involving the latter, however, often

[1] Cf. figure no. 7. These brooms were used by the Bobangi and the Mboshi in a similar way. Cf. E. ZORZI, *Al Congo*, p. 386.

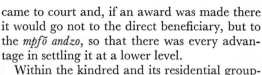

came to court and, if an award was made there it would go not to the direct beneficiary, but to the *mpfõ andzo,* so that there was every advantage in settling it at a lower level.

Within the kindred and its residential groupings, arbitration also played a role. Thus if two half-brothers of the same father but of different *ndzo* quarrelled, the father attempted a reconciliation, and called in both *mpfõ andzo* only if he failed. At a higher level, the village leader also arbitrated in conflicts between members of his settlement, even if murder was involved. The defendant in any of these situations had the choice, he could choose the court. Many village leaders did not like to arbitrate in serious matters involving witchcraft, bloodshed, or murder, for fear of creating a rift in the settle ment. So they would decline a proposition for handling the matter locally and call in the squire, or even a squire of another domain. The case was then still handled within the settlement rather than at the *mbali* and was still the squire's court and even compensation for murder, by the transfer of persons, could result.

There were thus slightly different groups involved all the way from a simple household quarrel to the squire's court. But the court was always the standard of justice, because it existed and any matter could always potentially be brought there. The evolution of a case of conflict was determined not so much by the nature of the case itself, which could deal with matters of trade, theft, adultery, matters involving marriage payments, quarrels, bloodshed, or murder, but rather by the stubbornness with which the parties stuck to their positions. Typically enough the hardest cases to settle out of court were matters dealing with women, including murders which most often had to do with women. Then the case went not only to court, but could be dragged from court to court. A typical instance was a case in which a certain Ngampa had a quarrel with Bankwa. He went

Fig. 7 A judge's broom of office: *onia*

to De Chavannes to settle it, while Bankwa went to the NGEILIINO, the most important chief of the crown.[2] The case involved a woman, probably adultery. Each party chose its court. Obviously Bankwa felt that he would get a better hearing because he had a better case with the Tio lord, while Ngampa banked on friendship with De Chavannes. The latter of course had no status as a squire but was considered the equivalent of a lord. Each party felt that the lord he had chosen was, for one reason or another, superior in prestige and power to the other so that the judgment could be enforced only by his lord and not the other one.

To claim that the lords, as representing the king, could be appealed to above the village headmen or the squires and as a first instance in important matters is to distort the process completely.[3] Everything depended on the parties and their determination to win the conflict or, on the contrary, their desire for arbitration and compromise. Therefore no clear judiciary structure with set levels of appeal existed at all. If a case was lost in one court, the loser could either pay or bring it to some more powerful authority, usually a lord, try to get it reversed in his favour and hope that the lord would enforce his court's decision. This procedure reminds one of the tactics of involvement in feuds and wars. It was a legal battle, but a battle nevertheless. The fluidity of the judiciary was its most typical feature.

Courts met when everyone involved was ready and often one or the other party waited a day or a week for witnesses or for the other party to arrive. Usually, even if the matter had been brought to two courts at once as in the Chavannes case, parties did not risk remaining unrepresented and would send defenders. Both parties frequently brought their *mpfõ andzo* or at least a mother's brother and any other relatives they felt were needed to assist them.

All being in readiness, the court opened its proceedings in the morning or early afternoon. Its 'president', the lord or squire, had his broom in his hand and at least two *amieene* as co-judges. The police of the court were provided by the speaker of the chief, if he had one.[4] The parties chose the *amieene* councillors they wanted to represent them among the personnel of the court. Often there were four, two for each side. The *amieene* could not refuse to represent a party. The defender had first choice. 'Personnel of the court' consisted of anyone in the audience which always included the older men of the settlement. Each party looked for a convincing orator and someone who could cite the right precedents. Yet *amieene* were not just attorneys, they helped to decide. Indeed it has happened that a court met without the squire or lord and four *amieene* tried the case. Everyone sat on the *mbali* or under a shed

[2] CH. DE CHAVANNES, *Avec Brazza*, p. 236.

[3] *Coutumes*, p. 41.

[4] CH. DE CHAVANNES, op. cit., p. 179. At the Pool this 'bailiff' wore a grass collar, had the iron bell of the lord presiding and held a rod.

with a 'bench' of the president of the court and the councillors on one side and the parties on the other and the trial could begin. Usually parties divided into two clusters at the other side. The audience stood where they liked all around the cleared space, but not behind the 'bench'.

The president then rose and opened the proceedings with a hallowed formula such as: *Ankani nkani mbuur amwaamwo*: 'Everyone now for himself', which was used more by pleaders than by the president, or *Woolo mana, mana ashili; mba lipfira ya nwẽẽi iloo kina*: 'Take some, leave some; those who one tries to deceive also see!' which meant 'think before you speak'. Then the contest began. The parties hoped to trip each other up and triumphantly gain the case. Yet the trial went on in an orderly fashion. The president began by hearing the complaining party, stating the case. Of course the councillors knew all about it beforehand and had in fact often discussed the case together when meeting for another trial. But this was official. Now the defender rose and rebutted. The hearing went back to the first party again until the charges and rebuttals were quite clear. The first statements were made by the plaintiff and defender in person, the follow-up being left to silver-tongued relatives, who knew how to electrify the audience with a clever proverb or could launch a catchy song. This was important since the audience could very well sway the judgment. Sometimes the speaker was interrupted briefly by a warning proverb from his own ranks or mockery in song or wit by the opposition. These songs and proverbs could hardly be called judicial rules as the following examples show:

'the master, the master, the master of the palaver, he knows it within the belly', a good one to open rebuttal with, meaning 'you cannot cheat me' (proverb).

'Take the animal that is seen on the hill' (good argument) (song).

'The bug will catch him first' (a warning, pay attention or you will lose the palaver) (song).

'If you go to the king, you cross the river Tsuubi' (money must be prepared before the trial) (proverb).

'This one says: everyone for himself; you say that you provided a fowl with its dress. The dress of the fowl, Nzã gave it' (meaning: 'you lie; prove it') (proverb).

After the opening sparring had slackened and the positions were clear, the time was ripe for one of the *amieene*, paid by his party, to suggest that his side should go to *ipfuuna*. That meant leaving the *mbali* and going into a huddle with his party, there to discuss whether to claim this or that, give in on some point or stick it out. Usually the councillor advised moderation while the original client was rather hot-headed. The relatives were often the decisive voice at *ipfuuna*. The spokesman returned, often sang a song prefiguring what was to follow and then stated the position of his clients. If the proposal was interesting, the other party went into *ipfuuna* on its own and it was common for courts to have a succession of *ipfuuna* in which the parties adjusted their claims and counter-claims and inched closer to an agreement. They could meet in *ipfuuna* both at the same time and send messengers from one to the other. The essential work of the *amieene* was thus to arrive at an agreement by common consent. They were also called *antsuo* which Sims translated correctly as *ncuo*: 'go-between, interpreter, spokesman, translator, judge, peace maker, middleman in the trade'. The same spirit is evident from his: *lano* 'judge, condemn; talk one to another'; *lana andoo*, 'judge', *ngalano*, 'peace maker, orator'. *Ipfuuna* served to effectuate this mediation which was so essential for a good settlement.

The legal reasoning used made much of reasoning by analogy. By 1963 at least a real jurisprudence existed,[5] with specific rulings being cited on tariffs or fines, e.g. for adultery. Much less clear was the role of jurisprudence in deciding what constituted an offence and what did not. The law was not divorced from the general feeling people had about norms. Legal norms were social norms and the feeling for justice seems to have been stronger than technical points. Playing on loopholes in the law seems not to have occurred.

Procedural rules were clear: no testimony irrelevant to the case could be brought up and this included testimony about the character of the parties, if the individuals were known to members of the court before the hearing. Sometimes such evidence was listened to, but never was one allowed to go into previous court cases the defendant or plaintiff might have defended. Thus one could not argue that the man's position was weak because he was quarrelsome and was always taking things to court, etc. When irrelevant material came up, the speaker was stopped by the president or the *amieene* of the other party.

Witnesses could be heard at almost any time after the opening statement and were called by the interested parties. Their depositions carried greater weight than most oaths or any other evidence except the ordeals. For oaths were also heard (Sims: *mukii*; 'oath'; *loo mukiu*; 'swear an oath'). People swore on their mothers, their cloth, their hair, Nzã, the *apfu*, the ashes of the dead. But it was only when they swore on the deceased elders of their kindred or *ndzo* that the oath was taken seriously. And to swear by Nkwe Mbali, the national *nkira* of the king, was considered absolute proof of the truth.[6] Proof by ordeal was even

[5] On jurisprudence or substantive law no data from the period were available, except for the general feeling that things were then what they were in 1963, but gradual changes in these matters could have occurred, much more unnoticed than in the formal procedure of witnesses and oaths, which are also said to have remained unchanged between 1880 and 1963.

[6] For the minor oaths see Calloc'h, p. 249; E. COART, A. DE HAULLEVILLE, *La religion*, p. 216, described a private oath. Both persons swallowed some earth and said: 'May the earth which has received this oath kill me if I lie.' Such private oaths were not acceptable. They were more in the nature of a private contract about an item that should be done.

better. The *ĩkwà* of a hunter was usually only brought in cases of accusations of witchcraft and had to be substantiated by further ordeals. All proofs were called *mpiõ*, a technical term. The validity of 'proof' was acknowledged when one party traced a line of kaolin on the arm of the other, or one party made a payment to the president who then traced a *mpiõ* line on the arm of the other.[7] A party could also deposit a payment, such as an *ibuunu* before the court as an indication of the truth of their statement. A last form of evidence in proof was a confession of lying called *ikia*. This was accepted without further question.

Thus between *ipfuuna*, the hearing of witnesses or the provision of other proof proceeded and each exposition was followed by new proposals and new *ipfuuna*. The proceedings were necessarily long. For if a court was a contest, it was also a place where a solution had to be found to the conflict. An imposed solution was sometimes necessary. More often the court knew that it could not really enforce the decision since it had no police force. The usual pattern was to leave the execution of the sentence to people at the hearings, designated then and there, but they were more witnesses to the sentence than responsible for its execution. Only great lords with more than just a few retainers had the power to enforce their court's decisions. So an imposed solution was impractical in most cases and mutual agreement had to be reached. This would then be announced as the verdict of the court by the president. In many cases the whole procedure amounted to a protracted bargaining between the parties with the court acting as a go-between.

When finally, sometimes after days of palaver, an agreement was in the offing, or when it became evident that no side would yield, the councillors for each party went off for a last time with their clients, then all returned and the councillors together now reached a decision which they communicated to the president of the court. The latter had to accept their opinion. These *amieene* were supposed to rule about innocence or guilt regardless of client, but one rather suspects that the *amieene* for each party held out for a settlement most favourable to their client, because they had espoused that cause all along and perhaps because they were paid by that party, for the defending party paid the *amieene*. The venality of judges was part of the system, and in 1963 at least some Tio said that even an innocent man might try to pay heavily to convince the *amieene* of his innocence, citing cases and amounts, for this was done quite openly.

The president then announced the judgment preceding his words with a song and a flourish of his broom *onia*. The song, always the same, ran: 'Man is your kin. Man speaks, currency does not. If you die, your friend will bury you, currency will not; currency is naught; don't forget your friend for currency. Each one on his own now: if you take

[7] A. MAURICE, *Stanley*, p. 123. Stanley drew such a line, from wrist to shoulder on Ngaliema's arm to back up the latter's statement that he had not sold the country.

one way, the other will stay' and pronounced the verdict, usually a fine. To announce a verdict was 'to cut the palaver' *tsira ndoo* (Sims: *cira andoo*; 'decide or settle a matter'; *cira*, 'cut'). The fine *iã* was the compromise reached by the parties or, if there had been none, it was an imposed solution 'cutting' the affair. Both the judge and the parties knew that there would be an appeal somewhere else, because the losers would refuse to pay and the winners would have to have the verdict renewed. Or perhaps the losers hoped to reverse the verdict. But the judge could also proclaim recourse to an ordeal, such as *lindaa* for thieves or the poison ordeal for witches, which could not be refused by the parties. To refuse was to admit guilt outright. The fine then went to the winning party as compensation.

The judge also announced the court costs to be paid to him, the president of the court. These were *ikwor'onia* ('the handle of the broom') or *itieeri*, just like the name for the first pieces of cloth paid as bridewealth. The amount of the court costs varied from court to court and reflected directly on the position and the relative power of the judge. They charged what they could, given the competition of other courts.[8] It used to be about one *ibuunu* for the court of a small lord or that of an important squire at a time when bridewealth was from 20–5 *ibuunu*. Both winner and loser had to pay the sum specified and half went to the judge, the other half being the official payment of the councillors.

In addition to the fine, the president of the court added another sum to be paid not to the winner but to him. This was always proportionate to the total fine and might be as much as about one eighth of the total.[9] It was attributed to the judge alone, being part of the *iã* and not court costs. Legally it can be seen as the fine paid for having created a public disturbance. Its counterpart should have been the possibility of having the verdict carried out. But all the judge could do and would do in cases as serious as witchcraft was, if he was a small squire, either to have the guilty party murdered by his *amieene* after having warned the lord of which he was a *nkani*, or to send the matter itself to the court of the lord. The lord then announced in court that he would have the witch killed. Whereupon the witch and his followers left the area to go and put themselves under the protection of one of the biggest lords in the land, such as MUIDZU. Ngateo remembered having heard of exactly such a case.

If the decision was to sell a person as a slave or to kill him, said Ngateo, such a sentence was rarely announced in public. The judge preferred to wait and catch the culprit by surprise *but publicly*. He was then killed or a grass ring was put around his neck and he was shackled

[8] In 1963–4 court costs at the royal court were 1,000 Fr CFA, 850 at Lord Mayala's court at Bouambé and 750 at courts of other big lords.

[9] In a case of adultery for instance 17,500 Fr CFA went to the husband and 2,500 to the judge, and this was also considered part of the fine.

and sent with one of the *mpfõ*'s men to be sold at Mpila. But Miandoo disagreed. A court did not have right over life and death. Obviously however the right of the mightiest seems to have prevailed. Ngateo remarked that formerly only great lords would dare to execute someone. For if a smaller lord or squire tried, a feud would erupt against him. Fear of the power of a lord alone could prevent this. Also only a great lord could sentence a smaller one and that without even holding a *mbali*. He set a fine and if it was not paid, he attacked the capital of the small *mpfõ*, captured some of his people and sold them into slavery. On the other hand, cases where *mpfõ* were plaintiffs and others defendants were often settled out of hand. It all depended on the actual might of the judging lord. If he was strong enough he might for instance ask for a woman in payment for a goat that had been stolen from him. His very arbitrariness was the measure of the power of a great lord.

This arbitrariness of the system itself explains the pattern of appeals. The parties appealed to a more powerful lord. Thus they increased the stakes since the court costs were higher and the fines were much heavier. But the winner was also more assured that the sentence would be carried out. Usually the lines of appeal followed the relations of dependence of the chiefs. One appealed to the lord whose *nkani* was the squire who had settled the case previously. Ultimately the most important or stubborn cases ended in the court of MUIDZU or the royal court headed by the NGEILIINO and NGAASAA, first wife of the king. No appeal was possible once one of these courts had reached a decision. There was thus no judiciary unity in the kingdom and could be none. Accepting cases in appeal meant vying with other lords for superiority. If this had been allowed at the highest levels, the kingdom would fall apart. A dissent between MUIDZU and NGEILIINO for instance would pit all the lands north of the Lefini against all those south of that river. Moreover those two lords were powerful enough to enforce their verdicts, even by war.

Courts existed to resolve conflicts. But because conflicts between great lords could not be settled peacefully, a thorough or more regular organization of the judiciary structure itself became impossible.

A few nineteenth century cases involving great lords show how power influenced settlement and shows the bargaining involved in reaching one. In one case the court of NGOBILA tried to settle a trade dispute between Janssen at Mswata and ivory traders from the right bank. But Janssen would not agree. A second trial was held when NGOBILA himself presided over the court and finally Janssen was persuaded to add 50 *mitako* to the price he had paid before. In another case, a squire Makole tried a Zanzibari who had entered a house without call, and had been wounded by the irate owner, whereupon he had shot the man. The Zanzibari was sentenced to be killed, but that was only a first declaration. After protracted bargaining a fine was agreed upon by both parties. The case of the war between NGOBILA and NGEILIINO Opontaba shows even more strikingly how power and justice were related. First Janssen negotiated a truce and a peace-settlement between the parties, whereupon both agreed to submit any future cases to his court.[10]

Along the river and at the Pool there were mixed Bobangi/Tio courts for mixed villages. The councillors were men who had sat in the audience at numerous Tio and Bobangi cases, so they knew the differences in customary law. But in major cases the Tio lord ruled. Thus a Bobangi who had killed another Bobangi near Mfwa was fined 500 to 600 *mitako* by the Tio lord.[11] The French very soon tried any cases which involved their men and their possessions. Thus a few months after his installation De Chavannes clapped a local person in jail for having stolen a boat and handled the case all by himself, despite the protests of the Tio lord.[12] As time progressed Europeans on both sides of the Pool began to take over more and more serious cases.

Court procedure also ruled councils. Travellers have described them and the *ipfuuna* have been noticed although not understood. The bargaining character of such meetings and the need to arrive at a common stand were also overlooked. Thus the Tio remember that at the meeting at which Iloo gave some of his earth to Brazza and signed the treaty, the chiefs Opontaba and Ikukuri both advised him at an *ipfuuna* not to do so, whereas it seems that the NGANSHIBI was in favour of the treaty.[13]

2. *Okuu inquest*

Witchcraft could be blocked without finding the witches within a kindred or *ndzo* by the inquest or ritual *okuu*. When a person was seriously ill, his *mpfõ andzo* would be called by a close relative, the father, if he still lived, or a brother, to come and hold *okuu*. The *ndzo* on the father's side was also present. Often the local squire came as well. The gatherings usually consisted of men only, perhaps fifteen or so in all. The procedure of *okuu* was that of a palaver. Either the *mpfõ andzo* or the father of the patient opened with a 'Now each one for himself' and

[10] CH. DE MARTRIN DONOS, *Les Belges*, II, pp. 66, 115–17, 134.

[11] E. ZORZI, op. cit., p. 404, for mixed villages; E. DUPONT, *Lettres*, p. 257 (Mfwa: the rationale was that blood had been shed on the lord's territory).

[12] E. ZORZI, op. cit., pp. 437–9; CH. DE CHAVANNES, op. cit., pp. 220–1. It was on 30 or 31 October 1884 a few months after his installation. NGIA, the lord and Opontaba the NGEILIINO had tried to take the case in hand (rather in the fashion of NGOBILA with Janssen) but De Chavannes had dismissed their intervention.

[13] H. BRUNSCHWIG, *La négociation*, p. 33, relates that Makoko told him to stand aside so that the Tio could discuss their position. Also L. GUIRAL, *Le Congo*, pp. 291–2, where the palaver went over the amount of goods that should be given to chiefs NGEILIINO and NGAALIÕ and their counter-gift to Guiral. Cf. also C. COQUERY, *Brazza*, pp. 348, 350 and CH. DE CHAVANNES, op. cit., pp. 179, 371–5. Calloc'h had p. 166: 'tenir conseil': *kura ipfuna* and 'conseil': *i-pfuna*; also 'deliberation' p. 180, *i-pfuna*; Sims: *ipfuni*, 'secret, conspiracy' underlines the privacy of *ipfuna*.

summarized the situation. X was ill and there had been suspicions. He went into the social history of the relatives of X, and accusations which had been thought about himself, the complaints he had against lack of respect other members had shown, and then he left for *ipfuuna*. He returned with a payment of beer or wine and a small sum for 'the head of the ill person(s)'. This was a disclaimer of witchcraft and a promise not to bewitch in the future, even if one had done so in the past. The drink was shared and accepted whereupon the leader of the other *ndzo* sang a song or said a proverb showing he accepted the statements made.

After this the party went to *ipfuuna* and made its declaration, prefacing it again with a proverb or songs. Similar payment for 'the head of the ill person' was made and, if necessary, the head of the *ndzo* or of the father's *ndzo* executed some symbolic action showing that all was now finished. Thus in 1963 the *mpfõ andzo* once put some pimento on the face of the sick person and poured some water in front of the house of the other head for the father's *ndzo*. Very often the *ngàà* who was handling the patient was there and would receive some drug to use in the cure of his patient. On occasion the *ngàà* could call an *okuu* if he felt that there was witchcraft in the *ndzo* or *ibuuru*.

Similarly *okuu* could also be held when a man's hunting was consistently unsuccessful. That too indicated witchcraft, and could be the work of women as well as of men. So women were called to the *okuu* if they were suspected. In one recorded case of 1963, a mother's brother accepted the responsibility, explained why he had put this witchcraft on his nephew, gave a token of good faith to the latter and received in return the promise that when luck in the chase changed, the nephew would pay him a specified sum of money.

Okuu were reconciliations between allied *ndzo* and other *ibuuru* members whose grudges might have led directly or indirectly to illness or bad luck at hunting. Often 'foreign witches' were thought to take advantage of quarrels within an *ibuuru* to kill and escape suspicion. *Okuu* was also an occasion to formulate grievances and air suspicions which were accepted by all parties. The formal promise to live in harmony and the reassertion of kinship solidarity went along with a reaffirmation of unity towards the outside and its 'stranger witches' who were often formally warned at the *okuu*. At the same time *okuu* was a ritual destined to boost the morale of the sick person and his close relatives. Both in its aim of overcoming rifts and reaffirming unity and in its role as a healing ritual the inquest differed from the court whose procedures it adopted.[14]

[14] Cf. Appendix No. 11 for several cases of modern *okuu*. *Okuu* certainly goes back to the 1880s although dictionary indications are uncertain and no writers report about it. Its existence of old was claimed by all Tio who were asked about it. The fact that the institution exists all over the Bateke world, including the Kukuya (BONNAFÉ, personal information) rather supports these assertions.

3. *Ordeals*

Several ordeals were in use and all the important ones, especially the poison ordeal, were ordered by courts. The major forms were the introduction of pepper into the eyes, the ordeal of the red-hot knife or of the ring in boiling oil and the poison ordeal.[15] In the pepper ordeal, the eyes of the patient were not supposed to get inflamed when chili pepper was rubbed in them. We do not know on which occasions it was used. The ordeals of the red hot knife (Sims: *za ikuiku*, *za nkanku*, 'to undergo (eat) hot knife ordeal') and the ring ordeal, *lindaa* (Sims: *lindaa*, 'ring') were used mainly by men to show that they were not thieves and by women that they were not witches.

Lindaa was well remembered at Mbe and had been in use until just before 1963. A woman nicknamed *lindaa* who was over eighty years old and died in 1964 had undergone it no less than three times. She had been the third wife of a squire, who accused her of bewitching him as he had no success at hunting. Every time she 'ate' *lindaa*. The preparations consisted in making a fire with *kuru*, a kind of camwood, and pouring two bottles of oil in a pot put on it after which the copper ring was put in the pot. The woman approached saying: 'You fire, if I am not guilty diminish' and it diminished. She took the ring without burning her fingers. If a person was guilty it was believed that the fire instead of diminishing, flamed up and could even engulf the guilty person. Three times the woman *lindaa* escaped with shouts of admiration from the bystanders. If she had been burned her husband could have killed and burned her as a witch without further ordeals, only forfeiting the *litsũ*. In a well-known case of theft, on the other hand, the man who underwent *lindaa* burned his fingers. He was then condemned to reimbursement and left the area in shame.

A slightly different type of ordeal was that of the palm-kernel. Someone rubbed a palm-kernel on his head and threw it in the water. If he was not *ndoo*, i.e. victim of witchcraft, it went to the bottom. Otherwise it floated. If he was *ndoo* they made *kaa* to protect him and tried to uncover the witch. This was much more a form of divination than a true ordeal.

The poison ordeal was the test *par excellence* to detect and punish witches and male adulterers. Women did not take it. There were two ways of bringing men to undergo the ordeal. First the party who had lost a member and had gone to its diviners and received *ĩkwa* proof from a hunter, went to the court, which delegated an observer to go with

[15] Calloc'h, p. 207: 'épreuve', mentions: 'of the red-hot knife', *imbyel'a mbaa*; 'of boiling oil', *nju a mali* (this is the ordeal with the ring), 'because one becomes too wealthy', *lyeme*; 'pimento in the eyes', *lidzi*. He did not include the poison ordeal which he cites p. 200 *wa nkaya*: 'empoisonner officiellement'. The *lyeme* and *lidzi* ordeals were not mentioned elsewhere.

them to a *vàà mbulu*. If the man was guilty the *vàà* announced formally in front of the accused: 'you, you are a witch'. Then the man had to take the test. Within the same *ndzo*, a *mpfõ a ndzo* could also request it and, if the circumstantial evidence was strong, the accused had no choice but to undergo it. If he refused and was not a wealthy man he could be sold by order of the squire or lord (usually the latter) and half of the proceeds went to the squire or lord. If the man was wealthy and refused to take the test he and his *ndzo* paid for a replacement for the deceased person. This was sometimes far more expensive. Thus Ngaliema had to buy off an accusation at Mpila against one of his nephews by paying seven slaves and one tusk. Stanley adds: that if he had been poor he would certainly have been burned.[16]

If the test (Sims: *ibuunu*, 'poison test'; *nkee*: 'poison') called *nkei* was taken[17] the accusers would put up three men as pawns and lose them to the accused if he turned out to be innocent. Otherwise the *ibuuru* of the accused would pay a person to compensate for the death of the person killed by the witch.

There was also *iuula*. *Iuula* was a payment of great value deposited by both parties before the test. Many times the guilty party would much prefer to pay the fine than to drink *nkei* and perhaps lose both his life and *iuula*. Proceedings with regard to adultery often started as follows: A accused B; 'If you say, you did not steal my wife, drink the poison; if you live you get X; if you have stolen my wife, you pay the fine agreed upon by the court (usually equivalent to a slave) and you get the *iuula* back'.

The poison itself was drunk in the evening within the house and was given in a shallow piece of pottery. The accused drank three times and then vomited for three or four hours. When the sun rose he went to the bush, sat down and drank one or more calabashes of water. Then he jumped three times in the rope. After that he was presumed innocent. The guilty person would not vomit, or not as much, and would certainly die when drinking the calabashes of water in the morning. In that case an autopsy was performed and the *ifi* or witchcraft substance taken out and hung in a tree as proof. The body was burned to destroy the *okwii* of the witch.[18]

Accusations were frequent. Both Ngateo and Ubwoono remembered an average of three to four cases per year in their youth. Almost none

[16] H. STANLEY, *The Congo*, I, p. 380.

[17] The existence of the test is attested by C. COQUILHAT, *Sur le Haut Congo*, p. 59 and CH. LIEBRECHTS, *Léopoldville*, p. 534 as well as H. JOHNSTON, *Grenfell*, II, p. 689. None of the sources gave any details, probably because none was an eyewitness.

[18] The ceremonial or ritual of the test is only described by Tio informants in a sketchy way, perhaps because they were small children when they saw the last cases, perhaps out of reticence with regard to anti-ordeal laws in force by 1963. Whatever the reason, there is not enough evidence to even estimate how elaborate the ordeal was as ritual, let alone to discover what its ritual meanings were.

of the accused refused to drink because they wanted to be cleared by the test for good. The test did not really perform this because it was believed that if the *ifi* was lodged in the calf of the witch he would not die. The second time he took *nkei* some of the poison would be rubbed on his leg. If he survived that he was truly innocent.

The proceedings took place under the supervision of the squire or lord. He sent a knowledgeable man to fetch the plant but it was to be prepared for the test by the kindred of the accused, so there could be no disavowal of it later. According to Ba, if a person was accused by a fellow member in the *ibuuru* and refused to drink, he was killed without more ado. Ubwoono recalled persons caught and bound with iron-strong ropes made of raphia palm thread and burned by being thrown in boiling palm-oil, without any ordeal. From the *lindaa* cases cited it has been seen that women could be killed in this way after the *lindaa* test. Most cases seem to have occurred within one *ibuuru* and several *ndzo*.

It seems clear that the intervention of the squire or lord was always required when a 'stranger', i.e. someone who did not belong to the *ndzo* or *ibuuru*, was involved. It was believed by all Tio informants that the accused always requested the ordeal in such a case to clear his name. If he did not, the squire would not order the test at all. The aggrieved party would then try to take the accused by surprise and shoot him, thus starting a feud.

The poison ordeal was the expression of serious conflict. Accusations were levelled only against men, that is only men drank it. It happened several times a year in a neighbourhood and it seems to have involved the leaders. In fact it was the most used and potent weapon in the struggle for leadership and even in 1963 Tio leaders were very well aware of the potential of a witchcraft accusation and the test. Yet lords or even squires seem not to have drunk it much, partly because they headed the courts who ordered the tests and partly because a weaker party, a commoner for instance, would never successfully accuse them in another court unless the lord there was much more powerful than the accused squire or lord. As a matter of course, competing lords accused one another of witchcraft and refused to take a test. If some lord attempted to force another to take the test, there would be war first. As for lords of the very highest rank, no one really doubted that they were witches and they may have boasted of it.[19] So accusations and ordeals were the main weapons at the level of intra-settlement quarrels or even conflict between village leaders, just as feuds were the expression of conflict at the level of settlement against settlement or war at the level of squires and lords.

The poison ordeal not only detected a witch, but killed him, in which

[19] W. BENTLEY, *Pioneering*, I, p. 346. Ngaliema in effect challenged anyone to stop him being a witch, if he was one.

it differs from all other divination techniques or ordeals. By 1958 there were alternative techniques for ferreting out and make witches innocuous. There was a ritual for witch hunting which was supposed to flush out all the witches in a settlement, and there are reasons to believe that it was an old technique.[20] This ritual was used when crisis after crisis had brought the tensions in larger settlements to breaking point. Demoralization became very great and the people yearned for something that would, in one stroke, do away with all the *apfu* spirits, so that death, illness, and misfortune could be checked. The situation must be described from recent cases since older data are not available. In settlement X, an epidemic struck in 1958. Seven children died and people began to accuse the official leader of the settlement. In desperation the latter called Mp a renowned Kongo *ngàà* of Brazzaville. On his arrival he asked all the women to bring firewood to the place where he would divine and put the settlement right again. The head of the settlement presented the leaders of each of the quarters and Mp put a rope around their necks. He then asked for a gun and began stalking through the settlement. Suddenly he saw an *apfu* behind O's house. It fled into Mw's house, the *ngàà* went after it and came out with a wooden statuette taken there. He returned to the plaza singing: 'Say to the *ngàà*, the charm is clever, oh the *ngàà*.' When the song was over he told the head that all his men were not there and that the one who was missing was the witch responsible. He waited for a while and then set out to fetch the witch. He went straight to Mw's house, found him in front of the dwelling, took him by the arm and brought him back. The next morning the younger brother of Mw accused him as well. The *ngàà* Mp had forecast that they would find cooking pots with Mw's charms buried on the other side of the river, but the villagers did not go to unearth them. Two days later Mw left the settlement with his three wives, his younger brother and one wife, one other man, one woman, and their children. They formed a new settlement some twenty-five miles away. The younger brother who had accused him had been the victim of Mw earlier in a rather serious case of adultery. As for Mw, he had been an up and coming *ngàà* before but this case finished his further career.

In another case, there had been a split away from the settlement two years before, some children had died and a general malaise was growing because a lesser leader was blaming the leader of the quarter where

[20] No informants claimed this, nor are there other indications in the travellers' accounts except vague statements about the power of the *ngàà*. But the Tio never accepted or developed anti-witchcraft movements which were typical for the populations of Central Africa and especially those of the lower Congo, Gabon, and the Kwilu. If this technique of witch hunting existed there was no need for anti-witchcraft movements. This accounts for the situation. Perhaps CH. LIEBRECHTS, op. cit., p. 535, that a culprit was always found for the misfortune of important men, might refer to this, but more likely it deals only with the poison ordeal.

it had happened. In addition this leader was overshadowing the head of the whole settlement. After the death of the child of the lesser leader, the head called in a famous *ngàà* S. The *ngàà*, on his arrival, accused the leader of the quarter, his brothers, and one other man in his quarter, thus completely taking the side of both the head of the settlement and the lesser leader. He then waited until the evening, went out then to the house of the incriminated major leader and began to destroy all the divining and healing material that leader had. He even attacked the house and a tomb behind it. The followers of the leader prevented him from going on with this and a scuffle followed. Then S decided that he was going to kill the *apfu*. He gathered the four accused men, put them on the plaza under mats. Then he stalked right and left in the settlement shooting from time to time. Whenever he 'saw' an *apfu*, he danced slowly near to it and shot. If he missed he took up the pursuit until he came back triumphantly, having shot one. This went on for the whole afternoon. The crowd fascinated just followed and saw nothing. The climax built up and then he shot with buckshot at the men under the mats, missing the first one, hitting the second one in the buttocks. When he came to the third one, the major leader involved, the latter's sons just prevented him. Suddenly panic gripped the crowd and everyone fled. After this the career as *ngàà* of the major leader involved was finished. The head of the settlement decided that two of his brothers should leave, but not the main leader, because he had too many direct kinsmen. The prestige of the quarter involved was shattered. From having been the centre of the settlement it became peripheral and was still trying to make a comeback several years later.

Witch hunts were climaxes to social dramas which had been building up for years, triggered off by a number of deaths and often leading to a major political realignment and a new social equilibrium in the settlement. For the common people the ritual heralded a period of peace and good fortune after the desperate struggle between the heroic *ngàà* and the forces of evil was done. For the leaders it was a desperate climax involving the loss or gain of all, save life.

Of all the techniques for solving strife discussed so far witch hunting comes closest to open violence. They were all peaceful resolutions of conflict but all implied the threat of violence and their prolongations were feud and war. This was evident in the court structure and witch hunting. It also was true for poison ordeals whose results, were not forgotten by the losing party which was often out for revenge. It was even true for *okuu*, because if that failed and the patient died, the reconciliation was over. So violence was just under the surface. Courts and ordeals which attempted to say who was right and therefore designate a winner, were more in danger of violence than *okuu*. *Okuu* and the ordeals were similar in that they tried to root out the cause of misfortune. They differed from the courts in their religious dimension.

This however made them matters of life and death, setting the stage for violence if death followed.

4. *Feuds*

Tio easily came to blows. A charm for winning fist fights, *inkooru*, was much in demand. It seems to have been usual for people who were not related or neighbours to go from arguments to blows, from blows to woundings and finally, sometimes, to murder. This immediately started a feud which might escalate into war. The very existence of feuds and their frequency were a sign of the weakness of the political structures and of the key position the social structure retained in the overall organization. This was also shown by the fact that the major roles of squires and lords were modelled after those of the leaders of kin-groups, the village headmen. For whenever a person had been killed, kinship solidarity was stronger than political control. There had to be a feud. The major causes for murder were, said LIPIE, the non-payment of *litsũ*, adultery, divorce, also theft. Accusations of witchcraft sometimes led immediately to feud. Thus LIPIE's mother's brother was accused by his wife's family of bewitching his wife so that she was ill. He did not call for *okuu*, but for a fight saying: 'If we are guilty, one of ours will die, if you are guilty, one of yours will die' and LIPIE's elder brother killed someone from the other side. The people involved in a feud were kinsmen of the deceased but not all kinsmen were involved. The members of the *ibuuru* who lived in the same settlement led the feud. The whole *ula* joined the feud, whether relatives of the deceased or not, even if the victim had no blood relations among his co-villagers. His wife's brother might lead the feud for him, if, for instance, he lived in her village. In addition mother's brothers, brothers and fathers had to join even if they lived in other settlements.

If the murderer and the victim were closely related there might be no feud. If they belonged to the same *ndzo* no compensation could be paid, since it could not be paid by the *ndzo* to itself. No feud was possible either. The victim's kin outside the matrilineage might be profoundly unhappy, but there was nothing to be done. If victim and aggressor belonged to the same *ibuuru*, lived in the same village but were of different *ndzo*, a feud did not usually erupt. The village leader called in the squire and the latter discussed the matter with the two *mpfõ a ndzo* involved. They agreed on the *mbuma* (Calloc'h: 'prix d'un homme tué par accident', *mvumi*, p. 300), i.e. the person who was to be paid in compensation. The *wookuru* was not directly implicated, so none of his villagers would resent and thus possibly leave him.

If the persons belonged to the same *ibuuru* but lived in different villages and were of different *ndzo* or lived in the capital of a squire, the latter did not settle the matter but preferred to call in a foreign squire to judge or rather arbitrate the case. Thus no one could blame him and leave his territory. If the parties were unrelated by blood but lived in the same village, the *wookuru* might attempt to settle the matter alone first or he could call in the squire and the *mpfõ andzo*. Whatever he did, he would act quickly to prevent a feud from starting within the settlement, since that would destroy it.

The word *omviira* for feud seems related to the verb *oviira*: 'to give back' (Sims has: *vira, bvira*; 'return, revenge' when followed by *ibaa, ibila, kwani*). *Kwani* meant 'revenge; obstructive fetish'. Essentially a feud was an attempt by the aggrieved party to kill the murderer (Sims: *itwii*; 'murderer, poisoner' and *itui*; 'madman') or one of his *ibuuru*. That was a direct feud.

Indirect feud *impfõ* occurred, said Ubwoono, when the aggrieved party went to take a hostage from a third village or even wounded or killed someone there. The conflict spread because the third village was supposed to take sides with the aggrieved party against the accused party. Miandoo held that the third village involved was usually the settlement of the main lord in the area. With his superior force he could then oblige the accused party to pay compensation for the person killed in the aggrieved party's village and in his own residence. Thus the wife of a man in Ntsaa had committed adultery. The culprit fled, pursued by two men from Ntsaa. He arrived at the tomb of NZÃ MBÃ at Mpiina Ntsa, which was a sanctuary, where he thought he was safe. But the pursuers killed him 'on the very tomb'. The people of Mpiina Ntsa felt this involved them in the feud since they had given the victim asylum. They started *impfõ* by killing a person from MUIDZU's Mpõ Olõ's village (before 1914). That was the end of the feud as far as Mpiina Ntsa was concerned. Now the feud lay between the people of Ntsaa and Mpõ Olõ. They then involved a major lord as third party.

In another celebrated old case, two men from different villages together found a tusk which they hid. Each went back home. After a while one went to his village leader claiming the tusk was gone and that his partner had stolen it. The accuser belonged to Mwaari, the accused to Ongia. Now the men of Mwaari simply took a hostage at Ãsa. The latter village asked the people of Ongia the reason for it all. They then ranged themselves with the forces of Mwaari. Ngateo's father's father fought for Mwaari, which dates it before 1900. There were two dead, both from Ongia. The fighting stopped because the horn was blown indicating that there was no more gunpowder. Then the lord MUIDZU intervened. He took both squires and made them drink maize beer together as a sign of reconciliation. The thieves of the tusk paid a fine, the hostage from Ãsa was released and the dead people were 'not counted'—no compensation was paid for their death.

Ngateo called this *mvulu atso*, a form of war. *Impfõ* to him was yet another form of feud. A village had a quarrel with another one, not over murder but over something like *litsũ*, and took a hostage from the other village. Then both villages could fight 'a war of the limits', a collective duel. After that the squire of the domain judged. This normally happened only within one domain. Miandoo cited such a case in the war of MBULANKIO versus Nkwia. Nkwia lost a man, then killed one from MBULANKIO and then took a hostage at NGANDZIÕ's, who was the major lord in that area. This forced him to intervene and judge the feud.

Whatever the terminology it is easy to visualize how a feud, once started might never finish, since each party always wanted to take revenge for every new casualty in the feud. The indirect feud was the institution which could stop feuds from dragging on forever. The third party was usually a squire or a lord and if it was not powerful enough, it appealed to a great lord who had enough men in his settlement to burn down the villages if they did not stop. The lord would send an envoy to call the people to court. If one party refused he took the side of the other one together with the third village involved, if it was not his own, and that was overwhelming. If someone of the lord's settlement had been killed he began a 'war of the borders'.

An escalating feud was always *impfõ*. If it erupted between two lords it might easily be war unless a very powerful lord intervened immediately. The lords were also supposed to intervene rapidly after two people had been killed on the same side without compensation. The lord waited for the third death and then set a fine, threatening to kill all he could in the village if they did not pay it. Mbali heard as a child of a case where the lord did not intervene, however, because the score was two dead for A and one for B. The ruthlessness of the lords is also shown in the case where Isu, MUIDZU (around 1910) simply kidnapped two women from squire Mbwili, sold them and kept the gains to himself, despite the fact that he had been involved in the first place because his wife's brother had been killed by Mbwili. The *ndzo* of the dead man received nothing.

On the Mbe plains squires and lords ended by going to the Mbe of the king if the feud's proportions continued to swell, involving too many deaths or two squires or lords. The king sent some wine or beer to the opposing headmen or *mpfõ*. They had to drink together and so formally end the fighting. After that they turned to arbitration. North of the Lefini MUIDZU performed this role. The Tio felt that a whole *ibuuru* might be wiped out, at least in one settlement, if the feud remained unchecked and a run-away feud might escalate to involve the greatest lords. Thus it seems that the war between Opontaba and NGANDZIÕ, which became evident by 1884, grew out of a feud. Actual fighting still occurred shortly before 1898 and the enmity still survived in 1963.

The dangers of prolonged feuds explain the savagery with which the great lords enforced their verdicts. If one party did not stop but killed one more person, the lord attacked the village, sold all the members of the offending *ibuuru* he could find into slavery and destroyed the settlement. This a MUIDZU in Ngateo's father's time had done in a feud between Abili and Mbe Isala, where there had been two and three dead respectively. The one with the three dead did not accept the settlement. It already involved a lord NGEIMPÃW (Abili) and NGANDZIÕ, a squire for Mbe Isala, so it had been war. MUIDZU just wiped out Mbe Isala with the help of NGEIMPÃW.

A murderer was not always supported by his group, as the case of Lipwo of Imba showed. Lipwo's wife was taken by the squire of Aniã, named Ndzoo. The aggrieved husband stole by night to Ndzoo's house and started to burn it. When Ndzoo fled, Lipwo shot him dead and fled to Imba near Djambala. Aniã started a feud, caught Lipwo outside Imba and just cut his throat over a big stone. That was the end of the feud because his kin did not support him, either for fear that Aniã was too strong for them or because the case was not good enough. A very similar case in 'the rubber period' (1900–14) tells of a husband whose wife had been stolen by a squire. He killed the squire and fled to Aku. The party of the murdered man at Aba first told MUIDZU so he would not intervene. Then they sent men to Aku where the residents claimed not to have seen the murderer. In fact he was there in hiding with his mother's brother. But when he went out, he was ambushed and his head was cut off and put in the squire's compound at Aba. The fact that the man was not originally from Aku or—in the other case—from Imba may have been decisive.

Feuds were not pursued either if the murderer was a known madman or in case of accident. In the latter eventuality a court would set the damages in *mbuma* to be paid: usually a person to be given to the other kin-group, but on the Pool it could be paid in goods. At Kinshasa around 1900, it was 10 *luni* or 200 *ntaa*, a gun and one or two goats and a few chicken, the animals being court costs.[21] Costermans had seen fines of up to twenty men among the Mfunu.[22] Also cases in which persons were only wounded did not necessarily turn into feuds. The squire common to both villages held his court first in the village of the victim. If the others refused to come, he moved there and set the fine in agreement with their village leader. If different domains were involved, the squire of the aggrieved party 'judged' first and if the aggressors did not come he went to his colleague in the other domain and they all went to the village where the attack had originated and settled the fine there.

Feuds, and especially indirect feuds, were a great threat to life. Thus when security was threatened settlements, even when not involved,

[21] A. MAHIEU, *Numismatique*, XXI; 928 No. II, p. 20.

[22] P. HERMANT. Van den Plas and Costermans (certainly before 1908, probably in 1899) had it that 'feuds were a thing of the past on the Pool'. The courts were headed by the village headman.

abandoned any sites they might have in the open to hide in the deep woods. Feuds also stopped normal intercourse and thus hampered local trade.[23] The interruptions to the production of subsistence goods were of much greater consequence. Even though stocks of cassava in the ground would be available, the eruption of a feud during planting or harvesting seasons could be disastrous. Not enough data are at hand to know the frequency of feuds nor the distribution of this frequency over the seasons. Most of them may well have been limited to dry season actions.

5. *War*

War involved groups of people fighting in the open under the leadership of a squire or a lord, whereas feuds were ambushes set by a few people and, if led at all, led by a village headman. War was most often feud prolonged on a larger scale. The Tio recognized two sorts of war: the collective duel, known as *mvulu ondil antsii*: 'war of the limits of the domain' and war on a larger scale, waged without any restriction which involved lords and the king.

The causes of war were those of all conflict, court cases as well as feuds. Accusations of witchcraft and differences concerning women were foremost. Guiral's dictum about the Tege that palavers about women caused most of the wars holds for the Tio too.[24] Rival men accused each other of witchcraft, while women and slaves were the most precious items persons or groups possessed. So that Guiral's opinion was also voiced by Tio such as Mbiinu Mbiinu and NGAMPO, both squires. Another frequent cause was the theft of goods or the running away of a slave or a woman. If it was a slave, the wronged party tried to kidnap a wife of the squire or lord to whom the slave had fled as a hostage and war ensued. If it was a woman, *litsũ* was claimed from her kin, who then joined the wronged husband to force the squire or lord to whom the woman had fled to give her up. He could not lose face as these women were *õke ampu*, so war followed.

The most common causes for war were a feud between competing chiefs or simply an open struggle for predominance between them. Perhaps a classic case was the war between NTSUULU and Ngaliema, after Ngaliema's brother had killed one of the men of NTSUULU. There were ups and downs and finally Ngaliema was forced out of

[23] L. GUIRAL, op. cit., p. 193. Nhango the Kukuya chief could not send his men to the Jinju of 'Nhemp'hourou' because one of the latter's wives had fled to him. This was cause for a feud and since both were chiefs a state of war followed.

[24] L. GUIRAL, op. cit., p. 173; CH. LIEBRECHTS, op cit., p. 531; P. HERMANT, op. cit., p. 291. Liebrechts listed as causes of war: cupidity, the spirit of fetishism, (witchcraft accusations?), women, e.g. if a woman felt ill and was not brought to her mother's village the husband could be accused of witchcraft and cause a war. Costermans (Hermant) cited return of bridewealth (*litsũ*). 'They try to avoid the reimbursement which among the Mfunu often led to war between the villages.'

Kinshasa and fled to Mfwa.[25] This constituted a bid for power within a neighbourhood (the seven villages of Kinshasa) and a feud and a war. Another cause for war could be the boundaries of domains. Two squires had succeeded only shortly before to the domains and claimed that they did not know where the boundary was. So they fought 'a war at the limits' to settle the matter. The ignorance was only a pretext since at least their *amieene* knew the boundaries; it was a simple attempt to seize control over more people and tribute. Land, of course, was of little value by itself. Great lords fought for absolute predominance. Around the king fighting brought his first lord Opontaba into conflict with NGANDZIÕ and Ikukuri and NGAMPO. The stakes involved were control of the centre of the kingdom. So they are mentioned in the general political history of the period along with the war by king Ngaayüo against Impe and those of MUIDZU. In the 1880's both MUIDZU and NGEILIINO were trying to establish a clear domination over all other lords, north and south of the Lefini. MUIDZU succeeded and NGEILIINO failed.

To achieve their political aims great lords supplemented their own militia, that is, the people of their residence, by slaves and perhaps by auxiliaries led by squires who were *nkani* to the lord. As for the king he had no national army, his settlement was small and he had to rely entirely on the armed forces of his lords. The armament consisted primarily of guns and the major limitation to war was provided simply by the availability of gunpowder. Goods had to be exported in order to acquire both guns and the precious powder. Also the best soldiers, one's slaves, were bought with wealth. As a consequence the great lords had to trade. The most important political figures, NGEILIINO Opontaba, NGAALIÕ, NTSUULU, NGOBILA, NGANTSU, NGEIMPÃW, NGWAMPOLO, Ngaliema,[26] were all traders. The evidence for MUIDZU, NGAMPO, Ikukuri, and NGANDZIÕ is not so clear, although they too obviously depended on guns and gunpowder. Estimates of the number of guns lords could put into the field varied from twenty or so for a Mfunu chief or a Bobangi boat to two hundred for NGAALIÕ, the strongest force on the Mbe plains and the same number, or perhaps more for Ngaliema.[27]

[25] H. STANLEY, op. cit., I, pp. 348–50.

[26] ibid., p. 290. Ngaliema was powerful because he had bought guns, slaves, and powder with his wealth.

[27] H. BRUNSCHWIG, *La négociation*, pp. 38, 47, gave several estimates and counts for boats (all around 20 guns). *Mpfõ* Mpuma Njali of the Mfunu, probably a squire, had 20. A. MAURICE, *Stanley*, pp. 112, 151, has estimates of 100 first, then 200 for Ngaliema, which would put him on a par with NGAALIÕ, of whom Brazza says that he had so many guns (pp. 38, 200) that people believed he made them. Figures for others on the Tio plains do not exceed 50 to 300. At the Pool C. COQUILHAT, *Sur le Haut Congo*, p. 57, estimated a total of 1,000 guns at end of 1882. CH. DE MARTRIN DONOS, op. cit., II, p. 126. L. GUIRAL, op. cit., p. 226, estimated 400 to 500 guns at Mfwa, but

It would be false to identify power with either numbers of soldiers or the number of guns. Differences in armament both in guns and in other weapons had to be taken into account and questions of morale were important in any situation of war. The guns were flint-locks, old European weapons refitted, usually at Liège. Shot was copper or lead slugs of varying sizes, the heaviest at the Pool and west of it. *Kiele* (iron slag) was also used on the plains. By 1889 around a hundred Snider rifles with cartridges were in use at the Pool. But because of the cartridges needed they were less liked than the flint-lock guns. The gun-powder came from war arsenals in Europe to the coast and hence to the Tio in kegs of standard size. The greatest single variable in the efficacy of flint-lock guns was the shot used. Great care was taken of guns, especially the Sniders, and the mechanics of guns were quite familiar.[28] Other arms were stabbing spears, knives, and battle axes. Spears (Sims: *yuo*) were commonly of two types, one with a long heavy blade imported by the Bobangi and one, used more for fishing, with a barb (Sims: *ikia*, 'spear barb'). There was a great variety of knives and one standard type of battle axe.[29] Bows and arrows were not used. Cannon was known but no longer in use.[30] Defensive structures included hiding the settlement in the woods and building palisades, *õkari*, all around it. Sims also has: *pfula*: 'road fenced on both sides' besides *ikoo*, 'fence, palisade, obstruction'. These types of fortifications were both reported

---

given the circumstances this almost certainly included most of the people of Mpila. It could well be close to the total strength in guns on the north side of the Pool. Stanley's estimates are not always reliable as can be gathered from their variability. He also tended to equate numbers of available soldiers with the number of guns. 200 guns for Ngaliema is one of his lower figures. Our estimates from all the data are then about 1,000 on the Mbe plains, and the channel, 400–500 on the north side of the Pool and a slightly higher number south of the Pool. But numbers at the Pool must have varied much with the trading season. Ten big boats might make as much as 200 guns' difference.

[28] On guns G. SAUTTER, op. cit., I, p. 372; A. WAUTERS, *Le Congo*, pp. 173–4. C. COQUILHAT, op. cit., p. 59; CH. LIEBRECHTS, op. cit., p. 529. H. BRUNSCHWIG, op. cit., pp. 47, 48. Calloc'h, pp. 225–6, gave forty-four terms for parts of guns and actions relating to their use; Sims gave sixteen such terms in his Tio-English.

[29] C. COQUILHAT, op. cit., p. 59, speaks of varied forms of knife. Sims lists: *lipe*, 'matchet'; *ibiu*, *izwali*, 'swords'; *ilumbu*, *(M)unku*, *Ibuna*, *mbiele alala* as types of knives, and *ibia* as the battle axe with *ibiele* as a hatchet. TH. MASUI, *L'état indépendant*, p. 81, spoke of seven or eight types of knives, all of the same general form but in different shapes; spears were by then imported from the upper river. H. STANLEY, op. cit., I, p. 411 (on spears' shorter and more rounded blade at the Pool), I, pp. 296, 299 (on knives which showed European influence in their structure, one-edged, handle disposition), CH. DE MARTRIN DONOS, *Les Belges*, I, p. 456 (for drawing of battle axe).

[30] Sims has: *tiene*, 'cannon'. Since one cannon of the eighteenth century or earlier was unearthed in Kinshasa (now University museum) with its shot, the term may antedate the arrival of Stanley. Apart from the cost and the difficulty of moving such armament over the paths of the lower Congo, it must have been almost of no value in war.

by Brazza along with palisading of the lord's compound. At the Pool Bentley and Augouard reported fences around the whole of Ntamo and straight across the road near Mfwa.[31]

The morale of the troops was probably much more important than their armament. Here charms were important. Sims listed *ikwiu*, *mpiu*, and *muboo* of which the latter was probably a charm for sharp-shooting. Stanley quoted one to become invisible when hard pressed in war and at Mbe this was known as *ĩkwi*. One could fly away if the enemy attacked. The charm consisted of grilled leaves in a *pfura* package along with camwood and was carried on the back. But the charm would not work if it was dropped on the ground. Bullets could be added to it and a metal point. This ensured that the enemy would be struck by the gun and the knife, spear or axe of the wearer. This type of charm was so common that its name was sometimes used for all war-charms. Yet another type *imbuuni* was a collective charm to make certain no one in a war party would be killed. This was ascribed to the Ngenge, but it is likely to have been in use elsewhere as well.[32] The king's Nkwe Mbali, which gave him the power to order the lions of the country to destroy his enemies, was a potent weapon and belief in the *nkobi* was also important. *Ngàà* could make special preparations such as the one of Mbã, a lord of former times, who wore a black cloth with two *nki andzo* and the skin of a civet-cat to enable him to overcome the magic of the enemy. In all the factor of war magic favoured the wealthy, who could attract renowned *ngàà*, and the successful since each success confirmed the efficacy of their *nkobi* and charms. It also gave a great advantage to the king in comparison with any single lord.

Preparations for all types of war were identical. The war bell *nkùnkùli* or *bà* was sounded, the men converged towards the settlement, women and children were hidden if an attack was feared and the war dance *iboolo* was performed on the plaza. Then the men left for the battle called *mvulu* (Sims: *mvulu*, 'battle, war'). Their leader was the squire or lord and there was no special organization of the forces. In a 'war of the borders' both sides formed a line of attack. W. Bentley describes this type of advance. One man would leave the line and in front of it wave his spear in the air, or throw his knife up, singing and dancing, challenging the enemy. The others behind repeated the song. Then there was a general advance with the shouts of *bura*, *bura* 'go back'. This went on and meanwhile the wings of the line tried to surround their opponents.[33] Besides this frontal attack, serious wars often

[31] H. BRUNSCHWIG, *Les cahiers*, pp. 167–8, 170; W. BENTLEY, op. cit., I, p. 350; D. NEUVILLE, CH. BREARD, *Voyages*, p. 213. The straight fence served as a barricade behind which the warriors of Mfwa grouped themselves.

[32] For Mbe Angõ who was specialized in hunting charms which are of the same order. Cf. CH. LIEBRECHTS, op. cit., p. 533; H. STANLEY, op. cit., I, p. 381.

[33] W. BENTLEY, op. cit., I, pp. 352–5. This was a show of force rather than an actual attack. It aimed at keeping Bentley out. A significant detail: Bentley bought

involved night attacks (Sims: *imfumi* = *impfõ* an escalated feud) and ambushes (Sims: *ansima*).

In the 'war of the border' the procedure was set. After the war dance and at the agreed time the warriors left for the battlefield, a site in the savannah, selected by agreement of both sides and burned down previously. The site lay in the border area, i.e. between the woods of one camp and those of the other. The women came along and camped behind the line to prepare food and drink for the warriors, while a brave chief went ahead of his men and the more prudent chief stood by and told them to go ahead. The fight began and was stopped as soon as one of the parties blew the horn *mvuli*. This meant someone was wounded or killed, or else that one side had run out of powder. The warring parties then left for home. The *amieene* of the side which had lost a man went to the other squire and peace was concluded. Blood money was set, the squires drank wine together and war was ended.[34] For a while the losers were full of shame (*odzwa*) until they won another contest.

The 'great' wars were different. A war between NGOBILA and Opontaba, the NGEILIINO, started in 1883, over Parrey who had died at Opontaba's but left his goods in Mswata where NGOBILA simply took them. Opontaba wanted them turned over to him, NGOBILA refused and it was war. NGANTSU the nephew and ally of Opontaba collected all the warriors he could from the surrounding villages who assembled carrying guns, spears, axes, knives and a flag (this was after 1880). Two or three hundred of them joined Opontaba's court and all proceeded to the bank of the Congo opposite Mswata, looking for boats to cross. But only one boat was found, since NGOBILA had brought all the others to his bank. So Opontaba camped while NGANTSU went to fetch a hundred more warriors. Opontaba had built a grass hut camp. The women of his establishment were busy around it, while many soldiers were buying food from women who had come from the villages to the camp. When Janssen arrived there was a picturesque hustle and bustle. The camp was not very well watched since no sentries had been posted. Still NGOBILA was afraid that the force might cross and with the help of Janssen overcome him. Opontaba on the other hand needed Janssen's help to cross the river, so there was no battle. NGOBILA crossed over to bargain and the inheritance of Parrey, cloth, weapons, and knick-knacks, were handed over to

on the battle field three spears, two knives, and two arm-rings from the enemy. Even there a good opportunity for trade was not lost upon the Tio warrior.

[34] Brazza invented another way to make peace by planting a tree in a hole into which both parties threw some bullets to bury war. H. BRUNSCHWIG, *La négociation*, p. 48. The tree was to be a flagpole. This was imitated at least once by Mgr. Augouard. A. REDIER, *L'évêque*, pp. 139–40, J. DE WITTE, *Vie*, p. 31. It is not clear if he copied Brazza or if this was by now 'custom' (1885) and that NGAALIÕ had proposed it. Salvoes of musket fire and special closed mouth singing had been added.

Opontaba.[35] The forces of Opontaba and his ally NGANTSU might have tried to surprise Mswata and stormed it to take captives, for in the bigger wars captives were taken. Thus in a war of Mwaari a captive was sold by the squire of that place to NGANTSU, perhaps one hundred miles away. The bigger the lord, the greater the victory, the more captives to be sold. Still, no Tio remembered a war in which more than five or six prisoners were taken.

If the first attack failed, peace offerings were very often made and accepted. The overtures were made through higher lords. If they were disregarded the great lord could attack the recalcitrant side as MUIDZU did at Mbe Isala. In the Mbe area the king could order peace. He would threaten to destroy the settlements of the warring factions and could order his major lords such as NGAALIÕ, NGANDZIÕ, or NGEILIINO to accompany him. As one text had it: 'They were his "younger brothers" and they may help the king, their elder brother.' They were certainly also inspired by the prospect of loot. By a combination of forces the king could stop even the NGEILIINO, his first lord.

It is evident that the Tio were not organized for protracted fighting. The immediate causes of war were often feuds involving lords and settlement was sought after one battle had been fought. The rare exception was a battle which gave a decisive victory, because weaker parties gave way. A typical case was Opontaba's attack under king Mbandieele (perhaps 1893–5) against Mpiina Ntsa. Ikukuri and a local squire of Itiele had joined Opontaba. The attacked parties fled 'because a lord of the court at Mbe is important'. Opontaba burnt the houses, but the fields were left intact as always and in the absence of people he may have taken the livestock or eaten it. But there had been neither prisoners nor casualties and Mpiina Ntsa soon recovered.

In the folklore a few massacres were reported such as when a village had hidden its women and children in a deep pit in the woods. An enemy soldier passing by threw some boiling water in the hole which hit someone who cried out. The people thereupon were all killed. It seems very unlikely ever to have happened. For in the rare case of total victory the losing party lost its settlement, some of its people, most of its guns and it dissolved because the followers of the defeated chief deserted to other settlements where they had kin. But even this was so rare that no actual case was remembered at all. Normally wars like feuds were fought out in the open, either as a collective duel on some day at some prearranged spot or as a fight where one major clash decided the issue. But ill-will often continued after the reconciliation had taken place and war easily erupted again, so that one can speak of hostilities lasting many years.

Under these circumstances politics of achievements for Tio lords

[35] CH. DE MARTRIN DONOS, op. cit., II, pp. 124–34.

consisted first in acquiring a power base in guns and slaves, even if it was only a small one. Once he had that, the lord did his best to make his *nkani* participate in war and he built up a system of alliances with other lords of equal status to assure their collaboration or neutrality. Diplomacy backed up by the threat of force, remained the most influential tool for increasing one's position. Wars could not be dragged out, and all lords were anxious for a settlement to occur because of the inconvenience, but also because of their fear that one of the warring parties might become so strong that he would be a danger to all the lords in the area. So conflict was fuelled by personal ambition, very imperfectly controlled by courts, erupted often into the violence of feud and war, and was settled effectively by arbitration after the war, because the rules of war prevented great losses and made wars indecisive. In the end the sword yielded to the word.

6. *The impact of conflict: slavery*

Whenever serious conflict erupted, in whatever form, it always resulted in the transfer of persons: women in marriage to forge alliances or slaves as compensation. Thus conflict, even more perhaps than the market economy, led to the maintenance and perhaps increase of the number of slaves in society. Thus it contributed with the effects of the market economy to sharpen the distinctions between the social estates at this level, while replacing the distinction between aristocrats and freemen by one between rich and poor. Non-ruling aristocrats had become undistinguishable from commoners and the rare commoner like Ngaliema who had built a power base was assimilated into the aristocrats. To be born an aristocrat was a potential advantage. The true upper estate or class was that of the powerful and wealthy as opposed to the free, but poor, middle class.[36] In fact there was a clear polarization and it looked as if the three estates were on the way to being replaced by only two classes since among the poor the distinctions between dependent and free persons were such that slavery was perhaps no more than adoption, as will be seen.

There were five categories of dependent persons, according to the way in which they had been acquired. They could be bought, they could pledge themselves, they could have been pledges for others, they could be clients or they could be persons transferred to pay a blood debt. The *mbuuru waatioo* or bought person could have been sold by his *ndzo* to settle a debt, perhaps for adultery or for atonement after refusal to drink *nkei* or after witchcraft had been proved, or again as a prisoner of war, or to pay a fine levied after the conclusion of feud or war or, on occasion, kidnapped. Trickery was sometimes also involved. Ngateo

[36] We can speak of classes in this context since they differed in way of life (upper class as opposed to the others), income and fundamental rights (slaves not free). The one feature still missing was a difference in education.

told a story, which had been familiar on the coast before, according to which a village head or a squire always had a walking stick with him with which to prod the mat on which he was invited to sit. For a mirror was concealed beneath it, so that the man sitting on it broke it and was fined a slave by his host. No doubt the story was a cliché but it translated the reality of arbitrary fines major lords could levy when they needed wealth.[37]

Most of these slaves were not war captives but persons sold by their mother's brother.[38] If this man needed wealth he went to the father of the child to ask for help. If the father could not help it was then proposed to sell the child, his sister's son. This always needed the approval of the *mpfõ andzo*, since it was a loss for the whole lineage and nephews 'from afar' or classificatory nephews could never be sold in this way. Some Tio held that even if the father could not help he might veto the idea of selling the child. But if the child fell ill the uncle would not come for *okuu* and would thus virtually leave the boy to the witches. If the nephew was a man accused of witchcraft but refused to take the poison ordeal he could be sold without further ado. Aristocrats, some thought, could not be sold, but one well authenticated case of this is on record.

The person to be sold was led to a squire or lord fairly far away from the place where he or she had lived and would be proposed to the chief. He alone had the right to buy first. If he did not but someone else in the settlement did, the latter first paid the chief 1 or 2 *ibuunu*. Most slaves were sold at known markets such as at NTSUULU's, at Mpila, at Ntsei, among the Kukuya, at NGANTSU's, or to the Laari, although Tio informants emphasized that they did not sell to Kongo or Lari. One case is known where a person originally from the lower Lefini was sold in the area of Ãsa (Masa) in Mpũ and undoubtedly others were also sold in the country itself. The slave, usually a young boy, was not supposed to know that he was to be sold and tricked to go to the market. He was inspected carefully before he was bought, one more indication of the impact centuries of slave trading had left. He would still believe that he was being looked over to discover some illness but often he was then already shackled (Sims: 'shackles, stocks', *ncuo*) or chained (Sims: *lingaña*, 'chain, fetters'). The buyer took the slave away. If the new master was a Tio and he often was, the slave became an adopted child to him, calling him *taara* and being called *mwaana*. He was placed in seniority along the other children according to the date of his acquisition. Any child born after that was his junior, all the ones born before were his seniors. He was however not a *nnaana* or *mbwei* or

[37] H. BRUNSCHWIG, *La négociation*, pp. 30–1. NGANTSU sold his brother's child to obtain the wealth to buy from the king a brass collar, which he had no right at all to do. Cases of the seizure by a lord of his own people and their subsequent sale are known, but it was always stressed that they were rare.

[38] ibid., p. 28.

1. King Iloo (Makoko of the Bateke). Photograph taken by G. Brazza, 1884. Reprinted from E. Zorzi, *Al Congo con Brazza*. Rome, 1940.

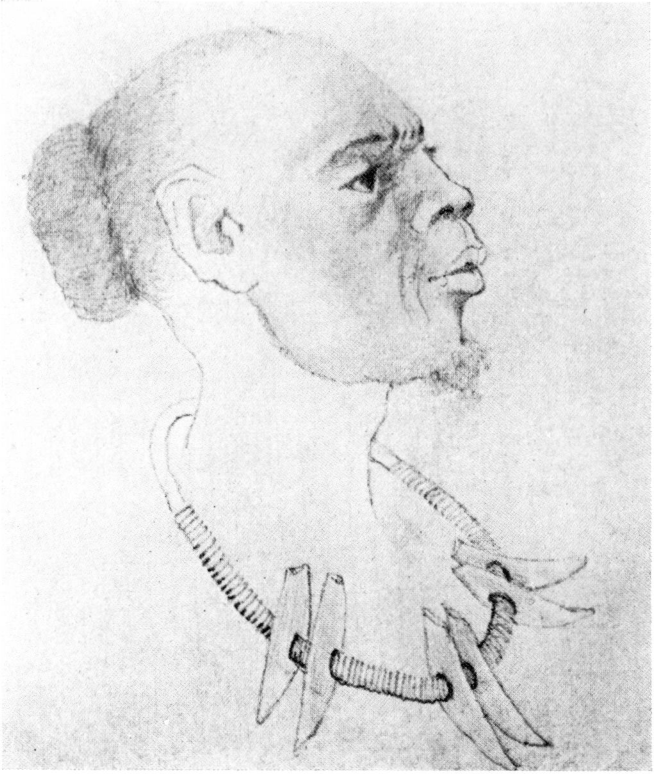

2. NGEILIINO Opontaba, 1884. Reprinted from Ch. de Chavannes, *Avec Brazza. Souvenirs de la Mission de l'Ouest Africain mars 1883–janvier 1886*. Paris, 1935.

kinele for them but *ibuun i'taara*. The adoption therefore was incomplete. In a normal household the slave (Sims: *(M)unkere*, 'slave'; Calloc'h, p. 191: *mu-kyere*, 'domestique') was a servant and could be called to do all sorts of work, but it is not clear if he did women's work if a man and vice versa. When the master died the slave became free and would be in charge of the division of the inheritance between the children of his master. If he was senior enough, he inherited himself. Indeed he could even succeed to the political position of his master. The case of Ikukuri who was succeeded by a slave, after having sold his own nephew who became a squire after his master died is no more exceptional than that of Ngaliema who inherited together with his two brothers (true or children of the master?) the wealth of his master Bamankua and thus started his career.[39] His position was stronger than that of the children because he also belonged to his master's *ndzo* and inherited with the *baan'ankieli*.[40] As long as his master lived, though, a slave remained dependent and could, for example, be resold. He was not free. He could earn a living, say by trade, but paid a tithe to his master and the latter could always kill him, which was undoubtedly rare but did happen. Opontaba thus tried to kill a slave boy. Wanton killing was disapproved and rare, since the slave could always be sold.[41] Moreover he retained from his earlier status the prescriptions on exogamy, so he could marry in his adopted family and often did. In fact most female slaves were married by their masters.

The career of slave was thus uncertain but not inhuman. The master was obliged to provide for his marriage and pay bridewealth if the slave could not, to feed and house him, as well as 'to put him a way of obtaining his own livelihood'.[42] Yet he was certain of his position only after his master's death. A person who feared his master could flee to the squire who then reimbursed the owner, which he had to do to maintain his prestige, or he kept the man but did not reimburse. This often led to an attempt by the master to abduct a wife of the squire. Or the squire might send the *mwaana* back, which was rare. A man could be sold back to the one who had sold him first, which freed him. This

[39] The well-known Ikukuri case was checked with descendants. For Ngaliema, cf. H. STANLEY, op. cit., I, p. 348.

[40] Yet Sims has *(M)umbura* 'slave issue belonging to the master'. The word means offspring. Perhaps slaves did not become free at the Pool; perhaps the term was applied only to slaves belonging to non-Tio, especially Zombo.

[41] CH. DE CHAVANNES, op. cit., pp. 244–5. It was evident that slaves were sacrificed, probably at the burial of important squires and lords. On the other hand in this case it looks as if Opontaba wanted to avenge himself because the boy had run away. The local squire NGIA stopped this attempt. Opontaba had first tried to sell the boy to De Chavannes. Cf. CH. LIEBRECHTS, op. cit., p. 530; *Coutumes*, p. 26, said they were killed when they did not behave well.

[42] H. JOHNSTON, *George Grenfell*, p. 685. TH. MASUI, op. cit., p. 81. Johnston noted that Ngaliema had been bought for a plate and ended up the wealthiest man in the whole trading system!

seems to have happened only during the early colonial period. It is worth mention here because that action was called *litsũ* exactly as if it was a reimbursement of bridewealth. Indeed the similarity between slavery and transfer in marriage holds, even in the realm of prices. Thus Ngateo held that the price of a slave in one case in his father's time (say 1890) was about 20 *ibuunu* and bridewealth was 18. Conviction of witchcraft and the fine for murder were also 20 *ibuunu*, as was the price for adultery with a squire's wife, although squires usually asked for a woman as a fine rather than *ibuunu*. These cases prove that the sale of slaves was part of a sphere of transfers of persons and as such equivalent to marriage.[43]

Mbuur anji, *mbuur ampfõ*, or *isã* (Sims: *isaña*, 'follower, attendant'; *ncana*, 'slave'), was a man who sold himself to a lord or to the king either because he could not pay a fine or be given the bridewealth to marry a girl. There was a slight difference in status with the *mbuuru waatioo* in that when the *isã* fell ill, one would call his original *mpfõ andzo* to conduct the *okuu*. The man was not a slave since he kept both his *ibuuru* and his *ndzo*, but he had sold his liberty of movement and his labour. This could be called contract-labour. Many of the attendants and slaves of great lords seem to have been *isã*.

Ntsuo was any person handed over as a pledge (Sims: *ncua*, *ncuo*: 'hostage, surety, person or thing in pledge'; but Calloc'h; p. 301: *bu-nsua*, 'protection'). As long as a person was in pawn he was a *mwaana* of the creditor. They could sometimes be taken by force when a debt was not settled as happened to two children caught by Ngaliema.[44] Persons were left in pawn only at the markets, with squires, lords or the king. Often the creditors defaulted and the *ntsuo* remained in that situation forever.

Nkani was a term used for a group of people, more rarely an individual, who came to put themselves completely under the protection of a lord or king. The same term designated subordinate squires or lords paying tribute to a higher lord. When illness and death had so destroyed a *ndzo* that people felt that they no longer had the spiritual power to protect themselves against witchcraft, they went to the lord or

[43] The case was one in which Ayangu had killed a person in the village of Ngateo's father and was fined a slave or 20 *ibuunu*. Of the fine (as for a witch or adultery) half went to the squire; the other half was compensation. Parallel marriage payments were then 10 *ibuunu* to the wife's *ndzo* + 2 for her father + 6 to her father to follow after marriage. He claimed the fine for adultery was 10–12 *ibuunu* for an ordinary woman. Other sources put the fine at one slave however, even for a commoner's wife. In all these cases, save adultery, the receivers of the fines had to use them to buy people as replacements, thus making the link between the transfer of slaves and women complete.

[44] C. COQUILHAT, op. cit., pp. 62–3; H. STANLEY, op. cit., I, p. 493; the children belonged to the Hum squire Ngamberenge. A. MERLON, *Le Congo*, p. 28. A creditor could take a few slaves of his debtor as pawns and tie them by the ankle to his own men. When on the road the slave wore a yoke held by a man who followed him.

king, gave him a girl, called *nkani*, without bridewealth. He became then *mpfõ andzo*, took over the conduct of *okuu* and avenged any members of the group who were subsequently killed or bewitched. When a woman *nkani* of the king died, the witch was always detected quickly and smothered without further ado. In addition the lord or king assumed the position of the *mpfõ andzo* in matters of vendetta, bridewealth payments, *litsũ*, inheritance questions, and whatever came up. The members of the group were thus not slaves but like *isã* had bargained away their liberty. Two informants, one of which was Abili Ndiõ, believed in fact that they were called *isã* as well.[45]

In addition to this case individuals became *nkani* when they took refuge with a great lord or king, after having committed a murder, or having been accused of witchcraft and fearing to be sold as a consequence, or because they were isolated. Thus a Tio Laadi in Mbe simply gave his daughter to the king. In cases of refugees accused of murder or witchcraft the lord then paid the equivalent of a slave and the *nkani* was practically an *isã*. The relationship did not end with the death of the lord, for the heirs of the *nkani* girl took over the obligation. In turn the *nkani* performed any services the lord or his heirs might require from them.

A last type of dependent person was the *mbuma* paid in compensation for a person killed before or during a vendetta. The fine for a dead person was equivalent to a person and could be called *mbuma* as well. The person given as *mbuma* did not assume the victim's precise social and personal status. He had to be of the same sex as the deceased, and adult if the latter was adult. If the victim had been *mpfõ andzo*, some day the replacement became *mpfõ andzo*, but Miandoo disagreed strongly. He felt that never could such a person lead the *ndzo*. The *mbuma* lived in the village of the victim and that was the essence of replacement, he argued. Also called *mbuuru waasobi*, 'exchanged person' he became part of the *ndzo* of the deceased: *maa amaamee*, 'mother of my mother' as Abili Ndiõ said. *Okuu* was done for him by the new *mpfõ andzo*. He was therefore adopted at least as much as a bought slave. This category also included persons handed over to the party of the victim after the accused in the other camp had refused to drink *nkei* and was not himself sold into slavery.

A *mbuma* person had to be paid for every time someone had been killed by witchcraft, i.e. for every death, if the culprit did not belong to the *ndzo* of the victim. In the latter case it was mostly paid in currency and in this case a person to replace the deceased was not bought with it but the sum was divided among the members of the *ndzo*. The currency, usually *ibuunu* on the plains, was, however, likely to

[45] L. GUIRAL, op. cit., p. 296. A man came to ask 'great fetish' from the king because his wife was ill. It could only be a *nkani* and not an *isã* who had his own *mpfõ andzo*.

be reinvestment in the transfer of other persons: bridewealth, payment of fines equivalent to a person, and the like. Cases of homicide, even accidental homicide—as when a messenger was killed during his errand—were handled like cases of witchcraft and *mbuma* in currency was paid by the responsible party. Thus the one who had sent the messenger paid. Unlike the case of feuds, compensation in the form of transfer of an actual person could not be insisted upon, except when someone had been actually killed.

Mbuma for a woman was never paid and feuds were never undertaken for this purpose, if the guilty party agreed to pay *litsũ* counter-bridewealth for the deceased. Again this is a striking illustration of the unity within the sphere of transfers of persons, whether in marriage or not. In the case where two half-brothers of different mothers fought and one killed the other, the murderer also simply paid the *litsũ* for the mother of the other.

Slaves were acquired in numbers by the traders. Sims notes it thus: *ngaankali*, 'trader' and *ngankali*, 'slaver' which is the same word.[46] Trade was no longer fed by the demand for export at the coast but internal demand, as well as the demand on the commercial routes for carriers and soldiers, remained strong. Every *ndzo* which lost someone tried to replace the loss. In general it is also clear, however, that there was a flow of people upwards to the lords and wealthy men with a corresponding weakening of kinship groupings at the base. The average *ndzo*, the average localized *ibuuru* was losing more people than it gained, the average lord, and especially the wealthiest and mightiest lords were gaining dependents. So that the movement in slaves contributed rapidly and strongly to the creation of the new two social classes. At the Pool or at Mswata where the imbalance was strongest so few free men were left that Sims could say that *mfumu* meant both chief and free person.

Trade was not the source of Tio slaves. It did, however, bring foreign slaves into Tio society. Slaves were procured directly by the methods of resolving conflict. The insecurity produced *nkani* and *isã*, the feuds and fines *mbuma* and *ntsuo*, war prisoners who became *mbuur waatioo* like persons who were sold because of a fine. Wars were not fought mainly or only to capture people for sale. The lords who sold their own subjects, the kidnappings, the trickery to make men pay fines were clearly the exception. The *ntsuo* taken as pledges in the market places in return for ivory were the ones who were redeemed most easily. So by 1880 at least, trade was not directly responsible for the production of slaves in a way comparable to conflict. It could be argued that the slave trade had produced an increase of penalties for settlement of conflict and thus

[46] Cf. Chapter X. For evidence of sale on the plains to Lari, cf. H. BRUNSCHWIG, *Les cahiers*, pp. 167, 169, 170, 172, for Jinju and Sese, involving even one case of kidnapping. Slaves were also offered *for sale* thus confirming that the Tio did buy slaves as well as sell them.

had been responsible for the situation. The contrary argument is at least as plausible. The Tio were the only population in this region who sold their own freely, because of the customs relating to conflict.

Yet there is a link between trade and conflict. The existence of the great Congo commerce had fed the ambition of men while the need to have guns with which one could defend oneself and increase one's status also required ivory or slaves. The ambition of the leaders at every level, beginning at the kinship level, the interests of every group from the *ndzo* and the localized *ibuuru* upwards, led to more demands for the transfer of persons and a faster transfer. Thus conflict was not the cause of trade or caused by it, but both reinforced one another, and probably had done so for centuries.

The most typical feature of the resolution of conflict in Tio society remained perhaps the transfer of persons which always accompanied it. The Tio kingdom, whose formal structure is presented now, had clearly failed to provide for an orderly protection of all, because of the lack of an effective centralization to check feuds and wars, to organize courts in an orderly sequence of importance and to institute a true bureaucracy. More specifically this lack was due to the total absence of any centralized police or army and to the absence of control from a single centre over the sale of weapons and gunpowder.

Chapter XIV
The King and His Realm

THE king, *õkoo*, was distinguished from all his chiefs. He alone was *õkoo* for the Mbembe, the Boõ, the Jinju, the Wũ, and a portion of the populations living around the Pool. Kingship referred to the widest political unit the Tio knew: the realm. It was the expression of a complex common ideology, which justified the existence of the kingdom and gave meaning to it; it was associated with a way of life and a role and it was the cornerstone of a system of authority which the king sanctioned. Thus the ideology of kingship, the royal way of life, the king as a ruler and succession to the crown form the subdivisions of this chapter. It does not deal with the historical evolution of the office under Iloo I, but only with its institutional features at that time and follows therefore logically on the similar presentation of the squires and the lords.

Before we embark on the description of kingship ideology, the following chart of the major titles is given as a guide to the web of ties which linked the ruler and his lords.

CHART 18

The major lords in relation to the King

title	*role at royal installation*[a]	*characteristics of office*
1 *superior lords*		
NGEILIINO	nominated king, sent him into ritual seclusion	First Lord; collected all *ingkura* for king; head of royal court, south of the Lefini
MUIDZU or NGANDZUUNU	minor role in installation	collected *ingkura* in realm north of the Lefini; head of supreme court north of the Lefini
ÕKOO NGENGE	—	Ruler of the NGENGE, loose association with realm
2 *ritual*		
NGANSHIBI	initiated king in seclusion 'open' charm Nkwe Mbali	—
MOTIIRI	initiated king in seclusion	—
LIPIE	'prayed' spirit Nkwe Mbali sent holy water to court	collected *ingkura* among southern Sese
NGAMBIÕ	royal smith. In control of royal fire	—

[a] A fuller description follows in the next section of the chapter.

title	*role at royal installation*[a]	*characteristics of office*
3 *royal household*		
NGAASAA	initiated with king. First wife, ritual complement of king	Head of royal court, south of the Lefini; regulated distribution of food at court
WAAFITIEERE	Second wife. Ritual keeper of kitchen	—
4 *major territorial lords*[b]		
NGANDZIÕ	nominated king, sent him in to ritual seclusion. Built royal enclosure	*Nkani* of NGEILIINO. Collected *ingkura* on large part of Mpũ and Mbe plateaux
NGAMPO	ritually built royal kitchen	*Nkani* of NGEILIINO. Collected *ingkura* in large part of Mbe and Mpũ plateaux. In charge of food supply to capital
NGAALIÕ	kept a perpetual fire	*Nkani* of NGEILIINO. Collected *ingkura* at Pool and in western Mpũ. Military commander of king, could succeed as king
MWANGÃW	assistant of NGEILIINO	unimportant
NGOBILA	—	*Nkani* of NGEILIINO. Ruled over river Congo from the Alima to the Pool
NGANTSU	—	*Nkani* of NGEILIINO. Unimportant but his position at Mpio a Bwaani in the 1880s gave him power
MAMPIELE	—	*Nkani* of NGEILIINO. Controlled passage over the river Lefini
NTSUULU	—	*Nkani* of NGEILIINO. Collected *ingkura* around the Pool
NGEIMPÃW or NGAAKULI	ritual playing of *kuli* ball	*Nkan i*of MUIDZU. Collected *ingkura* on eastern half of Mboõ plateau
NGWAMPOLO	—	*Nkani* of MUIDZU. Collected *ingkura* among the Jinju
NGANKUO	—	*Nkani* of MUIDZU. Collected *ingkura* among the Jiju. Head there of a local title system
MUNGWO or OPUU	—	*Nkani* of MUIDZU. Collected *ingkura* among the north Sese on northern half of Mboõ plateau

[b] No hierarchical order is intended here. Ranking takes first NGEILIINO's *nkani* by area, then MUIDZU's *nkani*. Offices which involve ritual duties are listed first.

1. *The ideology*

The sovereign was king because he was the 'master' of the national *nkira*, Nkwe Mbali. This male[1] spirit held sway over the whole kingdom and the fourth day of each week was named in its honour. On that day people did not go out into the forests or work the fields because *apfu* and *ikwii* roamed the earth, all because of Nkwe Mbali. Therefore it might be argued that the extent of the kingdom can be traced by the extent of the belief in Nkwe Mbali and that in turn by the extent to which people called the fourth day Nkwe Mbali rather than *mpika* or *mpiu*. By this criterion the Ngungulu, Kukuya, Laadi, Fumu, and populations bordering on the Pool did not belong to the kingdom nor possibly the Mfunu and even the Ngenge. The area over which *ingkura* was collected was bigger than this though.

Nkwe Mbali meant 'the court of the lion'. He lived in the Falls of the Lefini near Mbã. There the LIPIE was the minister of Nkwe Mbali's cult. When the king sent goats, white fowl, or *imbuunu* LIPIE sacrificed the animals and offered the cloth by throwing it into the river. His prayers were not different from those addressed to any other *nkira*. They mentioned not only the names of the king but those of all the major living chiefs. They were performed mainly when there was much illness in the realm. The king then distributed kola nuts to the squires so they could offer them to the *nkira* in their domains. The same thing happened if rains failed. The king was a squire for the whole country and his ties to the land were similar to those of the squires and therefore different from the ideology attached to the lords. Beyond this the king prayed for the illness of his enemies and this would be granted if they had really harmed him. It was the equivalent of a curse. It was believed that Nkwe Mbali was essentially just and that arbitrary demands of rulers would not be fulfilled.

At Mbã, just opposite the Falls there was a flat rock in which six anvils had been stuck. One middle one represented the king, next to him one was for LIPIE and the two on the sides were for Jinju and the Boõ Lords. Each morning LIPIE visited the spot and if he saw an anvil loosened, he would know that the lord, king, or himself whom it represented was about to die. He also touched the objects thrown by the cataract on to the hallowed shore near by. With these he could make packages called *ibili* and distribute them for a fee to village leaders who came to beg for them, thus linking their prestige to the kingship and Nkwe Mbali. On occasion the kindred of LIPIE assembled there, drummed and sang for Nkwe Mbali to be granted new objects to replenish the national charm. This was also called Nkwe Mbali and was kept at the capital by the NGANSHIBI and his *ibuuru*. All this dupli-

[1] Affirmation by Oshiakunu, an informant used by A. Masson Detourbet for her declaration that the spirit was hermaphrodite. A. MASSON DETOURBET, *Le tissage*, pp. 74–6.

cated perfectly the organization of worship common for any *nkira*. This charm was housed in a shrine as big as a house and was contained in a huge bale. Its contents were and are still secret. The 'openers' prayed there, sacrificed, and danced when this was required. Kola and blood were given to it. Each time a king died, the contents were believed to have been diminished and at the accession of the new king LIPIE had to send new materials to replenish it, to make the new king strong and the kingdom healthy. Around the package objects of *unũ* had been assembled as they are around *nkobi*. They included copal and conus, but also a huge copper plate, a sword of 'medieval facture', a set of animal skins, calabashes, and some wooden statues,[2] as well as arm rings in copper and black metal (probably lead) which was the metal of Nkwe Mbali and the king. Near the bale there was also an offerings stone to spit the kola on and shed blood.

Whenever a king was installed, he had to go through a long ritual called *lisee* by which he became 'master' of Nkwe Mbali. After it he needed lustral water from the Falls with which to 'cool' the realm when the fire of witchcraft, disease, or famine was destroying it. It was said that the first king came to the first LIPIE and asked for water and the charm. This is the only myth relating to Nkwe Mbali. This water was very important to the king, and once when he was asked to bring it but was unable to do so because he was ill, LIPIE brought on an armed expedition by king Ngaayüo. LIPIE himself could not collect it—only his *otioolu* or his children could. He carried it to the court. In addition the giving of water required the payment of a handsome fee to the LIPIE and sacrifices at Mbã to Nkwe Mbali. Nkwe Mbali was believed to be the first of all *nkira* of domains and the others were his 'wives', just as the squires were believed to be the 'wives' of the king, meaning his subordinates. In the world of spirits this mirrored the hierarchy existing among men.

The Falls were also the abode of the *ikwii* of all deceased kings. When a king died, his shade followed the Lefini upstream to the Falls and stayed there. Led by Nkwe Mbali all the spirits of the past kings travelled under the current of the Lefini to a spot nearest to the point where the new king was when he went into his ritual seclusion, *lisee*. They examined the candidate and approved of him. Thus the cult of Nkwe Mbali included the cult of the royal ancestors.

[2] L. GUIRAL, *Le Congo*, pp. 289, 295, saw these objects in Iloo's own house and was told that they were kept there because of the prestige and the security of the king for 'the charm is all mighty'. That Nkwe Mbali really existed then as a charm and a cult is proved first by the testimony of the LIPIE in 1963 who had taken over from his mother's brother some time around 1910. The mother's brother had succeeded his own father. Indirectly Brazza testifies to it in H. BRUNSCHWIG, *Les cahiers*, pp. 172–3, with the confusion he made between the Falls of the Lefini and the name Mokoko by the tie linking the king to the Falls, i.e. Nkwe Mbali. H. BRUNSCHWIG, *La négociation*, pp. 22, 25.

The cult of Nkwe Mbali involved a ritual, which was performed on each Nkwe Mbali day at court. LIPIE at the Falls took the little *ntsa* horn which he always wore attached to his forearm and with which he could stop rain, to whistle to the spirit. Nkwe Mbali was alerted and listened to the prayers. The same ritual was performed two days later on the other sacred day, *okwe*. On the same days NGANSHIBI prayed near the charm after having blown his *nshibi* whistle. For this occasion he wore the prestigious *nkã* red blanket, the tail feather of the rooster, sat on the skin of the *nzobo* wild cat which was reserved for the king and himself, also wore a *ntsa* whistle and a special type of arm-ring called *ikara*. He offered wine and kola to the package and then went to the king. He whistled on the *ntsa* whistle and if the king answered inside his house by blowing a similar whistle, he sounded the *nshibi* for the second time and was also answered by the king. NGANSHIBI derived his title from this *nshibi* whistle which he and the king alone could use. After this he could enter the house, give the *mpfõ* salute of homage, sit down and ask how the king felt. The answer given, both chewed kola together and ate. The king was supposed to remain in his house seated on the same spot all day long flanked by his ritual wives NGAASAA and WAAFITIEERE, his eyes decorated with the magic kaolin which enabled him to see in the invisible world and the red *ngula* to see in this world. He wore a hat with the red feather symbolizing the violence of authority (*nkuo*, 'plantain-eater') and that with the white rooster meaning leadership.

This description was obtained in 1963 from the NGANSHIBI who had succeeded to Ngalifourou. In 1963 this ritual was no longer observed and some details do not correspond with the observations of Brazza, for in his diary at the court there is no sign of a perceptible rhythm of royal seclusion each fourth day. The first of September he noted that towards the evening the king's men went to his house and started by making leaves explode by holding them between index finger and thumb and then hitting them with the flat of the other hand. They beat the iron bell and whistled on the king's 'fetish' horn. Then they whistled on the horn of the antelope (*ntsa*) next to the fetish 'which is always near the king's door'. Then the king shook the wooden bells (*libi:* 'rattle') on which he always spat kola nuts and the first draught of palm-wine, to call his ancestors to warm themselves during the night at the fire in his house. On 3 September the same ritual was performed. This seems to indicate that the ritual was held at both days of Nkwe Mbali and *Okwe*.[3]

[3] H. BRUNSCHWIG, *La négociation*, pp. 27, 28. The ritual seems to be that of Nkwe Mbali. As for the king's movements he stated, p. 28, that when the king did not come to him, he went to the king and did not record after that where the interviews took place, save on some dates. It is possible that Nkwe Mbali was on 1, 5, and 9 September. The king did come out on 7 September to visit Brazza who was ill, ill enough in fact

A number of avoidances went with the cult. The aristocrats could not come near Mbã and no one of the kindred of LIPIE could ever become squire or lord. The two orders were kept entirely separate. Avoidances linked with kingship stressed the king's relation with the life-giving forces of Nkwe Mbali. He might not see a coffin or a tomb, he left any place where someone was ill for fear of contagion. But he could touch blood whether human or animal. He could not walk without footgear, except for his toes, nor sit on the bare ground and was usually carried in a litter for fear his power would scorch the earth. He could not cross the Congo river or see the Pool, but he could travel by boat and cross the Lefini and Nkéni rivers provided he put a red blanket over his head and did not gaze on the rivers. The same was true with regard to the tiny brook Ngampe near NGANTSU's, a place where some held the *nkobi* had come out of the ground and which others felt was the special abode of Obuu. He could not eat caterpillars of the *atsiere* variety, nor buffalo meat, nor meat of the big black *nka* antelope. He could not go to war. He could not ever drink without covering his face and observing the proper ritual. Unlike the lords he ate in seclusion and 'not even a small child could watch him, for he was Nkwe Mbali'.

Besides the positive rituals of his installation, the ritual for the sacred days, the drinking ritual, a symbol, reminded him constantly of his sacred qualities. A perpetual fire was lit in his kitchen when he became king and was kept burning there by his second wife WAAFITIEERE who was also the only one who could cook for him. His sacredness found expression in the belief that he lost his virility after having passed through *lisee*. He was still allowed to sleep with his wives but the power of kingship had destroyed fertility. He would not beget children. Given the opposition between sex and sacredness this fits very well in the general pattern.

The power of Nkwe Mbali was expressed in another way. The king had the specific power to summon the lions of the country and send them out to destroy those who defied him. Even in 1960 a campaign of rumour had it that the then king was sending his lions to destroy parts of Brazzaville and to remind all who was the master of the land. The

---

not to have made any note on 8 September. On 9 September he visited Brazza who was well enough to reciprocate. If on the other hand Nkwe Mbali fell on 3, 7, and 11 September, as on 29 August the king may have remained secluded on all these dates except 7 September, when Brazza was ill. The minimum is then that the king could break the rule of seclusion when it was felt imperative. All the great meetings took place on days which were neither the supposed dates for Odzuo or Nkwe Mbali. To this extent then the rhythm of sacred and profane days was real.

In the description of NGANSHIBI there is mention of anklets in cloth with cowries or a cowry collar (p. 22). He also wore a collar with two teeth of a lion (p. 22) and on another day a hat decorated with lion's nails [*sic*], both elements associated directly with Nkwe Mbali. Note that Brazza's descriptions were made during presumed profane days, so the absence of the feather and bracelets is not surprising.

Tio had and have the greatest fear and respect for lions. From time to time people are killed by the prides which roam this territory. Each incident of this nature was magnified, told, and retold with a scarcely imaginable awe for the king of beasts. For instance the Mfunu explained that the Catholic mission had left their territory at Tua because a lion ate one of the sisters. The story was quite untrue but was believed by all. At Mbe every one closed their doors at night for fear of the lions. When one European who resided there for a few years did not, he was admired because his sorcery must have been very great indeed. The symbol of royal power was the lion skin. Only the king could sit on one and then only on sacred days, perhaps only on Nkwe Mbali. If a lord refused to forward a skin to the king, it was an act of open rebellion. But no such case was remembered in 1963.

The fear of the king's powers was real. Guiral said that the Mokoko had no temporal power; 'he is the great féticheur, the spiritual chief, and if I may be allowed the expression, the Pope of the Batékés'.[4] De Chavannes talked about the fear which his fetish inspired and the deference all had for him. Even the NGEILIINO, Opontaba, talked to him only in kneeling position and all prostrated themselves with great respect when he covered himself to drink.[5]

He had the power to make it rain in torrents, destroying crops and houses when his wrath was aroused. This was only a warning before unleashing the lions. In this his power was exactly the contrary of that of the lords and squires who stopped rain. But it also meant that no one could stop him. No magic whatsoever could prevent his lions, his rains, or lightning and the curse of his staff. For if he hit someone with his staff the person inevitably died.[6] Kingship was in this the epitome of witchcraft. The fierceness of the king was also expressed in folklore by a tale that was widespread in West Central Africa. When the king wanted to rise he took two spears, put them on the necks of two slaves and thus rising killed them.

Tremendous spiritual power was acquired during the ritual seclusion which followed a king's nomination, the *lisee*.[7] But first the question of the royal *mpiini* or life force had to be settled. The king sent his object *mpiini* to the ruler NGIA who lived near Gamboma in Ngungulu

[4] L. GUIRAL, op. cit., p. 293. He made it quite evident that the king's immediate authority did not go beyond his capital and some did not even obey there.

[5] CH. DE CHAVANNES, *Avec Brazza*, p. 370. Even Brazza, for whom it was not very diplomatic to say this (since he held to the supremacy of the king and the existence of a state in order to give value to the treaty), said that 'his influence was of a religious nature'. N. NEY, *Conférences*, p. 158; Cf. P. AUGOUARD, op. cit., pp. 28–9.

[6] H. BRUNSCHWIG, *La négociation*, p. 28.

[7] A king did not necessarily perform this immediately after nomination. Kings since Ngaayüo have been so terrified of it that they never went into seclusion. This was the official reason for the deposition of king Ntsaalu in 1964. Only after the *liséé* could the king wear his brass collar with the 'twelve points'. Before he wore only a simple collar with lion's teeth as the major lords were also allowed to do.

country. If the correct object was not sent, the latter rejected it, until the right *mpiini* was received. By this act the king put his life in the hands of the NGIA. After this the NGIA could always send messengers to ask for gifts when he was 'eating goods', in fact to ask for tribute. If the king refused, NGIA could 'cut off the head of the royal *mpiini*' thus killing the life force of the king. Because of their connexion a NGIA could not touch the king, or vice versa. Sometimes NGIA came himself to the capital, but, unlike royal lords, he did not need to come for the *lisee*. This curious relation was remembered in 1963 mainly by the Ngungulu but some elders questioned in Mbe did not deny it, but stressed that the NGIA kept the *mpiini* in trust just as other people might entrust their *mpiini* to their mother's brothers, so the *ngàà* will not be able to find it, a practice which was unknown at Mbe anyway. Yet this relation in which the king was clearly subordinate was attested in the 1880s.[8]

On the appointed day the king went into hiding and the NGEILIINO sent the MWANGÃW to find him. The latter found the king and beat him with a broom. Sometimes, said Ibalico, the beating was hard enough to break an arm or a leg, which seems exaggerated. According to LIPIE the NGANDZIÕ went out to catch the king and then handed him over to the MOTIIRI and the MWANGÃW who put him in the *mfula*, the house of *liséé* for nine days' seclusion. He went with his first ritual wife, NGAASAA, and a small child.[9]

That same day the king entered *lisee*, his new fire was lit by the royal smith, the NGAMBIÕ. The flame was produced by striking a piece of flint against a metal hook and catching the spark in an inflammable mixture of cotton shreds and palm-oil. Once it burned the MOTIIRI ran naked from his house, when all the other houses were still closed and lit a fire in the newly built kitchen between three anvils he planted there. The kitchen was built by the NGAMPO and would be the precincts for the WAAFITIEERE, who from now on was to cook the king's food there and bring it to the *lisee* each day. The NGAMBIÕ

[8] C. COQUERY, *Brazza*, pp. 339–41. Dolisie said: '. . . Guia, the famous chief who would be the suzerain or the friend of Makoko' and Ponel 'N'Guia Comonguiri, their great chief, who with Makoko shares power in the Batéké countries'. The ambiguity comes through nicely. Ponel compares them to the Pope and the emperor in Europe.

[9] Apart from the Tio informants M. IBALICO, *Quand et comment on devient Makoko*, was the only source. A. LEBEUF, *Aspects de la royauté*, pp. 464–5. Certain divergences exist between the different accounts. Thus some held NGEILIINO responsible for putting the king in *lisee*, while others championed NGANDZIÕ. This was linked with a power struggle that was going on from 1950 or 1952 onwards. LIPIE seemed best placed to give an objective view. So it probably was NGANDZIÕ. WAAFITIEERE, said Lebeuf, was not installed with the king but visited him every day and she is probably right. But she was definitely not responsible for the sacred objects. That was for MOTIIRI and NGANSHIBI. Only Ngalifourou, WAAFITIEERE of Ngaayüo had taken over the role of NGANSHIBI, hence the confusion. The terminology of Ibaliko is not always correct. He used Fumu in places or even Kongo terms.

was also responsible for making the great royal collar with twelve points and the king's fly whisk.

The king was in the *lisee* with NGAASAA and one of his small children who brought the cushion *likuba* (Sims: *likuba*; 'sack, bag, pillow'), stuffed with charms on which the king was to sit. If he left the hut with NGAASAA and eventually WAAFITIEERE to answer Nature's calls the child replaced him by sitting on the *likuba*.

Every single day MOTIIRI and NGANSHIBI visited him to show him some of the sacred objects associated with Nkwe Mbali, and which were kept in the basket *Ngia Ngombu* by Motiiri during the interregnum. These included sets of rings and collars, the red blanket *nkã*, the red costume *mbie*, and the hat *káá*. A. Lebeuf spoke of a throne on top of which a stone from the waterhole in the forest of the WAAFITIEERE was put, nine anvils for the eight major title holders and WAAFITIEERE, the *kuli* ball which came from NGAASAA's kindred and the Nkwe Mbali containing the frontal bone and the right little finger of each of the preceding kings.[10] These were all brought by the WAAFITIEERE. But she is clearly in error. The NGANSHIBI was responsible for this set. WAAFITIEERE in any case also entered the house daily to bring food.

Each of the royal cult objects had its own name or names, its secret meaning and its avoidance, called *ikià*. MOTIIRI handed one object after the other to the king starting with the most innocuous ones such as the bracelets, *mbielembiele*, *libia*, a ring, *ndzal ankori*, a bracelet for the upper arm, the *nkã* blanket, etc., proceeding to higher and more potent objects and ending on the sixth day with the *anõ* rings which destroyed the king's virile potency and the *káá* hat with the feathers of the plantain eater, called perhaps erroneously MOTIIRI by Ibalico, which with the great collar were the major insignia of the king. Anyone who wore it had to have avoided since birth any form of elephant meat, so that candidates for the crown always avoided this meat.

A. Lebeuf reported that the king and NGAASAA had to fight with all their strength against the powers in these objects and could only appropriate them when they overcame them. If the king did not die before the third day of *lisee*, he would, it was felt, survive and outside the people feasted, though they were still fearful. True enough by the third day he was safe, because that meant Nkwe Mbali and the royal

[10] A. LEBEUF, op. cit., p. 465. It is possible that the charm Nkwe Mbali contained this, but considering that the Tio eluded several inquisitive foreigners who wanted to know the contents of the Nkwe Mbali, it may be one of the fables invented to satisfy that curiosity. In any case the *nkobi* of Kongo chiefs do contain these objects. Much of the inquiry was made at Ngabe among outspoken supporters of Queen Ngalifourou who combined the duties of NGANSHIBI and WAAFITIEERE. These were not clearly separated at her death since the new male NGANSHIBI did not receive the Nkwe Mbali charm which remained with Abamudzu, a woman relative of Ngalifourou at Ngabe.

ancestors who had hovered around the *lisee* since the beginning had accepted him. But the giving of objects went on, and for each of these the king had to pay more and more, so that when he emerged most of of his wealth had been transferred to MOTIIRI and through him to the great lords of the crown. On the sixth day he also received the great brass collar with the twelve points. It was rumoured that to take this he had to condemn by witchcraft twelve of his kin to death, so as to make the power in the collar real. Others claimed that the king could not be a witch and if he was, the collar would prevent him from getting up and he would die. NGAASAA also received such a collar. On the next to last, the eighth day, the two most fearsome rituals took place. The king was to draw a sword and swear that the lords would be his 'children', that he would not exterminate them. By the way he drew his sword the NGANSHIBI and MOTIIRI knew how long he would reign. He also ate human flesh this day. This was brought by NGANSHIBI. While the king ate NGAASAA was not allowed to move at all and the king was forbidden to turn. When he had eaten, he said: *woolooolooloo*. The way in which he ate and spoke indicated to NGANSHIBI how he would rule and if he would last in the office or not.[11] This was a magical act setting the king apart from and above all humanity, as incest did in many other states.

Each day he was in seclusion, the king was washed and clothed by NGANSHIBI and MOTIIRI and each day the NGAMBIÕ steeped his iron tools in water, brought the water and sprinkled it over the king. Then he put a red blanket *nkã* over the fire in the *lisee* house and blew on it. The fire, fuelled with leaves on hot charcoal, produced a lot of smoke which was blown over the king's body to fumigate it and make it strong, which was also the aim of the sprinkling.

After this the 'coming out' was organized. During *lisee* the lords of the crown who had not been there for the beginning of the seclusion arrived. The day began by the making of a new fire in the same fashion as on the first day and this was to be the perpetual fire for the king's reign. At the same hour he had entered the house he was to leave it. The crowd massed in front of it and he emerged leaning on the boy who had sat on the *likuba*, the NGAALIKUBA. Homage was now paid to the king, after the insignia were all given to him in public. People crawled on the ground and the aristocrats touched their leopard skins with their hands to greet him. Then came the *inkinkira* ceremony. Each lord of the crown approached the king and gave him an emblem associated with his title, thus recognizing him. They also probably performed the great *mpfõ* greeting. In return the king made a handsome

[11] Data from NGANSHIBI. This ritual meal may be the origin of the persistent reports that the Tio and especially their king were cannibals. These began in the sixteenth century and were still current in the 1880s. Cf. A. REDIER, *L'évêque*, p. 149 (Mgr. AUGOUARD, 1885).

gift, the *inkinkira* proper. NGANSHIBI may then have put the king on the stone of the charm Nkwe Mbali, according to Ibalico, and blessed him. After which the royal drums began to play. The king got up and in the midst of praise singing he performed a solo dance in front of them all. After this a popular feast ended the day. Then the king remained in his palace for three days, while all the people of the capital could pillage and steal where they wanted to.

Each year there was a commemorating ritual called *imwooni*. The king sat on his *likuba* and began the feast by having his own royal rhythm played on the drums and dancing to it, as did the lords of the crown, who were there, and then the royal wives and children, after which the ordinary people danced. *Imwooni* was a ritual, for it was done to make the country 'strong' and, if a very good year was expected, it could be omitted.

At a superficial level the ritual of *lisee* as a *rite de passage* is evident. But the full meaning of *lisee* will only be evident the day the contents of Nkwe Mbali charm are known and when we have the complete inventory of objects given with their names, meaning, and sequence; in short when the teaching done at *lisee* becomes public.

An important feature of *lisee* was that it presented the ideology of the titles in the realm, i.e. the formal system of levels of authority. There were, it was believed, twelve lords of the crown, that is lords who had titles associated with *lisee* and this theory of the realm. Each of these titles was characterized by certain specific duties with regard to the king, with corresponding insignia and privileges. Such a system of titles existed in the whole Teke area. Thus Calloc'h translated pp. 134–5, 'autorité' by giving the set of titles for the Fumu. They are also reported from the Kukuya, Jiju, Mfunu, Ngenge, Ngungulu, although the number of titles is not always identical, nor is the rank or some of the titles themselves. Thus the first rank among the Tio: NGEILIINO was the last one among the Fumu.[12]

[12] The Fumu ranks were *MUKO* (*MUKOGO*); *NGALIEME* (*NGALIEO*); *NGANZYEMO* (*NGANZYEO*), *NGAKU*, *NGABA*, *NGAMPAGA* (*NGAMPAO*), *MVULUNGIA*, *NGA ILINO*, eight in all like the number. A. LEBEUF, op. cit., p. 464. She list's the king's speaker, the head of the weavers, the head of the smiths, and the heads of the four major areas of the kingdom. This information does not coincide with that of either Ibalico or our informants. It may have been provided by Oshiakunu. There is no relation with a myth, as Lebeuf has on pp. 466–7, a myth which was told to her by Oshiakunu. In particular the role of the weavers, and Oshiakunu was one, in this structure is greatly exaggerated.

M. IBALICO, op. cit., p. 30, had outside of the ranks NGAIMPA or the president of the rituals of *lisee*. Then NGAILINUU, minister of war and MWANGÃW, his messenger; ANKUO, the minister-priest (NGANSHIBI?) NGANDUNU or MUIZU, collector of tribute; NGA IMPO, looks after food and the kitchen for the king; NGANTSU, border guard; NGOBILA, naval commander; NGANDZIÕ, gives the *nkampa* (*nkã*) on the day the king goes to *lisee*, MUNGO in charge of providing the descendants of Iloo I with leopardskins; WAFI INTERE, priest of Nkwe Mbali; NGALIEME who filled the interregnum of the king; MUTIRE, prime minister, in charge of royal hat; NGALIFOUROU, in charge of household. Some points are

The relation between the events at *lisee* and the titles of lords of the crown is as follows. NGEILIINO the first lord, squire of the ground on which the capital, Mbe, stood, gave the king the white rooster feather and the red blanket. NGANDZIÕ made the royal enclosure *liko*, decided when the king would go to *lisee* and preceded the king on tour. NGAMPO built the royal kitchen and provided food for the capital, as Ikukuri in fact did, when he held the title. MOTIIRI gave the clothing and made the royal hat. NGAMBIÕ forged the collar, made the fly whisk, lit the new fire, lived behind the king's house, and kept the royal baldric of cowries. If the king was ill he treated him with 'the water and the fire' as during the *lisee*; he could also start the perpetual fire again, if it went out. To accentuate his ritual character he had to make a new fire for himself every Nkwe Mbali day and eat only what was cooked on it. NGANSHIBI was the keeper of the Nkwe Mbali charm, assisted the king during *lisee*, and ruled during the interregnum. MWANGÃW, an aide of NGEILIINO, escorted the king to the *lisee* and showed him the assembled lords when he came out. NGAALIÕ was the king's military commander and the only lord who could become king subsequently; he also had a perpetual fire. Then came three lords from north of the Lefini: NGAAKULI, who opened the deliberations of a council of chiefs by playing with the *kuli* ball, NGANDZUUNU or MUIDZU, a viceroy for the territory between the Mpama, the Nkéni and the Lefini. The first two came to *lisee* together with NGANKUWO, lord of the Jiju. Then there was LIPIE who was not present at the *lisee*. His closest connection with it was his relation to the spirit Nkwe Mbali; moreover the king could only drink water from Mbã after his initiation. The water had to be mixed with that of the Lake Sisõ near Impei and whenever the pot crossed a river, water was added to symbolize how, over a period of time, the lands of the king had grown, how peoples of different origins had come to range themselves with those who had already accepted the rule.[13] Thus the number of lords of the crown was twelve without LIPIE and IBOONO, who 'lived near the king'. Some informants did not count IBOONO or NGANKUO and one added NGANTSU. It was obvious that there had to be twelve and that only over the last four names mentioned would there be some disagreement.[14]

---

obviously wrong in M. Ibalico's list concerning WAAFITIEERE and Ngalifourou, which was not a title at court. For the rest compare with our summary which was obtained for the titles kept south of the Lefini from the title holders and north of the river from children or close relatives of title holders. M. N. OBENGA, *Le royaume*, pp. 39–40, obviously follows Ibalico closely.

[13] M. IBALICO, op. cit., p. 32. It is scarcely believable that the king could *only* drink this water. In any case he drank mostly beer or wine.

[14] Ngateo included IBOONO, a minor title held by his wife. No others did. The Jiju all include NGANKUWO, the major lord in their area. No one included LIPIE

Among these lords of the crown clearly the ritual specialists were NGANSHIBI, MOTIIRI, NGAMBIÕ, and LIPIE. All the others were mainly secular lords. All these office-holders were squires except NGANDZIÕ, MWANGÃW, and NGAMBIÕ, and all except MWANGÃW and IBOONO also held *lisee* where they were initiated.

The theory seems to have supposed a simple structure in which the land was divided into provinces for some lords of the crown, while others performed ritual duties. Under the province came the chiefdom. But nothing was further from even the ideal norm in the 1880s. For the possession of *nkobi* had altered the whole situation. The kingdom really had two concurrent constitutions: one based on kingship and its authority and one on the ranking of *nkobi*.

Two titles given to women, wives of the king, were most intimately linked with the nature of royalty. NGAASAA was the first wife. She had to originate from a kindred whose 'wood' was Itoo, north of the Lefini. Hence her other title WAAFITOO, 'she who comes from Itoo'. She could not be an aristocrat, but was, as the Tio pointed out, the highest of the commoners. She went through *lisee* with the king and wore the brass collar. When she died the king should not survive her and was killed for he could not rule without NGAASAA. If he died she was washed ceremonially at the end of the mourning period by MOTIIRI and NGANSHIBI and underwent a sort of *lisee* in reverse so that her insignia could be washed and taken away. She then received the name Ngontsuo and a new identity.[15] But she could never remarry. Her title meant 'master of the cereals' and she was supposed to ensure their fertility. Since women were the main agricultural producers this position, as held by the first woman in the land was the counterpart of the role of bringer of fertility which was the king's.[16] NGAASAA was chosen late in life, since she should not conceive children. She slept ritually with the king each night before Nkwe Mbali and on the day of Nkwe Mbali or *Okwe*, she sat next to her consort and also offered kola to the *libi*. Her place was on the right hand of the king while the WAAFITIEERE was on the left. Lebeuf claimed that her maternal uncle had to be the owner of the *kuli*, i.e. NGAAKULI or NGEIMPÃW (the two titles belonged to the same person). But this conflicts

but all held him to be very important. NGAATALI added NGANTSU but he had a particular bias as Mbembe and on the river there was a movement for including NGOBILA. The number twelve did not interfere with the counting in all accounts. Perhaps there were never twelve clearly recognized lords of the Crown.

[15] The king had to die because he could not go through *lisee* twice yet could not have a NGAASAA who would not have gone through *lisee*. A. DOLISIE, *Notice*, p. 245, mentioned the belief but added that he did not think Iloo had been killed (smothered) as a consequence, although he died somewhat later.

[16] H. BRUNSCHWIG, *La négociation*, p. 28. Brazza noted that she gave the cassava, groundnuts, and maize of abundance to NGEILIINO.

with the information that she had to be a commoner, since he was always an aristocrat.[17] In the 1880s she was honoured and all travellers mention her title. She sat near the king in palavers. Indeed she was supposed to judge in his place in court cases. She presented food to the king on a copper plate. When she gave something to someone it had to be received on the back of the hand, a mark of extreme respect. She was either the daughter of a major Jinju lord (Guiral) or of a great lord with much influence on the left bank of the upper reaches of the Congo, i.e. a Ngenge lord or king. For P. A. Augouard she, more than the king, directed the realm.[18]

WAAFITIEERE, the king's second wife, had to belong to a kindred which came from the wood Itieere. The name means 'she who comes from Itieere'. But she could also come from Itoo. She may have belonged to the same kindred as the NGANSHIBI although the relations between the two have been confused ever since Ngalifourou who was WAAFITIEERE took the other office as well. She was in charge of the kitchen of the king. Her status was less exalted than that of NGAASAA. Not only did she sit at the left side, but her death was of no consequence to the king and if he died there was no special ritual to desacralize her. For she had not been in *lisee* with the king and did not wear the collar. The day before Nkwe Mbali she could not touch the king and on the day of Nkwe Mbali she lit his pipe. She was not supposed to have children by the king and the only case remembered by Abili Ndiõ when this did happen, the child died soon after birth. In sharp contrast to NGAASAA, in the 1880s, no one mentioned her. Reports that she handed out the major emblems to the king after he emerged from *lisee*, because they belonged to her kindred, do not seem correct. This was NGANSHIBI's role.[19] Finally she could remarry after

[17] A. LEBEUF, op. cit., pp. 463–4.

[18] L. GUIRAL, op. cit., pp. 290, 296, 297, 300; E. ZORZI, *Al Congo*, p. 386; CH. DE CHAVANNES, *Avec Brazza*, p. 370. Guiral would seem to be more correct. N. NEY, op. cit., p. 334; ZORZI, opp. p. 448, had a photograph of her taken in 1884 by J. DE BRAZZA. P. AUGOUARD, op. cit., p. 28; A. VEISTROFFER, *Vingt ans*, p. 109; D'UZES, op. cit., p. 103.

[19] B. MAMBEKE-BOUCHER, *Ngalifourou*, p. 28, where it is also incorrect to state that she was on the right side of the king when he emerged from *lisee*; the hermaphrodite Nkwe Mbali of the same author does not seem correct. Neither was there any information corroborating that she was no. 4 in 'occult power' (NGANSHIBI on the other hand was certainly most important in this respect after LIPIE and before MOTIIRI). The statement that she was title no. 10 in absolute ranking has little meaning, given the variability of the ranking. This author does have better information than YOULOU KOUYA, *Une adoratrice*, also written to commemorate Ngalifourou. A. LEBEUF, op. cit., p. 464, also clearly confused NGANSHIBI and WAAFITIEERE. That a water hole near Itieere had been the place where the first couple of men emerged from the Earth has not been confirmed elsewhere. M. N. OBENGA, *Le royaume*, p. 35, only claims that she proclaimed the king's name to the *nkira* and the people when the elect left *lisee*.

the death of the king and was expected to work in the fields like any other of his wives (*angaana*).

A. Lebeuf has presented NGAASAA both as a twin of the king and as an image of the primordial couple. Our data indicate that she was rather his female counterpart or perhaps mirror image. WAAFI-TIEERE's role was much less important. In fact she was only part of the royal structure because she was related to NGANSHIBI.

One more major ritual expressed the ideology of kingship: the burial of the king. According to A. Lebeuf only the two titled women and the major lords were told the news of his death. Two of the lords cut a piece of the frontal bone and a little finger to be put in the Nkwe Mbali charm. The king was buried in secret on the spot where he died. The news was only made public nine days later. During that time an image of the king was fashioned clothed and ornamented with the royal collar, and was put in the catafalque. It was the substitute which was buried facing east if the predecessor had faced west, and the burial was preceded by the sacrifice of some slaves whose arms and legs had been broken. For nine days after the burial no productive activity was allowed until some title holders had given WAAFI-TIEERE (NGANSHIBI) a special offering.[20] The meaning of this ritual is not entirely clear. It is not because of the long period of exposure that the substitution was made, since the body could be preserved, as is known from other cases.[21]

2. *The King's appearance and his court*

The royal insignia which only the king could wear, or which were associated with kingship proper were not numerous. He sat on the lion's skin, wore the brass collar with the 'twelve points and for him the royal drum was played with the royal rhythm on the day of Nkwe Mbali'. He wore the feathers of *libobõ* and *nkuo*, with or without the *káá* hat and the *ãnõ* rings in an unknown metal covered with cloth.[22] The

[20] A. LEBEUF, op. cit., p. 466. Substitute burials were not unknown in Africa, e.g. in Benin. None of our informants would tell us about a royal burial except to claim that it was like the burial of any other aristocrat only bigger with *ndzo ancweli* on the catafalque and a year's interval between death and burial. The possibility of sacrificing slaves was not denied. The mound on the tomb was different from other such mounds, it was decorated and Ubwoono held that an effigy of the king in clay was left on the tomb.

[21] M. N. OBENGA, *Le royaume*, pp. 38–9, says the king's body was preserved like that of the chiefs. He is the only author to stress the meaning of the royal demise: with it the essence of all life was destroyed and existential chaos followed it.

[22] The name *ãnõ* is probably related to *manuma*, the well-known name for the Lunda supreme insignia, an arm-ring often made of human sinews. This is the only trace of Lunda influence found here. Its relation to the loss of virile potency by the king is also reported for the Lunda chiefs of the Kwango. The other insignia are either unique to the Tio (collar, pelt), very widespread (the system of feathers) the drum, found in the north (the broom *onia*) or among the Kongo.

káá hat was decorated with one feather of each bird whose feather was an emblem for one of the titles at court. He leaned on the *likuba*. Of these the lion's skin recalled the name (*nkwe*) of Nkwe Mbali and symbolized the subordination of all the chiefs who forwarded to him the lion skins they found on their lands. Even MUIDZU sent these and also, annually, a number of leopard skins, the sign by which squires and lords recognized the king. For the Tio the lion's skin was the emblem that the king was 'master of the land'. The twelve so-called points of the collar represented the great lords who depended on him, the *káá* hat the emblems of these lords. In all these the king was presented as the overlord who ruled over a whole system. The leopard skins of the lords corresponded to his lion's skin, the collars he gave them thereby delegating his authority[23] to his collar, the feather corresponding to the title, and to his hat and his two feathers *nkuoõ libobõ*. *Nkuo* was considered the king of birds and the red colour of its feathers was the king's red *ngaabie*, also the colour of his costume *mbie* and this was the highest of reds. The red of the lords was only *tsuula* (*ngula*), followed by the inferior *ncincu* (hematite), and *ndobo* (yellow) reds. The red blankets *nkã* were of the *tsuula* class. *Libobõ*, the nightjar, seems to have been the symbol of witchcraft and mystical power in the world of birds. Like the brass collar and the skin it was the expression of the king's occult power.

Other emblems proper to the king alone were the skin of the *nzobo* civet-cat, the *nshibi* horn shared with NGANSHIBI, and his litter covered with the skin of the red *mfini* straight-horned antelope, which was also linked with NGANSHIBI since the litter, carved out of a tree trunk, floated down the river Congo, together with a house and NGANSHIBI to come to the king.[24] These recall Nkwe Mbali.

The king could and did wear insignia which were common to all great lords, such as the adze, the *lie* bead, a collar with several lion's teeth, the fly whisk, conus, copal, the *mvuba*, the white rooster feather, skullcap, the red blanket *nkã*, leopard skins. The walking stick had the

[23] H. BRUNSCHWIG, *Les cahiers*, p. 173, where De Brazza expressed for the first time his belief that it was the sign of being a squire, but was given by the king as delegation of his authority. NGANDZIÕ, NGAALIÕ, NGEIMPÃW, and N'MAMBALI (NGAMPERE?) among others had it. Cf. p. 191. On investiture with the collar A. DOLISIE, *Notice*, pp. 44–5; CH. DE CHAVANNES, op. cit., p. 368, for the significance these collars assumed in the diplomatic struggle between French and Independent State. Despite the claims of De Chavannes it seems that collars were made and worn by the Mfinu, Fumu, and perhaps the chiefs of Mpila without reference to the king at all. *Coutumes*, p. 42, for symbolism of the twelve lords.

[24] H. BRUNSCHWIG, *La négociation*, p. 24. This house (probably a shrine?) is unknown from elsewhere. The whole is remarkable since it is the only myth linking kingship with the north, confirming evidence from the distribution of certain insignia, like the *onia* and the title *õkoo* itself, which is clearly akin to *bokoko*, 'village leader, elder' of the Mongo languages. CH. DE CHAVANNES, op. cit., p. 63, mentions the litter.

special power to kill his enemies, there was a *wara* bracelet with seventeen spirals covered by iguana skin, worn on the upper arm and ornaments with cowries, the latter two similar to those of lords but more elaborate and reserved for the king.[25] Then there were all sorts of *unũ* objects, among them single and double bells without clappers, single bells with clappers, rings of elephant's hair, all manners of imports. In this category the various gifts of the French missions were quickly promoted and displayed at various audiences. Among the *unũ* objects was at least one trophy of war—a paddle captured by the king from the Bobangi when he warred against them as a youth.[26]

Etiquette and court behaviour were much less typical of the king alone. He wore a long fingernail and walked on his toes, which gave the appearance of limping.[27] People often addressed him as Nzã, but that address could also be used for great lords. The drinking ceremonial and the salutes of homage, either the great homage or the lesser salute, were identical to what happened at the courts of lords, so was the etiquette concerning the announcement of the king by music, his entrance, and the disposition of the assistance and dignitaries at audiences.[28] All this

[25] Cf. H. BRUNSCHWIG, *La négociation*, p. 28 (the king claimed he alone wore cowries, but NGANSHIBI did too). Information on the *wara* ring came from Ngateo. It may be that this was the *ãnõ* already mentioned. Brazza mentioned the *lie* bead. *Oli* (copal) was chewed by king and lords to 'cool' the country; conus also had a mystical power, but was not connected with Nkwe Mbali. If they were thrown on the ground the *ikwii* would send illness (LIPIE). The two objects were kept in the shrine of Nkwe Mbali. The other emblems common to lords and king are mentioned in descriptions and some shown in illustrations or photographs.

[26] H. BRUNSCHWIG, op. cit., p. 28 (paddle); the bells were played when the king went to an audience and one bell with a clapper was affixed to the door of the compound (p. 22). Among the older imports the 'medieval sabre' and the big copper dish were the most outstanding. The sabre was known in 1963 as 'Brazza's sabre' showing how Brazza has taken the place of a culture hero in Tio consciousness. Each of the successive descriptions of the court shows new objects, recent gifts, being displayed. The costly cloth the kings wore also falls in the group of *unũ* objects. The very long pipe with two heads lighted by WAAFITIEERE can also be included in this group. On the adze, H. JOHNSTON, *The River Congo*, pp. 298–9, claimed it belonged to the king, whereas CH. DE MARTRIN DONOS, op. cit., II, pp. 14–15, attributed the same object to Opontaba, the NGEILIINO. E. ZORZI, op. cit., p. 386. P. AUGOUARD, op. cit., p. 28, lists the new objects of *unũ* displayed after the French visits to 1885: flags, the Treaty, a shield, tapestries. M. N. OBENGA, *Le royaume*, p. 37, whose short list of emblems (*bitoo*) includes a wrapper.

[27] N. NEY, *Conférence*, p. 335; L. GUIRAL, op. cit., p. 290. The fingernail was not noticed. It was a sign that the king did not work and even more a symbol of his vitality. P. AUGOUARD, *Le Congo*, p. 29; D'UZES, *Le voyage*, pp. 103–4. Note that other Tio sometimes let the little fingernail grow as well.

[28] On drinking: H. BRUNSCHWIG, op. cit., p. 28; CH. DE CHAVANNES, op. cit., p. 160; On homage: N. NEY, op. cit., p. 324 (*mpfõ* salute); H. BRUNSCHWIG, op. cit., p. 29. That this was different from the normal salute is made clear, p. 39; CH. DE CHAVANNES, op. cit., pp. 148, 156, 163, 160, where he claimed the *mpfõ* salute was more modest than the *ntsii* salute. The homage had a living meaning as shown there p. 178, when Opontaba took the hands of the people who did homage to him and placed them in the hands of Malamine saying: 'take'.

only showed that the king was a lord, but the salute of homage was the clearest expression given to the people of the submission of even the highest lords to the monarch.

In the 1880s the king was not very wealthy and his estate reflected this. His capital of Mbe was small, his royal enclosure *iko*, built like that of the lords contained only his own two houses and those of his wives who were few in number. Augouard counted only twelve of them and attributed eight slaves to him. In 1884 Pecile called the whole capital 'a small village, with houses falling in ruins and not very prosperous looking'.[29] Obviously the king did not have the wealth displayed at the Pool or by the followers of his major lords. But there was wealth in Mbe and it was displayed on great occasions. A description of one of these follows.

In the centre of the village red drapes had been spread above a small plaza, one next to the other so as to form a sort of pavilion to shield us and the royal court of Makoko from the sun.

As soon as we had placed ourselves under this dais, one saw magnificent skins of tigers (leopards) and lions brought from the royal house, on which the very august person of Makoko was to seat himself.

After twenty minutes or so of waiting the sound of two drums which were beaten with slow and well marked beats and of a bell that preceded them was heard which like the drums measured with its ringing the slow progress of H. M.

And here is Makoko now coming from the front of his house. An old, thin and worn out man with a pleasant figure, walking on the points of his toes, clad from top to bottom with several wrappers of different sorts of cloth and colours, worn one over the other. Around the neck he had his great collar and in addition a beautiful necklace in imitation hard stones (imitation Middle Ages) which was sent to him some time ago by the Commandant (Brazza). Because he is bald, he wears a sort of skull-cap or *beretta da camera*. It is a cap decorated with needlework forming designs of various colours. It is work of the country.

In front of him comes a man bearing his sceptre (a bit of moulded glass which are used for the railing of staircases in Europe, on top of a brass stick, the whole a gift of Ballay) and another man with the bell. Ngassa, his first wife, also decorated with the great collar, follows him; then all the other women and children, kin, etc.

He sets himself on the skins leaning his elbow on a cushion (*likuba*). The bell, the stick and a broom (*onia*) of a material I don't know, are put in front of him. . . .[30]

Similar descriptions are given elsewhere. The protocol was not

[29] E. ZORZI, op. cit., p. 388; J. DE WITTE, *vie*, p. 32; A. REDIER, op. cit., p. 147. Pecile summed up Mbe (Zorzi, p. 386): 'un piccolo villagio, colle case cadenti e d'aspetto non molto prospero'. See also L. GUIRAL, op. cit., pp. 289, 294–6 (royal compound and house). N. NEY, op. cit., p. 329 (drawing of the two royal houses by J. De Brazza, 1884).

[30] E. ZORZI, op. cit., p. 386 (1884: handing over of the treaty).

always identical but the whole royal household was always present. In 1880 the king was preceded by four pages, carrying a red serge wrapper, one of whom wore an old European suit. The king wore a cloth, armlets and anklets, the skull cap with two very long (*libobõ*) feathers, and followed his wives. He had only one wrapper. NGANSHIBI followed him with the medieval sword and a magic shield. The king seated himself on a carpet, about four yards one foot square, with a pattern of blue and red squares on which a travel-rug had been put, above which a lion's skin was to provide the seat. The *likuba* was near-by. The audience gave homage. A few days later the order of procession had varied when Opontaba came to court: the women followed the king. Opontaba did not do homage and he did drink. Both his salute and his drinking were certainly breaches of etiquette showing the great power he had achieved. A late visitor in 1885 saw the king clad in a magnificent red cloth with golden flowers, leaning on the *likuba*, which was then made of European cloth. He wore the collar and held a sceptre. The NGAASAA sat at his feet.[31]

From the different descriptions however it is clear that in 1880 the king possessed some valuable *unũ* objects and that the royal ceremonial existed. French gifts from 1883–5 were immediately displayed showing the king's increased wealth and power. After 1885 the magnificence must have declined again. There is little doubt that the great lords especially could outclass the king and that the show in 1880 was modest, as modest as the capital itself. In fact it was a direct reflexion of the power position of the king. For he might be the 'Pope' of the Tio, but was he a ruling sovereign?

3. *The King as ruler*

The kingdom was a concept which found its expression mainly in the collection of *ingkura* tribute. There was a high court of justice at the king's capital, but it was one of two and NGAASAA, together with the first lord NGEILIINO, presided over it. A legislative council did not

[31] H. BRUNSCHWIG, *La négociation*, pp. 22, 25. A pavilion made of eight red cloths shielded the assistants when Opontaba arrived. For June 1885 (Augouard) E. REDIER, op. cit., p. 145; P. AUGOUARD, op. cit., pp. 28–9. The first meeting was formal, the 'notables being present'. It was held in the king's hall of receptions. Other descriptions of the 1884 treaty are CH. DE CHAVANNES, op. cit., pp. 156–62 and drawing of the audience; E. ZORZI, op. cit., pp. 389–90, described the distribution of French gifts to NGEILIINO, NGAALIÕ, and NGANTSU in 1884 a few days after the audience where the treaty was handed over. The scene was splendid. The entry of the king was similar to the earlier description. The king drank, then danced, and then the palaver began. The lords did homage to the king. Cf. also N. NEY, op. cit., pp. 231–3; pp. 332–5 (J. De Brazza). L. GUIRAL, op. cit., pp. 286–7, was received without much ceremonial; pp. 289–92, a reception shed is described. The king held a brass and copper sceptre, wore only one cloth but had a seaman's whistle around the neck. A wooden statue (charm) stood near by and the lords wore approximately the same costume as the king.

exist, although it is clear that on matters of great import, the great lords near Mbe did meet, as for instance after the case of the stolen *nkobi* of Ikukuri. There was no common army, the forces of the lords of the crown near Mbe acting as such when required—and willing. But tribute did come from all the corners of the kingdom, going from squire to lord to higher lord and finally to NGEILIINO. The channels along which this flowed indicated the hierarchies and the whole formal structure of the kingdom.

The king ruled from his capital. However modest it might be, it was the capital (Sims: *mbee*, 'chief's town') and it was appropriately guarded. No one was allowed to approach the settlement unannounced. At fixed places along the access routes, halting places (*itsuuli*) were found. There were three on the road to the lands north of the Lefini, one to the Congo river and probably several on the road to the Pool. At each stop the traveller had to send warning ahead and could proceed only if he received permission to do so. Each of the routes was under the control of a lord who could stop the travellers. MAMPIELE controlled the Lefini and as such announced Brazza's arrival at Bouambé to the Court, NGEILIINO guarded access from the Congo river and NGANDZIÕ that from the Pool. Anybody who violated these rules and arrived at the capital in spite of them, was immediately fined, if he had not been ambushed before that.

Three lords lived in the capital itself: NGANSHIBI near the king, MOTIIRI at the opposite end, and NGAMBIÕ behind the king's palace. This may still have been the practice in Nduo, Iloo's settlement. It was also the duty of the other major lords of the crown, especially NGEILIINO and NGAALIÕ to live there, but in the 1880s they had founded a big settlement across the Gamboma river. On the Mbe plateau, about a day's distance away, two other major lords NGAMPO and NGANDZIÕ also had their headquarters.

This disposition of lords explains how the king could perform his major secular role: as a ruler. He might leave his lords alone and mediate between them when a war had broken out between them as between NGEILIINO, NGAMPO, and NGANDZIÕ by 1884. This mediation could be effective since, apart from his supernatural powers, he had authority to call on every other lord or squire anywhere to come to his rescue. In practice, Merlon's summary opinion that the king had around his village five others governed by major lords and ruled by messengers, is close to the truth.[32] Royal messengers went frequently from the court to the major lords. They did not carry orders, but information and called in the lords for advice when it was needed. As mediator between the lords the king could receive one lord one day,

[32] P. MERLON, *Revue*, p. 141. P. AUGOUARD, op. cit., p. 28, held that NGAASAA dominated the king and ruled: *divide et impera*; cf. A. VEISTROFFER, op. cit., p. 109; D'UZES, op. cit., p. 103.

another the next and come to a compromise or at least some balance of forces. As a king he could ask a lord to collect tribute or lead a trading expedition or both. Political crises threatening the whole kingdom were rare or absent because of its great spread and the low population density. So a co-ordinated rule by messenger was possible as long as the lords did not live too far away. These messengers were received with great respect. Thus a son of the king brought a wrapper giving the protection of the king to lord Opontaba and was received by the first lord of the realm on his knees.[33]

The king, too, could travel. It is said that Iloo travelled around the realm once a year near the end of the dry season,[34] probably to collect tribute. It was by travelling that he kept in touch with the lands north of the Lefini and his viceroy MUIDZU. During the years 1880–5 Iloo does not seem to have ever moved out of his Mbe, except for short visits[35] but his successors after 1899 certainly did, since one of them was nicknamed 'the wanderer'. His predecessors did also—at least one of them was known to have died when travelling.

As a secular ruler the king was clearly the first of the lords, but not the mightiest, at least not in terms of the resources he held in his own capital. He could not be more affluent than his NGEILIINO since the income from tribute and fines was divided into two parts, one of which was kept by the first lord. Other sources of income were the sale of brass collars, i.e. probably a price paid by lords when they were installed[36] and the free labour the king could command by asking lords, especially NGAMPO to provide it. Since no one at Mbe cultivated, that lord provided the royal capital with the food it needed even though the supply was rather irregular.[37] His dependence for food did not allow him to have surpluses or to trade in any foodstuffs. In fact the king was not a trader, even though his kinsmen were and ivory was occasionally sold for him by his *angabira* of whom there were only seven or eight.[38] Yet there was some wealth at the capital, since Iloo

[33] CH. DE CHAVANNES, op. cit., p. 162; The cloth was a safe-conduct. The king frequently sent messengers to Chavannes (ibid., pp. 190–275). Sometimes these were royal relatives (p. 274); also H. BRUNSCHWIG, *La négociation*, p. 30. From the detailed account of De Chavannes and the general notes of Guiral it is clear that the king did rule by mediation and constantly sent messengers to different lords. The mediation did not always succeed and L. GUIRAL, op. cit., pp. 293–4, remarked that this explained a lack of political unity in the positions of the chiefs.

[34] B. MAMBEKE-BOUCHER, op. cit., p. 27.

[35] CH. DE CHAVANNES, op. cit., pp. 162–3, for a visit to Ikukuri.

[36] H. BRUNSCHWIG, op. cit., pp. 30–1 (NGANTSU paid one slave for his collar).

[37] ibid., p. 23. The king mentioned his plantations of cassava. So residents of Mbe did cultivate. This would agree with Ngateo's remark that labour could be commanded by the king to help his wives with their fields if need be. Such labour came from other villages, stayed for the task (less than a fortnight) and was also employed in repairing houses, fences, cleaning, and perhaps clearing paths.

[38] J. DE WITTE, op. cit., p. 32. The eight slaves were perhaps *angabira*. As for trade that was perhaps conducted by his messengers to the Pool, but there is little trace of it.

was able to provide Brazza with fifty yards of imported cloth and three hundred local wrappers.[39] All this agrees with the observations made at state audiences. These durbars were on a scale compatible with his rank, but not exceeding what other lords had to offer.

Beside his role as a mediator between and co-ordinator of political action by the lords the king was also the squire of *nduo* and the headman of Mbe. His domain Itieere, included Ndua forest, one of the forests from which ancestors of kindreds aspiring to the throne had to stem from. It included Ibali, where many graves of lords and kings were located. A small establishment watched over them.[40] Beyond this and because of the lack of water, the domain had no inhabitants. The king himself lived in another domain belonging to NGEILIINO.

The king also acted as headman of Mbe. His relatives clustered around him as around any village leader. As such he had a council and *amieene*.[41] We do not know if he addressed his villagers at dawn and at dusk as other leaders did. Mbe was not just an ordinary village for few worked because they were all relatives of the king. The residents would go out and claim food in other settlements. They traded as well and expected to be housed and fed on their travels because of their status.[42] Among the royal women the king's sisters and mothers were not given special treatment. The king's daughters, however, were married without bridewealth for they belonged to 'all the Tio' and kings moreover could not be under *litsũ* counter-bridewealth obligations to their subjects. The king in turn could not marry any daughters of his major lords, 'for they were his children'. Perhaps these lords were too powerful to be allowed to enter into an egalitarian brother-in-law relationship with the king. But the major lords of the crown did send women from their domains to be wives of the king. Even a squire might send such a woman if she had caught the king's eye. In fact few gave women and since king Iloo no monarch had more than twelve of them.

One should not dismiss too lightly the king's role as headman. For in this he acted a basic role in Tio social and political life, which was very close to his role for the lords. He handled the inhabitants of Mbe and they were his kin in the fashion of a village leader. Like any headman he had to cope with lesser leaders in his settlement. So that behaviour

[39] D. NEUVILLE, CH. BREARD, op. cit., p. 116; H. BRUNSCHWIG, op cit., p. 30, where he alludes to this.

[40] L. GUIRAL, op. cit., pp. 301–3. The site had been used for some time. Iloo and Mbandieele would no longer be buried there but in a near-by wood at Nkoo. LIPIE, NGAATAALI, Ntsaalu, and Ngateo all agreed. NGAALIO Ikwa who succeeded Ngalie, the lord Brazza knew, was buried at Ibali and apparently so were NGANTSU and, according to one version, Opontaba. Ibali was not thought to be a place where all the kings that ever ruled had been buried. It was *en vogue* before Nkoo, probably because of the first king buried there.

[41] L. GUIRAL, op. cit., pp. 295–6; H. BRUNSCHWIG, op. cit., p. 33; P. AUGOUARD, op. cit., pp. 28–9. Some cassava was planted near by in 1885.

[42] L. GUIRAL, op. cit., p. 297.

associated with kinship served as a model for political behaviour. The lords were the king's 'children' or his 'wives' and he was their '*wookuru*'.

4. *The royal succession*

Anyone who belonged to the *baamukaana lilimpu* and who had had one ancestor whose kindred claimed origin in the woods of Ndua, Mbe aNdzieli (near Mbe), or Ikie was eligible. Ibalico spoke of six 'branches' named *impio, ison, onzala, impan, inkui, konsan.*[43] Moreover Ngaayüo maintained that only *baana be iboolo*, i.e. patrilaterally linked persons could be chosen. So far as is known, however, this rule was not observed for any succession after Iloo I. Nor did the kings have to be chosen from each of the three kindreds in any form of rotation. The choice was in the hands of the NGANDZIÕ 'the foremost child of the king' and the NGEILIINO jointly. Any squire or lord except NGAALIÕ was excluded and so was anyone who ever ate elephant meat. Yet Andibi was a squire.

From the known data since the accession of Iloo, descent in all-including mixed-lines prevailed. All the candidates, moreover, with the exception of Andibi and Ngankia Mbandieele were closely related to Iloo as *mbwei, mwaana ankieli*, or *otioolu.* A candidate had to have at least one king among his ancestors and this had to be proven. It is doubtful if this was an absolute rule, considering the case of Ngankia Mbandieele where this condition was, it seems, lacking. As for a rule the NGANSHIBI mentioned that only one whose *taara* had been king could become king and never one whose *nkaa* had been, that is virtually reversed by the data. In practice moreover a suitable person who was not wealthy would be eliminated because he would not be able to pay the lords at *lisee* and Ngateo as well as Mbiinu Mbiinu mentioned it explicitly.

It is clear that the election of a king was the occasion of much wrangling. For the last three kings before Iloo II were chosen by the NGEILIINO, although Ngalifourou as *chef de canton* and the French administrators were more than influential. The last king was a candidate of NGANDZIÕ and the *Jeunesses révolutionnaires* and both NGANDZIÕ and NGEILIINO agreed on nominations for kings earlier than and including Andibi, although one Mundzwaani, a son of

[43] M. IBALICO, op. cit., p. 30. Inkwii was the name of the king's quarter in Mbe and Ibalico notes, p. 32 that Ntsaalu's 'branch' was that one. His names are not 'forests', the Tio do not have names for lineages nor does anyone record them as such. It seems most likely that they were names of villages in which persons who later became kings were leaders. On the three forests Ntsaalu who came from Ndua and NGAALIÕ claimed that only this forest counted. NGANDZIÕ excluded Ikie, but all other informants (mainly Ngaayüo, NGAMPO, LIPIE, Ngateo) agreed on the three. LIPIE both knew and was not directly interested. M. N. OBENGA, *Le royaume*, p. 36, repeats Ibalico, but understands the names as referring to 'clans'!

Ikukuri was simply named by the French. It is evident that from the onset of the colonial period the influence of the French altered the whole process profoundly[44] and so it becomes difficult to know what actually happened.

According to LIPIE, the two lords NGANDZIÕ and NGEILIINO consulted with NGAMPO and NGAALIÕ and absolute agreement was needed. The choice of these four could be vetoed first by LIPIE who would see if the candidate would 'last' or not and in the latter case would advise the taking of another candidate. NGANSHIBI, the regent during the interregnum and MOTIIRI also had a possible veto said NGAATALI. Since the interregnum lasted for almost a year because the dead king had not yet been buried, there was time to jockey for positions, and finally agree on a common compromise candidate. Or, on the contrary, one man could eventually force the electors to take him, as seems to have happened at the time of Iloo's grandfather.

Once the man was known, he was told by the NGEILIINO, made a pretence of running away, was caught by MWANGÃW, beaten by the lords and the people. While the person was slapped, he was told: 'This the last time we can hit you freely; later when you will be king, you will not know us anymore.' Then the candidate was given a red blanket *nkãw* after which there was dancing for days. But before the public ceremonies, the chosen man was given the choice to turn the nomination down.

One source had it that the new king was to be a 'pure' Tio from the Congo river, had to be elected on the tomb of the deceased king and only from among the councillors of the former king. One of the main *ngàà* communicated with the late ruler's soul who then designated his successor. In this way Ngankia Mbandieele was chosen to succeed Andibi.[45] If this was true at all it was probably a part of the nomination rituals.

After having ruled for a short while, the new monarch was summoned and put into *lisee* by NGANDZIÕ. If the pattern of events after king Ngaayüo's death is any guide, there was much bickering over this. The lords wanted the king to be initiated as quickly as possible and the latter wanted to postpone *lisee* as long as he could. In fact *lisee* was designed to follow closely upon the nomination, since the opening ceremonies of *lisee* were identical with the nomination ceremonies.

The status and institution of kingship forms, with those of squire and lord, the focal institutions of the political structure. Each of them involved a status, a way of living, emblems and an ideology justifying authority. So much is similar between them that one would be tempted

[44] A. DOLISIE, op. cit., pp. 45–6. He already recommended Ikukuri before 1894.

[45] *Notice sur les Bateke* (Costurdié?) document dating from 1936–8. G. VERVLOET, *Un peu de Folklore*, p. 29, held from indirect sources that the king was elected by his 'Council of notables' to whom the rightful heir was designated in dreams.

to consider them images copied one from the other. The secular role was perhaps a mere extension of that of the leader of a residential kinship group, while the mystical dimension could be seen as an extension of the squire's relation with the *nkira*—lords and kings would then be merely magnified squires. But this view does not stand up to scrutiny. The relation between land and the person at the level of the squire is not duplicated closely, the roles of king and lords in coping with conflict are not found at the level of the squire, and kingship epitomizes a legitimacy of authority best seen at the ritual *lisee*, which stresses the delegation of authority from kingship to the lords, whereas the lords took pride in the autonomy of their power and authority as linked with the *nkobi*. Kingship was not lordship at a higher level. It was the cornerstone of the whole system.

5. *The formal structure of the realm*

The extent of the kingdom in the 1880s as reflected by the giving of tribute is not evident. In the north the Ngungulu north and south of the Nkéni did not recognize the ruler at Mbe as a political overlord, simply as a major foreign king. The Tio king could even be considered to be just a subordinate of the NGIA, overlord of the Ngungulu, in a way similar to the Ngungulu lords because he sent gifts to NGIA, just as at Mbe the Kukuya could be considered dependents of the realm because tribute from their two overlords reached Mbe. The king was not recognized by the Tege, but he was by the Jiju. In the west most of the Tio Laadi did not acknowledge the monarch's rule although the people living east of the Ndouo river gave tribute to the lord of Nkoo who paid tribute. In the south-west different lords paid tribute as far west as Mindouli and along the river Foulakari. Despite a strong sense of local autonomy the lords around the Pool were also tributary through their overlord NTSUULU of Kinshasa. North of the Black river NGOBILA collected from the Mfunu, but only from those of the territory of DUMU, not of TUA nor of Mbe Ngana, even though TUA did trace the origin of his authority to the king. But TUA no longer paid tribute. North of the Kasai the Ngenge all paid tribute to their own king at his Mbe, but it is not clear whether the latter sent tribute to the king of the Tio.[46]

[46] The theoretical boundaries were set by the limits within which tribute was paid, as is the Tio view. The writers based themselves on effective visible authority of the king or on the delegation of powers they assumed from the wearing of brass collars. In addition the diplomatic interests of the International African Association were not to recognize any authority to the king at Mbe beyond the plains of Mbe proper, while the French tried to represent this authority as stretching as far as possible. Indications are; H. BRUNSCHWIG, op. cit., p. 21, where Brazza gives the extent as stretching from the mouth of the Nkéni river to the rapids below Kinshasa and westwards to Ngamfourou (NGWAMPOLO?); W. BENTLEY, *Pioneering*, I, p. 334, seems to indicate a well marked boundary at the Foulakary river. At Linzolo the first Catholic mission,

The realm corresponded closely to the cultural and linguistic boundaries the anthropologist recognizes, with the possible exception of the Mfunu, the Fumu, and the populations around the Pool. Correlation with geographic features is also evident. The distribution of the populations shows a major nucleation around the Pool, where as many Tio lived as on the whole plains of Mbe, Mpũ, and perhaps Mboõ. Other nucleations seem to have existed around Mbe and the channel near Mpio aBwaani and Mswata, on the plains of Djambala near Ndolo, on the Mboõ plains near Abili, and perhaps on the western part of the Nsah plateau and on the Nkéni near the residence of NGIA. The Kukuya plateau was much more densely populated than the others. It is not surprising that major nucleations of population should correspond to more autonomous centres of political power. This holds for the Kukuya and the Ngungulu ruled by NGIA as well as for the area of Abili where MUIDZU and NGEIMPÃW resided, while the king controlled the nucleation around Mbe. But NGWAMPOLO on the Djambala plateau depended on MUIDZU and the dependence of the Pool on Mbe is a major anomaly in the pattern. If the economic circuits of trade are superimposed on the political territory, the anomaly of the Pool stands out even more. The wealthiest part of the kingdom was not the residence of the king, who only controlled, albeit imperfectly, the markets of Mpio aBwaani and Mswata and the traffic in the channel. These facts are obviously linked with the great autonomy the lords enjoyed. Only that made the situation acceptable to them. Thus only its mystical prestige enforced kingship.[47]

The formal political structure was visible in the collection of *ingkura* or tribute from the *nkani*. This was done in general, once a year, although the king could call for more in food when he needed it. At

---

the territory, which was Fumu, may or may not have belonged to the realm; since the NGAALIÕ with whom Mgr. Augouard made peace may have been the local Fumu title or the lord of Mbe. D. NEUVILLE, CH. BREARD, *Voyages*, p. 177, specified that the king's authority was not recognized two days west-north-west of the Pool in the direction of Djambala (information Brazza, 1880–1); p. 213, the Foulakary was given as boundary between the Batékés (Fumu) and groups related to the Kongo (Augouard, 1881). At the Pool the situation is well known. The king had little authority, least at Mpila and Ntamo. Nevertheless Brazza did meet NGAALIÕ who was on a trading and tribute collecting expedition with headquarters at Kinshasa. But Brazza, H. BRUNSCHWIG, op. cit., p. 54, recognized that the authority of the king was limited to the only privilege of having his lords from Mbe given food and tribute by the local lords, squires, and traders.

[47] The situation had arisen out of a protracted historical development. Kingship had most of its roots on the Mboõ plains and may have moved the centre of the realm south of the Lefini after the markets of the Pool began to assume great importance during the late sixteenth or the seventeenth centuries. The increased trade during the early 1880s still led to such a movement since NGANDZIÕ abandoned his former location to shift his residence to the south and closer to the route from Mbe to the Pool.

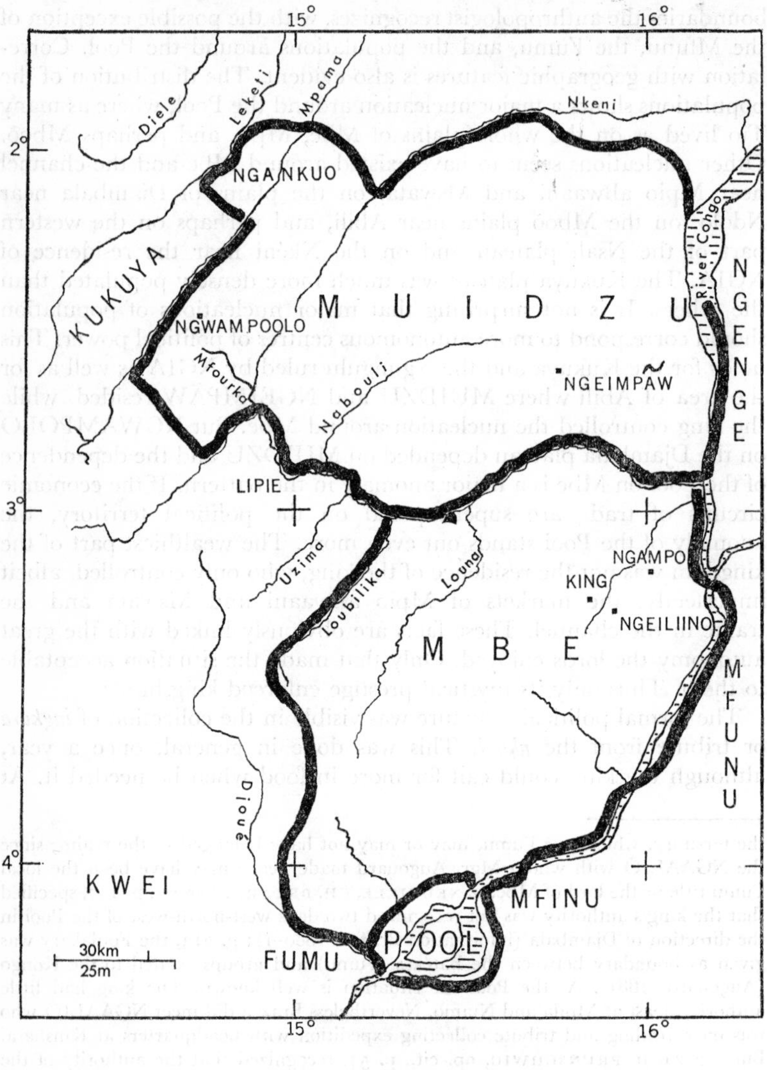

Map 12. *Political Nucleations*

▬▬ : Limits of nucleations and region of Pool

■ Lipie : Residence of some of the major lords

MFUNU : Names of peoples

MBE : Names of Nucleations

3. Ngaliema. Reprinted from H. M. Stanley, *The Congo and the Founding of its Free State*, Vol. I. London, 1885.

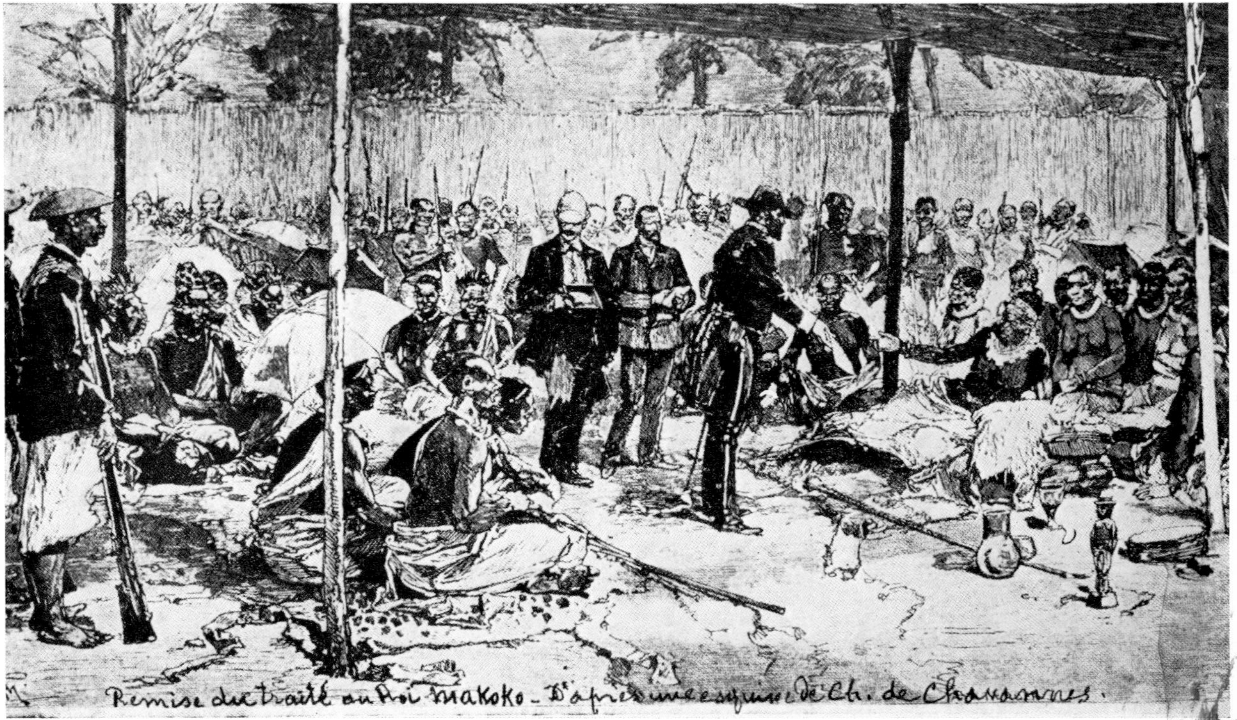
Remise du traité au Roi Makoko - D'après une esquisse de Ch. de Chavannes.

4. Brazza at Court, 1884. Reprinted from Ch. de Chavannes, *Avec Brazza. Souvenirs de la Mission de l'Ouest Africain mars 1883 – janvier 1886*. Paris, 1935.

each level of collection from the squire upwards each of the authorities kept half of the collected goods for themselves and with this bought slaves, married wives, or attracted followers by gifts to increase his settlement. The contents were meat, fish, goats, fowl, kola, mats, pipes, double or single bells, raphia squares or wrappers and, according to Ngateo, even *nji* and copper *ngiele* which were currencies. Crops were given only by the settlements near the capital. In each domain, for each squire, the amount was something like one goat or ten mats, or in a small domain it could be as little as a fowl or a few kola. NGAMPO asked from a well populated domain as much as 100 to 200 kola, 1 goat, 2 fowl, 5 or 10 *ikala* mats and residents complained about the amounts. In fact the amount was not specified. It was up to the lord to bring tribute to his overlord and to the squire to bring it to his lord. If it was not enough the amount was refused and more had to be brought. The frequency with which it was brought was also irregular. If squires or lords did not send for any a long period and did not heed suggestions, they might be attacked by their overlords. The fluidity in all this reminds one how close to the use of naked power this political system remained. Brazza recorded that certain settlements, peopled by ex-slaves of the king paid a goat, or goats to each passing envoy from the capital and goats and slaves to major lords. Opontaba received in 1884 tribute from NTSUULU and Bankwa of Ndolo consisting of a piece of blue cloth, a bundle of *mitako*, and two other lengths of cloth; Lekibu, squire of Kingabwa, wanted to pay a blue cloth as well but was told that he was a *nkani* of NGAALIÕ. He knew this quite well, but apparently felt that the situation required him to pay the NGEILIINO as well. From the greed shown by some of the Tio lords one suspects that they tried whenever possible to extract the maximum.[48]

There was a formal chain of command over *nkani* who brought tribute to a specified overlord. Theoretically this chain could never change. In practice the conflicting claims of the major lords on *nkani* indicate, as one suspected, that they tried to acquire *nkani* and to prevent previous *nkani* from going to another lord. The case of Lekibu indicates that smaller squires sometimes paid to two lords, especially if they were powerful and near by. The relation of *nkani* was also expressed in the homage *nkani* made through the *mpfõ* or *ntsii* salutes to their overlords and in the fact that the latter sent a length of cloth or raphia cloth to be 'attached' to the catafalque of late *nkani*.

Thus a theoretical structure of the kingdom with various levels of overlordship emerges which can be listed and mapped, showing

[48] H. BRUNSCHWIG, op. cit., p. 55 (goats, slaves), p. 54 (NGAALIÕ had two hundred soldiers with him. He was there for a year, living off the land and trading. Brazza expected him to be replaced by NGEILIINO or NGANTSU. (The former did indeed travel to the Pool later); CH. DE CHAVANNES, op. cit., p. 349 (tribute paid by NTSUULU. Bankwa, Lekibu); L. GUIRAL, op. cit., pp. 254–5, 300–1 (greed of both NTSUULU and the king).

Chart 19

The chain of tribute among major lords

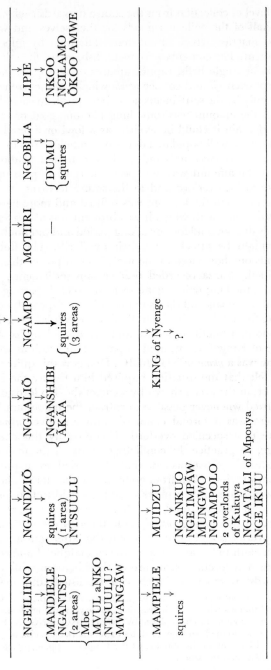

KING
↓
NGEILIINO
↓

NGEILIINO	NGANDZIÕ	NGAALIÕ	NGAMPO	MOTIIRI	NGOBILA	LIPIE
↓ MANDIELE, NGANTSU (2 areas), Mbe, MVUL aNKO, NTSUULU?, MWANGÃW	↓ squires (1 area), NTSUULU	↓ NGANSHIBI, ÃKÃA	↓ squires (3 areas)	—	↓ DUMU, squires	↓ NKOO, NCILAMO, ÕKOO AMWE
MAMPIELE ↓ squires	MUIDZU ↓ NGANKUO, NGE IMPÃW, MUNGWO, NGAMPOLO, 2 overlords of Kukuya, NGAATALI of Mpouya, NGE IKUU		KING of Nyenge ↓ ?			

Key: capitals: Titles; ↓ : indicate relation of lord to nkani.

provinces and cantons in the realm. At the top of the structure were some lords of the crown, the ones who had least ritual significance. The chart (page 400), gives the hierarchy at the level of overlord. But it must be remembered that all overlords sent tribute to NGEILIINO.

Note that the structure is angled so that even the most humble squire paying to NGEILIINO became equal with MUIDZU because the latter who collected from all the lords north of the Lefini and even transmitted gifts from the two Kukuya overlords represented in fact the apex of a system similar to the one led by NGEILIINO south of the river. Further it is remarkable that NGAMBIÕ had neither domain nor *nkani*. He was a 'woman' of the king and lived with him. Most of the lords at the second level only had squires, sometimes substantial numbers of them, under their command. If the model were to be built from the bottom up MAMPIELE, MOTIIRI, NGAMPO, and NGANDZIÕ would be demoted, which reflects correctly the territorial importance of the first two, but not of the others whose holdings formed huge blocks.

The above reflects primarily the point of view of the central organization at Mbe. Locally things were seen differently. To cite one case, the Fumu north of the Pool depended on a minor lord called MPUYA KUFUMU. He was said to communicate directly with the king, receiving royal messages, before anybody else did around the Pool. He commanded, both transmitting messages and collecting tribute, three other chiefs in the Brazzaville area, including NGIA or Mfwa, and paid his tribute in the dry season every two or three years to the king at Mbe. When a new MPUYA was named the king came to the area to give him three leopard's teeth, the collar, the fly whisk, and a knife of honour shaped like a crescent (a Bobangi model). Ibalico who collected these data stressed that it was an 'autonomous state'. He overlooked completely the position of the NGEILIINO.[49]

The hierarchy as it existed was clearly the outcome of particular historical events, rather than any logical attempt to organize the territory. If some areas such as the southern part of the plateau of Djambala under NGWAMPOLO (N'Gamfourou?) was a geographical and population unit and thus 'made sense', it was not so on the plains of Mpũ for instance when NGANTSU collected from a few tiny domains around the Gatsou lake, while NGEILIINO's *nkani* MANDIELE governed the rest but shared parts of the northern Mpũ with both NGANDZIÕ and NGAMPO. Such a situation could only be the outcome of a competition between the major lords.

[49] M. IBALICO, *M'bouya kou M'Foumou*, pp. 49–52. At the time of his writing (1954) political tensions were opposing the NGAMABA as the title was known then to the King in the city of Poto poto. This certainly coloured the presentation somewhat. It is known from direct written sources for instance that NGIA (Mfwa) was dependent on NTSUULU (Kinshasa) and through him on either the NGEILIINO or perhaps NGAALIÕ. Also M. N. OBENGA, *Le royaume*, p. 40.

Map 13.

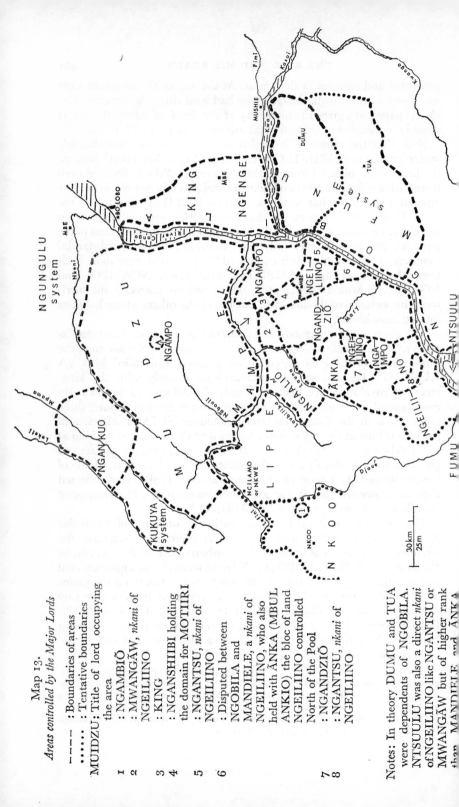

Areas controlled by the Major Lords

- - - - : Boundaries of areas
• • • • • • : Tentative boundaries
MUIDZU: Title of lord occupying the area
1 : NGAMBIÕ
2 : MWANGÃW, *nkani* of NGEILIINO
3 : KING
4 : NGANSHIIBI holding the domain for MOTIIRI
5 : NGANTSU, *nkani* of NGEILIINO
6 : Disputed between NGOBILA and MANDIELE, a *nkani* of NGEILIINO, who also held with ÃNKA (MBUL ANKIO) the bloc of land NGEILIINO controlled North of the Pool
7 : NGANDZIÕ
8 : NGANTSU, *nkani* of NGEILIINO

Notes: In theory DUMU and TUA were dependents of NGOBILA. NTSUULU was also a direct *nkani* of NGEILIINO like NGANTSU or MWANGÃW but of higher rank than MANDIELE and ÃNKA.

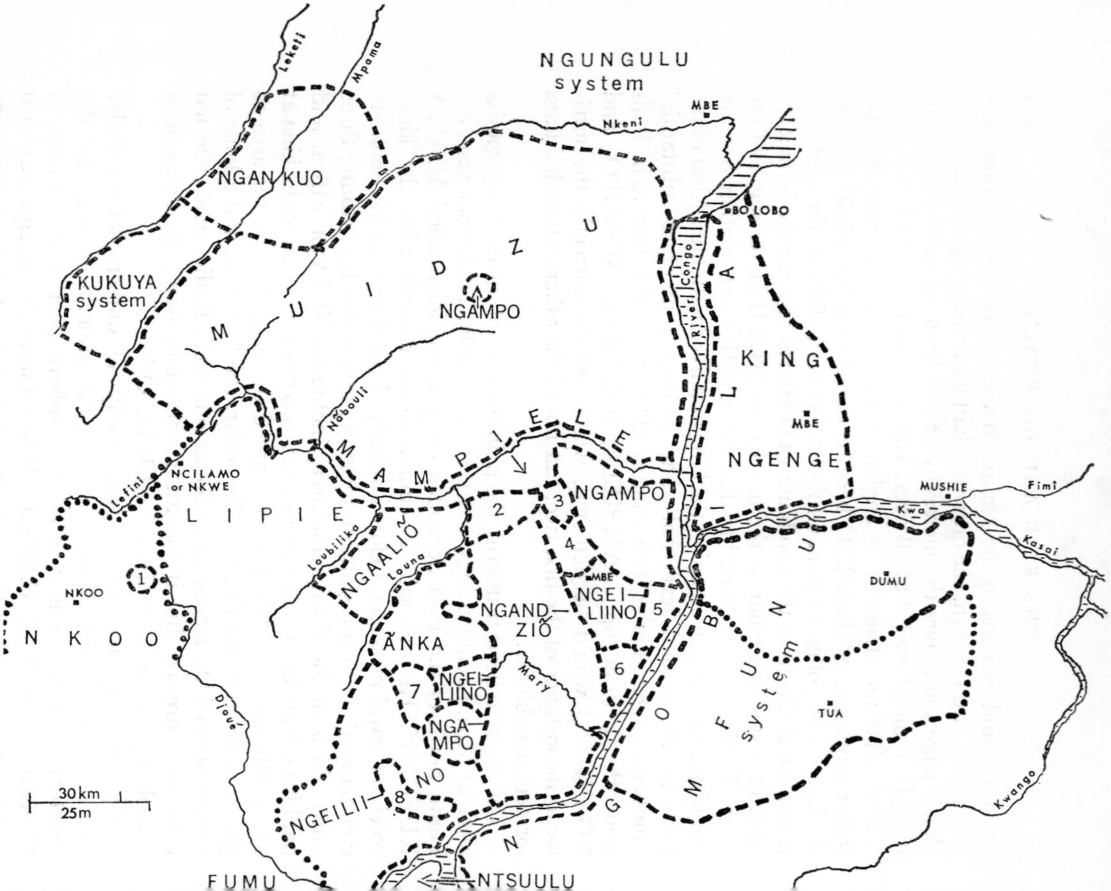

Governing consisted of collecting tribute, in defending *nkani* when they were attacked and in sending messengers with orders to the *nkani* about whatever matters might come up. At the top the king could communicate directly, presumably with the ten overlords listed in the diagram. But this orderly picture clashes violently with the data cited about conflict. Was this whole theoretical construct then without value? Or are the data about wars and feuds for instance misleading about the rarity of such events, which would make them exceptions?

Evidently wars were not raging all the time. Only two conflicts are mentioned: one at NGOBILA in 1883 and one at the border between Kukuya and Jinju in 1882.[50] But the story of the career of Ngaliema and his struggle with NTSUULU or the tensions between NGEILIINO, NGAMPO, NGANDZIÕ, and NGAALIÕ on the plains of Mbe, along with the references to fortifications, hidden villages, etc., strengthen the impression that there was considerable insecurity. One must dismiss part of the ethnographic picture as having little value. For instance to speak of cantons or provinces would do violence to all the facts as they are reported by travellers. To dismiss it completely was not correct either since tribute was collected, the king did receive food from the surrounding villages and the traditions stress the genuine authority over lesser lords and squires of the major lords.

The dilemma can only be solved by a recourse to concrete data. The paradox between the two points of view arises from the relation between authority and power in a society where actual power quickly tended to become established authority. In other words the impact of historical events was immediate and decisive. Moreover it should be obvious that the Tio political structures did not evolve in a vacuum during the 1880s. The arrival and gradual take over by Europeans should also be considered. Hence the need for a chapter dealing with the actual historical development of the kingdom in Iloo's reign.

The recording of these events however is also accidental. It highlights certain episodes, deals with certain parts of the realm more than others and concentrates mainly on the years 1880–5. Therefore a general view of the actual structure of the realm by 1880–2 needs to be presented first. Another compelling reason for this is that since titles have been presented in the abstract as parts of the structure to which they formally related, we need to see who occupied these positions and how far the actions of the office-holders corresponded with the theoretical ranking.

Traditions and writers agree to the following ranking of major lords in terms of power. The traditional view as given by LIPIE and NGAATALI who both knew the end of the period was: (i) NGEILIINO, (ii) NGAALIÕ or NGANDZIÕ, (iii) the one not mentioned

[50] CH. DE MARTRIN DONOS *Les Belges*, II, pp. 124–34; L. GUIRAL, op. cit., pp. 192–3.

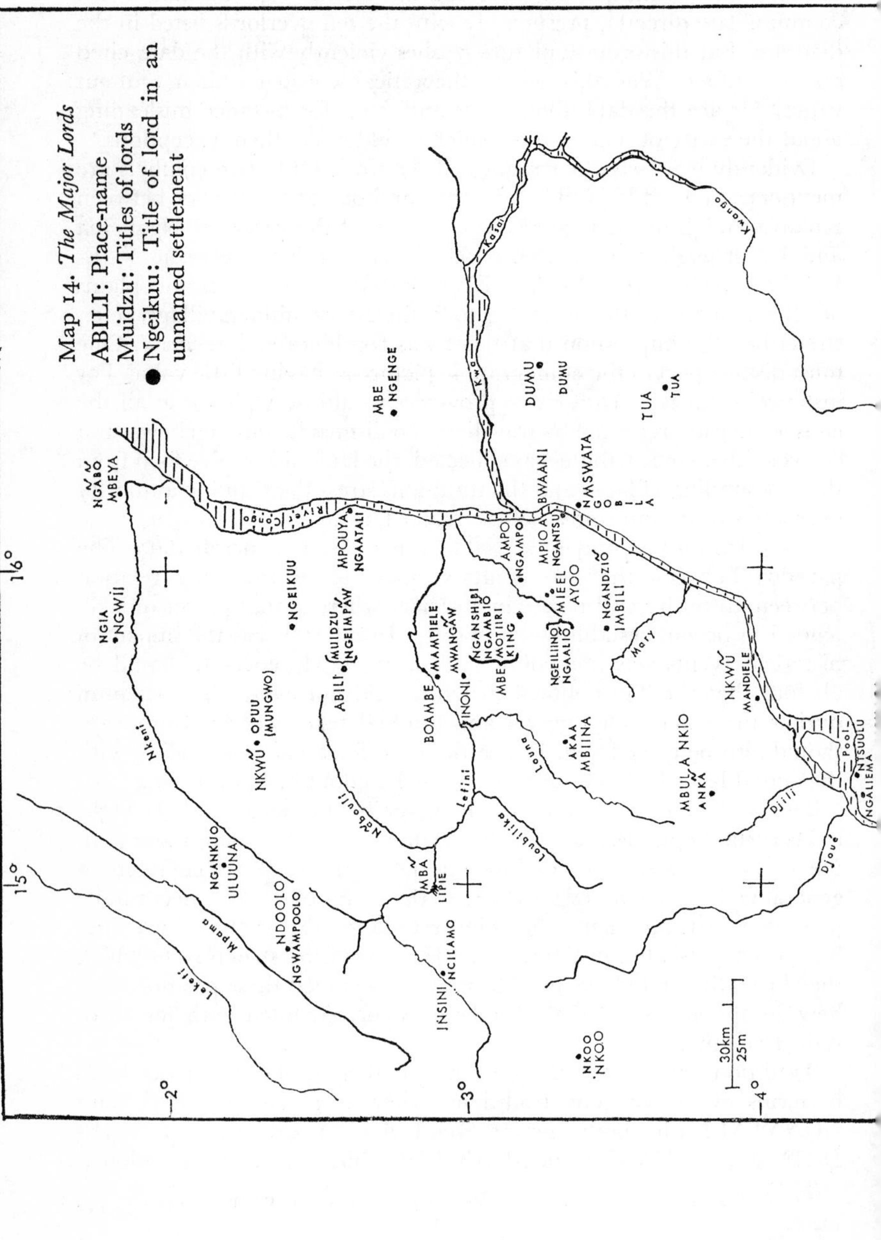

Map 14. *The Major Lords*
ABILI: Place-name
Muidzu: Titles of lords
● Ngeikuu: Title of lord in an unnamed settlement

under (ii), (iv) NGAMPO, (v) NGANTSU. The data ranked only the lords south of the Lefini. The inclusion of NGANTSU which entirely corresponds with the opinions of the writers, is remarkable. He was vying with NGOBILA for control of the 'channel'. The main difference between informants and all the written sources is the high rank given to NGANDZIÕ. The French neglected him completely until they returned to the court in April 1884 and were made aware of his status. Since they had brought gifts only for NGEILIINO, NGAALIÕ, and NGANTSU, they were forced to send belated presents to NGAMPO and NGANDZIÕ. Later events from this reign and the next indicate that the ranking of LIPIE and NGAATALI is correct.

The following table indicates what is known about the persons holding offices during the period.

From the chart a remarkable fact emerges, which was not given by Tio in explaining the political structure. All the chiefs of the area of Mbe were related by descent. The concept *baamukaana lilimpu*, or aristocrat, amounts in this case to an '*ibuuru* in which one inherits', a small kindred. Details about later kings and their claims of origin confirm this since many can claim both Ndua (like Iloo) and Ikie or even Mbe aNdzieli. Their genealogies included kings on both sides of their ancestry.

The chart explains and is completed by a remarkable record made by Brazza which was given in the form of a list of names. It represented a genealogy starting with the grandfather of Iloo and following a text about kingship from his time. According to it NGWAMPOLO, NGEIMPÃW, and NTSUULU were also related to the king, the first as father's brother's sons, the other as father's brother. This also involved MUIDZU who was always an elder close kinsman of NGEIMPÃW. The only title thus left out is NGOBILA. Thus the nature of the common cohesion between the lords, their common interests in kingship as a kindred, the nature of their personal links with it become much clearer. The king ruled by messenger and the messages were concerned with averting clashes between lords, or other such threats to peace, and with the collection of tribute. The divisions between the lords on the Mbe plateau are similar to divisions which are also found in kin-groups, such as when the pair of brothers NGEILIINO and NGAALIÕ is opposed to maternal relatives NGAMPO and NGANDZIÕ. In part the groupings are different, as when NGANTSU sided with NGEILIINO Opontaba. But the factor of close links of kinship to the king was of paramount importance in explaining how the kingdom could and did function. More than the ideology of kingship close kinship was the common bond between the autonomous lords.

This brings out a crucial feature of the king's rule to which little attention has been paid so far: his prerogative to appoint major lords. No case from the reign of Iloo is known, but both before and after kings

CHART 20

The known major lords of the 1880s

title	*date*[a]	*name*	*kinship relations*	*residence*
*KING	1880	Iloo	—	(Nduo; Itiele)
*NGEILIINO	1880	Opontaba	'brother' of king (Guiral, 284, 302)[b]	(Mieel a Yoo)
*NGANDZIÕ	1884	Ingulangula	matrikin of Opontaba (Miandoo)	(Imbili)
MUIDZU	—	Mpia or Inkul aNtso	?	(Abili)
NGEIMPÃW	1880	—	'brother' (Ba) or *otioolu* of MUIDZU (Ba)	(Abili)
NGWAMPOLO	1880	Ngamfuru ?	?	(Ndoolo)
*NGAALIÕ	1880	Ngaaliẽ	'brother' of king and Opontaba (Guiral, 284) Bwabwa Njali on Djoue was his nephew	(Mieel a Yoo)
*NGAMPO	1880	Ikukuri	*mwaan ankieli* of king and Opontaba (Guiral, 298)	(Ampo)
*NGANTSU	1880	Ngantale	*mwaan ankieli* of king and Opontaba (Guiral, 298)	(Mpio a Bwaani)
*NGAMBIÕ	1880	?	brother of king (Brunschwig, 30)	(Nduo)
NGOBILA	1880	Ngantiele NgeImpãw	?	(Mswata)
NTSUULU	1880	Ngaekala Ntsuvila	his son, title NGIA ruled Mfwa (Guiral, 227) his brother Ngako had been ruler of Ntamo (Brunschwig, 54)	(Nshaasa)
—	1877	Itsi Ngaliema	none	(Ntamo)
MAMPIELE	1880	Ngampere	his nephew was squire nearby (Brunschwig, II, 172)	(Bouambe)

[a] Date of first mention in documents.

[b] L. GUIRAL, *Le Congo*; H. BRUNSCHWIG, *La négociation*; H. BRUNSCHWIG, II: *Les cahiers*.

exercised this prerogative. King Ngaayüo once went with the whole court north of the Lefini to appoint a new MUIDZU. Apart from the gifts he received from lords who wanted various titles, the occasion allowed him to appoint a relative and someone among his relatives who would balance the factions at court more equally. He acted thus both as king and as the leader of a kinship group.

With these devices at his disposal the king with his court ruled effectively over the right bank of the Congo river between the Lefini and the Djoué, while MUIDZU governed the regions between the Lefini and the Nkéni. The plateau of Djambala with NGWAMPOLO and the Jiju of NGANKUO, like the Fumu, the Laadi, and the lands of NGOBILA were not under the king's direct control and beyond, the king of Mbe was only a reputation or a name. So that the realm in effect comprised those lands where the fourth day was really called Nkwe Mbali.

Chapter XV
The Kingdom under Iloo

IN the period of Iloo's reign Tio society altered visibly only in its political and economic dimensions. Even there events had an immediate impact only on the commercial structures and on the political relations at the level of kings and lords. Political and economic institutions provided the 'superstructures' of the whole social fabric and linked the Tio neighbourhoods together while relating them to areas around the kingdom. It is just because they were overarching structures that events had a more immediate effect upon them. The impact of events compels us to present a detailed historical sketch of the period. For the purposes of clarity the data will be separated in a section dealing with politics and the political structure, followed by a section devoted to economic history. It is not the intention to present a complete political and economic history of the establishments of Europeans in the area. The account remains strictly tied to Tio affairs. Hence much material dealing with European political and economic development was left out, as being irrelevant to the narrow field of Tio affairs.

1. *The political developments*

How and when Iloo came to the throne is unknown. He had ruled for many years before 1880 and was very probably ruling long before 1877.[1] The most important lords at Mbe, in the channel and along the Pool were all in office or in power by 1880 and survived at least to 1892, except for NTSUULU who died a year or two earlier and the lords of the Djoué and Mfwa, BWA NJALI and Mfwa who died in 1884. But the NGEILIINO, NGAALIÕ, NGAMPO, NGANDZIÕ, NGOBILA, NGANTSU, and Ngaliema of Ntamo lived during the whole period. This gave a certain stability to politics since the factor of differing personalities was practically kept constant.

Only one leader in this area was not an aristocrat. He was the famous Ngaliema, a run-away slave, taken in by a new master at Kinshasa

[1] He was old in 1884 when Pecile (E. ZORZI, *Al Congo*, p. 224) called him 'povero vecchio'. Cf. his photograph, ibid., opp. p. 148. This made a reign of some length possible. The fact that he or others never claimed that he was not king when Stanley arrived in 1877 makes it possible that he ruled then. Perhaps he came to the throne in 1870 or 1875. Even by 1920, as the available documents show, no one knew who had ruled before him, which may indicate a long reign. Very soon after his death apparently however he assumed the status of a 'founding hero'.

around 1872[2] who succeeded to his master, feuded with NTSUULU, fled to Mfwa, returned to Ntamo, made an alliance with the Hum, was co-leader of Ntamo with Ngako when Stanley visited in 1877 and sole lord there after.[3] He owed his fortune to the ivory trade, and provided a spectacular demonstration of the link between wealth and power.

Stanley's descent of the Congo river, where he was ambushed, probably by NGOBILA was the first known major event of Iloo's reign, after Ngaliema's rise.[4] Two years later in 1879 NGAALIÕ, whether on his own and in agreement with his brother Opontaba, or on orders of the king is hard to say, came to the Pool with two hundred men, a strong force, to trade and to collect tribute. Perhaps he was following up earlier attempts by Opontaba himself which had led to a certain resistance from NTSUULU.[5] Brazza, though, represented this situation as habitual and suggested that NGANTSU, NGEILIINO, and NGAALIÕ rotated in residence at the Pool.[6] NGANTSU does not seem to be much in the picture but NGEILIINO and his brother had certainly established themselves on the Pool. The lord MANDIELE who commanded the villages on the Mpũ plains near the entrance to the Pool at this time, was a close relative of theirs.[7] The situation

[2] E. HANSSENS, *Les premières*, p. 7, gives the estimate of 1872. By 1877 he was co-ruler of Ntamo, but still perhaps a shade behind Ngako. Cf. H. STANLEY, *Through the Dark Continent*, pp. 536–8 although Ngankono of Mpila called Ntamo the village of Itsi.

[3] There are several differing versions about the early career of Ngaliema. All agree that he was a slave, traded, quarrelled with NTSUULU, and rose to prominence. How he succeeded in obtaining the lion's share of the ivory trade is unclear although Hanssens does mention that he bought slaves from the Zombo caravans, reversing the previous pattern. W. BENTLEY, *Pioneering*, I, p. 460, confirms. It seems then that a more systematic acquisition of slaves, and a better management of their activities is partly responsible for this. His diplomatic skills were also remarkable.

[4] The general history of the area has been well studied before 1886. The most relevant books are those of Stanley, Maurice, De Chavannes, Brazza (Brunschwig, Ney) Guiral, Pecile (Zorzi), for contemporary documents and De Chavannes, Brunschwig, Coquery, Luwel, as recent studies. But none goes much beyond early 1886. De Chavannes' second book was much less concerned with the Tio area and gives little detail. The best overall views are the article of Liebrechts on Léopoldville (1887–9) and Dolisie's (1893 about the situation in 1892). Detail must be gathered from travellers. The historiography understandably deals mostly with the establishment of the colonies and activities relating to it. We can assume that these are well known and concentrate on the political evolution in Tio territory and what is known at present about the commercial evolution.

[5] M. LUWEL, *Winton*, p. 237, where it appears from Saulez's inquiry that there had been fights between Opontaba and NTSUULU in past years for the payment of tribute. This must have happened before 1882 and probably before NGAALIÕ arrived with his troops in 1879. Tribute was due to Opontaba and this is why the agents of the International African Association were anxious to have him on their side, for this fact justified the claims of the French on the south bank of the Pool.

[6] On NGAALIÕ and the rotation, cf. H. BRUNSCHWIG, *La négociation*, p. 54.

[7] A NGEILIINO and his 'brother' married two sisters with the same father and one branch took the title MANDIELE and stayed at the Pool. The other kept the office of NGEILIINO, according to the MANDIELE of 1963. Since no genealogy or

indicates the concern by the lords of Mbe for the Pool, the main source of wealth and new power.

Brazza appeared on the plains in the summer and first tried to secure a plot of land from Ngampei, a squire north of the Lefini. He was duly sent to Mbe, undertook negotiations and signed a treaty on 10 September. The text of the treaty transferred sovereignty to France since its first sentence ran:

'King Makoko, who is sovereign over the lands lying between the mouth of the Lefini and Ncouna (Pool), having ratified the cession of territory made by Ngampey for the establishment of a French station and moreover ceded his hereditary rights of supremacy . . .'[8] It has been argued that the king knew quite well what he was doing, but it seems clear that he only wanted to cede land for the establishment of a commercial station. Ondono confirmed that the king gave Brazza a piece of earth as a sign of the transfer, but also wanted to enter into blood brotherhood, a common practice between trading partners. Opontaba and Ikukuri were consulted along with NGANSHIBI and NGANTSU, perhaps also with the lords resident at Mbe: MOTIIRI and NGAMBIÕ. Both Ikukuri and Opontaba, who were apparently on good terms with each other at this time, advised the king to refuse the cession says Ngateo. But after discussion, the king had his way. In return for the cession, and this is not apparent from the documents but evident from the tradition, Brazza promised trade goods and the benefits which trade would bring along with a general alliance. He seems to have left two more papers at Mbe. The way the Tio understood it one of these was to be sent to Brazza if the king needed something, probably goods, the other if there was difficulty and the king needed military help.[9]

One can only guess at the reasons which led Iloo to overrule the advice of the two lords. Possibly he wanted an ally to counter-balance the overwhelming power of a faction composed of NGEILIINO, NGAALIÕ, and NGAMPO, a power which accrued to them from their trading activities and their establishment on the Pool. Almost certainly he hoped that the station would be set up at Nduo[10] and, when this could not be obtained, that he could still control the flow

---

succession was available the date remains unknown and it could have happened after Iloo. But this is unlikely given other data about the NGEILIINOs.

[8] A. REDIER, *L'évêque*, p. 76. What the Tio ruler was to be given in compensation is not indicated in the treaty.

[9] H. BRUNSCHWIG, op. cit., p. 11. Tio tradition in ONDONO, *Souvenirs*, and by Ngateo. The two letters became a major motive in the tradition about the death of king Mbandieele in 1898. That a commercial station was involved cannot be doubted from the text of the Treaty of (N. NEY, *Conférences*, pp. 160–1), the passus cited from the treaty of 10 September and the notebooks of Brazza. All the Tio kings and lords talked about was a commercial station.

[10] N. NEY, op. cit., p. 159. With regrets he agreed to the location on the Pool.

of trade more directly if the French brought their goods without middlemen to the Pool. The fear of being faced with two hostile European parties, Stanley and Brazza, may have influenced his decision. He wanted at least one ally and in any case his decision was reached only after consulting with the *ikwii* of his *nkaa's nkaa*, something which may indicate support for his position from NGANSHIBI.[11]

Brazza left for the Pool and with the help of NGAALIÕ obtained lands between Mpila and the Djoué, i.e. much of the territory of Mfwa, and planted the flag at Okila. The marks of NGAALIÕ, NGIA Sã (Scianho Ngaekala) and the further unknown 'chiefs' Jouma Noula Ntaba and Ngaeko (Ngako, NTSUULU's brother?) were placed on another treaty on 3 October.[12] The omission of NTSUULU, the overlord for the whole area, is of interest. He may have sent his brother Ngako in his place. In any case Sã was his son.

Brazza left Malamine on the spot and went away to the coast. Within the next months Malamine could not obtain food at Mfwa and moved to Kinshasa where NTSUULU received him well. There was even talk of marrying NTSUULU's daughter. Malamine seems to have understood the mechanisms of Tio politics quite quickly, learned to speak the language and begun to dress like the Tio. He did not trade but hunted big game for NTSUULU. All this happened before February 1881 when the missionaries Bentley and Comber arrived. These were well received by Ngaliema but repulsed by the men from NTSUULU. Malamine mediated but they had to leave. It is obvious that by now Stanley was identified with Ngaliema and the French with NTSUULU. The foreign competition had aligned itself perfectly with the local oppositions. These ran across the Pool. BWANJALI (Bwabwa Njali) and NGAMPA were competitors at the Djoué ferry, as Mfwa and Mpila were on land. BWANJALI and Ngankono of Mpila allied with Ngaliema against NGAMPA and NGIA, then the son of NTSUULU.

This best explains the reception of both Mgr. Augouard and Stanley in July–August 1881. The situation was not that clear-cut however. Stanley was accepted at Mpila by Ngankono but another leader of the same settlement, Ntaba, probably the one who had signed the treaty of October 1880, managed to sway the other 'big men' there and Ngankono could not prevent a blockade of foodstuffs. Then Stanley received some food from NGAMPA showing that the latter was mainly concerned about his competition with BWANJALI and thought he could steal a march on the latter, whose closer proximity to Mfwa seems to have deterred him from selling food. NGIA led the opposition to

[11] ibid., here the king claimed that he wanted friendship with Brazza, to avoid having to fight two European factions at once. Brazza had consistently painted Stanley as the enemy.

[12] Text in N. NEY, op. cit., pp. 160–1. 'Scianho Ngaekala' could be Sã who was then NGIA and who died in 1884.

Stanley and Ngaliema, not so much perhaps because of the treaty with Brazza, as was assumed, but because Stanley was considered to be an ivory trader, whose friendship with Ngaliema might alter the situation of commerce and hence the balance of forces considerably. In addition the traders from the lower Congo did all they could to convince the Tio at the Pool that the arrival of the Europeans would be disastrous. They feared of course the loss of the carrying monopoly.[13]

The situation remained essentially unchanged until late in the year Ngaliema bowed under the pressure of his trading partners and subordinate chiefs. He then turned against Stanley's advance, but the latter now obtained support from the Hum who had been completely frozen out of the markets for a long time. Ngaliema's attempts came to naught, so he turned again to support Stanley, once the latter had convinced the other leaders of Ntamo that only a commercial station was to be put up and that their country was not sold to the Europeans. Whereupon Léopoldville was founded on 1 December 1881.[14]

On the Mbe plains, meanwhile, 1881 probably saw the beginning of a very serious rift among the lords. Ikukuri, the NGAMPO had become wealthy—how is still a mystery—and acquired the *nkobi* of NGAMPO. Like Opontaba he was a forceful personality and perhaps a better orator. Both were by far the ablest lords on the plains. According to tradition Opontaba was ambitious even beyond the limits expected from Tio lords, fierce and brutal. Tradition stresses that he did not feel bound by custom and pressurized other lords with war, tried to isolate the king and took all the tribute he could.[15]

The opposition which was perhaps unavoidable began with a quarrel between NGANTSU and Ikukuri over the inheritance from their common father. NGANTSU also was full of drive. Guiral could not forbear to remark: 'Nganchon unfortunately cannot repress his pirate instincts'.[16] The quarrel apparently erupted over women or slaves.

[13] C. COQUERY, *Brazza*, pp. 114–15; D. NEUVILLE, CH. BREARD, *Voyages*, pp. 212–17 (Mgr. Augouard), pp. 264–85 (Bentley and Comber) from the original publications: A. MAURICE, *Stanley*, pp. 90–8, for a summary of Stanley's adventures. Stanley stated clearly, p. 96, that Ngaliema believed him to be an ivory trader, pp. 92–3, makes it evident that a formal alliance with Ngaliema was achieved after much bargaining. Cf. also H. STANLEY, *The Congo*, I, pp. 290–312. P. 298, Ngankono claimed 'Makoko' was only a chief but richer, with more guns and more people than anyone at the Pool, a rather surprising statement because Makoko's *personal* wealth was not great, he had few personal followers and hence guns. So Ngankono in fact confirmed the dominant position of the whole Mbe establishment. Cf. also p. 311, Stanley's evaluation of Ngaliema's wealth minus slaves at about £4,800 and, p. 309, the opposition of Kongo and Zombo traders to the establishment of Europeans.

[14] A. MAURICE, op. cit., pp. 109–24. Léopoldville was founded 1 December and the *En avant* launched 2 December; H. STANLEY, op. cit., I, pp. 323–56.

[15] G. SAUTTER, *Le plateau*, p. 158, for a reflexion of the traditions about Opontaba; A. DOLISIE, *Notice*, p. 46, for a portrait of Ikukuri; CH. DE CHAVANNES, *Avec Brazza*, pp. 160–1, 216–17, for Opontaba and a drawing opp. p. 160.

[16] L. GUIRAL, *Le Congo*, p. 298. He also 'looked intrepid and intelligent'.

It was a classic little war. NGANTSU attacked Ampo at night, probably with some damage. Ikukuri retaliated by stealing NGANTSU's wives and showed himself easily the stronger, although his successor of 1963 claimed that he had only about fifty guns. NGANTSU was forced to abandon Mpio aBwaani, his residence, and to take refuge with the Bobangi. That was the situation when Guiral arrived in May 1882.[17]

At the Pool Léopoldville was slowly consolidated and it was not until 9 April that Stanley renewed blood brotherhood with Ngaliema and his trading establishment was functioning well. He could then hand over and leave for NGOBILA where he arrived on 26 April and negotiated for ten days with NGOBILA, NGANTSU, and a Mfunu lord Stanley calls 'Gandelay'. NGOBILA abandoned his pro-French stance and the flag to side with the newcomers. NGANTSU also changed sides and begged for a station at Mpio aBwaani.[18] Janssen was left at Mswata. Around the same time Guiral had arrived at the Pool to relieve Malamine and bring him back to Gabon, abandoning the Pool. He met Stanley at Mswata, proceeded to Mbe and then to Franceville. The situation seemed to have turned completely in favour of the International African Association and NGANTSU's attitude is quite understandable.

At Mbe the situation was tense. Opontaba had decided to intervene against Ikukuri on behalf of NGANTSU and NGAALIÕ tried to moderate him. The king was rather leaning towards Ikukuri who provided his residence with food. Opontaba hoped that Guiral would go to war with him, but was rebuffed. Obviously Guiral had arrived in the middle of a crisis. The king himself was unsettled enough to complain about Opontaba's hostility.[19] The situation evolved predictably to a point. Opontaba sided openly against Ikukuri and followed NGANTSU in opening negotiations with the International African Association. On 12 December he signed a treaty with Valcke in return for many goods, such as NGANTSU had been receiving regularly since May, and even became a blood brother of Valcke. The latter had taken this course because the king had not allowed him access to Nduo. NGAALIÕ had shed his hesitation and followed Opontaba both in the war against Ikukuri and the dealings with the Association. Chavannes made the charge that Valcke wanted Opontaba to 'suppress' the king and replace him and indeed the agents of the Association seem to have believed that the former king was dead and

[17] ibid., pp. 282, 297–8.

[18] A. MAURICE, op. cit., pp. 173–6; H. STANLEY, op. cit., I, pp. 405–7. CH. DE MARTRIN DONOS, *Les Belges*, II, pp. 14–16.

[19] L. GUIRAL, op. cit., pp. 282, 288, 291 (Opontaba had a better carriage than the king; NGAALIÕ looked very cunning), pp. 293–4, 297–8. (The king said he would not take sides; Guiral believed he was not unhappy to see the discord); p. 299 (accusation of king).

that Opontaba had replaced him. Which makes it not impossible that the latter had started the whole plan. But if he did, he dare not carry it out, which shows that the overall authority of Iloo was really greater than Opontaba's power. It also confirmed that the rift between king and first lord had turned into an uneasy hostility.[20]

In January 1883 Janssen at Mswata had a quarrel with ivory traders dependent on Opontaba and took them prisoner. There was almost an uprising against him at Mswata because the people feared an attack by Opontaba. But the matter was settled and in February Janssen went to Opontaba's and confirmed the promise made by Valcke that the Association would send agents to 'Mbe'. The good relations remained. In April or May 1883 Opontaba gave refuge to Parrey, a leader ousted from Mswata and wanted to make war on Mswata but Janssen arbitrated and obtained a promise that henceforth conflicts between NGOBILA and Opontaba would be brought to him. The incident showed that the fear of the people in Mswata a few months earlier had not been groundless. Opontaba espoused the interests of NGANTSU who was a rival to NGOBILA.[21] It also showed that the presence of a European agent was a great asset, since an invasion of Mswata was prevented by Janssen.[22]

Meanwhile it seems amazing that with their superiority in armament and followers NGEILIINO, Opontaba, NGAALIÕ, and NGANTSU did not overrun Ikukuri. The 'war' must have been limited to skirmishes either because that was how the Tio made war or for fear that the king might side openly with Ikukuri and NGANDZIÕ and the lords north of the Lefini with him. Moreover after December Opontaba may have waited in vain until May 1883 for a European resident after which he could attack Mbe itself. We do not know, although the latter hypothesis seems more likely. By May 1883, however, Stanley apparently judged that a return of the French was not to be feared and preferred to use his staff for new foundations up river. This occurred not long after the war with NGOBILA. Thereupon Opontaba seems to have decided to go to Mpila about two months later, possibly to renew talks, possibly simply to collect tribute.[23] He and NGANTSU must have felt disappointed when they saw that NGOBILA on the channel and Ngaliema on the Pool were taking long leads over NGANTSU and NTSUULU. He was not yet fully committed to Stanley. In January,

[20] CH. DE CHAVANNES, op. cit., pp. 216–17, 376–7, for the Treaty. STANLEY, op. cit., I, p. 509 (blood brotherhood); pp. 508–9: in May 1883 Stanley declared that Makoko had been incapacitated and Opontaba replaced him as a regent . . .

[21] H. BRUNSCHWIG, op. cit., pp. 34–5, showing this rivalry already in 1880.

[22] CH. DE MARTRIN DONOS, op. cit., II, pp. 18, 62–81, 124–34, 508–9. H. JOHNSTON, *The River*, p. 149. No wonder NGOBILA believed Janssen to be his good fetish.

[23] H. STANLEY, op. cit., I, p. 509. These were the 'altered circumstances' Stanley alludes to.

after the visit of Valcke, he had travelled to the Pool and seems to have advised the lords there not to allow new European stations or else to remain in the French camp, while negotiating with the Europeans.[24] He had not yet put all his eggs in one basket, perhaps because his allies at the Pool were Ngaliema's enemies. Meanwhile the departure of Malamine from the Pool seemed to make it possible for the Association to negotiate for the establishment of a station at Mfwa or Kinshasa and thus obliterate the effects of Brazza's visit. Yet little progress was made by them between May 1882 and May 1883, mainly because the relations between Ngaliema and NTSUULU were constantly verging on open hostility. In January 1883 Braconnier tried to obtain treaties and was well received at NTSUULU's perhaps because of Opontaba's presence at the Pool, but Bankwa of Ndolo blocked the signing of a treaty. Ngaliema, meanwhile, was not on good terms with the Europeans any more because he felt, ever since the foundation of Mswata, that he might lose his position as an intermediary on the market, so he tried to block as much as he could further trips up river. When he learned in January 1883 of the good relations between Opontaba and the Association he even tried a food blockade of Léopoldville, but it failed.[25] Only an ineffective post was built at Kimpoko in February.[26]

By April the relations between the Léopoldville station and all the Africans were thoroughly bad. Stanley on his return from the upper river heard Ngaliema accuse Valcke of treating him as a common slave and threatening to trample him. Braconnier did not care to see anyone, etc. The Africans were thus not only upset about their position in trade; they were also reacting to European disdain and contempt. These feelings played their role when Stanley attempted during the same month to sign a treaty with NTSUULU. Bankwa again swayed the assembly and no treaty was signed. But this was temporary and soon a station was founded there.[27] In July this led BWANJALI to ask for a post. It was founded but withdrawn soon after, when the commander became mad.[28]

Soon after this the French appeared again, first near the Pool in September, and then Ballay settled at NGANTSU's in November, and

[24] C. COQUILHAT, op. cit., p. 120.

[25] ibid., pp. 60, 61, 62–3, 68 (finally Ngaliema helped Coquilhat to get two boats but they were received from Makabi, his rival at Ntamo), pp. 94–100. E. HANSSENS, *Les premières*, pp. 5–13.

[26] C. COQUILHAT, op. cit., p. 103.

[27] H. STANLEY, op. cit., pp. 495–6. H. JOHNSTON, op. cit., p. 210. Bankwa's arguments were that soon after a treaty many white men would come and Kinshasa would be lost. Ntamo already belonged to the white man. Johnston thought Bankwa had lost the palaver. C. COQUILHAT, op. cit., p. 117, was formal about Bankwa's success.

[28] C. COQUILHAT, op. cit., p. 117; H. STANLEY, op. cit., II, pp. 53–5. W. BENTLEY, *Pioneering*, p. 30, noted that the French were stopped short of Mfwa by BWANJALI in September. Despite the mishap he remained an ally.

founded a French station there. The king still seemed loyal to him, but wavering because he had so few goods to give in comparison with the Association. He received him well and his 'dignitaries' renewed their allegiance to Iloo and to France. The king moreover to him was 'an old weakened impotent man, almost without power'.[29] Obviously he was wrong. Iloo had maintained his position against Opontaba's encroachments. The situation then remained at stalemate until the arrival of Brazza's second mission in April 1884. The king signed the ratification of the treaty on 10 April. For him it was a considerable victory. His enemies Opontaba, NGAALIÕ, and NGANTSU were there, forced to agree, forced to do homage on their knees.[30] No wonder that the king exulted: '*Ngangwa*, Truly here is the one they proclaimed dead. Here he is. Here is the one they proclaimed poor. Here are his gifts!'[31] The gifts for the king alone consisted of eight hundred fathoms of cloth, guns and all kinds of objects, whereas the three lords NGE-ILIINO, NGAALIÕ, and NGANTSU received half of that amount. No wonder that the king was completely taken aback by these gifts.[32]

The king was so elated that he told Brazza he would mobilize all his people, with all his charms and everyone would follow to burn the settlements at the Pool on the right bank and on the left bank if Brazza was not well received.[33] The next two weeks were spent in settling the quarrels between Ikukuri and Opontaba as well as taking care of an opposition now first mentioned between NGANDZIÕ and Opontaba. Ikukuri was paid the slave which had started the war in 1881. In any case it also transpired that Ikukuri with the help of NGANDZIÕ had probably been stronger than his enemies. Still for him as for NGANDZIÕ and the king, the return in strength of the French was an unexpected major, and it seemed, complete victory.[34]

On 2 May Brazzaville was founded and on 9 May Opontaba arrived with Malamine, goods news from both Ikukuri and NGAND-ZIÕ and eight squires of lords they had passed on the way from Mbe. On 21 May the cession of land for Brazzaville was enacted at a palaver directed by Opontaba. NTSUULU, Bankwa, Lekibu, NGAALIÕ, NGIA were there. At another meeting on 18 May the brass collar had been given to NGIA who succeeded to his father, deceased some months before. The French position had been presented there to the squires and lords of the north bank including BWANJALI, Ngankono, and

[29] C. COQUERY, op. cit., pp. 115–16.

[30] N. NEY, op. cit., p. 232; CH. DE CHAVANNES, op. cit., p. 160.

[31] With slight variation the two texts in N. NEY, op. cit., p 231 and CH. DE CHAVANNES, op. cit., pp. 159–60. Also C. COQUERY, op. cit., pp. 342–3.

[32] E. ZORZI, op. cit., p. 389.

[33] C. COQUERY, op. cit., p. 343; E. ZORZI, op. cit., p. 388, but p. 417, in July he desisted and talked only of sending Opontaba instead.

[34] CH. DE CHAVANNES, op. cit., pp. 162–3, 166–7, 174–5. E. ZORZI, op. cit., p. 390; C. COQUERY, op. cit., p. 343.

four others, including one Bobangi, who all received the brass collar.[35]

But the king's victory was short-lived. An intense struggle developed among the Europeans on both sides of the Pool and the Association placed all its reliance on Opontaba who with their help was able to resume his opposition to the king very shortly afterwards. By 24 May he was still impressed with the fresh arrival of more than five hundred Adouma, but in June he was receiving gifts from the Association again, as well as from the French. Taxed with this he told Chavannes: 'I know full well that the Europeans of the two banks who are quarrelling today will end by coming to terms at our expense; meanwhile I take from both hands'.[36] This assessment so soon after the return of the French certainly shows his political astuteness, but also the probability that the Tio too settled some of their conflicts in a similar fashion.

In July Brazza complained that the three lords who had opposed the king now were full of kindness for him, trying to gain him for the cause of the IAA. Brazza countered with the same tactics. In addition Opontaba seemed to receive more goods from the IAA. Now the situation had changed in that the allied lords tried to get the king on their side hoping they might get the better of their enemies Ikukuri and NGANDZIÕ in this fashion as well as gaining wealth by it.[37]

These tactics did not help. Brazza evidently convinced the king that Opontaba was still trying to depose or kill him and the king was furious with Opontaba. The rift widened between the king and the lords as each side's European councillors incited them to act. In the latter half of July the king reassured Brazza that he would follow Opontaba with an army if the latter ever went back to the Pool, which allowed Brazza to leave Mbe by 1 August after some hesitation. Just after he had left, Opontaba announced that he was coming back to the Pool and arrived there in August.[38] The king had not followed him and thus lost face.

As the weeks went by the tension heightened. Mbe received a garrison to defend the king and Opontaba, it was said, was receiving guns from the Association. By October Iloo was asking De Chavannes to kill Opontaba who, it was rumoured had found a perfect poison and would do away with the monarch as soon as he came back to Mbe. De Chavannes meanwhile tried to get Opontaba back to Mbe, for he mainly feared his proximity to Léopoldville. In November the king

[35] CH. DE CHAVANNES, op. cit., pp. 173–81, 371–5.

[36] ibid., p. 185 (Adouma); p. 192 (citation). Brazza left for Mbe 5 June (p. 190) and Opontaba 15 June, after having been called back by the king (p. 192).

[37] C. COQUERY, op. cit., p. 346, dated July. This seems though to be the same letter as the one DE CHAVANNES, op. cit., p. 193, alludes to by saying there was 'un véritable complot d'interêts contre l'autorité de Makoko' which arrived 24 June. If not the same letter, both describe the same process.

[38] CH. DE CHAVANNES, pp. 199 fn. 1 (and 198 for date), 203, 204, 205, 208 (events at Mbe according to letters from Brazza).

was less alarmed, because Ikukuri had reaffirmed support for him.[39] The equilibrium at Mbe which had been alarmingly out of joint with the neutrality of Ikukuri, was righting itself again.

Encouraged De Chavannes sent Malamine to Mbe with gifts for NGAALIÕ in the hope of detaching him from the coalition. By the end of the year it was clear that this was not succeeding. In addition Makoko did not want to recall Opontaba to Mbe and thus De Chavannes could not prevent him from staying at the Pool.[40]

The situation remained unchanged during the first months of 1885 except that Opontaba's anger deepened. In January he threatened open war against the French and the king, but his allies, notably NGIA began to demur because he was taking too much wealth. On the other hand the Association supported more and more Opontaba's claims to tribute in their territory. A quarrel at Mbe between the French soldiers and the men of NGANDZIÕ was arbitrated and settled by the king, who needed the support of both. The agents of the Association were trying to make treaties with NGANTSU and BWANJALI and NGAMPA at the ferry.[41]

Finally Opontaba seemed to be decided to leave, which heightened the fears of the king again, despite the fact that NGANDZIÕ seemed to have put himself in readiness for war. This was the situation when the Act of Berlin came to be known at the Pool and the tensions between the Europeans on the left and right bank eased forthwith.[42]

The rapidity with which the situation altered is remarkable. A few days after the announcement De Chavannes left for NGANTSU's. The lord assured him that he had not followed NGAALIÕ or Opontaba in their opposition and was sent to Mbe to convince the king that there was no longer any reason to worry about the return of Opontaba who was now only a day away from Mbe. He too must have left soon

[39] ibid., pp. 212, 213–14, 218, 219, 220, 223. Ikukuri made his position known between 15 and 20 November. This was connected with a trip from NGANTSU to Mbe by J. De Brazza who told the king that Opontaba was receiving guns from Capt. Saulez and advised him to ask Ikukuri and NGANDZIÕ to open hostilities, according to E. ZORZI, op. cit., p. 439 (Pecile, 5 November).

[40] ibid., pp. 223–4, 225, 230–1, 234, 236, 237. Meanwhile Opontaba was pressuring all the tribute he could get from the people at Mfwa and Mpila. Tempers flared and Malamine was not well received at Mpila any more. In January NGANDZIÕ and Ikukuri were still supporting the king and NGANTSU seemed to disengage himself slightly from Opontaba's position, no doubt, because of the French station in his residence. Opontaba was robbing the caravans which brought food to Brazzaville and talking of burning down the villages. M. LUWEL, op. cit., p. 185. Because of the food situation Ngankono asked for a treaty with the Association in December.

[41] CH. DE CHAVANNES, op. cit., pp. 241, 245, 247–9, 251; M. LUWEL, op. cit., p. 237 (De Winton on Opontaba's rights in February); C. COQUERY, op. cit., pp. 346–7. NGANTSU declared modestly to the envoys of the Association that he was fourth after the king, NGEILIINO NGAALIÕ.

[42] CH. DE CHAVANNES, op. cit., pp. 259, 264, 266, 268, 272, 274, 276. The Act of Berlin was known by De Chavannes on 13 April 1885.

after 13 April. Because 'the situation was now quiet' the European posted at NGANTSU's was relieved by an African auxiliary imitating thus the Independent State which had already turned the post of Mswata at NGOBILA's over to two Zanzibari soldiers. Coming back from a trip up river in July 1885 De Chavannes checked at NGANTSU's found everything quiet without any news from Opontaba, and later in July NGAALIÕ came to NGANTSU's to salute De Chavannes who was passing and to assure him that all was peaceful at Mbe while there was still a soldier there. De Chavannes sent some gifts to the king, NGAASAA, NGANTSU, and NGAALIÕ on 23 July and after this Iloo was practically forgotten by the French. On 19 June the Congo Independent State confirmed to NGOBILA that there would no longer be a post there. By October NGANTSU's was abandoned and, in the next year, so was Kwamouth.[43]

A period had ended. Another had already begun. In the excitement about the tensions on the plains and around the Pool, the progressive implantation of De Chavannes at Brazzaville had not been particularly noticed. At the end of October 1884 De Chavannes had refused to let either Opontaba or NGIA judge in a case about the theft of one of his boats. By January 1885, a Tio squire came to him to have a case tried, because his opponent had gone to Opontaba, a day later De Chavannes arbitrated in a case of a lost boat his men had found and less than two weeks later he ordered Opontaba to spare the life of one of his slaves. Already by the end of November 1884 men and, mainly, women had come to him to complain about the excessive pillage by Opontaba.[44] All these incidents meant that gradually the administration of justice was coming in French hands. For the Tio this was the normal behaviour of a lord. For the French it was the start of their administration, so that when in August 1885 NGAMPA tried to prevent the French from organizing a free ferry, Veistroffer burned down the village and NGAMPA obtained only cold comfort from Brazza.[45] Even before April 1885 another movement had begun which was gradually to drive most of the Tio from the Pool. Because they did not hire themselves out for labour, Brazzaville relied on Kongo Lari workers. The first mention of a Lari food caravan, which in previous years would have been stopped before arriving at the Pool, dates from 20 December 1884, but it was not the earliest such caravan. Lari workers are mentioned by January 1885.[46]

From 1883 to 1886 the political situation on the south bank of the

[43] ibid., pp. 280–3, 311, 314–15. P. AUGOUARD, *Le Congo*, p. 19; A. VEISTROFFER, *Vingt anneés*, pp. 91, 109.

[44] ibid., pp. 220–1, 225, 236, 239, 244–5, 255 (a case of theft in March 1885).

[45] ibid., pp. 322–4, 326–7. C. COQUERY, op. cit., pp. 128–9; A. VEISTROFFER, op. cit., pp. 96–100.

[46] CH. DE CHAVANNES, op. cit., pp. 230, 237. C. COQUERY, op. cit., p. 462, for the 1886 report of Pradier explaining why the workers were Lari.

Pool varied only in that gradually Kinshasa like Ntamo came more and more under European control, especially after the French had arrived at Brazzaville while relations between Europeans and Ngaliema continued to deteriorate slowly. Much more attention was being paid to NTSUULU who had to be kept from joining the French alliance. So a stream of gifts went to NTSUULU from June 1884 to April 1885 while Ngaliema was being taken for granted. The latter still felt insecure about Léopoldville and asked Stanley when he was passing in January 1884 to stress again to his subordinates that the people at the station should act correctly towards Ngaliema.[47] As for NTSUULU his attitude was rather ambiguous. He maintained good relations with the French and accepted presents from them, yet he let his sons insult Brazza when the latter visited Kinshasa the day afterwards. With the Association he took the line that he did not have to pay tribute to Opontaba, which was known to be false. No doubt he was like Opontaba 'taking from both hands' and biding his time. More careful than Opontaba and less powerful he managed to do so well that when the outcome was known both the Congo State and the French still believed he was their ally.[48] As for Bankwa the third major leader south of the river, he did not manifest himself at all.

Because the Europeans no longer needed to worry about African allies after April 1885, they also became brutal, burning Lemba, the Hum's paramount chief's residence in January 1886. Data on Tio politics became very much scarcer after 1885. On the south bank Liebrechts who directed Léopoldville from 1887 to 1889 only noted that 'the Teke are submitting themselves perfectly to the authority of the State'.[49] They accepted the inevitable and turned themselves even more than before to commercial pursuits. A report from 1886 about Brazzaville also concluded that the populations were fairly peaceful and would stay like this, as long as their commercial privileges were not threatened.[50] Indeed all the incidents which were to oppose Tio and Europeans at the Pool after this were, it seems, directly connected with trade. A series of incidents between Bobangi and the French broke out after the death of Laneyrie, head of the station in January 1887. The Lari caravans who brought food to the station were attacked. A soldier sent to Mpila to requisition cassava was killed and the French retaliated by burning down Mpila which resulted in thirty-eight deaths. After this relations between the inhabitants and the French remained strained for a year or so.[51] A little later strains developed

[47] H. STANLEY, op. cit., II, pp. 189–91.

[48] M. LUWEL, op. cit., pp. 166–8, 186, 237.

[49] CH. LIEBRECHTS, *Léopoldville*, p. 527; *idem*, *Congo*, p. 192 (the Teke were calm); R. BUETTNER, *Reisen*, pp. 223, 262. The Hum chief had blocked the carrying of food to Léopoldville.

[50] C. COQUERY, op. cit., p. 462.

[51] *Le mouvement géographique*, 1887, No. 12, May, pp. 49–50. CH. DE CHAVANNES,

again in Kinshasa. The Tio were accused of being responsible for the periodic food shortages and later Ngaliema was even accused of having managed to achieve a monopoly over the supply of food. Because of lacunae in the data it is unclear as to what actually happened but by 1888 NTSUULU left Kinshasa for Mfwa, later Bankwa followed and in the summer of 1892 Ngaliema fled as well after Ntamo was burned by the Europeans.[52] Obviously by 1888 Brazzaville looked safer and perhaps commercially more interesting to these leaders. By the end of Iloo's reign only Lekibu remained with a Tio settlement at Kingabwa and remnants of the former populations at Ntamo and Kinshasa. Already the Bobangi, and especially the Bangala, had established their supremacy.

After 1888 the administration in Brazzaville asserted itself in new ways. It represented the king in granting brass collars to local lords and began to tax people, representing this as something 'like' the tribute they paid to the lords. They paid without difficulty and thus it is likely that they stopped paying to the king, and perhaps to his lords as well. By 1890, if not before, the area of Brazzaville, for all practical purposes, did not belong to the kingdom any more. The lords and leaders who had emigrated from the south bank had to apply for settlement to the French and in 1891–2 NTSUULU died. Bankwa who moved around 1890–2 succeeded and Ngaliema died only a few months after he crossed the Pool in 1892. Bankwa was proposed for paramount chief of the Pool area by delegation of authority from the administrator of Brazzaville.[53]

After July 1885 data on the political situation on the Mbe plains are

Le Congo, pp. 42, 70. The Laneyrie incident must be what CH. LIEBRECHTS, *Congo*, alluded to when, p. 192, he spoke of the difficulties the Tio had caused at Brazzaville. Chavannes is formal in accusing the Bobangi. For unrest, cf. J. DE WITTE, *Vie*, p. 40. The thatched mission roofs were set on fire more than once late in 1887 and early 1888. But then Father Augouard had collaborated with the punitive expedition. These events did not solve the food problem and in 1888 part of the station's personnel at Brazzaville had to be dismissed because the men could not be fed. Cf. *Le mouvement géographique*, February 1888, p. 208.

[52] A. DOLISIE, op. cit., pp. 44–5; W. BENTLEY, *Pioneering*, II, pp. 143, 226. Several groups from Ntamo had already left before even NTSUULU crossed, probably in 1887; TH. MASUI, *D'Anvers*, p. 61 (unhappiness of Ngaliema at Ntamo; half blind and hampered in his trade); C. DE DEKEN, *Twee jaar*, pp. 59, 60 (monopoly of food by Ngaliema; forced to flee to Brazzaville. Dated December 1892, whereas Masui was May 1892). M. STORME, *Ngankabe*, pp. 21–2 (fled imposed labour at Léopoldville). J. DYBOWSKI, op. cit., p. 52, for NTSUULU at Mpila in 1891 and D'UZES, *Le voyage*, p. 71, for the destruction of Ntamo and the crowning of Ngaliema (27 August, 5 September 1892).

[53] A. DOLISIE, op. cit., pp. 45–7 and n. 52; A. VEISTROFFER, op. cit., p. 143, about new difficulties with NGAMPA makes it clear that Dolisie still could not afford to antagonize the Tio too much yet even then. D'UZES, op. cit., p. 90, still comments in 1892 on the fact that the collar of Makoko gave the French their authority in palavers at Brazzaville. J. DYBOWSKI, *La route*, p. 52 (1891) on the ease with which the Tio came to have court cases settled.

almost totally lacking. Veistroffer visited them in November 1885 and received an escort of fifty men, perhaps provided by Ikukuri. Then one hears of a note that all went well there in 1888 and that the administrator of Brazzaville made the king provide the collar for investiture after NTSUULU had crossed. No European came to the plains. Their reputation of infertility and very low density of population guarded them against any form of French occupation.[54] How the rift between NGEILIINO, NGAALIÕ, and NGANTSU against the other lords evolved remains unknown from the texts.[55] When Iloo died in June or November 1892 they were still all living. Opontaba died around 1895 and NGANDZIÕ, perhaps, in 1897. They were enemies until then and beyond, since their sons carried on the tradition of hostility. On the other hand both NGAALIÕ and NGANTSU seem to have dropped out permanently from the coalition by the summer of 1885. The first had always been half-hearted, the latter was supervised too closely by the French boats which always stopped there. As for Ikukuri in 1892 he was so quiet that it was not known if he was still alive or not. By 1895, in any case, he was either deceased or completely disengaged from the feud he had started in 1881. The tension between the king and Opontaba also vanished, probably because Opontaba's power was seriously weakened and, when Iloo died, Opontaba was not even accused of having anything to do with it.[56] As for NGOBILA, the other main lord for which data were available, he remained steadfast in his allegiance to the Association and the Congo State and became more and more wealthy. Recognized as a 'great chief' by the colonial administration his internal position at Mswata and his rule over the surrounding Mfunu was securely backed by the State. This became even more evident when Ponthier crossed the hinterland with troops on a punitive expedition against the Mfunu and the Ngenge in 1891.[57]

What is known of the political history of the kingdom even for the period 1880–5 is still very limited. No indications whatsoever as to the

[54] CH. DE CHAVANNES, op. cit., p. 153 (July 1888, he stopped at NGANTSU's to make certain all was well at Mbe. In April 1888 (p. 134) Fondère arrived at Brazzaville having crossed the western plains. He found them sterile, except for the Kukuya plateau. A. VEISTROFFER, op. cit., p. 109.

[55] The large escort given to Veistroffer in 1885 may mean that Opontaba had rallied to the king. D'UZES, op. cit., p. 103, commented how Makoko still did not understand in 1892 why he was neglected.

[56] Traditions from Miandoo and NGAATALI; A. DOLISIE, pp. 45–6; P. AUGOUARD, *Lettres*, III, p. 16 (Iloo died in 1892); B. MAMBEKE-BOUCHER, *Ngalifourou*, p. 28, dated it from November and cited a tradition incriminating the next king Mbandieele in alliance with a Kukuya lord. It is of interest that it was not attributed to Opontaba.

[57] E. DUPONT, *Lettres*, p. 235; A. DELCOMMUNE, *Vingt années*, I, p. 219 (1888); TH. MASUI, op. cit., pp. 72–3 (May 1892; recognized great chief); C. DE DEKEN, op. cit., p. 73 (31 December 1892) and Mswata was still flourishing as ever. A village nearby had been burned by the punitive expedition of 1891 and was still in ruins. M. STORME, *Ngankabe*, pp. 22–4.

evolution of politics north of the Lefini is available. Still the data do allow us to draw certain conclusions with regard to the functioning of the political system.

South of the Lefini there were two major and one minor nuclei of political activity: the area of Mbe, the Pool and Mswata. Connexions between all these existed but they formed almost autonomous sub-systems and the same is probably true for the areas north of the Lefini, since no lords from this area became involved in the dissensions around Mbe. A sign of both the connexions and the relative autonomy is the attitude of Opontaba who in 1882–3 was both an ally of Stanley in the channel region where he espoused the cause of his underlord NGANTSU, and an ally of the French, or at least much more ambiguous in the Pool region, where he espoused the cause of NTSUULU. Because of developments at Mbe he also later took the side of the Association on the Pool, abandoning NTSUULU, but hoping that the Association would win its power struggle and reinstate him as overlord of NTSUULU. Thus a first characteristic of the system was that because of the autonomy of the sub-system, and this was due itself no doubt to the great distances involved, the politics of the major lords were strongly influenced *locally* by the situation in the sub-systems. There was no question of a 'national policy', not even of a consistent policy for one lord.

But the situation had a certain dialectic in it. The evolution of politics at Mbe took precedence over the evolution in the other sub-systems and ultimately could and did influence the other local situations. NGANTSU had to take the side of the Association to a certain extent although his interests were opposite to those of NGOBILA, the ally of the Association. NTSUULU was abandoned by Opontaba. The two cases show the two opposite solutions for situations where conflicts of interest arose between the sub-system of Mbe and the local ones. Either the underlord aligned himself (NGANTSU) with the position of the overlord or he broke with him and tried to gain a complete autonomy (NTSUULU).

Conflicts between lords presupposed only two opposing camps. In theory all allies of one lord in conflict with another should immediately take his side when conflict erupted. But this was not so. First Opontaba took a certain time to decide his position after the quarrel between Ikukuri and NGANTSU had erupted. When he shifted to support NGANTSU his reasons were not that the latter was closer to him than Ikukuri, for he was not, but that Ikukuri was the stronger and therefore more of a threat to him personally. NGAALIÕ who lived in the residence of Opontaba should immediately have sided with him, but he took time about it. It also took time to forge the Ikukuri NGANDZIÕ alliance which was not automatic.

From this it appears that serious conflicts among lesser lords had a tendency to escalate and that the major lords did not hurry into a conflict but saw where their interests lay. So the longer a conflict lasted, the more it escalated. But conflicts among small lords like BWANJALI and NGAMPA could remain at a low level for years. It also appears that major or minor lords would try to remain neutral and in a position for arbitration if they felt that their interests were not menaced. An escalating conflict always menaced the interests of the major lords because in the long run victory for one party made it so strong that it could then become a menace. Still, support from allied overlords or underlords was by no means to be expected in all situations.

The impact of personalities is also obvious. Opontaba was a politician of the first rank and seems to have been determined at one moment to overthrow the king or kill him or isolate him. He wanted the monopoly of power in the Mbe and all other sub-systems. In contrast his brother NGAALIÕ who was as strong militarily as he was had clearly no appetite for such ambitions and always played a minor role, another example of the impact of personality on structure and events in the whole career of Ngaliema. But then the system itself promoted the emergence of strong personalities.

The position of the king differed. Kingship was more important than actual power. So that when the political equilibrium was really upset the king could simply ally himself with the strongest party and Brazza suspected Iloo sometimes of wanting to change sides and go over to Opontaba.[58] When there was a lull in the power struggle as in 1880 he could take a position which was disapproved of by his major lords, as when he signed the treaty. This an ordinary leader could not do, witness Ngaliema who had to repudiate his agreement with Stanley. The king's position was that of the arbitrator 'par excellence', hence he was not to be drawn into the conflicts of his lords. Iloo tried to play this role when Opontaba had chosen to come out against Ikukuri. But he could only act if there was already some equilibrium between the forces of the warring parties. He seems to have thought wrongly in 1882 that Ikukuri would be crushed, felt threatened by the increased power that would accrue to Opontaba and came to an outspoken hostility that made mediation impossible. He did not have the military forces of his own required to fight Opontaba and, as Tio tradition has it, remained completely powerless because neither Ikukuri nor Opontaba 'would listen to him'. In such a case there was one last recourse open to him and he took it: to form a coalition against his enemy Opontaba. This seems to be the mechanism by which NGANDZIÕ was drawn into the war. The most extreme alternative, the calling of MUIDZU and his lords from north of the Lefini, may have been considered but was not set in motion.

[58] C. COQUERY, op. cit., p. 120.

The coalition of lords against an enemy was in effect the same principle of operation as the one familiar to end feuds under the threat that a superior coalition would attack the party which did not observe the truce. But the power of the king went beyond this. There was the fear of Nkwe Mbali, a major deterrent. There was the possibility at least that men from the opposing camp might desert their lords if the king asked them to. Both of these may actually have prevented Opontaba from attacking him in 1883–4.

Military power, whether the lords or the king are involved, was the foundation of actual authority as is abundantly clear from the predominance of Ngaliema over all others at the Pool. Yet it was a precarious form of power. Armies of a few hundred men, perhaps all armed with muskets might be formed and yet their interventions seem strangely inoperative. How was it after all possible for Ikukuri to withstand his enemies and even get the better of them with less men and guns, perhaps with only a third of the forces opposed to him? it could be that NGANDZIÕ redressed the balance somewhat, but not to the extent of outstripping NGAALIÕ and Opontaba, for NGAALIÕ was known to have by far the most guns of any lord on the plains. Battles rarely occurred and were ineffective. A raid on Ampo left NGAMPO's power practically intact. A counter-raid resulted in the kidnapping of a few women. Obviously the Tio way of waging war was very different from a European conception. Ambushes were the only form of warfare and an advantage was apparently never fully exploited. Long periods of calm passed between attacks and for all the talk of villages that were to be burned down, only the French and Free State agents did it. The conclusion must be that the rules of warfare, implicitly recognized by all, limited the damage to such an extent that campaigns became mere demonstrations of possible power. No one wanted to go beyond this, for fear of suffering as much harm as he had inflicted himself. Thus the struggle for power was decided more by attitudes, beliefs and impressions than by actual military victory. This explains why the conflicts were so drawn out, why the equilibrium of power shifted after all only slowly and why a normal pursuit of ordinary occupations was possible, why and how so much continuity through time was found in the exercise of political power. There was political rule despite the lack of centralized institutions because the balance of power shifted so relatively little. The key to this rule lay effectively in the hands of the supreme arbitrator, the king.

One could object that the personality of Iloo, who often seems to have vacillated between different possible policies, was a coincidence which was responsible for this situation. If say, Opontaba or Ikukuri had been king, things might have been different. There is no direct rebuttal to this, but since kings were arbitrators they had to conciliate and could not but act rather like Iloo. The intrusion of competing Europeans on the scene, foreigners with great power who fanned the dissensions among Tio leaders exasperated the tensions, as Coquery has noted. Yet, even so, no real warfare erupted.[59] The nature of politics and the means it used forbade it.

The data show how the political system changed. The basic roles of squire, lord, and king underwent only slow modifications. The rise of a Ngaliema changed something in the image of the lord. It showed that great leaders need no longer be aristocrats. Ngaliema had no title and never received one. So the change was minimal. Forceful personalities could and did upset the ranking of titles, however. Opontaba certainly extended the privileges of the NGEILIINO while NGANTSU made an important title out of a relatively insignificant one. So it is in the functions and ranking of secular titles that the kingdom could change most. In the long run this was the lasting effect of personalities on the structure.

2. *The economic evolution 1880–92*

The market economy is described in terms of the practice of 1880–2. Not much change took place in the first years of the European presence. Stanley opened a shop on 25 March 1883 and sold trade-goods, the first day for Ł500, the second for Ł 300. But only on 9 April could he buy ivory from Ngaliema, after which the trade in that commodity became well established. But as Guiral remarked in May the Europeans could only buy from the Tio and in effect in the first year only from Ngaliema.[60] This alone was a considerable achievement. Stanley had overcome the resistance of the caravan leaders from the coast and opened a road of his own which shattered the Kongo and Zombo monopoly. He was now prepared to break the monopolies up river. Trade was important to him. He saw in it the certain way to befriend the local powers and to drive de Brazza from the Pool, if he only had goods. His greatest fear was the lack of good commercial agents and the possible competition of commercial companies who only had to follow his tracks.[61] This only happened in May 1886 and until 1887 no commercial steamer had been launched to break through the Tio and the Bobangi monopolies, although each trip by a government steamer upstream did bring some ivory back, at least since 1883. Until then the Tio monopoly remained intact. The places where Europeans had

[59] ibid., pp. 118–21. We do not fully share her view of Iloo as someone who had not followed the evolution of the country or Opontaba as the leader of the 'dynamic wing' among the Tio.

[60] H. STANLEY, op. cit., I, p. 380; A. MAURICE, op. cit., pp. 150–2, 135, Stanley already complained that he would have to bypass the Tio if he wanted cheap ivory; so he thought a station should be built in 'Wyyanzi'; p. 148, he remarked that he could only cover expenses by the ivory trade if he went beyond the Bobangi as well. L. GUIRAL, op. cit., pp. 245–7. WHYMS, *Léopoldville*, p. 25.

[61] A. MAURICE, op. cit., pp. 115–18.

shops attracted people and their leaders also became more prosperous. NGOBILA and Ngaliema were the first to benefit. In May 1883 Stanley found that Mswata had grown unbelievably in the last thirteen months and now numbered 1,500, as against 290 or so at the end of the previous year, and NGOBILA was making more profits from his sales of food because the needs of Léopoldville were already outrunning the capacity of local supply, despite the opening of a good market near the station in 1883.[62]

The other features of the activity in 1883–5 were the considerable gifts of cloth and other goods to all sorts of squires and lords and the high prices paid for goods. When the French appeared on the river again in 1883 and in 1884 they hoped to stop the desertion to Stanley's camp in this way. This period ended rather abruptly in the summer of 1885. With the exception of Ngaliema and NGOBILA, the other lords all had benefited by it. But Ngaliema had by then already sent caravans to the coast, increasing his benefits on the trade.[63]

Now a situation arose in which the foreign traders tried to carry their ivory by boat from up river and thus bypass the Tio. A. Thys remarked shrewdly that in 1887 the African trade in ivory was still very important because much ivory was still sold to Kongo or Zombo caravans whose transportation prices were much less than those of Europeans since they used 'slaves or subjects' for the carrying. As for all goods of greater bulk and lesser value the position of the African traders was so strong that they could only be outpriced with the construction of the railway. Even for ivory in March 1889 Europeans at the Pool bought only five tons and three still went to the African caravans.[64]

[62] CH. LIEBRECHTS, *Léopoldville*, p. 522. The first trader Gresshoff known as the 'Sun king' and representing NAHV. Cf. R. BUETTNER, *Reisen*, p. 222. Daumas-Béraud and Sanford followed quickly. H. STANLEY, op. cit., I, p. 511; TH. MASUI, *L'état indépendant*, p. 81 and E. HANSSENS, op. cit., p. 14, for the earlier estimates of 200 and 290. The latter may have been an actual count by Janssen and Stanley's figure is inflated. Still a later source records the increase. A. DELCOMMUNE, op. cit., I, p. 219 gives it in 1888 as 700. WHYMS, op. cit., pp. 173, 27. W. BENTLEY, op. cit., I, p. 461, photo opp. p. 463.

[63] Chapter XI, fn. 20; CH. DE CHAVANNES, *Avec Brazza*, pp. 139–275 and E. ZORZI, op. cit., pp. 381–449, for 'the battle of presents' and rising prices. R. BUETTNER, op. cit., pp. 222, 227; 237, he commented on the wealth of NGOBILA 'who had used the station to the utmost advantage'. By October 1885 it was totally abandoned.

[64] A. THYS, *Au Congo*, pp. 44–5; CH. LIEBRECHTS, *Léopoldville*, pp. 524–5; W. BENTLEY, op. cit., II, p. 36. C. COQUERY, op. cit., p. 471, for massive trade by Kongo in salt, guns, and powder at unbeatable prices (1886). The situation in 1892 had not changed much. Greater quantities of rubber were now sold on the Pool all through the Tio and the caravans. Cf. TH. MASUI, *D'Anvers*, p. 61 and TH. MASUI, *L'état indépendant*, p. 411, for statistics. Only in 1889 did the State begin an active campaign to collect rubber, and production shot up after 1891. From 1887 to 1891 the production had risen from 30 tons to 131 and went down again to 123. This means that in rubber the production at the Pool increased from nil to perhaps 30 tons between 1883 and 1887. For 1892 see *La tribu*, p. 123.

The Tio traders did not accept the change in patterns passively. First they apparently managed up to 1892 to keep the intermediary role at the Pool, forbidding Bobangi to sell to Europeans.[65] They also explored new opportunities. For a while Ngaliema organized his own ivory caravans to the coast, shrewdly taking advantage of the abolition of the monopoly in this direction. But the rulers in Manianga did all they could to stop his caravans, including robbing them. He seems then to have dropped the venture.[66]

But then there were great gains to be made in the trade of foodstuffs. NGOBILA grew very rich on supplying the Pool and the steamers. In Kinshasa and Brazzaville food shortages were chronic during this period, despite plantations and attempts to force the Tio on the south bank to cultivate. More and more attention was given by the traders of Kinshasa and Ngaliema to the possibilities of this trade; their prices increased and the sources of supply were monopolized. Finally, by 1892 Ngaliema had the complete monopoly of food imports for Kinshasa, a situation which led to his being ousted, because he tried to enforce his monopoly and the state tried to break it. In fact the emigration of all the Tio leaders was related to the food situation. Since the Hum all cultivated the station commandant tried to enroll Tio labour by force which resulted in the first migrations from 1888 onwards.[67]

By the end of the reign of Iloo there were no great Tio traders left in Kinshasa, but in Brazzaville they had held their position and on both banks most of the goods still went through their hands, with the excep-

[65] A. DOLISIE, op. cit., p. 49, where the French had surrendered to the extent of making this obligatory; CH. LIEBRECHTS, op. cit., p. 525 (1889).

[66] E. DUPONT, op. cit., pp. 213, 263.

[67] On NGOBILA, E. DUPONT, op. cit., p. 235. He was so wealthy he had proposed to buy a trading steamer (less than a year after they had been launched). A. DELCOMMUNE, op. cit., I, p. 219. They also traded in ivory; C. DE DEKEN, op. cit., p. 73 (complains about the dearness). W. BENTLEY, op. cit., II, p. 167 (NGOBILA traded for several months at Kinshasa, between 1884 and 1887). Food shortages remained chronic. CH. DE CHAVANNES, *Avec Brazza*, p. 206, mentioned them already in August 1884 and before that Malamine had already left because food was scarce. The last mention we have is from January 1889 (CH. DE CHAVANNES, *Le Congo*, pp. 182–3). The affray after the death of Laneyrie in 1887 seems to have turned around the trade in foodstuffs (ibid., p. 42). At Léopoldville, CH. LIEBRECHTS, op. cit., pp. 527–8, accused the Tio of being responsible for the food shortages. He levied labour among them for the needs of the station thus provoking their migration to Brazzaville. Also pp. 505–19 and *idem*, *Congo*, p. 191. C. DE DEKEN, op. cit., p. 60, on Ngaliema's leaving after the struggle for the monopoly over food; p. 59, when he was gone a food market was opened in October, probably supervised by state officials. The first difficulties about food dated from early 1883 (C. COQUILHAT, op. cit., p. 100) when Ngaliema tried to stop sales to Léopoldville. The same tactic had already been used by the Hum against Ngaliema in October 1881 (H. STANLEY, op. cit., I, pp. 306–7). The supplies after 1882 always ran behind the needs. Witness the prices charged in 1887; E. DUPONT, op. cit., p. 213. D'UZES, op. cit., p. 71. By April 1893 there were seventy-five Europeans in Léopoldville and the food crisis was not yet overcome.

tion of ivory. Even there, their share in the market remained big enough so that they were able to enforce the maintenance of the value of ivory in cloth despite the depreciation of the *mitako* and its artificially increasing value in European currency.[68]

The evolution of trade in Brazzaville paralleled the development of Léopoldville. The first concession was requested by Gresshoff who had quarrelled with the Congo State and built his firm up in Brazzaville. Daumas-Béraud and Sanford followed.[69] A Portuguese trader who also settled at Brazzaville began to send out his Vili agents over the plains, thus beginning a competition with the Vili caravans which was to lead in the next two decades to a stream of Vili and 'Senegalese' traders hawking from village to village. Otherwise Brazzaville remained comparable to Kinshasa, down to the setting up of a food market, opened there in October 1891.[70]

Only on the plains must the period after 1885 have meant a loss in income, because of the serious losses in tribute. Nevertheless the ordinary people could sell tobacco as before or now send food in increasing quantities to the Pool. No real hardship seems to have developed, before the arrival of the *Compagnies concessionnaires* and this was linked, as all serious further economic developments in Congo Independent State were, to the development of the railway. Until then, and despite the presence of European trading societies, nothing much changed. But on the whole the volume increased. Thus ivory went from 98 tons (all at the Pool in 1885) to 204 by 1892 for the Free State, while by February 1893, 37 steamers for both colonies were plying the rivers, not counting another 40 steel boats. How under those circumstances the Bobangi trade still managed can only be explained by the serious cost price differences in their favour.[71]

Other differences which the Europeans had brought to the Pool was the notion of wage-labour, which the Tio did not adopt, except to hire their slaves out and the establishment of the *mitako* as a universal means of exchange. The introduction of wage-labour was only one aspect of the latter change.[72]

A last major development at the Pool and perhaps in the interior was the outbreak in 1889 of a serious epidemic of smallpox. Half the personnel of the post at Brazzaville died; perhaps more in the interior since vaccination stopped the epidemic at the Pool. After 1887 sleeping

[68] Cf. Chapter XI, 2 prices; 'fluctuations of price'.

[69] CH. DE CHAVANNES, op. cit., pp. 78, 87, 101, 103, 124, 226 (services rendered by Gresshoff). Cf. M. FROMENT, *Un voyage*, p. 215, fn. 1.

[70] CH. DE CHAVANNES, op. cit., p. 263.

[71] *La flotille*, pp. 34–5; *L'ivoire*, pp. 42–3; E. TRIVIER, *Mon voyage*, pp. 45–8. There were fifteen steamers in January 1889.

[72] Cf. Chapter XI, currencies (*mitako*); C. COQUERY, op. cit., pp. 208–10, 203–8 (opening of communications and trade tied to the administration did not affect the Tio).

sickness began to appear. Both these scourges must have seriously affected the demographic evolution of the population.[73]

The reign of Iloo had seen the arrival of the Europeans and the establishment of states on the European pattern. Yet for the Tio the changes while momentous, did not drastically alter either their economic way of life, even in trade, or their political order, leaving everything else relatively untouched. One cannot conclude with Coquery that the involvement of Tio politics in the scramble for Africa aggravated the crisis of the Tio state, a crisis in the weakening of political cohesion and the weakening of the ruler's authority. First it is uncertain that this cohesion had been any different for perhaps a century or more. Furthermore the king lost the tribute and the control over the Pool area only but remained undisturbed in all his other lands. His relations with the lords seem not to have changed fundamentally. As for the economic life, apart from the evacuation of the south bank by most Tio, the only changes had been an increase in the wealth of chiefs first, up to 1885 and of traders during the whole period. The commercial dynamism remained intact.[74]

These conclusions however are based on a certain evaluation of the previous situations in Tio history, while also foreshadowing further developments at later times. Hence the need for an historical section sketching out previous trends and following social change.

[73] A. VEISTROFFER, op. cit., pp. 141–2; E. TRIVIER, op. cit., pp. 40–1. CH. DE CHAVANNES, *Le Congo Français*, pp. 182–3.

[74] C. COQUERY, op. cit., p. 117, assumes perhaps a great degree of cohesion than was warranted, which led to (p. 121) the conclusion that the conflicts between lords had now led the kingdom to the brink of dissolution. Our interpretation of the political system has been very different; Coquery's conclusions about the economic effects (p. 211) were based on the notions that they clung to the slave-trade and to sterile thesaurization. This has not been confirmed by the analysis of the economic institutions. Hence the substantial differences between her and our conclusions.

Part II
Conclusion

TIO political and commercial institutions overshadow all the other structures in the society. Both presupposed all the institutions at the neighbourhood level and transcended them; more especially both were extensions of the social and economic structures in the neighbourhood. These political and commercial institutions did not however form a single organized whole such as those at the lower level. Trade and political structure were more independent from each other.

The area to which they referred was different. The political system faded away beyond the plains, the Pool and the Congo river, whereas commerce was part of a worldwide system and within it a network stretched from the ocean to the ends of the navigated river stretches of the Congo and its affluents. Because its area was much wider, trade was much less a Tio affair than politics. In spite of the size of the area involved, however, the internal cohesion of the commercial economy was greater than that of the kingdom and it was more sensitive to change. The political structure was more of an outgrowth of the social institutions than the commercial sector from subsistence economics. The independence of the trade sector and the kingdom as structures was clearest from the fact that both systems revolved around a different hub: Mbe was the political capital and the Pool the commercial one.

The typical features of both the structures which extended over the neighbourhoods can be explained by geographical and historical factors. Geography explains why the Pool was the centre of a network tying navigation on the rivers to the coastal areas; the nature of the plains and their low population density have much to do with the extreme decentralization within the kingdom. The position of Mbe as capital is the result of historical accident and the sensitivity of both political and trade affairs to historical events is best explained, both by reference to the much wider areas affected by them and by the fact that a few crucial personalities had so much influence in running both, which was a result of the structures themselves; moreover fluctuations of the world market affected trade almost directly.

The political structure was unique. A kingdom without a central army or a unified set of courts, central councils, central administration, delegation of authority from the top down, where at least two ideologies competed (kingship based on *nkira* and lordship on *nkobi*), where rule at each level was most reminiscent of leadership in a kinship unit.

The kingdom did not even present a unified policy towards the outside, e.g. towards the Europeans.

The system included a set of regional sub-systems each with centres and periphery, themselves an agglomeration of domains. Government worked itself out in each of these through competition between different lords and nowhere did a single lord dominate a whole region. The political structure as a whole was based on the core statuses of squire, lord, and king. Because there was only one king, the sub-system of Mbe differed from all the others.

Cohesion between the regions seemed absent, yet there was some co-ordination. Links between them existed because the lords of the crown from north of the Lefini and from Mbe came to the *lisee* of the king, because of the *nkani* system and the collection of tribute, because the king installed and sometimes chose his major lords. Political affairs of one region affected those of others. Now lords at Mbe sided with their *nkani* in a regional quarrel and their position at Mbe shifted as a result; now the position of the major lord at Mbe forced a shift in stance within another region. A dialectic movement between the regions thus existed.

The Mbe region was more than equal to the others. Cohesion within it was perhaps stronger than within other sub-systems. Kingship was responsible. The king kept in touch by messenger with the lords, consulted all, yet decided alone, whether he rallied to the opinion of a majority or stood against all. As arbitrator of the lords he strove to keep the balance of power adjusted so it afforded him maximum leverage. Because lords were cautious in choosing a faction when a major rift was developing, scope for manoeuvring and policy setting action was possible for the common arbitrator, the king. The latter's position was also strengthened by the protection of Nkwe Mbali, the allegiance the common man had towards the monarch and the fact that the king's lords were the king's kin. So the sovereign did not rule alone, nor rule by council and yet the sub-system at Mbe formed a cohesive enough whole to affect policies in other sub-system more than it was affected by them; it gave some direction to the whole.

Within the core of the kingdom two groups of regions existed: the area north of the Lefini and the area south. Relations between sub-systems in each group were more intense than between groups. The escalation of feuds and wars ultimately involved the centre of each group: MUIDZU north of the Lefini and the king south of it and each group had a separate supreme court.

Between these two constellations relations were limited but existed. Constellations such as the Kukuya, the Ngungulu, the Ngenge perhaps a Laadi Nkoo and Mfunu did not really belong to the kingdom, mainly because of the extreme tenuousness of relations with Mbe.

Within each region, the domains were made a coherent whole by the domination of common lords who stopped feuds and wars, to whom tribute was paid, and who provided common protection against outside attack. Squires could transfer their loyalties from one lord in the region to another and any one chose the lord of his liking when appealing against court decisions. This explains why the region was not in danger of splitting apart in areas controlled by a single lord. A constant network of ties crossing each other prevented this.

At the level of the domain the political structure was a simple outgrowth of the social organization. In politics at all levels a strong projection of leadership practices at the kinship level united the political to the social system.

Politics were based in last resort on a balance of power at each level above the domain. War was restricted in scope and methods in such a way that sudden upsets of an existing balance were unlikely. So decisions were reached by bargaining and points gained by superiority in apparent rather than proven power. Apparent power included the numbers of guns, slaves, followers, the size of a settlement, wealth, number and quality of alliances, and mystical support. These factors could change, but their nature and variety made change relatively slow, thus preserving the delicate web of regional and interregional arrangements. The sluggishness of war was the key to the whole system since it alone provided the necessary stability on which ultimately the autonomy of the lords, the operation of government in each sub-system and the existence of the kingdom itself was based.

Commerce had transformed the Pool area. Here no subsistence economy remained, nor was it peasant agriculture, or a market economy in European terms. The Pool was more a port of trade, rather like nineteenth-century Whydah and after 1882 the presence of Europeans increased the similarity. The absence of a universal money standard, so that several sub-spheres segmented the market and labour could not be hired, nor land sold, was the core feature in which this differed from the European market economy.

The heart of trade was the ivory, slave, cloth, guns, gunpowder circuit operated only by the leaders. The operation of this circuit required many men and the capital. The social organization associated was the township where a large number of slaves provided labour and defence. So there were few leaders and they made the highest profits, thus enabling the town organization to survive and expand. Other inhabitants traded in other stuffs and women mainly had a circuit of food markets. Because of the townships and the core circuit operations two social classes began to replace the three estates and opposition between men and women may also have grown.

The impact of the commercial economy along the river was great. On the plains it affected the subsistence economies less. Production techniques were somewhat changed. The technology there was impoverished, the production of cassava increased and that of maize decreased. The trade was directly responsible for the growing imbalance of the share of men and women in agricultural labour, even though this may have been somewhat tempered by an increasing production of tobacco. Malnutrition may have been slowly on the increase as a result. But the basic patterns of food production, the composition of social units and the values associated with these patterns remained only slightly affected. Among themselves, people of the plains still shared food rather than sell it. The subsistence economy was not autarchic however and depended more and more on the commercial eocnomy to acquire the means for defence, hunting, and prestige. There was a serious impact on the political structure, as is shown by the tendency of lords to build their residences on the pattern of those existing at the Pool. This influence of commerce contrasted with the successful resistance of locally produced goods in the sphere of social payments, although even there imported cloth began to appear.

The small scale society was affected most by the prevalence of a growing set of values in the overarching structures, which ran counter to those prevalent in the neighbourhoods. The ideals of rivalry and ambition clashed with the notions of harmony and good fortune for the community. The core of the commercial economy was the market and within it, bargaining set the price. Bargaining in conflicts was also the core of the political system. Achieved status almost ousted ascribed status and the flexibility of the commercial and political norms contrasted with the greater rigidity of social norms. The deep tension between the desire to be peaceful and the wish to be great led to the concomitant social dramas of perennial witchcraft suspicions and accusations. Whether the overarching sectors had or had not created the drive for ambition is irrelevant. Ambition by 1880 was the cardinal force which powered them. The effects were felt so much that the essence of integration in Tio society as a whole had become that the lord and the entrepreneur were now the models for the village-leader.

The political structure affected culture by enriching its symbols, patronizing literature, and spreading the language and ideas of the court. All this remained Tio. Trade however brought more spectacular effects. It introduced foreign conceptions, objects, behaviour, and beliefs all along the river thus bringing Bobangi, Hum, Kongo, and Tio cultures closer together. The Pool especially seems already to have started its role as the repository of a more complex cultural tradition which diffused from there to the political centres and the villages.

Change from 1880 to 1892 especially affected the superstructures of trade and politics. Europeans were nudging the Tio leaders out of the ivory circuit and the latter shifted to take control of the trade in foodstuffs and perhaps salt. The currency became money, and the abolition of monopolies on trade routes brought the Pool that much closer into contact with world markets. The Tio leaders lacked the incentive for accepting it as a means to hire labour, since that meant the loss of their slave capital, but they did hire their slaves out. The Europeans further replaced the lords at the Pool and took that region out of the kingdom. The damage remained limited however, because of the great autonomy of the sub-systems within the realm. Further evolution only came after 1898 when European interference sought to force changes in the patterns of subsistence production and local government.

Part III

A Perspective Through Time

Chapter XVI
Tio Society to 1880

SO far Tio society has been described during a short moment in time. Our conclusions concerning the existence of a closed small society and of overarching structures as two distinct parts of the society can be cross-checked by using an historical approach. The understanding gained so far can be increased by showing exactly how the different institutions and structures described had evolved and interacted in the past before Iloo's reign. To achieve this it is not necessary to go through a detailed examination of each historical question connected with the Tio past. A sketch showing the major events and the general evolution will show how the society as a whole evolved. Hence also an approach which narrates the changes within the structures, rather than a chronological order which could obscure institutional development. Therefore sections on the origins and first growth of the political system and on migrations are followed by discussions of the evolution of the commercial economy and the political system after which changes in the neighbourhood structures—subsistence economics, kinship structures, and the few data available about religion, are presented. Next the concluding chapter will probe the questions raised by looking at the other end of the historical continuum. What change and how much social change has occurred since 1892? How did change affect the various structures and how do these data affect our analysis of Tio society in Iloo's times? At the same time this investigation will show what the gross impact of the colonial period on the Tio has been.

1. *Origins of the Tio and the Tio kingdom*

From time immemorial the Tio have dwelt on their grasslands and they have been organized as a kingdom from remote times, since the king is already mentioned by 1507 in the first written document about them.[1] According to tradition the Tio have always lived on the plains and there always was a kingdom. 'They have been a human pier around which the migrations of other peoples have turned or which they have battered.'[2] Confirmation for the long span of time involved since the settlement of the plains by the Tio comes from toponyms. The names of villages, forests, rivers, and other natural features recur over and over

[1] D. PACHECO PEREIRA, *De Esmeraldo Orbis;* Cf. D. PERES, *Esmeraldo*, p. 171. *Emcuquanzico:* =*õkoo* a Jinju. (Mukoko Ansiko.) Note the mention that this country was very far from the coast and 'we do not know of any profit to be had there'.

[2] G. SAUTTER, *Le plateau*, p. 128.

on all the plains including those occupied by the Tege and the Mfinu, and the mixture of names on each plateau is similar to what is found on the others. Such a mixture can only be the product of criss-cross movements which have been going on for centuries, especially the names of forests and rivers or streams which are more stable than others are convincing in this respect.

The origins of the Tio remain a matter for speculation. The testimony of their neighbours who all claim to have arrived after the Tio were already settled, and especially the Kongo traditions from Manianga,[3] only allow us to state that there were Tio in this general area by the thirteenth century. Only archaeological excavation will eventually be able to advance our knowledge further.[4]

The Tio had evolved on the spot or brought with them the notions of squire and domain which are very general in Central Africa. These domains were the basis from which the political structure evolved. Kingship may have been developed on the plains or the notion was perhaps borrowed from the forest peoples to the north. In any case, it was closely linked with kinship since the royal title *õkoo* is derived from *nkoko*: 'village elder, lineage elder, head of a tribe (if the society is completely organized on kinship)' a current term in the central and western Mongo language.[5]

If it is accepted that the worship of Nkwe Mbali is as old as the kingdom itself then the fact that the six anvils there represent only Boõ and Jinju chiefs, the priest himself, and the king, implies that the kingdom arose on the plain of Nsah or perhaps the grasslands of Djambala. Mboõ or Nsah is also indicated by the Kukuya habit of describing the Tio kingdom as the state of the Buma (Boõ) and also by reference to the old historical sites, the forest of Mpiina Ntsa[6] the forests of Itoo, Ikie, Ndua, Itieere, and Mbe Andzieli associated with the kings and their first two wives. This includes the northern part of the plains of Mbe. The involvement of the Jinju is shown by the fact that their name in Kikongo, Ansiku, was the name under which the people were known by their western and southern neighbours in the sixteenth century.[7] As

[3] A. FU KIAU, *N'Kongo*, p. 108; J. CUVELIER, *Traditions*, pp. 479–80.

[4] A scatter of relatively late sites is known from the Mbe plains. Pottery, seeds, and remains of metal may yield the necessary clues. The Tio do not melt iron now, but they did.

[5] The term in its most general meaning is 'elder'. Cf. for instance G. VAN DER KERKEN, *Les populations*, I, p. 176 (Nkundu) for the use of the term as head of a 'tribe'. C. COQUILHAT, *Sur le Haut Congo*, p. 57, noted the derivation.

[6] A huge funeral mound at Mpiina Ntsa was attributed by Ngateo and Ubwoono to Nzã Mbã but others tended to credit the first king with it. It should be excavated. Cf. YOULOU KOUYA, *Une adoratrice*, p. 55. The place is not far from the falls at Mbã.

[7] Ansiku is certainly Jinju. Cf. W. BAL, *Description*, n. 87, pp. 168–70. The correspondence with Jinju is regular (the Jinju are still called Ansiku by the Kongo) and PH. CURTIN, *The Atlantic*, table 26, p. 97, gives the form *Enchico* (Spanish 1548–60) which is the closest to Ajinju.

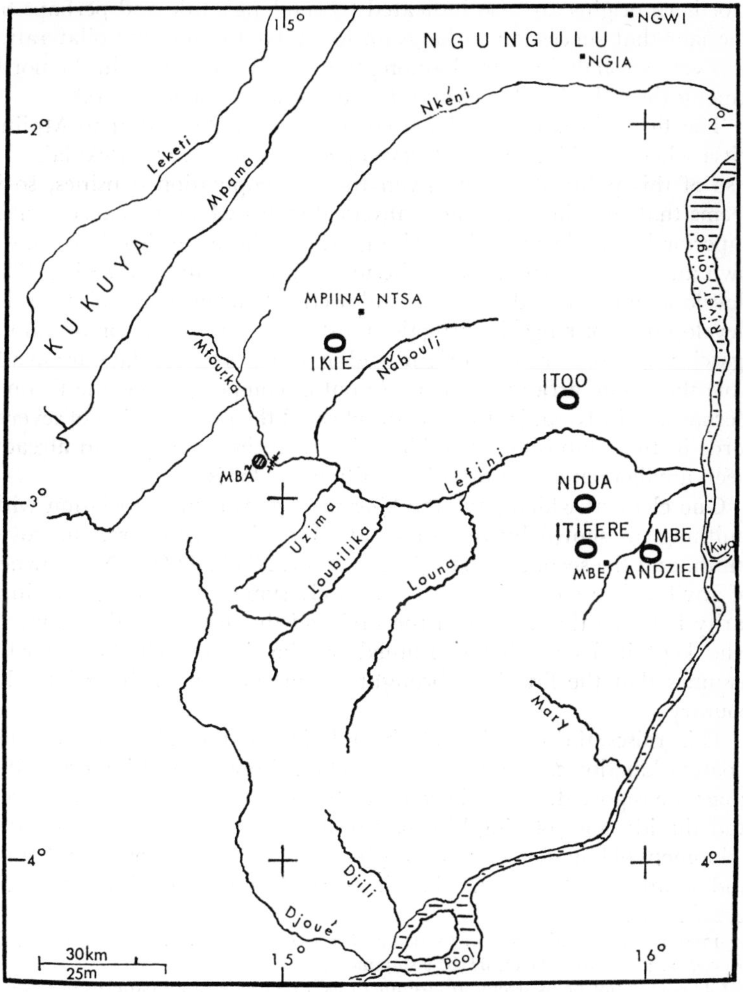

Map 15: *Sites connected with Early History*

o : Forests of origins of kings, NGAASAA, WAAFITIEERE
● : Residence of Nkwe Mbali, near waterfall

for the origin of kingship two claims are made, one linking them to NGIA at Ngwi, in Ngungulu country while the other held only that NGANSHIBI drifted down the Congo river with the king's litter.[8]

[8] Claim made by NGIA at Etoro not far from Ngwi. The relations between NGIA and the king in terms of *Mpiini* could be a retention of a former link. NGIA is attested

Northern origins are also indicated by the king's title and perhaps by the fact that succession to kingship was bilateral and that bilaterality was very strongly ingrained among the Tio. It is also thus in the north among the Mboshi, Bobangi and in the whole Mongo group.[9]

The first Tio king may have come from the Ngungulu to Mpiina Ntsa where the kingdom first developed. Conquest cannot explain the rise of this political system given the low population densities, so it seems that the king-lord had a mystical status which was accepted as superior by the local squires who gradually began to legitimize their own authority in part by titles bestowed upon them by the king. The development of a modest tribute followed. At one or more points in the development of kingship struggles must have developed, for we find a 'gate' system of 'forests of origin' and in all cases where data are available these gate arrangements arose out of competition for the throne. Perhaps, as in Kasanje, the system reflected the participation of several lords in the establishment of kingship. If so the domains had already been amalgamated in unstable coalitions by lords.

One element which gave the king prestige was his association with smithing, as shown by the anvils at Mbã, the sacred fire, the royal smith, and the second title in the kingdom: NGANDZUUNU, 'owner of anvils'. The connexion may be purely symbolic stressing the similarity between the 'master of the fire' and the 'master of the country' who kept it from being consumed by the fire of evil. One hardly assumes that the first king brought the art of iron smelting into the country.

This raises the question of the relation of the Tio, Kongo, and Loango kingdoms, where similar relations between smithing and the kings are reported. It is believed that the Tio was the earliest of these[10] and the ideology of kingship may well have influenced the later development of kingship south of the Pool (Mbata) and among the Kongo and Loango to the west. The diffusion of better techniques to melt

---

by 1700 as a powerful ruler; L. JADIN, *Le Congo*, p. 492 (82). H. BRUNSCHWIG, *La négociation*, p. 24, for NGANSHIBI's statement.

[9] This may not be as strong an argument as it seems, because patterns of descent may have changed over the huge time periods involved. But the size of the bilateral 'pocket' in the forest area indicates at least a certain age. Note also that succession among the Mongo was patrilineal. Here the Tio resemble the Kongo. The vicinity of matrilineal organizations is invoked to explain this.

[10] O. DAPPER, *Beschrijvinghe*, p. 219: 'All the blacks who live near the sea have derived their rights, laws and privileges from those of the Pombo.' The Nguunu tradition may be a myth. A proverb well known from the Tio to the coast stresses that all are descendants of Nguunu. The Tio explained it as meaning that they were all men, whether Tio, Kongo, or Vili. At the coast R. LETHUR, *Etude*, p. 21, says the name referred to a woman who would have been the ultimate ancestor of Tio, Kongo, Woyo, Vili. There is no reason to believe in an old kingdom of Nsundi, called Nguunu which would include all of these peoples with the Pfuunu and Nzabi as E. ANDERSSON, *Contribution*, p. 10, n. 1, did on the strength of this proverb alone.

ores helped. The Tio worked the ores in the Mindouli area and even earned the Kongo appraisal: *Bateke bateke nzundu*, 'The Tio sold the anvils'.[11]

2. *Early population movements*

The early Tio occupied the plains, perhaps a point or two south of the Pool and the areas west of the Pool and north of the Congo river, now known as the mining district of Mindouli and the region of Manianga or Mazinga, which gave them a considerable extension in the lower forested areas of the headwaters of the Niari. The heartlands on the plains were not densely populated and the countryside in the sixteenth century must have looked much as it does today.[12] Given the assumptions that the pattern of Tio settlement was similar to what it was in the 1880s, and this is born out by toponymy because personal names (of village-leaders) and place names form only one set, one can understand how overpopulation set in rapidly. The plains people had adapted to their environment and emigration for them was a search for a similar environment. The process is well described by one tradition relating how the Ngenge left. These were followed by the Mfunu and both migrations were finished at the latest well before the middle of the seventeenth century.[13] In a similar fashion the Mfinu and Tio spread in several 'waves' to the plains south of the Pool and east of the Nsele until they encountered opposition on the southern margins on their environment in Dikidiki and Lula territory. This too was an early migration.[14] The Hum near the lower Kwango similarly emigrated and

[11] J. CUVELIER, op. cit., p. 480. The dating and the spread of the art of iron smelting, developments in techniques used and the age of the workings in the copper area of Mindouli-Boko Songho all await archaeological research. This paragraph represents merely a hypothesis. An alternative one would be that all kings in the area inherited this link with smithing from previous lords and squires and that it would go back to the introduction of the art of melting iron.

[12] W. BAL, op. cit., pp. 55–8. Lions, herds of black (savannah) buffaloes and before 1583 even black rhinoceros prove that this was a very open savannah as it is now. Lopes leaves no doubt: 'They (buffaloes) err in infinite numbers in the deserts of the kingdoms of the Anzique.'

[13] On Ngenge migration cf. Appendix no. 13. Even the Tege, said Ngateo, came from the Mboõ plains. On Ngenge, Mfunu see F. GUSTIN, *Les populations*, p. 6, tradition by NGOBILA; S. LECOCQ, *Rapport*; S. LECOCQ, *Chefferie*; S. LECOCQ, *Meko*; TECHY, *Enquête*; AUGUSTEYNS, *Note*. War played a role in one version only. In all others famine was paramount. For the date the citation of the Mfunu title MFUNINGA and of the GIRIBUMA title (Ngeli Boma proving the existence of the Boma kingdom which came into being after the Ngenge arrived) by O. DAPPER, op. cit., p. 217 (FUNGENO still a variant for MFUNINGA in 1963), p. 218 (GIRIBUMA or GIRING-BOMBA). Data probably taken from Herder in 1641–2. The episode of five Portuguese merchants arrested in 'Okanga' and brought to the court at Mbe seems to indicate that the whole Mfunu and Hum area was still under some control by the king (G. CAVAZZI, *Istorica* v. II, p. 90, German ed.).

[14] Cf. LEKEUX and JORIS in F. PEIGNEUX, *Projet*, and the latter; J. LAMBERT, *A propos*, for eastern-most Mfinu.

this migration to the area known as Okanga after 1600 was finished by then.[15] All these migrations involved the settlement of previously unpopulated or very sparsely populated areas of the same type as the plains in the heartland.

But other sets of migrations involving the Tio have also been reported. The Yans, the Ding, the central Kuba claim, probably with some reason, to have left the area of the Pool to migrate to their present locations. These movements were certainly concluded by the sixteenth century since the last may have been the Kuba who arrived in their present habitat before 1600. These were movements of many people as well, but usually by boat and under the leadership of a form of chiefs. Thus they differ from the migrations by people of the plains and rather represent the effects of other forces, in the Kuba case apparently first the closeness of Europeans, later the Jaga. The Tio as such are not involved, but a later set of emigrations clearly involving only aristocracies of the Yans, Hungaan, and perhaps some Ding. The Yans movement might perhaps be situated between the fifteenth and seventeenth centuries, i.e. again at the time of the population movements to the plateaux beyond the core, with which they are not to be confused.[16] Yans or Hungaan rulers have some typical Tio customs and institutions.

With this last movement, ideas about Tio chiefship also spread, a movement comparable to the vast diffusion of the *nkumu* ideology which spread over much of the forest areas in the Middle Congo basin, and from which the Tio notions may perhaps derive. However unclear the total picture still remains, it intimates movements of diffusion spreading political 'models' over huge areas. So the likelihood that the Tio developed their whole ideology by themselves in splendid isolation on the plains, without being influenced or influencing the world outside is nil. Right from its birth the kingdom was culturally outward-looking; an ideology and presumably a structure open to the outside.

[15] H. ROULIN, *Les Bateke*, deals with this in detail. Okanga was understood by the Tio as *Ok' anga*: 'leader of the large village'. It is said to be a Mfinu and Hum term for the leaders of their big settlements. The prefix alone indicates a Tio dialect, Mfinu or Hum/Mfinu. For Ocanga cf. W. G. L. RANDLES, *L'ancien royaume*, pp. 13, 23. The name occurs after 1595.

[16] The literature about these movements is ample. The earlier movements involving transfer of populations are also attested by the linguistic situation. This confirms that the rivers were the channels of migration.

For the later movement of aristocracies cf. G. DE PLAEN, *Les structures*, pp. 41–3, 46–7, and Hungaan: E. TORDAY, J. JOYCE, *Note*, p. 297. All authors confused both the population and the aristocracy movements among the Yans. Typical Tio features are found in emblems, terminology, and vocabulary. These could be diffused and not brought by the immigrant chiefs, because all these features form compact distributions between the Hungaan and Tio. The one exception may be the *ndzo ancweli* of the Tio and Yans overlords. This is also a feature more likely to have been carried with the migrant chiefs rather than diffused later.

3. *Trade and its developments*

Even before the Portuguese arrived in Kongo there was trade in that kingdom since the unified currency, the *nzimbu* was already in existence. It is likely that articles traded included salt from the coast, iron and copper from Nsundi and Manianga, fish, different styles of pottery and baskets, as well as the fine raphia cloth from the north and east. The Tio were involved, certainly, in the ore-producing area and probably along the Pool and the Congo. The trade dealt in local products on a small scale and involved perhaps not much more than exporting surplus goods for which a neighbourhood was famous, such as a style of baskets, mats, or pots, in return for other goods of this type. The area of the Pool had some importance by 1491 even though Pacheco Pereira did not know of any profit to be made there. For in that year the Kongo king asked Portuguese help to fight the Anzique, perhaps the Hum, perhaps the Tio, near the river.[17] It is also possible that the Pool was already of some commercial value because a group of fishermen, the Bale, came from the area of Bolobo to settle first on the Mbamu island and then south of the Pool under a leader called NGOBILA, 'king of the waters'.[18] Fear of enemies was given as a reason for this movement away from the upper river, but the attraction of the Pool may have helped.

Very soon, by 1529, Mpumbu, the area south of the Pool, inhabited by the Hum (Mubumbi)[19] was mentioned in documents as the major slave-market and it remained so for centuries. Before 1560 at the latest,

[17] Probably at the Pool. Cf. W. BAL, op. cit., p. 84, n. 273, p. 200. The opinion which held that the war was fought at Nsanga and Mazinga near Manianga is not really tenable.

[18] G. SAUTTER, *De l'Atlantique*, I, p. 365, after M. IBALICO, *L'origine*, pp. 37–9. Tradition held that the Babali (Bale) were Ngungulu and started just south of the mouth of the river Nkéni. They fled from their overlord Mokemo who pursued them to Mbamu. The chief of the rebels took the title NTSUULU. *Babali* is derived from *Ibali*, meaning the Congo river in Bobangi and perhaps Ngungulu. The form *Ibare*; closer to Bobangi *ebale* was known to the Portuguese by 1620. Slaves came from that 'country'. The tradition noted by Ibalico had already been recorded in 1698 by Caltanisetta. Cf. F. BONTINCK, *Diaire*, p. 133 and M. D'ATRI, *Relation*, p. 66. The reason given then was that they did not want to pay tribute to Makoko. But since they did pay in the 1650s and were south of the river, the Ibalico version may be more correct. Whatever happened, they arrived before the reign of King Affonso I since their leader, the NGOBILA (later it would be the NTSUULU) was baptized. Cf. F. BONTINCK, op. cit., p. 134. This dated it before 1506. The migration belongs to the fifteenth century at the latest. The expedition of 1491 to the Pool may have had a connexion with the installation by these Babali or a later refusal by them to pay tribute to Kongo.

[19] A. BRASIO, *Monumenta*, I, pp. 525–7; (1529); ibid., II, p. 38 (1540: which is clear; F. BONTINCK, op. cit., p. 120 and fn. 140). *Mubumbi* = Hum and is derived from Mpumbu. Note that the plains north of the Pool were also called Mpumbu in Kikongo, Mpũ in Tio, and the Tio who inhabited them were Awũ, in Kikongo also Bawumbu.

Tio slaves were reported in Colombia. In the seventeenth century Ansiku were to become a special class of slaves in Brazil, thus showing how many were being imported there by then, for the Kongo did not export their own people if they could avoid it, while the Tio seem to have readily exported their own. It seems that the nature of slavery, a form of adoption, helped. The Tio were not only getting rid of their own criminals, but also of free persons, if the price was right. No moral qualms were involved since it was believed the buyer would treat the slave as the Tio treated theirs. In addition a number of other slaves from areas beyond the Tio must also have been labelled Ansiku since they came through the same market.[20]

The first period of trade with the Kongo was interrupted by the Jaga invasions. Before 1560 slaves seem to have been exported by the route to San Salvador and thence to the coast along with ivory, palm-cloth, and redwood, while *nzimbu*, wines, salt, cloth, and beads began to travel in the other direction. After 1575 when the kingdom of Kongo was restored and the Jaga ousted, the trade went to Luanda. But the Jaga have played a role in this reorganization of the trade, not only because of the weakening of the Kongo kingdom but because of their activities after 1575. Groups established themselves between the Pool and Loango, north of the river. By the 1620s they were allies of the king of Loango and had occupied the small state of Bungu. By the middle of the century large numbers of them lived in the Nsundi province of Kongo or just beyond and the two sections became active in the Loango trade which begins, it seems around 1575. One group, the Yaa, formed an intermediary between the West Teke and the Kunyi on the way to Mayombe, while another the Bahangala, a name probably derived from Imbangala, a Jaga ethnonym, occupied the mining district of Mindouli. Numbers of them were still recognizable by the 1650s but like the Bahangala were to be absorbed culturally by the Nsundi and sent with them into the Tio territory near the mines, beginning with Manianga and Mazinga. There the newcomers slowly assimilated the local Teke and by the 1660s this economically crucial area was firmly in their hands.[21]

[20] C. CURTIN, op. cit., p. 97. One or the other may have arrived well before 1548 in Colombia. For Brazil J. RIBEIRO, *O Elemento Negro*, p. 24. I am indebted to Miss M. Karasch for information about Tio slaves in Brazil. These were called Angicos. On slaves from beyond the Tio country W. BAL, op. cit., p. 34, 'to offer slaves from Nubia, country which lies at the borders of their territory'. Major Tio exports listed by Lopes there and pp. 32–3, were slaves, ivory, and raphia. The Tio brought them to the Pool or within the kingdom Kongo. Goods imported p. 34, were *nzimbu*, salt, ornamental cowries (p. 173, fn. 97), but also Portuguese imports such as silk, linen, glassware (beds). Furthermore he mentioned p. 32, copper, red wood, grey wood, and again raphia. This seems to relate to the area of Mindouli and the upper Niari. By 1583 the kings of Kongo had a guard of Tio: W. BAL, op. cit., p. 120, probably slaves.

[21] W. G. L. RANDLES, op. cit., p. 23 (Bungu); p. 142 (*Gangala* = *Bahangala*, which clearly is *Imbangala*); O. DAPPER, op. cit , pp 216–18 (*Muyako* = evidently later *Yaa*

The seventeenth century, then, saw the functioning of two routes to the Pool, one from Loango, the other from Luanda. Imports and exports remained the same on both save that Portuguese wine was less in demand and the Dutch sold fire-weapons and gunpowder and bought copper for export. On the northern route raphia cloth was the currency and on the southern *nzimbu* remained paramount. At the Pool both were undoubtedly used by 1583. Other major differences were that the southern caravans were equipped by Portuguese with Portuguese capital and led by their agents, the *pombeiros*, whereas the Vili organized the caravans to the Pool from Loango, probably on the trust system with Dutch capital and perhaps with Jaga help. Both caravans relied heavily on slave carriers, involving slaves which were not destined for export, at least on the northern route, since slave exports were minimal until the 1660s. Dutch demand after 1637 led to a gradual increase of the number of slaves from about 300 annually to 3,000 annually by 1670. On the route to Luanda, the only figure available from Kongo alone claims 5,000 to 6,000 slaves by 1656 but the number used to be higher. So slaves went to Luanda, not to the Loango coast. How many left the Pool, how many among them were Tio, is unknown. Three thousand a year from the Pool, perhaps half of these Tio, would seem to be a high figure.[22]

Thus further changes took place in the 1660s. By now the Tio did not exploit the mines any longer and slaves began to arrive in great numbers at the Loango coast, while the exports to Luanda dwindled. The chaos created in the Kongo kingdom after 1665 explains this shift. The Vili took over the trade in the south and the Soso and Zombo began to follow the Vili example after 1750, carrying their goods mainly to the coast between Ambriz and the mouth of the Congo river. Vili caravans by now were large and settlements of Vili for temporary purposes sprang up at various points in the Kongo domains, no doubt after the model of the temporary settlements which they had begun to make before 1660 in the mining area of Mindouli for extracting iron and copper themselves. The slave trade now grew by leaps and bounds until 1750 and then remained stable until the Napoleonic wars, with exports on the Loango coast ranging from 14,000 to 18,000 slaves a year while imports became more and more similar to the nineteenth-century

and *Yaami* since *-k-* in second position drops in Tio); pp. 159, 220, Jaga between Loango and Pombo.

On the Loango Trade, cf. PH. MARTIN, *The Trade*, all and p. 151 (Yaa), p. 143 where argument that mining district became Nsundi between 1610 and 1660 at the latest. But Nsundi then was largely Jaga as, e.g. J. CUVELIER, O. DE BOUVEIGNES, *Jérôme*, all. The first mention of an area called Manianga and probably markets there in F. BONTINCK, op. cit., p. XXXIX (lands of Munhangi, which he identified with Moenhe Mugi, but we believe to be more likely Manianga).

[22] PH. MARTIN, op. cit., and W. G. L. RANDLES, op. cit., pp. 173–82, summarize the available data on trade from Loango and from Luanda and Kongo.

patterns. Cloth, guns, and gunpowder were the mainstays with finished iron goods and salt following. It is estimated that between 1750 and 1800 perhaps as many as 50,000 guns a year reached the Loango coast.[23] Of those slaves perhaps one fourth were Tio or related to the Tio and one sixth were Bobangi by 1786.[24]

With the increase in demand and a series of events on the upper river the trading network had been constantly expanding from the Stanley Pool upstream. By 1698 the traders of the Pool knew about the lower reaches of the Kasai and certainly went as far as the Alima, since NGIA, who ruled near Gamboma, is mentioned. The mention of Degranpré proving that a century later the Bobangi were partners in the trade as well indicates that now slaves were coming from at least as far as the mouth of the Ubangi river. In the Alima area the eighteenth century saw an immigration of Bobangi and population movements among the Mboshi who seem to have been pushed up river, producing in turn other movements of which the effects were felt deep into Gabon. Scattered indications confirm a great extension of the network on the rivers. For instance the pottery unearthed at Mafamba near the mouth of the Kwa is so rich in its variety of form and decoration, even more than the pottery of NGOBILA at Kingabwa, that the only valid explanation would be that at least the patterns came from a wide variety of sources on the middle Congo and Kwa rivers. Then various imports in the Kwa and Lake Leopold II area confirm that trade was felt there. Again archaeological investigation could clarify this point more directly.[25]

[23] PH. MARTIN, op. cit., p. 153. The number seems very high, but two to three guns were paid per slave exported. Even 30,000 a year, the minimum figure acceptable still remains impressive. On trade 1670–1800 besides PH. MARTIN, cf. W. G. L. RANDLES, op. cit., pp. 201–5; P. D. CURTIN, op. cit., p. 266, for overall peak in the slave trade 1700–1850 for all of Africa. As an example of early Vili caravans cf. F. BONTINCK, op. cit., p. 23, 49 fn. 35. For three years this group of Vili seems to have stayed at the Kongo court of Bula-Lemba, north of the Congo to supply the king João with guns.

[24] PH. MARTIN, op. cit., p. 150, after Degranpré. Add to her reference his pp. viii, xxiv, and II, p. 38. Note that his proportions were valid for Loango only while the estimate of 14,000 to 18,000 slaves exported a year was valid for the whole Loango coast. One cannot therefore take 1/4 of these figures and claim these to be the Tio exported. 4,000 a year from the Bateke group is too high and so is 3,000 'Bobangi'. Perhaps half of those would be more correct. Tio slaves in the eighteenth and nineteenth centuries came to be known as Monjorros, Moncongues (in part only) and 'scratch-face'. Enough were exported to produce again a recognizable population in Brazil. Monjorro is linked with Monsol, an area in the kingdom, near its capital already mentioned by Dapper (before 1660).

[25] M. N. OBENGA, *Le royaume*, pp. 33–5; J. EMPHOUX, *Mafamba*; H. VAN MOORSEL, *munteenheid* and collections at Lovanium Museum for Kingabwa, where objects from the seventeenth through to the middle of the nineteenth century were unearthed. The volume of the trade at the Pool can be imagined when one of the local lords there, was able to buy a marine cannon and have it dragged to Kinshasa! Note from Van Moorsel that at the turn of the eighteenth century, wealth was still hoarded at least in *nzimbu*.

After the decline in trade during the Napoleonic wars a revival in slave exports took place which reached its peak perhaps in the 1830s and then dropped off rapidly, after 1840. A few slaves were still exported along the lower Congo by 1860 but now legitimate trade, especially the ivory trade, had taken over, so that from 1860 to 1880 ivory was the key commodity on the Pool market.[26]

The nineteenth-century slave trade clearly involved a route from the Yaa to the Tege and beyond as Koelle's data indicate, a route which may well have existed before. Tio internal data indicate that before 1800 the Bobangi already brought goods from Europe to Ntsei and the indications about the Bobangi–Tio strife show clearly that these struggles occurred between 1820 and 1840 or 1850, i.e. during the renewed massive export period of slaves. The latter were not wars in the European sense of the word, but raids and counter-raids in the channel and along the Pool. The Bobangi tried to settle in this area and break the Tio monopolies, most notably by an attack on Kinshasa, which was helped on that occasion by lords and their followers from the Mbe plains.[27] The last wars were remembered as having been exceptionally fierce since there were seventy-five deaths. For Merlon the Tio war forbade overland travel to the Bobangi and kept the markets on the Pool. The Bobangi however got the upper hand on the river.

The gradual decline of the slave exports, the fact that ivory had always been an export as well and the additional truth that slaves were

---

Other finds are known from the Kwa and Lake Leopold II area but not yet published.

[26] PH. MARTIN, op. cit., p. 160; P. D. CURTIN, op. cit., pp. 260–2 (Ambriz partly received its slaves also from the Pool); W. G. L. RANDLES, op. cit., pp. 205–9. Even in the peak after 1826 the maximum of 1750–1800 was not reached again.

[27] For Koelle, P. D. CURTIN, op. cit., p. 256, fig. 23. The Tege route went as far north as the Mbeti around the Equator. On Bobangi 'wars' cf. H. BRUNSCHWIG, *La négociation*, pp. 28, 37 (a Bobangi version claiming that formerly they could not go down river further than the channel and had to trade at Mbe). E. ZORZI, *Al Congo*, p. 387, on Iloo's participation; A. DOLISIE, *Notice*, p. 48. Tio tradition in 1963 was clear that these were 'wars' conducted by individual lords or groups of lords against individual Bobangi chiefs or groups of chiefs. The *terminus ante quem* is the expedition to Kinshasa in which Iloo himself participated when young. Data on generations from Dolisie (Bobangi generations) also make it clear that the events happened before 1840, 1850 at the latest, and after 1820. Dolisie's note about the beginning of the trade by Bobangi four generations ago agree with Degranpré if one generation was taken at about twenty-five years to thirty years. The agreement between these estimates and the peak of the slave exports is striking. Cf. also a Nunu source on Tio/Bobangi wars in HENDRICKX, *L'asservissement*, p. 5. The Bobangi party came from near Kwamouth at Kapanda, attacked Kinshasa, did not succeed and asked Nunu help from Dwantole, the first remembered Nunu king. A second war was 'won' but they still could not settle there. In 1880 Bokoko, the fifth remembered king was ruling. At twenty years a reign this puts it in 1800, at ten years a reign around 1840. It is likely that it happened in between these extremes which correlated with Dolisie and the *terminus ante quem*. A. MERLON, *Le Congo*, pp. 25–6. No blood money had to be paid for a Bobangi killed on land or a Tio on the water after this war.

useful as carriers and retainers so that an internal market took over some of the numbers previously exported, all made the transition at the Pool from slave to legitimate trade smooth. There was no crisis and no slackening in the volume of the trade. The diversity of regional commodities traded, moreover, was probably always an important part of the trade and gave it its additional flexibility. So the exports of ivory increased and also those of tobacco. Whereas tobacco was a rare commodity at the Pool in 1698 it reached Ambriz in appreciable quantities by 1870. Tobacco came from the Tio plains where it thrived better than anywhere else. The trade is also remembered by the Tio. Other products, with the probable exception of copal were too bulky for export in relation to their value per lb, so that, for instance, groundnuts of which the Tio had provisions were not worth carrying.[28]

The currencies in use changed during the nineteenth century, or perhaps in the seventeenth century. Imported cloth was certainly added to the raphia cloth already in the eighteenth century and metal currencies began to succeed each other. After lead, it was *ngiele*, copper, and finally the imported *mitako*. The latter were certainly not used before the establishment of legitimate French and British trade on the coast around 1850. Probably it may have gained favour because of a steady depreciation in the *ngiele*, similar to the depreciation later of the *mitako* itself.[29]

The market at the Pool as a centre for regional trade antedates the sixteenth century. It was drawn very early into the orbit of the slave trade, partly no doubt because of its geographical position, but at least in part because the institutions dealing with slavery among the Tio were favourable to an extension of the trade. After this the trade was affected by the Jaga invasions and by the collapse of the Kongo kingdom, not in its essence, only in the organization and the direction of trade routes. Demand increased according to world demand and the trade grew regularly, reaching a considerable volume after 1750. The commercial economy was developing in itself, not as a result of other sectors in social life.

The Loango trade affected the Tio of the plains more than the trade from the Pool to the south. So that if changes in the volume of trade or in the commodities carried by the Loango trade precede related

[28] M. D'ATRI, op. cit., p. 64. Salt from the sea was also rare; CH. JEANNEST, *Quatre années*, p. 77. The volume of legitimate trade increased in value so that by 1884 Anstey evaluates the value of British trade at two million pounds; cf. W. G. L. RANDLES, op. cit., p. 205 and fn. 1. For new uses for slaves cf. H. BRUNSCHWIG, op. cit., p. 55 (slave villages in Mpũ).

[29] Cf. Chapter XI, 'currencies'. Note that beads had once been common currency as well and remained so in Manianga. F. BONTINCK, op. cit., p. 110, for region of Mbinza in Mpumbu not far from Pool in 1698. Whether another metal currency ever preceded lead is unknown. It could have been iron or copper. No trace appears about this in the literature.

changes in other sectors, these are caused by the commercial economy because they are both subsequent and related. Indeed such changes did occur most strikingly in the political sector.

4. *Political developments*

Regularly in the scarce documents before 1575 one hears about the Ansiku and the people of Anzicana. By 1561 the Lord of Chiquoco, whose people came to Nsundi to trade was said to want baptism with many of his people.[30] The impression was left that he was certainly a great king, since he had many people. He did not seem a threat. Yet one or two kings of Kongo, Bernardo I in 1567 and Henrique I in 1568 are said to have died in a war against the Anziku, and in Pigafetta they are represented as a very war-like people.[31] One is tempted to represent the kingdom then as 'strong' and possessing an efficient army. Yet in documents of this period there is already a contradiction. Some texts extol the greatness of the kingdom, others mention several countries of the Anziku or even claim that the kingdom was small. Lopes speaks of the 'deserts of the kingdoms of the Anzique' using a plural. The paradox seems to indicate that even then there were autonomous areas governed by different lords.[32] The kingdom may never have been a cohesive co-ordinated whole. The confusion recalls the quarrel when the French opposed the Agents of the Congo Independent State in the 1880s. It is probably due to the same fundamental cause—the extreme lack of cohesion in the kingdom.

If the kingdom was so decentralized why then did the Jaga not over-run it? Given the nature of life on the plains, the size of the territory,

[30] A. BRASIO, op. cit., II, p. 478. Some priests were prevented from going there in 1584; ibid., IV, pp. 369–401. Other early references date from 1548 and 1549, as well as 1529 and 1540.

[31] W. G. L. RANDLES, op. cit., p. 141, after Pigafetta Lopes; W. BAL, op. cit., p. 104, mentions only Henrique I; p. 206; fn. 293, for Bernardo I who may have been killed by the Suqua, an unidentified group. If one reads Cuqua, it could refer to the Tio of Makoko or a Hum group with a *Mukoko*. Since Henrique I died in 1567 or 1568 and the great Jaga invasion dates from 1568 there is probably a connexion. Either the Jaga killed him, the Jaga invaded the kingdom because of the confusion following the event, or there were already Jaga in Anzique. The latter seems the more likely, since it explains why he was reportedly killed by the Anzique. On the armament and skill in war of the Anzique, cf. W. BAL, op. cit., pp. 33–4. R. DELGADO, *historia*, I, p. 244 read *Suqua* as *Cuqua* = Makoko; Also his vol. III, pp. 110, 443.

[32] Cf. W. G. L. RANDLES, op. cit., p. 23 (it was never tributary to Kongo). Randles quotes sources up to Dapper and a source from before 1600 claiming the country was bigger and more powerful than either Kongo or Angola. Yet another text of 1656 says that it is 'the most miserable kingdom in the area'; W. BAL, op. cit., p. 58, for the citation from Lopes, p. 34, for a mention of loyalty to their lords in the plural, p. 32, for a distinction between Ansiku and Anzicana, a Latinized derivation and Bal's comments, pp. 168–70. It is clear that Lopes included the Hum in Anzicana. L. JADIN, J. CUVELIER, *L'ancien Congo*, p. 168, n. 1 for a declaration by Lopes that it was only a small kingdom.

the low density of population, is it not surprising that they left the grasslands alone. They overran the western Teke and they may have occupied part of the area around the Pool and mixed with the peoples there. The relations between Jaga and Tio are documented by Dapper whose sources all date from before 1660 and after 1640, when he is not copying Pigafetta Lopes. (1583) After mentioning that the king had thirteen kings under him, which may be an echo of the twelve lords of the crown, he went on with a description of the Jaga. He was so mixed up that he wrote in one place that both peoples seemed to live in the same area and elsewhere he wondered if the Tio were not perhaps the 'true' Jaga.[33] This may reflect not only the certain presence of Jaga among the western Teke but also their presence around the Pool.

The sources do not allow one to conceive of the kingdom as a unified centralized state. Yet one text, again from Dapper, runs counter to this view. It is the statement that the king of the Tio kept a strong standing army against Muyako (Yaa), his enemy.[34] Given all we know this seems totally unlikely and Dapper must have misunderstood his source, which itself was based on rumour. It is yet another piece of 'europeanization' of African conditions.

Even after 1560 the Tio king wanted to enter into direct contact with European traders and missionaries, the latter passing in Tio tradition as *õndiele ãtoni*, or 'Europeans of St. Anthony'. Rome organized a mission to the area and as a result of these plans Father Montesarchio arrived in February 1655 at the Pool, stayed for a few weeks and was succeeded in 1698 by two other missionaries who made a very short stay at the Pool again. They stayed with a lord NGOBILA who ruled over what seems to be Kinshasa. From their descriptions, an idea of the political structure at the time can be gathered.

In 1655 the capital, elsewhere designated as Monsol or the area of Monsol was located on the Mbe plains since it took two days by water and three overland to reach it. Even if these numbers are reversed, the location would be about the same. There was evidence of contact between the king and NGOBILA. In 1655 a son of the king happened to be at NGOBILA's and the king sent messengers to fetch Montesarchio. The latter did not want to go further and left NGOBILA in a hurry. As a result NGOBILA seems to have suffered some displeasure from

[33] O. DAPPER, op. cit., p. 182. The king was the most powerful in Africa. Immediately after this sentence, he spoke about the Jaga. Pp. 217–18, he speaks again of the Tio Mokoko, mentions that the Fungeno between Congo and Kwango belonged to his kingdom, and p. 218, mentions the capital Monsol, two hundred miles from the (Loango) coast. Perhaps the Meticas (Teke, Tio) are the true Jaga, he thinks p. 218; p. 180, he declares that Jaga and Anziku are reported in the same area. R. DELGADO, *Historia*, I, p. 398, n. 35, cites a 1779 source which speaks of the Jaga of Anzika with others who live east of them, which would be in the area of the Pool, unless he meant the Yaka of Kwango.

[34] O. DAPPER, op. cit., p. 218.

the king. Another indication of an earlier period showing that the king had some authority, is the story of how five Portuguese traders travelling through Mfinu country were brought by the lord of the area, MFUNINGA, a tributary of Makoko, to the capital and released after lengthy negotiations.[35] By 1698, however, the NGOBILA was said no longer to pay tribute to the king, but to the Duke of Nsundi. In the long run this was temporary since the NTSUULU in the nineteenth century was once again tributary to the Tio king.

It can be inferred that the authority of the king was bolstered by the ideology of authority linked to the system of titles of which NGOBILA is one. Three major Tio emblems were mentioned in this context: the *ndua* feathers, the lion skin ornaments, and the famous brass collar of investiture. No *nkira* was observed, but it is very likely that this sort of thing was carefully hidden from zealous missionaries, who did not hesitate to destroy such objects. NGOBILA had his 'féticheurs'. Scanty as it is, the evidence allows the statement that the power of the lords, Dapper's under-kings, was autonomous to a large degree, but that they derived their legitimacy and its mystical sanction from the royal ideology.

As to the appearance and way of life of the lords themselves, NGOBILA carried a whole set of emblems and *unũ* objects such as a red cape, baldrics of lion's skin decorated with *shiba* feathers, conus, brass collar, brass chain, adze, arm-rings, a sceptre coloured with red camwood, a bell of office, in short what the typical lord was wearing in the 1880s with the exception of the *ndua* feathers and the hat. In the 1880s only the king could wear *ndua* feathers and use lion's skin, while the hat, which covered a bun, already typical for the Pool area by 1698 but only for lords, was the most important emblem of office. NGOBILA could never take it off, which made for some difficulty when it came to baptizing him. By 1880 chiefs wore hats but could take them off. Since authority or *mpu* is derived from *lipu*, hat, the 1698 data can be taken seriously. There have been therefore minor shifts in a lord's emblems. Some like the bun became general wear, some, such as the hat, lost their meaning, some ceased to be worn, such as the lion baldrics and the *ndua* feathers reserved later for the king, while others seem to have retained their meaning without much change. Trends on the Pool between 1698 and 1880 have been for lords to share more with lesser squires and even ordinary men and, surprisingly, to abandon some of the regalia to the king. However, even in 1880 they wore emblems which were not found elsewhere and reflect not only a cultural difference, perhaps, but also a relatively greater distance from kingship. This should not surprise us, since the lords of the Pool in the seventeenth century were NGOBILA at Kinshasa and the Hum overlord at Lemba. NGOBILA, as the excavations at Kingabwa have shown and the texts

[35] F. BONTINCK, op. cit., p. XXV.

confirm, ruled over the most important market inland, a market apparently not counter-balanced as yet, by the rise of other market places on the northern shores of the Pool. The Loango trade had not yet made a deep imprint. Later the dispersal of markets would reduce NTSUULU's power.

Political dynamics on the Pool foreshadowed nineteenth-century situations. There were competitors for the title NGOBILA, both in 1655 and 1698. In 1698 a war was being fought between the Hum chiefs of Lemba aided by the three main 'vassals' of NGOBILA and the latter. This war was apparently as protracted as those of the nineteenth century. Damage was also limited. The foes of NGOBILA burned his capital and he fled to Ntamo without loss of life. From there he organized a come-back, there was a fight 'at the limits', at the river Lukunga, and some men were killed among the foes. Both sides sought allies, not by taking people as hostages, but by buying heads of settlements to assist with troops. A mercenary solution, to be expected in the area of a great market.

NGOBILA was a lord, not a squire. He had *nkani*. Unfortunately the reciprocal obligations of *nkani* and lord are not attested, but for the fact that when the *nkani* had chased him from his capital they installed another contender as NGOBILA. This means that they could not conceive of themselves as free of bonds with some NGOBILA and implies an institutional relation in which a NGOBILA was overlord.

Another typical feature of Tio politics, the practice of marrying sisters or daughters of leaders to other leaders, was also in evidence. On both trips the missionaries were entreated to marry girls or at least to have intercourse with them so their relatives would have 'children of the *ngàà* of the Pope'. One recognizes the policy which led NTSUULU to marry his daughter to Malamine or Ngaliema's matrimonial career.[36]

At the level of the major lords on the plains one indication from oral tradition may be added. When a major war was breaking out each lord and the kings could presumably call up their *nkani* with all their men. An army was formed near the Mbe of the lord by the arrival of all these contingents. It would march only when it was believed enough men had been gathered for a successful campaign, an arrangement which recalls similar practices among the Kongo.[37] The efficiency of such a system was obviously minimal. The campaigns could only be short, *nkani* might rebel, change sides, be bought off, as happened with NGOBILA'S 'vassals'.

[36] For 1655 cf. J. CUVELIER, O. DE BOUVEIGNES, *Jérõme de Montesarchio*, pp. 93–5, 104–17; O. DE BOUVEIGNES, *Jérõme*, all; F. BONTINCK, op. cit., pp. 115–35 (Caltanisetta) and pp. XXVI–XLV, for discussions of the mission to the Tio, NGOBILA and his capital; M. D'ATRI, op. cit., pp. 35–70. The expression *py*, *py* on p. 67, meaning 'quiet', makes it certain that these people spoke Tio, for it is still the same.

[37] Appendix No. 13. Tradition by Eloge.

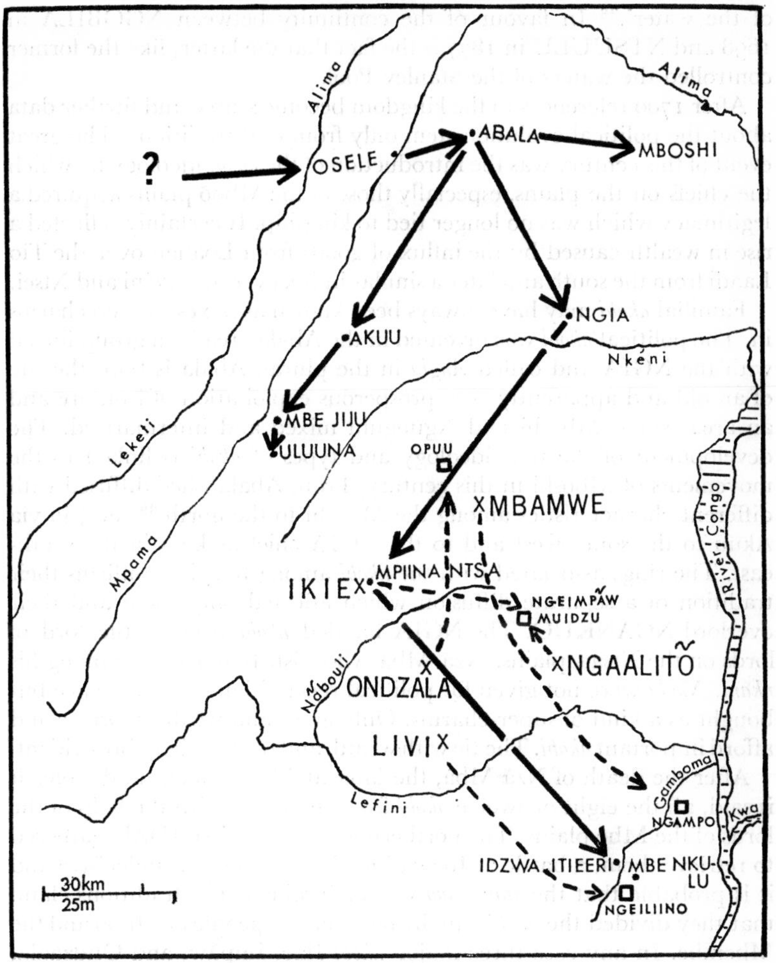

Map 16. *Diffusion of the nkobi*

⟶: Direction of diffusion
× : Residence of the major *nkira* and their names
□ : Residence of owner of major *nkobi* and their title
- - →: "Movement" of *nkira* to *nkobi*

NGOBILA in 1698 seems to be the predecessor of the lord who ruled with the title of NTSUULU in the 1880s while the NGOBILA then was settled at Mswata in the channel. The title also occurred among the Ngenge where the NGOBILA lived at Tshumbiri and controlled the river Congo there. The function of the title in all cases was associated with control of the river and they all claimed to be 'king (master) of the water'.[38] In favour of the continuity between NGOBILA in 1698 and NTSUULU in 1877 is the fact that the latter, like the former controlled the waters of the Stanley Pool.

After 1700 references to the kingdom become scarce and further data about the political evolution stem only from oral traditions. The great event of this century was the introduction of the *nkobi* ideology by which the chiefs on the plains, especially those of the Mboõ plains acquired a legitimacy which was no longer tied to kingship. It certainly reflected a rise in wealth caused by the influx of goods from Loango over the Tio Laadi from the south and later a similar influx over the Nkéni and Ntsei.

Familial *nkobi* may have always been known as boxes to keep charms in. The political *nkobi* was invented in the Abala area by a group linked with the NGIA and called *Angia* in the plural. Abala is both the site of an old and apparently very prosperous exploitation of iron ore and an area where Mboshi and Ngungulu mixed and intermarried. The development of the new ideology and types of *nkobi* is linked to the movements of Mboshi in this century. From Abala *nkobi* diffused with different characteristics among the Mboshi to the north,[39] the Jiju via Akuu to the south-west and to the NGIA chief or king in the south-east. The rings associated with the *nkobi* among the Jiju confirms their tradition of a separate diffusion which affected only them and their overlord NGANKUO. The NGIA handed *nkobi* over to the lord of lords on the Ntsaa plains, Nzã Mbã who distributed them among his *nkani*. *Nkobi* were not given for political recognition of dependence but bought as a kind of super-charms. Only great and wealthy lords could afford important *nkobi*. The tie with wealth and trade is therefore evident.

After the death of Nzã Mbã, the king at Mbe reacted and stole, it is said, all the eight or twelve *nkobi* from the north with the help of the lords of the Mbe plains. The northern lords led by MUIDZU gathered to retrieve them, a battle at Idzwa itieeri near Mbe was indecisive and it is probable that the *status quo* was maintained. The traditions claim that they divided the *nkobi* equally between the people of Mboõ and the Mbembe. In any case three major *nkobi* Ikie, Impãw, and Ondzaala, remained on the Mboõ plains and two only, Livi and Mbamwe, were held in the south. After this the major *nkobi* spawned smaller *nkobi* for

[38] F. BONTINCK, op. cit., pp. XXXIV–XXXV, 128. Caltanisetta claimed the title in Tio was *Ngongo Vila Ntinu Amaria*, which contained at least one Kongo word; in Kikongo it was Ne Ngobila. We think he mistook the Tio for Kongo and vice versa. It would then mean that Ngobila could be translated as king of the waters. But it does not mean that in Tio. King of the waters = õkondzaadza.

[39] Mboshi history remains almost unknown. The data in J. ERNOULT, *Afrique*, pp. 35–7, are doubtful because they seem to confuse Mboshi and Bobangi. The date is a guess and might be closer to Bobangi dating than to Mboshi. Only an inquiry in the area may elucidate these points. Since the events of the area caused considerable movements and political changes over a vast region of Congo Brazzaville and Gabon, such a study is urgently needed.

the *nkani* and gradually the royal ideology became diluted, even among the smaller squires, and lords. As late as the middle of the nineteenth century or even the 1880s *nkobi* were still the focus of political quarrels and LIPIE asserted that they caused several wars.[40]

When did all this happen? An approximate date for the battle might be 1840, which does seem very late. As for the life of Nzã Mbã the only dateable element in it is that the Bobangi did trade on the market at Ntsei at the end of the eighteenth century.[41] The most remarkable fact about the evolution is that it did not go from south to north but the reverse. One would have expected that those squires or lords who were most involved with the Loango trade would have made such a move first, closest to the overland road from the Pool to Loango. The situation shows then that it was not enough to be wealthy and autonomous to invent the ideology. The set of specific circumstances evolved at Abala triggered this off and its spread, with the acceptance of the *nkobi*, is due to the effects of the Loango trade, once the first invention was made.

The Kukuya did not take the *nkobi* ideology of the Mboõ, mainly because they had undergone a political transformation of their own during the same period. Why the Jiju did not take to *nkobi* is less clear, but could be attributed to the tense relations existing between their NGWAMPOLO and the MUIDZU of the Mboõ.

Tradition has also kept a vivid portrait of Nzã Mbã. The name was both a title, and a name. It meant 'The Creator of Mbã' a rather prestigious title to take, even if the Tio did address major chiefs as Nzã. Other similar praise titles are known, such as 'king of the waters' and Nzã baari, 'Creator for the people'. This lord lived at Mpiina Ntsa and was related on his mother's side to MUIDZU of whom he was an *otioolu*. On father's side he was also related to a lord Sã, a Tio or Ongia, forest Mboõ, in the neighbourhood of Mpiina Ntsa.[42]

Great stress is laid in the traditions on Nzã Mbã's wealth and *unũ* objects: 'He received Toby jugs from the NTSUULU on the Pool, in white and black designs and one was blue, yellow, white with a handle.

[40] Data from the different versions about *nkobi* in Chapter XIII, The Lords. Cf. and J. VANSINA, *The Kingdom of the Great Makoko* for more detail. Unfortunately the editors left the map out so that the text is difficult to follow. Hence cf. Map No. 17. Evidence for the spread from north to south is given by the fact that the *nkira* are all located north of the Lefini.

[41] LIPIE and Ubwoono both claimed the battle took place when their grandparents lived and their father too. Ubwoono's father was old when he was born. If one accepts these data at face value it is hard to put the date earlier than 1840, and 1850 would seem more likely. But there may have been confusion between *taara* and the *taara* of *nkaa*. A date after 1750 and before 1800 is most likely for the diffusion of the *nkobi* to the Mboõ. Excavations of the mounds at Mpiini Ntsa could provide better information. The movement of the *nkobi* may be linked to the foundation of a new form of overlordship among the Kukuya which is dated by P. BONNAFÉ around 1750.

[42] All data about Nzã Mbã came from LIPIE, Ubwoono, and Ngateo, the latter two being descendants of this lord having lived at Mpiina Ntsa.

Sherds of five or six of these are still on his imposing tomb.' There was a glass, an anvil, a royal hat and a brass collar with twelve points like the one of the king, a huge single bell and an equally impressive double one.[43] He could not be seen by ordinary folk, whom he received seated behind a curtain of mats; he ate only maize porridge *okaa*, never cassava, and it was brought to him by a woman who presented the food on her knees and no one could watch him eat at all. His drinking ceremonial was most refined, etc.

All these objects of *unũ* came from trade both with Mpila and Ntsei. One Bobangi chief was his blood brother and watched over him when he was dead and lying in state. He had kinsmen among the Wũ and perhaps at Mfwa. He fought for ivory and slaves. When he sent his hunters out they had to return with ivory or be sold themselves. His Tswa were constantly hunting elephants and not buffalo. He made war on NGEIMPÃW, the areas of Ntsaa and Mwaari, for the slightest excuse to steal ivory and make captives, but nevertheless he stuck to the type of warfare called 'war at the limits'. His Tswa also traded for him in goats, ivory, and tobacco with the Ngungulu and the Bobangi could fish in the Nãmbouli river, provided they gave him half of their catch. The colourful detail of the traditions shows again and again that he did not neglect a single source of income and had even started to orient production to the market economy by exporting tobacco and having his hunters go mainly after elephants.

As a politician he fought other lords: 'He often made war with his brothers and uncles.' In short he managed to become *wookuru* or leader of all the lords, including MUIDZU. It was by the number of guns and the number of retainers, including bought slaves that he rose to this position. He seems to have been the first lord on the Ntsaa plains to have consequently organized his domains and his residence to maximize wealth and derive the utmost political advantage from it.

Later other *mpfõ* followed. Ipubi in the area of Bouambé gained renown both for his cruelty and for an attempt to make and police a road from there to the Kukuya. Another famous lord was Sã. Their exploits were magnified and remembered for the marvellous stories they made. So these data must only be used as descriptions for a period, the height of the slave-trade either before 1800 or after 1820, and not strictly as historical events, for many known clichés are mixed in them. There was a person Nzã Mbã referred to by Ubwoono's father as *nkaa* and Ngateo's knew that NGANDZIÕ Ntsu ankare's father, Ngwaayulu called the younger half-brother of Nzã Mbã, *nkaa*. These data allow us to date his life at the turn of the nineteenth century, and because of trade conditions the floruit could be estimated at 1820–40, unless two generations were coalesced so that it falls well into the eighteenth

[43] Ubwoono kept his tomb for some years and claims remains of all of these objects were still visible there.

century. To us this seems the most likely.[44] The genealogical connexions are also important to show that this was a real person and not a mythical first king. For some informants such as king Ntsaalu, he divided the *nkobi* and may have been king. This deformation stems from the glory of the Nzã Mbã legend itself. If he was so powerful, so wealthy, he could only be king.[45]

Later in the nineteenth century the data became better. Brazza collected information and a skeleton genealogy in 1880, while Guiral knew that Iloo's father and grandfather had been kings. From the traditions a few names are remembered and the following reconstruction is proposed.

CHART 21

Kings before Iloo

names in receding order	*remarks*
Iloo	lived at Nduo, not Itiele
Ngoolua?	One informant, Ovulamo remembered the name
Nge ilieele?	*nkaa* of Andibi, in generation preceding Ngaaÿuo which makes him of the same generation as Iloo. Remembered only by Nge Impio
Pieele	Possible father of Iloo. Lived at Nduo. A. BASTIAN, *Die Deutsche Expedition* heard a Teke king was called Gancucu or Gambieri or Gamanbieri (I, p. 328).[a] Brazza said he lived at Mbenga, probably Mbe Ngõ nearby Nduo
Ncu acumpfiri	
Opontaba	Probable grandfather of the NGEILIINO Opontaba and hence of Iloo. Lived at Mbe Nkulu. Fought at Idzwa itieeri
Ngantso	The name most remembered. Contemporary of Nzã Mbã. Probably lived at Ibali[b].

[a] The information dates from a period before 1873 without further precision. The mention of 'one' Tio king makes it look as if he had died and the mention of Gancucu (Makoko, *õkoo*) makes it certain it is not the MAMPIELE.

[b] A detailed discussion of all information would take too long. Kings have been included without a question mark if at least two independent witnesses testified to their existence.

[44] Calculating that a father was thirty years old when his son was born and all the links to be in the male line, this would give with coalescing 1735 (since Ubwoono was born around 1890) for his birth date and say 1765–1800 or so the period of most intensive trade, including the participation of the Bobangi in it. Obviously it could be later, but not much earlier. A date after 1820 for his death would seem unlikely also since trade was not brisk between 1800–1820.

[45] MAMPIELE and Ntsaalu thought he had been king but Ntsaalu said: 'For some he was king, for others not.' He thought he was because of the *nkobi*. Some seem to have made Nzã Mbã a sort of mythical first king. The title would lead (and related himself to Nzã Mbã) he should know. It is still possible nevertheless that an early king lived at Mpiina Ntsa and perhaps founded the kingdom there. Only serious excavations will tell. There should be a tomb of the nineteenth or eighteenth century and perhaps a very early one, antedating 1500.

The person of king Opontaba is recalled as the time when Mbe Nkulu, where ruins are still visible, was at its heyday. The site is big and the legend about the mothers tying bells around the necks of their children so they would not be lost, is told as an indication of this. The NGAALIÕ gave the following description:

> The king lived there with his wives and some people. MOTIIRI lived behind him. Then the lords of the crown lived at eight points around this centre with their *nkobi*. It is what was called the eight branches. When they danced they gathered at the centre. All twelve *nkobi* were there and my 'father' (probably the *taara* of his *nkaa*!) saw this. All the *nkobi* from north of the Lefini were here . . . Mbe Nkulu was abandoned because of a great famine. There were too many people and so they were ordered to leave. NGOBILA lived there too, and the Ngungulu, Mboshi (?) and Bobangi all came to trade there. They called it Mieelayoo (the Name of NGEILIINO's settlement in 1880). There were twelve villages and the meeting place was in the middle.

The ruins show that there was a great settlement there with indeed apparent kernels separated one from another, but only perhaps three of these were found. The settlement of the NGEILIINO in 1880 was the descendant of this 'Old Mbe'.[46]

King Opontaba had built it and he was the king who fought the northern lords about the *nkobi*. The people from the north were led by MUIDZU Mpio. Either they settled at Mbe Nkulu as well or they were defeated and Opontaba appointed successors at Mbe. Whichever it is, it is obvious that Mbe Nkulu corresponded to a period when the Bobangi did not go much to the Pool, but stopped at Mbe. Brazza recorded the story from the Bobangi point of view, probably according to Mballi Michima. Trade went overland and the goods came to Mbe. Few Bobangi went all the way to the Pool. Gradually the Bobangi fished and hunted less on the plains.[47] Later more of them went down river until they carried most of the trade and the trade overland, or by Tio canoes, dwindled.[48] Obviously this period two generations before Iloo[49] was a high point of royal prestige coming just after a low point caused by the spread of the *nkobi* and the wealth accumulated on the

[46] Mbe Nkulu means old or ancient Mbe.

[47] This recalls the story of the Bobangi who fished for Nzã Mbã on the Nãmbouli and another one by Brazza according to which they stopped going up the Lefini after an accident. H. BRUNSCHWIG, *Les cahiers*, p. 177. P. 211 seems to indicate that Laadi went to 'Macoco' via Awey (Akwei). Even in 1880 apparently some Laadi arrived as far east as NGANTSU's (ibid.).

[48] H. BRUNSCHWIG, *La négociation*, p. 37. It is clear that there always was trade by water, but that about two generations before Iloo the Bobangi managed to get through in larger numbers than before. This did represent a loss for the kings as Brunschwig, points out p. 12, but in fact Mbe's wealth came more and more directly from the Pool. At Mbe Nkulu as later it may have been mainly the lords who enriched themselves.

[49] Opontaba as a name could only be inherited by an *otioolu* who was Iloo's brother or cousin called 'brother', his NGEILIINO Opontaba.

Mboõ plateau. It did not last long. The Bobangi began to attack Tio parties on the river and beat off the efforts of the Tio to prevent them from going downwards. Mbe as a trading centre declined, perhaps even before Opontaba's death. A conservative calculation puts Opontaba at about 1810–20 just before one calculates the Bobangi 'wars'. This implies then that the date given for the battle of Idzwa Itieeri has to be put earlier as well.

The forces which allowed Opontaba to recover are not known. The forces which led to the downfall of Mbe Nkulu may have been partly famine and partly the Bobangi breakthrough, but NGOBILA also cited incessant wars between the lords and Miandoo tells that one of the lords there, Linganu, sold his own people, from his own town, so they left him. A combination of all these factors may explain the decline. But the last straw which forced Iloo's father, probably Pieele, to leave for near-by Ngõ was the revolt by what seems to be a competitor for the crown. He had nominated his brothers and his nephews as lords and now, says Brazza, sent them out in the country to block the rebel who had been defeated, but lived 'a little farther away'. In practice he lost the control over the lords he and king Opontaba had had. This, thinks Brazza was the reason why the king became a suzerain instead of being an absolute monarch.[50] Obviously the interpretation was Brazza's. Tio traditions and earlier sources, as well as the general configuration of those vast underpopulated reaches all seem to indicate that the kings were never very much in control of their lands, whether their lords lived at Mbe or not. As for the rebel 'nephew' he cannot be identified but he was apparently backed by the MUIDZU, a classical situation, which shows again the reality of the two political constellations which constituted the kingdom.

The breaking up of Mbe Nkulu was nevertheless felt as a serious setback, as comments by chief Ngampei indicate.[51] Pieele had obviously exercised greater authority than his successors and the nomination of his brothers and 'nephews' to the major titles shows it. Among his 'brothers' on the skeleton genealogy one recognizes NTSUULU and a 'Ngheliba' which recalls a 'Gilibe' mentioned by Koelle as a place among the Boõ.[52] Other brothers are MBULANKIO, a title in Mpũ,

[50] H. BRUNSCHWIG, *La négociation*, p. 29. Quarrels and wars 'at the limits' were also causes for the decline. Miandoo remembered a long tale about a war between Mbe Nkulu, the royal settlement and Mieel ayoo. The lords who fought it are not named, but the later presence of NGEILIINO suggests that he was fighting against the royal settlement.

[51] H. BRUNSCHWIG, *Les cahiers*, p. 189. It is obviously not possible that Ngampei proposed that the Europeans should oust the king. So the speech was edited somewhat either by the translator or by de Brazza.

[52] S. W. KOELLE, *Polyglotta africana*, 2nd group . . . 'a town Gilibe one and a half day from the river Mobale (clearly the Congo)'. NGELIBE or NGALIBE may have been a title.

and the unidentified Okila and Nganiu, perhaps personal names. Unless the latter was NGANDZIÕ. To make appointments he had to wait until the occupant of the title had died so that his father king Opontaba must already have inaugurated the policy. In any case the fact that NGEIMPÃW and 'Nganfuru' (NGWAMPOLO) appear on the list indicates that he exercised influence on politics as far away as Ndoolo near Djambala, the Pool, and Abili in the heart of the Mboõ plains. This was no longer the case under Iloo when the whole plains of Mboõ and of the Jinju seem to have kept few ties with Mbe.[53]

If one can assume a gradual decline from Opontaba's reign to Iloo's, in part because of the Bobangi break through and later because of quarrels among the lords, still Pieele, perhaps around the middle of the century, held effective control over nominations. It may have been this very policy which led to the revolt by a 'nephew' from another royal gate.

From 1850 onward, to 1875 or so, the situation of the king deteriorated further, mainly because NGEILIINO had succeeded in keeping Mieel a yoo intact as a large settlement in which NGAALIÕ also resided. Both the king and his NGEILIINO continued to pay great attention to the Pool. The king settled slaves on the road to the Pool, probably after ivory had become the most important export by 1860 or so, while NGEILIINO and NGAALIÕ spent much time there exacting tribute. NGEILIINO also established a branch of his house as the MANDIELE. By 1880 when Brazza arrived, it looks then as if the king was isolated from many of his lords in strong opposition to what had once been the situation at Mbe Nkulu.

Despite the apparent decline, however, one must also stress that, at least since the eighteenth century, the autonomy of the Pool, the plains of Mboõ and Mbe is apparent and that even at Mbe Nkulu the king's power was not strong enough to prevent local wars. So that the deterioration was much more relative than Brazza assumes. On the other hand the king kept the prerogative of naming lords and exercised it after 1892. It was perhaps because of the fact that no important lord died between 1880 and 1892 that the impression of weakness seemed so much greater than at other times. For ultimately, the very lack of cohesion protected the position of the king and kingship. Trade might make the lords of Mboõ and the Pool powerful, a new ideology could even arise in competition with the royal ideology, but the obligations of the lords towards the king were so few, the practice of war remained unchanged and the interest of competing lords all ensured that the system itself was so little of a constraint that it was left unchallenged.

Whether or not there were structural cycles underlying the relations

[53] H. BRUNSCHWIG, *La négociation*, p. 29. The kinship relations indicated by Guiral make certain that it is a skeleton genealogy as well as the expression: 'his brothers and nephews'.

between lords and the king is still not clear. Opontaba's and Pieele's policy of granting the nominations to their closest male kin may have happened before at times when kingship was more dominant. Such a policy would entail gradual estrangement over the generations until a monarch succeeded in regrouping the major titles in his *ibuuru* again. Or the policy may in fact have been fairly continuous, certainly on the Mbe plains, perhaps for the Lefini and the Pool, as it was in the kingdom Kongo. The fact though that the NGOBILA's of the seventeenth century were not said to be close relatives of the king militates against it. As for the more general evolution one can only say that the king's influence was greater from the 1620s to the middle of the century than at the end of it, when it was less than at the middle of the nineteenth century. The documentation does not allow us to say more about this problem of recurrence.

5. *The evolution of neighbourhood structures*

An evolution in the production of agriculture is attested by the origins of the cultivated plants themselves. It is evident that maize was introduced during the sixteenth or early seventeenth centuries and began to oust millet from the forest fields. Its higher resistance to humidity and its much better yield in forest conditions than millet would explain this success, even though millet had been cultivated primarily in the savannah fields. Still there were certainly forest fields since the term *ngwuunu*, 'field', is found in many Bantu languages, more specifically as a field in the woods.

Later in the seventeenth century, cassava came to be accepted at the Pool and was gradually replacing the cultivation of yams there. By 1698 chicouangues or cassava bread was made there in the form of loaves.[54] Planting cassava had advantages: yield was better than that of yams, the bread could be used on commercial expeditions as a 'canned food', it could be kept for two years, minimizing famines stemming from droughts or rains, it did not require storage, its cultivation could be left almost entirely to the women so that men could pursue other occupations, such as trade. Its relatively early appearance then on the Pool in the form of loaves is not surprising. Its disadvantage was its low nutritive value. But along the Pool and the river this did not matter so much, mainly because these people ate fish almost daily. From the few indications available before Brazza's period, it seems that cassava did not oust maize from the dominant place in production before the reign of Iloo even though it had become equal to the other crop. There may thus have been a gradual extension of women's farm work as against men's farm work ever since the late seventeenth century. At the Pool it is evident that the division of labour changed more drastically, with the men devoting themselves more to trade and navigation.

[54] F. BONTINCK, op. cit., p. 127.

Women's share of the work was also increased by the introduction of groundnuts which partly replaced the *voandzea*. By the end of the nineteenth century tons of groundnuts were produced but *voandzea* also held its own. Both plants had probably gained a relatively greater place in the diet than two centuries before. As for minor new crops these were often trees planted by men or plants kept in the dawn-gardens. Their effects both on the diet and the distribution of labour was not pronounced. Their role in keeping a mentality of experimentation with new crops alive, especially among the women, is not to be underestimated. These same dawn-gardens where before Brazza's time some cabbages had found their way, was the experimental station for taro in the twentieth century.

The innovations in terms of plants were furthered by better yields, fewer pests, lesser climatic risks, and other advantages for cassava. But they did not presuppose the acceptance of new technology or new food habits, since maize replaced millet and was handled like it, groundnuts replaced *voandzea* and cassava yams. Poisonous yams had been used before so the treatment of poisonous cassava was not new. Most of the recipes were obviously old although the *kwanga* of chikouangue may have been an invention.

Tobacco was not a replacement for another plant. Perhaps the Tio had smoked other, non-cultivated leaves before since at least three varieties of these were known in Mbe by 1964. Whether smoking was or was not a habit, it had become one very quickly. But the spread of the plant was slower than that of the other American cultigens because, we think, of the lack of experience with this type of crop. By 1698 the people at the Pool were craving for the weed but did not apparently cultivate it.[55] Yet by 1880 they not only planted it on the plains but exported the product to the Pool and to the coast, when the slave trade declined and via Ntsei to the Lukolela area and further up the Congo. This implantation dates from the eighteenth century, the surplus of exports from the nineteenth. It required forest soils and hence male labour. Its cultivation may thus have somewhat checked the visibly glaring imbalance between men and women, except along the Pool where the women gradually abandoned all cultivation save for some little cassava and planted tobacco for sale.

For agricultural production responded somewhat to the demands of trade. The Sese like the Kukuya[56] seem to have intensified the cultivation of the raphia palm, to produce the cloth which was in such

[55] M. D'ATRI, op. cit., p. 64.

[56] O. DAPPER, op. cit., pp. 159, 218. 'Boekkamele' or 'Bukke meale' (Bukamila?) was part of the kingdom and the Tswa were the hunters. They sold the tusks to the 'Jaga' (clear from context these are the Yaa). It is hard to believe they ever traded themselves. Their lords or squires most probably did. The area was the home of the Tio Laadi and forested. They were the carriers to the Yaa and part of the tusks may have come from the Sese, Jinju and Boõ.

demand on the Loango trade route after 1600 and thereafter tobacco and cassava in unknown proportions. This movement was of course slow and of much lesser amplitude on the plains than at the Pool and along the river, since at the Pool, subsistence production in agriculture practically disappeared.

Production of animal or other raw commodities only changed marginally in that smoked fish and buffalo meat from the plains were well received at the Pool. Hunting elephants however became better organized. Already in Dapper's day it is clear that the Tswa *angabira* were used primarily to hunt elephants by the lords and the stories about Nzã Mbã are even more explicit. Yet on the Mbe plateau for instance, the pachyderms were not really hunted systematically and hundreds lived quietly in the gallery forests of the Lefini. Why? The rule obliged anyone who had killed an elephant to bring both tusks to the squire, in return for which he would receive half the benefit after deduction of all costs of going to the lord, sending messengers to the Pool, etc. Such a regulation was not a strong incentive for ordinary men to do much more than set elephant traps, because of the great risk involved in hunting, even with the adapted *tswala* spears shot from a gun. The lords had an incentive as they could send Tswa and those *angabira* who were not occupied with messages, chores, etc. A slave establishment designed to hunt elephants alone was never created, no doubt because slaves could be sold or used later in a better fashion on other jobs. For after 1800 the supply of ivory from the north made it better business to trade as middlemen than to hunt. Certainly this was so for the Pool.

The most obvious impact of the trade was the change in craft production. The bows and arrows known in the sixteenth century[57] gradually disappeared, replaced by guns; local salt, if it was ever produced, was replaced by imports from the Kwa and from the coast; the smelting of iron ore which was carried out until perhaps the middle or end of the eighteenth century was totally abandoned. The ore and many of the finished products were imported. Cloth did not oust raphia because of the difference in spheres of circulation but glassware and European porcelain were competing with the fine pottery along the rivers and the site of Mbe Nkulu seems already to contain much less beautiful Mfunu ware than older sites. Indeed the NGOBILA of 1698 drank, not out of a calabash but from a Dutch Majolica pot.[58] Boats, paddles, fishing gear, and weapons were bought from the Bobangi.[59]

But the disappearance of certain arts and crafts, was not the only effect of trade on technology, since at the Pool the production of pottery actually increased. What happened for the whole economic area between coast and Equator was a specialization in the production of those

[57] W. BAL, op. cit., pp. 33–4. [58] F. BONTINCK, op. cit., p. 128.

[59] For evidence of these questions see J. VANSINA, *Tio—Voix Muntu.* There is archaeological and linguistic evidence besides written documentation.

commodities which had the strongest position on the market. The smelting was done in Nsundi, the preparation of raphia cloth among the Kukuya, pottery along the river, tobacco on the plains, salt in the Kwa, mats and baskets on the plains, etc. An autarchic system of crafts in the neighbourhood had been badly disrupted. That this sector of the neighbourhood economy was most affected is not surprising: the larger trade developed in part from it to begin with.

There is no doubt that the changes in the subsistence economy were all visibly linked to preceding change in the commercial sector. With regard to the evolution in social structure, the bilateral and matrilineal structures seems to be very old since Montesarchio mentions sons and nephews in one breath. Settlements were probably already clusters of kinsmen grouped around leaders, which explains why the names for villages are also often personal names. Polygyny was practised but little is known about marriage. Slavery as an institution existed, we think with all the variants recognized later. The major development in this seems to have been the practice of exacting the fine of a slave for small offences. Yet fines in slaves were usually only imposed for compensation after a murder had been committed and in adultery cases. Yet because witchcraft could be invoked, diviners could find a man guilty and make him pay slaves as Ngaliema did when his nephew was thus accused at Mfwa. It is also evident that slavery may have led to an increase in feuds and warfare, especially by the greater lords, and an increase in accusations of witchcraft. If the latter is true then tensions would increase in the communities since an accusation creates as much anxiety as it dissolves. The one certainty in this matter, however, is that the Tio clearly did not believe any more that slaves were to be adopted by the Kongo or Loango traders who bought them up, since they inspected them exactly in the same way as was done at the coast.[60]

The harems of over a dozen wives observed around the Pool in the 1880s developed only after 1700.[61] The need for alliances with surrounding lords cannot explain these. They were an indication of prestige, perhaps, but they were also most certainly a work force which produced

[60] J. CUVELIER, O. DE BOUVEIGNES, op. cit., pp. 104, 114, 116–17; F. BONTINCK, op. cit., p. 133 (mentions a son being sent as envoy). Obviously the Montesarchio texts are indirect evidence only (the sons and the clan of the NGOBILA were indignant about the actions of the competitor) but in the context of all known data, they are acceptable. The 'clan' mentioned (p. 117) was obviously matrilineal. Therefore the competitor was not matrilineally related.

On marriage the only indication is F. BONTINCK, op. cit., p. 129, where the people hope the priests would give some European cloth to women who would be their concubines. On polygyny, J. CUVELIER, O. DE BOUVEIGNES, op. cit., p. 116; on position of wives of NGOBILA, F. BONTINCK, op. cit., p. 121. One of his wives had a 'vassal' of Mbangu beaten for having stepped on her wrapper and this led to the war between NGOBILA and his *nkani*. A lord's wife then was obviously more obeyed than later. The oldest report on Tio slaves is W. BAL, op. cit., pp. 34–5.

[61] J. CUVELIER, O. DE BOUVEIGNES, op. cit., p. 116.

for their husbands, either tons of food as the thirty wives of NGOBILA did in the 1880s, tobacco, which may have been what they planted at the Pool, or pottery and marketing which were their other occupations there. One might also expect that such women would give numerous children to the husband, swelling his immediate *ibuuru* to an impressive size. In addition, because most of these women were slaves, the children belonged to the *ndzo* of the father as well. But being children they had many more rights and more freedom than slaves, which must often have thwarted the leader of the group; not to mention quarrels between groups of half-brothers. A point of diminishing return was quickly reached on this as compared with the constitution of a group of bought slaves, so that the basic reason for the harem remains economic. A clear social effect was the loss of influence of wives who thus lost much of the social position that their sisters had enjoyed in the 1690s. This on the Pool, along with the division of labour and its changes on the plains, contributed, we think, to the estrangement between men and women which is so typical for Tio society.

The indications given are clearly limited. The sources do not tell us about changes in kinship structure and cannot throw light on the relation of change in the subsistence economy and changes in the composition of the social groups or in social institutions, at least beyond the hints given.

Some data about Tio belief show first that the major beliefs were old. The huge spread of the terminology for religious specialists and witchcraft as well as charms, which is common Bantu and the huge spread over Central Africa of the belief in witch-substance, and of the name Nzã are all indications that these beliefs are of great age and indeed if Lopes does not mention them, Montesarchio and, after him, the fathers of 1698 do. The belief in *nkira* is evident from a mention by Montesarchio, who gives an explanation of the eastern Kongo for the reason he was mistaken for a *nkira*. A number of institutions including the poison ordeal, the use of magic in war and on markets, the existence of specialized religious personnel are all mentioned and are all again probably of great antiquity.[62] *Ikwii* and *apfu* are both derived from stems 'to die' and indicate that at one time the latter referred to ancestors. One may assume that ancestor worship existed, if one accepts that one text of Dapper refers to the Tio and not to the Jaga.[63]

[62] The terms *ngàà, ndoo, ngeiloolo* (from *loko*) *bvaa* or *vàà* are all reflexes of common Bantu words. W. BAL, op. cit., p. 35, where Lopes only said the Tio were 'pagan'; J. CUVELIER, O. DE BOUVEIGNES, op. cit., p. 115. *Banchita* (*ankira*) were said to Montesarchio to be ghosts from the other world. The NGOBILA of 1698 did not come out on the nsona or fourth day. Cf. F. BONTINCK, op. cit., p. 124. Other details on religion there pp. 124–33 (note avoidances) and J. CUVELIER, O. DE BOUVEIGNES, op. cit., pp. 114–18 (CAVAZZI, *Istorica*, II, p. 90, on divination attributing illness at Makoko's capital to traders).

[63] O. DAPPER, op. cit., p. 182. The indications on religion come after those he

The general concepts may have been similar but their application was different. Dapper says that the sun was the greatest God of the Tio and Ngateo believed it had been so. For Dapper the sun was male, the moon female and in the present Tio classification this is still so. But the sun for a long time has been no longer a *nkira*. Similarly it is known from the *ãnkira* women that formerly *nkira* occupied some of the 'slots' in belief which are now, by 1963, occupied by ancestors. It is obvious that the proportion of cases of misfortune attributed to spirits or to witches or to ancestors may have varied and probably did in the past. If so such changes were probably unconscious and gradual. Its jurisprudence was divining and the evolution in the answers of diviners to given situations would lead the evolution in belief, just as the evolution in the use of objects or actions in curing probably led the evolution in symbolism. On all this we lack data, or rather indications are so faint that one can see the continuity, but not the change.

The overall impression remains then that the structure of the neighbourhood changed very little, except for the subsistence economy, and here all changes derived from the commercial economy. One could call the small closed society the 'cold' society impervious to history. It only reacted to dynamic situations outside itself and these situations are connected with economics. One would be wrong, because in contrast to the political structure and certainly to the commercial sector, there are almost no valid data about change with regard to the social structure and the religious institutions especially. What the data mainly indicate is a difference in attitude of both the outsiders, the writers and the insiders, the Tio, about structures belonging to the neighbourhood and the overarching structures. The outsiders participated in trade and entered the society via the political structures. The insiders were conscious of the personality factors involved in political action and even so remembered fairly little of it. Changes in the neighbourhood were considered either unimportant by them or went unnoticed because they were very gradual or unconscious. Outsiders thought the structures of the neighbourhood too unimportant to report on them.[64] Even when dealing with subsistence economics, the data on change have been inferred mainly from botanical or linguistic evidence. The scraps of data on religion show some change in beliefs at least. Only in the kinship organization can no change be shown at all.

---

copied from Pigafetta and before he mentions Makoko and talks about the Jaga. He says: 'Everyone has his idol which he adores and charms especially for war. . . .' That idol in every home is probably the known *itio* which the Kongo called *biteke*. *Ikwii* is a normal derivation of *-kwa* to die and *a-pfu* has the stem of *li-pfu*: 'death' (Sims) and is identical with *a-pfu*: 'corpses'. Both terms go back to the same Common Bantu root and it seems that *akwii* was coined when *apfu* had fallen into partial discredit. At one time in an undetermined past many ancestors were supposed to be the agents of witches and a new term had to be invented for blameless ancestors.

[64] And in the seventeenth century they only visited one atypical settlement.

With regard to trade, a commercial economy must be postulated from the early sixteenth century at the latest. It developed in conjunction with and received its impulse from the world market. The political structure seems to have changed with a loss of royal prestige in the later eighteenth century and a gain in the nineteenth, but the gain had been lost by 1880. But the kingdom was so uncentralized that the greater or lesser influence of its centre, the king, on the regions was of little impact compared to the autonomy of the regions at any time. In fact we may argue that there was little genuine dynamism in the system and that even the introduction of the *nkobi*, which consecrated *de jure* what had been autonomy *de facto*, is not comparable to the kind of dynamics occurring in the commercial sector where cumulative changes took place since at least 1530 and where change may well have been irreversible. The commercial sector is the 'hot' structure reacting most to events and trends, whereas the political structure occupied a middle ground between the neighbourhood structures which it incorporated and the much wider commercial sector.

It is certain that Tio society by 1880 had undergone many changes and belies the title 'traditional society' which might be bestowed on it. It was a society both very old and relatively young, a society in flux. The only documented but perhaps the strongest continual input which maintained this flux was the commercial economy.[65]

[65] Not mentioned in the text is the practice of cannibalism attributed by all early authors to the Tio. By 1880 the only cannibalism was eating of human flesh at the *lisee* of at least the king. Many of the old observations may merely apply to witchcraft. But it seems evident from F. BONTINCK, op. cit., p. 134, that there was cannibalism at the Pool and that the local Tio 'ate' persons killed by the poison ordeal and persons killed in war among the enemy, both probably for ritual reasons. O. DAPPER, op. cit., p. 182, attributed this to the Jaga, mixed with Anziko. But Montesarchio confirmed it for the Pool. Cf. O. DE BOUVEIGNES, op. cit., p. 107. If they did eat their enemies in the real sense and not the magical meaning of the word, they had stopped this practice by 1880. Since only the Jaga did this, the hypothesis of a Jaga mixture with the population of the Pool gains in credibility from it. Note that in the 1880s the missionaries still believed the Tio were cannibals. Cf. P. AUGOUARD, *Le Congo*, p. 29; 'but above all they avidly eat the feet and hands of the corpses to be buried, to preserve them from the evil spirits and protect them from the enemies'. Cf. even in 1892 D'UZES, *Le voyage*, p. 90. Yet at this time it is practically certain the Tio were not cannibal at all.

Chapter XVII
Social Change Among the Tio of Mbe (1880-1964)

DURING the reign of Iloo I the Tio kingdom became a part of a larger whole which was to evolve into French Equatorial Africa and later into the Republic of the Congo. Gradually Tio political history becomes more and more unreal as the new political structures took over one function after another of government. A similar evolution took place with regard to economic organizations, certainly in the commercial sector. Other major trends such as demographic movements also show that Tio history became merely an increasingly smaller part of the wider history of the Congo. A detailed discussion of this process should be placed against a background of the general evolution with the Congo and, since it was felt that this no longer related directly to the subject of this book, such a study was not undertaken.[1] Yet a view of the main evolution of social change since 1892 is relevant since it helps to place the relative interrelations between the different segments of society, as they have been described for the reign of Iloo, into perspective.

To achieve this, the situation of 1963–4 was simply contrasted with the situations existing at the end of the nineteenth century and in some cases data on the actual periods of change could be obtained. Before discussing social change itself, however, it is still necessary to give a wider view of the major events which shaped it during this lapse of time.

1. *The major events*

Mbandieele succeeded to Iloo in late 1892. He was a half-brother or paternal cousin of the late king and the French may already have exercised some influence on the nomination.[2] During his reign the major event was the fighting which broke out after Opontaba's death

[1] This is not to deny that such a study would be useful. On the contrary, there is scope for a thorough examination of the Tio group under colonial rule provided it be based on an exhaustive examination of the written documentation and considered as a part of the wider study about the gradual amalgamation of different ethnic groups into the new whole. Contrasting case studies between different parts of the country would shed a great deal of light on what was actually happening in this respect.

[2] A. DOLISIE, *Notice*, pp. 44–7, deals with the most suitable successor to Iloo. Since B. MAMBEKE BOUCHER, *Ngalifourou*, p. 28, mentions that Mbandieele came from Mpila he may well have succeeded with the active help of the French.

between his sons and NGANDZIÕ and the latter's sons. NGANDZIÕ seemed to have become more and more important to Tio politics and had just resettled his residence on the direct Mbe–Pool road. He had come to Mbe to influence the choice of a new NGEILIINO. But the fighting did not go his way, although it was a short struggle in which few people were wounded or died and seemed indecisive. In any case NGANDZIÕ lost influence and then proclaimed that everything would collapse soon after his death.[3]

Indeed very few years later, in May 1899, Mbandieele died.[4] The administrator of Brazzaville had gone to the Lefini to claim land for one of the *compagnies concessionnaires* which had just been founded[5] since the completion of the Matadi–Léopoldville railway had made the Pool accessible for the export of bulky crops such as rubber. As a result of the notification to the king about the loss of his lands north of the Lefini an affray broke out and the administrator had to retreat to Brazzaville. A military patrol returned, killed a dozen Tio and beat up the king who was taken to Brazzaville to die there. His successor Ikukuri (not the lord of that name), had to go to Brazzaville to receive the investiture. It was clear to all that the Tio king was no longer sovereign. The reign of Mbandieele also saw the total ruin of the Tio position at the Pool. With the arrival of the railway they were now driven from the foreshore of the lake, except at Mpila, because the shore was allotted to the European trading houses. Their business went to the new trading houses who could now handle the bulkier imports and exports. The Tio reverted to fishing or left Mfwa to go inland and turn to subsistence agriculture north of Brazzaville.[6] At Brazzaville their place

[3] According to Miandoo. This was the final act in the feud between Ikukuri and Opontaba, but the first in a new rift the effects of which were still visible and locally important in politics in 1964. The battle itself is once again a typical example of Tio warfare.

[4] Date and details in *Bulletin de l'Afrique Française*, 1899, p. 426, as the Tio revolt, dated June 1899; M. IBALICO, *Ou il est question*, pp. 66–7 (Tio version); P. AUGOUARD, *Trente-six années*, pp. 16–19 (Augouard version, probably correct on facts, not on interpretation); *Mouvement géographique*, 1899, XVI, No. 21 of 21 May 1899, XVI, p. 269 (cf. date). If the date is correct the sources confused Iloo and Mbandieele. Mbe at the time counted only *thirteen houses*, i.e. practically only those of the royal household.

[5] The only *compagnie* in this area which occupied the area between Nkéni and Lefini, according to F. ROUGET, *L'expansion coloniale*, opp. p. 628 and p. 642, was the *Société de l'Ongoma* but there must be a mistake. It is certainly the *Compagnie agricole commerciale et industrielle de la Lefini*, cf. map No. 1, S. AMIN, C. COQUERY-VIDROVITCH, *Histoire économique*, *in fine*. No doubt the monograph of Mme Coquery about the *compagnies concessionnaires* will shed more light on this. It may be that the companies were not involved, but that an attempt to recover poll tax led to the fight. Cf. A. VEISTROFFER, *Vingt années*, p. 211 on poll tax, 1897–1900.

[6] G. SAUTTER, *De l'Atlantique*, vol. I, maps pp. 380–2; text pp. 379, 383–4. By 1898 Bankwa successor to NTSUULU had abandoned the vicinity of Mpila to go to Kintélé, beyond the Djili.

was taken by Kongo from the Kinkala area who were willing to work as hired labour.

The Tio have not remembered the dramatic death of Mbandieele in its perspective but tied it symbolically, perhaps, to the treaty with De Brazza. Brazza, it said, had left two papers, one written in blue, one in red. If there was trouble at Mbe the king should send the red letter to Brazzaville to ask for help. His nephew Ngaawuli thinking there might be money in it sent the letter, the administrator came. When he arrived Ikukuri, the NGAMPO, shot in the air to welcome him, but the administrator believed it was an attack, people were killed and the king was wounded. Brought to Brazzaville he refused treatment and died.

Ikukuri, the next king, was nicknamed Opfulipfa because he did not remain at Mbe but led a roving life through his lands. The French government does not seem to have cared much about him and his succession by Ngaayüo, probably in 1907[7] was not recorded in any printed source. Ngaayüo ruled until 1918. The two reigns are remembered by the Tio as the 'epoch of rubber' and the First World War, ending with a huge epidemic. Internally a serious quarrel broke out between king Opfulipfa and his NGAMPO Ikaa, who had succeeded to NGAMPO Ikukuri. The NGAMPO allied himself with the new NGANDZIÕ and the king, even at Mbe Ngõ where he lived, was only supported by Mieel a yoo where the NGEILIINO Ashiambã and NGAALIÕ the later Ngaayüo lived. The situation of the early 1880s in reverse!

Ngaayüo was NGAALIÕ under Opfulipfa. He was a forceful personality and not very long after his accession he tried to reassert his authority over the Mboõ plateau, apparently abandoned by the French government as well as by the *Compagnie* which had attempted to operate there. The old MUIDZU Mpo Olõ or Inkuo had died and he wanted to install Isu as the next MUIDZU against considerable opposition. He managed to unite the lords of Mbe for this purpose. Isu paid a tusk for the title, more than the others were offering. The king also relieved both the incumbents of the titles NGE IMPÃW and OOPOU, gave OOPOU to the former incumbent of the NGE IMPÃW title and NGE IMPÃW to a favourite of his who had also paid for the service. Obviously the net effect of this was to show to the Boõ that the king was still master.

From this and chronologically related stories of feuds it is quite clear that there was no French control whatsoever in the area. But in 1912 the French founded the post of Mpala to supervise the plateau and the post of Kindongo to 'administer' the plateaux of Mpũ and Mbe. Some time afterwards Ngaayüo got involved in a quarrel with the village of Impe, which was accused of having killed a relative of the

[7] For the date of Ngaayüo's accession. Cf. Dossier 90, archives Moyen Congo, 18 June 1934.

LIPIE. Ngaayüo went to occupy Impe and took all the fowls there. Hence the name: 'the war of the fowls' in Tio tradition. The village was burned and all their livestock taken as booty. The inhabitants went to Mpala to complain and Ngaayüo was captured by a patrol and jailed at Mpala. Liberated some time later he returned to Mbe but decided to leave there because it was land under the jurisdiction of Kindongo (Indoo). He fled to Ngabe which was still controlled by Brazzaville, i.e. not administered.[8] There he died during the epidemic of influenza or dysentery in March 1918.

With him the monarchy totally collapsed. He was the last king to undergo *lisee*, the last to have at least a modicum of autonomy. His successor died on his return from Brazzaville and it was believed had been poisoned by the WAAFITIEERE, Ngalifourou, who now managed to be officially installed as *chef de canton* by the French. For years the throne remained empty. With the authority of kingship also went control over the lands north of the Lefini. No one there ever bothered again about kingship. The new ruler under the French became the *chef de canton*, usually residing at Ntsaa.

At the Pool this reign saw the complete defeat of even the last vestiges of Tio prestige or influence. Nsundi pushed far to the north occupying Fumu land and the whole area to Pangala, backed by the administration at Mayama, for they collected more rubber and brought it to the markets. Only on the plains did the Tio remain unchallenged.[9]

The decision of Ngaayüo to settle at Ngabe with almost all the Mbembe, all fleeing Kindongo, could not have been taken at a worse time. There had been serious epidemics of smallpox before, but at Ngabe there was endemic sleeping sickness, which killed at a high rate. In addition the place was malaria-infested and developed both the 1917–18 dysentery epidemic (from Tanzania) and the 1918–19 pandemic of Spanish influenza. All of this wiped out the original Ambembe to the point that from an estimated five hundred Mbembe in 1915 or so, only eleven men and women were descendants in 1963–4.

[8] Data on the wars mainly from LIPIE who went with the king on both occasions. M. IBALICO, *Ou il est question*, pp. 67–8 gives details over the end of the war of the fowls. Ngaayüo fled from Mpala to complain at Brazzaville, got nowhere and was returning to Mbe when he heard soldiers of Mpala were waiting for him there. He fled to the Belgian Congo and returned later to Ngabe.

[9] G. SAUTTER, op. cit., I, p. 419 fn. 4, p. 384. By 1910 the Tio language was still important enough to be used in instruction by the missions west of the Pool. By 1918 Calloc'h's grammar and vocabulary had become completely useless in the area; *Les marchés*, p. 101, map for situation in 1916 and pp. 94–5. By 1916 (p. 98) the Kongo Lari and Nsundi in the *Circonscription du Djoué* cultivated for the 15,000 adults of Brazzaville almost all of which belonged to Kongo groups as well. There remained Mpila and two hamlets, later incorporated in Poto Poto for the Tio: Total number of adults less than 800 which was the total in 1899 for all Brazzaville Lari workers included.

The population of the Mbe plateau proper, north of the Blue river was wiped out.[10]

These reigns were the age of rubber. Theoretically taxation went back to before 1899, but it was not enforced on the plains. Now it was to be enforced especially after 1912. Taxes apparently could be paid in rubber, goods could be obtained from travelling traders against rubber, rubber seemed to be the new staple commodity, ousting even ivory from its place. People took advances in goods or could not pay their tax and soon a feverish hunt for rubber began. Somehow the choice became to gather rubber or to be jailed or to flee to Ngabe.[11] Only a few could find work at the new *postes à bois* for the steamers along the Congo or began to seek work in Brazzaville.

The 1920s were the 'years of the machine', the period during which the Congo–Océan railroad was built. Everywhere except in the *Circonscription du Pool* there was intensive recruitment of forced labour for the construction of the railway, begun after 1925. This provided the incentive for many Tio to drift from the Mboõ plateau southwards towards Inoni on the Mbe plains. Practically the whole population of the plains today is the product of this migration which lasted until the early 1930s. Already by 1928 the administration was complaining about the fact that the new king encouraged people to settle and thus escape recruitment.[12] Ultimately the migration movement culminated in the settlement of a king Ngankia Mbandieele, chosen among the immigrants who founded a new Mbe on the plains in 1934.

In spite of the complaints of the recruiting officers the office of king had deteriorated even further in the 1920s. First Ngalifourou prevented any nomination. Then around 1928 an elderly man Mundzwaani was installed and was deposed a good year later, because his NGAASAA had died, but also because he displeased the French administration and the NGEILIINO with whom he had a quarrel. The latter seems to have been helped by the *chef de canton* Ngalifourou. The administration

[10] Figures for the earlier period come from the village distribution and estimations given in Chapter I. The survivors in 1963 were adults only. They included at Imbãw NGAATALI, the NGANDZIÕ and Ngiina; at Ngabe Avila, Abamudzu, MOTIIRI and Ntsaalu; at Mbe Mbiinu Mbiinu, the NGANSHIBI and his twin brother and even NGANDZIÕ. The latter was half Wũ however.

[11] A part of Tio traditions, cf. *Marchés indigènes*, pp. 96–8. No dates for the developments are given there, but evidently the 'deuxième période' went to 1907 or so and did not start before 1900. The administrator who wrote this report blamed the trust system of the Portuguese, Vili, Sierra Leone, and Senegalese traders (all called Senegalese by the Tio) but the necessity for taxes was also a strong incentive. Note from the report that only markets 'of the first order traded in anything but food and that was then mainly in cloth'. By 1916 most of the rubber did not even come to the market any more. Cf. also S. AMIN, C. COQUERY-VIDROVITCH, op. cit., p. 46. 1906 was the peak year, equalled by 1920.

[12] G. SAUTTER, *Note sur la construction, passim*, for the building of the railway and p. 248, fn. 84, for the report of 10 September 1929 about the emigration. Cf. Appendix No. 4, 5, for emigration, according to Tio evidence.

then unilaterally installed Ngamvaala whose Lari wife became NGAASAA at Oka not far from Kindongo, 'to be close to the French'. After about a year he died. Then Andibi was picked, apparently by Ngalifourou and ruled from 1931 to 1934. During his term of office the lords at Brazzaville claimed complete independence from the puppet kings at Ngabe and so by the end of his reign Andibi was left with three 'terres' containing about 750 people: the northern plateau of Mbe. The king had become even less than a *chef de canton*.

The re-establishment of Mbe by Ngankia Mbandieele who acted on the orders of an official who wanted to see a village on the road to Ngabe[13] did not restore the prestige of kingship, for he like Andibi seems to have been completely dominated by Ngalifourou who had force on her side. Nor did the situation change when Nkima succeeded and when Ntsaalu took office until the death of Ngalifourou in 1956.[14]

During the great depression of the 1930s the roads were built and some encouragement was given to the planting of cash crops such as bananas in Djambala or tobacco on the Mboõ plateau. At Mbe and on the plains of Mpũ the major revenue came from selling cassava for Brazzaville and hunting buffalo, whose meat also went to the city. By this time Mbe had firmly come within the orbit of the city. Many went to work there as unschooled labour to return when one of their relatives became king, or when they were older and had some savings. Not many worked on the *postes à bois*. In fact Mbe like the other villages on the plateau of Mbe had become a sleepy small village from which youth escaped when it saw the chance.[15]

After the Second World War, which made almost no impact on this area, an attempt at economic development was undertaken by founding in 1948 an agricultural station at Inoni which was to experiment with mechanized agriculture and the suitability of the plains for extensive stock breeding was examined. Both these efforts came to naught and of the Inoni experiments there remained by 1964 only the habit of hiring a tractor to plough the women's fields at Mbe. During

[13] M. Bousculé, says the unanimous tradition. The Mbe of 1963 developed from this settlement in 1934–5. First it was the quarter Masala, then under king Nkima (1939–48) Lifura Mbaa was built and Inkwii followed after that. Uluuna was not founded by a king but by emigrants from Imbãw in 1962–3.

[14] The dossier 90 from the *archives du Moyen Congo* of 18 June 1934, of 15 May 1936, n.d. (1937–40) (probably by Costurdié) recapitulates data to the reign of Ngankia. Tio information is plentiful as well. On Mbe in 1933 before the resettlement, cf. V. BABET, *Exploration*, p. 38. For dates, beyond documents cited, see M. SORET's forthcoming genealogy, also L. PAPY, *Les populations*, p. 116 photo b. (burial o Nkima in September 1948). Ntsaalu succeeded in December and was deposed in April 1964. In 1948 (p. 121) Mbe still was not bigger than 'a dozen houses'. G. VERVLOET, *Un peu de folklore*, pp. 28–9, dates the burial of Nkima on Sunday 12 September 1948. He makes it clear that Nkima had never been 'approved of' by Ngalifourou and lacked authority.

[15] L. PAPY, op. cit., pp. 127–9.

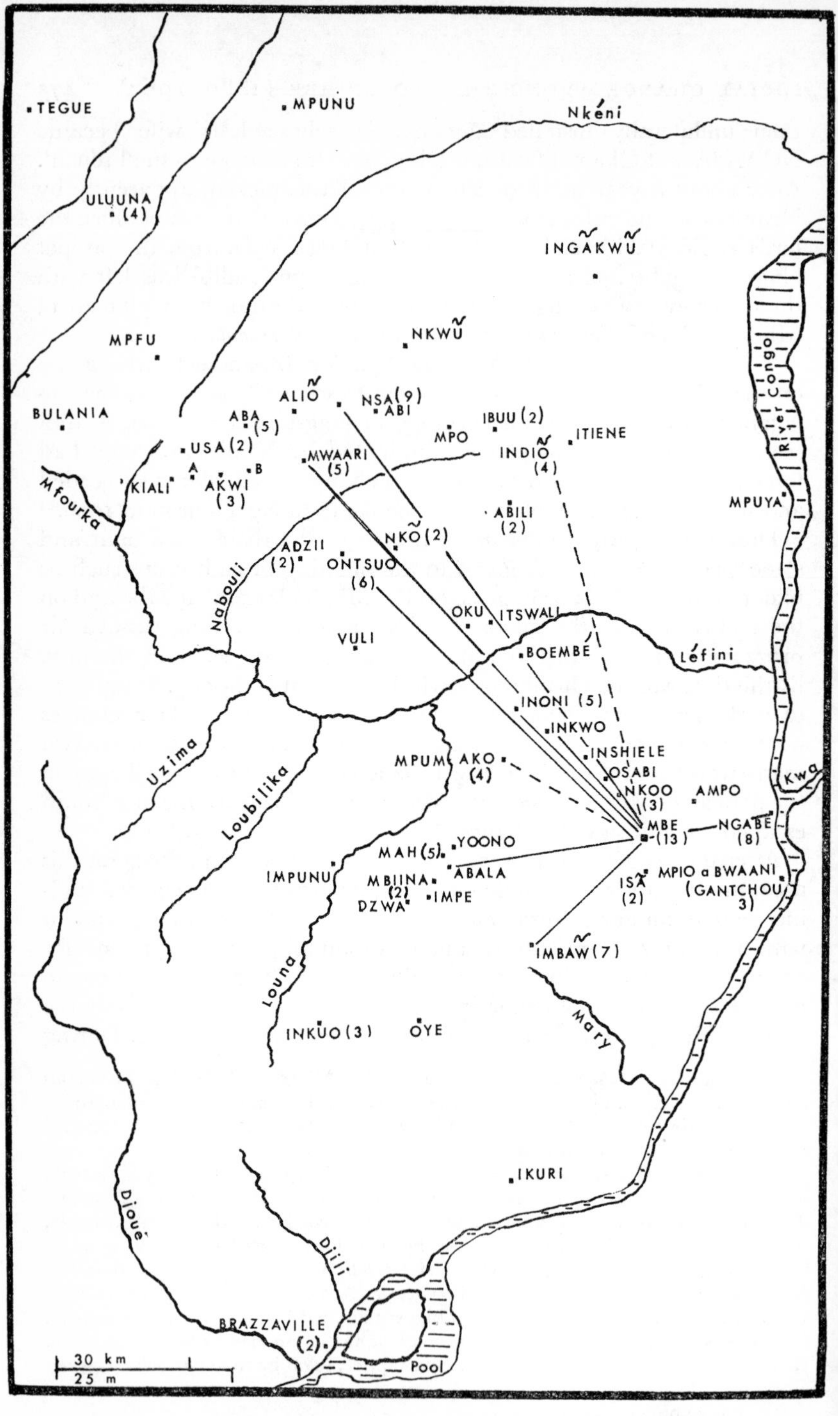

Map 17. *Origins of the Inhabitants of Mbe* (1963)

A : Ongia B : Mpiina Ntsa no. 2 (3)

Mbe (13) : The number indicates the people now in Mbe born there

- - - - : Links Mbe with the village of origin of four residents

——— : Links Mbe with the village of origin of five or more residents

the same period a school and a dispensary were first built at Ngabe and then another school at Mbe. Otherwise the development was limited to the establishment of a mission post at Mbe, but that was abandoned by 1962 for lack of converts.[16]

After the war the French government tried to restore some of the former lustre to the position of king and after the death of Ngalifourou, Ntsaalu even paid a formal visit to France. The *chef de canton* who had replaced Ngalifourou was not able to continue to play her domineering role and by 1957 kingship looked attractive again, mainly because possession of the title carried the advantages of a salary, a car, and an official residence. This certainly was part of the explanation for a deep rift which had already developed in Brazzaville before 1952, shortly after Ntsaalu's election, between backers and antagonists of the king. The situation developed into an attempt by opponents still including the NGANDZIÕ and a number of lords, among whom the lord of Bouambé was the driving force, to depose Ntsaalu. This quarrel became part and parcel of the political life which was vigorously developing in Congo in the 1950s and ultimately led to the ousting of the king on 20 April 1964. He was replaced by Iloo II. It must be stressed, though, that this remained a very minor aspect of Congolese politics and that the king had not regained any authority at all. Kingship by the 1950s and certainly after 1960 had largely become a folkloristic survival for most of the Congolese, excepting those at Mbe and Ngabe.[17]

After the war, more and more Tio went to live in Brazzaville and the pattern whereby younger men left and older persons returned affirmed itself. There were few 'Batéké' in Brazzaville, however. The 1955–6 census bore out the fact that they were at a disadvantage educationally with regard to others. 22 per cent of the unskilled labour and 15 per cent of the household help were Tio and only 4 per cent had achieved the position of office workers. A strong contingent was still fishing as their forefathers had done and others were gardeners. The establishment of schools on the plains or the practice of sending children to school in Brazzaville developed only very gradually. By 1963 the situation was unchanged except that hunting buffalo was no longer possible, that several young men at Mbe worked as unskilled labour for modern road construction projects and that one was on a scholarship in France and others were away at primary or secondary school.[18]

[16] L. PAPY, op. cit., pp. 129–30; Earlier mission work had been limited to the fringes of the plains and partly on the Mpũ plateau.

[17] On political developments, cf. the documents for the 1950s in *dossier* 90 and observation. On Ngalifourou and her cult, cf. YOULOU KOUYA, *Une adoratrice*; B. MAMBEKE BOUCHER, *Ngalifourou*; ANON., *Enterrement*; and *dossier* 90 relating to her death, succession problems, and the funeral.

[18] Cf. Appendix No. 8, 9 (Crafts and children away at schools outside Mbe). Census figures for Brazzaville and discussion in G. SAUTTER, *De l'Atlantique*, I, pp. 572–3, 391, 396–9, 421, 423.

Yet after independence an effort was made to help the local population of the Mbe plateau. A dispensary was finally built, the school was expanded and gave first-rate education to children, as well as classes for adults and a new technical school was set up. The impact of these institutions on the population was still slight.[19] The population was, however, much more aware of national events and developments than a mere few years earlier. This was not only the result of the emergence of national politics and elections, independence and subsequent events, nor only of the improved roads and the mobylettes which enabled a few younger persons to travel to and from the city. Above all awareness of the outside world was coming to Mbe via the cheap transistor radios.

From the above it is evident that the turning points in the development of Tio society after 1892 were first the economic collapse of 1899 and its sequels: the ages of rubber and of the machine and later the political collapse of 1918. For a while Ngalifourou succeeded in providing a new rallying point for Tio pride but she represented a typical colonial force. The old world can be said to have died in 1918. After this a task of political and economic integration into the new units proceeded. Economics again went faster than politics and Mbe found itself after 1934 soon a remote suburb of Brazzaville. Political integration into the Congo state was slow in the colonial period, but was proceeding more rapidly after independence. By 1963 the old overarching structures had completely disappeared and had been replaced by completely new structures. Compared with other parts of Congo the evolution had been slow, no doubt because of underpopulation.[20]

[19] In 1962–3 177 pupils attended the grade school at Mbe: 108 boys and 69 girls. These included children from all over the northern plains. Most children at Mbe attended classes. But three to six children per year only obtained the Certificate. Only ten children were pursuing studies in secondary school and one could expect in 1964 only one or two of those to succeed. One was pursuing post secondary school in France, but was not progressing very well. Given the low total number of the population involved these results were not negligible.

[20] Cf. the comments made by G. SAUTTER, *Le plateau*, pp. 161–6, about the economic consequences of under-population. Transportation problems led to the failure of Inoni, to the modest output of tobacco for the SEITA and in general made Mbe the least administered area perhaps in the whole Congo. The transportation problems themselves were caused partly by the nature of the terrain, partly by lack of manpower to keep the roads in good condition, which was itself a consequence of the low density. The under-population was such that Inoni succeeded in absorbing all available labour for 100 km around the experimental station. In the 1960s the road surfacing activities on certain stretches of the great south–north road also drained the whole available labour force.

The cost of administration per inhabitant was and is still higher than in almost all other areas of the Republic. The small Mbe school absorbed all the children of the whole northern plains, which meant that most of the children who came from outlying villages had to be boarders and obviously there was no money for a boarding

The change had gone deeper. The whole social, economic, and ideological fabric of society was affected. These deeper changes are now to be discussed. None of them seems to have really begun its evolution before 1920. Apparently one of the roles of the two wider systems had been to shield the neighbourhood from change. With their collapse this evolution began.

2. *Social change*

Kinship structure in 1964 were still the single most important social institutions for most Tio of the Mbe neighbourhood.[21] Changes within the social structure have been a gradual blurring of matrilineage and kindred. The *ndzo* gained in importance because the Europeans assumed that the Tio were matrilineal and most *mpfõ andzo* became *chefs de village* responsible for collecting taxes, furnishing labour when required, and information for the census, which were the three major if not only functions of the administration besides the administration of justice. Another factor promoting the *ndzo* was the matrilineal organization of both Lari and Nsundi who became the reference elite for the Tio in relation to the modern world. With the disappearance of feuds and wars the *ibuuru* lost some of its crucial functions. It declined also because the French did not use the settlement as a basis for their territorial organization. It was a strange paradox for a European administration that their *chefs de village* were not necessarily heads of settlements, and if they were, they could only order directly members of their matrilineage!

Yet the *ndzo* did not simply grow and oust the *ibuuru*. For since 1900 or so the share of the wife's father in the bridewealth increased constantly until it had become larger in many cases than the *ndzo's* share of the bridewealth. As a result marriage affairs no longer concern the *ndzo* alone. All palavers about bridewealth or *litsũ* now involve the wife's father, and at least his *ndzo*, very much. But it goes beyond that

school, so they were taken in by local inhabitants, carried food for the whole week when they arrived on Mondays and often went hungry. The dispensary was built in 1963 and began operation in 1964 as a maternity centre. The cost of the buildings and equipment was out of proportion to the number of patients. The ten beds at the maternity centre were expected to be able to take care of all cases on the whole northern plateau. As for the technical school which had started in 1963–4 its number of pupils varied between ten and eighteen.

[21] This section deals only with Mbe and its neighbourhood. Changes on the Nsah plains were parallel except for the greater importance the cultivation of tobacco has assumed. At the Pool the fundamental changes have been a return first to subsistence agriculture (called gardening) and fishing, the hiring out of labour, and later the acceptance of many tenets of Christianity and the emergence of urban ideals and standards of life. Because of the competition by immigrants the Tio find themselves in a precarious economic and social condition. Only a few men, who were still 'owners of the land', had been able to convert part of their land into cash and then trucks, establishing themselves as traders.

since the father's share seems to have been spread to his *ibuuru* and not only his *ndzo* and to a certain extent this may even have happened on the wife's mother's side. In other words the *ibuuru* gained ground there.

Why this development occurred remains unclear. It seems to be connected with attitudes towards the bridewealth itself. For the economic spheres so typical for the 1880s have largely disappeared and all payments are at least valued in terms of money. Since goods were inherited in the *ibuuru* and still are, its importance has grown in relation to the amount of goods to be inherited, and bridewealth is assimilated to it. Since most of the Tio remained very poor this development has not been dramatic, beyond the effect on bridewealth. Finally the fact that most boys in an increasing number since 1900 hire their labour or sell products such as, first, rubber, later tobacco to find the means to marry, must be considered too. The origin of bridewealth, the means of payment even, have increased the commercial attitude towards it and hence the stake of the *ibuuru* in it. The net effect has been a blurring of distinctions between *ibuuru* and *ndzo* and, in 1964 at least, a slight advantage to the *ndzo*. But with increasing wealth the blurring should be of advantage to the *ibuuru*.

Another important change has been the gradual disappearance of the oppositions between generations. The whole system of alternate generations was breaking down, at least with respect to marriage. Marriages to small babies or *otioolu* were no longer practised. The age of marriage for men was younger than before but for girls it had slightly increased. The bridewealth circulation was disturbed. First young men found their own bridewealth or married on credit, a common occurrence at Mbe by 1964 where one boy had succeeded in having several wives by making only minimal down-payments. As a result of this a shortage of women was felt, since the ideal of polygyny persisted and since most men still tried to have two wives, even though only a smaller number of them achieved this goal.[22]

The competition for women and the example of the Lari led in the 1920s to the assertion by sisters' sons that they should inherit their mothers' brothers' wives and many began to call them *okali*, when the husband was out of earshot. Cases of actual inheritance happened and were on the increase, it was said in 1963. Obviously this broke down the whole pattern of circulation of women in alternating generations and of goods in the opposite generations. It also made *litsũ* practically impossible in cases where inheritance by sisters' sons had taken place. In the other cases still, the great majority of *litsũ* was claimed sooner than it used to be and the portion given to the children of the deceased became smaller, since it was felt that the need to keep the *ibuuru* united was much less pressing than the acquisition of goods to acquire wives with. Another sign of the pressure for women and the consequent dis-

[22] Cf. Appendix No. 6 (polygyny at Mbe and Ampo).

turbance of the generation structure was the tendency for younger brothers to give up their wives to their elder brothers.

To confuse the situation even further, more and more women refused to be inherited at earlier ages than before and rather tried with success to find for themselves new husbands who then handled the repayment of bridewealth themselves. The greater independence of women also manifested itself in the fact that for marriage the agreement of the girl was by now absolutely necessary. The practice of running away as *okẽ ampu* to a chief had vanished but the new emphasis on the girl's consent balanced this.

Other signs of the increased competition for women was the rise in adultery which nearly all older men pointed out. Of course, this might be just a case of growing moral indignation with age and a defence of their privileges. Yet it is true that the fines for adultery were much less than before since slavery had been abolished and young men could usually pay the fines levied, even though such an event set their proposed marriages back by a considerable time. For the fine was still heavy enough to take a good part of the amassed bridewealth. The rise in adultery, and it was quite common for young men in Mbe to have affairs with married women, is also to be attributed to the lack of other outlets for sex. It seems that the number of *ãkãw* women, who being unattached could take lovers, had dwindled. There was too much opportunity to remarry and pressure to do so for them to remain unattached for long. On the other hand divorces were probably increasing. The reasons for divorce were usually not only an unsatisfactory sex life but an increased bitterness of women about men since they had to take up more and more of the total production within the household and resented the small amounts of money given to them by their husbands. This of course ties in with the increase in adultery, for most women who filed a suit for divorce already had lovers.

At the same time some aspects of the marriage alliance which had been significant before became less so. There were much fewer 'closed' marriages, i.e. marriages with people who were already affines in the *ibuuru* or *ndzo*, marriages of two brothers with two sisters and the like. These, like the great polygyny, had been most marked among political chiefs and their status had been much reduced. Yet in general the need to secure safe alliances with kin-groups that could be trusted in times of stress such as feud of war, had gone and with it much of the practice of planning marriages for children. Most of the boys chose their own partners and most of the parents or uncles did not even object any more, provided no incest was involved. On the other hand most marriages were still endogamous in the neighbourhood, in fact 76 per cent of them were. Men and their kin still felt that it was useful to 'know' the bride's kin and vice versa, but the determining factor seems to have been simply the fact that most available partners younger people met regularly belonged to the neighbourhood. This was even true when the young men went to Brazzaville, because they would cluster in the streets of Ouenzé where the Mbe neighbourhood was predominant.[23]

Obviously the structure of marriage had changed deeply. The giving of women in marriage was still conditioned by the payment of bridewealth, even though perhaps the sums involved had risen less than the cost of living.[24] This relative decrease is borne out by the increasing numbers of marriages 'on credit' and the relative decrease of the amounts in relation to wealth that could be earned elsewhere. In short bridewealth was no longer the single greatest amount of wealth transferred. The breakdown of economic spheres was responsible for this. The fact seems amazing because women were more in demand and the supply was scarcer. But women are not any commodity and demands of high sums were tempered by the fact that most young men would offer only so much and their relatives would stand by them. There was a constant rise in demands and offers, but we think it did not match the general increase in the cost of living. Psychologically, though, it seemed as if the cost of bridewealth was rising, especially when new demands were compared with *litsũ* for payments made sometimes twenty years earlier. Add to this that recipients of bridewealth also had to disburse funds on other occasions and were more and more afraid to be caught in a situation of divorce provoked by the girl so that they would have to reimburse double the stakes. Ultimately the growing independence of both boys, because they were wage earners, and girls, because they could always marry again and run away if coerced, is the basic dynamic behind the situation.

Payments for bridewealth still sanctioned an alliance between groups and *okuu* was still the major sanction behind it. But the alliance involved the two *ibuuru* more than before and tended to be already ended in the next generation either by the inheritance of the woman or *litsũ*. The four generation deep pattern of exchange had given way to a two generation deep pattern.

Beyond this the significance of the alliance itself as the true meaning of marriage had diminished. Whether literate or not—and by 1963 most young men were semi-literate in Mbe—all younger people had

[23] Cf. Appendix No. 6 (data about marriage: Endogamy within Mbe). Note that the exogamous marriages almost all involved people at Brazzaville so that the combined percentage of endogamy on the plateau and marriages at Brazzaville rose to 90 per cent of all marriages. The remaining 10 per cent mostly married on the Nsah plateau.

[24] This happened among the Mfinu. Cf. J. PAUWELS, *La dot*, pp. 7–9; Tables II, III, and compare with general depreciation of Congo currency. Listening to discussions about *litsũ* at Mbe it was evident that even though an index for the rise of the cost of living was calculated when reimbursement was discussed, this was felt to be lower than the rise in the cost of living.

been influenced by the ideals of marriage as companionship and the marital relation itself was beginning to be the most important feature of marriage at least for the young, and paradoxically this is related to the increase in adultery and divorce. For the Western ideal had to coexist with the traditional notions about the role of women and the worsening division of labour between men and women.[25]

By 1963 changes in marriage patterns went deeper than overall change in the kinship system. They will, no doubt, themselves bring further change in the kinship structure. They themselves seem to flow mainly from both changing economic conditions and a profound change in values, both being introduced from outside.

Patterns of settlement also changed. Geographically villages were regrouped along the roads in the 1930s so the available labour could keep them up and roads had therefore to follow available water supplies. The village assumed a different appearance with the introduction of the Lari square houses and the practice of grouping houses along a rectangular court. The leader of the village occupied one of the short ends, the men lived along the longer sides of the rectangle, women's houses were grouped behind those of the men, and the last side of the rectangle was open towards the road.

The larger villages, the residences of lords and squires had melted away to become typical small settlements of related kin. For with the decline of their power and wealth their attraction also faded. Only the new Mbe showed how succeeding kings could still attract people. Another change was that many of the smaller settlements which had been located in or near the denser woods to escape harm from warfare now settled in the open, so that Mbe apart, there was no longer much distinction between the settlement of a titled man and that of any other leader. In fact apart from Mbe the biggest settlement on the plains was founded by a man whose trade in tobacco had attracted kinsmen.

The structure of the villages and especially of Mbe can still be wholly understood by the former criteria. There was a leader and other men with their nuclear families followed him. At most one could see here and there an empty house belonging to some young man who was away working. Some children were absent, because they were at school in Brazzaville. But by and large everything was explained in the old idiom of leaders and followers. The internal dynamics as shown by village history showed a continuation of the struggles for leadership, the accusations of witchcraft and their periodic catharsis by the spectacular smelling out of witches. And yet the whole structure could also be explained differently.

[25] This is evident from Appendix No. 6 (data about marriage: Divorce at Mbe). Most divorce occurred after the couple had been married six months and before a full year had elapsed. Mutual incompatibility and not problems of alliance were therefore the major cause of divorces.

For by 1963 most men in every village had spent some time at Brazzaville or along the Congo river being employed as unskilled labour. Their careers showed that the pattern of movement had been and still was one which had led them from village to city and back to these villages. The oldest example in Mbe was certainly Mbali who left for the city in 1914 and came back during the Second World War when one of his relatives had become king. He was then of an age which commanded respect in the countryside, but not in town. On the contrary employment became more and more difficult and the attraction of going back to the rural areas and their norms was definitely higher than the prospect of staying in town.

Most of the other leaders of wards at Mbe or villages elsewhere had not been to Brazzaville themselves. They had come during the migration of the 1920s and early 1930s south of the Lefini and then drifted with their settlements towards Mbe. Of the four wards at Mbe this was true for two. The head of one came from Ngabe and had always been at court there, but did a little trading on the Congo river as well. The head of the last ward had not gone to Brazzaville but had worked for years at a logging station for steamers on the Congo river. As for the two biggest villages outside Mbe, making up three wards, all the leaders came from Ngabe or accompanied the migration of the 1920s.

It was not so much these leaders who exemplified the new pattern as the younger people. There, scarcely a man had not been to town or had at least been a trader, so that in all correctness one can state that, given the top leaders on the plateaux as poles of attraction representing the former order of things, kingship and all, their followers all came from the city. Some still went back and forth between Brazzaville and Mbe, others had left Brazzaville because they hoped the opportunities for making a living were better on the plateau, some felt they now had a higher status and were entitled to more consideration on the plains, some had simply left the city because they had been unemployed for years.

In short then, the settlement pattern of the plateau cannot be explained without reference to Brazzaville. The mechanics of settlement were the old ones, the reasons for settling were different. Moreover all the dynamic young men left these settlements to try their luck working in or near Brazzaville or at school. The plain of Mbe was fast becoming a rural backwater, losing its best elements to the city and expecting mostly older people to return from it. A better illustration of the predominance of economics, at least economic expectations, could hardly be found but it should not make us forget the importance of the excitement of urban life as a factor of attraction.[26]

[26] Cf. Appendix No. 4 (origins of the population of Mbe) and Appendix No. 5 (notes on the political history of Mbe since 1934) as well as the diagrams No. 1–2 (Mbe) and No. 4–5 (leadership in Mbe). People went to Brazzaville to find work, for the night-life, to go to the cinemas, to be smart. They contrasted the city with the 'dull' life at Mbe.

Even though a thorough demographic study was not made, the data we have show that the people lacking in these settlements were the boys between ages sixteen or so and twenty-five. The situation was much more pronounced in the smaller and also duller villages than in Mbe. At Mbe itself a range of semi-modern occupations soothed the self respect of many. As for men over twenty-five many of them had come back because they had married, perhaps taken two wives, they could swagger for a while with their earnings and hoped to become successful in trade or as artisans.[27] Most of them were not succeeding very well, but they were respected by their peers at Mbe and that was what mattered.

In economics, even in subsistence economics the changes have been great. At first sight agriculture seems to be much what it was, hunting looks no different, patterns of labour or consumption may not look much modernized. Yet there is a fundamental change. The economy, all of it, has become a money economy.

In agriculture the main developments were first the gradual decline then total abandoning of maize in favour of cassava, a trend which was completed well before 1920. Perhaps the need for collecting rubber was partly responsible for this, although at Mbe it was believed that the young men collected most rubber, while maize was a crop cultivated by men in the *ngwuunu*. Also between 1900 and 1914 the practice of hiring out one's labour became acceptable and French coin was introduced as an all-purpose money. From the 1920s some taro was introduced from the Lari but the plant did not gain a wide acceptance, perhaps because it needs a forest environment. By 1963 a few stands of a dozen plants or so were still found in or around dawn-gardens. No other changes seem to have taken place until well after the experimental station at Inoni had been created. Some time later it was realized that tractors could plough the fields for all the women of Mbe in a day or two and in the 1960s a tractor was hired for the purpose each autumn. Obviously it had to be paid for and the payment came from the sale of cassava. Every month or so a truck would lumber up the escarpment to the plains and take whatever produce there was. Most women were able to prepare a 100 lb bag every month. This pattern of trade developed only after the escarpment from Brazzaville had been asphalted, which was finished by 1962. A further simultaneous development was the

[27] For modern trades, cf. Appendix No. 8 (new trades in Mbe); for people absent from Mbe, cf. Appendix No. 9 (persons who have left Mbe). They amount to 10 per cent of the population at Mbe. Young people were 12 per cent of all young people; the others were married women (36 per cent of exogamous marriages are reflected here). The attraction of Brazzaville was most evident for men: eleven men were there as against two at Ngabe, one at Djambala, Gamboma, and Pointe Noire each. The one in France was not counted since he had not been in Mbe for a very long time.

For obvious reasons it is not possible to publish detailed career histories including motives for going to Brazzaville or coming back.

acquisition by two Tio of Brazzaville of some trucks bought with gains on land speculation. These came to get the produce on occasion. At other times three of the traders at Mbe hired a truck in town to take away a full load. This did not happen very often because the rent asked for such a truck was high (21,000 Fr CFA per trip). Most of the time then, it was a lorry belonging to either a European or a Lari firm which visited the plains, and went to Ngabe and back with cassava.

This participation of women in the cash-crop economy required a serious increase in work. It seems that well before the practice of selling *fufu* had come into being, women had been selling the excess of the groundnut crop at Brazzaville, as they may already have begun on the channel in Iloo's time. To produce *fufu* (cassava-flour) however was quite a different proposition. They calculated in 1964 that they could fill a 100 lb bag with four *mutete* (headloads) of cassava. One *mutete* took 2 afternoons to prepare before it could go to *idzia*. One *mutete* occupied an *idzia* hole for 3 days. Then the product had to be chopped up and ground finely because the trader took only fine *fufu*. They were expected to produce one bag every 3 weeks when the traders came along. This meant that they had to find 8 afternoons for the preliminary preparation, 12 days of *idzia* time and perhaps another 4 or so afternoons to finish the product. In time it cost them as much as 12 afternoons or more out of 21 days, over 25 per cent of all their time and 50 per cent of their afternoons. This was not counting the time it took to plant the excess quantity of cassava required and tend the extra acreage of fields.

In former times they did not prepare *fufu* but only *ito* as they did for home consumption. This saved considerable time. But the demands of the traders required this adaptation. For all this they were paid by the bag, which was not weighed and at the time of the fieldwork the government was trying to bring the prices down on the Brazzaville market. This should have been achieved by cutting out middlemen or part of their profits, but the effect was a low price per bag. Women made a regular income from this which helped in the household, but apparently they had to hand over most of this to their husbands. The ill feeling between men and women becomes quite understandable under those conditions!

After 1945 the Tio were asked by the administration to plant tobacco and seeds were distributed. Tobacco had been a crop on the plateau for a long time and one might have expected that the improved plants would yield handsome returns for the growers. They did not. Tobacco was planted in the *ngwuunu* by most married men but only one person, the poorest, or at least socially the least accepted person in Mbe, was growing it on a commercial scale. He alone possessed a shed for curing the leaves and presumably netted returns from the sale. Despite this lack of production most men, including the young ones who were most averse to cultivating a *ngwuunu*, agreed that a manageable field would yield to a man more money than one could gain at Brazzaville as an office-worker. They would not do it, however, because they said the soil was too poor. Yet twenty-five miles away at Okiene all the men planted tobacco after the example of their old village leader and no one could say why the soils of Mbe would differ from those at Okiene. Still one man in Mbe cultivated his tobacco at Okiene. The cultivation of tobacco was an example of the influence of prestige on economic production. The professions such as trade in cigarettes or wine, tailoring, carpentry, or bicycle repairs were considered much more of a gentleman's occupation at Mbe. Okiene was too small to have these services, which explains why all the men there cultivated the crop.

After the gradual abandoning of maize the men at Mbe spent more time hunting. They began to use steel cable traps with improved results and sold the antelope meat and even more buffalo meat to the city. After 1960, however, the area around the settlement was declared a reserve and a guard was installed to prevent poaching, at least on a large scale. At the same time the local guns were seized by the administration and this source of income fell totally away.

To make some money the younger men, including the younger married men turned to other occupations. A diversity of 'specializations' sprang up. In one ward the men made and sold mats, several men turned to the fabrication of modern furniture in basket-work, a few became tailors, a few retailers of either general stores or wine and spirits. All except the last two types worked only on order which left them idle most of the time. The older men however still cultivated their *ngwuunu* while practising crafts such as healing, singing, or smithing. By 1963 two men in one ward at Mbe had just begun making curios for the market in Brazzaville, carving out small tables with intricate legs. The income from all these trades as well as what was left of the income by hunting with nets in free areas was pitiful.

Outside of Mbe these new crafts did not exist. And the old ones were dying out. At Ngabe, where most men still fished and made money from it, there were only two women potters left and they could make only crude vessels. For the whole plains there was one weaver, not counting one who lived across the Lefini and one carver of statuettes. Mbe and the area of Inoni met the new demands for services.

The most striking features of the situation were a specialization in goods and services which reflected the individualism of Tio men as much as their economic uselessness, a loss of the former crafts which had made the neighbourhood self-sufficient for many articles, and above all a complete disparity between men and women's labour. By 1963 most money earned at Mbe was earned by women, and most women handed their earnings over to their husbands or used them to pay for the needs of the household. Yet they were still considered by the men as inferior beings. Working all day, every day, with inadequate nutrition, they were at the same time undernourished and very bitter about men in general, especially about the younger men without *ngwuunu*. Only one of the younger men realized this and had begun to cultivate along with his wives. The others were aware of the strain as were the elder people, but no one worried enough to do much about it. No one apparently saw the relation between the increasing bitterness in the discussion of cases of adultery or divorce or their increasing frequency and the situation created by the new division of labour.

At the same time the demand for consumption goods had begun to include many foreign items. French wine and spirits had replaced local beverages as completely as imported cloth had ousted raphia. Houses were larger than before, especially men's houses and contained several rooms. They were made in wattle and daub. A few of the young men back from town had begun to cement their floors and put up tin roofs over their houses as well as shutters in front of the newly accepted windows (without window panes). But in 1963 only two or three houses in Mbe had these refinements. Women needed lamps, pails and other, often plastic containers, soap, perfume, and an occasional bauble. Men used razor blades, cigarettes, and yearned for a bicycle or even a mobylette or a transistor radio. The latter items were still rare and only one radio was really owned by an inhabitant of Mbe. But the village also housed a few other Congolese who were teachers at the school, warden of the game reserve, and male nurse. They had these and other objects and some of them lived in government-built housing. These men together with less than five local young men, back from the city and owners of a mobylette were the modern intelligentzia at Mbe and set standards of living not only for all the other inhabitants but for all other Tio on the plateau.

The introduction of an increasing demand for more and better machine-produced consumer goods was throwing the local economy ever more out of joint. The available income could not possibly keep up with the new needs. And completely new problems had arisen. Married women pondered how much time to spend at the *idzia* or on the preparation of cassava for sale as against how to budget their time for other crops which were not saleable. The one young man who had decided to farm cassava for sale along with his wives and the older man who had gone in wholeheartedly for planting tobacco were, with the women, living examples of a new economy where the division between market economy and subsistence economics had completely vanished. There was only one economy now with various production processes. The bright young lads who had come back from city employment or the workers at the main road, like the salaried Makoko, all belonged to one economy and most realized it by now. Obviously the situation in 1964 was still very labile but it could only be described in terms of a modern money economy spread over a nation in which the Mbe plateau was only a backwater.

The same intelligentzia which had helped to expand the 'need' for many modern things at Mbe represented the outside world and progress in Mbe. When the child of one of the local Tio members died, it was buried in a coffin, even though the mother ran away shortly afterwards, partly out of protest against this. The child had been alternately treated at the hospital in Brazzaville and by local healers and a proper *okuu* had been held. It was the victim of an epidemic of measles, a new disease for the Tio. The whole tragedy illustrates the role and the problems of such a new intelligentzia living in the familiar old rural surroundings, a role which was very different from the situation in the cities.

These few Tio and the personnel of the schools and the dispensary had conducted, and were still conducting, campaigns for more hygiene; they let the people listen to the radio and brought back more news from Brazzaville where they spent weekends. Thus they brought to the plains not only new goods, but new ways of life and especially new ideas and values. The extent to which these were catching hold of the imagination of all younger people was astonishing, for after all the country had only been independent for three years, and before independence there had been no models to follow. There had been a European missionary in Mbe and one European settler at least at Ngabe, but the Tio could not see how the style of life of those people could relate to their own. But the Congolese were different. Two men were Tio of Ntsaa whose kindred was well known to all. The others had plausible backgrounds and had become what they were through education. Then there were still other Tio of whom they heard at Mbe whose education had brought them to very high positions in the Congo.

The Tio had never adopted Christianity or any of the African religions derived from it. The underpopulation of the area had made the missionary effort not worth while until very late. Moreover early resistance on the Mpũ plateau had convinced the missionaries that there was not much hope. The impact of modern life on this remote plateau had not prompted the desire for a new foreign cult. In fact much had happened which had strengthened the old religion. For many years it had functioned quite openly and witchcraft was involved as the explanation for the epidemics up till 1920. LIPIE said that the people at the old Mbe had died because they had too many and too powerful charms. Then the administration forbade the poison ordeal and it was abandoned fairly quickly, but *lindaa* remained and the other rituals were still practised as usual. Along the Congo river some Christians came, but also the new charms from everywhere: charms to kill your enemy and charms to become wealthy. Both were increasingly in demand. The first was a means of defence for an individual who could not ask for the poison ordeal any more, the other was needed as the money economy spread more and more. Even so it is said that the new charms came in only by 1944. Christianity was also believed to be a set of charms whose *ngàà* were the *Ngàà* Nzã, the missionaries. But these charms were European and therefore useless.

After 1944 the administration apparently discouraged all healing and all ritual and attempted half heartedly to prosecute some *ngàà* for fraud. This policy drove religious practices underground. But after independence, all the rituals were openly held again at the villages and the most spectacular public witch huntings date from these years. Little had changed in the religious outlook. Perhaps some Christian notions about Nzã had been accepted by many pagans, perhaps the role of the *nkira* had declined compared with that of the ancestors, a development quite in line with the decline of the squires, but the belief in Nkwe Mbali was still intact. It was also true that French wine could be used in sacrifice instead of the old maize beer or palm-wine, but these were small changes when it is considered that the whole *Weltanschauung* had remained the same. The belief in witchcraft had perhaps even been strengthened, the variety of charms had become greater, the desire for *ngolo* remained the deep basis of all aspirations, even of the ambitious ones. Even the young people had not been affected by European religions or modern ideologies enough to claim that they were not knowledgeable about rituals, let alone to proclaim that it was all superstition or even less to abstain from participating in the rituals. They were just as religious and apparently in the same way as their elders. Yet there were elements of a new ideology. The best illustration was perhaps the case of the child which was being cured by a dancing *ngàà* while the medical nurse was giving it an injection in the arm. Much modern medicine has been accepted by the Tio. They send people to the hospital at Brazzaville or now to the dispensary at Mbe. They have especially accepted injections which was a way of treating the body unknown before. They will take European drugs. But they do not yet believe in the ideology of European medicine. 'There may be microbes', said the king, 'but my Nkwe Mbali is stronger than all of them.' In any case people are still ill because they are bewitched and have to be cured by eliminating the witchcraft.[28] So the effects of

[28] The medical situation at Mbe in 1963–4 was not good. About half of the population was sick or in poor health. Unfortunately no statistics are available. The major prevalent diseases were for children: helminthiases, kwashiorkor, general anaemia and dangerous epidemics of measles (killing often because of pulmonary complications), and whooping cough. The adults suffered most from pulmonary diseases and T.B. as well as a form of conjunctivitis. Consultations and drugs at the dispensary were free and every two months a doctor visited from the city. In addition regular programmes to fight leprosy and sleeping sickness (almost eradicated) were in progress. Besides this a great number of 'fevers' were listed, which could not be elucidated for lack of laboratory equipment. Teaching about hygiene and the enforcement of laws dealing

medicine on ideologies have been small. In fact one would not expect medical knowledge or acceptance of medicine to have made much difference. The new ideology emerges from the wishes of people, from their dreams. They see the examples of upward social mobility around them and they want a brilliant career, if not for them, at least for their children. The children go to school and along with the teaching of the three R's they are infused with an attitude which diverges from the religious ideology, even if it does not clash with it. After all when lightning struck the school, the *ngàà* had to cool the building! Still the school begins to sow doubts and when the brightest children go to Brazzaville, as they have to do for secondary school and upwards, many parts of the religious outlook are lost.

The ideology is changing also because of what people hear over the radio. Political propaganda attempts to foster an ideology of its own. It expounds the belief that the good life for all can come and what must be done to make it come. In a very simplified form a whole philosophy of society is thus brought to the inhabitants of Mbe, and all who listen to the radio, day after day, gradually take it in. By 1963–4, then, several ideologies lived side by side none excluding the other. The ideology of the nation and its mystique of development completed and was actually replacing the old political ideologies of *nkobi*, *nkira* and perhaps even Nkwe Mbali. The mystique of scientific achievement found a place next to the belief in charms and the good life was still to be attained by eradicating witches. The development here had been more cumulative than in the social structure or in economic organization where change of the pre-existing institutions had been great, but cumulative change is also a dynamic evolution.

The old political structure was practically dead in 1964. The old methods of solving conflict had vanished by 1914 or so as far as feuds and wars were concerned. The poison ordeal was abandoned in the 1920s, criminal law was taken over by new national courts. The latter were accepted because murderers went to jail for life and that said an informant is the equivalent of killing them. Civil law and the palaver have not changed much, except that there is always recourse to a court in Brazzaville. Otherwise appeals and arrangements in 1963–4 were still as chaotic as ever, more so, perhaps, since the court at Mbe had just become a court like any other. Slavery was gone so that both retainers and compensation in the most serious conflicts had vanished.

As for political status, already in 1933 a squire in the Mbe area saw an immigrant settler who refused to give the haunch of animals killed. Nothing happened. Now squires were still given some meat from

with hygiene had little effect. But obviously the presence of so many sick people in such a small population did maintain suspicions of witchcraft or sorcery at a high level.

the hunt by most men, but beyond that they were just village leaders. The same was true for lords, provided they headed a village, for some did not. The wealth and followers which had made their way of life so different and glamorous was gone. Fancy funerals were only held for kings or for Ngalifourou. There remained the king, but no king had been through *lisee* since 1918 and none had had the holy water from Mbã. Their spiritual appeal as well as their prestige had never recovered from this and from their treatment by Ngalifourou. The court was no longer a real centre of attraction. At Mbe the king lived like a stockholder on his income. The way of life of the younger people with their cement floors and green shutters was much more impressive.

For the new reference group, the new centre of local power had by this time become the modernizing group in Mbe. Its power came from its example. True there was still much talk of strife between some lords, but the locus of power lay in Brazzaville and the apparent power by which compromise was reached or victories won was the power of the State. The struggle which had begun after Ntsaalu's accession to the throne in 1949 ended with his deposition in 1964. He was actually removed by the *Jeunesse révolutionnaire* from Brazzaville and his successor was a young man.

This short review of social change since 1880 confirms the previous analysis. There were two levels of structures in the society. The larger political and economic organizations were shielding the neighbourhood from the outside world, while they let innovations filter through. Once they were destroyed, by 1900 for the commercial organization, by 1918 for the political system, local society began to change. The new political organization was first the colony, then the republic. The new economic system was the money economy. They provided the dynamics for local change. Most of the evolution can be connected with the development of the unitary money economy. The political organization, however, also exercised a powerful influence by destroying the former organization, by creating a new territorial structure, by creating Brazzaville as a pole of attraction and lately by its proposition of a new ideology.

At the local level the kinship structures have barely altered. Yet the idiom of kinship and social ties based on it is being used to regulate relations between city and rural areas. The stratification in social estates and the two classes of the 1880s are gone while the new stratification, brought into being by the upward social mobility assisted by education, is as yet scarcely visible on the plains. The premise of inequality rooted in the principle of generations and age was under serious challenge. The national youth movements accelerated this tendency. New forms of economic integration were being felt, even though the economic integration in the market economy fell little short of being chaotic. In the ideologies the changes were cumulative, so that the old religion had not altered much. Perhaps the high incidence of disease was in part responsible for this.

The three interrelated systems of kinship, agricultural production and household consumption, rituals and religion changed least, remarkably but not surprisingly. They were most integrated one with another and formed the core of the Tio social system. But they were beginning to become part of larger social, economic, and even ideological organizations. The whole neighbourhood became a rural suburb of Brazzaville. Underneath the unchanging images of rural life, deep changes were taking place because of its adaptation to the new city and the new state. This alteration of the essential character of the neighbourhood justifies the labelling of the whole process as a mutation of society.

Part III
Conclusion

THE institutions and structures of Tio society while operating together in a neighbourhood or small scale society clearly fall into two blocks: an integrated set of structures, covering all aspects of life whose geographical basis was the area occupied by a village and its neighbours as opposed to the much wider structures. The latter as opposed to the former were disparate. The overarching structures acted culturally and socially as a shield protecting the small scale society from change and as a sieve through which change was introduced.

With regard to change a rule might be postulated: the greater the geographical area covered by an institution, the greater the chance of change. Thus the commercial organization varied most, followed by the political structure, while the neighbourhood changed least and most slowly.

Two forces contributed to give to Tio society its most typical and original features: the special environment and the steady expansion of the commercial system. The plains were indeed a special environment. Water was scarce and this more than anything else seems to have prevented other populations from occupying the plains, even in our century. Yet the scarcity of water explains the low density of population only to a degree. For adaptive techniques had been developed by the Tio and after all, many villages could have settled, strung out along the banks of the few rivers. Sautter's thesis that the lack of water was only a relative obstacle to a dense occupation of the plains[1] is warranted. His contention that the low density of population was the effect of depopulation by the slave trade, which was itself spurred by the need of foreign imports for conspicuous destruction at burials, is not, however, convincing. The plains had been sparsely populated ever since the 1580s, well before the great era of the slave trade. The destruction of goods at funerals was more limited and happened more rarely than has been thought.

For the Tio, the plains are not underpopulated. Indeed in times preceding the great expansion of the slave trade, one records one emigration after another from the plains. For the Tio there had been overpopulation. The notion of overpopulation is relative to a society and an economy: Tio society used land very extensively. The social and political forms of competition presupposed large tracts of unused lands, so that any loser could flee and settle on his own, without fear of destruction. The Tio leaders, like Caesar, preferred to be first in

[1] G. SAUTTER, *De l'Atlantique*, p. 971, n. 2 and *idem*, *Le plateau*, *passim*.

Helvetia than second in Rome. The whole social and political organization was predicated on a low density of population. Bilateral residential descent groups could only operate if scission and separation were possible, political autonomy, so typical for the lords, was only possible if the centre of the realm was far away. It does not matter which came first, although it must have been a low population density. What matters is that by 1880 all the institutions were geared to a low density of population. Even in the value system the typical Tio features of strife, individualism, and ambition were all linked to the existence of open spaces where one could strike out anew. The Tio attitude was that of a frontiersman not of a new frontier such as the American Far West once was, but of a familiar unchanging frontier like the Sahara was for the Tuareg. This complex of values was expressed not only in social strife, political competition, economic entrepreneurship, and bargaining, but in the praise-songs, the burials which varied in lavishness with status, the rituals to become *ngàà* or to cure, where each person affirmed his individuality in his own way with his own variants. Its clearest expression was the mobility of the men. Adult men left villages if they felt unprotected, because misfortune had struck, because wives or children languished or had died: in fact because they were dissatisfied to live with the other men there. Tio restlessness was not mere romantic feeling for the open spaces: it was the result of tension in social relations between adult men whose individualisms led to clashes. Either a man gave up and became a protected person, a slave, or he quarrelled.

The environment did not alter and the density of population may not have altered much over the centuries. For after the emigrations the slave trade probably drained enough Tio from the plains before 1860 to maintain a very low overall density.

The other original feature of the environment was the presence of the Stanley Pool and the great river system which led to it. This later provided an ideal highway for transportation and fostered trade. Some form of commercial exchange had undoubtedly existed since remote times. From 1530 the Pool area was connected up with a world-wide commercial system: the Atlantic slave trade.

The steady expansion of the trade in slaves and ivory since the 1530s provided the second force bearing on Tio society. A dynamic input from Europe, starting in the sixteenth century, reached a steady level of pressure by the last part of the eighteenth century. The developing commercial organization fostered changes in production by allowing some crafts to fall into disuse, by introducing new crops, some adaptive changes in production such as an increased level of production for cassava and tobacco in the nineteenth century or the previous expansion of the cultivation of raphia in the west, by creating a port of trade at the Pool, divorced from subsistence agriculture, with its own forms of settlements and social structures, and by introducing the *nkobi* ideology into the political system. Like the impact of the environment, the impact of external trade can be found in all aspects of life. It was so serious that in the 1880s the ecological balance between man and his environment on the plains was disturbed. Not only because of a glaring discrepancy in the division of labour between men and women and its consequences, but because the pressure to grow more cassava led to more malnutrition on the plains which lacked the supply of proteins fish provided along the watercourses. Then the appearance of large scale epidemics of first smallpox then sleeping sickness, dramatically underlined the unsettling effects of the commercial system.

This primacy of economics as a dynamic generator of change in Tio society for the last centuries before the arrival of the Europeans on the Pool was not necessarily inherent in the nature of Tio society, since it was the result of a major foreign input into the Tio universe, an input which kept up pressure for centuries. For beyond the two forces mentioned a *tertium quid* must be invoked to account for other features of Tio society, even such original characteristics as the mixture of a bilateral system of organization with a matrilineal system. The data only allow us to state that this third force was constituted by the strong continuity in transmission within Tio society and by the ethnic environment in which the Tio lived. Each new generation grew up in the society of its elders and took over most of it, although with more change than is usually believed. When change seemed desirable the practice of other surrounding peoples could provide the example which was then restructured to fit into the society. These processes of transmission and change existed even though no direct documentation allows us to prove them beyond a few illustrations.

This has been an attempt to describe a society at a given period in time. Whether it has succeeded or not must be left to the appreciation of the reader. If it has, similar research should be undertaken in other societies before the last eyewitnesses disappear and the traditions are lost. The image given by the monographs, based on fieldwork, using the 'ethnographic present' and describing 'traditional society' can be made much more precise by going back to documentation of the period before effective colonization took place. True there is little use in contrasting this study in detail with 'classical' monographs, because there simply does not exist such a monograph for the Tio. Conclusions therefore must remain tentative. But is is clear that the description of the political structure in operation and the role of war, the analysis of the spheres in the market economy, the data about prices and volume of trade can only be recovered from historical data.[2]

[2] A small example of the kind of error made by relying over much on interpretations given at the time of fieldwork is the following. By 1948 the Tio believed

This is likely to be true elsewhere, for all societies in Africa lost their autonomy and closed character so that their economic structures also underwent great change. It is further evident that the image we now have is one of a society much less integrated, much more in a state of flux, much less isolated from its neighbours than appears in other monographs. How far is this a reflexion of the Tio situation and not of a difference in the data used to write the monograph?

Similar research we undertook among the Kuba seems to lead to similar results: the operation of the political processes had changed beyond recognition since precolonial times and the commercial role of the Kuba in the Kasai was not clear from data observed in 1952–6. The impact of colonial activities on agricultural production, settlement patterns, inheritance had been more varied and greater than one would have predicted; on religious rituals and ideology it turned out to be less and in different ways. This and other experience seems to confirm that great insight can only be gained from historical study of these questions, rather than by guessing at what may or may not be lacking in the approach used hitherto.

The idiosyncracies of Tio society may have some comparative value for the theory of anthropology. On a more general level, the suggestion that each structure in a society has a sphere of its own in space and time and that susceptibility to change is directly correlated to the geographical size of that sphere may prove helpful and will have to be examined in relation to theories of social integration. Perhaps this study may further our understanding of the complexity of societies and lead us to refine the social models we all use now. If so, this book will have achieved the aim of every descriptive monograph.

---

that a duly installed king could not reign for more than four years before dying. Cf. G. VERVLOET, *Un peu de folklore*, pp. 28–9. In 1963 a similar belief was still held at Mbe, but the length of reign was only described as 'short'. One is tempted to postulate from this some kind of ritual murder associated with divine kingship of some sort. But it is evident that the belief arose after 1918 and was fostered both by the death of Ankono (Ngatino) who was to succeed king Ngaayüo and the behaviour of Ngalifourou. As keeper of Nkwe Mbali she knew better. But as *chef de canton* and *de facto* ruler she had no advantage at all in discouraging these rumours. On the contrary, she seems to have spread them herself.

Appendix No. 1

Informants

A. *List*

1 Abamudzu, Ngabe: woman, middle-aged. Mainly about pottery and Nkwe Mbali.

2 Abili Ndiõ: woman, old. Major source. Came from Abili.

3 Alaatsã: man, middle-aged. General, hunting.

4 Andzabi Jacques: young man. Jiju traditions. Came from Djambala.

5 Angõ: Okiene: man, older, general.

6 Akontali, ÃNKÃ: seen at Mbe. From MbulaNkio, man, middle aged, political, Mpũ, general.

7 Antsala: man, younger. History of Mbe, general.

8 Ba: man, middle-aged to older, major informant. Came from Nkwũ on Ntsaa plains.

9 Bara Jean: man, young. Ngungulu affairs. Was a travelling Ngungulu from Gamboma.

10 Bilankwi: man, middle-aged to older; smith. Major informant.

11 Iyini: Ampo: man, older; weaver. On Mbe history and weaving. General. *Litsũ.*

12 Ikoli: Imbãw: man, younger; *ngàà*-healer. On sacrifice and religion. Witnessed a treatment by him.

13 Ilanga Dominique: man, middle-aged. Tege. On Tege society compared with the Tio.

14 Itambali: Ngabe: man, middle-aged; fisherman. Fishing techniques; settlements on the river.

15 Lãwe: Inoni: woman, old; mainly on *lindaa.*

16 Likubi Marcel: man, middle-aged. Major informant.

17 Lindzandza alias avion: Mpenenke: man, middle-aged. General, religion.

18 LIPIE: Mbe but he came from Mbã: man, very old. The single most important informant. Died in April 1964. Keeper of the cult of Nkwe Mbali. Excellent memory.

19 Maalimwa: woman young to middle-aged. General and fields, women's work, etc. Much by observation.

20 MANDIELE: Mbe but from Mandiele. Political and Mpũ, general.

21 Mayala François: Bouambé: General, kingship.

22 Mbalawa: NGAATALI: Imbãw: man, very old; squire. Mbembe. Major source.

23 Mbalewari: Mbe and Imbãw but he was from Mpũ: man, older. General about Mpũ.

24 Mbali: man, older. Major source.

25 Mbali Henri and Bobo Antoine: Kwamouth (Mfunu): younger men: Mfunu migrations. (They were related to Mfunu lords.)

26 Mbiinu Mbiinu: man, middle-aged to older. Squire of Mbe. Major source. Mbembe.

27 Mbuma Daniel: Ngabe: young man, child of Ngobila: General; Title NGOBILA.

28 Mbusa Albert: Gamboma: man, middle-aged: On NGIA and Ngungulu society.

29 Mbusa Pierre: Ipwene (lez Etoro): man, younger: On Ngungulu society.

30 Miandoo: Imbãw. Man, middle-aged to older. Major source.

31 Mielani Jacques: Ngabe: Man, younger. On NGAMBIÕ, whose brother he was.

32 Mpaani: man middle-aged. Major source (Mbe: Uluuna); Jiju society (from where he came and would succeed to a title. All of Uluuna was Jiju in origin).

33 MOTIIRI: Ngabe and Mbe: man, middle-aged. General, titles, *liséé*.

34 Mpio Marcel: man, young to middle-aged. General.

35 Musala François: man, middle-aged. Guardian of the peace. General.

36 Ngaakã: Okieene: man, older. Major informant.

37 NGAALIÕ: Mbe but from Mbiina in Mpũ: Man, middle-aged to older. General, titles, *nkobi*, situation in Mpũ.

38 Ngako Fidèle: young man. Secretary to king. General.

39 NGAMPO: Ngabe: man, older. Major informant.
NGANDZIÕ: see Ntsuankare.

40 Ngankuni of Masende: Gamboma: younger man. Ngungulu society.

41 NGANSHIBI: man, middle-aged (born 1912/17). Major informant. *liséé*, Nkwe Mbali, Ngalifourou.
NGAATALI: See Mbalawa.

42 Ngaayüo: Ngabe: man, middle-aged. General. Wars, palavers.

43 Ngaayüo Bernard: man, young. Served as interpreter and most of information supplied by him was traced to its sources.

44 Ngadzo André: Kwamouth: man, young. Ngenge related to 'king of the Ngenge': Ngenge society.

45 Ngambulu: woman, older: *ngàà mbulu:* religion.

46 Ngamwa and Ngaanyono: Ngabe: women, mother, and daughter. The oldest was quite old, wife of NGOBILA and of Nunu extraction. General, NGOBILA, Nunu *nkobi*.

47 Ngateo: man, older. Major informant. Originally from Mpina Ntsa. Had an excellent memory.

48 Ngeimpio: man, middle-aged, twin of NGANSHIBI: General.

49 NGIA: Ngwi near Etoro: man, older. NGIA. Ngungulu society.

50 Ngie Albert: Ngabe: youngerman: Ngungulu society

51 Ngokabi: Ngabe: woman, older: general.

52 Ngontsuo: woman, middle-aged (married before 1942). NGAASAA of Nkima. General, NGAASAA.

53 Ndumiana André: Inga: man, young. Ngungulu society.

54 Nguye Victor: Gamboma: man, middle-aged; related to GÃBÕ. Ngungulu society and lords.

55 Nkia Philippe: Kwamouth: man, younger; Mfunu society and migrations.

56 Nkobo Raphael: Kwamouth, man, younger; child of NGOBILA: general.

57 NgeIkiere: man, older; originally from Bulanga lez Ndoolo near Djambala: Jinju society, wars. General. Major informant.

58 Ntsaalu Alphonse: man, middle-aged; king. Political structure; history.
59 Ntsuankare: NGANDZIÕ: Imbãw: man, younger. General. Titles especially NGANDZIÕ.
60 Okaana Samuel: Ngabe: man, older. General.
61 Okondzaadza: man, older; praise-singer; major informant.
62 Ondzala Gilles: man, younger; trader. Culture change; social changes.
63 Onka Boniface: man, younger. General. Work of *chef de village*.
64 Oshyakunu: Itswali: man, middle-aged; weaver. Weaving and worldview.
65 Otswaani: Isasiba: man, older; general.
66 Ubwoono: man, older. Major informant.
67 X: elders of the Mbe of GÃBÕ. Ngungulu society.

B. *Spatial distribution of information.* (Cf. Chapter I)

1 The period in the field was spent at Mbe, except for a fortnight at Imbãw and at Ngabe. Visit to Gamboma, the *mbe* of GÃBÕ and the *mbe* of NGIA.
2 The list above shows the major informants from other areas. It should be remembered that most of the persons in Mbe were Boõ immigrants or Jinju (e.g. Okondzaadza). The major data were checked with Jiju, Ngungulu, Tege, Wũ information. The Ngungulu are different on many points and Tege society may also differ. The others are all practically identical with few variations for the southern Wũ. The Kukuya have been studied by P. Bonnafé. Their society differs considerably, perhaps more than Ngungulu society. The few data available about Ngenge and Mfunu indicate great similarities with ways of life at Mbe. One interview with a western Teke shows their society to be quite different. Since the man had resided at Mbe for several years, the testimony seems valid.
3 Direct observations of *litsũ*, palavers, *itsuua*, *ãngkira*, burials, dedication of huts to ancestors, prayers to *nkira*, curing, and daily life were observed at Mbe. Palavers and fishing were seen at Ngabe. Palavers and curing of illness were observed at Imbãw.

APPENDIX No. 2

Relative Chronology used at Mbe

1877: Passage of Stanley.
1880: Arrival of Brazza. Treaty signed at Nduo (Mbe) September 10.
1882: Comet.[1]
1884: Return of Brazza. The Senegalese Samba with him that year was well known at Mbe.
1892: Death of Iloo.[2]
1895–6: War between the children of NGANDZIÕ and those of NGEILIINO at death of Opontaba.
1899: (June) Death of Mbandieele. War of the blue and the red pencil. NGAMPO Ikukuri was dead by then.

[1] Comets and eclipses after D. J. SCHOVE, *Eclipses*; R. GRAY, *Eclipses*, p. 260.
[2] For dates relating to kings cf. Chapter XVII, section I. If 1899 and 1892 are certain all the other dates to 1947 are given by later documents and there may be errors, of a few months to a year. We suspect that 1907 is too late for the accession of Ngaayüo but it is the date given in 1934.

1907: Accession of Ngaayüo.
1910: 18 May: Halley's comet.[3]
1912: Foundation of Kindongo and Mpala.[4]
1914–15: Recruitment of soldiers.
1918: March. Death of Ngaayüo. Dysentery epidemic.
1918: July. Death of Ankanho. Epidemic? Rule of Ngalifourou.
1918: November. Epidemic of Spanish influenza at Brazzaville.[5] It ended only by March 1919.
1919: 27 May: eclipse of the sun.
1919–20: Post of Mpala abandoned for Gamboma.
1925–8: Worst recruiting for the railroad.[6] The 'Age of the machine'.
1928–30: Mondzouani.[7]
1930–1: Ngamvwaala at Oka.
1931–4: Andibi. He died 13 January.
1934–9: Ngankia Mbandieele.
1934: Resettlement of Mbe.
1935: 15 March. Death of the Gouverneur-Général Renard in a plane crash in Ngenge country.
1939: Election of Nkima.
1939: September, Second World War began.
1940–4: 'The reign of Eboue'.
1945: The war ended.
1947: November. Death of Nkima.
1948: September. Nkima buried.
1948: December. Ntsaalu installed.
1949: Decoration of Ngalifourou and Ntsaalu.
1956: 20 April Death of Ngalifourou.
1957: 3 March. Burial of Ngalifourou.
1959: February. Riots in Brazzaville.
1960: 15 August. Independence of Congo.
1963: August. The revolution.

[3] Observed in Brazzaville. Cf. P. AUGOUARD, *Trente-six années*, III, No. 322, p. 379.

[4] They did not exist in 1906 but G. SAUTTER, *De l'Atlantique*, I, p. 180 has them in 1913. It is probable they were founded in 1912.

[5] J. DE WITTE, *Vie*, p. 87. The celebration of the Armistice of 11 November was postponed until 2 March 1919 because of the epidemic.

[6] G. SAUTTER, *Le chemin de fer*, pp. 233–4 (end of construction 13 April 1934), pp. 243, 246, 248, n. 84. A report of 10 July 1929 said that Tio fled to the Mbe plateau under the protection of the king. The movement included several hundred Tio.

[7] Other relative dates were calculated from genealogies (older than X, younger than Z, for whom a firm date could be established) and from movements of villages, especially those of persons who became later kings or village leaders. Thus Ngankia Mbandieele was said to have lived for about ten years in the area of Inoni before moving closer to Mbe and that happened only during Andibi's reign. This would put his crossing of the Lefini as early as 1922, during Ngalifourou's personal rule.

APPENDIX No. 3
Census data

1. *Mbe*: (14 November 1963)

wards	*men*	*women*	*children*	*totals*	*leaders*
INKWII I	11	22	35		Mbiinu Mbiinu
INKWII II	6	7	9		none
NGANSHIBI	3	3	6		NGANSHIBI
King	1	8	6		King
total INKWIT	21	40	56	117	
ULUUNA	7	7	6	20	Mpaani
LIFURA MBAA I	11	19	39		Okondzaadza
LIFURA MBAA II	2	2	7		Mbali
total LIFURA MBAA	13	21	46	80	
MASALA I	5	5	7		Bilankwi
MASALA II	3	5	8		Ubwoono
MASALA III	17	24	37		Ngateo
totals MASALA	25	34	52	111	
grand total	66	102	160	328	

Comments: The competing wards for leadership were INKWII I, LIFURA MBAA I, and MASALA III.

1 The latter had been weakened by defections in recent years. The heads of these wards were respectively Mbiinu Mbiinu; squire, Okondzaadza and Ngateo: both *amieene*. MASALA II and III co-operated closely, but MASALA I was quarrelling with them.

2 Foreigners living at Mbe were not included (3 teachers, 1 medical nurse, 1 game warden, and their families).

3 Persons absent at the date of the census are not counted.

2. *Other settlements*

	men	*women*	*children*	*totals*
AMPO (9 December 1963)	7	9	6	22
(16 January 1963) NGABE: quartier 'Est' (quartier sud and quartier nord, mostly non Tio, were not included)				
ward: MFUBA	2	2	6	10
ward: AMPO	18	21	50	89
ward: LIFURA MBAA	6	12	17	35
ward: MASALA	2	3	3	8
totals NGABE	28	38	76	142

	men	women	children	totals
IMBÃW				
(25 February 1964)				
ward: KWOLI	9	14	14	37
ward: ÃTORO	9	14	16	39
totals IMPÃW	18	28	30	76
OKIENE (13 December, 1963)	13	14	24	51
MPENENKE (21 March 1964)	4	8	11	23
IDZULU (IMBALI)				
(21 March 1964)				
ward: IMBALI I	3	5	4	12
ward: IMBALI II	1	2	5	8
ward: IMBALI III	1	6	2	9
totals IDZULU	5	13	11	29
OSABI				
(3 January 1964)				
ward I	1	2	3	6
ward II	2	5	0	7
totals OSABI	3	7	3	13
ISASIBA (3 January 1964)	4	3	4	11
totals all villages:	82	120	165	367

Comments: Persons absent at the date of the census are not counted. No adult/child ratio can therefore be deduced since most of the absentees are children at school. For Ngabe which has a grade school the figures for children are therefore much higher.

3. *Ratio men/women*

Mbe:	66 men	102 women	64·7% men per 100 women
villages:	82 men	120 women	68·3% men per 100 women
totals:	148 men	222 women	66·6% men per 100 women

Comments: Evidently the ratio is to be explained by the differential in ages of marriage. It makes widespread polygyny with two wives possible. Overall there are one third more women than men.

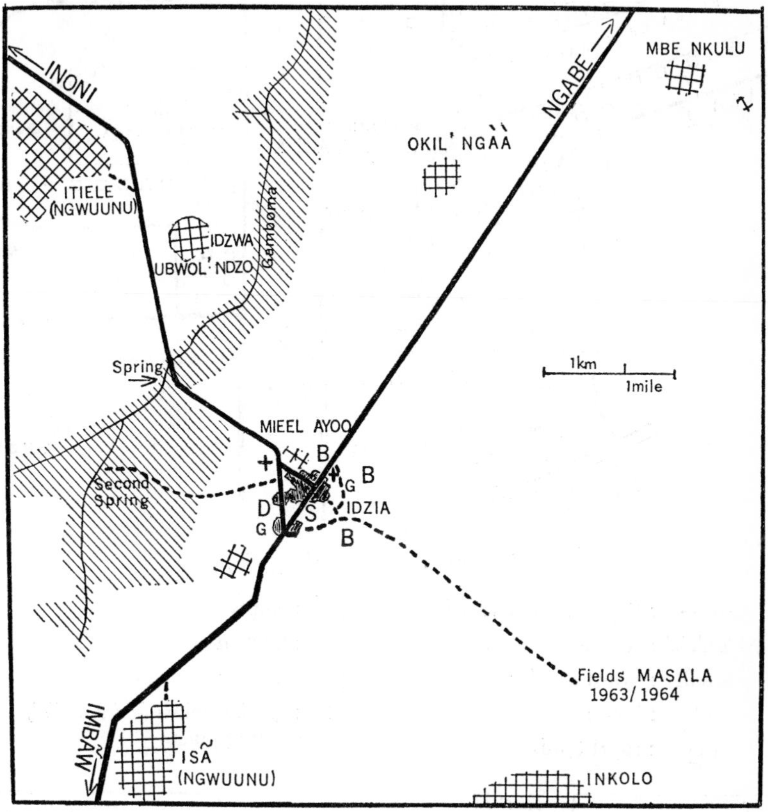

Diagram 1. *Mbe and Environs* (1963)

INONI: Place names
——— : motor roads
- - - - : major paths
S : Schools
B : Banana plantations
+ : Mission stations (abandoned)

D : Dispensary
G : Garbage disposals
: Mbe Proper
: Woods
: Gallery forest of the Gamboma river

Note: The cemetery is located in MIEEL AYOO.

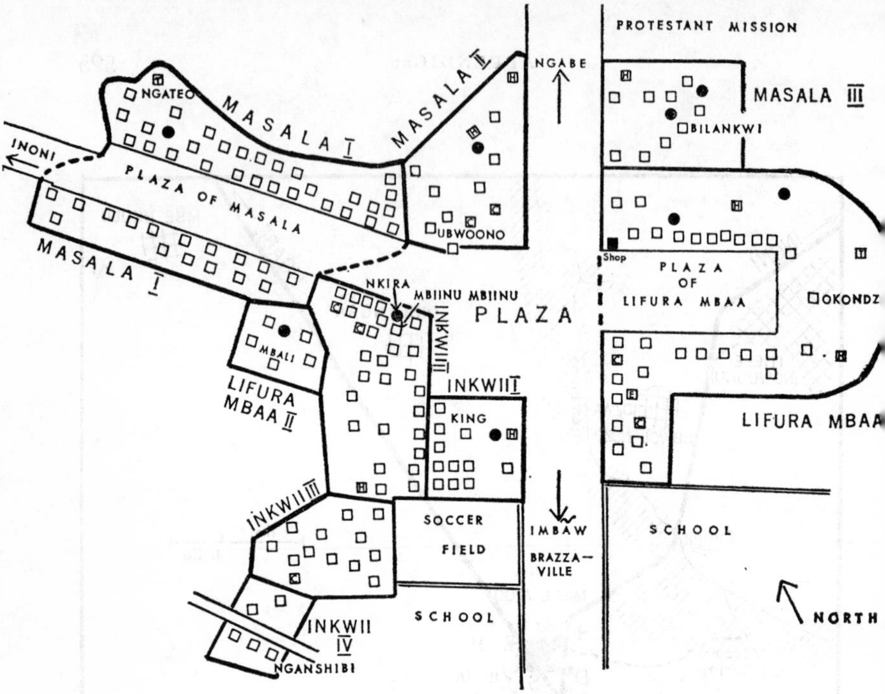

Diagram 2. *Plan of Mbe* (1963)

——	: Boundaries of Wards	E	: empty
MASALA	: Names of wards	C	: kitchen
Mbali	: Ward Leader	H	: hangar
□	: house	●	: special points (*nkira*, *nkiini*, meeting place)
T	: royal tomb		

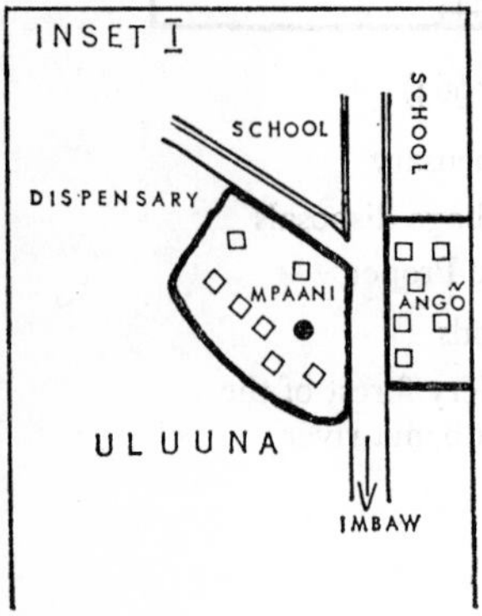

Inset II

- ▨ : Masala I–III
- ▥ : Lifura Mbaa I–II
- ⁘ : Inkwii I–IV
- ⊞ : Uluuna I–II
- - - → : motor roads

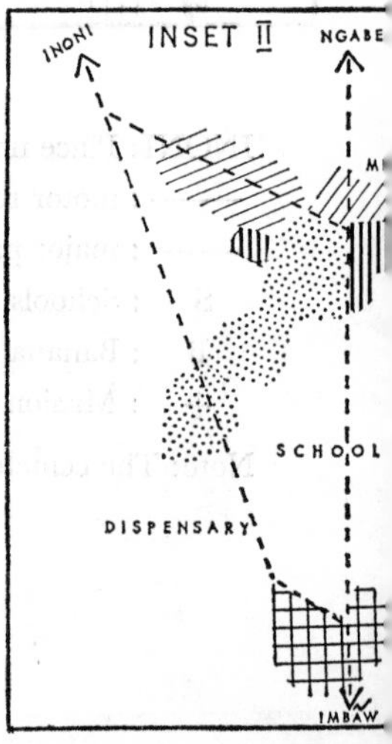

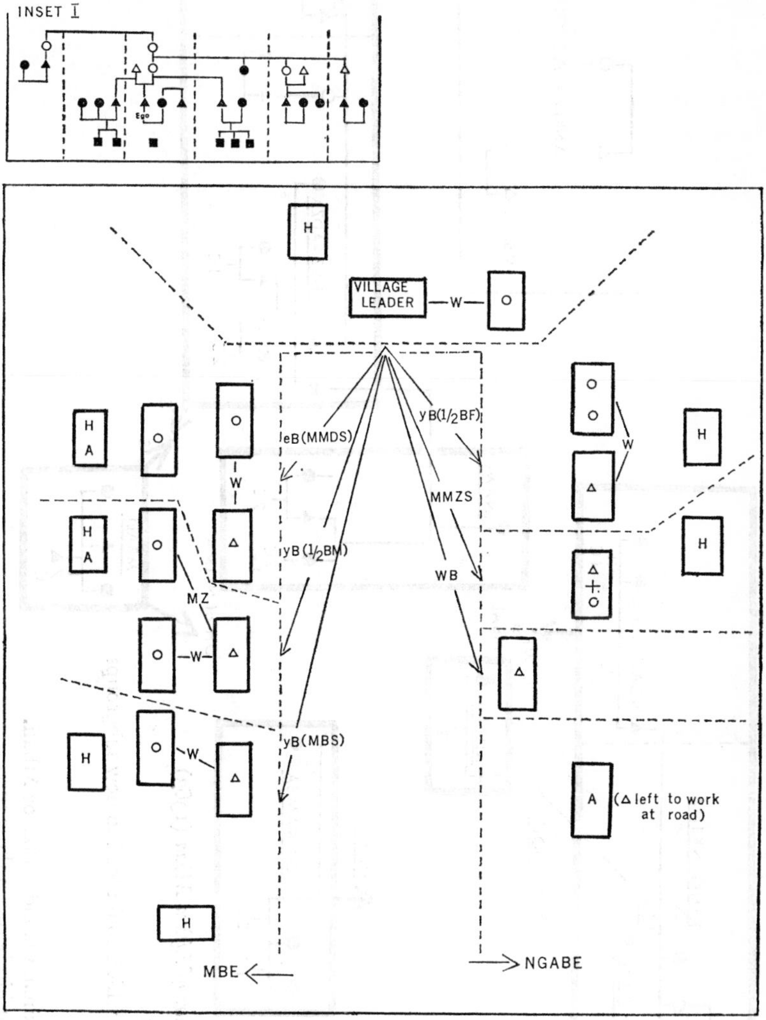

Diagram 3. *Plan of Ampo* (1963)

- - - - : subdivisions of compounds

——— : relations between village leader and others between compounds relations between persons and heads within compounds

H : Hangar   Δ : Men

A : Abandoned   O : Women

Inset: Genealogical relationships to Headman who is designated as Ego

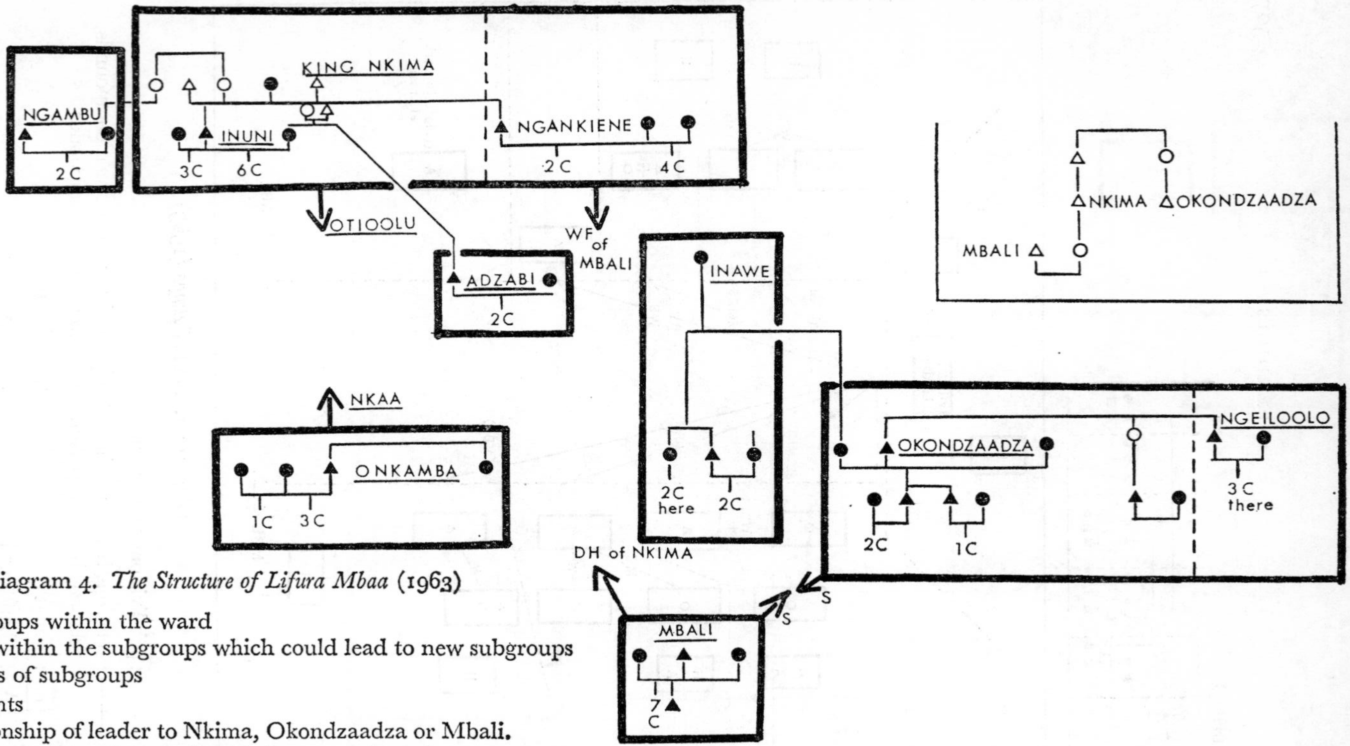

Diagram 4. *The Structure of Lifura Mbaa* (1963)

□ : subgroups within the ward
---- : splits within the subgroups which could lead to new subgroups
<u>Mbali</u> : leaders of subgroups
●, ▲ : residents
→ : relationship of leader to Nkima, Okondzaadza or Mbali. The inset shows the relationship between those three.

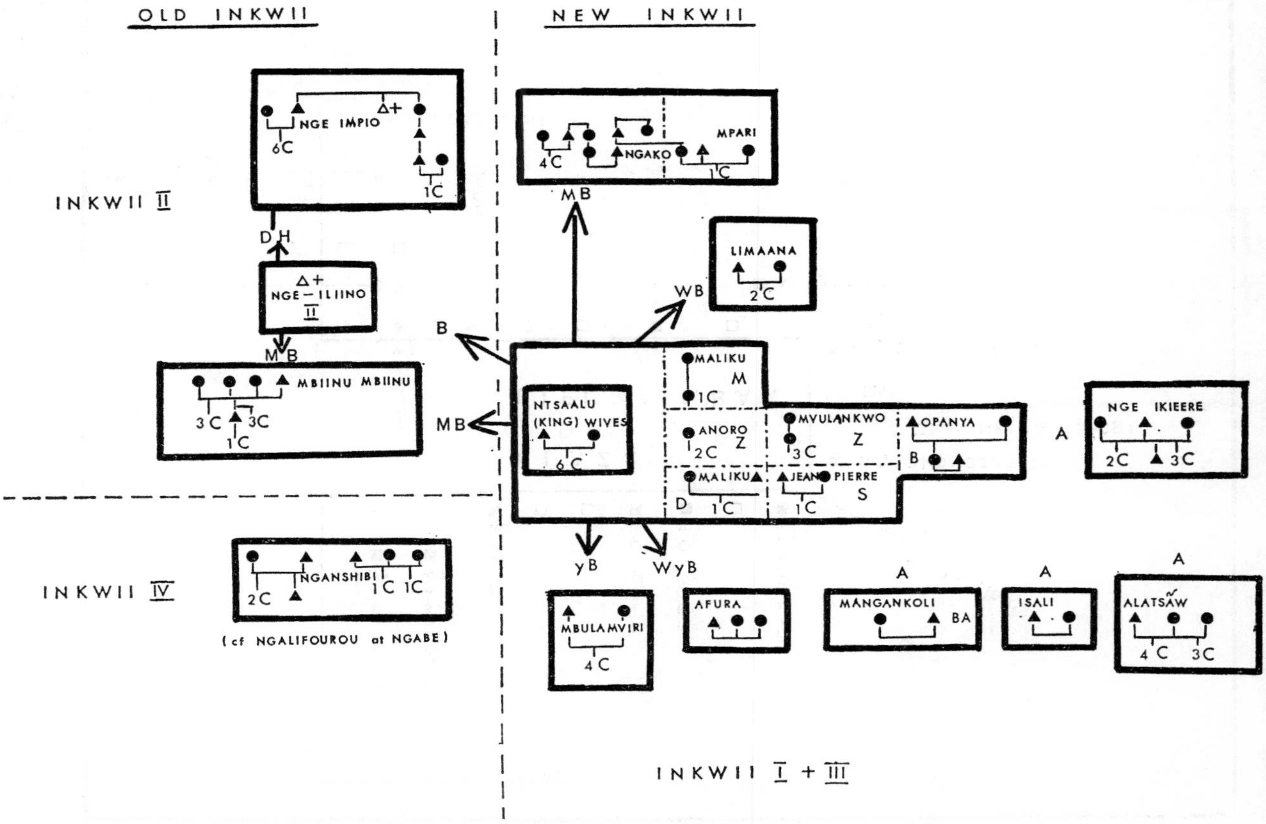

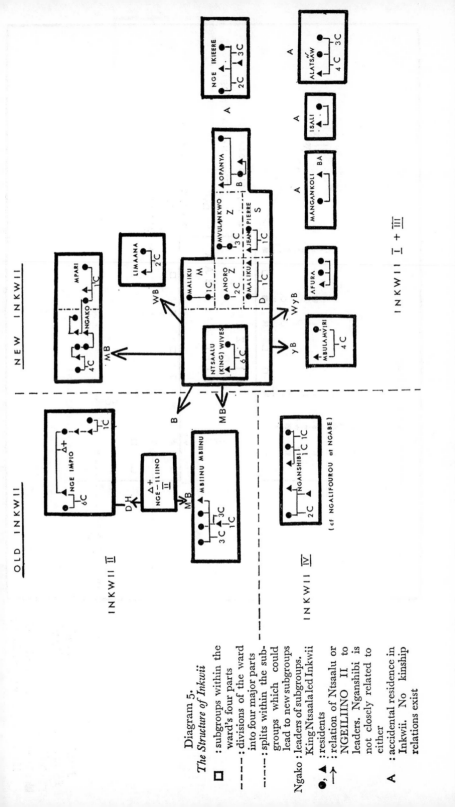

Diagram 5.
The Structure of Inkwii

- □ : subgroups within the ward's four parts
- – – – – : divisions of the ward into four major parts
- –·–·– : splits within the subgroups which could lead to new subgroups
- Ngako : leaders of subgroups. King Ntsaala led Inkwii
- ●, ▲ : residents
- → : relation of Ntsaalu or NGEILIINO II to leaders. Nganshibi is not closely related to either
- A : accidental residence in Inkwii. No kinship relations exist

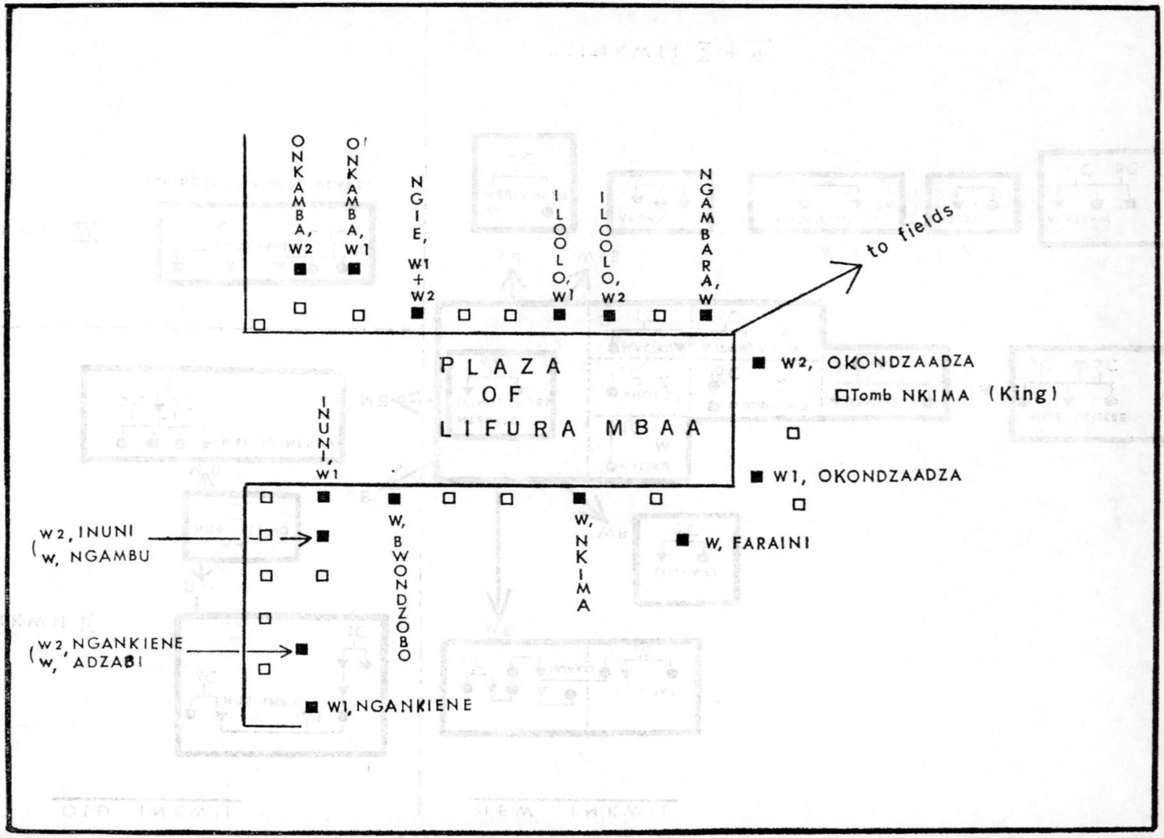

Diagram 6.
Location of Married Women of Lifura Mbaa I in the ward (1963)

□ : Men's houses
■ : Women's houses and their identifications (e.g. W1 Inuni)

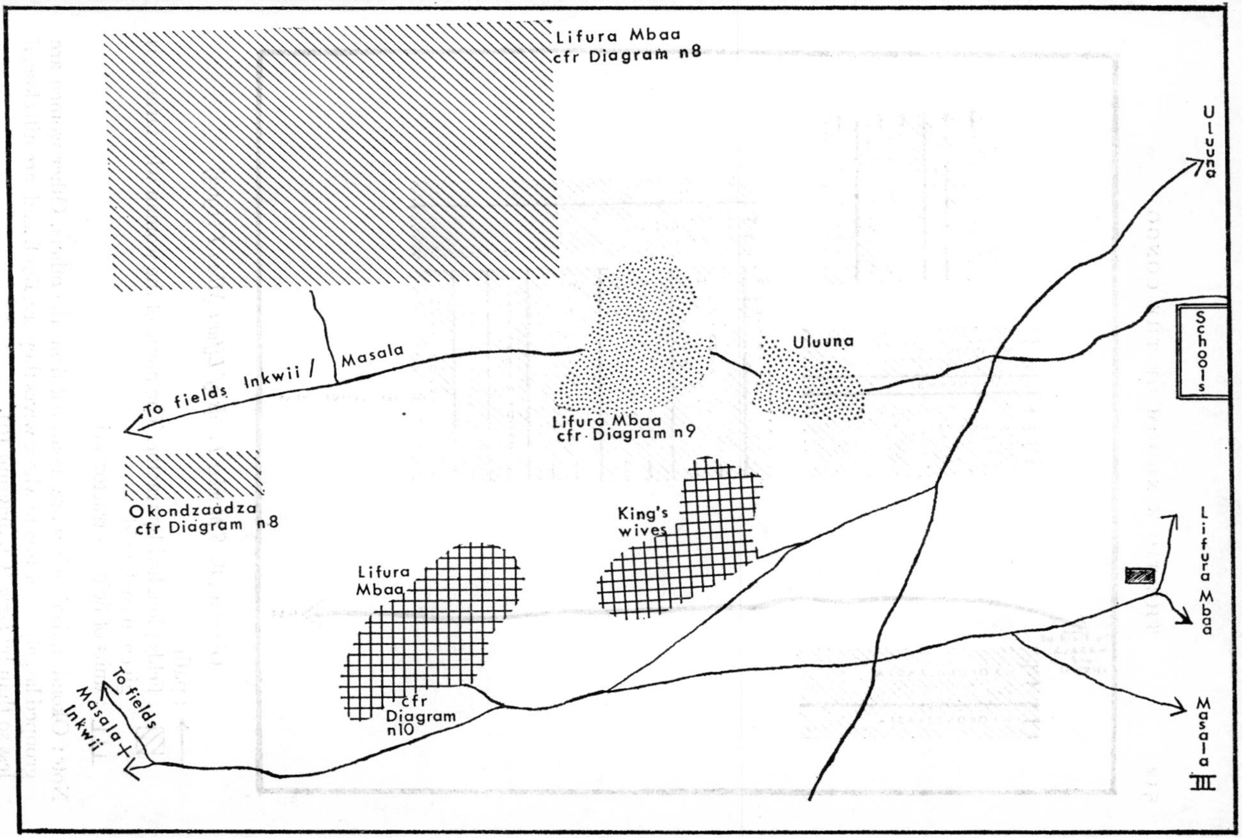

Diagram 7.
Location of Fields and
Idzia of Lifura Mbaa (1963)

- ——— : paths
- : September fields of Lifura Mbaa (Cf. Diagram 8)
- : February Fields of Lifura Mbaa (Cf. Diagram 9), and of Uluuna
- : *Idzia* of Lifura Mbaa (Cf. Diagram 10) and of the king's wives

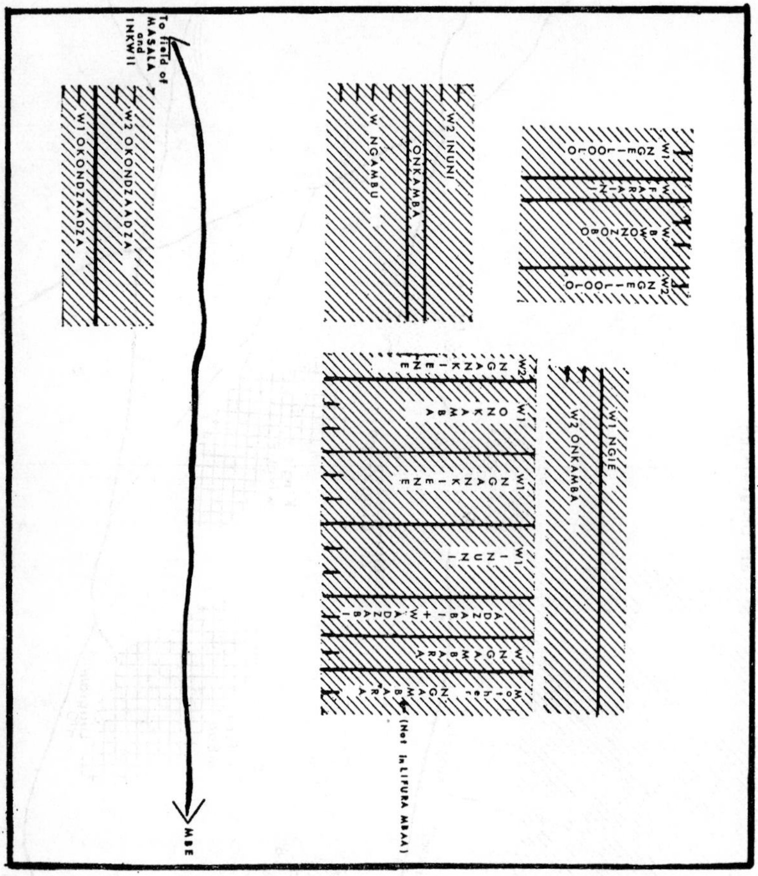

Diagram 8. *September Fields of Lifura Mbaa I* (1963)

⟶ : path

▨ : fields ploughed by tractor. The name of the woman who farms it is given in each field

ꓕꓕꓕ : units of fields in tractor strips

Note: Okondzaadza's wives are separated from the others. Other women are grouped largely according to whose wives they are. But friends are still close, if less so than by *idzia* (Cf. diagram 10).

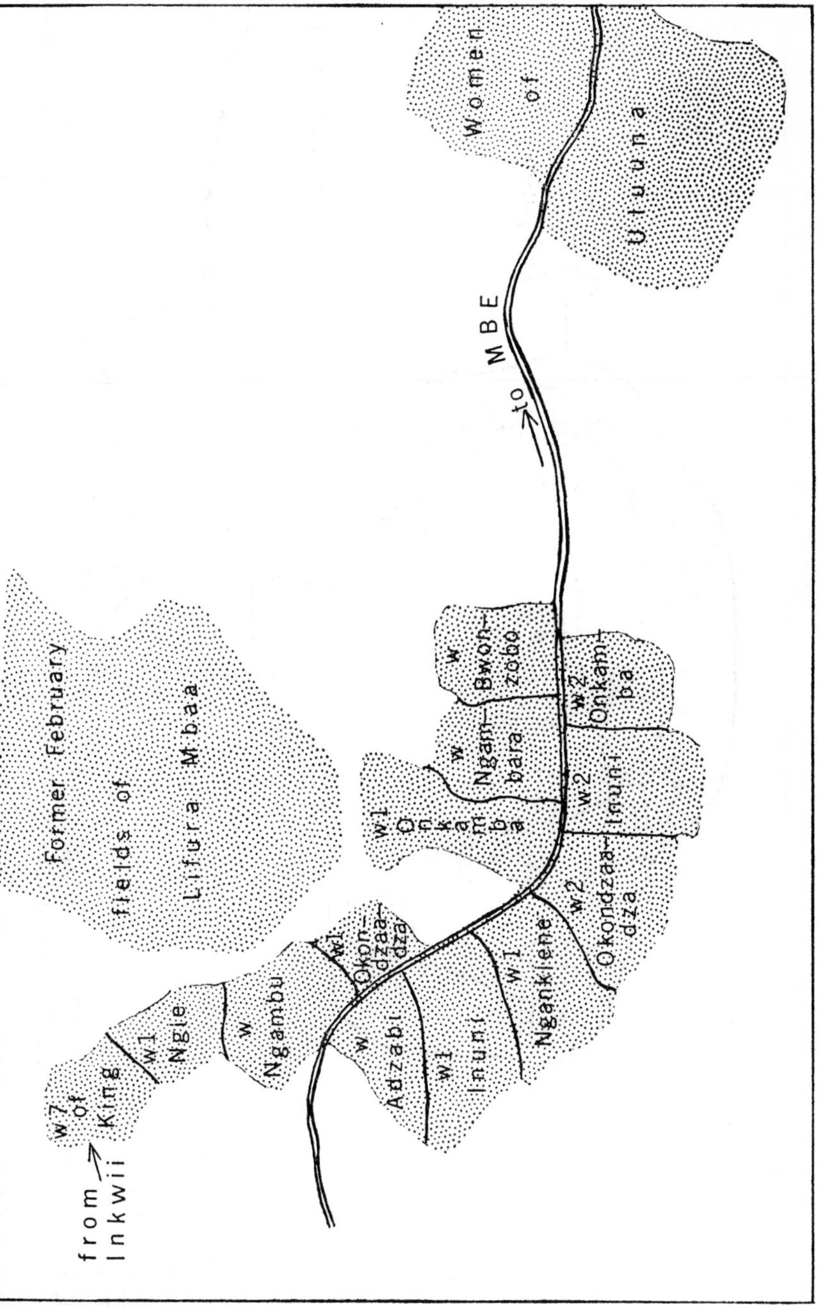

Diagram 9. *February Fields (òkala) of Lifura Mbaa I* (1964) ═ : road ⁙ : field with name of owner

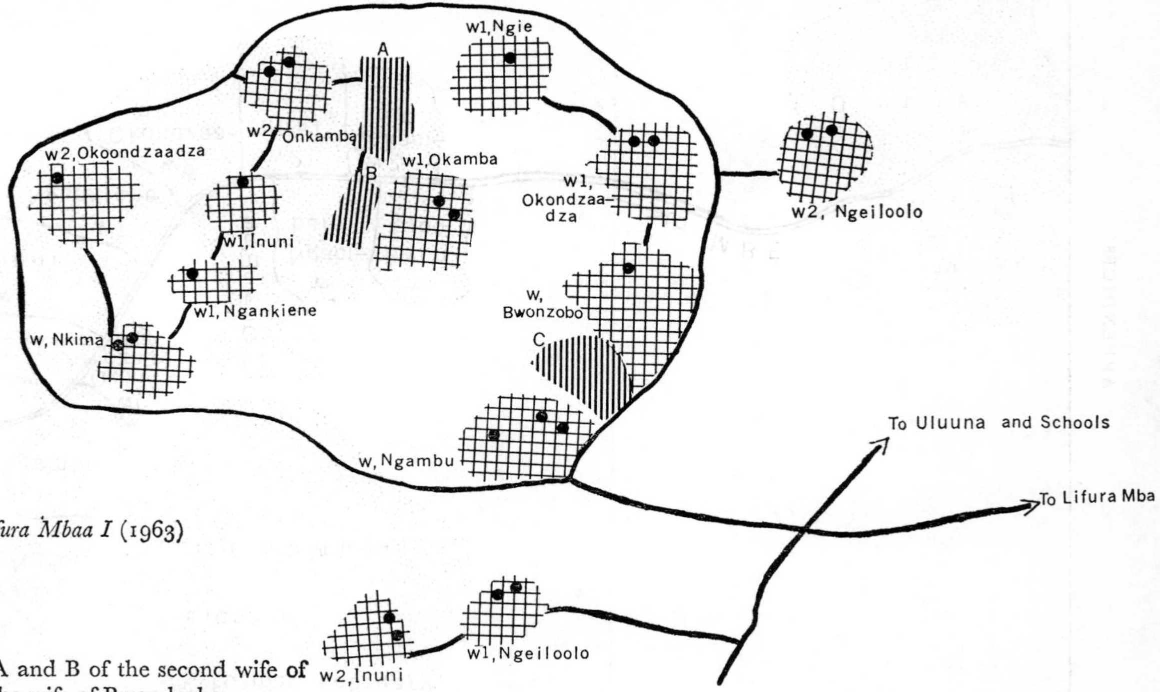

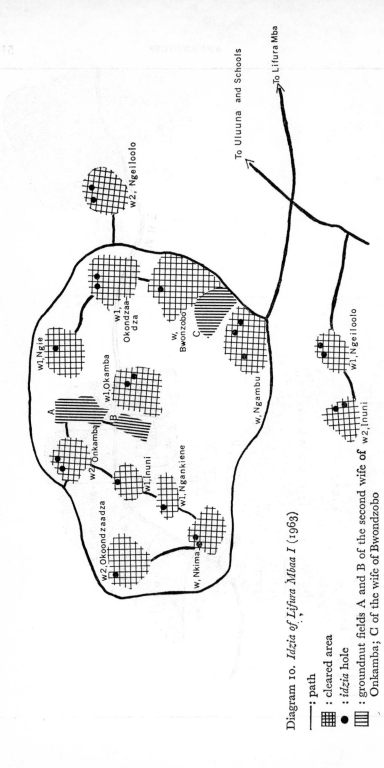

Diagram 10. *Idzia of Lifura Mbaa I* (1963)

——: path

▦ : cleared area

● : *idzia* hole

▥ : groundnut fields A and B of the second wife of Onkamba; C of the wife of Bwondzobo

APPENDIX No. 4

Origins of the Population

1. *By plateau affiliation*

A. MBE

ward		*Boõ*	*Mbembe*	*Jinju*	*Wũ*	*Jiju*	*Ngungulu*	*Sese*	*Tege*
INKWII									
men		8	5	1	1			2	
women		9	10	4	2	1	1		
total		17	15	5	3	1	1	2	
ULUUNA									
men		1				5			1
women		1			2	3			
total		2			2	8			1
MASALA									
men		22						1	
women		14	2	11	1			3	
total		36	2	11	1			4	
LIFURA MBAA									
men		11		2	1		1		
women		10	2	6		1		1	
totals		21	2	8	1	1	1	1	
MBE Totals									
men		42	5	3	2	5	1	3	1
women		34	14	21	5	5	1	4	
totals		76	19	24	7	10	2	7	1
	%	52	13	16·5	4·8	6·8	1·4	4·8	0·7

Comments:

1 Totals are not equal to the total men and women of Mbe, because all adults were not questioned.

2 Everyone listed the plateau of his father.

3 Note the difference between wards especially for men. INKWI has a strong influence of Mbembe, ULUUNA is Jiju, MASALA and LIFURA MBAA are mostly Boõ.

4 Notice how geographical proximity has distributed proportions of women especially Jinju girls married by the men when they were still mostly on the plains of Ntsaa and a new influx of Wũ girls.

5 The distribution reflects widely different backgrounds of informants.

B. IMBÃW

ward:		*Boõ*	*Mbembe*	*Jinju*	*Wũ*	*Jiju*	*Lari (Kongo)*
ÃTORO		2	14		6		1
KWOLI			9	1	12	1	
totals		2	23	1	18	1	1
	%	4·3	50	2·2	39·1	2·2	2·2

Comments:

1 The contrast with Mbe is striking. This is the continuation of an old Mbembe settlement. The proximity to Mpũ (it is a 'border village') explains the number of Wũ; the one Jiju is a person left by ULUUNA at Mbe, which used to live at Imbãw. Only 8·7% of the population came from north of the Lefini while at Mbe only 17·8% came from south of the Lefini!

2 The distribution between men and women is not given. Most Wũ were women and most men Mbembe.

3 Informants gave the plateau of the father as origin, as in Mbe.

Note: The data and genealogies taken in other villages for other purposes indicate that they all follow a pattern similar to Mbe, with the exception of Ngabe where the Dzindzali population has increased the % of Mfunu, Ngungulu and Tege.

2. *Birthplace of inhabitants* (place and number of inhabitants born there)

regions:	*INKWII*	*ULUUNA*	*MASALA*	*LIFURA MBAA*
Mbe neighbourhood	[Inkwii 6 Mbe 6 Ngabe 7] Ngantsu 3 Isã 1 Viõ 1 Imbãw 3	[Imbãw 4]	Mbe 2	Mbe 4
			Ampo 1	[Nkoo 3 Osabi 1 Inshiele 1 Inkuo 1]
Inoni neighbourhood	Ndua 1 Inoni 1 Boembé 1 Itswali 1 Oku 1	Inoni 1	[Inoni 3 Mpumako 2]	Mpumako 2

regions:	*INKWII*	*ULUUNA*	*MASALA*	*LIFURA MBAA*
Mpũ	Mah 2		Mah 2	Mah 2
	Dzwa 1			
	Inkuo 2			
	Brazzaville 1			
		Mbiina 1		
		Impe 1		
			Yoono 1	
			Oye 1	
			Ingunu 1	
			Ikuri 1	
				Abala 1
				Anka 1
Ntsaa plains	Adzi 1			
	Ontsuo 1		Ontsuo 5	
	Itiene 1			
	Indiõ 1		Indiõ 3	
	Nkwũ 1			
	Ntsaa 2		Ntsaa 3	Ntssa 4
	Usa 1		Usa 1	
			Ibu 2	
			Abili 2	
			Mfura 1	
			Ingãkwũ 1	
			Mpo 1	
			Mwaari 1	Mwaari 1
			Abi 1	
			Aba 3	Aba 2
			Akwi 2	Akwi 1
			Mpiina Ntsaaa 3	
			Kiali 1	
			Ongia 1	
				Vuli 1
				Nkõ 2
Djambala plains	Bulania 1			Mpfũ 1
Jiju plains		Uluuna 4		
Tege		Tege 1		
Ngungulu			Mpunu	

Comments:

1. This table confirms the previous one, but tells much more. For each of the wards past residence is shown by concentrations of places, which have been put in boxes. INKWII resided near Mbe and Ngabe and takes its name from a former village near Mbe. ULUUNA resided first at Uluuna (Jiju) from where it took its name and then at Imbãw. MASALA came from the plains of Ntsaa, south of Ntsaa-Ngo moved to Inoni neighbourhood and then to Mbe. LIFURA MBAA came also from Ntsaa, but moved to Nkoo and later to Mbe.
2 Other origins are mostly those of wives. The influence of Mpũ is remarkable.
3 Note the wide spread of origins reflecting both the mobility of the population and the attempt to spread marriages. 4–7 are the highest numbers and indicate a period of residence of twenty years or more in a given neighbourhood.

---

3. *Migrations of wards and ward heads until the settlement in Mbe*

1 Early movements

Relations between the plains of Ntsaa and Mbe are old. During Ngaayüo's reign Itsu was installed as MUIDZU at Ntsaa and took his relatives with him. They did keep their ties with the people here. Even at the time of Iloo there was contact and intermarriage since Iloo's NGAASAA came from Jinju.

2 Masala

A. The original leader of Masala was Ayu. He lived with Ngankia Mbandieele, Ubwoono, and Ngateo, at Ontsuo. Because of a quarrel with a local lord over ivory and the recruitment, Ayu and Ngankia Mbandieele left for Inoni where Ayu's wife's father lived. In this area Lisia, his mother's brother's son was an important person since he was MWANGÃW and ruled part of Bouambé.

After 1931, when Andibi became king, Ngankia Mbandieele moved with Ayu and Ubwoono who had rejoined the party at Inoni, in Ngambiõ near Imbali.

In 1934 Ngankia Mbandieele became king and leader of Masala. He moved to Idzwa Itieeri, quite near by.

In 1934 or 1935 he came to Mbe, which was inhabited only by an old man NgeIbiõ and his two wives, the only remnant of the pre-1918 Mbe. The place was indicated by a European who wanted them to be near the road.

In 1939 Ngateo came from his father's village to take over the leadership after Ngankia's death; Ubwoono declined to do it.

B. Bilankwi, the present-day leader of a part of Masala, left Ntsaa for Brazzaville to look for work in 1931–4. He found none, heard that his kinsman might become king and joined Ngankia at Ngambiõ and went from there to Mbe. Ngankia was his wife's father, but his mother's father also came from the Mbe area and had married the sister of MUIDZU Isu and followed her then to Ntsaa.

3 ULUUNA

The leader Mpaani followed his mother's brother who had come as a wood-cutter from Uluuna in Jiju to the Congo opposite Imbãw; he married and settled at Imbãw. Mpaani followed him and took over after his death. Mpaani's sister's son and the sister's son of the latter followed each in turn. They left Imbãw for Mbe around 1955.

4 LIFURA MBAA

A. Nkima used to be the leader. He left the area of Aliõ around 1925–9 to join his sister's son Lisia, the MWANGÃW, who had succeeded to his mother's brother at that time and was the wife's brother of some one who lived at Bouambé. Lisia indicated Nkoo as a settlement for Nkima. He remained there until the death of Ngankia perhaps in 1939 (Cf., Dossier, 90, archives du Moyen Congo; letter of 15 May 1936 mentions him).

When Nkima died in 1947 Okondzaadza took over. He had rejoined Nkima at Nkoo after Okondzaadza's father died at Aliõ. They were 'brothers'.

B. Mbali's father came from Ibaana near Inkuo near Inoni. But Mbali was born at Ntsaa (around 1890–2). He was drafted during the First World War, demobilized and worked at Brazzaville. Later he moved to Inoni where Ngankia Mbandieele and Ayu lived and he followed them. He had first come back to Inoni because his father's younger brother still lived there. This move took place after Andibi became king in 1931 but before Ngankia moved to Ngambiõ.

With the arrival of Nkima at Mbe, Mbali found closer relatives in that group than he had among the Masala group. Okondzaadza is a classificatory sister's son. But his preceding history explains why he kept separate from Lifura. Mbaa was and is still settled in Masala.

5 INKWII

Inkwii consists of at least four parts: old Inkwii of Mbiinu I, the compounds of king Ntsaalu, the settlement of NGANSHIBI, and the new Inkwii without a definite leader in 1964.

A. Mbiinu Mbiinu succeeded as leader to the last NGEILIINO, Mpiere, who was his mother's brother. The latter came from Mpio aBwaani (NGANTSU's) where he had settled after the preceding NGEILIINO Oshiãmbãw who had left Mbe before or along with king Ngaayüo had settled at MANDIELE's at Kwũ and died there. Mpiere came back to Mbe after Ngankia had settled there probably in 1935–6.

B. Ntsaalu and his immediate household moved from Ngabe after he became king in 1949.

C. NGANSHIBI moved after the death and burial of Ngalifourou in 1957.

D. All the small groups of new Inkwii were attracted by king Ntsaalu, except for a friend of Bilankwi. They all arrived apparently after 1957. Bulamviri came because Ntsaalu was his mother's brother's son and settled 1958–9; Amfura, a trader from Brazzaville was sister's son of Ntsaalu and moved in in 1962; Nge Ikieere came from Inoni where he had been ill. Cured by a *ngàà* in Mbe he moved there in 1959–60. He was born at Bulania near Djambala town, left to follow his wife and lived in Itswali with his wife's brother. Misfortune drove him to Inoni where his half brother of the same father lived.

E. A special case is Ba. He settled soon after 1934 but lives in new Inkwii. He originally came from Nkwũ to Bouambé to trade and settled after misfortune at Nkwũ. He married and followed Bilankwi who had married his wife's sister. He did not go to Masala III however and stayed on his own.

6 Leaders and followers

It is obvious that Lisia triggered off the immediate migration from the Ntsaa area but that sporadic movements had been going on in both directions to and from the Ntsaa plains for a long time. These in time became one way migrations, because of the harshness of recruiting for the railway and the lesser degree of administrative control south of the Lefini.

One can show from the biographies of all men in Mbe that they 'followed' someone who followed one of the leaders mentioned. They left because they experienced misfortune (children or wives died by witchcraft or they were ill), including trouble with Europeans. They came because their relative was well off (MWANGÃW, king . . .) and because of the relative lack of control by the French administration in this area.

7 Growth by quarters in Mbe was then as follows:

MASALA 1934–5 from Ntsaa; old INKWII 1935–6 from Ngabe; LIFURA MBAA 1939 from Ntsaa, Ntsaalu's INKWII from Ngabe 1949–50; ULUUNA from Jiju (Imbãw) 1955; NGANSHIBI from Ngabe 1957; New INKWII after 1958. The date about migrations and origins are confirmed by the biographies and Tables I and II above.

8 Migration

Similar data indicate that Okiene, Ampo, and Osabi were linked with the MASALA migration. Isasiba moved on its own from Aba on the plains of Ntsaa via Mpumako and arrived in the area at Ampo in 1931–4. The leader left for Idzulu then Nkoo (before 1939) and stayed behind when Nkima of LIFURA MBAA went to Mbe. This movement involved Jinju and its first leader was Mbaakuo who crossed the Lefini in the early 1920s because one of the first Europeans at Djambala, Mushielimwa, made the people work much too hard.

APPENDIX No. 5

Notes on the Political History of Mbe since 1934

From 1934–5 to 1939 Mbe still remained small. Ngankia Mbandieele's only competitor for leadership was Ubwoono, who was not interested. Outside of MASALA the NGEILIINO Mpiere had to be reckoned with but no rivalry between the king and Mpiere is reported. Mbali already had his household and was then outside the mainstream of leadership.

By 1940 Nkima was king and had brought LIFURA MBAA. MASALA was now led by the newly arrived Ngateo and around this time Mbiinu Mbiinu succeeded to Mpiere as leader of INKWII. The village became more and more dominated by the MASALA section which was the biggest and least unified at the time. Bilankwi, who may have hoped to lead the ward after Ngankia's death, was uneasy about Ngateo's predominance.

After Ntsaalu's arrival Okondzaadza and Ngateo became the *amieene* of the king and with the consolidation of LIFURA MBAA and its ally Bilankwi, MASALA'S leadership came more and more to be challenged. Over the years Ntsaalu failed to provide leadership to integrate INKWII which could therefore not compete with the two other groups. By 1958 or so a fraction of MASALA left under Ngaila after a quarrel with Ngateo and settled at Ampo. Still MASALA remained dominant until Bilankwi the king and Okondzaadza hired a *ngàà* in 1961–2 to investigate witchcraft. He designated several leaders of MASALA and Ngateo's power was broken. But the king asked him to remain, for if MASALA had left, a good third of the population would have gone. So gradually his influence rose again.

ULUUNA never participated in internal politics in Mbe and paid as much attention to the situation in Imbãw, from where they came, as to Mbe. Their localization apart from the main village helped them to retain their autonomy.

By 1963–4 it was evident that besides the older leaders, younger men had formed followings within each ward, so that one could foresee, especially in LIFURA MBAA, struggles for later participation in leadership. The patterns followed exactly the competition of leadership which could be expected in any village. The major difference at Mbe was the presence of small splinter-groups not attached to any of the two or three big wards. Thus the cases of Mbali, Bilankwi, Ba, every older man in New Inkwii, NGANSHIBI, and even part of ULUUNA led by Angõ. If Mbe had been an ordinary village all these splinter-groups would have settled a mile or so away from the others. They obviously stayed because of the schools and the dispensary. This is also the reason why ULUUNA came to Mbe. It indicated the impact of modern institutions on the former residence groups.

APPENDIX No. 6

Data on marriage (Mbe)

1. *Spread of marriages at Mbe* (in numbers of girls)

origins: wards:	*MASALA*	*LIFURA MBAA*	*INKWII*	*ULUUNA*	*Totals*
married in wards:					
MASALA	6	2	3		11
LIFURA MBAA	3	2	3		8
INKWII	1	2	5	1	9
ULUUNA		1			1
totals	10	7	11	1	

Comments:

1 ULUUNA was a recent arrival and was not yet connected by marriages with the other wards.

2 The totals show that about as many girls were given in marriage by each ward as received in marriage although MASALA and LIFURA MBAA each gave one more to INKWII than they received in total. The even spread between giving and receiving is remarkable on the whole. It confirms an interpretation of marriage as an exchange.

3 Note the high endogamy within MASALA and LIFURA MBAA which are the oldest and most cohesive wards in Mbe.

2. *Marriages of women born at Mbe*

(No. 1 took into account all girls born to parents residing at Mbe).

origins: *wards:*	*MASALA*	*LIFURA MBAA*	*INKWII*	*totals*
married in wards:				
MASALA	*1*	1		2
LIFURA MBAA	1		2	3
INKWII	1	1	*1*	3
unmarried[1]				2
village MBIINA				1
totals	3	2	4	

Comments:

1 Of the nine married girls only one married outside Mbe. MASALA and LIFURA MBAA spread the available girls over the two other wards while INKWII did not enter into an alliance with MASALA. ULUUNA was too recent to have girls of marriageable age yet.

2 MASALA gave one girl more than it received, LIFURA MBAA gained one and INKWII lost one to MBIINA. On the whole the results are comparable with the previous table, except that the ward endogamy is scarcely discernible as yet. The endogamy within Mbe is 8–9.

3. *Endogamy within Mbe*

(a) Women of Mbe parents married at Mbe: 28
 Women of Mbe parents married elsewhere: 14[2]
 % of endogamy: 66·6%

(b) Women of Mbe parents married in the region (including Ampo, Osabi, Idzulu): 32
 Women of Mbe parents married out of the region: 10
 % of endogamy for the region (neighbourhood) 76%
 % of alliances with Brazzaville 14%

4. *Divorce at Mbe*

(a) Length of marriage before divorce both for men and women.

months or years	*number of cases*	*comments*
1 month or less	3	
2 months	1	
3 months	1	
4 months	2	
6 months ±	5	almost a unit of time
7 months	1	
8 months	4	
9 months	1	
10 months	1	

[1] One was divorced, the other was born in the old Mbe, (pre-1918) and a widow.

[2] Cf. Table: Persons who have left Mbe.

months or years	*number of cases*	*comments*
11 months	1	
less than one year	12	also a unit of time
1 year	33	also a unit of time
1 year two months	1	
1 year six months	2	
2 years	4	
2 year two months	1	
4 years	1	
6 years	1	

....

or: six months or less:	12
six months to one year:	53
over one year to two years:	8
over two years:	2

The crucial period lies then between six months and one year after marriage. Divorce is clearly a problem of adaptation between spouses and affines.

(b) Divorces and marriages terminated by death, in relation to all marriages.

	marriages ended by divorce	*marriages ended by death*	*existing marriages*
persons over 45	30 or 37·5%	33 or 41·25%	17 or 21·25%
persons under 45	46 or 38·65%	19 or 16%	54 or 45·35%
totals	76 or 38·19%	52 or 26·13%	71 or 35·68%

Comments:

1 The percentages of divorce for persons under and above forty-five years of age are close. The presumed increase may be slight, but bigger than shown since there is more time to divorce for younger people. On the whole the table shows a stable proportion.

2 The closeness of the % for over and under forty-five-years old with regard to divorce may substantiate table (a). Most divorces occur shortly after marriage.

(c) *Divorces related to present day marriages*

	number of divorces	*number of marriages*
persons over 45	30 (64%) (1)	17 (36%)
persons under 45	46 (46%)	54 (54%)
	76 (52%)	71 (48%)

Comments:

1 Compare with previous table. This index of divorce does change in time hence the higher percentage for over forty-five-years old.

2 The index, just like the index of divorces as a % of all marriages terminated, its complement, is not nearly as good an index as (b). The % for divorces as a % of all marriages terminated lies at 59% or 47·6% for over forty-five-years old and 70% for the under forty-five-years old, because so few marriages were terminated by death in that group.

5. *Polygyny at Mbe and Ampo: number of men with one wife or more*

number of wives:	*1*	*2*	*3*	*8*	*total men*
wards:					
MASALA	14	6 (3)	1 (1)		21
INKWII	11	6 (5)	1 (1)	1	19
LIFURA MBAA	5	6 (3)			11
ULUUNA	3	1			4
AMPO	6	1 (1)			7
totals	39	20	2	1	62

key: (3) etc. Indicates the numbers in the group of men who are old, at least over forty-five.

Comments:

1 The person with eight wives is the king.

2 Note the proportion, well over 50%, of old men among those who have two wives; only two really young men had been able to marry two wives; most of the older men had inherited one. All old men with three wives were old (in other villages too) and had inherited at least one wife.

3 Very strikingly polygyny is both widespread and limited to two wives. The % of polygynous men is 37%, just a little higher than the excess of women over men and the % of women is 57% of all married women. Few men are not married and few have more than two wives, which explains the first percentage. The second indicates that a woman has more than an even chance of belonging to a polygynous household.

APPENDIX No. 7

Poverty and Kinship according to Genealogical Evidence

Data are presented here to show that in 1963–4 poor people also tended not to have many kin. A poor person's genealogy was compared with that of a man of about the same age and without any political position in Mbe. The following results obtain. Job is poor compared to Everyman.

A. Job's kin

generation differences	*names unknown*	*names known*	*totals*	*comments*
+2				all unknown
+1	3	5	8	(3 alive, 5 dead)
0	6	14	20	(17 alive, 3 dead)
−1	6	6	12	(12 alive)
totals	15	25	40	(32 alive, 8 dead)

Note: He knows twenty living relatives by their name of which seven are affines and thirteen consanguineal kin. But in fact he has continual contact with seven kinsmen, affines included: six co-evals and one in the generation +1. That excludes six children of his and his brother.

B. *Everyman's kin*

generation differences	*names unknown*	*names known*	*totals*	*comments*
+3	4		4	(4 dead)
+2	5	3	8	(2 alive, 6 dead)
+1	11	27	38	(33 alive, 5 dead)
0	5	35	40	(32 alive, 8 dead)
−1	17	21	38	(34 alive, 4 dead)
−2	9	6	15	(14 alive, 1 dead)
totals	51	92	143	(115 alive, 28 dead)

Note: 72 of the living kin are consanguineal and belong to his *ibuuru*, 34 are spouses of members of his *ibuuru*. The members of the *ibuuru* are almost all known by name and with fully two-thirds of these he seems to be in regular contact or with about 50 old people. Small children excluded makes it at least 30 others, over four times more than Job.

C. *Comment*

Other genealogies confirm this image. Poor people have far fewer relatives than others. In part this situation reflects the fact that people with relatives can always expect a minimum amount of help and will not be labelled poor as a consequence. In part the reverse is true. Rich or influential people recall more relatives (especially by name) because more relatives visit them or live with them. The role of kinship as a system of social security is clear. And wealth was often acquired with the help of a large kin-group.

APPENDIX No. 8

New Trades in Mbe

quarter	*occupation*
Lifura Mbaa	1 trader
	1 carver of small tables
	1 hairdresser but is not paid for it
	1 small trader, farmer of cassava and tobacco for export
Masala	1 housebuilder
	1 maker of beds
	1 rural policeman
	1 trader and tailor
	1 trader, worker for road company and baker
	1 gardener when there was a mission, mason, trader and palm fruit-cutter
	1 servant at the palace
	1 boy chauffeur
	1 tailor
	1 small trader, mechanic (bicycles, mobylettes), tailor
Inkwii	1 small trader
	1 trader in wine
	1 chauffeur
	1 nurse (not practising)
	1 secretary to king
	1 female nurse
	1 trader and tailor
	1 servant at the palace
Uluuna	—

Comments:

1 The combination of specialities and the degree of specialization (bedmaker!) explain why there are mostly only one for each occupation. Only one woman had a 'modern' occupation. All these specializations with 3 exceptions were part-time and brought few economic returns.

2 As against the 22 new traders there were 26 specialists in old trades (including kingship) so that 48 men or over 64% of all men (66) are so qualified.

3 Predominating new trades were tailor and trader; predominating old trades *ngàà*, musicians, and hunters. The new trades were all in the hands of younger or middle-aged men, the old trades, with the exception of some of the musicians, were practised by older men.

4 Most women worked about one week in three for preparation of cassava meal for export; none of the part-time trades for men gave them this much work. Again one sees confirmation for a division of labour whereby women do the productive work while men use their occupations as status symbols.

APPENDIX 9

Persons who have left Mbe. (31 *December* 1963)

men or boys	*women or girls*
1 office worker, Brazzaville	1 girl pupil, secondary school, Mouyondzi
1 soldier, Brazzaville	2 prostitutes Brazzaville
1 unskilled worker, Brazzaville	6 women married in Brazzaville, almost all married to Tio
1 mechanic, Brazzaville	2 women married to Ampo
1 trader/weaver, Brazzaville	1 woman married at Osabi
1 teacher Ngabe	1 woman married at Idzulu
1 teacher Pointe Noire	1 woman married at Ontsuo
6 pupils secondary school, Brazzaville	1 woman married at Ngalidzõ
1 pupil secondary school, Gamboma	1 woman married at Inoni
1 pupil secondary school, Djambala	1 woman married at Osala
1 pupil school, Ngabe	
totals 16 men or boys: all young	17 women of various ages

grand total: 33 compared to population of 328 or 10%

Comments:

The attraction of Brazzaville is evident. Beyond that the range is spread:

1 both for girls marrying as for the others is quite limited.

2 shows only three men have positions requiring some education, but eight boys and one girl were in schools which were giving them an equal or better education.

APPENDIX No. 10

A palaver: *Onka's divorce.*

actors: AMVII and IKUUNU (wife's fathers to ONKA), the wife's mother, OKIÕ his wife, NGAAYÜO, (wife's brother), OYUNI (wife's mother's brother) ONKA, MPAANI (his mother's brother), and ONGKAANA (his sister's son).

judges: NGANDZIÕ, squire NGAATALI, MIANDOO, BALEWARI, NGWAMBAA.

court: NGANDZIÕ's court at Imbãw 29 February 1964 to 1 March 1964 in appeal from the king's court at Mbe. The court held its hearings on the *plaza* of the village in front of chief NGANDZIÕ's house, the supporters of Onka sat on their left and the wife's kin on their right. There were almost no spectators since the village is quite small.

1. *Paying the goats: adultery and divorce or divorce only?*

NGWAMBAA: Ikuunu has come, there he is.

ONKA: Who is Ikuunu? Who owes me or not? Who owes you?

Thereupon he asks for two goats, one for adultery and one for divorce.

IKUUNU: Why should I give two goats?

ONKA: One for the divorce, one because you gave your daughter Okiõ to another man.

NGWAMBAA: I took one goat [*for the divorce*].

BALEWARI: Why do you still hold to that. Get a living goat.

ONKA: Why do you say *one* goat. Who will give the other. Ikuunu must give two of them.

AMVII: How? You ask for two goats. One goat is enough for I must pawn the girl [*ntsuo: for lack of money to pay the goat, the girl would be left as pawn with the lord*].

ONKA: Two are needed.

AMVII: True, it is true Onka; the way you are talking is correct. I answered only one goat.

ONKA: Listen, this is my palaver. If there are not two living goats, 2,500 Fr CFA will be needed for the two goats.

IKUUNU: Who has goats for sale here? [*he wants to buy a second one, giving in to the argument*].

Nobody had a goat for sale.

BALEWARI: You must pay 1,000 Fr CFA for a goat.

ONKA: Two goats are needed.

AMVII *calling* NGAAYÜO: Go, get a goat in the village.

ONKA: Two goats are needed: one for the divorce, the other because he has benefited by the adultery of his daughter. When I went to him for explanations, he told me to ask for a goat.

SOMEBODY: There must be one goat. If you want two, we will need to pawn your girl [*to leave her with the lord as pawn*]. Just send a man who will go and fetch a goat.

On the side: IKUUNU *to* NGAATALI: Sell me a goat.
NGAATALI: There is one at the village; it costs 2,500 Fr CFA.
IKUUNU: I'll give 2,000 Fr CFA.

ONKA: I took the girl when she was small. There must be two goats.

NGWAMBAA: Let him explain that to lord NGANDZIÕ! [*It is not customary; one gives only one goat back at divorce, the other one was asked for adultery, but in divorce cases adultery is not usually counted*].

NGANDZIÕ: What do the judges say? Onka asks for two goats. What do you say?

ONKA: There was a man Impiini who has committed adultery with the woman. When the adultery was paid to me, they had not given the customary goat. That is why I still ask it.

NGANDZIÕ: So, one goat for the adultery with Impiini and one for *ipwooro* [*here the payment of divorce*]. Listen Onka. You are my uncle, I am the chief. Listen, money never finishes.

NGANDZIÕ: One goat for Impiini; as for *ipwooro,* I don't know yet. After this, perhaps there will be another goat.

ONKA: Two goats.

NGANDZIÕ *sends the matter to* AMVII *who says*: Listen and I must say, I don't say for nothing, chief/I answered: 'one goat'. If he sticks only to two goats, I don't speak.

NGWAMBAA: There is one goat, Onka.

ONKA *sings*: If you hunt a mythical animal, the mythical animal runs away; the animal is me [*meaning: 'If you cannot speak, the argument is lost for you'*]

Ankanınkani mbuur'amwamo: The goat is for everybody, why do you keep it back? [*in every similar case, such a goat is given*].

NGANDZIÕ *to* ONKA: One goat is right. They established the adultery Impiini *in flagrante*?

ONKA: Yes.

MPAANI: That adultery was never paid in public.

IKUUNU *wanted to speak but all prevented him.*

AMVII: If you tie a rope around me there is a reason.

ONKA *talks about the money of the adultery fine that has not been paid yet. But if a bit of it has been paid he cannot insult anymore.*

ONKA: In this business I am the king's enemy [*he had brought the matter to the court of a political enemy of the king*].

MPAANI: Since the matter had been badly handled at Mbe, you went to NGANDZIÕ to follow it up. [*Earlier at Mbe the judges had refused to grant a divorce, because* ONKA *had said he wanted his wife back.*]

ONKA *to* AMVII: There remained 5,000 Fr CFA.

NGWAMBAA: Where are those 5,000 Fr CFA?

OKIÕ: I spent the 5,000 Fr CFA.

2. *Divorce: does Okiõ ask for a divorce or not?*

NGWAMBAA: Go to your husband.

The woman went to ONKAANA, *the sister's son of* ONKA. *He told her to go to her own husband but she does not, thus refusing him.*

NGWAMBAA: Onka, the 5,000 Fr CFA [*still due for the adultery payment*], your wife spent them.

ONKA *rhetorically*: So when there is a divorce here or in the canton of Djambala, it is different there and here. Since they do not want to pay, the bride-wealth will return to them perhaps?

All in the assistance: That is not it. [*When everyone interrupts, they shout all together, get up, mill around; the protagonists* ONKA *and* IKUUNU *face each other, etc.*]

IPFUUNA I

The wife's side wants to go to Ipfuuna (*away from the plaza*).

AMVII: Since we refused to pay 6,000 Fr CFA the lord will say that the matter cannot be settled. On 5,000 Fr CFA we will give 2,500 Fr CFA. [*The woman agreed to give* 2,500 *Fr CFA. The others agreed. They return to the court.*]

AMBII: *Ankana* etc. . . . : This is how the elders left the matter. Ngwambaa, it was 5,000 Fr CFA. . . . The woman has given 3,000 Fr CFA and spent 2,000 Fr. She will give 2,000 Fr for *ibwooni* [ipwooro *when paid by a husband to a wife or vice-versa*] *because he has seen* Impiini. [Ipwooro *was to be paid because the wife had refused to tell the name of her lover.*]

ONKA: I don't take it. The 2,000 Fr CFA she gave me was for the poison ordeal. Now they have refused the poison ordeal. [*It is customary to back up a statement by a promise to take an ordeal such as* lindaa *in a case like this. Earnest money* iuula *to this effect is given. If afterwards the ordeal is refused by the party who proposed it, the earnest money is lost to them.*]

The people all started shouting: Onka, you refused the 3,000 Fr CFA your wife was giving to you? [*They started pressuring him on this point which would establish his bad faith.*]

ONKA: It is true. Give me now my *tike* [*i.e. The woman asked for a divorce, so double the bridewealth must be repaid. The doubling is called* tike].

The assistance refuses this.

NGANDZIÕ: You must not count the *tike.* MPAANI *agrees and* NGANDZIÕ: Let us talk about something else.

3 *The adultery case*

ONKA: *Ankana . . .* [*He gives a little stick to the judges as a sign that adultery has been committed.*]

IKUUNU: It is correct. Onka did request a payment for adultery from me.

NGWAMBAA *interrupts*: Impiini had come to this court. He wanted to drink the poison ordeal. Impiini had stated that there needed to be a witness to drink the poison ordeal. So *iuula* [*earnest money for this*] should be put up and the party which lied would lose it. Good. At that time then both Onka and Impiini had put up 100 Fr CFA. And then Impiini who had begun by denying everything admitted he had committed the adultery and that Ikuunu, father of the girl had given her to him. This is very serious. The witness to *iuula* had been Ngie Ubo.

NGIINA (*child of* NGAATALI) *sings*: The ears listen to the words of the people. [*Tell the truth.*]

AMVII *told about a similar case and concluded that when the matter was handled first* IKUUNU *had lied. Ngie Ubo had been the witness and* ONKA *had taken the* 200 *Fr CFA earnest money.*

BALEWARI *sings two songs*: Listen you all; Listen to these declarations. [*He added that* ONKA *had then demanded 50,000 Fr CFA of* IKUUNU.]

IKUUNU: I did not know anything about this adultery. I had not given my daughter to Impiini.

NGANDAZIÕ *repeated the testimony of* NGWAMBAA *concerning this point and told* IKUUNU *and* OYUNI (*the wife's mother's brother*) *that if they continued their obstruction he would call* IMPIINI. *If he confirmed what* NGWAMBAA *had told,* IKUUNU *and* OYUNI *would be in the wrong*: and after that, you will still say that the chiefs are bad [*even though it is your own fault*].

NGWAMBAA: For this *iuula* business NGAALIÕ was there.

OKIÕ: My father did not receive anything from Impiini.

NGWAMBAA *and* BALEWARI *explain the first judgment about this to* NGANDZIÕ.

ONKA: Impiini gave 4,000 Fr CFA and two bottles of wine to Ikuunu. Now NGANDZIÕ you are the lord, what do you want? [*How will you set the fine for adultery?*]

AMVII: You Onka, you are mixed up in many cases. Have you ever seen a divorce in this court? You know that when a divorce case is complicated by adultery, the latter is a matter of little importance.

NGANDZIÕ *told* AMVII *that he was to leave the village in a few days* (*and could not see the matter dragged out*). *He turns to* ONKA *and talking about cases he had judged quotes*: A path without dew, is the one a man follows say the ancestors. Onka tell us, how much you want for a fine?.

ONKA *wants to speak* but NGAATALI *interrupts*: Listen Onka. . . . *He repeats what* NGANDZIÕ *said to hint that he should not ask too much.* [*The road without dew, is the road people usually take.*]

ONKA *angry*: Ah, all I say, you don't want anything about it.

MPAANI *sings*: *Ankani . . .* : Now all this is over. Onka you can speak. [*He advises* ONKA *as a Mother's brother to cool his temper and state the amount.*]

ONKA: First settle the adultery and the goat before we talk about the bride-wealth.

THE PEOPLE: That is true, that is good.

4. *Divorce: the matter of* tike.

NGANDZIÕ: An *uva* of 50 Fr CFA [*the usual amount*] had been given. Since everybody was not there, I'll explain the matter.

IKUUNU *explains that the 50 Fr CFA were for* uva.

NGANDZIÕ *refuses this interpretation.* OKIÕ *had paid the 50 Fr for* tike (tike *meant that the woman was asking for a divorce. Formerly* tike *was also called* uva, *like the first payment of bridewealth.* IKUUNU *was playing on words*). *He talked to* OKIÕ: If a man talks with a woman in the bush are you saying that you return home? No! (you have a lover). Why did you give *tike*? Did you not think ahead of time at home that you would have to pay *tike* and did you think that Onka's sister's son (Onkaana) would pay the bridewealth? You did not give *uva* but truly *tike*.

OKIÕ: I did not refuse my husband. When I stayed with him I was the wife of his sister's son. I am the wife of Onkaana. To stay with Onka is like two boys together. [*He is impotent.*] If he had said that the woman should go to Onkaana I would not be giving *tike*. If he agrees that I should stay with his sister's son, I withdraw *tike*. Moreover the 50 Fr CFA is not *tike*. Onka had obliged me to pay as *ipwooro*. Give me wine he said. I had given 50 Fr CFA for the wine (*ipwooro*). That is not *tike*. If I have to return to the husband, I can still accept this. [*She wants* ONKA *to divorce so her kin will not have to pay double the bridewealth back.*]

NGANDZIÕ *repeated what* ONKAANA *had told before. He no longer wanted the woman, there were too many disputes with her kinsfolk.* ONKAANA *had refused the woman*: If it is not like this, . . .

ONKAANA *reaffirms the statements made by* NGANDZIÕ *and refuses the woman*: Tell me Okiõ, what happened. We will tell it to the judges. There must be a yes or a no.

OKIÕ: Me and my husband are like a woman and her mother-in-law. I do not refuse my husband I gave him the wine, because he said I could not remain with two husbands.

NGANDZIÕ: You want to return to Onkaana?

OKIÕ: Yes.

NGANDZIÕ: If your mother's brother says: 'You want to go to Onkaana and I don't want to, what then?

OKIÕ: I am still on good terms with Onkaana.

NGANDZIÕ: And the 50 Fr CFA were the *tike*?

OKIÕ: No, the 50 Fr CFA was for the wine.

Interpretation

[*It is explained that if the husband refuses the woman he will give the* tike *but not the* uva, *which had been paid as first down payment on the bridewealth to the wife's father and symbolizes the bridewealth. If the woman refuses the husband, she must pay the* tike *and* uva. *Formerly the presence of* uva *made out who was refusing whom. If the woman asked for divorce the bridewealth would be doubled, otherwise the simple amount is paid.*]

5 *Establishing the divorce.*

NGANDZIÕ (*coming back*): Before we go on, get the 10,000 Fr CFA, otherwise I leave. [*He walks to his house. He fined the woman 10,000 Fr CFA so she would go back to* ONKA *to frighten her.*]

OKIÕ *refuses to pay.*

AMVII: For 10,000 Fr CFA you must call me behind the houses and tell me that you want 10,000 Fr CFA for this or that. As it is, in public, I can't give it.

NGANDZIÕ: Good. If there are no 10,000 Fr CFA I can't say a word.

NGWAMBAA: Here, when a *ngàà* cures someone, if the ill person does not heal, must the fee be given? [*In this case it must so the* ngàà *will continue the cure; they must pay so* NGANDZIÕ *will continue to judge.*]

NGANDZIÕ *to* ONKA: Where did you marry her?

ONKA: At her father's village.

NGANDZIÕ *to* OKIÕ: When lords talk, they do not talk wildly. That money, those 50 Fr CFA, which you have given to your husband, that is the *tike*. Was it not your plan to have Onkaana say: 'It is the wife of my mother's brother, it is he who gave her to me.' When they ask if you have given the *tike* you refuse the husband and Onkaana will then pay the bridewealth.

OKIÕ: They judged the matter in Mbe. I have been ill for ten days. Okaana said that I had been ill for ten days and that he would ask to get out of this. Otherwise he was leaving her to go to Etswali. After a while, if he found a job there building the road, he would have her called. But first he had to work so he could repay the bridewealth to her father. Once the money was there he would pay her father and her mother's brother. They would pay the father secretly. That was what Onkaana had told her.

ONKAANA: Tell the truth.

OKIÕ: Onkaana worked at Inoni. I went to visit him there. He had returned to Mbe, but could not find work there. When all was settled Onkaana refused me. I did pay *tike* so Onkaana would pay the bridewealth. He refused that too.

NGANDZIÕ: Onkaana also refused. Whether it be at the king's court or at Brazzaville or elsewhere a lord must always ask several times [*to know the truth*]. Onkaana had refused, saying that relations were not smooth with the relatives of the woman. Now if you had given me the 10,000 Fr CFA, I would have advised you well. [*He would have advised* ONKA *to keep quiet and to her to return to* ONKA.]

BALEWARI: Listen. Yesterday it was a matter of the child of Mpaani [*the woman* KIELIKO, *another divorce case*] and the woman took her husband again before the session of the court. But at the session she refused him nevertheless? You, Onkaana does not want you. If you have to return to your husband, will you refuse?

OKIÕ: If it is to return to Onka, I'd rather have my neck cut! ! !

NGANDZIÕ: All of you, see how I judge. If I lie, you would say that I only talked in favour of Onka (which is not true). We establish only who is in the right. I had refused all Onka's words. Now the matter of *tike* must be cleared up.

BALEWARI *wants to explain that there are three sorts of adulteries and payments, citing cases. But the audience stopped him from talking.*

NGANDZIÕ: Listen, Amvii and another one, Okiõ will go with you to *ipfuuna*.

OKIÕ: Nine years without knowing my husband and they still tell me to return!

IPFUUNA II. *Ipfuuna* for Okiõ:

Three times AMVII *asks her to drop the divorce suit. She refuses three times exclaiming finally*: Has the lord never seen a woman refuse her husband?

They return

AMVII *sings*: Tell your mother to find food for you; the family is broken up.

ONKA *answering sings*: The pole which grows roots is the strong pole.

AMVII: The woman refuses. She refuses because her husband gave her to his sister's son and that she had not known her husband since nine years. She has given *uva*. He will count the amount of the bridewealth. She added: 'Why must people suffer? The marriage was broken a long time ago. Have you never seen a woman refuse her husband?'

ONKA: I must return to the village to eat.

ALL: *Ah, non!* We will judge now.

6 *Settling the compensation for adultery.*

ONKA: You are going to settle this business for me. My wife refuses me. Bridewealth must be taken. [*He takes two sticks and puts them on the ground.*] That is for the adultery, that is for the goat. Once I see those payments I'll count the bridewealth.

IKUUNU: I accept for the goat, not for the adultery.

NGANDZIÕ: You can't refuse. It is the custom.

BALEWARI: Listen to me. There are three sorts of adulteries . . . [*The others interrupt but he finishes*]: Formerly then *tike* was what 'killed' people.

NGWAMBAA: *x speaking for* ONKA: 40,000 Fr CFA for the adultery.

He gives NGANDZIÕ *a stick.*

IKUUNU *recalls old cases to prove that in cases of divorce adulteries were not paid.*

ALL THE JUDGES: Ikuunu if you agree to pay, we continue; otherwise not.

NGANDZIÕ: If I was involved I would be very friendly with my father-in-law. For bridewealth is a good institution since there is *tike*. So the marriage will not break up lightly. 'The thing of anger is money.' Count the money first.

AMVII *repeats what* BALEWARI *said about the three ways in which there can be adultery. The others interrupt him as they had done with* BALEWARI.

THE OTHER JUDGES *to* IKUUNU: Take the sticks for the goat and the adultery and go to *ipfuuna*.

IKUUNU: This is not customary. [*But he picks* NGWAMBAA *and* BALEWARI *as advisors and goes.*]

IPFUUNA III. *Ipfuuna* for proposing compensation.

Present are IKUUNU, NGWAMBAA, BALEWARI, *and* MIANDOO. IKUUNU *proposed 5,000 Fr CFA for the adultery and 1,000 Fr CFA for the goat. The judges/advisers added 10,000 to make it 15,000 Fr CFA for adultery.*

They return. They want to send someone to go and kill a goat at NGAATALI's [*his settlement was half a mile or so away*] *but* ONKA *stops the messengers. Confusion.*

NGWAMBAA *explains the discussion at* Ipfuuna *and put sticks in front of* ONKA. *Since this was not the proper procedure* BALEWARI *took everything back and put it in front of the chief: one stick for the goat and three sticks of 5,000 Fr CFA each for the adultery.*

NGANDZIÕ *has it put in front of* ONKA. *Now the procedure is correct.*

ONKA: Can one buy a goat for just 1,000 Fr CFA?

THE OTHERS: No, that is not the question.

AMVII: Whether one pays a living goat or a goat in money is the same thing.

ONKA: Give me that back. I want a living goat and 30,000 Fr CFA.

NGAATALI: Onka when there is a divorce, does one ask 30,000 Fr CFA for an adultery?

NGANDZIÕ *annoyed*: Since you have adjudged 15,000 Fr CFA and since she has put the *tike* . . . adultery and divorce and ordinary adultery is not the same thing. At Djambala adultery is still different if the woman has confessed to the husband. In the *canton* of Djambala, in a case like this, they would already be counting the bridewealth. [*Adultery under the circumstances would not be thought very important there.*] But since you went to *ipfuuna* with a compensation estimated at 15,000 Fr CFA, that is too much in a case such as this. But my role is to add not to diminish the sum. I cannot do anything anymore now.

BALEWARI: Since we added, you should diminish.

NGANDZIÕ: Diminish how? Onka has seen the proposition. He would say that I am not impartial. And if I did this, all would blame me. For the goat he will give 1,500 Fr CFA. For the adultery Mpaani should judge.

ONKA *to his mother's brother* MPAANI: What did I do to the woman? Why always diminish the compensation? [*Angry he gets up and leaves.*]

OKIÕ: Good, if you don't settle the case, I leave and go where I want to. Nobody will have anything to reproach me with.

OYUNI *angry*: He gave his wife to his sister's son and now he wants a divorce. If he does not like this court, we will settle the matter at Djambala.

ONKA *comes back*: I will take the adultery at 25,000 Fr CFA.

THE WIFE'S FAMILY IN CHORUS: That we cannot accept.

MPAANI *who has taken the* onia *besom to judge* ONKA *who was walking around*: Onka, don't think that your mother's brother is going to save you. I have grown up in front of the eyes of NGAATALI, I cannot refuse NGAATALI's word; even when I am at Mbe I have to listen to NGAATALI.

ONKA *does not listen, but* MPAANI *goes on and talks about the case of* KIELIKO [*his daughter who was suing for divorce*]:

Now this court here is your court. If the lord rules, you must listen. There are many divorces. Today you speak, you receive compensation, they wake you up. All see how you are speaking. A matter about a woman is a matter of anger in your heart. Today it is your court. . . . When I give. . . . For an adultery before a divorce it is custom to take a small sum. You will say the price. Now you are talking in the forest [*wild talk*]. For the adultery you ask 40,000 Fr CFA. I do not refuse. . . . *Speaking to* NGANDZIÕ *he goes on*: For the adultery, I will judge. I say 10,000 Fr CFA adultery, and 2,500 Fr CFA for the court and let Onka count the bridewealth.

ONKA: The goat . . . I listened to my mother's brother. If there is a divorce, that the woman leave and if I come visit her she should prepare some food for me, because there are children between us. I want 20,000 Fr CFA for the adultery (so little because of the children).

AMVII: You always want to be right. Hõõ, hãã . . .

NGAATALI: You must listen to the words of others. Later you will marry here or at Uluuna. If you do not listen to anyone, nobody will want again to give you a girl in marriage.

ONKA: 15,000 Fr CFA and 2,500 Fr CFA for the lord; 12,500 Fr CFA for me.

NGAATALI: Count the bridewealth: 'The news from the father goes to the child, the news from the mother goes to the father.' [*A child follows the advice of his father and mother. The proverb was intended for* IKUUNU *to indicate the latter was wrong to take his daughter back.*]

MPAANI: 10,000 Fr CFA for the adultery, 2,500 Fr CFA for the lord; count the money that I see it.

The wife's party start a quarrel all talking at once.

ONKA: I want to count tomorrow.

THE OTHERS: No, count today.

ONKA: Tomorrow; I have not eaten.

THE OTHERS: Bring your list and the paper; we will settle tonight.

6 *Settling the amount of the bridewealth to be reimbursed.*[1]

Interruption. ONKA *left on his bicycle to fetch his accounts.*

IKUUNU: Good, let us count.

NGWAMBAA: First, pay the money for the court; each party 750 Fr CFA.

ONKA: Since I receive the money, it is good; otherwise I would die because of my wife.

IKUUNU *tries to make the 750 Fr CFA count as part of the sum awarded for the adultery of Impiini. It does not succeed. He gets up to fetch the money muttering to himself.*

NGANDZIÕ: Ikuunu, we are going to count the money now. You must tell the truth.

IKUUNU: All right.

The account of ONKA *is read, every point on it is discussed and the court writes down what the wife's family admits. There are discussions between* IKUUNU *and his wife, the mother of* OKIÕ, *and again between the latter and* OKIÕ. *Every person gives an account for the part of the bridewealth he or she has received in the order:* IKUUNU, *his wife,* OYUNI, NGAAYÜO *and the other brothers present of* OKIÕ. *This is also the order on the list of* ONKA.

One difficult case had to be settled. PIERRE, *brother of* OKIÕ, *had received 4,800 Fr CFA in tins of gunpowder to trade with in the then Belgian Congo. Must that amount also be doubled or not? They do not double it and take the amount CFA at the time for the commodity, not counting the benefit* [PIERRE *said he had sold at 1200 Fr. B. per tin which made 12,000 Fr CFA.*]

Follows the list of the other items as the court accepted them after much bargaining:

IKUUNU: 3,000 Fr CFA + one *ndzu anna* + six lengths of cloth + one goat or 1,100 Fr CFA.

IKUUNU'S MOTHER: 200 Fr CFA, one blanket and two lengths of cloth.

ANTSAANA (*brother of* OKIÕ): 3,500 Fr CFA and two lengths of cloth.

NGAAYÜO: 1,900 Fr CFA, One bit of a standard length of cloth and one length, one blanket . . . , two shirts, one repaired mosquito net.

[1] In this section and during the meeting of 1 March every utterance was no longer retained, since most of the talk was bargaining.

NGOKABI (*sister of* OKIÕ): 2,000 Fr CFA and one length of cloth.

ÕSHINU PIERRE (*brother of* OKIÕ): 4,800 Fr CFA for the gunpowder and one blanket.

MONGWO (OKIÕ's *mother's brother*): 3,500 Fr CFA and one blanket.

OYUNI: 1,500 FR CFA and one blanket.

The whole was set at 28,700 Fr CFA, thirteen lengths of cloth [with three bits counting for one], six blankets, two shirts, one ndzu anna, *one mosquito net [that was refused the next morning by the wife's kin]. The first of March the two shirts were evaluated at 700 Fr CFA together, so the money came to 29,400 Fr CFA, doubled making 58,000 Fr CFA.*

Before the meeting broke up three more reclamations were examined: NGAPELE (*son of* IKUUNU) *and* INGALI (*for whom they counted 900 Fr CFA*) *were absent. They are* mbalikali, *so this was not a matter for bridewealth. A man* NGEIBILI *received fifteen lengths of cloth, paid for him to the court at Mbe after a session of the court there. When the bridewealth would be repayed, and the date was set as of 15 April, the correctness of* ONKA's *assertion concerning this huge sum will be checked with* OKONDZAADZA *and other judges at Mbe.*

Then ONKA *announced he would claim 600,000 Fr CFA for the clothing given to his wife after marriage.* OKIÕ *protested that she had received only one wrapper since Queen Ngalifourou died.* NGANDZIÕ *asked both parties to pay* ikwor'onia: 'to catch something with the *onia* broom'. IKUUNU *and* ONKA *both paid 1,000 Fr CFA. (These are the court costs.)*

The next day the court assembled only at 14 h because the rain in the morning had broken up the meeting after it had barely started.

ONKA *asked for 700,000 Fr CFA for the clothes given to his wife shown by seven sticks on the ground.*

NGANDZIÕ *asked* NGAATALI *to judge and left,* ÕSHINU PIERRE *exclaimed that he never had seen such a demand.* BALEWARI, *angry gave him the sticks:* It is up to the judges to discuss the matter, not up to the parties. Even if the lord decided wrongly the judges would not accept it.

NGAAYÜO *helping* PIERRE: If you do not want to judge this, leave it then.

A general discussion followed.

MIANDOO: It is the work of the judges.

AMVII *told the woman's brother to stay put:* It is the lord and the elders who judge; don't fight like this. My sister divorced twice this way (by giving *tike*) and I found the money and it is finished.

BALEWARI: If it is too much one follows the customs and one diminishes. If Onka does not agree we will give you a testimonial. He'll go to another court even to Brazzaville if he wants to.

NGANDZIÕ *calls an* ipfuuna *for* ONKA.

Ipfuuna IV: *The amount of bridewealth to be asked by Onka. He left with* MPAANI *and* NGAATALI.

Coming back he falls back to 400,000 Fr CFA but asks to pay the adultery money first.

IKUUNU: If it is like that, wait until the day comes when we will be back with the whole wealth. Then we will see. [*If they did, there would be no longer any payment for adultery for the return of the bridewealth, even without the return of the clothing given by the husband ended the marriage and all their obligations.*]

ONKA *wants someone sent to Mbe to check on the fifteen lengths of cloth he paid there.*

IKUUNU: Let us pay half now of the remainder of the bridewealth and half when we come back. And we'll settle the fifteen lengths of cloth then.

MPAANI *to* ONKA, *angry:* The business is short. Now if you carry on like this again, I'll leave. [*He gets up, walks around and comes back.*]

IKUUNU: I dont have the money for the adultery. Once I have it, I will come back and we'll settle it then.

NGANDZIÕ *who was absent that morning sends a messenger to say that the money for the adultery must be paid first. Then the bridewealth will be settled. If necessary the wife's kin should despatch someone immediately to fetch the money to settle the adultery case.*

BALEWARI: You must take the 9,000 Fr CFA Ikuunu has [*four lengths of cloth and 5,000 Fr CFA cash*].

ONKA *takes it and all await* NGANDZIÕ. *But the judges take the money back: 2,500 Fr CFA for the court and 6,500 Fr CFA to* ONKA. *There remains to be paid another 3,500 Fr CFA.*

NGANDZIÕ *arrives.*

ONKA *repeats his demand for the clothing given to his wife and set at twice 200,000 Fr CFA or 400,000 Fr CFA.*

ONKAANA *counted 1,500 Fr CFA he had spent on the woman and one length of cloth for her sister* NGOKABI. *He wants to add this to* ONKA*'s demand. He also adds six lengths of cloth for the woman, and 200 Fr CFA given to* IKUUNU.

IKUUNU *accepted 1,000 Fr CFA of the 1,500 Fr CFA asked by* ONKAANA *but haggled over 100 Fr CFA in connexion with a demi john of wine sent to him by* ONKA.

BALEWARI *sings:* The thing that is given, are you looking for someone to inflict a fine?

NGANDZIÕ: The lord has no friends. If you bring him meat, he is a friend; if you bring him a case, he also agrees to hear it. You count 1,000 Fr CFA and seven lengths of cloth, Onkaana. But how [*by what right*] are you going to take them? What is the cause to take them? I will answer it [*there is no valid motive to the claim*]. If I have a younger brother and one of my wives stays with him; when the younger brother does not want her anymore, that she be given back to me. If the woman refuses the elder brother *and* the younger brother, one will start counting [the bridewealth]. The younger brother refuses the woman. Therefore he cannot double, since she does not refuse him. Moreover he cannot recover even the single amount! [*This referred to the relationship of* OKIÕ *and* OKAANA. *The latter had refused her first and in addition he was not the husband, so he had no real claim.*] The lengths of cloth and the money were gifts, not bridewealth. [*He refused* ONKAANA*'s demand and declared that* IKUUNU *would pay 1,000 Fr CFA but not the seven lengths of cloth.*]

The judges agreed.

OKIÕ: And even today, I am willing to go live with Onkaana.

They give the 1,000 1/2 CFA to ONKAANA.

ONKA *and* NGAAYÜO *start a violent discussion about the mosquito net, which is not acceptable and about a bicycle:*

NGAAYÜO: I had only borrowed his bicycle. The handle bars had been a bit damaged. Now he asks 1,500 Fr CFA for that, but he has not had the handlebars repaired.

The judges rule that since the handlebars were not repaired, the money cannot count. The bicycle cannot count.

BALEWARI: You must calculate the amount seriously. If Onka makes too much trouble, he will not remarry.

Meanwhile NGANDZIÕ *was off to inspect his motorbike. He came back and sent* ONKA *to* ipfuuna.

Ipfuuna V: *The amount of money for clothing to be asked by Onka*

On his return he proposed 125,000 or double 250,000 Fr CFA. The wife's kin asked ipfuuna.

Ipfuuna VI. *The amount of money for clothing to be ceded by Okiõ's kin.*

IKUUNU *started by declaring that there was only 56,400 Fr CFA instead of 58,800 Fr CFA for the bridewealth, or 55,000 Fr CFA without blankets or shirts.*

ONKA *sticks to 125,000 FR CFA for the clothing given and that is the sum not doubled.*

NGANDZIÕ *wants to send* ONKA *to* ipfuuna *again, but the latter refuses.*

NGANDZIÕ *takes up again the amount of 58,800 Fr CFA for the bridewealth.*

ONKA: For Kieliko, who was only married a few years [*and whose case had been settled recently*] they did pay much money. Here it must be much more. [*This marriage had held for fifteen years or more. He then left for* ipfuuna.]

Ipfuuna VII. *The amount of money to be asked for clothing by Onka.*

ONKA *on his return proposed for everything, bridewealth included 115,000 × 2 = 230,000 Fr CFA.*

The wife's kin went to ipfuuna.

Ipfuuna VIII. *The Amount of all costs of the divorce to be paid to Onka*

AMVII *announces they offer 60,000 Fr CFA doubled in all.*

NGANDZIÕ*'s secretary announces that is barely one length of cloth over the bridewealth. It is clearly not enough and there is a deadlock.*

NGANDZIÕ *follows a football match over his transistor radio; the others sit silent and sullen or listen to* MPAANI. *For thirty minutes* MPAANI *tells very well how* IKUUNI *refused to let him marry the latter's* otioolu *some time ago. But he had already received 3,000 Fr CFA as a gift. He must pay it back.* MPAANI *even tries to get the amount doubled. This will be the next case to be handled by the court.*

NGANDZIÕ: If you want to give the court your earnest money *itieeri* now, Mpaani, the court will tackle the case after this.

NGANDZIÕ: I will finish this case and all will go. We lords, if we are not clever, it won't do. In a marriage without children one cannot set 50,000 or 60,000 Fr CFA. When there are children. . . . When the woman has given *tike*, it is difficult. You the elders, you speak well. I listen. If you speak badly I see it too. Onka, if you win, it is thanks to me. As for your wife, that she is going to give you *tike*, if there had been no children we would all be famished [for the palaver could not be stopped, so huge would be the amount to pay]. Take the people, not their words. Onka you are lucky to get the bridewealth back for the woman. At my place they would not even give me that . . . I will speak. I, if one comes to court and there are children, I don't go to court. There is no way to talk too strongly about the woman. They [*the wife's people*] have planted 30,000 Fr CFA. When I say: you refuse, you will not say that my child has refused me. You will still be in the family. The woman refuses you, she has given *tike*. I cannot enter into the charms [*ãti*] of others. My wife and I we have made a charm for the children. The money that is best is children. Of the 60,000 Fr CFA I order 10,000 and 5,000 for the court. I have spoken.

ONKA: The children, that is good too.

BALEWARI: Make it short; we are hungry.

ONKA: For the 75,000 Fr CFA; the children are with it?

AMVII: For the adultery with that, it will make 80,000 Fr CFA. You can keep it all. For the children there is no problem. That will be arranged [*he must not give anything to the children and they will still recognize him as father, if he agrees to the sum*].

All start talking. Finally they add the six blankets without tike.

NGANDZIÕ: Pay half and go to *ipfuuna* to settle the day of payment.

Ipfuuna IX. *The Wife's kin settles the date for payment. Returning from* ipfuuna *they set the date of 15 April. They pay one out of the six blankets and the remaining 3,500 Fr CFA for the adultery.*

ONKA *agrees. Without a break the court then goes to the next case.*

The palaver was sitting as a court. One will notice that despite the apparent disorder the proceedings were structured and led by NGANDZIÕ who also rendered the decisions. From the example it can be realized how such a palaver could deal with any sort of matter and come to an acceptable decision for the parties involved. The procedural rules form a sort of Robert's Book of Rules flexible enough to be adapted to any circumstance in which decisions had to be reached.

APPENDIX No. 11

Okuu Cases

1 *Okuu for Mabumu, Mpilatsio, Waisolo*

A. *Actors:* Mabumu, Mpilatsio, Waisolo, children of Ngandziõ's full brother, being treated for madness by Ilanga Dominique, a *ngàà* from Uluuna.
Their 'fathers' Ngandziõ, Ubwoono, Angõ (a set of half brothers).
The *ngàà* Ilanga Dominique.
The Mother's brother Nduene.
The notables: Mbiinu Mbiinu (squire of Mbe), Okondzaadza, Mbali, NgeImpio Ba, Imã, Ngafula, Mpaani, Angõ.
Okuu held at Mbe 1 May 1964.

B. *Event*

Ngandziõ for the fathers: '*Ankana*, etc. When my brother died he left a wife and four children, two boys and two girls. Waisolo left his kin in the prefecture of Djambala. Ngandziõ asked him to come back. Ngandziõ later heard he was ill. Waisolo's mother's brother Nduene took care of him. Once he led Nduene, brought him to Ngandziõ. But after his mother's brother had been home for three weeks Waisolo fell ill. He was most days in the bush. When he came back he was mad.[1] They brought him to the *ngàà* Iooli, who specialized in

[1] This is exactly the way great *ngàà* find their calling. But not all lost madmen become *ngàà* as this shows.

treating madmen. Then Waisolo was healed. His sister who was at Brazzaville was lost. Mpilatsio then said: "I will go and kill the fathers, they have bewitched us." So when Ngandziõ heard the word "kill" he sent word to the *ngàà* Iooli that he should not bring Waisolo back to him, because we, the fathers, we are bewitching the children. He should be brought then to his elder brothers at Brazzaville.[2]

'A little while later Mpilatsio fell ill and became mad, after their mother had died at Brazzaville. Then Nduene who was their true mother's brother sent word to Ngandziõ: "Why did you turn my sister's sons away?" Ngandziõ answered that Nduene's sister's sons had turned their backs on them because they were witches. And even when their mother died, they did not send a note to Ngandziõ. And so he was unable to go to the mourning.

'A month later, around 2 am Mpilatsio knocked on my door. I opened. Since we saw the sick child all by himself, early in the morning, we called a *ngàà* to take care of him. When the illness grew and continued growing, Ngandziõ sent word to Nduene and the mother's brothers of the boy. Nduene said he would come. The other mother's brothers did not answer. The three fathers Ngandziõ, Ubwoono, and Angõ went to fetch another *ngàà*. Today, since you Nduene have come, you will make a good *okuu*[3] over my children, so the children will heal.'

Ipfuuna I: Ngandziõ, Ubwoono, Mbiinumbiinu and Okondzaadza went to one side. Coming back Ngandziõ gave 15 Fr CFA for 'the heads of the children' and a bottle of red wine. Then Okondzaadza repeated everything Ngandziõ had said.

Nduene for the mother's brothers: Nduene sang a song: *Isiese*, brother-in-law *isiese, isiese*, father *isiese*, (meaning he agreed). He then distributed a little of the red wine to all. All drank.

Ipfuuna II. Nduene, Okondzaadza, Mbali, Ba, Ngafula, Bilankwi, Ngeikieere. They stayed a long time. Nduene said: '*Ankana*, etc. and sang two songs: "butterfly come, I will take you away" and "the domain stays upright upright".'

Nduene: 'Ngandziõ, you are my brother-in-law. For your children there is no more root (no more *ndzo*). The witch, I am it, I their mother's brother. But I killed only my sister, their mother. For the children, that is finished today. Your children will heal, they will not die. When I speak all my *ikwii* are listening. It was me alone, nobody else. The younger people are "behind me". He spoke as he had done at previous *okuu*. He asked for a bowl of water from Mabumu and put pimento on Mpilatsio's face. Then he took a feather of the forest bird *nkoo*, *lisisõ*, an *opuuro* grass and pimento and mixed it and made a spot on the little *otsitiõ* tree which grows in front of Ngandziõ's house.

'He gave 50 Fr CFA to Mbiinumbiinu "for the heads of the children" and he gave *oshioonu* to the *ngàà* Ilanga Dominque.[4] Then he poured a bowl of water in front of the door of Ngandziõ and sang'.

After this Mpaani repeated all Nduene had said and okuu was ended.

[2] It is typical to see Brazzaville function as another Tio centre. All these relatives lived at Ouenzé in a few streets where all the plateau Tio live together as in a village in town.

[3] It is the father who calls for an *okuu*, but the mother's brother who performs it.

[4] *oshioonu* is this payment. The *ngàà* who is treating the sick person for whom *okuu* s performed, receives it. Usually it is a little stick.

C. *Comment*

This is a very typical *okuu* called in the proper way, for a sick child, even though it was not dangerously ill. The proper categories of persons were there (the squire and all the wardheads of Mbe even the secondary leaders!). The structure of the *okuu* also was typical. The fathers begin, end with *ipfuuna*, give the money for the 'head of the children'. Then the mother's brothers accept this, go to *ipfuuna*, make their speech, bless the sick person and give the pledge to the medicine man. In the second case all these elements are again found.

2. *Okuu* for Ndzaalindzali.

A. *Actors:* The younger brother of her second husband Miandoo, her husband Nkyino.
Her father NGAATALI, her son NGANDZIÕ.
Ndzaalindzali.
The *ngàà* treating Ndzaalindzali, Ikoli.
The uterine brother of the patient. About fifteen adults of the village.
At Imbãw, 28 February 1964.

B. *Background*

Ndzaalindzali had been ill for a long time and had done *itsuua* before. When her grandchild, the child of NGANDZIÕ died they gave a goat to NGAATALI. He refused it at first, accepted it later and sacrificed it to his *ikwii*.[1] A little later he had bad dreams involving her. A second goat was sacrificed and the second husband went to see a *ngàà* in the prefecture of Djambala. He put her in *itsuua*, but the illness did not end. So now she is at Imbãw under treatment by Ikoli.

C. *Events*

Miandoo speaks for the husband: 'Lioolo bwa, nkei akulu kiaa: stay quiet.[2] Ever since Ndzaalindzali was a girl, it was difficult for her to have children, but she had Ngokabi (absent from the *okuu*). She had consulted a *ngàà* who diagnosed *itsuua impuu* with a fever every four hours or so abating in the evening.[3] I was then *ngàà*. Around that time the former NGANDZIÕ died and she was to be inherited. But she refused the inheritance and married Nkyino, my younger brother. If his wife could not recover, one had to go far away.[4] But when she arrived at Nkyino's she was still ill. Nkyino did not have any family except me, who am his brother of the same father. Later we go to the *ngàà*. Nkyino is an orphan. So I say Ndzaalindzali must be healed by you (among us there is no

[1] This was done in serious cases for grown-ups. In 1964 for instance the mother's brother of a king's wife brought a goat to be sacrificed on the tombs of the king's *ikwii* as part of the *okuu*.

[2] The rest of the formula (*nkei akulu kiaa*) is not understood.

[3] This illness made a person become wan. The *ngàà* put leaves on the body of the patient, spit in the house, took the hands and executed a treatment with them. The cure was known as *mpuu* and the specialist as *ngàà mpunga*.

[4] Because only a foreign *ngàà* would make headway to find witches in the settlement where the leaders themselves were feeding on their charges.

witch and Nkyino had not paid the bridewealth yet). Otherwise, fathers take your daughter during the day, rather than letting her die at Nkyino's.'[5]

ipfuuna of the brother of Ndzaalindzali where he declared that he would give *intaaba shwè*, a special knot representing a goat. Coming back he could give this to NGAATALI. If the child still falls ill, we will go to the *ngàà*, otherwise you NGAATALI, you who have the *ikwii*, you will kill the goat. Ndzaalandzali must heal.' They came back from the *ipfuuna* with the *ngàà* who had gone with them.

The *ngàà* Ikoli said: *Ankana*, etc. and told what had been said at *ipfuuna* and then went on with a story about how he had asked all to come to *okuu* to find ways to cure the patient.

After this two persons complained that there was no wine to drink, as is the custom. The *nkieli*, who was representing the *ndzo* of the patient and had spoken at the *ipfuuna* said that he was tired about this *ndzo*, that the first time he came for *okuu*, he had told Ngamiele, the sister of NGANDZIÕ's father what to do. He had then complained to Ngamiele that she did not wish to recognize him as kin. She had acknowledged this and had given him 500 Fr CFA. And he had come for *okuu* then. But this *okuu* is the last he will come to. NGAATALI is the oldest and the squire (and he should protect people from witchcraft).

One of the spectators a certain Amviri retorted: 'Before you talk that way to NGAATALI, you must first advise your own family. Fetch the wine jug; come with that. When I must give kola nuts what is it with? It is NGAATALI who must give the wine and money to the *nkieli* so he can buy kola. That is the way we do it in our village. That is what I tell you.'

NGAATALI for the fathers: 'Who will loan me 500 Fr CFA here?' No one moves. He goes on: 'That child is mine. *Ngàà* you have well spoken. When that girl was with me she was healed. But now, it must be NGANDZIÕ who will ask his village [who will find the witch]. And here is 150 Fr CFA for the wine.[6] The *nkieli* gave him the goat's knot but NGAATALI refused it. The *ngàà* begged him to take it and finally he did.

Amvii said: 'They have given the knot of the goat so you NGAATALI at your village Ãtoro and you NGANDZIÕ at your Kwoli (both being Imbãw) will speak to your people. Balewari told NGAATALI he had received the knot of the goat because he was squire. He should advise the witch that he should go away now.

The *nkieli* told the husband of the patient to bring the bridal goods *itieeri* as soon as his sister was healed. Then he took a little earth, rubbed it on the body of his sister,[7] gave 100 Fr CFA as *oshioonu* to the *ngàà*. And the *okuu* ended.

D. Comments

This type of *okuu* involves the husband, who is the first responsible for his wife and has to call *okuu* and both sides of her kingroup. It is still her *mpfõ andzo* (her brother, here) who had to perform *okuu*. He did this essentially by promis-

[5] The usual expression for husbands of girl's fathers who accuse them implicitly of bewitching their daughers. In this case no bridewealth had been paid and it was felt this made it practically impossible for the husband to be suspected.

[6] He had been trying to get wine from us on the same day before the *okuu*. Obviously the 'Fathers' must give the wine.

[7] Normally ashes are used. But someone from another village could not use ashes.

ing a goat for sacrifice to the *ikwii* of the father, by giving the *ngàà* his pledge and by rubbing earth on his sister.

One also misses the self-accusation of the first example although it is very frequent in *okuu*. The fact of its absence is an index of greater suspicion between the mother's *ndzo* and the father's kin than if such an accusation had occurred. Clearly the brother believed NGAATALI was the witch. The latter accused someone in NGANDZIÕ's settlement, perhaps the husband or Miandoo, perhaps a 'political' witch from the outside.

The spectators play a more important role here than in the first *okuu*. This is typical. Despite the scenario all sorts of interruptions and discussions or comments involving spectators or even between spectators are allowed. The very flexibility of the inquest makes it much more convincing, than if it were just a formula.

Okuu was a strong moral help for the sick, who believed that the anointing by their *mpfõ andzo* could stop witchcraft, especially in cases where the witch 'confessed' and promised to relent.

APPENDIX No. 12

Succeession of the Kings since ILOO I

The following chart summarizes the information known. It is based on information received from descendants of all kings since Andibi, on the genealogy as presented by Ntsaalu, Ngateo, Okondzaadza, Mbiinu Mbiinu for Iloo, and Mbandieele, data which are corroborated by the indications collected by writers especially in the *dossier 90: archives chefferie Moyen Congo*, especially documents of 1934, and *Notice sur les Batékés*. Data for other kings come mostly from the same oral sources. The report of 18.VI.1934, which at first looked complete, turns out not to be trustworthy:

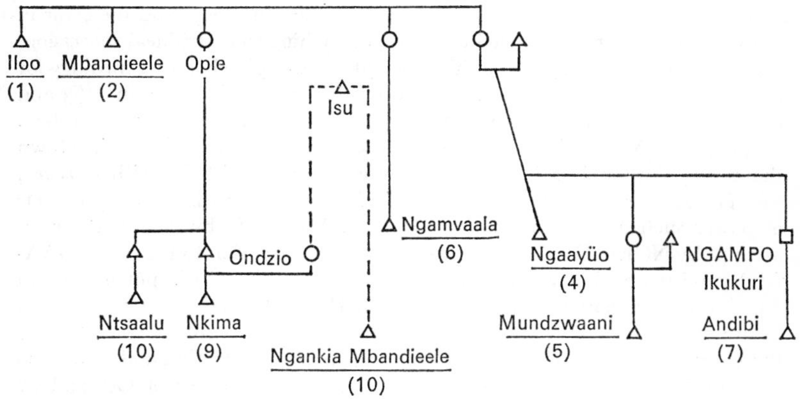

The ancestry of king Ikukuri, nicknamed Opfulipfa, is unknown. In fact his name was usually forgotten in lists of kings and this was already so in 1934. He was third in the list. As for Ngankia Mbandieele there is no visible link with Iloo at all, while the descendants of Andibi claim that he became king, not because of his link with Iloo but because his grand-parent had been king. That would have been Ngeilieele, and he would have ruled apparently before Iloo.

The vagueness of the genealogy becomes apparent when one realizes that it is said that kings Ngankia and Nkima were 'brothers' because they had a common *nkaa*, Isu, the famous MUIDZU installed by king Ngaayüo. In fact the link between Nkima and Ngankia seems to be the following:

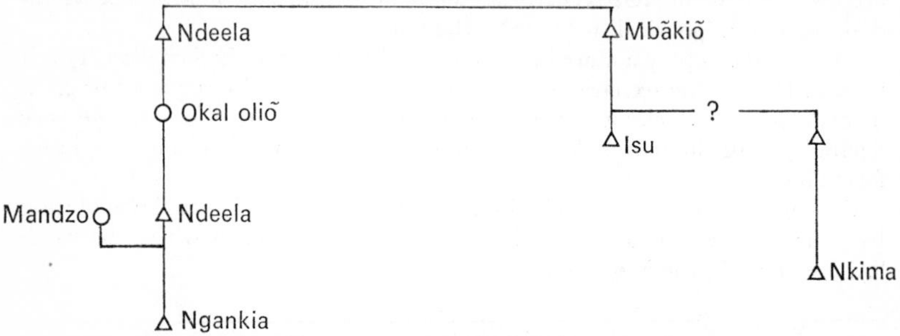

The connexion between Isu and Nkima is not even clear for although it is said Isu was Nkima's father's brother it may have been only a cousin. In any case the example shows for Ngankia how far the relationship was. Ambitious men can succeed by simply stressing that they are *mbwei* or *mwaana nkieli* or *otioolu* or *mwaana* without having to explain the degree of the relationship in detail.

Thus Ngankia succeeded because he was, the *Notice des Batékés* says, the 'police' of Andibi, not because he was closest in line for the succession. It was said that the soul of Andibi had appeared in dreams to the notables to designate Ngankia!

The fact that the succession was a combination of rights based on descent and sheer power play explains the vagaries in the genealogy, and the error in the 1934 document which tried to reduce everything to matrilineal succession. The Tio must have helped, since they invented a completely false genealogy for Ngankia Mbandieele's mother. His two brothers were still living in 1963 and from their genealogies (they were full brothers) the truth could be established.

A collation of what is known about the successions to the titles of the crown shows very similar situations. The successors can all be listed as either *nnaana*, *mbwei* or *mwaana nkieli* or *mwaana* or *otioolu*. But some successions were pure acts of power such as the nomination of Isu as MUIDZU by Ngaayüo, or an attempt by NGEILIINO Ngwomba to alter the succession to the title NGAALIÕ, an attempt that was foiled, just as the NGANDZIÕ did not succeed in appointing the man of his choice as NGEILIINO after Opontaba's death before 1896. The essential bilateral character of the successions comes out in the cases. Thus the NGEILIINO's succession went from Opontaba to Mpo aTaanu (relationship unknown). The latter was the father of Oshiambãw who was the mother's brother of Mpiere, alias Ngwomba who was the elder brother of Ngulangu. NGOBILA Ngantiene (who was the one living in 1880) had taken over from his 'mad' brother who had taken over from his *nkaa* and he was succeeded by his son Nkia. *Nkaa*'s would be all sorts. For MOTIIRI it was his father's father, for NGAMBIÕ it was his mother's father who did not want to leave the function to a girl, his daughter, and waited for his grandson.

For some titles as for kingship several gates are mentioned. In the situation of the title NGAMPO it was said that Ikukuri introduced a new 'gate' after he had stolen the *nkobi*. For MUIDZU too there were two gates and although the declarations are confused the situation was imputed to a MUIDZU living before the time of Iloo. Therefore it is likely that the 'gates' given for kingship also reflect rather summary take-overs.

The kings since Iloo all claimed origins in the Ndua forest, except Ngankia Mbandieele and Nkima who claimed the forest Ikie (through their common *nkaa* Isu!) as did Mundzwaani. Ngamvaala claimed Mbe andzieli. And *Notice sur les Batékés* specifically claimed that the latter had been nominated by the Commandant de Cercle without consulting the 'notables'. When talking about this at Mbe, it was moreover made clear that all the 'exceptions' could also claim descent through Ndua.

If anything, the effect of colonial rule upon succession practices seems to have been to prevent power plays and therefore to 'regularize' the successions. With regard to the crown this is not evident and all we know tends to indicate that succession before Iloo was neither more nor less 'regular' than after him. It teaches us also to be careful not to take tradition literally when it claims that the father and the grandfather of Iloo (and of Andibi!) have been kings.

The data about successions clarify how it was possible to come to situations like the one in 1880 when all major titles were in the hands of close kin of Iloo.

APPENDIX No. 13

Nzã Mbã: The nkobi*; war with the Jiju; the migration of the Ngenge*

By Eloge Dominique who heard it from Libara at Ibu, who is supposed to be the oldest person living on the Ntsaa plateau in 1963. Written down in French and Tio by Ngaayüo Bernard.

The story of Mvulibari or Nzã Mbã

The first Nzã Mbã was at Abili. He had his *nkira* in the wood of Abili. He was more powerful than all the Tio. NGIA saw how Nzã Mbã ruled over the whole country. And he brought him twelve *nkobi*, Nzã Mbã had eleven children and one child of his younger brother. All the children, there were twelve too. He divided twelve *nkobi* among his twelve children. The child of his little brother was called Mbã. He took his *nkobi* to Ndoolo to rule over the Jiju. One *nkobi* went to Akwi, one to *nkobi* to Ntsaa, one *nkobi* to Nkwũ, one *nkobi* to Mpiina Ntsa I, one *nkobi* to Mbe, one *nkobi* to Mbe Isala, one *nkobi* at Uluuna, one *nkobi* at Ãndzio, and the three other *nkobi* he (the story-teller) did not remember any more.

Nzã Mbã distributed all the twelve *nkobi* and gave the limits to each *nkobi*. After that Nzã Mbã called the twelve lords. When all the lords had arrived Nzã Mbã said that they were to choose a king. Among the twelve children Mbã of Ndoolo was absent. He had refused to come.

When everyone had gone back to their village and some time had elapsed

Mbã went some time afterwards to catch the Ngenge of the Belgian Congo.[1] The Ngenge have fled their settlement behind the village of Mbã. After this leaving no one, even if it were five or six hours after he had fled, could enter the village of the Ngenge again. If someone entered he could be killed and eaten.[2] Mbã stayed behind. He went after the people of Aba, killed some and burned the village. Now MUIDZU asked of his father Nzã Mbã: 'Why does Mbã come to make war in my land.' Nzã Mbã answered: 'He is the child left by my younger brother. I am powerless.'

After this Mbã went again to catch people at the village of Akwi. The leader of Akwi sent a message to Ntsaa and Nkwũ saying: 'Mbã attacks the leader of Akwi.' Now then, when Mbã attacked Akwi, the leader of Akwi and his people saved themselves thanks to his charms. When they had made a circle with the men and the leader of Akwi in it, the others (of Mbã) also formed a circle and began to shoot their guns.[3] When the gunners of Mbã had no more powder they sent a man to say that they had come to see if they (the people of Akwi) were strong.

So, when the lords of Ntsaa and Nkwũ arrived with their people (to help Akwi) the leader of Akwi said: 'They came to try me out.' And the two lords told him to leave Mbã, otherwise he was going to kill them (the people of Akwi) all.

Then, when they had left Akwi the children went to tell their father Nzã Mbã that they would wage war on Mbã. Nzã Mbã answered that he was the child left by his younger brother and paradoxically he had more power even than Nzã Mbã. So if they wanted to, all the children should bring each his men and each man his gun. Every *mpfõ* brought 5,000, 6,000, even 7,000 men.[4] When all were assembled with their guns Nzã Mbã said: 'Let us see if there are many persons assembled for the war', and they danced *Iboolo*.[5] When they had danced, there was an earthquake[6] and more than ten persons died trampled under the feet of the crowd.

Now then a councillor of Nzã Mbã said: 'If we go over there, all will find their death.' And because this councillor was a true *ngàà*, who can take the forest away, he was listened to. This councillor told Nzã Mbã: 'To wage war on Mbã, I must go ahead and you will give me all I ask: a staff with copper rings spiralling around it, a wrapper *ndzu a nna* with a red border, a knife that cuts with both sides, and a flywhisk.' Having taken all these things the councillor went to Ndoolo at Mbã's and arriving near his residence, the man became a very beautiful woman. She arrived in the village and asked where the house of the councillor of Mbã was. When they had pointed it out to her, she entered. The councillor of Mbã asked what her business was and she said: 'I was the wife of Nzã Mbã but he divorced me, now I come as *õke ampu* to Mbã.'

He told her to show what she had received there if she had been Nzã Mbã's wife and the poor woman showed all the objects she had received from

[1] The designation like many others is an anachronism.

[2] This becomes clear from the notes of the seventeenth century by Montesarchio and Caltanisetta. Enemy warriors were eaten.

[3] Again guns are an anachronism. The type of fighting seems to be typical for the nineteenth century.

[4] The numbers are poetic. Later numbers are expressed in hundreds and seem still overdone, but not so much.

[5] *Iboolo* was a dance performed just before going into war or battle.

[6] An earthquake provoked by the dancing of so many people.

Nzã Mbã. When the councillor saw this he went to tell Mbã that this woman had been at his father's Nzã Mbã and now came to him as *õke ampu* and that he should not take a wife of his father. Mbã refused saying: 'No, I must keep her. Let her come.' When the woman came he told all his wives to sleep at their houses, for he was to spend the night with the new woman. As the woman was a *ngàà* she had relations with him and he slept deeply. When midnight had arrived the woman got up and through the mystery of the magician she asked him when he was sleeping: 'When there is a battle against the enemies what do you take with you?' He said: 'When there is a battle I take my knife and two *kaa* tied with a black cloth with two *nki andzo* and the skin of the civet cat.' The woman took all these things and fled with them that very same night and transformed herself into a man. He was on his way long before dawn. When the morning came the favourite wife of Mbã asked herself why he had not awakened yet. The councillor of Mbã said that it was because he had a new wife. The favourite went to open the house and thus woke Mbã. Waking up he looked at the roof and saw that all the objects were gone and the woman too. So he ordered a pursuit.

When they ran after the woman they met the man and asked him if he had seen a woman on the road. He said 'No'. They asked him where he came from. He answered that he came from this small village and offered to join them in the pursuit. He ran behind them and finally they told him that they were tired and returned. He said that he would continue on his way. They came back and told Mbã that they had not seen the woman.

The councillor of Nzã Mbã told him: 'Give me two women' and I will tell you. He received two women and said: 'The charms of Mbã should kill us all. Before we start the battle with Mbã we must cut a palm-tree and everyone must trample it.' They put the palm-tree in front of the village on the way by which they were to leave. When they awoke around two in the morning, the youngest of his (Nzã Mbã's) children had already gone with his men and they went too trampling the palm-tree. The tree became like straw after all those people had passed over it.

When they arrived about ten kilometres from Mbã they camped and sent a man to Mbã to tell him that they had come to wage war upon him. And at five in the morning Nzã Mbã heard the guns resound at Mbã's and he asked: 'But who is that at Mbã's?' The other children said that it was the youngest child. He had gone with 500 people, he came back with 200 people. He told Nzã Mbã: 'Over there things do not look good.' Another child went with 600 people and came back with 400 people. He too said that Mbã would finish off all the people. The one from Mbe brought 800 persons and came back with 700. When he returned saying that it was of no avail they all went.

When they arrived a true war broke out. When Mbã was about to kill the one (lord) of Mbe he was changed into a woman. Mbã pulled her up and told his men to take that woman and to send her behind the lines. But the lord of Mbe answered that it was he who had been sent behind the lines and not a woman, and killed Mbã. He then returned to his father saying that he had slain him. Nzã Mbã would not believe him and asked for proof. He went back to cut off the arm of Mbã which had already lost a little finger (and could be

[7] The role of the lord as giver of women is very clear here.

identified). He brought it to Nzã Mbã who looked at the little finger which was cut off and believed it.

Because of these wars the Jiju do not get along with the Boõ because of their lord Mbã which the Boõ killed.

After the war they returned to the village of Nzã Mbã at Abili. On the way back they went to the country of the Ngenge. When they arrived there they made a census. If there were two people in the house they put[8] two; if they see five, they put also five persons, and so on until the end of the census and the Ngenge said that these men had come to kill them and not in friendship and their lord told his people to go and kill Nzã Mbã in the house of the lord of the Ngenge. They killed Nzã Mbã and the latter's men shouted: 'We are quiet and our lord Nzã Mbã is already killed.' And they in turn killed the lord of the Ngenge and the war began.

When the men (Ngenge) had suffered many losses they were compelled to cross the river Congo. When they had finished crossing like slaves, the corpse of Nzã Mbã was brought back to Abili and was buried there. At the spot where he is buried two people could not go without fighting among themselves, for he was fierce and his charms still resisted. But this is how the Ngenge went to the Congo; otherwise they were in the French Congo.[9] That is why they say they are Tio and now no one has taken over his power, because when the lord died in the war he had no time to explain his chiefly power so that people could take over.[10] And thus people have diminished on the Tio plains.[11]

[8] 'They put.' There is no indication of how this census was recorded. This is the only indication we found of any census taking in pre-colonial Tio society.

[9] The text states just the contrary. But the meaning is clear. The Ngenge now live on the bank of the Democratic Republic of Congo.

[10] This shows how Tio feel about the nature of lordly authority. The next sentence could equally well apply to the loss of people caused by the departure of the Ngenge or as an effect of lordly power running amok since no person could control it any longer. His power is the title of Nzã Mbã which did disappear and not that of the Ngenge who still have lords.

[11] The text is the only really long tradition encountered, except for one other text. Both dealt with wars and magic. It is obvious that this was remembered for its aetiological explanations (e.g. about the *nkobi*) but also and mainly for its value as a story.

Reference Material

I. *Printed sources*

ADAM, J., 'Note sur les variations phonétiques dans les dialectes batéké', *Première Conference internationale des Africanistes de l'Ouest, Comptes Rendus,* 1951, T.11, pp. 153–65.

ALLAIN, M., *Encyclopédie pratique illustrée des colonies françaises,* Paris, 1931, 2 vols.

AMIN, SAMIR et COQUERY-VIDROVITCH, C., *Histoire économique du Congo,* 1880–1968, Dakar/Paris, 1969.

ANDERSSON, E., *Contribution à l'ethnographie des Kuta* (Studia Ethnographica Uppsaliensia, VI), Uppsala, 1953.

ATRI, *see* D'ATRI.

AUGOUARD, P., 'A la suite de Mm. Stanley et de Brazza', *Missions Catholiques,* 1883, XV, pp. 37–42.

AUGOUARD, P., 'Journal de voyage de Brazzaville à l'Equateur', *Missions Catholiques,* 1886, XVIII, pp. 10–12, 17–21, 28–9, 56–7, 69–71, 80–3, 93–6, 103–6.

AUGOUARD, P. (Mgr.), *Trente six années en Afrique,* Poitiers, 1925.

AUGOUARD, P., 'Le voyage à Stanley Pool', *Missions Catholiques,* 1881, XIII, pp. 517–18; 1882, XIV, pp. 100, 113–16; 125–8, 140–1. Most of the text reprinted in D. NEUVILLE, CH. BREARD, Cf., below.

AVELOT, R., 'Les grands mouvements des peuples en Afrique; Jaga et Zimba', *Bulletin de géographie historique et descriptive,* 1912, XXVII, pp. 75–216.

BABET, V., 'Exploration de la partie méridionale des plateaux batékés', *Bulletin du Service des mines de l'A.E.F.,* 1957, No. 3, pp. 21–56.

BAL, W. ed., PIGAFETTA F., LOPES (1591), *Description du Royaume de Congo et des contrées avoisinantes,* Paris, 1965.

BALLAY, N., 'De l'Ogooué au Congo', *Bulletin de la société de géographie de Marseille,* 1885, IX, pp. 277–89.

BARBOT, J., *Voyage to the Congo River or the Zaire in the year 1700.* J. CHURCHILL, *A Collection of Voyages and Travels,* London, 1732, vol. V, pp. 499–522 (also in Pinkerton's Travels, London, vol. 16).

BASCOULERGUE, BERGOT, J., *L'alimentation rurale au Moyen-Congo,* Brazzaville, 1959 (A.E.F.: Service commun de la lutte contre les grandes endémies: Section nutrition).

BASTIAN, A., *Die deutsche Expedition an die Loango Küste,* Iena, 1874, 2 vols.

BASTIAN, A., *Ein Besuch in San Salvador,* Bremen, 1859.

BENTLEY, W. H., *Pioneering on the Congo,* London, 1900, 2 vols.

BITTREMIEUX, L., 'Enkele aantekeningen over de te weinig bekende Batéké's', *Congo,* 1936, II, 5, pp. 663–7.

BONGOLO, H., 'A propos des "coutumes indigènes dans la cité de Léopoldville" ', *Bulletin du C.E.P.S.I.,* 1947, XLVII, 5, pp. 36–6 (later in *Voix du Congolais,* 1948, IV, 22, pp. 16–19, and XXIII, pp. 55–60).

BONNAFE, P., *Un aspect religieux de l'idéologie lignagère. Le nkira des Kukuya du Congo-Brazzeville,* Paris, 1969. (Document de travail No. 1. Laboratoire de sociologie et de géographie africaines. I.A. No. 94.) (stencilled.)

BONTINCK, F., *Diaire Congolais (1690–1701)*, Leuven, 1970.

BOUVEIGNES, *see* DE BOUVEIGNES.

BRASIO, A., *Monumenta Missionaria Africana (Africa Ocidental)*, Lisbon, 1952–64, X + III vols.

BRUEL, G., *L'Afrique Equatoriale Française*, Paris, 1918.

BRUNSCHWIG, H., *Brazza l'explorateur. L'Ogooué 1875–1879*, Paris, 1966.

BRUNSCHWIG, H., 'Les Cahiers de Brazza (1880–1882)', *Cahiers d'Etudes Africaines*, 1966, 22, vol. VI, 2⁰, pp. 157–227.

BRUNSCHWIG, H., 'La négociation du traité Makoko', *Cahiers d'Etudes Africaines*, 1965, No. 17, vol. V, pp. 5–56.

BRYAN, M. A., *The Bantu Languages of Africa*, London, 1959.

BUETTNER, R., 'Die Congo Expedition', *Mittheilungen der Afrikanischen Gesellschaft*, 1886–9, IV–V, pp. 168–271.

BUETTNER, R., *Reisen im Kongolande*, Leipzig, 1890.

BURTON, R. F., *Two Trips to Gorilla Land and the Cataracts of the Congo*, London, 1876, 2 vols.

CALLOC'H, J., *Vocabulaire Français-Ifumu (Bateke), précédé d'éléments de grammaire* Paris, 1911.

CALTANISETTA, *see* DA CALTANISETTA.

CAMBIER, E., Lettre-*Revue illustrée des missions en Chine et au Congo*, 1889, vol. I, No. 8, p. 128; No. 11, p. 157.

CORDEIRO, L., ed., CASTELLO BRANCO, GARCIA MONDES DE — *: 1574–1620 Da Mina ao Cabo Negro*, Lisbon, 1881.

CASTEX, Dr., 'Vocabulaire comparé des principaux dialectes ayant actuellement cours en Haut-Ogooué', *Bulletin de la société de recherches Congolaises*, 1938, No. 26, pp. 23–54.

CAVAZZI, Gio Antonio (da Montecuccolo), *Istorica Descrizione dei tre regni: Congo, Matamba e Angola*, Bologna, 1687, German Translation, Munich, 1694; Portuguese translation by GRAZIANO DA LEGUZZANO, Lisbon, 1965, 2 vols.

CHABEUF, M., 'Anthropologie physique du Moyen-Congo et du Gabon méridional', *Bulletin et Mémoires de la société d'Anthropologie*, Paris, 1959, X (X), 2, pp. 97–185.

CHAPEAUX, A., *Le Congo historique, diplomatique, physique*, Brussels, 1894.

CHAVANNES, *see* DE CHAVANNES.

Chef de la circonscription du Djoué, 'Les marchés indigènes de la circonscription du Djoué en 1916', *Bulletin de l'Institut d'Etudes Centr'africaines*, 1956, II, pp. 91–109.

COART, E., DE HAULLEVILLE, A., *La céramique*, Brussels, 1907 (Annales du Musée du Congo. Série III–II, Fasc. I).

COART, E., DE HAULLEVILLE, A., *La religion*, Brussels, 1906 (Annales du Musée du Congo, Série III–I, Fasc. 2).

COQUERY-VIDROVITCH, C., *Brazza et la prise de possession du Congo (1883–1885)*, Paris, 1969.

COQUILHAT, C., *Sur le Haut Congo*, Brussels, 1888.

COURBOIN, A., *Bangala. Langue commerciale du Haut Congo*, Paris, 1908.

CUREAU, A., *Les sociétés primitives de l'Afrique Equatoriale*, Paris, 1925.

CURTIN, P. H., *The Atlantic Slave Trade: A Census*, Madison, 1969.

CUVELIER, J., *L'ancien royaume du Congo*, Brussels, 1946.

CUVELIER, J., 'Traditions congolaises', *Congo*, 1930, II, No. 4, pp. 469–87.

CUVELIER, J. (Mgr.), JADIN, L., *L'Ancien Congo d'après les archives romaines (1518–1640)*, Brussels, 1954. (Mémoires de l'Académie Royale des Sciences d'Outre-Mer. Classes des sciences morales et politiques, XXXVI, Fasc. 2.)

DA CALTANISETTA, LUCA., 'Relation sur le royaume de Congo 1690–1700', *Cahiers Ngonge*, 1960, No. 6 (a summary: complete text by F. BONTINCK).

DAPPER, O., *Naukeurige Beschrijvinghe der Afrikaensche gewesten*, Amsterdam, 1668.

D'ARTEVELLE, E., *Les N'Zimbu, monnaie du royaume du Congo*, Brussels, 1953.

D'ATRI, Marcellino, 'Relation sur le royaume du Congo, 1690–1700', *Cahiers Ngonge*, 1960, No. 5 (a summary).

DE BOUVEIGNES, O., 'Jérôme de Montesarchio et la découverte du Stanley-Pool', *Zaire*, 1948, vol. II, No. 9, pp. 989–1013.

DE BOUVEIGNES, O., CUVELIER, J. (Mgr.), *Jérôme de Montesarchio, Apôtre du vieux Congo*, Namur, 1951.

DE CHAVANNES, CH., *Avec Brazza. Souvenirs de la Mission de l'Ouest Africain. Mars 1883–Janvier 1886*, Paris, 1935.

DE CHAVANNES, CH., *Le Congo Français et ma collaboration avec Brazza 1886–1894. Nos relations jusqu'à sa mort 1905*, Paris, 1937.

DE CHAVANNES, CH., 'Voyage dans l'Ouest—Africain', *Bulletin de la Société de Géographie de Lyon*, 1886–7, VI, pp. 65–96.

DE DEKEN, C., *Deux ans au Congo*, Missions de la Chine et du Congo, 1897, pp. 438–42.

DEGRANPRE, L., *Voyage à la côte occidentale d'Afrique fait dans les années 1786 et 1787*, Paris, 1801, 2 vols.

DELAFOSSE, M., POUTRIN, Dr., *Enquête coloniale dans l'Afrique Française Occidentale et Equatoriale sur l'organisation de la famille indigène, les fiançailles, le mariage*, Paris, 1930.

DELCOMMUNE, A., *Vingt années de vie africaine*, Brussels, 1922, 2 vols.

DELGADO, R., *História de Angola*, Benguela/Lobito, 1948–55, 4 vols.

DE MARTRIN DONOS, CH., *Les Belges en afrique centrale*, Brussels, 1886, 3 vols.

DEMETZ, H., 'Les poteries des peuplades Batékés du Moyen-Congo', *Première Conférence Internationale des Africanistes de l'Ouest, Comptes Rendus*, 1951, vol. II, pp. 260–71.

DE PLAEN, G., *Les structures d'autorité des Bayanzi*, Leuven, 1969 (stencilled).

DE SOUSBERGHE, L., *Structures de parenté et d'alliance d'après les formules pende*, Brussels, 1955 (Mémoires de l'Académie Royale des Sciences d'Outre-Mer. Classe des sciences morales et politiques, NS. IV, Fasc. 1.)

DE WITTE, J., *Vie de Mgr. Augouard*, Paris, 1924.

DOLISIE, A., 'Notice sur les chefs batéké', *Bulletin de la Société de Recherches Congolaises*, 1927, VIII, pp. 44–9.

DOUGLAS, M., *The Lele of the Kasai*, London, 1963.

DUPONT, E., *Lettres sur le Congo*, Paris, 1889.

D'UZES (Duchess), *Le voyage de mon fils au Congo*, Paris, 1894.

DYBOWSKI, J., *La route du Tchad, du Loango au Chari*, Paris, 1893.

EMPHOUX, J. P., 'Un site de Proto et Préhistoire au Congo (Brazzaville): MAFAMBA', *Cahiers O.R.S.T.O.M.*, vol. II, No. 4, 1965, pp. 89–95.

ERNOULT, J., *Afrique d'hier et aujourd'hui: La République du Congo*, Brazzaville, 1961.

FELNER, A. A., *Angola*, Coimbra, 1933.

FROMENT, E., 'Trois affluents français du Congo: rivières Alima, Likouala, Sanga', *Bulletin de la Société de Géographie de Lille*, 1887, VII, pp. 458–74.

FROMENT, E., 'Un voyage dans l'Oubangui. De Lirranga à Modzaka', *Bulletin de la Société de Géographie de Lille*, 1889, II, pp. 180–216.

FU-KIAU kia Bunseki-Lumanisa, A., *N'Kongo ye Nza vakun'zungidila* (*Le Mukongo et le monde qui l'entourait*), Kinshasa, 1969.

GHYS, J., 'Étude agricole de la region batéké, batende, baboma', *Bulletin Agricole du Congo Belge*, 1934, XXV, pp. 114–27.

GOODY, J., *The Social Organization of the LoWiili*, Oxford, 1967 (2nd ed.).

GOUROU, P., 'Carte de la densité de la population', *Atlas du Congo Belge et du Ruanda Urundi*, Brussels, 1959, index No. 624.

GRAY, R., 'Eclipse Maps', *Journal of African History*, 1965, VI, 3, pp. 251–62.

GUIRAL, L., *Le Congo Français*, Paris, 1889.

GUTHRIE, M., *The Bantu Languages of Western Equatorial Africa*, London, 1953.

GUTHRIE, M., *The Classification of the Bantu Languages*, London, 1948.

HANSSENS, E., 'Les premières explorations du Haut Congo. Lettres inédites du capitaine Hanssens', *Le Congo illustré*, 1892, vol. I, pp. 5–7, 13–15b, 29–31, 37–9, 45–7.

HERMANT, P., 'Les coutumes familiales des peuplades habitant l'Etat Indépendant du Congo', *Bulletin de la société royale belge de géographie*, Brussels, 1906, XXX, pp. 149–73, 283–98, 407–38.

HOTTOT, R., 'Nomadism among the Bateke tribes', *Congrès international des sciences anthropologiques et ethnologiques, 1938*, Copenhagen, 1939, pp. 264–5.

HOTTOT, R., WILLETT, F., 'Teke Fetishes', *Journal of the Royal Anthropological Institute*, 1956, LXXXVI, I, pp. 25–36.

H.L., *Pêche*-Encyclopédie mensuelle d'Outre Mer, 1952, III, I, 27, pp. 335–8.

IBALICO, M., 'M'pouya kou M'Foumou, une dynastie qui se meurt', *Liaison*, 1954, No. 43, pp. 49–52.

IBALICO, M., 'L'origine des Batéké d'Impila', *Liaison*, 1955, No. 46, pp. 37–9.

IBALICO, M., 'Origine et sens des noms batéké', *Liaison*, 1956, No. 52, pp. 29–33, No. 53, pp. 41–4 (in continuation; see next entry).

IBALICO, M., 'La thérapeutique en fonction des noms', *Liaison*, 1957, No. 54, pp. 17–21 (end of preceding).

IBALICO, M., 'Ou il est question du royaume des Anzicou et de la station de Ncouna', *Liaison*, 1954, No. 44, pp. 65–8.

IBALICO, M., 'Quand et comment on devient Makoko', *Liaison*, 1955, No. 45, pp. 30–2.

IHLE, A., *Das Alte Königreich Kongo*, Leipzig, 1929.

JACQUOT, A., 'Précision sur l'inventaire des langues teke du Congo', *Cahiers d'Etudes Africaines*, 1965, 18, vol. 5, pp. 335–40.

JADIN, L., 'La Congo et la secte des Antoniens. Restauration du royaume sous Pedro IV et la "Sainte Antoine" congolaise (1694–1718)', *Bulletin de l'institut historique belge de Rome*, 1961, XXXIII, pp. 411–615.

JEANNEST, CH., *Quatre années au Congo*, Paris, 1883.

JOHNSTON, H. H., *The River Congo from its Mouth to Bolobo*, London, 1884.

JOHNSTON, H. H., *George Grenfell and the Congo*, London, 1908, 2 vols.

Le journal officiel, 3 December 1882. Text of the Treaty between France and Makoko.

JUNG, R., 'Piège à porc-epic', *Journal de la société des africanistes*, 1948, XVIII, pp. 129–33.

KJERSMEIER, R., *Centres de style de la sculpture nègre africaine*, Paris, 1937, vol. III.

KOELLE, S. W., *Polyglotta Africana*, London, 1854 ed., Freetown, 1963 (P. E. H. HAIR, D. DALBY, eds.).

LAIGRET, J., 'De quelques coutumes indigènes concernant les accouchements', *Bulletin de la Société des Recherches Congolaises*, 1925, VI, pp. 11–14.

LAMAN, K. E., *The Kongo*, Stockholm, 1953–62, 3 vols. (Studia Ethnographica Uppsalensia, XII).

LEBEUF, A., 'Aspects de la royauté Batéké (Moyen-Congo)', *Selected Papers of the International Congress of anthropological and ethnological sciences, 1960*. Philadelphia, 1961, pp. 453–67.

LEBEUF, A., 'Le rôle de la femme dans l'organisation politique des sociétés africaines', D. PAULME, ed., *Femmes d'Afrique*, Paris, 1960, pp. 93–119.

LEM, F. H., 'L'art de l'Afrique centrale', GUERNIER, E. (ed.), *L'Encyclopédie coloniale et maritime*, vol. V. *Afrique Equatoriale Française*, Paris, 1950, pp. 537–52.

LETHUR, R., 'Études sur le royaume du Loango et le peuple vili', *Cahiers Ngonge*, 1960, No. 4.

LEMAIRE, CH., *Voyage au Congo*, Brussels, n.d. (1894).

LEWIS, I. M. (ed.), *History and Social Anthropology*, London, 1968 (Association of Social Anthropologists, Monograph No. 7).

LIEBRECHTS, CH., 'Léopoldville', *Bulletin de la Société royale belge de Géographie*, 1889, XIII, pp. 501–36.

LIEBRECHTS, CH., *Souvenirs d'Afrique: Congo, Léopoldville, Bolobo, Equateur (1883–1889)*, Brussels, 1909.

LINDBLOM, G., 'A Noose Trap Appliance for the Capture of the Fruit-eating Bat of the Lower Congo Region', *Man*, 1928, XXVIII, pp. 93–5.

LOIR, H., *Le tissage du raphia au Congo Belge*, Brussels, 1935 (Annales du Musée du Congo Belge. Série III, Tome III, Fasc. I).

LOMBARD, J., 'Matériaux préhistoriques du Congo français', *Journal de la société des africanistes*, vol I, 1, 1931, p. 56.

LUWEL, M., *Sir Francis de Winton, Administrateur Général du Congo (1884–1886)*, Tervuren, 1964 (Annales du Musée Royal de l'Afrique Centrale, Série in 8°. Sciences Historiques No. 1).

MAES, J., *Fetischen of Toverbeelden uit Kongo*, Brussel, 1935 (Annales du Musée du Congo Belge, Série VI, Tome II, Fasc. I).

MAES, J., 'Les Lukombe ou instruments de musique à cordes des populations du Kasai-Lac-Léopold II, Lukénie', *Zeitschrift für Ethnologie*, 1938, vol. 70, 3–5, pp. 240–54.

MAES, J., 'Poterie du Lac Léopold II', *Artes Africanae*, 1937, pp. 20–44.

MAES, J., 'Le tissage chez les populations du Lac Léopold II', *Anthropos*, 1930, XXV, pp. 393–408.

MAES, J., 'La vannerie au Lac Léopold II', *Artes Africanae*, 1936, pp. 3–33.

MAESEN, A., 'Un art traditionnel au Congo Belge: la sculpture', *Les arts du Congo Belge et du Rwanda Urundi*, Brussels, 1950, pp. 9–33.

MAHIEU, A., 'La numismatique au Congo belge', *L'expansion belge*, 1928, XXI, No. 11, pp. 16–24; No. 12, pp. 13–15; XXII, No. 5, pp. 19–26, No. 8, pp. 29–32; 1929, XXII, No. 1, pp. 11–16. (Was also published as book later.)

MAILLOT, L., 'Notice pour la carte chronologique des principaux foyers de la maladie du sommeil', *Bulletin de l'Institut de Recherches Scientifiques au Congo*, 1962, I, pp. 45–54.

MALBEKE-BOUCHER, B., 'Ngalifourou, reine des Batékés', *Liaison*, 1957, No. 57, pp. 27–9.

MANSO PAIVA, Visconde de, *Historia de Congo* (*Documentos*), Lisbon, 1877.

MAQUET, M., 'Les populations des environs de Léopoldville', *Congo*, 1937, II, 3, pp. 241–58.

MAPULA, M., 'Les chefs disparaitront-ils?', *Liaison*, 1956, 52, pp. 16–18.

MARTIN, PH., 'The Trade of Loango in the Seventeenth and Eighteenth Centuries', in R. GRAY, D. BIRMINGHAM (eds.), London, 1970, pp. 139–161.

MARTRIN DONOS, *see* DE MARTRIN DONOS, CH.

MASSON DETOURBET, A., 'Le tissage du raphia chez les Batéké (Moyen Congo)', *Journal de la Société des Africanistes*, 1957, XXVII, I, pp. 67–99.

MASUI, TH., *D'Anvers à Banzyville*, Brussels, 1894.

MASUI, TH., *L'Etat Indépendant du Congo à l'Exposition Bruxelles-Tervuren*, Brussels, 1897.

MAURICE, A., *Stanley. Lettres inédites*, Brussels, 1955.

MENSE, TH., 'Anthropologie der Völker vom Mittleren Congo', *Verhändlungen der Berliner Gesellschaft für Anthropologie, Ethnologie und Urgeschichte*, Berlin, 1887, pp. 624–50.

MERLON, A., *Le Congo producteur*, Brussels, 1888.

MERLON, A., 'Les Noirs. Moeurs, Legislation, Croyances, Superstitions des peuplades du Haut Congo', *Revue du Monde Catholique*, 1892, V, No. 4, pp. 296–310.

MILETTO, Dr., 'Notes sur les ethnies de la region du Haut-Ogooué', *Bulletin de l'Institut des Etudes Centrafricaines*, 1951, II, vol. 2, pp. 19–48.

NEUVILLE, D., BREARD, CH., *Les voyages de Savorgnan de Brazza: Ogooué et Congo (1875–1882)*, Paris, 1884.

NEY, N., *Conférences et lettres de P. de Savorgnan de Brazza sur trois explorations dans l'Ouest Africain*, Paris, 1887.

OBENGA, Mwene Ndzale, 'Le royaume de Makoko', *Présence africaine*, vol. 70, 1969, pp. 28–45.

OLBRECHTS, F. M., 'Une curieuse statuette en laiton des Ba-Teke', *Congo-Tervuren*, 1955, I, 3, pp. 103–4.

ONDONO, 'Souvenirs de l'époque de Brazza', *Encyclopédie mensuelle d'Outre-Mer*, Paris, 1952, No. 7, pp. 14–15.

PAPY, L., 'Les populations Batéké (A.E.F.)', *Cahiers d'Outre-Mer*, 1949, II, No. 6, pp. 112–34.

PAYEUR-DIDELOT, J. F., *Trente mois au continent mystérieux. Gabon, Congo et côte occidentale*, Paris, 1900.

PERES, D., *Duarte Pacheco Pereira: Esmeraldo de Situ Orbis*, Lisbon, 1954.

PLANQUAERT, M., *Les Jaga et les Bayaka du Kwango*, Brussels, 1932 (Mémoires de l'Académie Royale des Sciences coloniales. Classe des sciences morales et politiques, III, I).

RANDLES, W. G. L., *L'ancien royaume du Congo des origines à la fin du XIXe siècle*, Paris, 1968.

RAVENSTEIN, E. G. (ed.), *The Strange Adventures of Andrew Battell of Leigh*, London, 1901.

REIDER, A., *L'évêque des anthropophages*, Paris, 1933.
RIBEIRO, J., *O Elemento Negro: Historia-Folklore-Linguistica*, Bibliotheca Historica, VIII, n.d., Rio de Janeiro (1930s).
ROBERTS, A., 'Nyamwezi Trade'; R. GRAY, D. BIRMINGHAM (eds.), *Pre-Colonial African Trade*, London, 1970, pp. 39–74.
ROUGET, F., *L'expansion coloniale au Congo Français*, Paris, 1906.
SAUTTER, C., 'Le plateau congolais de Mbe', *Cahiers d'Etudes Africaines*, 1960, II, 2, pp. 5–48.
SAUTTER, C., 'Les pêcheurs du Stanley-Pool', *Géographia*, 1958, vol. 83, pp. 21–8.
SAUTTER, C., *De l'Atlantique au fleuve Congo: une géographie du souspeuplement*, Paris, 1966, 2 vols.
SAUTTER, C., 'Notes sur la construction du chemin de fer Congo-Ocean (1921–1934)', *Cahiers d'Etudes Africaines*, 1967, vol. VII, pp. 219–99.
SCHOVE, D. J., 'Eclipses, Comets and the Spectrum of Time in Africa', *Journal of the British Astronomical Association*, 1968, vol. 78, pp. 91–8.
SIMS, A., *A Vocabulary of the Kiteke as spoken by the Bateke (Batio) and Kindred Tribes on the Upper Congo: I English-Kiteke*, London, 1886; *II Kiteke-English*, London, 1888.
SMITH, M. G., 'History and Social Anthropology', *Journal of the Royal Anthropological Institute*, 1962, vol. 92, pp. 73–85.
SOELLNER, CH., *Un voyage au Congo*, Namur, 1895.
SORET, M., 'Carte ethnique de l'A.E.F. Feuille No. 1, Brazzaville', Paris, 1955.
SORET, M., *et al.*, *Les coutumes II. Les Biens-La chefferie*, Brazzaville, n.d. (1961–3).
STANLEY, H. M., *The Congo and the Founding of its Free State*, London, 1885, 2 vols.
STANLEY, H. M., *Through the Dark Continent*, New York, 1878.
STORME, M., *Ngankabe, la prétendue reine des Baboma*, Brussels, 1956 (Académie Royale des Sciences coloniales. Classe des sciences morales et politiques VII, 2).
SURET CANALE, J. J., *Afrique noire occidentale et centrale. T.II L'Ere coloniale, 1900–1945*, Paris, 1964.
THYS, A., *Au Congo et au Kasai*, Brussels, 1888.
TORDAY, E., JOYCE, J., *Notes ethnographiques sur les populations habitant le bassin du Kasai et du Kwango Oriental*, Brussels, 1922.
TRIVIER, E., *Mon voyage au continent noir. La Gironde en Afrique*, Paris, 1891.
TUCKEY, J. K., *Narrative of an Expedition to Explore the River Zaire*, London, 1818.
VANDEN BOSSCHE, J., 'La poterie chez les Ba-Teke de Kingabwa', *Brousse*, 1953, IV, pp. 10–16.
VAN DER KERKEN, G., 'Les populations africaines du Congo belge et du Ruanda Urundi', *Encyclopédie du Congo belge*, Brussels, 1952, vol. I, pp. 81–200.
VAN MOORSEL, H., 'Bij een oude munteenheid gevonden te Kingsbwa', *Brousse*, 1953, IV, pp. 21–5.
VANSINA, J., 'Les noms personnels et structure sociale chez les Tyo (Téké)', *Bulletin des séances de l'académie royale des sciences d'Outre-Mer*, 1964, IV, pp. 794–804.
VANSINA, J., 'The Kingdom of the Great Makoko', in MCCALL, D., BENNETT, N., BUTLER, J., *Western African History*, Boston, 1969, pp. 20–44 (map is missing).

VANSINA, J., 'Religions et sociétés en Afrique centrale', *Cahiers de religions africaines*, 1968, II, 2, No. 3, pp. 95–107.

VEISTROFFER, A., *Vingt ans dans la brousse africaine*, Lille, 1931.

VERVLOET, G., 'Un peu de folklore africain', *Bulletin des Vétérans Coloniaux*, 1949, XXI, I, pp. 28–9.

WAUTERS, A. J., *Le Congo au point de vue économique*, Brussels, 1956.

WHYMS, *Léopoldville. Son Histoire 1881–1956*, Brussels, 1956.

WITTE, J., *see* DE WITTE, J.

YOULOU-KOUYA, H., 'Une adoratrice du Nkoue-Mbali', *Liaison*, 1957, 58, pp. 54–6.

ZORZI, E., *Al Congo con Brazza. Viaggio di due esploratori italiani nel carteggio e nel 'Giornali' inediti di Attilio Pecile (1883–1886)*, Rome, 1940.

ANON., 'L'Art congolais', *Belgique coloniale*, 1896, II, pp. 3–5 (pottery).

ANON., Notes in *Bulletin du Comité de l'Afrique Française*, 1899, p. 426; 1935, No. 4, pp. 209–10.

ANON., 'Les colliers', *Le Congo illustré*, 1893, II, pp. 163–4.

ANON., 'Commémoration du centenaire de la naissance de Brazza', *Encyclopédie mensuelle d'Outre-Mer. Documents*, 1952, No. 7, pp. 1–16.

ANON., 'L'enterrement solennel de Galifourou, dernière reine des Batéké', *Belgique d'Outremer*, 1957, pp. 381–4.

ANON., 'La flotille du Haut Congo', *Le Congo illustré*, 1893, II, pp. 34–5.

ANON., 'Galifourou, reine des Batéké va mourir au Moyen Congo', *Bulletin du Cercle Colonial Luxembourgeois*, 1956, XVI, pp. 13–14.

ANON., 'L'ivoire', *Le Congo illustré*, 1893, II, pp. 42–3.

ANON., 'La monnaie', *Le Congo illustré*, 1892, I, pp. 34–5.

ANON., 'Carte', *Le mouvement géographique*, 6 avril 1894, p. 1; No. 1, 1.

ANON., Notes in *Le mouvement géographique*, 1899, XVI, No. 21, p. 269.

ANON., 'La musique chez les nègres', *Le Congo illustré*, 1893, II, pp. 48, 66.

ANON., *Panorama du Congo*, Brussels, n.d. (1911–12), pp. 1–7.

ANON., 'Le sel', *Le Congo illustré*, 1893, II, pp. 135, 154–5.

ANON., 'Un peuple du Moyen Congo. Le peuple Batéké. Aspects de la vie économique', *Bulletin d'Information et de Documentation*, 1950, XXXXVII, pp. 1–3.

ANON., 'Les tatouages', *Le Congo illustré*, 1892, I, pp. 154–5.

ANON., 'Le tissage', *La Belgique coloniale*, 1896, II, p. 329a.

ANON., 'Les tissus', *Le Congo illustré*, 1893, II, pp. 210–11.

ANON., 'La tribu des Batéké', *Le Congo illustré*, 1892, I, pp. 122–3.

II. *Manuscript Sources and Others*

Archives du Moyen Congo: Dossier 90:

18 June 1934	Subdivision autonome de Brazzaville No. 571 à M. l'Administrateur en Chef Delégué pour l'administration de la colonie du Moyen Congo à Brazzaville. Objet: Situation politique du plateau Batéké.
15 May 1936	Note pour Monsieur le G.G. faite le 12 mai 1936 par le Directeur des affaires politiques.
1937–1939?	Notice sur les Batéké par le Directeur des affaires politiques et de l'administration générale.
pre-1940?	Notice sur les modalités de désignation et d'intronisation du Makoko. Anonyme.

27 June 1952 Le chef et les notables de M'Foa (District de Brazzaville) à M. le Gouverneur, Chef du Territoire du Moyen-Congo à Pointe Noire.

1952? Organisation de la Chefferie des Batékés-Sud temps primitif. Anonyme, but written by Africans.

1 Aug. 1952 L'Administrateur Maire de la Commune de Brazzaville à M. le Gouverneur du Territoire du Moyen-Congo. Refers to *Organisation*, above.

30 June 1954 No. 568. Directe B.H. 34 A/S Makoko et Galifourou par Chef bureau APAG.

1 Oct. 1954 à Inzouli. Les chefs de canton de terre et chefs coutumiers Batéké du District de Brazzaville (M'Foa-plateau Batéké) à M. le Gouverneur, Chef du Territoire du Moyen-Congo à Pointe Noire.

13 Oct. 1954 à Brazzaville. Chefs de canton M'Boulankio et canton Inteli et chefs des terres Imbama, Ngamaba et N'gampouy et de Mayala François, Lefini à M. le Gouverneur, Chef du Territoire du Moyen-Congo.

13 June 1956 at Brazzaville. Le Chef de District de Brazzaville à M. le Chef de la Région du Pool à Kinkala: objet: décès de la reine Ngalifourou No. 33/CF. 6p. signé illisible.

16 June 1956 Bulletin hebdomadaire de *l'Eveil de Pointe Noire*: 'Les rites funéraires ont commencé à N'Gabe ou la reine Ngalifourou sera enterrée en février', (A.F.P.) I p.

15 Jan. 1957 Chef de la région du Djoué, Directeur de la Délégation du Moyen-Congo à M. le Chef du Territoire du Moyen-Congo, Pointe Noire. Objet: obsèques de la reine Ngalifourou.

30 July 1957 No. 720 and No. 733 Inf. Brazzaville 34. Du 22.VII et 23.VII.1957. Activité politique a/a: du Makoko et activité politique au Chef de la Region du Djoué, I.G.S.S., S.L.P.

Archives du Congo Belge. Copies in Archives du Musée Royal de l'Afrique Centrale:

AUGUSTEYNS, 1932, Territoire de Mushie, 10 p. Territoire de la Lufima. Notes Complémentaires-Enquête de chefferie Tua (P.V. 18).

GUSTIN, F., 1924. Territoire Bikoro. Les populations du territoire de la Pama-Kasai. 16 p.

JORIS, G., 1937. Territoire de l'Inkisi. Etude sur la chefferie de Gana (not at Tervuren. At Kasangulu).

LAMBERT, J., 20 December 1959. Territoire de Kenge. A propos du rapport d'enquête sur la limite Sud Est du Territoire de Kasangulu, 6 p. (not in Tervuren. At Kenge).

LECOCQ, S., 8 September 1931. Territoire de Mushie. Enquête sur la chefferie Tua.

LECOCQ, S., 24 September 1931. Territoire de Mushie. Rapport d'enquête sur la chefferie de Dumu, territoire de la Lufimi.

LECOCQ, S., 1931. Territoire de Mushie. Enquête sur la chefferie Meko.

LEKEUX, 27 December 1937. Territoire de l'Inkisi. Note complémentaire sur les Batéké sud (not at Tervuren. At Kasangulu).

REYNAERT, —, Territoire de Mushie. L'asservissement au Congo. Tribu des Batéké, 26 p.

ROULIN, H., 1936–7. Territoire de Banningville. *Les Bayanzi et les Batéké* (very long manuscript. Over 200 p.).

SCOHY, A., 1939. Territoire de Bikoro. Notes sur la perle *nkangi* ou *nkange*, 4 p.

TECHY, 1933. Territoire de Mushie. Enquête sur la chefferie Ebale.

Dossiers ethnographiques du Musée Royal de l'Afrique Centrale:

Dossier anonyme No. 996.

Others:

BONNAFE, P., Oral information and manuscripts concerning the Kukuya.

DAELEMAN, J., Vergelijkende Studie van enkele Noordwest Bantoetalen. Leuven Lic. Afrikaanse taalkunde, 1956.

PAUWELS, J., La dot chez les Tyo (Teke): mécanisme et fonctions. Faculté de Droit de l'université officielle du Congo à Lubumbashi, November 1966.

SORET, M., Généalogie des rois tio depuis Iloo I (using Dossier 90 of the *archives du Moyen-Congo* cited, especially docts. of 1934 and 1936).

Index

T

Index

Note: Persons mentioned only as authors in footnotes are not listed unless their views are discussed. Sims and Calloc'h are mentioned only when the name occurs in either text or footnote and their data are specifically discussed.

Glossary of Tio Words

Note: Only words which occur at least twice and for which a gloss is not provided in the text are included.

ãkã: see *nkã*
ãkaãw: fiancée, 49, 86–7, 481
amieene: councillors, 321, 323, 342–6, 360, 363, 393, 503, 521
anõ: royal emblem (ring), 380, 386, 388n.
angabira: retainers of lords, 395, 392, 465
ãngkira: women possessed by the spirit of a shade, 45–6, 63, 224, 229, 230, 232, 468, 501
apfu: evil spirit, 40, 78–9, 170–8, 182–6, 191ff., 221–3, 226–8, 231–3, 238, 242, 344, 353–4, 374, 467, 468n.
ãti: charm, 126, 175, 180, 183, 195, 225, 229–31, 539
ãtoro: banana (sp), 110, 186, 192, 205
ba: war bell, 141, 165n., 362
baamukaana: 'those of a species', 34; *baamukaana lilimpu:* aristocrats, 76, 321, 394, 405
baana: see *mwaana*
bwoolo: plant (sp.) used for making colour, 113, 144
iã: fine, 321, 340, 346
ibili: charm for headman, 75, 76, 374
ibuunu: cloth currency, 88–90, 92, 93, 95, 97, 104n., 282–4, 287, 345–6, 366–9
ibuuru: kindred, 29, 34, 35, 40, 46, 47, 53n., 61, 82, 100, 101, 104, 142, 172, 238, 349, 351, 352, 355–8, 368, 370, 371, 374, 405, 463, 467, 479–82; *ibuur'imo:* 'same kindred', 75; *ibuur vyishiil iloo:* kindred for inheritance, 35, 39, 56
ibwooni: fine from wife to husband, 63–4, 529
idzia: hole to soak cassava: 5n., 64, 72, 80, 95, 109, 110, 112, 117, 148, 160, 162, 168, 486, 488, 511, 512, 514
ifi: witch substance, 171, 173, 351, 352
ĩkwa: proof of divination, 175–7, 345, 350
ikwii: shades, 39–46, 63, 78, 79, 125, 127, 170, 172, 174–8, 182, 183, 188, 190–8, 207, 211, 214, 217n., 218, 220, 221, 224–33, 235, 238, 319, 351, 374, 375, 388n., 411, 467, 468n., 540–3
ilibankie: tree (sp), 131, 191–3
iliri: whistle (sp), 183, 196
imiõ: drug, 174, 180, 183, 188, 191, 193–5, 200, 201n.
impfiri: witch substance, 171, 173, 226–39
impfõ: feud, 356–7
ingkura: tribute, 32, 320, 323, 328, 372–4, 390, 397
ipali: charm for wealth, 173, 194

ipfuuna: part of judicial procedure, 343–5, 348, 349, 529, 533, 534, 536, 538, 539, 540–2
ipwooro: fine between close kin, 57–9, 63, 64, 66, 67, 71, 528, 531
isã: client, 90, 368–70
isaani: group of brothers, 68n., 97, 100, 107
itieeri: stage of payment of bridewealth for marriage, 92, 346, 538, 542
itio: statue of shade, 40, 41, 43, 63, 127, 146, 176, 182, 232, 281, 468n.; *ititio:* small lid, 176
itiõ: group work, 81, 114
ito: gruel of cassava, 149, 196, 486
itsuua: woman's ritual, 64, 114, 160, 174, 176, 182, 184–7, 195, 196, 201, 206, 225, 229, 230, 236, 501, 541
iuula: pledge for poison oracle: 351, 529–30
kaa: amulet, charm, 41, 42, ill. 78, 173–7, 180, 191–4, 197, 224–5, 227, 230, 263, 350, 547
káá: royal hat, 380, 386, 387
kio: shrine, 40, 43–6, 63, 125, 233; *kia ngayuulu:* 'shrine on top of house', 45
kuli: ball, 164, 373, 380, 384
libi: rattle for shade, 41, 42, ill. 191n., 231, 384
libobõ: nightjar, 386, 387, 390
lie: hexagonal blue bead, 154, 269–70, 304, 334, 387, 388n.
likuba: cushion, 112, 318, 324, 380–2, 387, 389, 390
lindaa: oracle (sp), 177, 268, 346, 350, 352, 489, 529
lisee: initiation, king or lord: 229, 230, 233, 327, 375, 377–85, 394–6, 432, 469n., 473, 492
lisisõ: grass (sp), 77, 79, 182, 191, 192, 229, 231, 540
litsũ: return of bridewealth, 60, 69, 97–107, 319, 340, 350, 355, 356, 359, 368–70, 393, 479, 480, 482, 501
luni: currency of raphia: 283, 358
mã: my mother, 49, 51 (+ combinations of pronouns), 60, 208
mbaa: co-wife, 50, 54, 58, 59, 65, 180
mbali: courtyard of ruler, 77, 335–7, 340–3, 347
mbalikali: wife's sister's husband, 50, 54, 58, 91, 536
mboompo: plant (sp), 113, 219
mbula: *olivancillaria nana*, shells, 88, 141n., 206, 269, 283, 287, 309, 321
mbulu: jackal, 173, 175, 178, 183, 184, 187, 189, 196, 197, 228, 230
mbuma: person given as bloodprice, 355–8, 370
mbuuru: person; *mbuuru waasobi*, see *mbuma; mbuuru waatioo;* bought slave, 365, 368
mbwei: younger sibling, 48, 52, 54, 57, 58, 68, 69, 71, 96, 208, 366, 394, 544
mitako: brass rod currency, 88, 282–96, 299, 303–6, 308, 348, 399, 429, 450
mpfõ: chief, 91, 118, 131, 132, 332, 347, 357, 360n., 376, 381, 458, 546; salute for a chief: 335, 388n., 399
mpfõ andzo: head of matrilineage, 30–3, 46, 97, 98, 214, 220, 340–2, 348, 349, 351, 355, 356, 366, 368, 369, 479, 542, 543
mpiini: animal double, 199–202, 221, 224, 225, 233, 378, 379, 441
mpu: hat or power, 154, 332, 333, 453
mvuba: sign of authority in shape of anvil, 217, 326, 332, 335, 387
mvuli: antelope (sp), 36n., 41, 121, 123, 165, 363; *mvulimvuli*, its horn, 79

mwaana: 'child', 48, 50–2, 54, 56, 366–8, 544; *mwaan'ankaa*, 51, 52, 54: *mwaan'ankieli:* sister's son, 32, 34, 48, 51, 52, 56, 367, 394, 406; *mwaana we iboolo:* 'child of man', 30, 31, 46, 47, 55; *mwaana wuuke:* 'child of girl', 55, 67; plural is *baana*

nciele: child born in a special way, 118, 194, 204–6, 224, 225, 229, 230, 234

ncio: savanna field, 109, 110, 114–16, 118, 159, 160

ndoo: victim of witchcraft, 350, 467n.

ndua: bird (sp.), 45, 192, 334, 453

nduu: friend, 47, 48, 80n., 81, 82, 87, 91, 95

ndzo: matrilineage: 29–35, 38–46, 63, 68, 69, 82, 83, 88, 90, 95, 97–100, 102, 104, 105, 107, 172, 214, 216, 230, 233, 238, 318, 320, 340, 341, 344, 348, 349, 351, 352, 355, 357, 365, 367–71, 467, 479–81, 540–3

ndzo ancweli: special catafalque, 211, 220, 386n., 444n.

ndzu: raphia cloth; *ndzu atieeri;* 3 rows of cloth, 88, 144, 145n., 209; *ndzu anna* (4 rows of cloth, 88, 89n., 104n., 144, 145n., 209, 337, 535, 536, 546

ndzubi: papyrus (sp), 112, 131, 146

ngàà: healer, diviner, 153, 170–98, 222, 226–31, 236, 237, 303, 307, 315, 320, 334, 349, 353, 354, 362, 379, 395, 454, 467n., 490, 491, 495, 521, 526, 532, 539–43, 546, 547

ngáá + noun: 'master of', 'owner of': *see* personal names, titles, etc.

ngáàluu: younger sibling (address), 48, 152

ngáàyuulu: woman healer who passed through *itsuua*, 185, 186, 195, 206, 229

ngántsii: 313, 319, 320, 323

ngeiloolo: witch, 171, 206, 226, 467

ngiele: copper currency, 39, 88, 89, 145, 268, 272, 283, 284n., 285, 287, 294, 301, 326, 399, 450

ngili: avoidance, taboo, 36, 37, 118, 188, 189, 197, 234, 235

ngolo: Fortune, 170, 226, 237, 238, 240

nguboolo: mother's brother, 31–4, 49, 51, 52, 54, 56

nguõ: pluriarc, 165, 182, 232

ngwuunu: forest field, 109, 110, 112, 115, 116, 131, 159, 160, 162, 280, 463, 485–8

nji: small *olivancillaria nana*, 88n., 192, 269, 282–5, 290, 294, 304, 305, 309, 399

nka: antelope (sp.), 7, 121, 123, 200, 377

nkã: red cloth, 13, 88n., 103, 150, 152, 268, 376, 380, 381, 382n., 387, 395

nkaa: grandparent, 36, 45, 47, 48, 51–4, 57–60, 63, 65, 71, 84, 85, 90, 92, 97, 142, 394, 411, 457n., 458, 459, 460, 544, 545

nkani: tributary, 324, 327–9, 335n., 337, 346, 347, 360, 365, 368–70, 372, 397, 399–403, 432, 454, 456, 457, 466n.

nkei: poison for ordeal, 131, 172, 351, 352, 365, 369

nki andzo: type of cloth, 362, 547

nkieli: sibling of opposite sex, 48, 54, 57, 66, 208, 542, 544

nkiini: village charm, 77–80, 217, 230, 233

nkira: nature spirit, 45, 113, 118, 125, 170, 176, 184, 185, 187, 188, 191–6, 200–6, 210, 221–6, 229–39, 315–30, 322–4, 326–30, 330, 339, 344, 374, 375, 385, 396, 431, 453, 455, 467, 468, 490, 491, 501, 545

nkir'mbu: container for shrine (sp), 199, 200, 206, 224

nkobi: box for charms, 41, 42, ill. 63, 179, 180, 185, 186, 190, 196, 233, 324–32, 336–8, 362, 375, 377, 380n., 384, 391, 396, 412, 431, 455–7, 459, 460, 469, 491, 496, 545, 548n.
nkuo: plantianeater, 376, 386–7
nnaana: elder sibling, 48, 54, 57, 58, 68, 69, 71, 96, 172, 208, 366, 544
ntaa: raphia cloth (sp.), 88, 89, 96, 144, 209, 211, 268, 282, 283, 286, 290, 293, 304, 305, 358
ntsa: antelope (sp.), 7, 79, 92, 93, 121, 183, 185, 376
ntsee: antelope (sp.), 7, 121, 122, 125, 166, 317
ntsii: domain, 313, 326; salute for squire of land, 335, 338n., 399
ntsuo: pledge, hostage, 368, 370
nzimbu: *nji*, 283, 284, 445–7, 448n. (Kikongo)
obwooro: tree (sp.), 77, 113, 192
odzuo: day of the week, 167, 188, 205, 238, 265, 377n.
odzira: type of marriage payment, 90, 92, 93
okali: wife, 49–51, 54, 55, 58, 95, 480
õke: woman; *õke ampu*: chief's woman, 88, 90, 359, 546, 547; *õke wuu yumpfõ*: 'chief's woman', 77, 91, 481. These women marry by seeking refuge at a chief's court
okila: day of the week, 167, 188, 238, 265n.
õkoo: king, 8, 372, 382n., 387n., 439n., 440, 459n.
okuu: inquest for illness, 31, 37, 46, 63, 75, 90, 91, 100, 173, 174, 182, 184, 207, 229, 230, 233, 242, 319, 340, 348, 349, 354, 355, 366, 368, 369, 482, 489, 539–43
okwe: day of the week, 167, 187, 203, 216, 232, 238, 265n., 376, 384
olõ: husband, 49, 50, 54, 55, 58, 95
ondzali: brother in law, 50, 54, 58
onia: broom of office, 41, 326, 341, ill. 345, 386n., 387n., 389, 534, 536
osel'beene: type of charm, 180, 194
oshioonu: symbolic payment to healer, 188, 317, 540, 542
otioolu: grandchild, 47, 48, 51, 52, 54, 58–60, 65, 71, 85–7, 90, 97–100, 102, 105, 107, 322, 375, 394, 406, 457, 460n., 480, 538, 544
oto: tree (sp.), 77, 113, 217
õtsara: rattle for shade, 41, 42, ill. 174–6, 182, 184, 214, 231
pfura: magical package, 127, 174, 175, 179, 189, 194, 307, 362
taara: father, 48–52, 54, 196, 208, 366, 394, 457n., 460
tike: type of divorce, 103, 530–4, 536, 538–9
tookei: Father's sisters, 48, 52, 54, 56
tsuula: red camwood, 45, 127, 387
ula: settlement, 29, 38, 40, 62, 70, 82, 202, 355
unũ: prestige object, 154, 217, 266, 267, 269, 272, ill. 304–6, 318, 325, 326, 333, 375, 387, 390, 453, 457, 458
uva: earnest money in marriage, 92, 93, 531, 533
vaa: diviner, 174, 175, 178, 351, 467n.
vooro: raphia cloth (sp.), 144, 218
wara: bracelet of prestige, 114n., 326, 333, 388
wookuru: elder, headman, 75–9, 318, 319, 321, 355, 356, 394, 458

Vansina, Jan.

The Tio kingdom of the Middle Congo, 1880–1892. London, New York, Oxford University Press for the International African Institute, 1973.

xvii, 586 p. illus., maps, plans, ports. 23 cm. index. £8.00
B 73-07372

Bibliography: p. 549–558.

1. Bateke (Bantu people) I. Title.

276031 DT546.242.V36 301.29'67'24 73–164033
ISBN 0-19-724189-1 MARC
Library of Congress 73 [4]

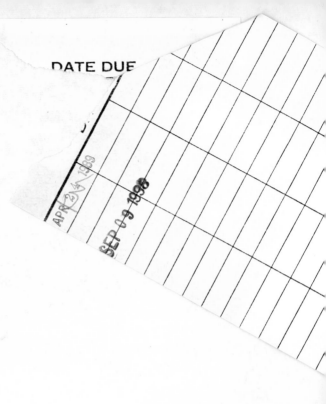